2018 中非纺织服装国际论坛论文集

Proceedings of 2018 Sino–Africa International Symposium on Textiles and Apparel

邱夷平　主编

Edited by Qiu Yiping

中国纺织出版社·北京

China Textile & Apparel Press · Beijing

图书在版编目(CIP)数据

2018 中非纺织服装国际论坛论文集 = Proceedings of 2018
Sino-Africa International Symposium on Textiles and Apparel：英
文/邱夷平主编. -- 北京：中国纺织出版社,2018.9
　ISBN 978 - 7 - 5180 - 5010 - 9

　Ⅰ.① 2… Ⅱ.①邱… Ⅲ.①纺织工业—中国、非洲—国
际学术会议—文集—英文 ②服装工业—中国、非洲—国际学
术会议—文集—英文 Ⅵ.①F426.8 - 53 ②F440.68 - 53

　中国版本图书馆 CIP 数据核字(2018)第 099612 号

策划编辑：符 芬　责任编辑：沈 靖　责任印制：何 建

中国纺织出版社出版发行
地址：北京市朝阳区百子湾东里 A407 号楼　邮政编码：100124
销售电话：010—67004422　传真：010—87155801
http://www.c-textilep.com
E-mail：faxing@ c-textilep.com
中国纺织出版社天猫旗舰店
官方微博 http://weibo.com/2119887771
北京虎彩文化传播有限公司印刷　各地新华书店经销
2018 年 9 月第 1 版第 1 次印刷
开本：889×1194　1/16　印张：28.25
字数：900 千字　定价：168.00 元

Organizing Committee of 2018 SAISTA
Chairman:
QIU Yiping   TBD

Committee Menbers:
GU Bohong   LI Jun   LI Min

QIN Xiaohong   ZHAO Mingwei

Advisory Committee of 2018 SAISTA
Chairman:
JIANG Changjun   President of Donghua University

Honorary Advisor:
TBD   Vice President of Bahir Dar University

LIU Chunhong   Vice President of Donghua University

Academic Committee of 2018 SAISTA
Chairman:
YU Jianyong   Donghua University, China

Committee Menbers: (Alphabetically Sorted By Last Name)
TBD   Bahir Dar University, Ethiopia

GU Bohong   Donghua University, China

Preface

Since the first Sino-Africa International Symposium on Textiles and Apparel in 2015, the Belt and Road Initiative has gained much greater momentum in promoting the social-economic development of the developing countries along the ancient Silk Roads under the leadership of President Xi Jinping. Significant progress has been made in our collaboration with these countries in terms of textile and apparel research, cultural and student exchanges as well as education collaboration. In this symposium, we intend to present more recent results of relevant research in the field. A total of more than 90 research papers have been submitted and most of them have been accepted for the proceeding and the quality of the papers has also been improved compared with the last three symposiums. These papers cover a wide spectrum of topics such as textile engineering, nano technology, textile materials, wearable technologies, apparel design and technology, textile management and marketing, and textile history. The authors come from more than 15 countries including African countries. This indicates that SAISTA 2018 has attracted substantially increased attentions from China and Africa as well as around the world. The symposium is attended by educators and professionals from Ethiopia, Kenya, Sudan, Zimbabwe, Tanzania, Uganda, and South Africa as well as China. About 20 presentations are given in the symposium. I believe that this symposium provides a great opportunity to review the latest progress of the collaboration and exchange in the textiles and apparel education and research among China, Africa and many other countries in the Belt and Road regions.

Professor YU Jianyong
Academician of Chinese Academy of Engineering

Contents

A Facile Method to Prepare Electricity Conductive Fabric and Its Application in Pressure Sensor ······ 1

Bending Properties of 3D Integrated Woven Spacer Composites with Hybrid Carbon/Glass Fiber ······ 5

Chemical Stable, Superhydrophobic and Self-Cleaning Fabrics Prepared by Two-Step Coating of
Polytetrafluoroethylene Membrane and Silica Nanoparticles ·············· 12

Mechanical Property Enhancement of Bead-on-String Electrospun Nanofiber Membrane ·············· 18

Mechanical, Interfacial and Electrothermal Properties of Nickel Coated Carbon Fibers ·············· 24

Mode I Fracture Toughness Behaviors of 3D Angle-Interlock Woven Composites ·············· 30

Natural Dye Extracted from Mexican Marigold Flower and Its Colorfastness Behavior on
Lyocell Fabric ·············· 35

Non-Isothermal Crystallization Kinetics of Novel PET/QE Composites ·············· 40

Novel Bio-Based Recycable Epoxy Resin and Its Application in Carbon Fiber
Reinforced Composite ·············· 46

Properties of Discarded Fiber/Polyurethane Flame Retardant Insulation Board ·············· 54

Recyclable Carbon Fiber Reinforced Polyimine Resin Composites ·············· 64

Stable Gold Nanoparticle Modified Fabric Was Prepared by PDA In-Situ Reduction ·············· 70

Through-Thickness Properties of 3D Orthogonal Woven Carbon Fabric Reinforced Composites ······ 74

Torsion Deformation and Damage of Bi-Axial Warp Knitted Composite Tubes ·············· 80

A Novel Cord-Shaped Supercapacitor with High Stretchability ·············· 86

Adsorption of Cationic Contaminants in Water by MXene Nanosheets/Alginate
Composite Fibers ·············· 91

Bending Properties of Zigzag Shaped 3D Woven Spacer Composites: Experiment and
FEM Simulation ·············· 100

Fast-Curing Halogen-Free Flame-Retardant Epoxy Resins and Their Application
in Glass Fiber Reinforced Composites ·············· 107

Development of Multi-Functional Cotton Using Fluorocarbon Resin ·············· 113

Optimal Scheduling for Mobile Device with Heterogeneous Energy Management Units ·············· 123

Optimization of Microwave Extraction Process for Pigment from Walnut Husk by Using
Response Surface Methodology ·············· 129

Separation Model of Dual-Beard Cotton Sample for Short Fiber Contents Measurement ·············· 139

Silk Fabric Protection Obtained via Chemical Conjugation Transglutaminase and
Silk Fibroin Reinforcement ·············· 144

Structural and Mechanical Properties of Silk Biomaterials Plasticized by Glycerol ·············· 151

Textile-Based Passive RFID Tag with Text-Meandered Structure ·············· 156

The Development of High-Performance Natural Ramie Fibers Reinforced Polylactic
Acid Composite via Surface Modification of Fibers and Composite Thermal Annealing ·············· 161

The Effect of Alkali Treatment on the Characterization of Apocynum Venetum Bast
Fibers and It's Weibull Distribution Prediction ·············· 167

The Effect of Chemical Degumming on Component, Structure and Properities of
Apocynum Venetum ……………………………………………………………… 173
The Influence of Woven Fabric Structure on the Characteristics of Capillary Action …………… 179
The Study of Omnidirectional Stretchable CNT/PDMS Electro-Heating Composite …………… 187
A Wearable Pressure Sensor Based on Facilely Prepared Carbonized Woven Cotton Fabric ……… 192
A Graphene-Based Yarn Strain Sensor with Low Electrical Hysteresis …………………… 197
A Novel Method to Test Moisture Dissipation of Woven Fabrics ………………………… 201
A Stretchable Woven Fabric Circuit: Fabrication and Application ………………………… 206
Quasi-Static and Tensile Impact Properties of 3D Angle-Interlock Carbon/Epoxy
Woven Composites ……………………………………………………………… 210
Design and Weaving of Three-Dimensional Woven Fabric with Rectangular Shape …………… 216
Dopamine Modified Wool Fabrics for Formaldehyde Removal ………………………… 221
Effect of Cryogenic Treatment on the Interfacial Properties of Carbon Nanotube Yarn /
Epoxy Resin Composite ……………………………………………………… 225
Effect of Garment Pressure from Running Compression Pants on Lower Limbs
Muscles Fatigue Threshold ………………………………………………… 230
Effect of Jute Fiber Modification on Mechanical Properties of Jute Fiber Composite ………… 237
Effect of Plasma Modification on Carbon Fiber Surface ………………………………… 241
Effect of Lay-Up Sequence on the Flexural Properties of CFRP Laminates ………………… 246
Effects of Nano-Silica Particle on the Properties of Phenolic Resin/Glass Fiber Composites ……… 252
Evaluation Surface Characteristics of Needle-Punched Nonwoven Polypropylene Sorbents ……… 257
Extraction and Characterization of Cellulose Nanocrystals from Ethiopian Corn Silk …………… 263
Fabric Classification Using Three Dimensional Drape Model ………………………… 268
Fabrication of Fiber-Based Woven Triboelectric Nanogenerators and Study on Influential
Factors for Output Performance ……………………………………………… 273
Fabrication and Properties of Apocynum Venetum Bast Fibers Reinforced Polylactic
Acid Composites ……………………………………………………………… 279
Intelligent Plantar Pressure Monitoring Insole Based on 3D Printing and Flexi Force
Sensor Technology …………………………………………………………… 284
Man's Web-Tailor-Making Shirt Demand Appeal to Integrated Technology and
Business Solution ……………………………………………………………… 289
Overview About the Co-Branding Development of Fashion Brands …………………… 294
Preparation and Properties of ZnO-Ag-CeO$_2$/PI Composite Films ………………… 301
Ramie Fabrics Fixed with TiO$_2$NPs for Formaldehyde Elimination ………………… 307
Research on Surface Properties of Cotton Fabrics Coated with Nano-TiO$_2$ Particles ………… 311
Research on Moisture Absorption and Transmitting Perspiration Performance of Cotton Fabrics …… 316
Study on Stress Relaxation of High Stitch Density Biaxial Warp Knitted Polyester Fabric
Reinforced PVC ……………………………………………………………… 321
Study on Properties of Bamboo Yarn Knitting Products ……………………………… 325
Study on the Integration of Sizing and Dyeing of Medium and Coarse Yarn ………………… 330
Surface Modification Analysis of Flaxseed Fiber Bundles ……………………………… 336
Temperature-Sensitive Garment for Real-Time Monitoring of Human Skin Temperature …………… 340

Tensile and Flexural Properties of Sisal Reinforced Unsaturated Polyester Composite:
For Furniture Manufacture ·· 345
The Effect of Different Female Body Shape Patterns on Marker Efficiencies at Dissimilar
Fabric Width in the Garment Production ··· 352
The Preparation and Hydrophobic Test of PTFE/PAM Electrospinning Membrane ···················· 357
The Study on the Variance of Fabric Drape Based on the Three-Dimensional Mesh Model ··········· 362
Using Different Mordanting Methods for Tencel Fabric Dyeing with Pomegranate Peel
Extracted Dye ··· 368
An Investigation on Crashworthiness of Carbon-Glass Hybrid Composites ·························· 374
Automatic Classification of Fabric Flatness Templates Based on Deep Learning ···················· 379
Classification of Scarf Printing Pattern Based on Perceptual Cognition ··························· 383
Design and Experimental Data Analysis of Four-Wing Split-Type Multifunctional Pillow
Based on Ergonomics ··· 388
Effects of Graft Modification on Water-Solubility and Adhesion Property of Chitosan for
Warp Sizing ··· 393
Fabrication of Electrospun PA6 Nanofibrous Porous Membrane ······························· 396
Incorporation of Metal Ions into Hydrogen-Bonded Polymer Complex Film ······················ 400
Influence of Polymerization Conditions on Grafting of Methyl Methacrylate onto Native Chitin
for Melting Spinning ··· 404
Pilling Image Grade Evaluation of Round Fabric Area with Deep Convolutional Neural Networks ······ 407
Preparation of Anti-Bacterial Cotton/Willow Non-Woven Composites via Needle
Punching Process ··· 411
The Present Situation of Cashmere Market and Consumer Behavior in Shanghai ···················· 415
Structure and Mechanical Properties of Polyamide 56 (PA56) Fibers ··························· 420
Study on Properties of Nano-TiO$_2$ Glass Fiber Cloth ······································· 424
The Ingenious Design in the Decoration of Ethnic Minority Costume in Southwest China ············· 427
Raw Material Analysis and Structure Properties Research on Hotan Traditional Etles Silk ············· 432

A Facile Method to Prepare Electricity Conductive Fabric and Its Application in Pressure Sensor

Ronghui Wu[1,2], Yifan Zhang[1,2], Liyun Ma[1], Weidong Yu[1,2] *

[2]*Department of Technical Textiles, College of Textiles, Donghua University, Shanghai 201620, China*

[1]*Key Laboratory of Textile Science & Technology, Ministry of Education, Donghua University, Shanghai 201620, China*

* *Corresponding author's email*: wdyu@ dhu. edu. cn

Abstract: Electronic fabric which combine traditional fabric with intelligent functionalities have attracted increasing attention. This research fabricated a flexible and wearable pressure sensor with conductive nylon fabric as electrodes and elastomer Ecoflex as dielectric layer. The nylon fabric was first treated by alcohol washing for 30 minutes, followed with radioactivation activated by $SnCl_2$. The conductive nylon fabric which showed a high conductivity of $0.268\Omega \cdot cm$ (square resistance) was made by megnetron sputtering with Ag. A self-made mould at the size of $1mm \times 1mm \times 0.5mm$ was used to make the dielectric layer of the fabric based flexible sensor. The flexible pressure sensor shows a high sensitivity of $0.6190kPa^{-1}$, a good linearity of 0.991 (R^2) under the pressure from 0kPa and 162kPa, and a quick response time of 0.801s. Also, the pressure sensor has a good stability, when press and reply for 9500 times, the capacitance loss rate is only 0.0534. The fabric based flexible and wearable sensor with good properties has wide potential applications and provided a prospect in the field of intelligent fabric for the acquisition of human motions and health data.

Keywords: Conductive nylon fabric; Megnetron sputtering; Pressure sensor

1 Introduction

Intelligent fabric which integrate various electronics such as sensors[1-2], energy harvesting device[3-4], antenna[5-6], into fabrics has attracted researchers considerable interest with the increasing development of advanced flexible and wearable devices due to the great potential applications in the smart, living, health care and medication in combination of big data and (artificial intelligence) AI. Conductive fabric can be made by Materials like conductive polymers, metals and metal oxide nanoparticles/nanowires, carbon based micron/nano materials, such as carbon particles (CP), carbon nanotubes (CNTs), carbon fiber and graphene, have been used and investigated. These materials are promising for a variety of applications including flexible optical and electronic devices, and chemical and biological sensors[7]. Generally, There are three types of sensing mechanisms for electronic textile based sensors, resistive[1-8], capacitive[2,9-10], and self-powering[11]. For the resistive sensors, a change in the electrical resistance occurs when the geometry of the textile deforms upon the application of strain and stress. However, the conductive layers are usually unstable during stretching or compressing because of the adjustments and damage of conductive elements.

The capacitive sensor is typically composed of a dielectric layer sandwiched between two conductive layers[12]. The variation of distance between two electrodes and dielectric constant when pressing would lead to the increasing of capacitance. In this study, we use a facile way to fabricate a kind of electricity conductive fabric by megnetron sputtering with Ag and make it into a fabric based capacitance sensor, using Ecoflex with high elasticity and resilience as the dielectric layer. The sensing properties of the textile based pressure sensor were measured and tested and the sensor can be used as wearable electronics to detect human motions.

2 Experiments

2.1 Materials

Plain woven nylon fabrics were obtained from Dongting Ramie Textile Printing & Dying Mill (Hunan). Two-component material Ecoflex was provided by Zhonghua Suhua Co., Ltd. (Guangdong). Alcohol, $SnCl_2$, Analytical purity, was supplied by Xilong chemical incorporated company (Guangdong).

2.2 Fabric treatment

Before magnetron sputtering, the nylon fabric was washed in the solution of acetone for 30mins, and then followed by alcohol washing for 30mins, followed with radioactivation activated by $SnCl_2$ for 10min.

2.3 Preparation of conductive fabric

Treated fabrics were dried at 60℃ in an oven for 2h to remove all absorbed moisture before sputtering. An Ag thin layer was directly deposited on the treated nylon fabric by magnetron sputtering at room temperature, and a sputtering incident power of 50W, for 30 min, under the protection of argon. A nenameled Cu wire was attached on the side of nylon fabric by conductive silver paste (DuPont 4929N) and conducting resin stabilizing the linkage segment. Conductive fabric with Cu electrode was then encapsulated by Ecoflex.

2.4 Preparation of Ecoflex based compression sensor

The double components of Ecoflex were mixed upcompletely before being poured into the self-made template with the size of 5mm × 10mm × 10mm. The prepared encapsulated conductive fabric was attached on the both sides of the elastomer Ecoflex.

2.5 XRD measurement of pressure sensor

To clarify the deposition of Ag nano-particles on the nylon fabrics, XRD was used to measure the characteristic peaks of Ag.

2.6 Property testing of the fabric based pressure sensor

The square resistance of the conductive fabric was measured by RTS−8 four-probe resistance tester.

Mechanical property and electricity response of the corresponding pressure sensor were measured through compression test of composites using a micro force tension meter Instron 5565A with a load cell capacity of 100N. The capacitance of the pressure sensor was measured by TH8090(Changzhou)(Fig. 1).

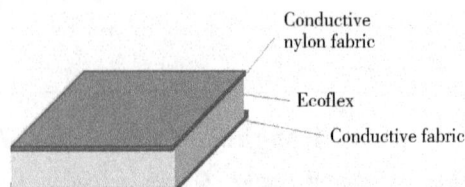

Fig. 1　Structure of conductive fabric based pressure sensor

3 Results and Discussion

3.1 SEM measurement and square resistance of the conductive fabric

The square resistance of the treated fabric was $0.268\Omega \cdot cm$, which shows a high electricity conductivity. This is because the nylon fabric has a high fabric density and the Ag nano-particles can be attached on the fabric after the activation. The SEM and EDS spectrums of the conductive silk fabric were showed in Fig. 2. From the SEM image, it can be shown that the weft and warp yarns were closed to each other, so that the fabric has high electricity conductive after coating with Ag nano-particles on the surface. The EDS spectrums show that the Ag nano-particles were distributed attached.

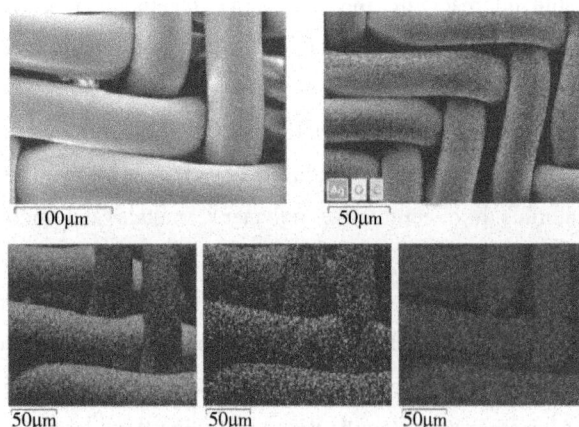

Fig. 2　SEM image and EDS spectrums of the conductive fabric after sputtering with Ag

3.2 Property measurement of the fabric based pressure sensor

The capacitance of the sensor (C_{sensor}) can be described by the following parameters: electrode area (S), dielectric thickness (d), and permittivity of the dielectric (ε). Equation (1) describes the change-in-capacitance due to variations in dielectric layer thickness

$$C = \frac{\varepsilon s}{4\pi kd} \qquad (1)$$

When a pressure was applied on the sensor, the distance between two electrodes would decrease. In addition to the dielectric thickness change, variations in the effective relative permittivity of the dielectric under the pressure loading also contributes to a change in capacitance. Fig. 3 shows the electrical response of the fabric based sensors. Measured sensitivities were 0.6913kPa^{-1} for the sensor, with a good linearity of 0.991 (R^2), in the area of 0 to 162kPa. With pressure increasing, the capacitance variation shows a relation of logarithmic function. From 600kPa^{-1} to 800kPa^{-1}, the sensitivity is 0.05643kPa^{-1}. This is because with the distance between two electrodes decreasing when pressing, more forces were needed to change the same quantity of capacitance.

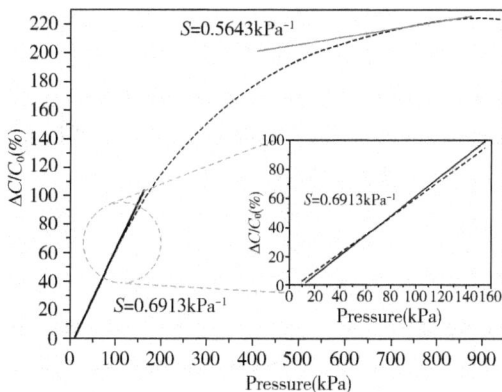

Fig. 3   Relative change in sensors' capacitance under pressure for the sensors consists of Ecoflex dielectric layer with conductive fabric electrodes

The elastomer named Ecoflex has a quick response to the applied pressure. Fig. 4 shows the capacitance variation when applying a certain distance of 0.6mm, with the corresponding load of 0.25N to the composite. The results show that the capacitance type sensor has a quick response time, which is as short as 0.801s. Also, it can be also showed that when a certain pressure and force was hold for 5 seconds, the capacitance response was very stable.

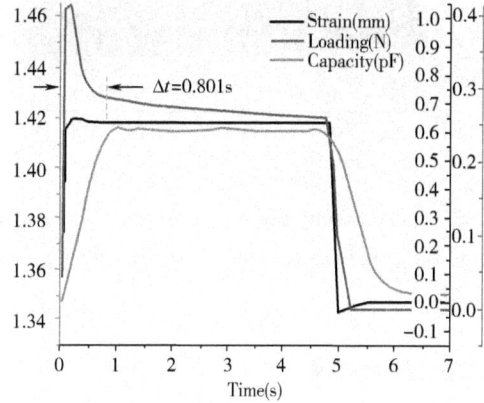

Fig. 4   Capacitance variation when holding the pressure sensor for 5 seconds with the displacement of 0.6mm

3.3 Cycle stability of the pressure sensor

The pressure sensor showed a stable response to the pressure of 100Pa and 10kPa, respectively, which is shown in Fig. 5. The conductive fabric based sensor can response to different pressure stably and validly.

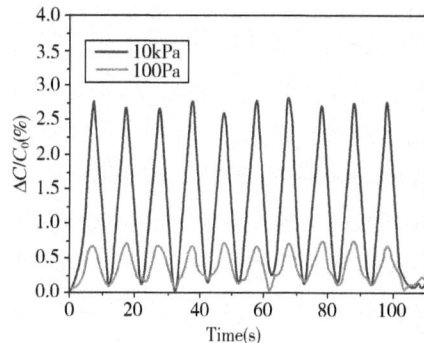

Fig. 5   The capacitance variation for 10 times under the pressure of 100Pa and 10kPa, respectively

A cycling test was carried out to measure the stability of the pressure sensor. It can be seen from Fig. 6 that the pressure sensor has a very good stability with the capacitance loss of 0.0534 when recycling for 9500 times. Also, it can be speculated that there is no damage and electricity loss for the conductive fabric and the bonding section of the electrodes.

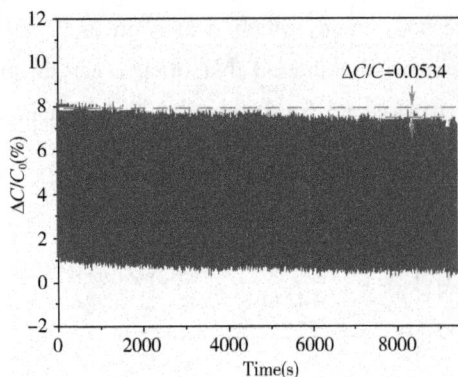

Fig. 6 Cycle stability test of the pressure sensor under the pressure of 10kPa for 9500 times, with the frequency of 0.5Hz

4 Conclusions

In this work, we fabricated a flexible and wearable pressure sensor with conductive nylon fabric as electrodes and elastomer Ecoflex as dielectric layer. The high conductive nylon fabric was obtained by magnetron sputtering with Ag nanoparticles. The nylon fabric was first treated by alcohol washing for 30 minutes, followed with radioactivation activated by $SnCl_2$. The conductive nylon fabric which showed a high conductivity of $0.268\Omega \cdot cm$ (square resistance). The double-component Ecoflex was mixed up completely and was poured into a self-made mould at the size of $1mm \times 1mm \times 0.5mm$, which was made into the dielectric layer of the fabric based flexible sensor. The flexible pressure sensor shows a high sensitivity of $0.6190kPa^{-1}$, a good linearity of $0.991(R^2)$ under the pressure from 0kPa and 162kPa, and a quick response time of $0.801s$. Also, the pressure sensor has a good stability, when press and reply for 9500 times, the capacitance loss rate is only 0.0534. The fabric based flexible and wearable sensor with good properties has wide potential applications and provided a prospect in the field of intelligent fabric for the acquisition of human motions and health data.

References

[1] Ge J, Sun L, Zhang F R, et al. A stretchable electronic fabric artificial skin with pressure-, lateral strain-, and flexion-sensitive properties[J], Advanced Materials, 2016, 28 (4): 722-728.

[2] Lee J, Kwon H, Seo J, et al. Conductive fiber-based ultrasensitive textile pressure sensor for wearable electronics[J], Advanced Materials, 2015, 27(15): 2433-2439.

[3] Hu L, Pasta M, Mantia F L, et al. Stretchable, porous, and conductive energy textiles[J], Nano Letters, 2010, 10(2): 708.

[4] Zeng W, Tao X M, Chen S, et al. Highly durable all-fiber nanogenerator for mechanical energy harvesting[J], Energy & Environmental Science, 2013, 6(9): 2631-2638.

[5] Chang H C, Liu C L, Chen W C. Flexible nonvolatile transistor memory devices based on one-dimensional electrospun P3ht:Au hybrid nanofibers[J], Advanced Functional Materials, 2013, 23(39): 4960-4968.

[6] Paul D L, Giddens H, Paterson M G, et al. Impact of body and clothing on a wearable textile dual band antenna at digital television and wireless communications bands[J], IEEE Transactions on Antennas and Propagation, 2013, 61(4): 2188-2194.

[7] Rajesh, Ahuja T, Kumar D. Recent progress in the development of nano-structured conducting polymers/nanocomposites for sensor applications[J], Sensors & Actuators B Chemical, 2009, 136(1): 275-286.

[8] Wang Q, Jian M Q, Wang C Y, et al. Carbonized silk nanofiber membrane for transparent and sensitive electronic skin [J], Advanced Functional Materials, 2017, 27(9).

[9] Atalay O, Atalay A, Gafford J, et al. A highly sensitive capacitive-based soft pressure sensor based on a conductive fabric and a microporous dielectric layer[J], Advanced Materials Technologies, 2018, 3(1).

[10] Li J F, Xu B G. Novel highly sensitive and wearable pressure sensors from conductive three-dimensional fabric structures[J], Smart Materials and Structures, 2015, 24(12).

[11] Pu X, Li L, Liu M, et al. Wearable self-charging power textile based on flexible yarn supercapacitors and fabric nanogenerators, advanced materials[J], 2016, 28(1): 98-105.

[12] Eaton W P, Smith J H, Micromachined pressure sensors: review and recent developments[J], Smart Materials and Structures, 1997, 6(5): 530-539.

Bending Properties of 3D Integrated Woven Spacer Composites with Hybrid Carbon/Glass Fiber

Liyong Wang[1,2,3], Fujun Xu[1,2]*, Yiping Qiu[1,2]

[1]Key Laboratory of Textile Science & Technology, Ministry of Education, Shanghai 201620, China

[2]Department of Technical Textiles, College of Textiles, Donghua University, Shanghai 201620, China

[3]Shihezi Fiber Inspection Institute, Shihezi, Xinjiang 832000, China

*Corresponding author's email: fjxu@dhu.edu.cn

Abstract: The face sheets of three-dimensional (3D) integrated woven spacer fabric have an important influence on the bending properties of the spacer fabric composites. The 3D integrated woven spacer composites with different ratios of carbon/glass fibers in the surface layers are designed and prepared. The bending properties of spacer composites with hybrid different content of carbon fibers are examined. Macroscopic morphology and microscopic morphology are studied to understand the fracture and failure mechanisms. The results indicate that the bending properties of the spacer composites are significantly affected by the carbon fibers that are intermingled into the surface layers. Compared to the spacer composites with pure glass fibers, as the carbon fiber content increases, the bending modulus increases by 14.82%, 17.49%, 37.39%, 46.18% and 51.11%, respectively, while the bending stiffness increases by 26.30%, 26.25%, 54.58%, 61.75%, 68.05% and 74.80%, respectively. The deformation and fracture of the compression face sheets are the main failure mode of the spacer composite. There is no visible deformation or fracture in the tension face sheets and the pile yarns. Linear elastic stages and brittle fractures are obviously observed during the bending process. The interfacial bonding performance of carbon fibers and resin is poor, and the fracture sections of carbon fiber yarns are uneven, and the phenomenon of delamination, degumming and extraction is prone to occur. Hence, the interfacial binding performance needs to be further improved.

Keywords: Three-dimension; Spacer composites; Bending properties; Hybrid; Failure mechanism

1 Introduction

The development of composite materials is more and more inclined to textile-based high-strength and lightweight designs[1-2]. Spacer fabrics are complex three-dimensional (3D) constructions, consist of two plane outer layers connected vertically by pile yarns or fabric layers[3], exhibit a great potential for weight reduction. To meet requirements of high performance and lightweight, in the past, many scholars have studied the mechanical properties of 3D integrated woven spacer composites. Wang et al.[4], Li et al.[5] studied the mechanical performance of 3D spacer composites by additional weave to strengthen the facesheets. The results showed that additional weaves can enhance the mechanical performances relative to the face-sheets effectively, especially for flexural and edge wise compressive properties. In addition, Wang et al.[6] indicated that the bending stiffness and edgewise strength increased with increased additional weave layer numbers, and for the flexural test, the effect of the additional weave became smaller after a certain layer number. Moreover, the distribution manner of the additional weave layers had little influence on the bending stiffness. Fan et al.[7] studied that the bending properties of 3D spacer composites with different thicknesses and spans along weft and warp direction, respectively, which indicated that the fracture process exhibits three stages: elastic deflection, shear failure by face-sheet crippling and plastic rotation, and the weak mechanical properties of the woven face-sheets were the main shortcoming of the spacer composites. Li et al. [8-9], Sadighi et al. [10], Jia et al. [11] investigated the bending properties of spacer composites on pile height, pile distribution density, warp/weft direction, and liquid nitrogen temperature, and the results revealed that the bending stiffness of spacer fabric composites increase with increasing pile height and the distribution density, and the bending properties in the warp/weft direction showed a significant anisotropic behavior, and the bending properties at liquid nitrogen temperature were improved significantly than those at room temperature.

As stated above, the study of the bending properties for 3D integrated woven spacer composites mainly focuses on the pile height, pile distribution density, the thickness of the surface layer, and the processing temperature of spacer composites and so on. The influences of hybrid intralayer on mechanical properties of spacer composites have been paid little attention. In the paper, the bending properties of 3D spacer fabric composites with different hybrid proportion of carbon/glass fibers in the face sheets are checked. By means of microscopy and scanning electron microscope (SEM), the damage and fracture morphology of the spacer composites after bending failure is studied. The influence of hybrid carbon fibers on bending properties and the failure mechanism is demonstrated. The aim of the paper is to present a oretical basis for future research and application.

2 Material and Specimen Fabrication

Fig. 1 shows the schematic structure diagram for 3D integrated woven spacer composites. It consists of two separate surface layers woven integrally by the interpenetration of pile yarns. The single pile can be viewed similarly the form of "goblet"-shape in warp direction, and the adjacent piles to resemble the "8"-shape, while the piles resemble the "1"-shape in weft direction.

In the study, the 3D integrated hybrid spacer fabrics were woven with E-glass fibers (Yarn type EDR13-300-386, Yarn fineness 300tex, Jushi Group Co., Ltd.) and carbon fibers (Yarn type T300B-3000-

40B, Toray Industries, Inc.), which were woven by reformed 3D loom. Fig. 2 shows the morphology of carbon and glass fibers.

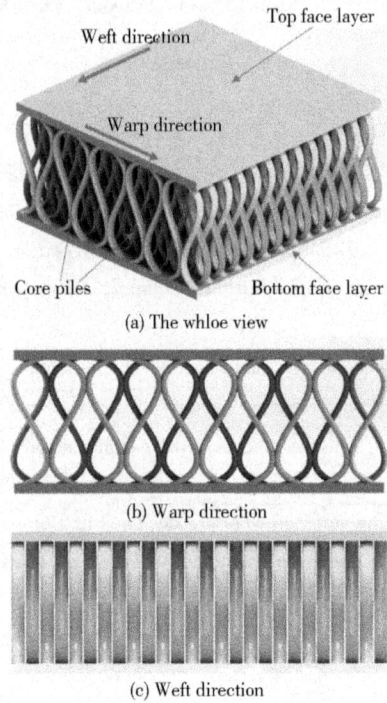

(a) The whloe view

(b) Warp direction

(c) Weft direction

Fig. 1   The schematic structure diagrams for 3D integrated woven spacer composites

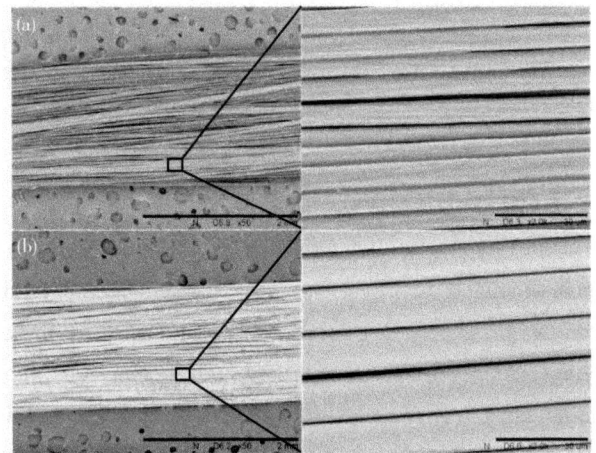

Fig. 2   The appearance of (a) carbon fibers and (b) glass fibers used in the spacer composites

Fig. 3 displays the configuration and morphology of seven types of 3D integrated woven spacer composites with hybrid carbon/glass fibers. It was clearly noted that the carbon fibers could be only found as weft yarns in the face sheets of plain weave, and the number of carbon fiber yarn was regularly increasing in the seven types of 3D integrated hybrid spacer composites. And the weft yarn sorting schemes of carbon fibers and glass fibers were different in seven different types of 3D integrated spacer fabrics: G, C/G/G/G, C/G/G, C/G, C/C/G, C/C/C/G, C, and the corresponding spacer composites were named as [G], [C/G/G/G], [C/G/G], [C/G], [C/C/G], [C/C/C/G], [C], respectively. During the manufacturing process, all the woven parameters were fixed except changing the sorting schemes of weft yarn to guarantee the comparability between seven types of 3D integrated woven spacer fabric composites. The preforms with different weft yarn were dropped with epoxy resin (JL‐235, Changshu Jiafa Chemical Co., Ltd.), using hand lay-up molding process. The mass ratio of epoxy resin and curing agent (JH‐242, Changshu Jiafa Chemical Co., Ltd.) was 100∶33. When the whole preform was uniformly wet, put it in the oven with pre-curing at 50℃ for 3h and curing at 70℃ for 7h. And then the composites were cut to ensure perfectly parallel along the weft yarn, and the specimen dimensions were 160mm × 30mm for bending tests. The detail parameters of bending samples tested were given in Tab.1.

Fig.3　The configuration photographs of 3D integrated woven spacer composites with hybrid carbon/glass fibers in the face sheets (a) face sheets; (b) weft direction; (c) warp direction

Tab.1　Details of bending samples

Type	Width (mm)	Height (mm)	Length (mm)	Surface layer (mm)	Weight (g)	Fiber volume fraction of face sheet in weft direction (%)
[G]	29.48	6.49	160.3	0.65	16.57	21.88
[C/G/G/G]	30.29	6.62	159.2	0.67	16.98	19.32
[C/G/G]	29.43	6.67	160.2	0.68	16.73	19.19
[C/G]	29.35	6.66	159.6	0.71	16.93	18.34
[C/C/G]	29.52	6.77	160.7	0.71	16.76	17.15
[C/C/C/G]	29.74	6.72	159.3	0.70	16.79	16.70
[C]	29.50	6.76	158.3	0.70	15.99	15.47

3　Experimental Procedure

The three-point bending tests on INSTRON 6957 testing machine in accordance with the standards of ASTM C393/C393M, ASTM D790 and Chinese GB/T 1456—2005. The cross-head speed is maintained at a rate of 3mm/min with the span length of 80mm. No less than 5 specimens were tested in weft direction, and the average values of the testing results are obtained. Before being tested, it was noticed that the bending specimens were ground to ensure horizontally parallel top and bottom sheets, and then the upper pressure head was ensured vertical for the tested samples and kept in the middle of span length in each testing process. The experimental procedure is shown schematically in Fig. 4.

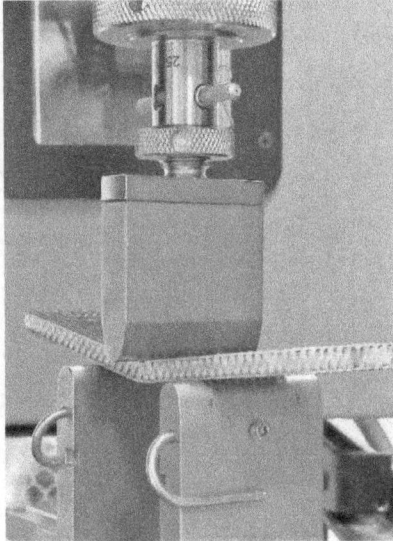

Fig. 4 The experimental procedure of bending test

4 Results and Discussion

4.1 Hybrid composites under bending load

Fig. 5 gives the load-displacement curves for seven types of 3D integrated woven spacer composites with hybrid carbon/glass fibers. It can be readily observed that the composites behave almost linear elastic properties in the initial stage of the curves, and then suffer obvious brittle fracture after running up to the peak load. The peak loads of different hybrid spacer composites are decreasing gradually with the content of carbon fiber increasing. This phenomenon is consistent with the law of weakest-link for composites[12]. Due to the large rigidity and brittleness of carbon fibers, the number of fractured carbon fibers increases dramatically with the increase of carbon fiber content in the bending test, resulting in the fact that the load that causes the fracture of the carbon fibers must be sustained by the unbroken glass fibers, which accelerates the destruction of the surfaces of the composites.

In addition, Fig. 6 shows the change trend of bending displacement and strain for different composites with hy-

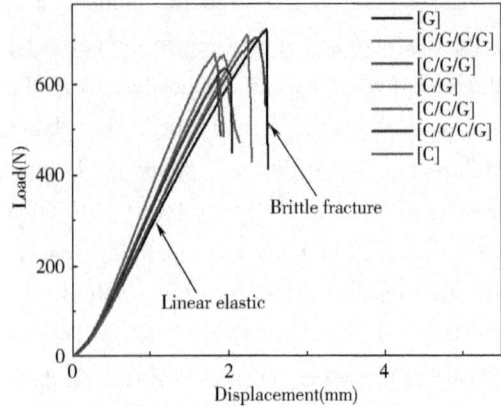

Fig. 5 The load-displacement curves for different hybrid spacer composites

brid carbon/glass fiber. It can be easily observed that the bending displacement and strain decline significantly with the content increase of carbon fiber. This also illustrates that, compared to the glass fibers, carbon fibers are easy to be damaged under the bending load, and because of the damage of carbon fibers in advance, the glass fibers are also damaged due to the excessive amount of bending load caused by the damaged carbon fibers.

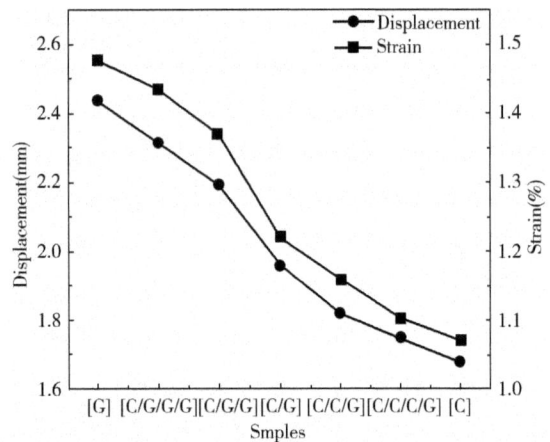

Fig. 6 Comparison of peak displacements and peak strains for different hybrid spacer composites

Therefore, the above-mentioned peak loads of the spacer composites with hybrid carbon/glass fibers gradually decrease as the carbon content increases.

Fig. 7 shows the comparison of the peak stress for different spacer composites with hybrid carbon/glass fiber. The stresses are calculated according to the following formula:

$$\sigma_f = \frac{PL}{2t(d + c)b} \tag{1}$$

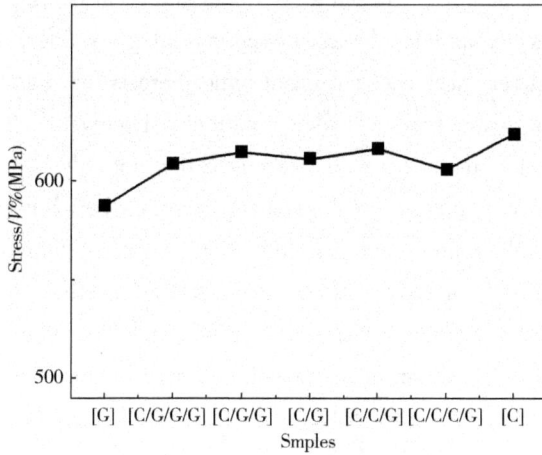

Fig. 7   Comparison of the peak stress for different hybrid spacer composites

Where σ_f is the facing bending stress, P is the load, L is the span length, t is the facing thickness, d is the spacer composite thickness, c is the core thickness, b is the spacer composite width.

From Fig. 7, it can be also noted that though the values of peak stress for different hybrid spacer composites are a certain extent of improvement and fluctuation, the increments of different hybrid spacer composites are not very significant. Compared to the [G], growth proportions of peak stress for different hybrid spacer composites are orderly 3.61, 4.53, 4.02, 4.82, 3.09 and 6.17 percentages.

Fig. 8 shows the comparison of the elastic modulus and bending stiffness for different spacer composites with hybrid carbon/glass fiber. The elastic modulus and bending stiffness are calculated by the following formulas:

$$E_f = \frac{L^3}{4bd^3}\left(\frac{\Delta P}{\Delta \delta}\right) \tag{2}$$

$$D = \frac{E_f(d^3 - c^3)}{12} \tag{3}$$

Where E_f is the elastic modulus, ΔP is the load increment of the initial line segment on the bending load-displacement curve, $\Delta \delta$ is the displacement increment at the midspan point corresponding to ΔP, D is the bending stiffness.

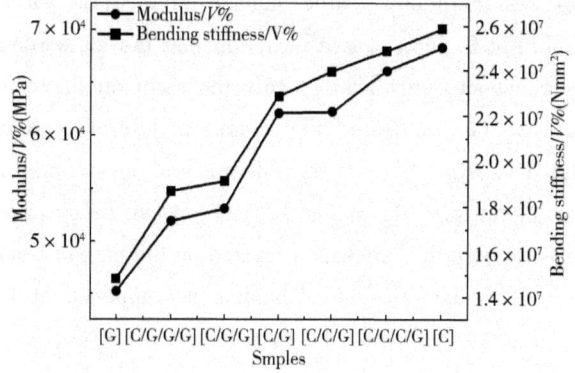

Fig. 8   Comparison of elastic modulus and bending stiffness for different hybrid spacer composites

From Fig. 7, it can be found that the variation trend of bending stiffness for different hybridspacer composites is consistent with that of elastic modulus, and compared with [G], the values of elastic modulus and bending stiffness for different hybrid spacer composites are remarkably increased with the increase of carbon fiber content[12]. Compared with the [G], the values of elastic modulus for different hybrid spacer composites are increased by 14.82, 17.49, 37.39, 46.18 and 51.11 percentage, respectively. While the properties of bending stiffness for different hybrid spacer composites are more significantly improved, and the values of bending stiffness are accordingly up by 26.30, 26.25, 54.58, 61.75, 68.05 and 74.80 percentage. The phenomenon mainly stems from the fact that apart from the property of carbon fiber itself, the deformation of glass fibers is, to a certain extent, restrained by carbon fibers woven into surface-sheets of spacer fabrics, and the inhibitory effect is enhanced gradually with the increase of carbon fiber content. Therefore, the elastic modulus of hybrid spacer composites increases gradually[13].

4.2   Failure mechanism of hybrid spacer composites

Fig. 9 and Fig. 10 show the failure modes of brittle fracture for [G] and [C] in the compression testing process, respectively. From the two figures, it can be obviously seen that the compression faces of [G] and [C] were broken, and cataclastic resin and fractured yarns were visible under the squeeze head. However, there was no visible damage to the tension faces of [G] and [C], nor was there any visible damage on the pile yarns. From Fig. 9 (c), it can be found that the glass fibers were not suddenly brittle, only the resin on the compression face appeared tiny cracks and turned white. But the carbon fibers were different from glass fibers in the lateral face. From Fig. 10 (c), it can be observed that not only the breakage occurred on the carbon fibers and resin, but also the delamination happened at the interface of the damaged carbon fiber and warp yarn. In summary, there is only the compression failure on the upper layer of the spacer fabric composites in the initial stage of bending damage.

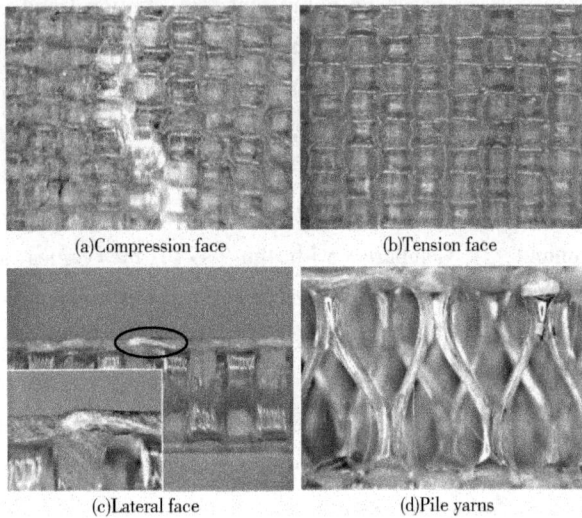

(a)Compression face   (b)Tension face

(c)Lateral face   (d)Pile yarns

Fig. 9　The initial fracture photographs of sample [G]

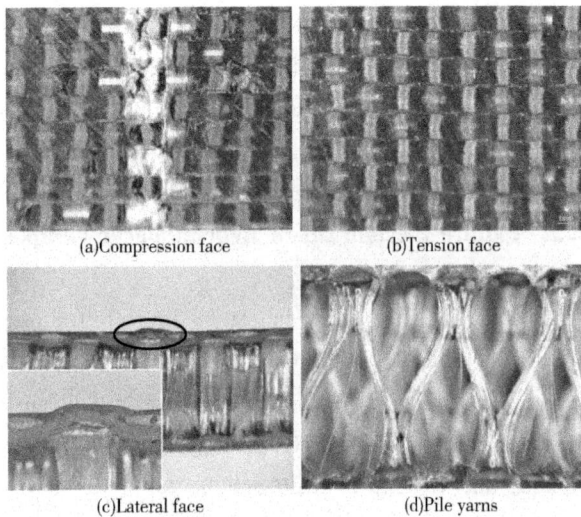

(a)Compression face   (b)Tension face

(c)Lateral face   (d)Pile yarns

Fig. 10　The initial fracture photographs of sample [C]

Fig. 11 and Fig. 12 show the fracture modes of glass fibers and carbon fibers in the compression face, respectively. It can be pointed out from Fig. 11 that the interfacial bonding between glass fibers and resin is relatively good, and the breakage sections of glass fibers are relatively neat and consistent, and there is few glass fibers extraction or delamination. However, from Fig. 12, it can be clearly observed that not only is there a serious question of degumming situation between carbon fibers and resin, but also there are more fibers extracted from resin. In addition, the destructive cross-sections of carbon fibers are uneven and the delamination phenomenon for carbon fibers is relatively serious. There are left over matrix without fibers after the carbon fibers are broken. This needs to show that the interface properties of the carbon fibers and the resin are poor.

Fig. 11　The SEM photographs of bending fracture for sample [G]

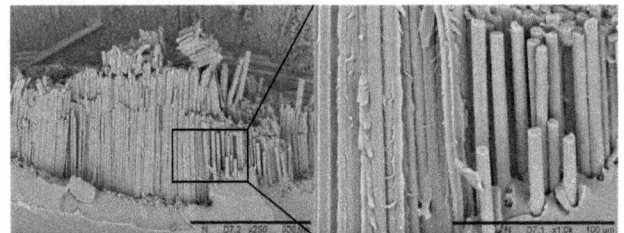

Fig. 12　The SEM photographs of bending fracture for sample [C]

5　Conclusions

The bending properties of 3D integrated woven spacer composites are studied by changing the fiber types and hybrid ratios in the face sheets. The results indicate that the load-displacement curves of different hybrid spacer composites reveal obvious linear elastic feature before the peak loads, and then brittle failure occurs in all composites. Moreover, peak loads, peak displacements, peak strains of all hybrid spacer composites gradually drop off as the increase of carbon fiber content. However, the stress of different hybrid spacer composites is not significantly affected by the carbon fiber content, but only slightly increased, while the variation of elastic modulus and bending stiffness for different hybrid composites is very obviously improved, almost straight rise. Compared to [G], the elastic modulus and bending stiffness for [C] are increased by 51.11% and 74.80%, respectively.

The examination and analysis of macro and microfracture morphology for different hybrid spacer composites indicate that the damage and fracture of weft yarn in the face sheets are the main failure mode, including the fiber extraction and fracture. The glass fibers and resin have good bonding properties in the interface, and glass fibers mainly appear fracture damage, and the broken cross-sections of glass fibers are relatively uniform. However, carbon fibers often easily suffer from fracture and delamination, and the fracture sections are uneven. The interfacial properties of carbon fibers and resin are very poor, need to be further improved.

References

[1] Mountasir A, Hoffmann G, Cherif C. Development of multi-layered woven panels with integrated stiffeners in the transverse and longitudinal directions for thermoplastic lightweight applications[J]. Textile Research J, 2013, 83(14): 1532-1540.

[2] Mountasir A, Hoffmann G, Cherif C, et al. Development of non-crimp multi-layered 3D spacer fabric structures using hybrid yarns for thermoplastic composites [J]. Procedia Mat Sci, 2013: 210-17.

[3] Abounaim M D, Cherif C, Flat-Knitted. Innovative three-dimensional spacer fabrics: a competitive solution for lightweight composite applications [J]. Textile Research J, 2011, 82(3): 288-298.

[4] Wang S K, Li M, Gu Y Z, et al. Mechanical reinforcement of three-dimensional spacer fabric composites [J]. Mat Sci Forum, 2010, 654-656: 2604-2607.

[5] Li D S, Zhao C Q, Jiang N, et al. Fabrication, properties and failure of 3D integrated woven spacer composites with thickened face sheets [J]. Mat Letters, 2015, 14(8): 103-105.

[6] Shaokai W, Min L, Zuoguang Z, et al. Properties of facesheet-reinforced 3D spacer fabric composites and the integral multi-facesheet structures [J]. J of Reinforced Plastics and Comp, 2009, 29(6): 793-806.

[7] Fan H, Zhou Q, Yang W, et al. An experiment study on the failure mechanisms of woven textile sandwich panels under quasi-static loading [J]. Composites Part B: Engg, 2010, 41(8): 686-692.

[8] Li M, Wang S, Zhang Z, et al. Effect of structure on the mechanical behaviors of three-dimensional spacer fabric composites [J]. App Comp Mat, 2008, 16(1): 1-14.

[9] Li D S, Zhao C Q, Jiang L, et al. Experimental study on the bending properties and failure mechanism of 3D integrated woven spacer composites at room and cryogenic temperature [J]. Composite Structures, 2014, 111: 56-65.

[10] Sadighi M, Hosseini S A. Finite element simulation and experimental study on mechanical behavior of 3D woven glass fiber composite sandwich panels [J]. Composites Part B: Engineering, 2013, 55: 158-166.

[11] Jia L X, Wang R, Liu J M, et al. Influence of reinforcement structure on the flexural properties of sandwich composite panels [J]. Materials Res Innovations, 2015, 19(1): 381-387.

[12] Manders P W, Bader M G. The strength of hybrid glass/carbon fibre composites [J]. J of Mat Sci, 1981, 16(8): 2246-2256.

[13] Zeng S, Jia Z, Hou B, et al. Tensile properties of unidirectional carbon fiber-glass fiber hybrid reinforced epoxy composites in layer [J]. Acta Materiae Compositae Sinica, 2016, 88: 172-177.

Chemical Stable, Superhydrophobic and Self-Cleaning Fabrics Prepared by Two-Step Coating of Polytetrafluoroethylene Membrane and Silica Nanoparticles

Tasixiang Yeerken[1,2], Hongling Liu[1,2]*, Weidong Yu[1,2]

[1] *Key Laboratory of Textile Science & Technology, Ministry of Education, Shanghai 201620, China*

[2] *Department of Technical Textiles, College of Textiles, Donghua University, Shanghai 201620, China*

* *Corresponding author's email*: hlliu@ dhu. edu. cn

Abstract: A superhydrophobic fabric with a novel self-cleaning ability and excellent chemical stability was prepared by two-step coating technique using an easily available material system consisting of Poly-*m*-phenyleneisophthalamide (PMIA), Polytetrafluoroethylene (PTFE) membrane and silica nanoparticles. Compared with the original fabric, the contact angle of PMIA fabrics varied from completely infiltrating to 130° after compounding with PTFE membrane through hot process. When the fabric was coated with PTFE particles and SiO_2 nanoparticles, the hydrophobicity was significantly enhanced with contact angle 154° and rolling angle 4° due to the role of low surface energy and rough nanostructures observed by SEM images. Furthermore, the coated fabric could withstand at least 300 cycles of abrasion without apparently changing its superhydrophobicity. The coating fabric was also very stable to immerse in different pH value solutions after 100 hours. There were slightly enlarging pores after the coating fabrics were attacked by strong H_2SO_4 (98%) and NaOH (40%) for one hour. The simple but effective coating fabric may be useful for the development of individual protective clothing for emergency rescue application.

Keywords: PMIA; PTFE; Chemical stability; Superhydrophobocity; Self-cleaning

1 Introduction

Chemical protective clothing for emergency rescue is personal protective equipment that people involved in the rescue operations. Due to the extremely complicated rescue environment, it is necessary to have excellent performances like resistance to chemical corrosion with super-hydrophobic and self-cleaning properties for high-grade clothing for chemical protection. At present, great efforts have been made to design superhydrophobic and self-cleaning surfaces through fabrication of appropriate roughness and low surface energy[1-4].

There were several strategies to improve the durability, such as cross-linking the durable coating layer[5], creating multi-scaled roughness on the substrate[6], establishing chemical bonds between substrate and coating[7] and endowing the coating with nanocomposite structure[8]. However, it is still a challenge to fabricate superhydrophobic fabrics with chemical durable and rapid self-cleaning properties at the same time through a low cost and time-saving method for commercial individual protection.

PMIA fabrics were mainly used as substrate due to its excellent chemical and mechanical properties in commercially protective clothes[9-11]. PTFE membrane or PTFE particles which owing to good hydrophobicity and excellent chemical stability performances were able to lower the surface tension through coating process[1, 12]. The superhydrophobic coating layer was achieved by SiO_2 modification through forming roughness on the surfaces[2, 13]. As far as we know, superhydrophobic modification which is suitable for preparing PMIA/PTFE fabrics which were obtained by hot press has been scarcely reported in recent research literature.

In this work, we used two-steps coating route to fabricate chemically durable fabrics with function of super-hydrophobocity and rapid self-cleaning ability. The coating was highly stable against H_2SO_4 (98%), NaOH (40%) for at least 1 hour and also withstood in strong acid/base solutions for 100 hours. Furthermore, the coating maintained superhydrophobocity after extreme physical abrasion with a specific self-cleaning ability. Thus, this durable and rapid self-cleaning fabric shows potential application in multifunctional protective textiles.

2 Experiments

2.1 Materials and characterization

PMIA fabric (plain wave, $170g/m^2$, thickness $600\mu m$) was supplied by Tayho Co., Ltd., China; PTFE membrane (Thickness $0.3\mu m$), PTFE dispersions (solid content 60%), PTFE powders with the average particles size of $1-3\mu m$ were purchased from DuPont Co., USA; Penetrant JFC and KH550 cross-linker were provided by Dow Corning Co., USA; silica (SiO_2) nanoparticles of 7nm in mean diameter was obtained from Aladdin Chemical Regent Co., China. Acetone, sulfuric acid (98%), NaOH were procured from Sinopharm Chemical Reagent Co., Ltd. Commercially available fabrics were cleaned with acetone and deionized water sequentially before use.

Flex SEM 1000 Scanning Electron Microscope was used to study surface morphology. The hydrophobicity was measured with Attention Optical Contact Angle Analyzer (DKSH Ltd., China). Contact angles were obtained at a room temperature measuring at least five different points of one sample. Abrasion properties were investigated through YG (B) 401E fabric leveling machine. Abrasive wool fabrics with a diameter of 140mm were used as abradants. A load pressure of 12kPa was employed, which was typically used for evaluating heavy duty upholstery usages. Fourier transform infrared spectroscopy was employed using Nicolet 5700 Fourier transform infrared (FTIR) spectra (Thermo Nicolet Co., USA) to examine the chemical composition and the change of surface functionalities. The UV transmittance of the samples was analyzed by U-4100 Ultraviolet Visible Near Infrared spectrophotometer (Hitachi, Japan).

2.2 Pre-treatment

The original MPIA fabrics were pre-treated in order to remove impurities on the fabric surface. NaOH and penetrant JFC (mass ratio 5:1) were added in deionized water with a decoction ratio of 20:1. Then the pre-treatment solution was obtained by placing in an oven which set 50℃, 1h. The PMIA fabrics were immersed in the solution and then was placed to dry in an oven for 1h at 50℃ after washed until the pH=7.

2.3 Preparation of composite fabrics

The composite fabric was composed of two layers, chemical resistant layer and waterproof layer. The procedure to prepare the composite fabric was schematically illustrated in Fig. 1.

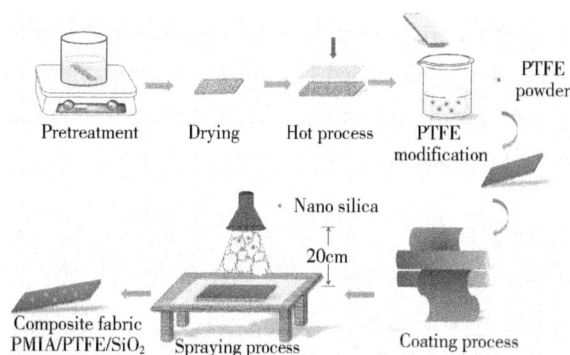

Fig. 1 Preparation procedure for composite fabric PMIA/PTFE/SiO₂

The chemical resistance layer was achieved by compounding PMIA fabrics with PTFE membrane under the condition of 180℃, 3MPa and 10min.

PTFE particles, adhesive polyacrylate (mass fraction 5:1:1) and 1mL KH550 coupling agents were mixed under stirring at room temperature for 30min. PMIA/PTFE fabrics were immersed in ready suspension for 3min and then placed to dry in an oven for 1 hour at 60℃.

Based on previous studies, a homogenous coating solution with SiO_2 (2%) was obtained after 30min ultrasonic stirring. Superhydrophobic surface was obtained by spraying process and then the final composite fabric was obtained through drying in an oven at 60℃ for 1 hour.

3 Results and Discussion

3.1 Chemical stability of composite fabrics

To prove the stability of anti-chemical properties, the liquid droplets 5 μL NaOH (40%), and H_2SO_4 (98%) were left on the composite fabric for 1 hour at room temperature. The liquid corrosion and penetration properties on the uncoated fabric and coated fabric surfaces were observed by SEM images as shown in Fig. 2 from the SEM images in Fig. 2 (b), it can be observed that PMIA fabric exhibited smooth surface even corroded by NaOH after 1 hour. At the same time, a porous membrane without visible single fibers was found after being corroded by oil of vitriol as shown in Fig. 2 (c), indicating the crosslinking of concentrated sulfuric acid with PMIA fibers led to the surface corrosion of the fabrics. When the PMIA fabric was coated with PTFE membrane, the holes eroded by acid were larger than those of base, Fig. 3. It was proved that the strong acid damaged PTFE membrane more than the strong alkali.

Fig. 2 (a) PMIA fabric; (b) Corroded by NaOH (40%); (c) H_2SO_4 (98%) after 1h

Fig. 3 (a) PMIA/PTFE; (b) PMIA/PTFE fabric corroded by NaOH (40%); (c) PMIA/PTFE corroded by H_2SO_4 (98%) after 1h

In order to further investigate the chemical stability of the composite fabric, the fabric samples were immersed in different solutions with the pH = 1 – 14 for 100 hour to study the weight loss rate in the acid/base environment. It can be seen from Fig. 4, the weight loss rate curve of original and composite fabrics at different pH solutions showed a trend of decreased and then increased by the changes of acid to alkaline. There was no obvious change in neutral pH range in both uncoated and coated fabrics while large in strong acid and alkali environment. For the composite fabric, the weight loss rate changed from 4.73% to 0 when the pH increased from 1 to 7, and then increased to 5.39% when the pH increased to 14. Under the same pH condition, the weight loss rate of the composite fabric was lower than that of the original fabric, especially in a very high or a low pH solution. For example, when the pH was equal to 14, the weight loss of the coated fabric (5.39%) was reduced by 49.58% compared to the untreated fabric (10.69%), indicating the improved chemical stability after coating process.

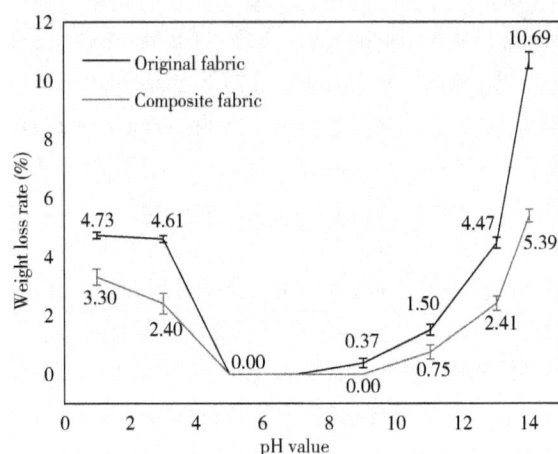

Fig. 4 The weight loss rate of fabrics at different pH (after 100h)

3.2 Superhydrophobocity

As shown in Fig. 5, the superhydrophobocity along with related SEM images of PMIA, PMIA/PTFE and PMIA/PTFE/SiO_2 fabrics. For the PMIA fabric, the contact angle was 11° due to the hydrophilic nature of PMIA fibers. As indicated in Fig. 5 (a) and Fig. 5 (d). Fig. 5 (b) indicated that the PMIA/PTFE fabric showed a enhancing contact angle of 130° due to the low surface tension of PTFE membrane, which was well known to obtain a good hydrophobicity with porous structures, Fig. 5 (e). However, when the surface of PTFE membrane was treated with SiO_2 nanoparticles, protruded roughness structure was formed on the surface according to Fig. 5 (f). Based on Wenzel's prediction, for the PTFE membrane, a hydrophobic surface with contact angle > 90°, roughness could enhance hydrophobicity[13]. Therefore, the distributed aggregates consists of further rougher nanostructures could be responsible for the observed quasi-spherical shape of water drops on the coated substrates with a high contact angle of 154°, Fig. 5 (c).

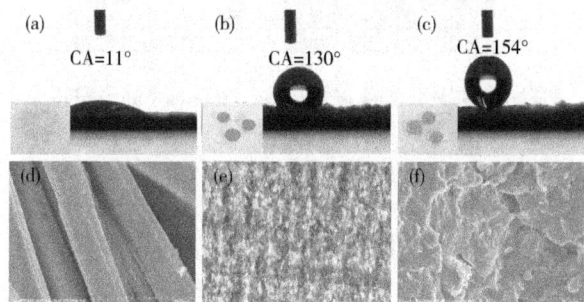

Fig. 5　(a) Contact angle of original PMIA; (b) PMIA/PTFE; (c) PMIA/PTFE/SiO₂ and corresponding photographs of blue-colored water on the fabric surface; (d) – (f) the SEM images of WCA of original PMIA, PMIA/PTFE, PMIA/PTFE/SiO₂

The dynamic wettability of the composite fabric was also measured at room temperature. It can be seen from Fig. 6(a) that the pure PTFE membrane has greater adhesion to water. After water-repellency modification, the hydrophobicity ability was enhanced significantly. Water droplets completely leaved without wetting or contaminating the coating surface, indicating the hydrophobic property was enhanced significantly after water-repellency modification, the low adhesion to the substrate surface, Fig. 6 (b).

Fig. 6　The comparison of dynamic wettability

3.3　Self-cleaning and waterproof performances

Fig. 7 showed the surface self-cleaning effect of the composite fabric finally obtained. After the drop of the methylene blue reagent powder on the coated fabric, the powder smoothly rolled on the surface without any stain immediately, indicating the good self-cleaning functions of the obtained fabric.

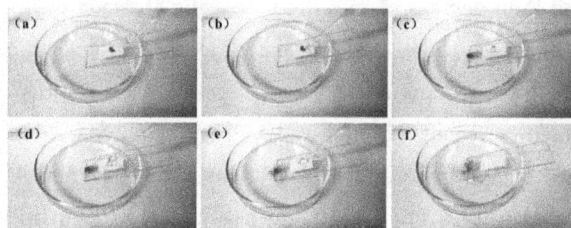

Fig. 7　(a) – (f) Self-cleaning ability of the PMIA/PTFE/SiO₂ composite fabric

The waterproof/breathable performance of coated fabrics were visually represented by observing the color change of the colored silicone[14]. As shown in Fig. 8, the hydrophilic characteristics of PMIA fabrics and the PTFE porous membrane structure led to inconspicuous allochroic silicone on the surface after 10 minutes. However, the allochroic silicagels on the surface of the composite fabric began to fade after 30 minutes. It showed that the gap of the composite fabric became smaller after being coated by PTFE and SiO₂ which affected the penetration of water vapor. Therefore, this fabric has potential applications in the harmful gas barrier fields.

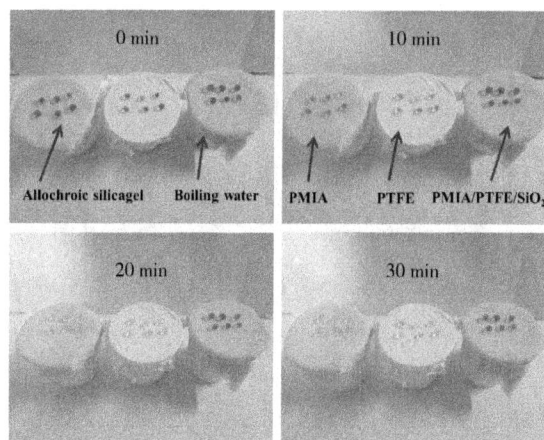

Fig. 8　Comparison tests demonstrating the waterproof/breathable performance of original PMIA (right), PTFE membrane (middle) and PMIA/PTFE/SiO₂ (left)

3.4 Abrasion durability

Fig. 9 indicated the effect of increased abrasion cycles on the contact angles and rolling angles of the composite fabrics. Contrary to the rolling angle, the contact angle of the coated fabric decreased firstly, then increased and then decreased with the increasing abrasion cycles. The results were largely related to the morphological structure of nano-silica formed on the fabric surface, which were seen from Fig. 10. For unabraded fabric, the contact angle and rolling angle were 154° and 4°, respectively, which were benefiting from roughness nanostructure of SiO_2 particles, Fig. 10 (a). As was shown in Fig. 10 (b), when the abrasion cycles were 100, the random aggregation of SiO_2 and PTFE micro-powders on the fabric surface were destroyed, resulting in corresponding the decrease of contact angle and the increase of the rolling angle. Furthermore, the further abrasion cycles, the nanoparticles formed a new stable rough nanostructure, and the hydrophobicity of the sample was restored with the contact angle 154° and rolling angle 6°, Fig. 10 (c). However, the continuing abrasion cycles could destroy the roughness again resulting in a decrease of the contact angle and an increase of the rolling angle as shown in Fig. 10 (d). Consequently, the composite fabrics still had a high contact angle of 140°, in which the rolling angle was 18° after 600 cycles of abrasion, indicating a good performance of mechanical resistance.

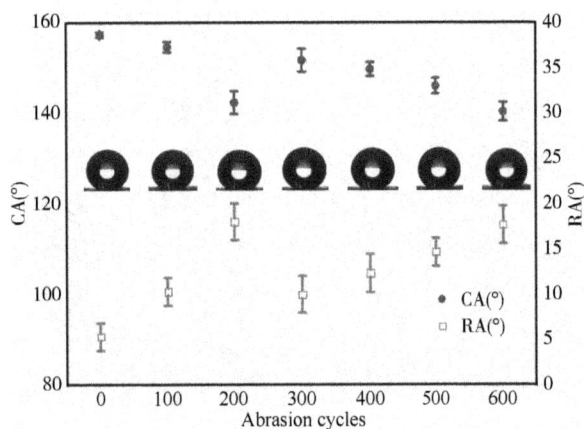

Fig. 10   SEM images of composite fabrics (a) 0 abrasion cycles, (b) 100 abrasion cycles, (c) 200 abrasion cycles and (d) 300 abrasion cycles

3.5　FTIR and UV analysis

FTIR analysis of (a) the original PMIA fabric and (b) PMIA/PTFE/SiO_2 composite fabric were shown in Fig. 11. Several characteristic absorption peaks were observed in the range between $1800 cm^{-1}$ and $700 cm^{-1}$ indicating the presence of some functional groups, such as C—F, O—Si—O and C=O in the sample. After the coating treatment, peaks at $1214.9 cm^{-1}$ and $1153.2 cm^{-1}$, which were known to the C—F bonds of PTFE have been obtained[1, 15] benefiting from the presence of PTFE coating. New peaks around $771.3 cm^{-1}$ were assigned to Si—O—Si stretching vibrations[16]. There was a stretching vibration peak at $1729.3 cm^{-1}$, which was contributed by C=O bonds[5]. These results confirmed that the introduction of PTFE membrane and modification with SiO_2 coating led to the formation of C—F and Si—O—Si bonds on the coating surface.

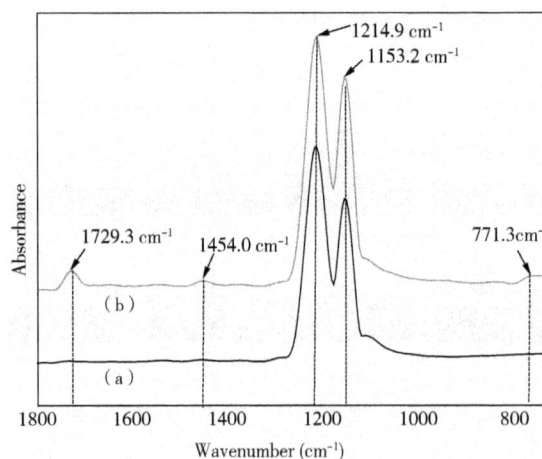

Fig. 9   Abrasion resistance performances of the composite fabric PMIA/PTFE/SiO_2

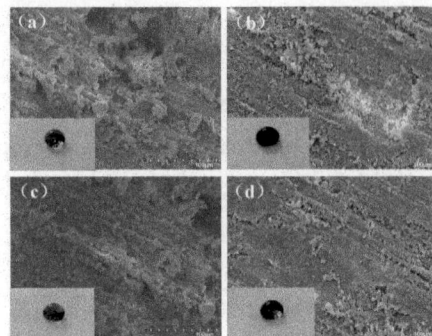

Fig. 11   FTIR analysis of (a) the original PMIA fabric and (b) PMIA/PTFE/SiO_2 composite fabric

4　Conclusions

The fabrication of chemical stable, superhydrophobi and self-cleaning composite fabric was realized by two-step coating process. The chemical resistantance was achieved through hot-pressing method compounded PMIA fabric with PTFE membrane. The superhydrophbicity and excellent self-cleaning ability with the contact angle 154° and rolling angle 4° were obtained via the combination of enhanced roughness and low surface energy derived from SiO_2. In addition, the obtained composite fabric exhibited long-term stability against strong acid/alkaline solutions for 100 hours and 300 abrasion cycles, which can still maintain its superhydrophobicity. The composite fabric also could withstand H_2SO_4 (98%) and NaOH (40%) solutions for up to 1 hour. The composite fabrics have a promising future in realizing the industrialization of the individual protective textiles for chemical protection.

Acknowledgements

This work was supported by the National Key R&D Program of China (No. 2016YFC0802802).

References

[1]Zhou H, et al. A waterborne coating system for preparing robust, self-healing, superamphiphobic surfaces [J]. Advanced Functional Materials, 2017. 27(14): 1604261.

[2]Luo G, et al. Preparation and performance enhancements of wear-resistant, transparent PU/SiO_2 superhydrophobic coating [J]. Surface Engineering, 2018(2): 139-145.

[3]Yu L, et al. Repellent materials. Robust self-cleaning surfaces that function when exposed to either air or oil [J]. Science, 2015(No.6226): 1132-1135.

[4]Li Y, et al. A facile and fast approach to mechanically stable and rapid self-healing waterproof fabrics [J]. Composites Science & Technology, 2016. 125: 55-61.

[5]Zhou H, et al. Robust, self-healing superamphiphobic fabrics prepared by two-step coating of fluoro-containing polymer, fluoroalkyl silane, and modified silica nanoparticles [J]. Advanced Functional Materials, 2013. 23(13): 1664-1670.

[6]Karapanagiotis I, et al. Facile method to prepare superhydrophobic and water repellent cellulosic paper [J]. Journal of Nanomaterials, 2015. 2015: 1-9.

[7]Xue C H, et al. Fabrication of robust superhydrophobic surfaces by modification of chemically roughened fibers via thiol-ene click chemistry [J]. Journal of Materials Chemistry A, 2015. 3(43): 21797-21804.

[8]Li Y, et al. Bioinspired self-healing superhydrophobic coatings [J]. Angew Chem Int Ed Engl, 2010. 49(35): 6129-33.

[9]Salter B, et al. N -chloramide modified Nomex ® as a regenerable self-decontaminating material for protection against chemical warfare agents [J]. Journal of Materials Science, 2009. 44(8): 2069-2078.

[10] Mao N. High performance textiles for protective clothing [M]. 2014.

[11]Perepelkin K E. Chemical fibers with specific properties for industrial application and personnel protection [J]. Journal of Industrial Textiles, 2001(No.2): 87-102.

[12]Weng R, et al. Spray-coating process in preparing PTFE-PPS composite super-hydrophobic coating [J]. AIP Advances, 2014. 4(3): 031327.

[13]Cao M, et al. Hot water-repellent and mechanically durable superhydrophobic mesh for oil/water separation [J]. Journal of Colloid and Interface Science, 2018: 567-574.

[14]Sheng J, et al. Tailoring water-resistant and breathable performance of polyacrylonitrile nanofibrous membranes modified by polydimethylsiloxane [J]. ACS Appl Mater Interfaces, 2016. 8(40): 27218-27226.

[15]Zhou H, et al. Superstrong, chemically stable, superamphiphobic fabrics from particle-free polymer coatings [J]. Advanced Materials Interfaces, 2015. 2(6): 1400559.

[16]Kim J M, et al. Control of hydroxyl group content in silica particle synthesized by the sol-precipitation process [J]. Ceramics International, 2009. 35(3): 1015-1019.

Mechanical Property Enhancement of Bead-on-String Electrospun Nanofiber Membrane

Wenru Cui[1], Tingxiao Li[2]*, Xin Ding[1,3]*, Jiyong Hu[1,3], Xudong Yang[1,3], Qiao Li[1,3]

[1] *College of Textile, Donghua University, Shanghai 201620, China*

[2] *Fashion College, Shanghai University of Engineering Science, Shanghai 201620, China*

[3] *Key Laboratory of Textile Science & Technology, Ministry of Education, Shanghai 201620, China*

* *Corresponding author's email*: litingxiao824@163.com; xding@dhu.edu.cn

Abstract: Electrospinning bead-on-string nanofiber with good mechanical property and drug release profile could be used as potential scaffold in tissue engineering. In the study, the mechanical property of bead-on-string nanofiber membrane was investigated. The morphology was examined using scanning electron microscope (SEM) and analyzed the effect beads number (BN) and the fiber diameter (FD) on mechanical property. Then solvents with different volatility were used to improve the mechanical property by decreasing the porosity of bead-on-string nanofiber membrane. Finally, the flat panel collector was replaced with a roller to improve the orientation distribution by changing the speed of roller in order. It was found that solvent HFP with a low vapor pressure could improve the porosity of electrospun bead-on-string nanofiber membrane from 80.05% to 70.65% compared with TCM/acetone mixed solvent. The strength of bead-on-string nanofiber membrane electrospun from HFP was 2.7 times of TCM/acetone, the elongation was 3.3 times of TCM/acetone. Improving the orientation distribution obviously by roller collector at 800rpm, tensile strength, Young's Modulus and elongation were further improved and the strength reached 8.08MPa, the Young's Modulus reached 151.32MPa and the elongation at break reached 233.44MPa.

Keywords: Bead-on-string nanofiber; Mechanical property; Bead number; Porosity; Orientation distribution

1 Introduction

Bead-on-string[1-2], as we all known, is a common phenomenon observed under appropriate processing parameters in electrospinning. The diameters of beads on continuous nanofibers are usually in micron level[3]. The final function of bead-on-string scaffolds was to encapsulate particle drug with micron-level diameter. The number of beads should be enough to encapsulate most of the particle drugs. As a novel drug-loading system, bead-on-string nanofiber scaffolds have excellent drug release property. But with the appearance of beads, their mechanical property would be deteriorated[4]. This defect will hinder the controllability of drug release in late period and the application of bead-on-sting nanofiber drug-loaded scaffolds in tissue engineering. But there are few studies on the mechanical property of bead-on-string nanofiber membrane.

The mechanical property of electrospun nanofiber membrane was greatly influenced by the fiber size distribution in the membranes, porosity, individual fiber orientation in the membranes and fiber-fiber interaction and entanglement of the fibers[5]. For bead-on-string nanofiber, the morphology of bead-on-string, the porosity of membrane and the orientation distribution are the key factors that influence the mechanical property of bead-on-string nanofiber membrane.

In this study, poly(lactic-co-glycolic acid) (PLGA) was chosen as the polymerto electrospin bead-on-string nanofiber membrane. The morphologies of bead-on-string nanofiber membrane, including the diameter of fiber and the number of beads, are influenced by the concentration of solution. The volatility of the solvent affects the fiber diameter, fiber-fiber interaction and the pores on the fiber surface, resulting in changes in the porosity of the nanofiber membrane and affecting the compactness of the nanofiber membrane[6]. And the individual fiber orientation in the membrane can be regulated by the collector. In the study, we chose a roller collector and changed the rotation speed of the roller to obtain different orientation distribution of the nanofiber in the membrane.

2 Experiments

2.1 Materials

Poly (lactic-co-glycolic acid) (PLGA, 50 : 50, M_w 93000) was purchased from Jinan Daigang Biomaterials Co., Ltd., China. The solvent of PLGA solution was chloroform (TCM) and acetone (analytic pure, Shanghai Lingfeng Chemical Reagent Co., Ltd., China) and Hexafluoroisopropanol (HFP, analytic pure, Shanghai Darui Fine Chemical Co., Ltd., China).

2.2 Fabrication of electrospinning nanofibers

The polymer solution was fed into a 2.5mL standard syringe and pumped at a feeding rate of 1mL/h. A voltage of 20kV was applied between the syringe needle and the collecting aluminum foil. The distance from the needle tip to the foil was 15cm. The spinning process was conducted at 25℃ ±5℃ and the relative humidity was 40% ±5%.

2.3 Morphology of nanofibers

The morphology of the electrospun nanofibers was observed by scanning electron microscopy (TM3000, Hitachi Co., Japan). The diameter of the fibers was measured by Image J software (National Institutes of Health, United States). The number of beads was calculated by drawing 5cm × 5cm square in Photoshop, placing 5 squares in the SEM image of the same nanofiber membrane, counting the number of beads in each square and calculating the average.

2.4 Mechanical property

The specimen was processed by the template as Fig. 1. The template was glued on the nanofiber membrane and was cut into rectangular pieces (10mm × 50mm) along the vertical lines.

The thicknesses of the specimens were measured by using a Digital Desktop latex thickness gauge (Shanghai

Liuling Instrument Co., Ltd., China).

The tensile testing was performed using a YG (B) 026G-500 Strength Tester at a strain rate of 10mm/min with a gauge length of 30mm. The specimens' width was kept to 10mm. 5 specimens of each membrane were tested and then calculated the average.

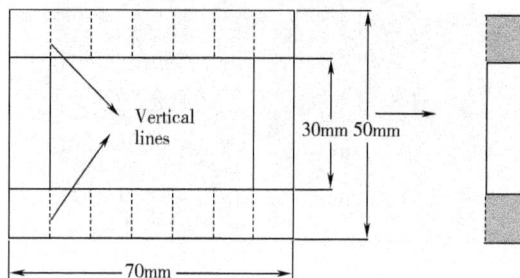

Fig.1 A paper template used to prepare tensile specimens of bead-on-string nanofiber scaffolds

2.5 Porosity of nanofiber membrane

The porosity of the specimens were calculated by the following Formula[7]:

$$Porosity(\%) = (1 - \frac{\rho_1}{\rho_2}) \times 100$$

$$\rho_1 = \frac{m}{V}$$

m——specimen mass (accurate to 0.01mg);

V——specimen volume;

ρ_1——PLGA standard density 1.22g/cm^3。

3 Results and Discussion

3.1 The effect of specimen morphology on the mechanical property

To investigate the influence of the morphology of bead-on-string nanofibers on its mechanical property, six series of solutions with different concentration were prepared as listed Tab.1. According to our previous study, a mixed solvent consisting of chloroform and acetone in a volume rate of 2 : 1 was chosen as the solvent. It can be seen from the Tab.1 that with the concentration increase, specimens from solutions 1, 2 and 3 show bead-on-string nanofiber as Fig.2 (a) - (c). Those from solutions 4, 5 and 6 shows smooth nanofiber as Fig.2 (d) - (f). Fiber diameter (FD), bead number (BN) and the mechanical property of nanofiber were also shown in Tab.1.

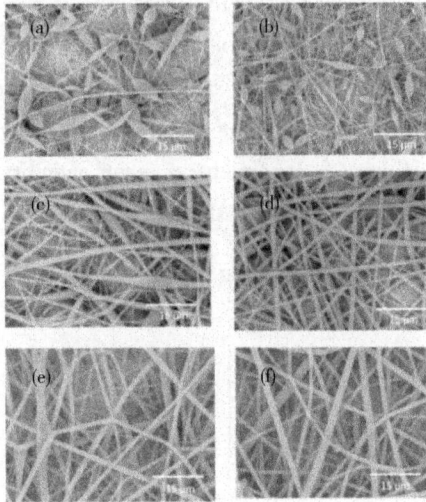

Fig. 2 SEM images of nanofibers electrospun from solutions with different concentration (a)120mg/mL; (b) 140mg/mL; (c) 160mg/mL; (d) 170mg/mL; (e) 180mg/mL; (f)190mg/mL

the specimens with smooth nanofiber, the tensile strength and elongation at break were enhanced significantly as the FD increases. For beaded nanofiber, the FD become finer and BN become more as the concentration of solutions reduces, which results in the deterioration of the tensile strength, Young's modulus and elongation at break.

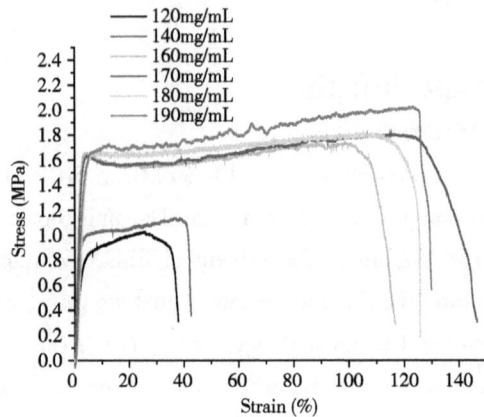

Fig. 3 Stress-strain curves of smooth and bead-on-string nanofiber

It can be seen from Fig. 3 that with the appearance of the beads, the mechanical property deteriorated. For

Tab. 1 The morphologies of nanofibers electrospun from PLGA solutions with different concentration

	Concentration (mg/mL)	BN	FD	Strength (MPa)	Young's modulus (MPa)	Elongation (%)
1	120	15800	0.21	1.028	31.6	24.6
2	140	13000	0.36	1.147	47.9	36.6
3	160	5400	0.57	1.814	64.7	114.9
4	170	0	0.923	1.736	74.83	98.29
5	180	0	1.07	1.833	54.95	104.06
6	190	0	1.4	2.025	56.75	122.23

3.2 The effect of specimen porosity on mechanical property

To investigate the influence of the specimen porosity on the mechanical property, two series of solvents (a: HFP; b: TCM: acetone = 2 : 1) were prepared as listed Tab. 2. The porosity and mechanical property was shown in Tab. 2. It can be seen that the volatility of solvent a is higher than of solution b from the vapor pressure as listed in Tab. 2. And the porosity of specimen prepared from solvent a is lower than that from solvent

b. Smooth nanofiber show as Fig. 4 (a) and (b), and bead-on-string nanofiber show as Fig. 4 (c) and (d), it's obvious that the fiber-fiber interaction prepared by solvent a are more than Fig. (b) and Fig. (d).

From the stress-strain curve shown in Fig. 5 and mechanical property shown in Tab. 2, it can be seen that, no matter it is beaded nanofibers or smooth nanofibers, specimens prepared from solvent a were significantly superior to that from solvent b. Because solvent a is less volatile, in the high-voltage electric field, the droplet

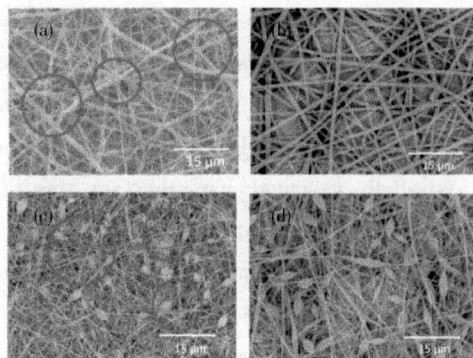

Fig. 4　SEM images of nanofiber electrospun from solutions with different solvent（a）HFP-Beaded；（b）TCM：acetone-Beaded；（c）HFP-Smooth；（d）TCM：acetone-Smooth

ber membrane structure is denser, which is helpful to enhance the mechanical property of specimen.

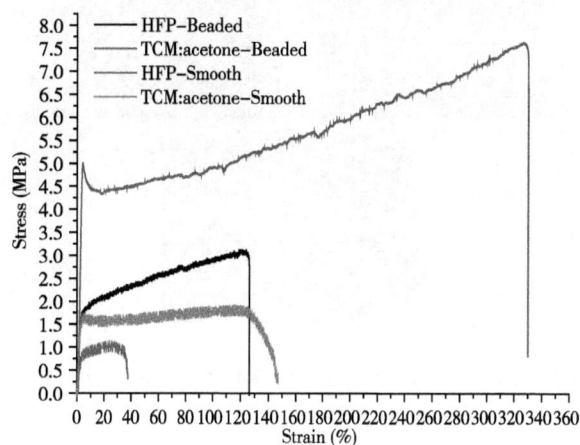

Fig. 5　Stress-strain curves of electrospun nanofiber

has enough time to form a well-structured fiber, and more interactions between fiber and fiber, so the nanofi-

Tab. 2　The volatility of solvent, porosity of fiber membrane and the mechanical property

	Solvent	Fiber type	Vapor pressure (mmHg)	Porosity (%)	Strength (MPa)	Young's modulus (MPa)	Elongation (%)
1	a	Smooth	119.9	67.63	7.64	200.01	325.26
2	b	Smooth	165.3	81.92	1.814	74.83	114.90
3	a	Beaded	119.9	70.65	3.13	50.7	121.72
4	b	Beaded	165.3	80.05	1.15	47.9	36.6

Notes：a：HFP；b：TCM：acetone＝2：1.

3.3　The effect of specimen orientation distribution on the mechanical property

To investigate the influence of specimen orientation distribution on the mechanical property, FD, BN and porosity were controlled by the experimental parameters. The roller collector was used in this experiment, the rotation speed of roller collector and the mechanical property were listed in Tab. 3. Increase the orientation distribution by increasing the rotation speed of the roller, including 0, 400rpm and 800rpm show as Fig. 6 (a) − (c). It can be seen that the specimen reached orientation distribution at the rotation speed of 800rpm.

Tab. 3　Roller speed and the tensile property of specimen

	Rotation speed (rpm)	Strength (MPa)	Young's modulus (MPa)	Elongation (%)
1	0	3.13	50.7	121.72
2	400	6.63	188.62	197.3
3	800	8.08	151.32	233.44

From the stress-strain curves in Fig. 7, it can be seen that the increase of orientation degree will significantly enhance the tensile strength, Young's modulus and elongation at break of the bead-on-string nanofiber membrane. With the increase in the rotation speed, the

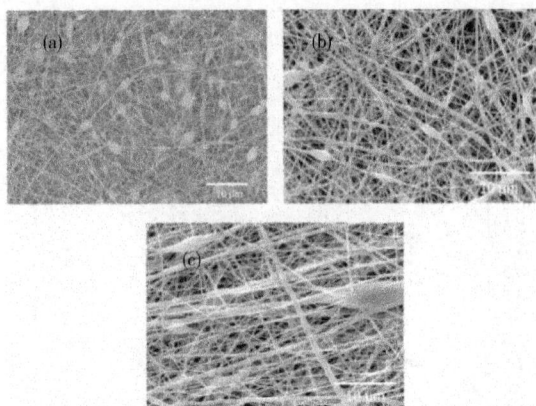

Fig. 6　SEM images of nanofiber with different rotation speed (a)0;(b)400rpm;(c)800rpm

degree of orientation was increased and the interaction between fibers was more. Besides, although the strength and elongation at 800rpm was higher than 400rpm obviously, the Young's modulus of the specimen at 800rpm was lower than 400rpm. So the rotation speed of the roller shouldn't be too high.

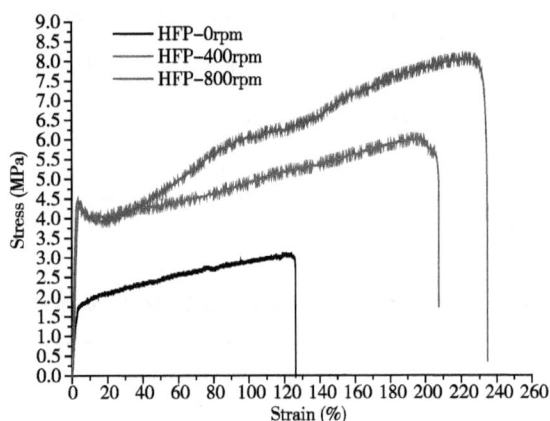

Fig. 7　Stress-strain curves of nanofiber with different rotate speed (0, 400rpm and 800rpm)

4　Conclusions

The mechanical property of electrospun bead-on-string nanofiber was greatly enhanced by adjusting the morphology of nanofiber, porosity, individual fiber orientation in the membranes and fiber-fiber interaction.

In the study of the influence of bead-on-string nanofiber morphology on mechanical property, 6 series of solutions were prepared by TCM/acetone mixed solvents. It was found that the BN was decreased and FD was increased with the concentration of solution increased. And with the appearance of beads, the mechanical property was deteriorated. Bead-on-string nanofiber had half the strength of smooth nanofiber and one fifth the elongation of smooth nanofiber.

To improve the mechanical property of bead-on-string nanofiber membrane, the porosity of membrane was investigated. It was found that the solvent with low vapor pressure (HFP) decreased the porosity of membrane compared with TCM/acetone. From the SEM of membrane, it can be seen the solvent with lower volatility facilitates the interaction between fibers. The strength of bead-on-string nanofiber membrane reached 3.13MPa and the elongation reached 121.71% prepared by HFP.

On the basis of last step, replaced the flat panel with roller and adjusted the speed of roller to improve the mechanical property further. It was found that fibers were orientation distribution at the rotation speed of 800rpm. The strength, Young's modulus and elongation were improved and the strength improved to 8.08MPa, the Young's modulus improved to 151.32MPa and the elongation improved to 233.44%.

References

[1]Bu N B, Huang Y A, Deng H X, et al. Tunable bead-on-string microstructures fabricated by mechano-electrospinning [J]. Journal of Physics D-Applied Physics. 2012, 45 (40).

[2]Versypt A N F, Pack D W, Braatz R D. Mathematical modeling of drug delivery from autocatalytically degradable plga microspheres—A review [J]. Journal of Controlled Release. 2013, 165 (1): 29-37.

[3]Li T X, Ding X, Sui X, et al. Sustained release of protein particle encapsulated in bead-on-string electrospun nanofibers [J]. Journal of Macromolecular Science Part B-Physics. 2015, 54 (8): 887-896.

[4]Li T X, Ding X, Tian L L, et al. Engineering bsa-dextran particles encapsulated bead-on-string nanofiber scaffold for tissue engineering applications [J]. Journal of Materials Science. 2017, 52 (18): 10661-10672.

[5]Baji A, Mai Y W, Wong S C, et al. Electrospinning of polymer nanofibers: Effects on oriented morphology, structures

and tensile properties [J]. Composites Science and Technology. 2010, 70 (5): 703-718.

[6] Megelski S, Stephens J S, Chase D B, et al. Micro- and nanostructured surface morphology on electrospun polymer fibers [J]. Macromolecules. 2002, 35 (22): 8456-8466.

[7] Vaz C M, Tuijl S V, Bouten C V C, et al. Design of scaffolds for blood vessel tissue engineering using a multi-layering electrospinning technique [J]. Acta Biomaterialia. 2005, 1 (5): 575-582.

Mechanical, Interfacial and Electrothermal Properties of Nickel Coated Carbon Fibers

Yanhong Cao[1], Fujun Xu[1,2]*, Sidra Saleemi[1], Yousong Xue[1], Mengwen Huang[1], Dongshen Ge[1]

[1] College of Textiles, Donghua University, Shanghai 201620, China

[2] Shanghai Key Laboratory of Advanced Micro & Nano Textile Materials, Shanghai 201620, China

* Corresponding author's email: fjxu@ dhu. edu. cn

Abstract: Various fundamental properties of nickel coated carbon fibers (Ni-CFs) were studied in this paper, using the carbon fibers (CFs) for comparison purposes. The mechanical properties were investigated by single fiber tensile test and Weibull distribution. The interfacial properties were investigated by micro-bond test to calculate interfacial shear strength (IFSS) and SEM images were observed. The electrothermal properties were characterized with an infrared camera to investigate the electric heating behavior. The average strength, modulus and IFSS of Ni-CFs were(2.05 ± 0.36) GPa, (102 ± 25.7) GPa and (34.72 ± 6.43) MPa, respectively, which is less as compared to CFs. Less variation and more even distribution of defects in Ni-CFs improved the mechanical and interfacial properties stability. The Ni-CFs can reach a higher equilibrium temperature than CFs at the same voltage. The average maximum temperature of Ni-CFs was (164.24 ± 7.32)℃ at the applied voltage of 1.75V. The Ni-CFs fabric and Ni-CFs/epoxy composites reached a maximum temperature of 91.6℃ and 58.1℃ at applied voltage of 2V, respectively. Ni-CFs presented excellent electrothermal performance and can be used as an electric heating material or electrothermal composite material.

Keywords: Nickel coated carbon fibers; Electrothermal properties; Mechanical testing; Micro-bond test; IFSS

1　Introduction

As a high-performance fiber, carbon fiber (CF) is a promising material in the engineering field. However, CF has a relatively low conductivity as compared to metals due to acertain size inherent resistance[1].

Nicke coated carbon fiber (Ni-CF) has characteristics of metal. In comparison with CF, Ni-CF has great application value in electrothermal materials due to excellent conductive properties[2]. Ni-CF conductive composites possess similar mechanical properties as of CF conductive composites, but significantly electrical conductivity.

Ni-CF has good mechanical properties, small thermal expansion coefficient and small specific gravity. Ni-CF reinforced composites have higher specific strength, specific modulus, specific rigidity, high temperature resistance[3], and good dimensional stability[4]. Nickel is a kind of wave-absorbing material, so the addition of Ni-CF in the composite material can greatly improve the effectiveness of electromagnetic shielding[5] and can be widely used in military, aerospace and electromagnetic shielding equipment. Ni-CF is light, soft and conductive. The cables made of Ni-CF not only ensure electrical performance but also significantly reduce the weight of the cables. Ni-CFs have excellent heat resistance and are suitable for the preparation of components for high-speed space shuttles. Ni-CFs can also be applied to magnetic thin films, small high-capacity capacitors, electromagnetic shielding of electronic equipment, functional components, and so on.

Like functional high-performance carbon fiber, Ni-CF not only retains the mechanical properties of carbon fiber such as high modulus and strength, but also has metal characteristics with excellent electrical conductivity. Having the advantages of excellent mechanical and electrical properties[6], Ni-CF is a promising electrothermal material and can be widely used in multi-functional composite materials. Various fundamental properties of Ni-CFs were studied for further research. The mechanical property was investigated by single fiber tensile test. The interfacial shear strength was calculated by microbond test. An infrared camera was used to find the electrothermal properties and electric heating behavior.

2 Experiments

2.1 Materials

Ni-CFs were provided by Suzhou Institute of Nano-Tech and Nano-Bionics, Chinese Academy of Sciences. As the raw material, each bundle of carbon fibers was weighed 0.8139 gram per meter including 12K single fibers. CFs were black and kept in close contact with each other due to strong bundling. Ni-CFs were silver and easy to disperse due to the loose fiber bundle (Fig. 1).

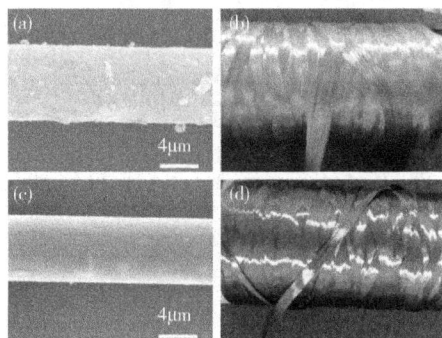

Fig. 1 (a) SEM images of CF; (b) CFs; (c) SEM images of Ni-CF; (d) Ni-CFs

2.2 Single fiber tensile test

The mechanical properties of fibers were measured by using a single fiber strength tester (XS (08) XD−3, Shanghai Xusai Instrument Co., Ltd.) at a gauge length of 10mm and a tensile speed of 0.5mm/min with a 3N load cell. Fiber diameter of each specimen was measured by using a polarized light microscope (ECLIPSE LV100 POL, Nikon) to capture a digital image and the nano measurer to take the average of 10 measurements.

2.3 Micro-bond test

The interfacial properties between fiber and matrix were measured by the micro-bond test by using a single fiber strength tester at a speed of 0.5mm/min with a 3N load cell and a special fixture. Mix epoxy resin and curing agent in a ratio of 3 : 1 evenly and place the beads on the fibers after 15min. The specimens were cured for 2h at 50℃ and post-cured for 3h at 70℃. Select an appropriate test micro-bond, which is about 8−9 times the diameter of the fiber, using a polarized light microscope. The interfacial shear strength (IFSS) was calculated according to the tested force, the measured fiber diameter and embedded fiber length.

2.4 Electrothermal property test

A set of voltages was applied and the corresponding current was recorded. The resistance of Ni-CFs and CFs were compared according to current-voltage curves.

The electrothermal property was characterized with an infrared camera to investigate the applied voltage-dependent electric heating behavior of Ni-CFs at a tested length of 10mm by applying constant voltage of 0.25−1.75V lasting for 120 seconds. The temperature-time curves of Ni-CF fabric and Ni-CF/epoxy composites were investigated by applying constant voltage of 2V lasting for 2 minutes. The infrared camera monitored the change of the temperature of the sample and captured the thermal images.

3 Results and Discussion

3.1 Mechanical properties

At least 60 effective data of the single fiber tensile test were obtained. The results were analyzed to compare the elongation, strength and modulus as presented in Tab. 1 and compared in Fig. 2 (a). When compared with carbon fiber, the strength and elongation of nickel coated carbon fiber decreased by 40% and 26%, respectively, while the modulus only decreased by 5.6%, which might be due to the weak mechanical properties of nickel coating. In addition, the slurry in surface of carbon fiber was removed at a high temperature in the nickel coating process, which could cause the loss of mechanical properties of carbon fiber, but the SD of all.

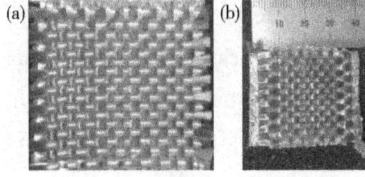

Fig. 2 (a) Ni-CFs fabric; (b) Electrode

Parameters were decreased, which indicated the nickel coating narrowed the mechanical property scattering of the fiber. The strength and modulus of Ni-CF were 2.05GPa and 102GPa, respectively, so nickel coating carbon fibers were still high-performance fibers.

Tab. 1 Mechanical properties of Ni-CF and CF

Fiber type	Diameter(um)	Force(cN)	Elongation(%)	Strength(GPa)	Modulus(GPa)
Carbon fiber	7.55	15.10	3.26	3.4	108
SD	0.43	3.46	1.01	0.83	30.6
Nickel coated carbon fiber	8.41	11.38	2.10	2.05	102
SD	0.36	2.12	0.68	0.36	25.7

The strength variation of Ni-CF and CF was evaluated by adopting a two parameter Weibull distribution. The cumulative probability of fiber failure $F(\sigma_f)$, at applied stress of σ_f, is given as[7-8]:

$$F(\sigma_f) = 1 - \exp\left(-L\frac{\sigma_f}{\sigma_0}\right)^{\beta} \quad (1)$$

Here, σ_f is the fiber tensile strength, σ_0 is the scale parameter, and β is the Weibull shape parameter. Eq. (1) can be rewritten as:

$$\ln(\ln(1/(1-F(\sigma_f)))) = \beta\ln\sigma_f - \beta\ln\sigma_0 + \ln L \quad (2)$$

$F(\sigma_f)$ can be calculated as:

$$F(\sigma_f) = \frac{n}{N+1} \quad (3)$$

Here, N is the total number of specimens, n is the accumulative order of tensile strength in ascending rank. Linear fitting the Weibull distribution plots for the strengths with $\ln(\ln(1/(1-F(\sigma_f))))$ as a function of $\ln(\sigma_f)$ in Eq. (2), as shown in Fig. 3(b), the shape parameter and scale parameter could be obtained by the slope and intercept, respectively, as presented in Tab. 2. The experimental strength in Tab. 2 was reasonably approximate to the scale parameter σ_0 which also means the characteristic strength. Shape parameter β characterizes the dispersion in fiber strength and larger β indicates smaller scattering. When compared with CF, the shape parameter β of Ni-CF increased, which implied less variation and more even distribution of defects. Therefore, the performance stability of nickel coated carbon fiber was improved.

Tab. 2 The Weibull parameters at a gauge length of 10mm

	Scale parameter σ_0	Shape parameter β
CF	3.749	4.445
Ni-CF	2.216	5.554

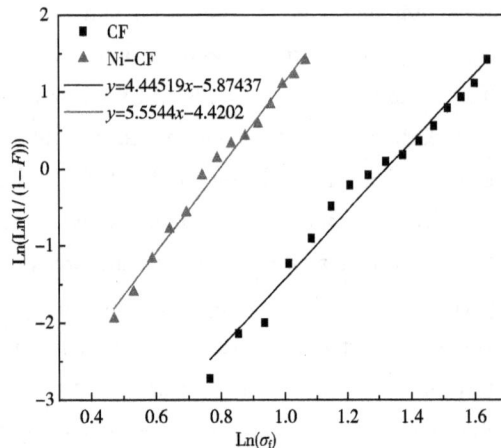

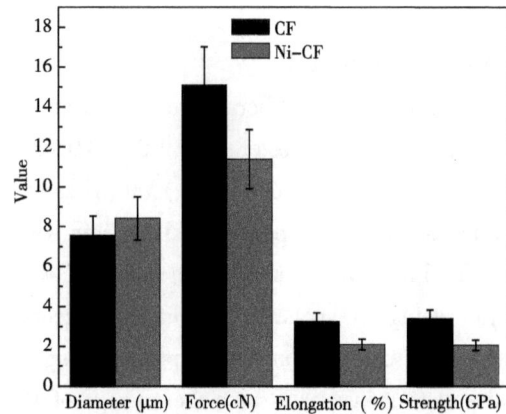

Fig. 3 (a) The mechanical properties; (b) Weibull distribution plots and linear fitting

3.2 Interfacial shear strength

At least twenty effective data of the micro-bond tests were obtained. The results were presented in Tab. 3. The interfacial shear strength (IFSS) between fiber and epoxy resin was calculated according to the given equation as[9]:

$$\text{IFSS} = \frac{F}{\pi \times D \times L} \quad (4)$$

Here, F is the maximum force recorded during the beads de-bonding process, D is the fiber diameter, L is the embedded fiber length by the beads and πDL is the embedment area.

The average IFSS of Ni-CF decreased with a smaller standard deviation which might be due to the less variation of defects and improved stability as compared to CF. The natural properties of the smooth surface of the nickel metal might cause the weak bonding between nickel coating and resin, thus decreasing the interfacial properties of the nickel coated carbon fiber.

Tab. 3 The interfacial shear strength of single fiber

	$D(\text{um})$	$L(\text{um})$	$F(\text{cN})$	IFSS(MPa)
CF	7.73	82.57	9.06	44.70
SD	0.27	13.31	3.25	11.73
Ni-CF	8.83	83.59	7.95	34.72
SD	0.76	14.55	1.96	6.43

The beads slipped significantly along the fiber axis after the Micro-bond test, as presented in the images captured by a polarized light microscope in Fig. 4. SEM images in Fig. 5 examined the failure surface of the micro-bond specimens. After interfacial de-bonding, beads broke at the end of the bond with the fiber as shown and marked A in Fig. 5(a) and a gap and void space were formed between micro-bond and fiber as shown and marked C and E in Fig. 5, which made the beads slip when imposing an external force, such as the slippage from A to B in Fig. 5(a). The surface of Ni-CF in Fig. 5(a) was still rough while the surface of Ni-CF was as smooth as the CF and there was a broken region in fiber axis as marked D in Fig. 5(c) after interfacial de-bonding. The end of de-bonded beads was rough in Ni-CF in Fig. 4(c) but smooth in CF in Fig. 4

(a). It was speculated that the interface between nickel coating and carbon fiber might be damaged besides the interface destruction between beads and nickel coating in micro-bond test.

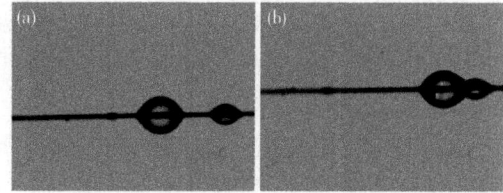

Fig. 4 Images of Ni-CF captured by polarized light microscope. (a) Before testing; (b) After testing

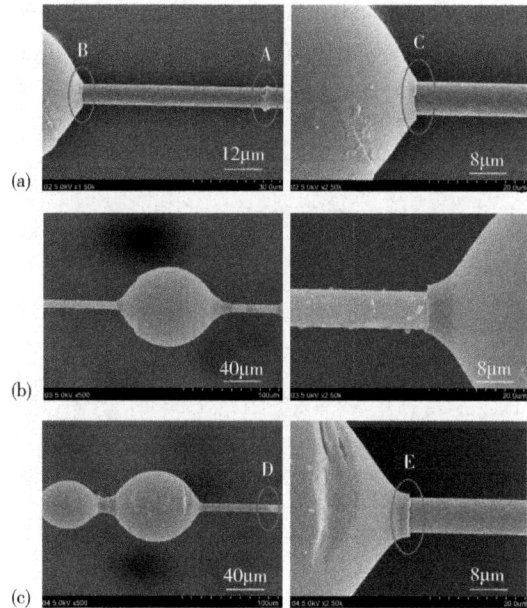

Fig. 5 SEM images of micro-bond specimens after interfacial de-bonding. (a) CF; (b)&(c):Ni-CF

3.3 Electric heating behavior

The current—voltage (I—V) curves of Ni-CFs and CFs were presented in Fig. 6. The electrical current increased linearly with the applied voltage, which indicated that the resistance of Ni-CFs and CFs maintained relatively steady[10]. The higher current at the same applied voltage indicated the smaller resistance of Ni-CFs. Thus, the conductive performance of Ni-CFs was more excellent.

Comparing the temperature-time curves of Ni-CFs and CFs at applied voltage of 0.5–1.75V in Fig. 7, the Ni-CFs can reach a higher equilibrium temperature than

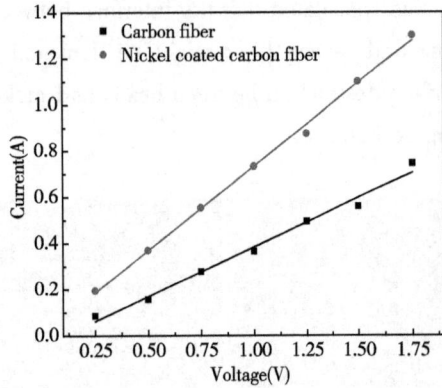

Fig. 6　Current-voltage curves at a tested length of 10mm

CFs at the same voltage. Infrared thermal images were captured. The temperature of Ni-CFs and CFs reached a maximum value within 20s and 10s, respectively, and then kept a relatively steady state in equilibrium. When the applied voltage was off 120s, the temperature of Ni-CFs and CFs decreased to the initial temperature within 30s and 20s, respectively. It implied that the temperature of Ni-CFs responded more slowly to applied voltage than CFs, which might be due to the loose bundle of Ni-CFs.

The maximum temperatures of five samples at applied voltage of 1.75V were presented in Tab. 4. The average maximum temperature of Ni-CFs was (164.24 ± 7.32)℃, and that of CFs was (139.06 ± 7.13)℃. According to the Joule's law, $Q = \dfrac{U^2}{R}t$, Ni-CFs with a smaller resistance can generate more Joule heat than CFs and reach a higher temperature at the same applied voltage and time, indicating that the electrothermal performance of Ni-CFs was superior to CFs.

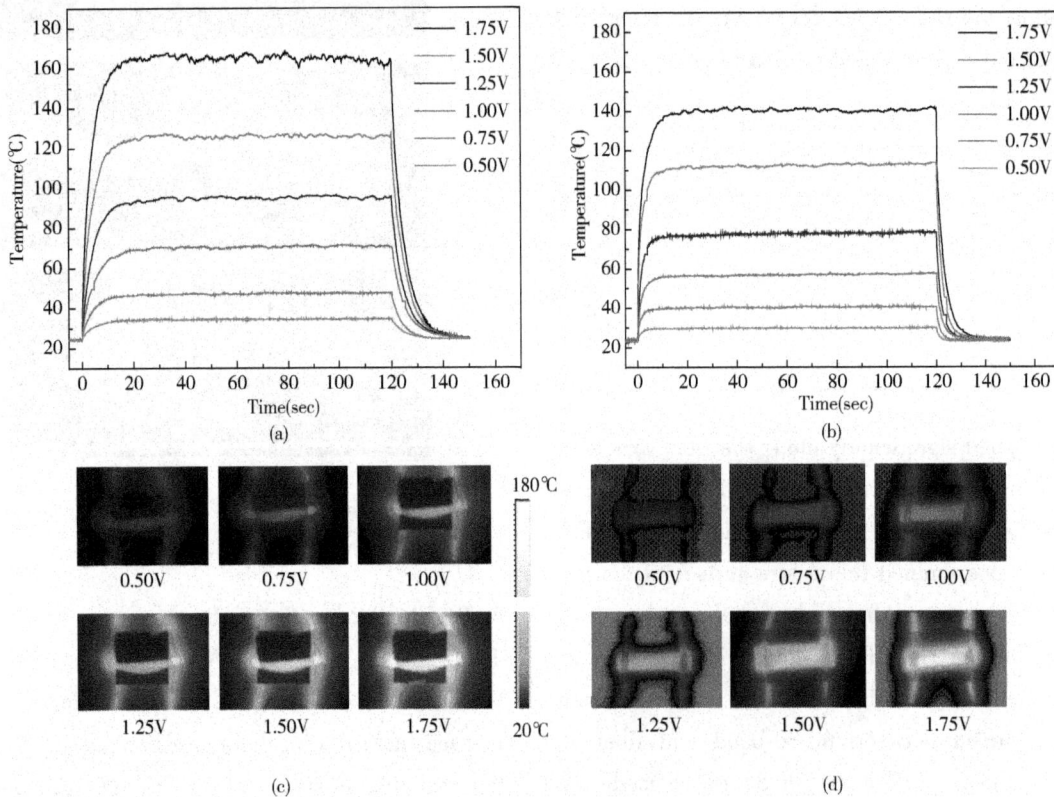

Fig. 7　Temperature-time curves of (a) Ni-CFs and (b) CFs; Thermal images of (c) Ni-CFs and (d) CFs

Tab. 4　The maximum equilibrium temperature at applied constant voltage of 1.75V

Sample	1(℃)	2(℃)	3(℃)	4(℃)	5(℃)	Average(℃)
Ni-CFs	168.6	162.8	156.9	158.4	174.5	164.24 ± 7.32
CFs	135.6	140.8	135.4	132.8	150.7	139.06 ± 7.13

The Ni-CF fabric and Ni-CF/epoxy composites reached a high maximum temperature of 91.6℃ and 58.1℃ at applied voltage of 2V for 6 minutes, respectively. The temperature-time curves and thermal images were shown in Fig. 8. Therefore, the Ni-CF can be used as an electric heating material and compounded to obtain an electrothermal composite material, applied to electric heating products such as electric heating floors.

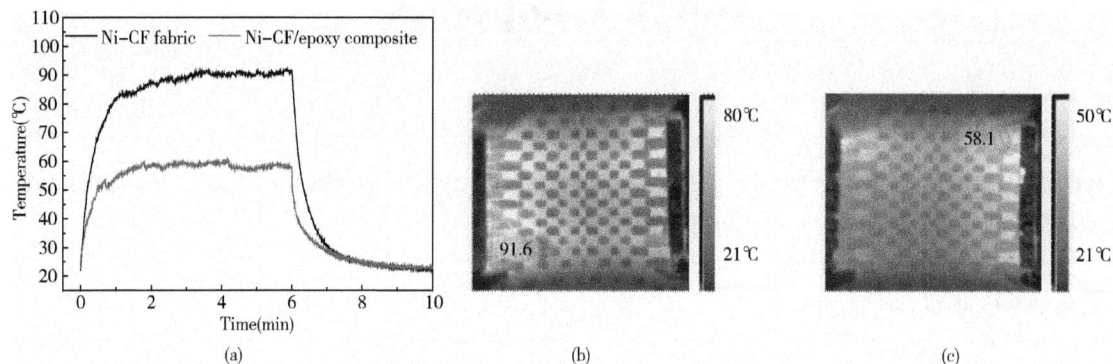

Fig. 8 (a) Temperature-time curves; Infrared thermal images of (b) Ni-CF fabric and (c) Ni-CF/epoxy composites

4 Conclusions

The average strength, modulus and IFSS of nickel coated carbon fibers were (2.05 ± 0.36) GPa, (102 ± 25.7) GPa and (34.72 ± 6.43) GPa, respectively, so nickel coating carbon fibers were still high-performance fibers. The strength and IFSS of Ni-CF decreased by 40% and 22%, respectively, while the modulus only decreased by 5.6%. Smaller standard deviation of mechanical parameters and larger Weibull shape parameter β indicated less variation and more even distribution of defects in Ni-CFs and stability of the mechanical property improved. The conductive performance of Ni-CFs was more excellent due to the smaller resistance. Ni-CFs can reach a higher equilibrium temperature than CFs at the same voltage. Ni-CF fabric and Ni-CF/ epoxy composites reached a maximum temperature of 91.6℃ and 58.1℃ at applied voltage of 2V, respectively. The Ni-CFs showed better electrothermal performance and could have a broad application in electric heating materials or electrothermal composite material.

References

[1] Liao F, Han X, Zhang Y, et al. Carbon fabrics coated with nickel film through alkaline electroless plating technique [J]. Materials Letters, 2017, 205: 165-168.

[2] Isaji S, Bin Y, Matsuo M. Electrical and self-heating properties of UHMWPE-EMMA-NiCF composite films [J]. Journal of Polymer Science Part B: Polymer Physics, 2009, 47: 1253-1266.

[3] Hua Z S, Liu Y H, Yao G C, et al. Preparation and characterization of nickel-coated carbon fibers by electroplating [J]. Journal of Materials Engineering and Performance, 2012, 21: 324-330.

[4] Hou X, Chen H Y, Xu C J, et al. Conductive nickel/carbon fiber composites prepared via an electroless plating route [J]. Journal of Materials Science: Materials in Electronics, 2016, 27: 5686-5690.

[5] Yang J M, Yang Y Q, Duan H J. Light-weight epoxy/nickel coated carbon fibers conductive foams for electromagnetic interference shielding [J]. Journal of Materials Science: Materials in Electronics, 2017, 28: 5925-5930.

[6] Han X, Zhou Y X, Wang Z J, et al. Influence of plating time on continuous nickel electroplating of carbon fiber [J]. Electroplating & Finishing, 2014, 33: 363-365.

[7] Zu M, Li Q W, Zhu Y T, et al. The effective interfacial shear strength of carbon nanotube fibers in an epoxy matrix characterized by a microdroplet test [J]. Carbon, 2012, 50 (3): 1271-1279.

[8] Deng F, Lu W B, Zhao H B, et al. The properties of dry-spun carbon nanotube fibers and their interfacial shear strength in an epoxy composite [J]. Carbon, 2011, 49: 1752-1757.

[9] Shao Y Q, Xu F J, Li W, et al. Interfacial strength and debonding mechanism between aerogel-spuncarbon nanotube yarn and polyphenylene sulfide [J]. Composites: Part A, 2016, 88: 98-105.

[10] Yan J, Kim B, Jeong Y G. Thermomechanical and electrical properties of PDMS/MWCNT composite films crosslinked by electron beam irradiation [J]. Journal of Materials Science, 2015, 50(16): 5599-5608.

Mode I Fracture Toughness Behaviors of 3D Angle-Interlock Woven Composites

Amna Siddique[1], Hailou Wang[1], Anvarjon Nishonov[1], Baozhong Sun[1], Bohong Gu[1]*

[1] *College of Textiles, Donghua University, Shanghai 201620, China*

* *Corresponding author's email*: gubh@ dhu. edu. cn

Abstract: Mode I interlaminar fracture toughness and related toughening mechanisms of three dimensional angle interlock composite were studied. Quasi static Mode I fracture tests were conducted using double cantilever beam specimen on an Instron tensile testing machine. Fracture process was recorded to reveal the effects of 3D angle-interlock woven fabric architecture on mode I interlaminar toughness. Critical strain energy release rates (G_{Ic}) were computed by "Area method", and presented it versus delamination length (*R*-curve). Fractographic study was carried out for confirmation of the mechanisms identified by fracture process. From fracture photographs, it was observed that primary structure failure occurred at resin-fiber interface, while other contributing toughening mechanisms were matrix cracking, matrix breakage, yarns bridging and pull out. *R*-curve showed a large increase in interlaminar fracture toughness with increase in delamination length. It was found that layer by layer reinforced composite structure was favorable to resist fracture to a large extent as confirmed by the fracture process and G_{Ic}.

Keywords: Fracture toughness; Strain energy release rate; Mode I; Quasi static; Double cantilever beam (DCB)

1 Introduction

Over the last few decades, there has been growing interest towards structural failure investigations. Interlaminar delamination growth is one of the prevalent failure modes in composites. In fact, it is a most critical life-limiting factor for composite structures[1-2]. Delamination may be introduced during manufacture or caused by damage events during service such as: bird strike, large hailstones, and impact damage events thus hampering structural integrity and durability[3-4].

Fracture mechanics approaches such as: fracture toughness measurement plays an important role in academic research interests as well as in structural design process, as it gives valuable data for design process[5]. Fracture toughness is defined as "a property which describes the ability of a material which contains crack to resist fracture"[6]. In fracture mechanics, strain energy release rate (G_{Ic}) is known as the most fundamental parameter to investigate structural strength and stability[5-7]. It is demonstrated that composites manufactured using 3D textile preforms suppress delamination limitation of fiber reinforced composites[8-10]. Specifically laminated woven carbon-epoxy composites are expected to have G_{Ic} propagation values approximately 0.6kN/m to 0.8kN/ m, whereas G_{Ic} values of 3D woven carbon/epoxy composites are in the range of 1.4–6.4kN/m[2-11].

This paper aims to assess the Mode I fracture toughness and related toughening mechanisms of composite reinforced with specially designed 3D AIWF without binder yarn. Load-displacement curve and *R*-curve will be given to show fracture toughness response of 3D AIWC. Strain energy release rates were measured by area method. Furthermore, fractographic analysis is carried out for deep understanding of toughening mechanisms. Fracture process is revealed with photographs and by clarifying their correlation to load displacement curve.

2 Experiments

2.1 Materials and specimens

3D AIWF with layer by layer angle interlocked structure

supplied by Torayca carbon fiber tows, was used as reinforcement. Tab. 1 reports specifications and Fig. 1 (a) shows sketch diagram of 3D AIWF. The 3D AIWF is composed of only warp yarns and weft yarns.

Epoxy resin (JA-02C) supplied by Changshu Jiafa Chemicals Inc. was used to saturate the reinforcement with the assistance of vacuum assisted resin transfer molding technique. Resin was injected into performs at 60℃. The curing procedure was carried out under following conditions: temperature 90℃ for 2hours, 110℃ for 1 hour, and 130℃ for 4 hours. The fiber volume fraction was about 32%. Fig. 1 (b) shows composite photographs.

Specimens were cut from composite plate, along weft direction. Dimensions and configuration of the test specimen are demonstrated in Fig. 2. A cut out was machined into the DCB specimens in order to insert steel loading fixture with hinge. Starter crack was introduced in the specimen by using a very fine hand saw.

Tab. 1　Structural parameters of 3D angle-interlock woven fabric

Parameter	Type of fiber	Weave density (ends/cm)	Thickness (mm)
Warp fiber tows	Carbon K 12 1 strand	4.7	12.6
Weft fiber tows	Carbon K 12 2 strands	3.6	12.6

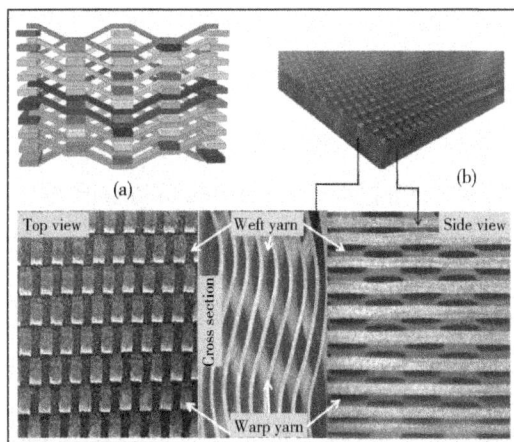

Fig. 1　3D angle interlock woven composite (a) Sketch diagram of 3D AIWF; (b) Photograph of composite

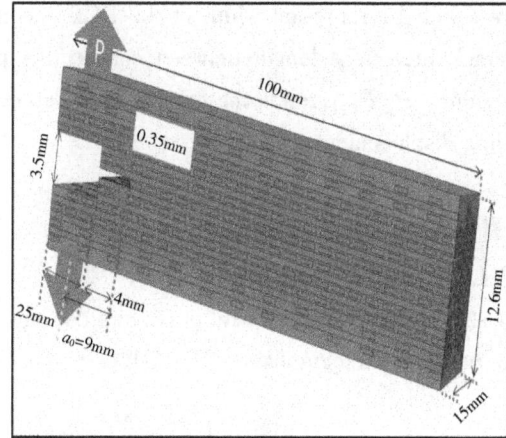

Fig. 2　Double cantilever beam (DCB) specimen

2.2　Mode I fracture toughness test (DCB test)

Quasi static DCB Mode I fracture toughness tests were conducted on Instron machine equipped with a load cell of 3kN capacity (Fig. 3). Three replicate specimens were tested at crosshead velocity of 2.5mm/min. The tests were conducted at room temperature. The delamination crack growth length was monitored optically using a camera (Canon DSLR). In order to read crack tip position during experiment, paper ruler with 1mm graduations was glued to side (across width) of the specimens starting from just below the starter crack tip.

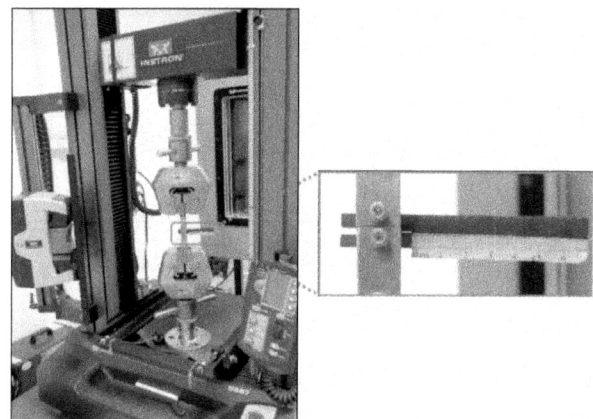

Fig. 3　Mode I DCB test

2.3　Date reduction scheme

Area method was used to calculate critical strain energy release rate (G_{Ic}) for crack growth. It provides direct measure of interlaminar fracture toughness.

G_{Ic} was calculated from the following expression[12]:

$$G_{Ic} = \frac{P_i \cdot d_{i+1} - P_{i+1} \cdot d_i}{2t\Delta a} \qquad (1)$$

Where t and Δa represent width of the DCB specimen and crack increment length between consecutive peak load points. P_i, P_{i+1} represent critical loads at corresponding displacement, d_i, d_{i+1}.

3 Results and Discussion

3.1 Load displacement curve

Fig. 4 shows load—displacement curve and damage evolution process photographs of 3D AIWC at specified points. Three major regions are highlighted on the curve. In the first region, the load versus displacement curve increased linearly until the crack initiates (Nonlinear Point), in the DCB specimen. This region represents the elastic deformation of the DCB specimen with linear rise in load. In the second region, nonlinear ascending behavior is observed for load, known as the crack propagation region and plastic deformation occurred in this region.

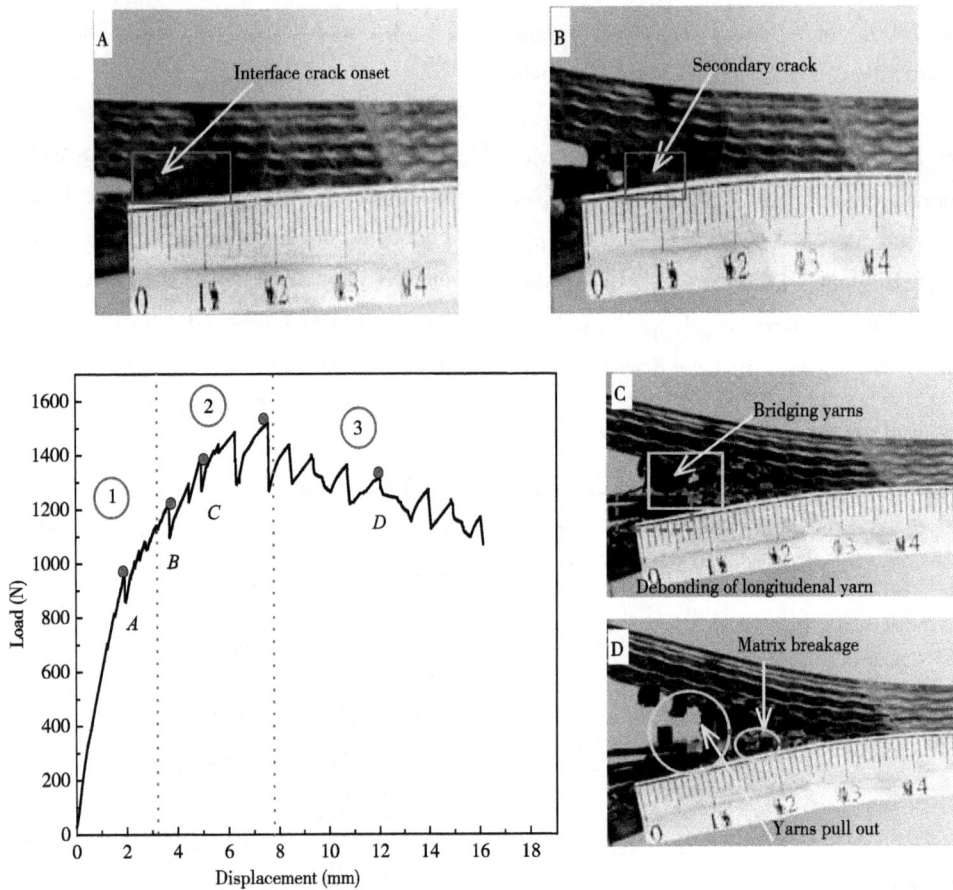

Fig. 4 Load displacement curve

The third region is the descending region which mainly starts after maximum peak load. Prominent increase in crack opening displacement rather than increase in crack length (crack arrest behavior) occur at the peak load as shown by Fig. 5. A big load drop with increase of displacement is seen directly after crack propagation.

3.2 Fracture process and toughening mechanisms

In Fig. 4, point A shows that crack initiation mainly occurred due to fiber/resin interface debonding. Point B shows occurrence of in plane secondary cracks, predominantly for the delamination length of $\Delta a \leqslant 6$mm. Point C shows bridging formation and debonding of longitudinal yarns from DCB specimen after the maximum peak load point. Point D shows increase in crack opening as well as crack length due to yarn pullout behind the crack tip (energy was dissipated at that point as shown by a load drop).

3.3 Fracture toughness data

Eventually, the results of mode I fracture toughness as function of delamination length (R-curve) are plotted

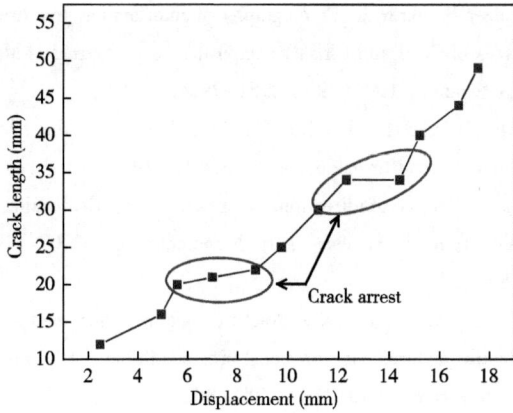

Fig. 5　Crack length vs. crack opening displacement

in Fig. 6 (a). The R-curve shows that fracture energy increased with crack extension gradually at the initial stage of crack propagation when crack length is less than about 20mm.

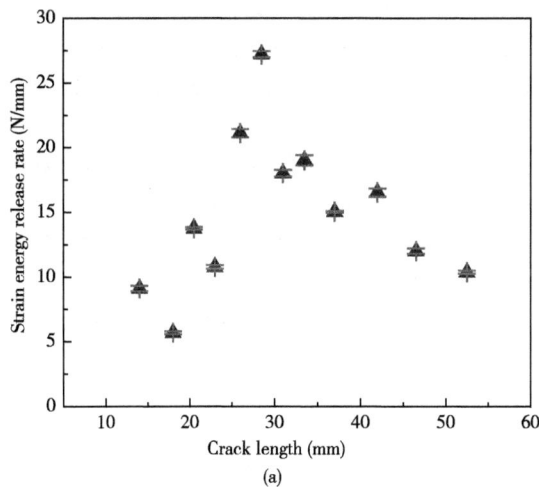

(a)

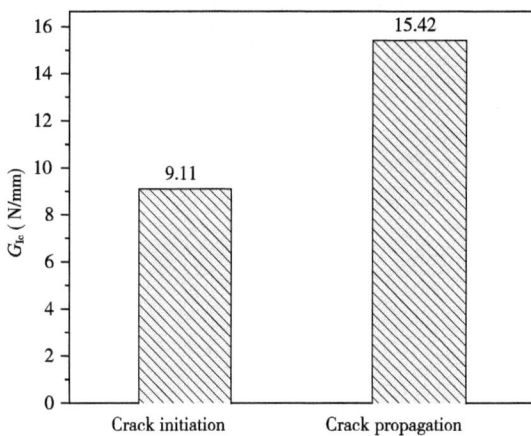

(b)

Fig. 6　Results from fracture toughness tests (a) R-curve; (b) Comparison of G_{IC} values for crack initiation and crack propagation

A comparison of crack initiation and propagation values of G_{Ic} is presented in Fig. 6 (b). G_{Ic} value for crack propagation is 60% more than G_{Ic} at initiation, attributed to structure of 3D AIWF.

3.4　SEM microscopy

Fig. 7 shows damage morphology from cross section and fractured surface of specimens. Fig. 7 (a) depicts the energy absorption mechanisms, such as debonding of undulated warp yarns from matrix layer along with resin cracking. Fig. 7 (b) shows extensive resin cracks on fractured surface.

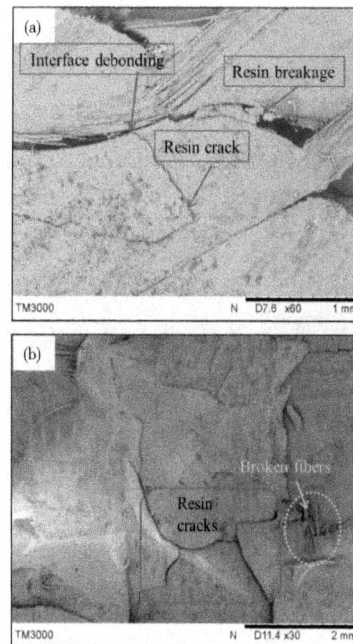

Fig. 7　SEM micrographs of the fractured DCB specimen　(a) Cross section; (b) Fractured surface

4　Conclusions

In this research work responses of Mode I interlaminar fracture toughness testing of 3D AIWC were evaluated by load—displacement curve and strain energy release rate. Photographs were captured during DCB test to reveal fracture process and toughening mechanisms. Further details of fracture were obtained by fractographic analysis, which confirmed the fracture mechanisms observed from photographs.

The following conclusions are obtained:

3D AIWC without binder yarn presents superior fracture

toughness properties compared to conventional laminated composites used in literature. The major contributing energy absorbing mechanisms are identified as: interface debonding, matrix breakage, yarns bridging, pull out and secondary cracks formation as well as their propagation. Undulated warp yarns act as binder and promote bridging there by increasing absorbed fracture energy. Hence, this structure offers better damage tolerance than laminated composites without compromising in-plane mechanical properties since there is no binder yarn. As binder yarns are assumed to affect in-plane mechanical properties of composites.

Acknowledgements

The authors acknowledge the financial support from National Science Foundation of China (Grant Number 11572085, 51675095).

References

［1］Sebaey T A, Blanco N, Costa J, et al. Characterization of crack propagation in mode I delamination of multidirectional CFRP laminates ［J］. Composites Science and Technology, 2012(72):1251-1256.

［2］Tanzawa Y, Watanabe N, Ishikawa T, et al. Interlaminar fracture toughness of 3D orthogonal interlocked fabric composites ［J］. Composites Science and Technology, 1999 (59): 1261-1270.

［3］Jin L, Yao Y, Yu Y, et. al. Structural effects of three-dimensional angle-interlock woven composite undergoing bending cyclic loading ［J］. Science China Physics, Mechanics and Astronomy, 2013(57): 501-511.

［4］Selzer R, Krey J. Fractography of interlaminar fracture surfaces of CFPI and CFBMI composites ［J］. Journal of Materials Science, 1994(29): 2951-2954.

［5］Morais A B D, Pereira A B. Application of the effective crack method to mode I and mode II interlaminar fracture of carbon/epoxy unidirectional laminates ［J］. Composites Part A: Applied Science and Manufacturing, 2007 (38): 785-794.

［6］Zhu X K. Advances in fracture toughness test methods for ductile materials in low-constraint conditions ［J］. Procedia Engineering, 2015(130): 784-802.

［7］Fanteria D, Lazzeri L, Panettieri E, et al. Experimental characterization of the interlaminar fracture toughness of a woven and a unidirectional carbon/epoxy composite ［J］. Composites Science and Technology, 2017(142): 20-29.

［8］Tamuzs V, Tarasovs S, Vilks U. Delamination properties of translaminar-reinforced composites ［J］. Composites Science and Technology, 2003(63): 1423-1431.

［9］Jia R, Kim Y K, Rice J. Comparing the fracture toughness of 3D braided preform composites with z-fiber-reinforced laminar composites ［J］. Textile Research Journal, 2010 (81): 335-343.

［10］Tanzawa Y, Watanabe N, Ishikawa T. FEM simulation of a modified DCB test for 3D orthogonal interlocked fabric composites ［J］. Composites Science & Technology, 2001, 61 (8):1097-1107.

［11］Fishpool D T, Rezai A, Baker D, et al. Interlaminar toughness characterization of 3D woven carbon fibre composites ［J］. Plastics, Rubber and Composites, 2013 (42): 108-114.

［12］Guenon V A, Chou T W, Gillespie J W. Toughness properties of a 3dimensional carbon epoxy composite ［J］. Journal of Materials Science, 1989(24): 4168-4175.

Natural Dye Extracted from Mexican Marigold Flower and Its Colorfastness Behavior on Lyocell Fabric

Sayed Yaseen Rashdi[1]* , **Tayyab Naveed**[2, 3] , **Ahsan Ali**[2] , **Yiping Qiu**[4] , **Wang Wei**[1, 5]

[1] *College of Chemistry, Chemical Engineering, and Biotechnology, Donghua University, Shanghai 201620, China*

[2] *Department of Technical Textiles, College of Textile Engineering, Donghua University, Shanghai 201620, China*

[3] *School of Fine Arts, Design, and Architecture, GIFT University, Gujranwala, Pakistan*

[4] *College of Textiles, Textile Science and Engineering, Donghua University, Shanghai 201620, China*

[5] *Saintyear Holding Group Co. , Ltd. , China*

* *Corresponding author's email*: sayedyaseenrashdi@ outlook. com

Abstract: In this study, the color of the Mexican marigold flower also termed as "Tageteserecta L" is extracted with the help of Soxhlet extraction. The extracted dye is applied on Lyocell fabricwhile using two mordanting methods (pre-mordanting and post-mordanting) for the evaluation of colorfastness. Mordant ferrous sulfate and mordant copper sulfate are used for the fixation of dye. The color shade (K/S 7. 812), washing fastness, light fastness, rubbing fastness and perspiration in all dyed samples are admirable (4–5 grade). The mordant ferrous sulfate has shown the higher K/S value and all other fastness results as compared to the mordant copper sulfate. Thus ferrous sulfate is more effective for color strength of the dye. Furthermore, the outcomes revealed that Tageteserecta Linn could be used for dyeing successfully in the textile industry as a natural colorant.

Keywords: Natural dyes; Lyocell; Colorfastness; Tageteserecta

1 Introduction

In recent years, due to the environmental awareness "Green Chemistry", the uses of synthetic dyes are restricted while natural dyes are endorsed. The reason is of their biodegradable nature and not harmful to living beings[1].

Marigold flower(Tageteserecta L) mostly exist in warmatmosphere and the color extraced is also a biodegrable. It was originated in south Asia but for many years, have been grown in Mexico, Peru, Ecuador, Spain, India and Chinafor the production of pigments. It is a herbaceous plantand cultivated as a garden flower. It has full of the stunning colors like yellow, golden to orange, red and mahogany color. Marigold plants are stout and branching and grow to the height of 1–3 feet and spread to 0. 5 feet[2]. Leaves are settled in conflicted patterns. The leaf vane length is less than 2 inches and tint of the leaf is green. Marigold flower (shown in Fig. 1) con-

tains compounds called carotenoids, where the lutein ($C_{40}H_{56}O_2$) is a natural pigment of the carotenoids. Fig. 2 displays the chemical structure of Marigold, lutein and its isomers zeaxanthin ($C_{40}H_{56}O_2$).

Fig. 1   Tagetes flowers (Erecta Linn)

The aim of this work is to examine the appropriateness of Mexican marigold to provide the abundant information about the extraction, dyeing behavior and color fastness properties in textile fields. The natural dye from the petals of Mexican marigold flower is extracted by using ethanol and water. This dye is applied on the Lyocell fabric along with mordants to investigate the effect on colorfastness. The difference in color shades, L^*, a^*, b^*, c^*, h^* and K/S values are examined through Spectra Flash-Data Color (SF-600).

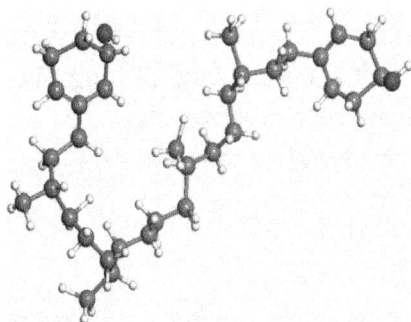

Fig. 2　Chemical structure of Lutein and Zeaxanthin ($C_{40}H_{56}O_2$)

2　Experiments

2.1　Materials and equipment

Mexican marigold flower (Tageteserecta L) was bought from the domestic market of Shanghai, China. 100% Lyocell fabric was gained from Hangzhou Xinsheng printing and Dyeing Co., Ltd. (Hangzhou). Chemicals; such as Ferrous sulfate, Copper sulfate, Ethanol, Sodium hydroxide, Formic acid, Lhistidine hydrochloride ($C_6H_{90}2N_3 \cdot HCl \cdot H_{20}$), Weighing balance, Water bath, Soxhlet apparatus, Hot air oven, Rotatory evaporator, Lab IR Dyeing machine, Data color were used in the experiment.

2.2　Raw material preparation

Fig. 3 has shown the preparation steps of the raw material. The petals from Mexican marigold flower were washed and dried. The dried petals were grinded into the form of powder and used for the extraction process.

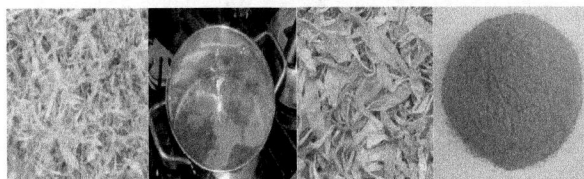

Fig. 3　(a) Petals in fresh cut; (b) Petals washed with water; (c) Petals dried with sunlight; (d) Petals in powder form

2.3　Soxhlet extraction method

A Soxhlet extractor is a piece of laboratory[3]. It is an apparatus which was invented in the year 1874 by Franz Von Soxhlet[4]. The Soxhlet carried out the filtration for the efficiency of separation of the solvent and residue. Ethanol was used as an organic solvent. The evaluated amount of feed (F) and dignified volume solvent (S) were taken in certain F/S ratio. The raw material (grinded powder of flower) was kept in a thimble of Soxhlet extractor and a condenser with a high flow rate of water is filled over it. A rotatory evaporator was used for the evaporation of the solvent and the remaining dye extract is weighed[5]. Fig. 4 has shown the mechanism of the Soxhlet extraction method. It was observed that the tint of the dye extracted was dark orange in color[6].

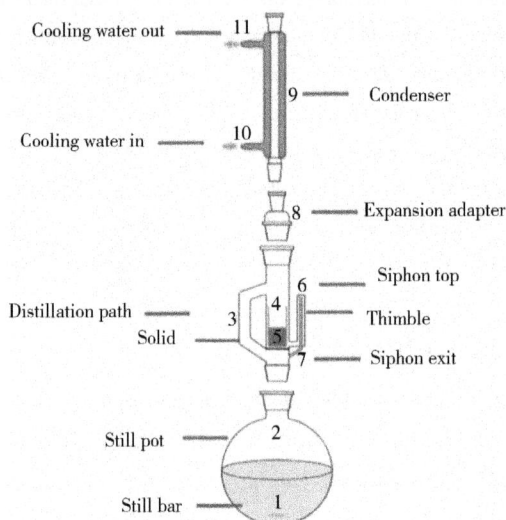

Fig. 4　A schematic representation of a soxhlet extractor

2.4　Dyeing process

The samples of Lyocell fabric were mordanted with ferrous sulfate or copper sulfate before dying. The dyeing process was carried out through two different methods i. e. pre-mordanting and post-mordanting. The mordant was dissolved in distilled water to make the liquor ratio of 1 : 40. The samples were dunked into this solution and were processed for 1/2 hour in Lab IR dyeing machine at the temperature of 90 ℃.

The dyed samples were taken out, squash and desiccated in a hot air oven. The different properties like color strength (K/S values), washing fastness (ISO 105 – CO3), light fastness (ISO 105 – BO2), rubbing (dry and wet) (ISO 105 – X12), and perspiration (ISO 105 – E04) were investigated.

3 Results and Discussion

3.1 Coloring on extracted dye and mordants

The dark orange color extract was obtained from the flowers of Tagetes erecta. The dye was applied on the Lyocell fabric samples with two mordants i. e. ferrous sulfate and copper sulfate. The different shades were perceived with the use of these two mordants from a solo dye. Tab. 1 has shown the coloring effect on dyed Lyocell fabrics through both mordanting methods at 90℃ temperature. Data color, SF–600 was used to measure the dye captivation concentration on the Lyocell fabric. Different color range was also found on Lyocell fabric by using L^*, a^*, b^*, C^*, h.

Tab. 2 has demonstrated L^*, a^*, b^*, C^* and h^* values of dyed Lyocell fabrics. The L^* value shows luminance in CIE-Lab color space and it values from 0 (darker) to 100 (lighter). The $+a^*$ value designates red and $-a^*$ values indicates green color, whereas $+b^*$ value directs yellow and $-b^*$ value specifies blue color[7]. Due to chemical mordants, the highest color value (K/S = 7. 812) was found with ferrous sulfate whereas the lowest color value (K/S = 0. 301) was found with copper sulfate in the post-mordanting method.

Tab. 1 Samples of dyed Lyocell fabric

Methods of mordanting	Ferrous suplhate	Copper sulphate
Pre-mordanting		
Post-mordanting		

Tab. 2 CIE L^* a^* b^* C8 h^* and K/S values of dyed Lyocell fabric

Mordant	Mordant method	K/S	L^*	a^*	b^*	c^*	h^*
FeSO$_4$	Pre-mordanting	6. 395	−22. 62	14. 24	38. 48	40. 72	−5. 03
	Post-mordanting	7. 812	−22. 72	15. 13	42. 40	44. 72	−5. 16
CuSO$_4$	Pre-mordanting	0. 846	−13. 62	−0. 26	10. 00	9. 99	−0. 47
	Post-mordanting	0. 301	−3. 78	−4. 33	3. 38	4. 92	2. 46

Fig. 5 has displayed the color shades (K/S) values of dyed Lyocell fabric through both mordanting methods at 90℃. The figure confirmed that color shade of Lyocell fabric with ferrous sulfate have higher value in both mordanting methods as compared to the copper sulfate. The dark orange curve line in the figure has represented the outcomes of shade difference in both mordanting methods while the copper sulfate (grey color line).

Thus highest color value (K/S = 7. 812) was achieved with ferrous sulfate in post-mordanting method and the lowest color value (K/S = 0. 301) was found with copper sulfate.

3.2 Color fastness properties of dyed Lyocell

Light fastness of many natural dyes, particularly which are extracted from flower parts are found to be humble to the standard[8]. Extracted dye from Mexican mari-

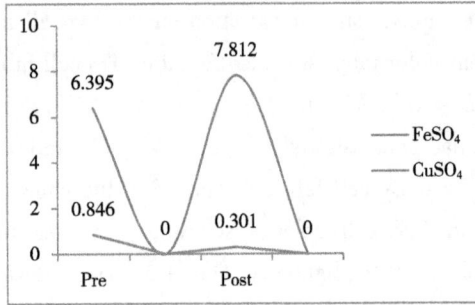

Fig. 5 *K/S* value of dyed Lyocell fabrics

gold flower contributed good washing, light, rubbing and perspiration fastness properties with the corresponding mordants. However, mordant ferrous sulfate has yield better results.

3.3 Washing fastness

Fig. 6 has revealed the result of the washing fastness. ISO 150−C03 was used. In the figure, usage of multiple fiber having six fiber strips has shown the effects of different staining on dyed Lyocell fabric samples.

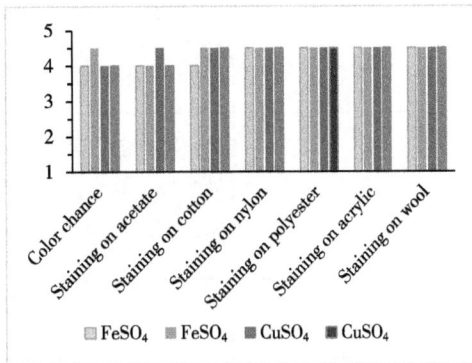

Fig. 6 Washing fastness of dyed Lyocell fabric

The mordant ferrous sulfate showed the utmost value of washing fastness in post-mordanting method. Further, the result of copper sulfate in both mordanting methods also has good to excellent grade (4−5). All the dyed samples have a slight change in their colors (4−5).

3.4 Light fastness

In Fig. 7, the dark orange color bars have specified the effect gained through ferrous sulfate while light grey color bars have recognized the treatment of Lyocell fabric samples with copper sulfate. The ISO 105−B02 standard was used for the outcomes. The copper sulfate has lower colorfastness than ferrous sulfate in both mordan-

ting methods. The differences observed were (4−5 : 4 and 6 : 4). The mordant ferrous sulfate has the highest consequences in post-mordanting method. It has determined that the Lyocell fabric in post-mordanting method with ferrous sulfate has excellent light fastness result (6).

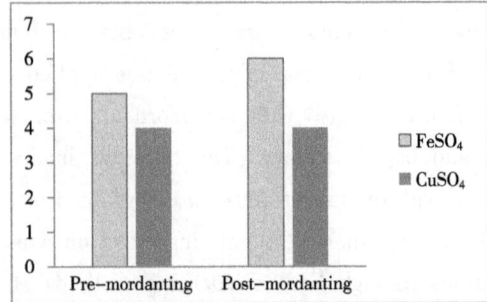

Fig. 7 Light fastness values of dyed Lyocell fabric

3.5 Rubbing fastness

The rubbing fastness (dry and wet) results of dyed Lyocell fabric (shown in Fig. 8) were obtained through "ISO 105−X12" standard. The general trend of rubbing fastness in both mordanting method was found similar. The result of dry and wet rubbing fastness with ferrous sulfate was (4−5 dry rubbing) in pre-mordanting method and (4 wet rubbing) in post mordanting method. The result depicted that there was a slightly change in dry and wet of ferrous sulfate. The respective bar has also shown good to excellent grade with copper sulfate.

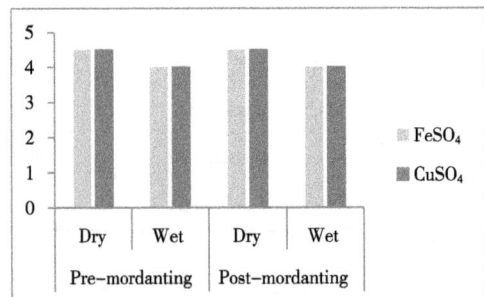

Fig. 8 Rubbing fastness (dry and wet) of dyed Lyocell fabric

3.6 Perspiration fastness (Alkaline and acidic)

Fig. 9 (a) and Fig. 9 (b) have shown the acidic and alkaline perspiration fastness out comes through the standard ISO 105−E04. It was found that samples treated with ferrous sulfate and copper sulfate exhibited good to excellent (4−5) perspiration fastness in both mordanting dyeing methods.

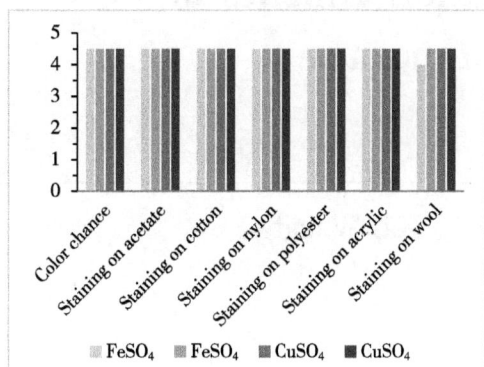

Fig. 9 (a) Acidic perspiration of dyed Lyocell fabric

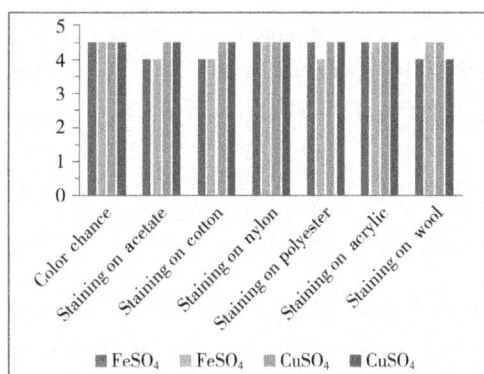

Fig. 9 (b) Alkaline perspiration of dyed Lyocell fabric

4 Conclusions

In this study the natural dye was successfully extracted from the flowers of Tageteserecta (Mexican marigold flower) through Soxhlet apparatus. Two mordants, ferrous sulfate and copper sulfate were used for dye fixation through pre-mordanting and post-mordanting methods. Experimental results showed that ferrous sul-fate mordant has better results of colorfastness properties and post-mordanting method was more effective than pre-mordanting method. Thus post-mordanting method with ferrous sulfate is a better choice (*K/S* 7.812) for dyeing of Lyocell fabric.

Acknowledgements

The research was supported by National Natural Foundation of China (No: 51403032).

References

[1] Alemayehu T, Teklemariam Z. Application of natural dyes on textile: a review [J]. International Journal of Research-Granthaalayah, 2014. 2(2): 61-68.

[2] Dawson T L. Biosynthesis and synthesis of natural colours [J]. Coloration Technology, 2009. 125(2): 61-73.

[3] Bhande R, Giri P. Extraction of garcinia Indica oil from kokum seed [J]. Management and Applied Sciences, 2017 (5): 724-728.

[4] Soxhlet F. Diege wicht saiialy tische bestimmung des milchfettes; von. 1879.

[5] Toussirot M, et al. Dyeing properties, coloring compounds and antioxidant activity of Hubera nitidissima (Dunal) Chaowasku (Annonaceae) [J]. Dyes and Pigments, 2014 (102): 278-284.

[6] Leon K, Pedreschi M F, Leon J. Color measurement in $L^* \sim a^* \sim b^* \sim$ units from RGB digital images [J]. Food Research International, 2006, 39(10): 1084-1091.

[7] Maha-In K, Mongkholrattanasit R, Klaichoi C, et al. Dyeing silk fabric with natural dye from longan leaves using simultaneous mordanting method [J]. Materials Science Forum, 2016, 857: 491-494.

[8] Samanta A K, Agarwal P. Application of natural dyes on textiles [J]. Indian Journal of Fibre & Textile Research, 2009, 34(4): 384-399.

Non-Isothermal Crystallization Kinetics of Novel PET/QE Composites

Qisong Lin[1], Shunhua Zhang[1]*, Kai Wang[1]

[1] *College of Materials and textiles, Zhejiang Sci-Tech University, Hangzhou, China*

* *Correspondence author's email*: zshhzj@163.com

Abstract: Novel poly (ethylene terephthalate)/clay composites were prepared by melt processing using novel natural clay Quantum Energy® (QE) powder as the modifier, and the non-isothermal crystallization kinetics of PET/QE composites were studied using DSC and WAXD. The results reveal that: QE powder exhibits an excellent performance as nucleating agents and elevates the crystallization rate of PET, decreases the activation energy with the increasing amount as well. It also can be assumed that the dispersion of QE in PET matrix possibly affects the interlayer spacing of QE and the nucleation effect during the crystallization process.

Keywords: Poly (ethylene terephthalate); Novel natural clay; Non-isothermal crystallization; Nucleation effect; Effective activation energy

1 Introduction

Poly (ethylene terephthalate) (PET) is a thermoplastic semi-crystallizable polyester with remarkable mechanical, thermal and chemical properties, having been widely used from fibers to bottle containers and engineering plastics, etc. Although possesses extensive applications, the interest for higher-performance applications of PET is still maintaining. Thus, a variety of modifiers were developed to enhance or broaden the properties of PET. Among those modifiers, natural or manufactured clay, due to its promotions on PET properties (thermal, mechanical, and barrier properties, etc.), has attracted great interest[1].

Recently, a novel natural clay material officially listed as Quantum Energy® (QE) powder, collected from Hamangun in Korea and further treated by calcination and unique fermentation, was incorporated into polyester fiber to develop a heat-generating fabric[2]. The thermal insulation, fast-drying performance and heat-generating performance of the fiber were improved and showed a promising prospects. In our previous study, PET/QE fiber showed superior moisture and ultraviolet absorption as well. Consequently, to provide a useful reference for the production, it is significative to study the crystallization process of PET with the addition of novel QE powder, which is crucial for the product morphology and its performance. Therefore, this work prepared PET/QE composites with twin-screw extruder and presented a detail work against the effect of QE to the non-isothermal melt-crystallization behavior of plain PET and the composites by using a differential scanning calorimeter (DSC) method. The crystallization mechanism of PET, as the key issue, was also discussed with the participation of QE powder.

2 Experiments

2.1 Materials

The PET ($\eta = 0.95$ dL/g) was obtained from Sinopec Shanghai Petrochemical Co., Ltd. (Shanghai, China) and Quantum Energy® (QE) powder was commercial product acquired from Quantum Energy Research Center (Incheon, Korea) with particle size range from 40 to 200 nm.

2.2 Preparation

All materials were dried in avacuum oven for 12h at

105℃ before using. The modification of the neat PET took place in a TSE−30A twin-screw extruder (Nanjing, China) with the melting temperature at 280℃, and 265℃ for extrusion. Amounts of QE powder such as 0, 1% and 2% were mixed with PET following added to the feeder of the extruder. The as-prepared extrudate was air cooled before chipped.

2.3 Instruments and Methodology

Non-isothermal crystallization was studied using a Perkin Elmer DSC 8000 under a N_2 atmosphere (20 mL/min). The sample was initially heated to 280℃ at 10℃/min and held for 5min to eliminate the thermal history, then cooled to 30℃ at a constant rate. Applied cooling rates were 5℃/min, 10℃/min, 20℃/min and 40℃/min, respectively. WAXD patterns were acquired on an ARL X'TRA powder diffractometer with Cu K_α radiation, and tested at an accelerating voltage of 45 kV and a current of 40mA. The scanning rate 2°/min was used over the 2θ range of 3°−50° for all samples.

3 Results and Discussion

3.1 WAXD analysis

WAXD patterns of QE powder and PET/QE composites are shown in Fig. 1. The QE powder shows a unique X-ray pattern with complicated reflection peaks, which similar to other natural clay minerals[3]. A characteristic reflection peak was found at $2\theta = 9.84°$, compared to PET/QE composites, which corresponded to an interlayer distance of 0.898nm(8.98Å). This peak became broader with the presence of PET, implying a decrease in the degree of coherent layer stacking of the QE by forming a more disordered system with PET. For the composites, when the content of QE was 1%, because of the intercalation of PET chains, the interlayer spacing increased and WAXD peak was shifted to lower angles in this region[4]. However, compared to the PET−1% QE sample, the peak shifting was not obvious for PET−2% QE, and that was due to the probably unsatisfactory dispersion in the polymer substrate, which also further discussed below. Neat PET exhibited a well-defined crystal reflection indicates that it possessed a triclinic structure[4]. Moreover, the incorporation of QE improved the crystallization performance of PET and

the crystal structure of PET was not changed, since no changes in peak positions were observed and the characteristic diffraction peaks for PET became sharp with the increasing loading of QE.

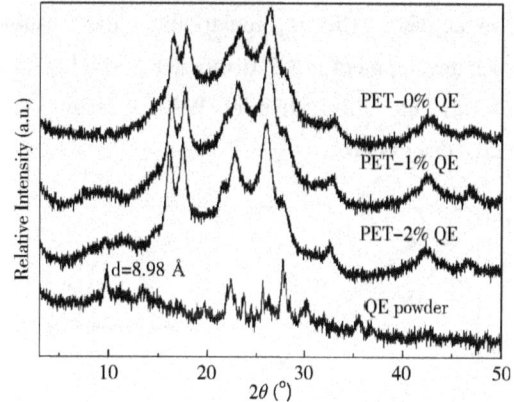

Fig. 1 WAXD patterns of QE powder and PET/QE composites

3.2 Nucleationactivity of QE powder

In order to assess the nucleation activity of QE, herein reference the Dobreva method[5], which quantitatively described the nucleation activity (φ) of foreign substrate in a polymer matrix. The φ can be defined as a ratio that represents the work decrement of three-dimensional nucleation during the crystallization in additives/polymer blend melt. The value of φ, ranges from 0 to 1, may manifests lower value when the foreign substrate possesses stronger activity, and is calculated as below:

$$\varphi = \frac{B^*}{B} \tag{1}$$

where B^* and B are the parameters during heterogeneous and homogeneous nucleation, respectively. Both B^* and B can be experimentally determined from the slope of equation:

$$\ln\beta = \text{Constant} - \frac{B}{\Delta T_p^2} \tag{2}$$

Where, β attributes to the cooling rates and ΔT_p represents the super cooling ($\Delta T_p = T_m - T_c$).

According to Eq. (2), plots of the $\ln\beta$ versus $1/\Delta T_p^2$ for neat PET and PET/QE composites are carried out in Fig. 2(a) and several straight lines are obtained. The values of B and B^* for neat PET and PET/QE composites are obtained from the slopes of these lines, respectively. Then, the nucleation activity is figured out from

Eq. (1) and plotted in Fig. 2 (b). The results indicate that QE has beneficial nucleation effect on PET crystallization. Besides, the curve shows a partly upward trend with the increase amount of QE (from 1% to 2%), which means PET−2% QE has slightly lower nucleation activity. This is, remarkably, can assume to the poor development of QE dispersion, which also consistent with the observation of WAXD results on the foregoing discussion.

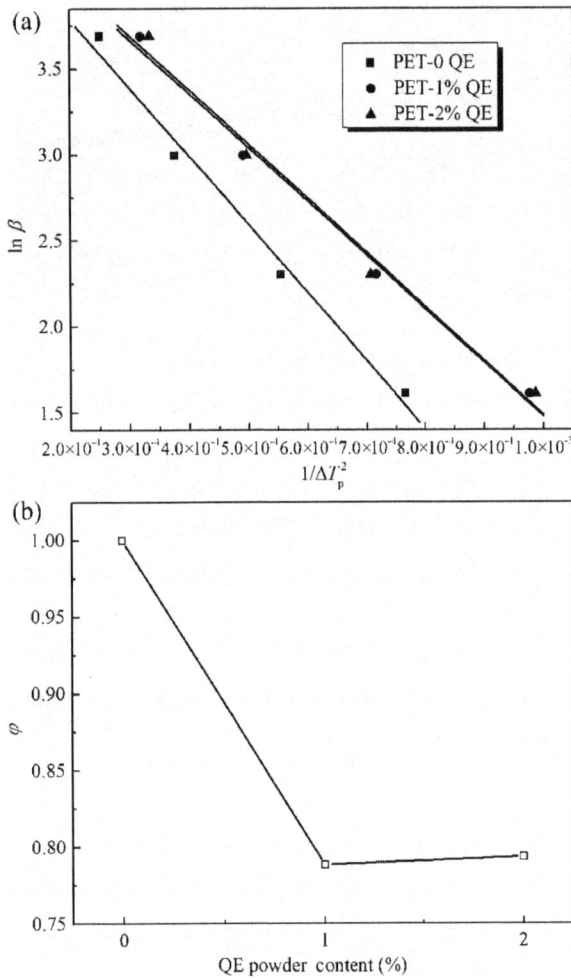

Fig. 2 Plots of the $\ln\beta$ versus $1/\Delta T_p^2$ for neat PET and PET/QE composites (a) and nucleation activity of QE in PET composites (b)

3.3 Non-isothermal crystallization kinetics

To clarify the non-isothermal melt crystallization kinetic, the DSC data acquired in selected cooling rates, PET−2% QE for example, has to be converted to relative crystallinity as a function of time and is plotted in Fig. 3 (a). The curves exhibit similar sigmoidal shape,

which indicating a quick primary crystallization during the early stage and a slow secondary crystallization at the later stage for all cooling rates and showing that higher cooling rate lowers the completion time for PET crystallization. In addition, same results were observed in neat PET and PET−1% QE as well, which were not presented for briefness.

Avrami model, anucleation-growth model that establishes the relationship between the relative crystallinity X_c and crystallization time t, can be usually used for the interpretation of isothermal crystallization kinetics and described as follows[6]:

$$1 - X_c = \exp(-Z \cdot t^n) \qquad (3)$$

Where, the exponent n is a parameter indicates the type of nucleation and the growth morphology.

It is notable that n value is a specific integer ranging from 1 to 4, and Z is a growth rate constant depends on both nucleation and growth rate parameters, in terms of the original assumptions of the theory. To analyze the non-isothermal crystallization behavior as well, Jeziorny extended the theory by introducing a correction factor β for the growth rate constant Z, and the factor is defined as the cooling rate[7]. The corrected Z_c can be written as:

$$\lg Z_c = \lg Z / \beta \qquad (4)$$

By substituting Z_c into Eq (3) and transformation, the derived Avrami equation as follows:

$$\lg[-\ln(1 - X_c)] = n\lg t + \lg Z_c \qquad (5)$$

Fig. 3 (b) shows various of the double logarithm plot of $\lg[-\ln(1 - X_c)]$ versus $\lg t$ for PET−2% QE at different cooling rates, which can be divided into two parts: the primary crystallization stage (fitted with straight line) and the secondary crystallization stage (deviated from the line). The same observation also carried out in all other samples. All n values, half-time of crystallization ($t_{1/2}$) and Z_c are obtained and listed in Tab. 1. For all composites, higher n values are figured out compared to the neat PET, except PET−2% QE at several cooling rates, which demonstrate the remarkable affection of QE on the crystallization mechanism of PET. In addition, PET−2% QE gives a low $t_{1/2}$ value for all cooling rates, which means QE can elevate the crystallization rate of PET composites. However, PET−1% QE does not show an obvious promotion on $t_{1/2}$ value and even lower at several cooling rates when compared to PET–0QE, implying that low quantify of QE has limited effect on crystallization rate. The values of Z_c are increasing with the increasing value of cooling rate for all samples, implying that crystallization rate is proportional to cooling rate. Moreover, compared to neat PET, similar to PET–2% QE, PET–1% QE shows high Z_c values at high cooling rates as well. This may be attributed to the better dispersion of QE in the matrix which contributes the excellent nucleation performance. Although Jeziorny method has been routinely applied to crystallization of polymers, the intrinsic value of the resulting does not accurately reflect the nucleus growth mechanism for the non-isothermal crystallization. Hence, Mo proposed a kinetic equation that combine the Avrami and Ozawa equations, defined as[8]:

$$\ln\beta = \ln F(T) - b\ln t \tag{6}$$

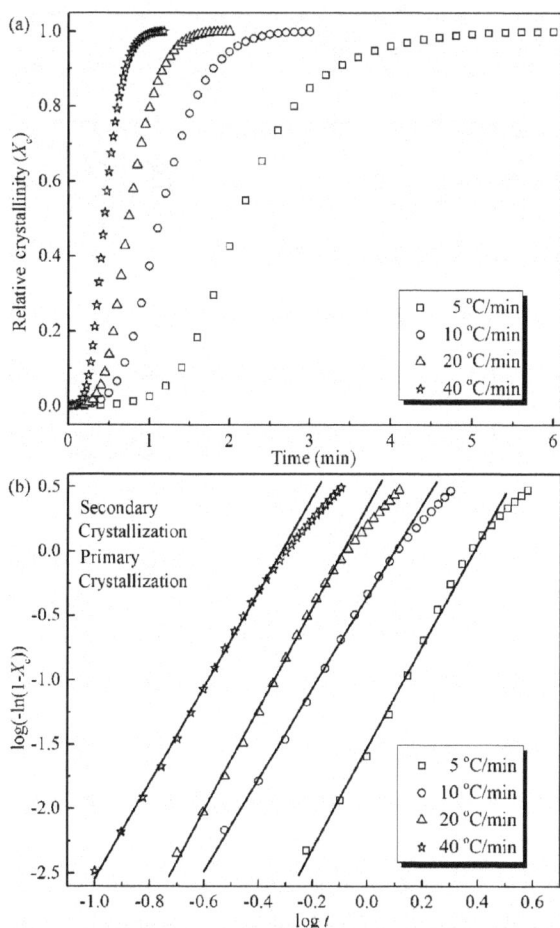

Fig. 3 Relative crystallinity functions of time for PET–2% QE (a) and its corresponding Avrami plots (b) at different cooling rates

Tab. 1 Avrami parameters of PET/QE composites

Sample	Avrami parameters	Cooling rate (℃/min)			
		5	10	20	40
PET–0QE	$t_{1/2}$ (min)	2.20	1.40	0.85	0.45
	n	3.83	3.92	3.97	3.40
	Z_c (min^{-1})	0.50	0.85	1.02	1.06
PET–1% QE	$t_{1/2}$ (min)	2.42	1.33	0.81	0.52
	n	4.00	4.22	4.62	4.45
	Z_c (min^{-1})	0.44	0.85	1.04	1.07
PET–2% QE	$t_{1/2}$ (min)	2.12	1.13	0.75	0.44
	n	3.95	3.56	3.95	3.71
	Z_c (min^{-1})	0.49	0.92	1.04	1.07

Where, $b = n/m$. n and m are the exponent for Avrami and Ozawa equations, respectively. $F(T)$ is a precise cooling rate when the measured system amounts to a certain relative crystallinity at unit crystallization time. And a linear line declares the validity of this method for PET non-isothermal crystallization when plots $\ln\beta$ versus $\ln t$ with a given relative crystallinity.

Herein, Fig. 5 is carried out according to Eq. (6) with the sample of PET–2% QE and a good linear is observed in all given relative crystallinity, apparently indicating that Mo's method is suitable for non-isothermal crystallization analysis in this work. And the detail $\ln F(T)$ and b values for all samples are also tabulated in Tab. 2. As it can be seen, the b values change moderately, which denote that all polymer chains are able to grow in three-dimensional.

Tab. 2 Mo parameters of PET/QE composites

Sample	Mo parameters	X_c (%)			
		20	40	60	80
PET–0QE	b	1.25	1.29	1.32	1.31
	$\ln F(T)$	2.29	2.57	2.84	3.17
PET–1% QE	b	1.32	1.34	1.37	1.39
	$\ln F(T)$	2.39	2.64	2.88	3.20
PET–2% QE	b	1.30	1.33	1.36	1.37
	$\ln F(T)$	2.18	2.45	2.69	2.98

Compared the $\ln F(T)$ values at a given relative crystallinity, unlike PET–2% QE possess lower values, PET–

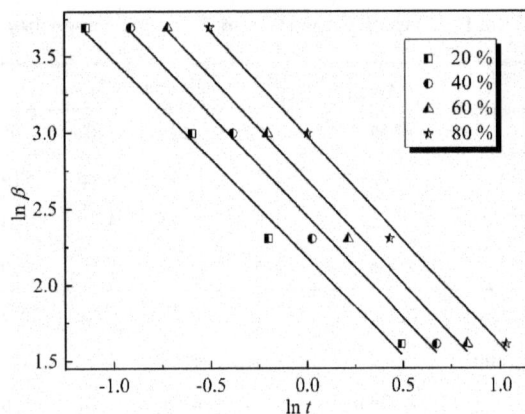

Fig. 5　Mo plots at given relative crystallinity for PET－2%QE

1%QE shows similar or even higher values than neat PET, which indicates the crystallization rate of PET increase with the loading of QE and that is consistent with the results of $t_{1/2}$.

3.4　Effective activation energy for non-isothermal crystallization

Apart from the description of the crystallization process, it is also significant to compute the effective activation energy of non-isothermal crystallization in polymers. Friedman's method[9], a differential iso-conversional method, is one of the most creditable methods for evaluating the effective activation energy and is based on equation:

$$\ln\left(\frac{dX_c}{dt}\right) = \ln A + \ln f(X_c) - \frac{E}{RT} \qquad (7)$$

Where, dX_c/dt set as the instantaneous crystallization rate as a function of time at a given conversion X_c, A is the pre-exponential factor and the function $f(X_c)$ describes the reaction mechanism. E and T denote the effective activation energy and its temperature at a certain X_c value, respectively. R is the gas constant. According to Eq. (7), $\ln\left(\frac{dX_c}{dt}\right)$ versus $\frac{1}{T}$ can be plotted at various values of X_c with the data recorded at all cooling rates, the curves should exhibit good linear and E value can be derived from its slope.

Fig. 6 exhibits the dependence of the activation energy on the relative crystallinity for all samples. It is clear that all curves follow an upward trend, showing that, as the crystallization developed, the hinder for segment diffusion and regular stack is increasing. Notably, at

low crystallization conversion ($X_c < 0.2$), PET－1% QE has lowest E value, which may be due to its higher nucleation activity can contribute to the crystallization and therefore, an inferior activation energy value appeared as the result at initial stage. However, the effective activation energy of PET－1%QE becomes higher than PET－2%QE when X_c develops above 0.3, and that is, indicating the complex crystallization behaviors, with unique mechanisms and different activation energy, are taking place at different degree of crystallization conversion, and there is also competition among those mechanisms during PET and its composites crystallized in different relative crystallinity. The increasingly difference between PET－1%QE and PET－2%QE in E value implying that the effect of nucleation activity is certainly not the key factor in high relative crystallinity region, therefore, as the final result, the higher quantity of QE shows lower activation energy and increases the crystallization rate of PET in the mid to late stage of crystallization in this work.

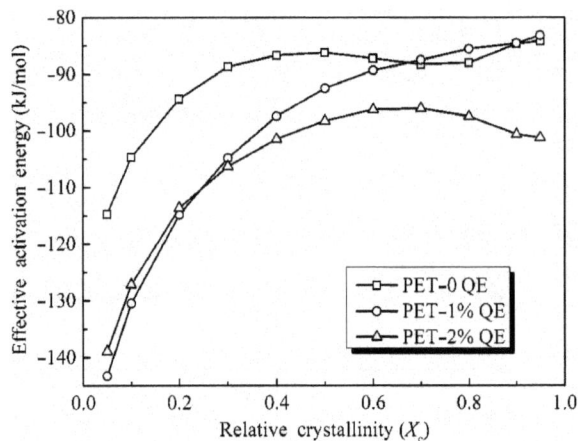

Fig. 6　Dependence of the effective activation energy (E) on the relative crystallinity (X_c) for PET/QE composites

4　Conclusions

In this work, we prepared novel PET composites with different QE powder content by melt blend processing, and with an emphasis on studying the melt-crystallization behaviors of PET/QE under non-isothermal cooling condition. The WAXD patterns of PET did not show significant change with the low loading of QE, indicating that PET in composites still possessed a triclinic structure, and furthermore, a shifting characteristic peak for QE illustrated that the interlayer spacing of QE changed due to the intercalation of PET chains, which also, determined by the dispersion of QE particles.

Further DSC studies revealed that the appearance of QE elevated the crystallization of PET, which demonstrated the beneficial effect of QE on PET crystallization. The Dobreva method clarified that QE powder played a main role in the heterogeneous nucleation, and the amount of QE was inversely proportional to the nucleation effect during the overall crystallization process, which may be owing to the dispersion of QE. However, the extensive studies with Jeziorny and Mo theories verified that the increasing content of QE followed a higher crystallization rate, moreover, the effective activation energies results showed lower values at secondary crystallization stage for PET-2%QE sample as well. Thus, an interpretation can be proposed that nucleation factor no longer possessed a pronounce effect on the later period of crystallization and the incorporation of QE powder could improves the crystallization rate of PET and decreases its effective activation energies.

References

[1] Farhoodi M, et al. Migration of aluminum and silicon from PET/clay nanocomposite bottles into acidic food stimulant [J]. Packag Technol Sci, 2014, 27(2): 161-168.

[2] Bahng G W, Lee J D. Development of heat-generating polyester fiber harnessing catalytic ceramic powder combined with heat-generating super microorganisms [J]. Text Res J, 2014, 84(11): 1220-1230.

[3] Calcagno C I W, et al. The effect of organic modifier of the clay on morphology and crystallization properties of PET nanocomposites [J]. Polymer, 2007, 48(4): 966-974.

[4] Cruz-Delgado V J, et al. Carbon nanotube surface-induced crystallization of polyethylene terephthalate (PET) [J]. Polymer, 2014, 55(2): 642-650.

[5] Dobreva A, Gutzow I. Activity of substrates in the catalyzed nucleation of glass-forming melts [J]. I. Theory. J Non-Cryst Solids, 1993, 162(1-2): 1-12.

[6] Lorenzo A T, et al. DSC isothermal polymer crystallization kinetics measurements and the use of the Avrami equation to fit the data: Guidelines to avoid common problems [J]. Polym Test, 2007, 26(2): 222-231.

[7] Jeziorny A. Parameters characterizing the kinetics of the non-isothermal crystallization of poly (ethylene terephthalate) determined by DSC [J]. Polymer, 1978, 19(10): 1142-1144.

[8] Liu T X, et al. Nonisothermal melt and cold crystallization kinetics of poly (aryl ether ether ketone ketone) [J]. Polym Eng Sci, 1997, 37(3): 568-575.

[9] Friedman H L. Kinetics of thermal degradation of char forming plastics from thermogravimetry: Application to a phenolic plastic [J]. J Polym Sci Part C, 1964, 6(1): 183-195.

Novel Bio-Based Recycable Epoxy Resin and Its Application in Carbon Fiber Reinforced Composite

Hui Zhang[1,2], Wanshuang Liu[1,2]*, Yiping Qiu[1,2], Yi Wei[1,2]

[1] *Collaborative Innovation Center for Civil Aviation Composites, Donghua University, Shanghai 201620, China*

[2] *Key Laboratory of Textile Science & Technology, Ministry of Education, Shanghai 201620, China*

[3] *Department of Technical Textiles, College of Textiles, Donghua University, Shanghai 201620, China*

* *Corresponding author's email*: wsliu@ dhu. edu. cn

Abstract: Permanently cross-linked epoxy resins have outstanding mechanical properties and solvent resistance, but they cannot be processed and reshaped once synthesized. This paper presents a new type of bio-based recycling epoxy polymer with dynamic covalent imine bond (EPI). The EPI was cured by the curing agent synthesized from lignin-derived vanillin. The EPI showed comparable mechanical and thermal properties compared with traditional epoxy resin. Through the exchange reaction of the imine bonds, the EPI can be repeatedly remolded without depolymerization and degrade in small molecule amine solution. Finally, The EPI was used to fabricate carbon fiber reinforced epoxy composite (CFRP). The CFRP demonstrated performance comparable to those of its commercial counterparts. More important, nondestructive retrieval of carbon fibers was realized through gentle depolymerization in the amine solution.

Keywords: Recycling epoxy resins; Carbon fiber reinforced composites; Imine bonds; Biopolymers

1　Introduction

Carbon fiber reinforced polymer composites (CFRPs) are widely used in aerospace, wind power, automotive, military, and electronics because of their lightweight, high strength, good fatigue resistance, and flexible structural design[1-2]. Currently CFRPs mainly use thermosetting epoxy resin as the resin matrix. This is mainly because the epoxy resin also combines excellent dimensional stability, mechanical strength, chemical resistance, and processability, in addition to lower cost. However, epoxy resin is a petroleum-based product. Due to the depletion of petroleum resources and the release of greenhouse gases from petroleum refining, the issue has attracted intensive attention from countries around the world, which has brought challenges to the sustainability of the epoxy resin industry. In addition, since the cross-linked structure of the epoxy resin is constructed by irreversible covalent bonds, it is difficult to recover, reprocess, and degrade after the destruction

occurs. Therefore, with the continuous increase in the amount of CFRPs, the environmental protection issues caused by it have getting more and more attention.

At present, the processing method for scrapped CFRPs mainly includes landfill, thermal cracking, crushing, and supercritical fluid methods. However, these treatment methods have problems such as environmental pollution and high equipment costs[3]. Therefore, developing important way to solve the recycling prg epoxy materials with recyclable functions is aoblems for CFRPs. An important strategy to prepare epoxy resins with recyclable function is to introduce dynamic covalent bonds with certain environmental stimuli-responsiveness in their cross-linked structures. Under the stimuli of specific environmental conditions (such as light, heat, electricity, mechanical stress, pH change, etc.), these dynamic covalent bonds underwent a reversible bond-bonding or exchange reaction process, resulting in rearrangement of the crosslinked structure, and therefore the material macroscopically exhibited recyclable functions such as self-repairing or reproducible forming[4-11]. For example, Saito et al. used the dynamic characteristics of Diels-Alder (DA) reaction to reverse decomposition at high temperature and re-addition at low temperature, prepared a self-healing epoxy resin containing DA addition structure[12]. Zhang and Rong used the mechanism based on the rapid exchange reaction of disulfide bonds catalyzed by tri-n-butylphosphine to develop an epoxy resin that can be self-repaired and reworked at room temperature[13]. However, these recyclable epoxy resins have lower T_g and poorer mechanical properties than conventional epoxy resins, and generally have a longer healing time and a low healing efficiency.

In this study, lignin-derived vanillin was used as raw material to prepare epoxy curing agent with imine dynamic covalent bonds. Through the curing reaction with the epoxy resin monomer, the imine dynamic covalent bonds were introduced into the epoxy resin structure. The cured epoxy with imine bonds (EPI) showed high T_g value (132℃) and comparable mechanical properties compared with traditional epoxy polymers. The EPI can be repeatedly remolded and has high-performance retention after three recycling processes. The EPI can also degrade in small molecule amine solution. After evaporating the amine, the obtained epoxy powder can be reprocessed to solid epoxy by hot press. Finally, The EPI was used to fabricate CFRPs. The CFRPs demonstrate comparable flexural properties to those of its commercial counterparts. What's more, nondestructive retrieval of carbon fibers was realized through gentle depolymerization in the amine solution.

2　Experiments

2.1　Material

Vanillin, tetrahydrofuran (THF) and ethylenediamine (EDA) were purchased from Sigma-Aldrich. Methylcyclohexane diamine (HTDA) was obtained from Shenzhen Yexu Industrial Co., Ltd. AFG−90 trifunctional epoxy resin with epoxy equivalent weight (EEW) of 100g/mol was provided by Shanghai Huayi Resin Co., Ltd. Ethylene glycol diglycidyl ether (EGDET) with

EEW of 154g/mol was supplied by Wuxi Lanxing Petrochemical Co., Ltd. T700 carbon fiber was purchased from Jiangsu Hengshen Fiber Material Co., Ltd. Diethyltetramethylimidazole (2E4MZ) was purchased by Hubei Yuancheng Saichuang Technology Co., Ltd.

2.2　Synthesis of the vanillin-based curing agent

15.2g (0.1mol) vanillin was dissolved in 40mL ethanol, and 38.4g (0.3mol) HTDA was taken into a three-necked flask (the molar ratio of vanillin and HTDA is 1:3). The solution of vanillin in ethanol is placed in a dropping funnel, then slowly dropped into the three-necked flask under magnetic stirring. The mixture was refluxed at 80℃ for 4 hours, under a nitrogen atmosphere. After completion of the reaction, ethanol, excess HTDA, and water generated during the reaction were distilled off under reduced pressure. A brown solid powder was obtained. Finally, the product was recrystallized from ethyl acetate and dried in a vacuum oven to give a yellow curing agent powder (the mixture of hardener 1 and hardener 2). The synthetic route is shown in Fig. 1.

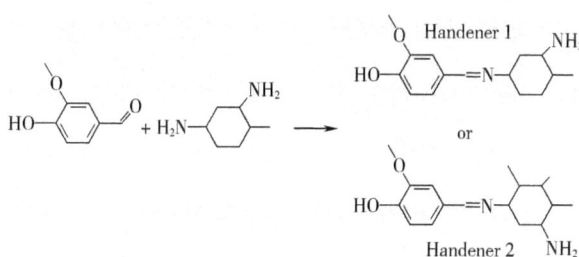

Fig. 1　The synthetic route of the curing agents

2.3　Curing with epoxy resin

AFG−90(60%) was mixed with EGDET (40%) to obtain low viscosity epoxy with EEW of 116.3. In a 250mL flask, 8.7g curing agent powder, 0.2g 2E4MZ (accelerator) and 40mL THF were added. After stirring for 15min, 11.63g diluted AFG−90 was added to the mixture (the molar ratio of the epoxy group to the curing agent is 3:2). The mixture was stirred for 30min to allow them to mix thoroughly. Then the well-mixed liquid was distilled under reduced pressure at 40MPa for 50 minutes to evaporate the THF solvent therein, afterword poured it into an aluminum mold and degassed in a vacuum oven at 50℃ for 30 minutes. Finally, it was cured in an ordinary oven (80℃ for 1h, 140℃ for 2h, 170℃ for 1h) to obtain EPI.

2.4 Reprocessing of EPI

The cured EPI was crushed into pieces in a multi-functional crusher, and ground into powder by Vibration grinding machine as shown in Fig. 2(b). Then the EPI powders were poured into a mold which was placed on a hot press machine, and heated the mold at 180℃ for 40min at a pressure of 5MPa to receive a Reprocessing molding which is shown in Fig. 2(a), we name it 1st Reprocessing sample. The 2ed Reprocessing and 3rd Reprocessing samples were prepared by repeating the processes.

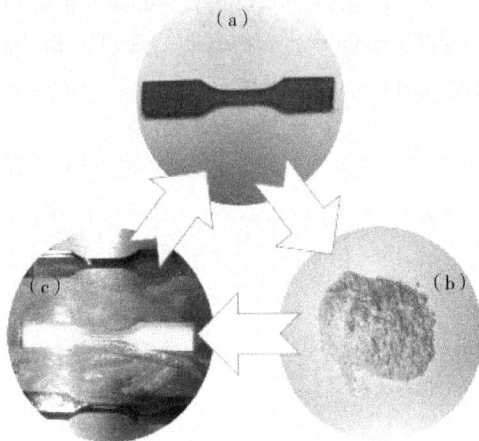

Fig. 2 (a) Repetitively shaped samples; (b) EPI powder; (c) Hot press mold

2.5 Fabrication of CFRP

In a 40cm × 30cm aluminum plate, 69.8g diluted AFG-90 trifunctional epoxy resin was mixed with 52.2g curing agent powder, 1.2g 2E4MZ and 250mL THF. Then carbon fiber fabric (26cm × 22cm) was immersed in the epoxy solution. Afterwords, the carbon fiber fabrics were dried in an oven at 80℃ for 8 minutes and carbon fiber prepregs were obtained. Eight layers of prepregs were stacked together and put on a hot press machine with a pressure of 0.2MPa. After curing (80℃ for 1h, 140℃ for 2h, 170℃ for 1h), CFRPs panel (CFRP-1) was fabricated, as shown in Fig. 3 (a). Another eight layers of prepregs were cured sepa-

rately in an oven (80℃ for 1h, 140℃ for 2h, 170℃ for 1h). After curing, the cured prepregs were stacked together and put on a hot press machine at a pressure of 5MPa for 1 hour, the obtained CFRPs was named as CFRP-2 as shown in Fig. 3(b).

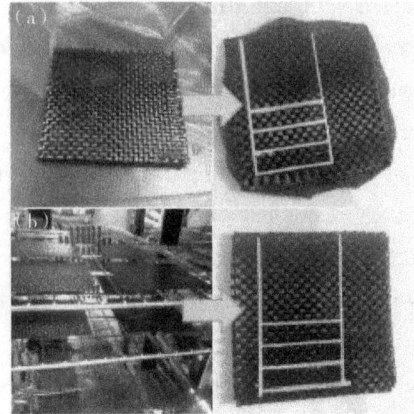

Fig. 3 Fabrication and photographs of (a) CFRP-1 and (b) CFRP-2

2.6 Characterization

Differential scanning calorimeter (DSC) was conducted on a NETZECH 214 at a heating rate of 10℃ min^{-1} using nitrogen as a purge gas. Dynamic mechanical analysis (DMA) was performed on a TA DMA Q800 at a frequency of 1Hz and a heating rate of 3℃/min. Fourier transform infrared (FTIR) spectra were recorded on a Nicolet 6700 FTIR spectrometer with the scan range of 4000－400cm^{-1}. NMR spectra were taken on Inova 400 and Inova 500 spectrometers in deuterated solvents (d-DMSO). Scanning Electron Microscopy (SEM) was observed on a Hitachi S4800 scanning electron microscope (SEM). Mechanical properties of the epoxy resin and CFRPs were tested on the universal testing machine 203B－TS (Shenzhen Wance). The tensile and flexural tests were conducted following ASTM D638 and D790, respectively. The GT200 Vibration Grinding Machine produced by Beijing Gelideman Instrument Co., Ltd. was used to make EPI powders. Hot press testing machine (HY-10TK, Shanghai Henghan) was used to prepared epoxy and CFRP samples.

3 Results and Discussion

3.1 Characterization of curing agents

Fig. 4 a shows the ^{1}H-NMR spectrum of the synthetic curing agent. The peaks at 8.2, 4.0, 3.8 and 2.0ppm are corresponding to hydrogen at f, a, b, m on the curing agent, respectively. The peaks at 7.3ppm, 7.1ppm and 6.8ppm can be assigned to the hydrogen at c, d, e on the benzene ring of the curing agent, respectively. The broad peaks between 0.7 and 1.8 correspond to hydrogen on the cycloaliphatic ring in the curing agent.

FTIR spectrum of synthetic curing agent as shown in Fig. 4 (b) reveals the characteristic absorption bands of the stretching vibration of primary amine and phenol groups at ca. 3430cm^{-1}, and a benzene groups ring stretching vibration band at ca. 1520 and 1600cm^{-1}. The band at 1640cm^{-1} can be assigned to C=N stretching vibration, indicating the formation of imine bond. The band at 1280cm^{-1} can be assigned to the stretching vibration of phenolic hydroxyl group. The results of ^{1}H-NMR and FTIR spectra confirm the structure of synthetic curing agent.

3.2 Curing and thermal mechanical properties of EPI

The curing of EPI was investigated by DSC in a non-isothermal mode. There are two exothermic peaks, which is because two groups (phenolichydroxyl group and primary amines) in the curing agent can react with the epoxy groups in the resin and the activities of the two groups are quite different. The activity of the phenolic hydroxyl group is relatively low, so imidazole accelerator is added. Based on the results of DSC, the curing program is set as 80℃ for 1h, 140℃ for 2h, 170℃ for 1h.

Storage modulus and loss modulus as a function of temperature for the cured EPI are shown in Fig. 5(b). The temperature at the maximum tan δ value is often taken as glass-transition temperature. As can be seen, the T_g value of cured EPI is 132℃. The storage modulus at room temperature is around 3000MPa, which is similar to the conventional epoxy and much higher than many reported recyclable epoxy resins.

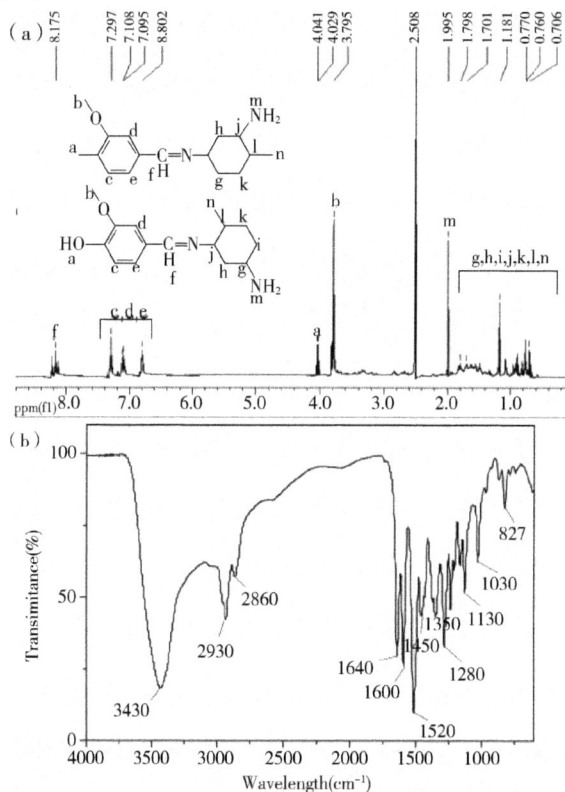

Fig. 4 (a)^{1}H-NMR spectrum and (b) FTIR spectrum of the synthetic curing agent

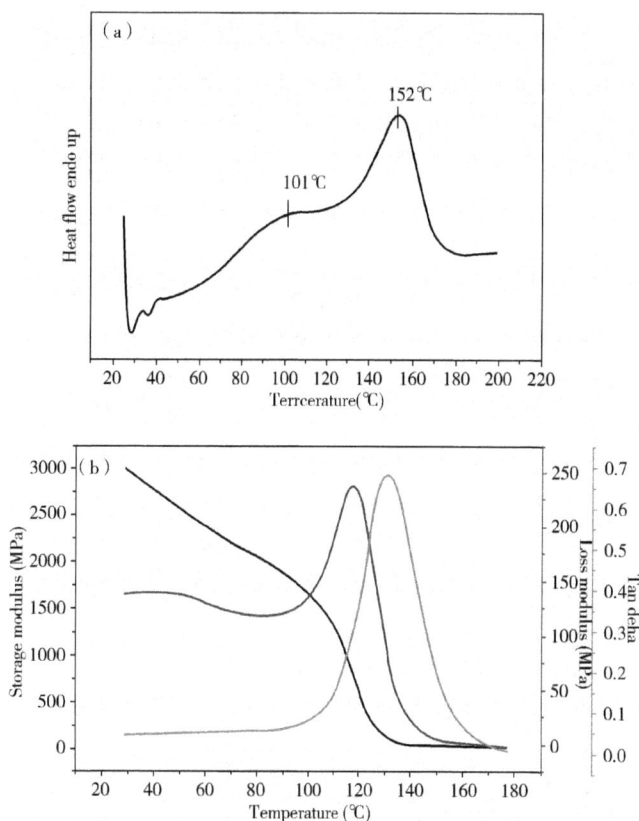

Fig. 5 (a) DSC heat flow scan and (b) DMA temperature sweep

3.3　Reprocessing function of EPI

The reprocessing of EPI is due to the fact that dynamic covalent imine bonds can undergo mutual exchange reactions. The principle is shown in the Fig. 6.

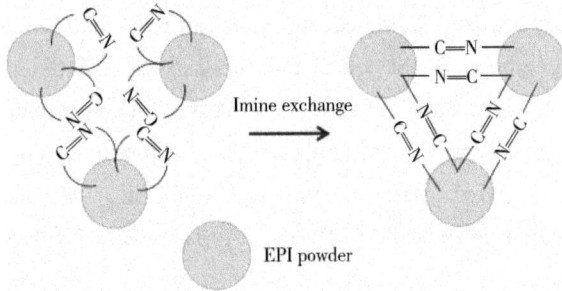

Fig. 6　Schematic illustration of the reprocessing process of EPI

Tensile tests were conducted on the original epoxy and the reprocessed epoxy samples. The tensile strength of the original and reshaped specimens is shown in Fig. 7. The reprocessing experimental parameters for the three types of samples are listed in Tab. 1. Tensile strength of the original EPI can reach 84MPa, which is slightly higher than that of traditional epoxy resins. The retention efficiency of 1st Generation can reach 93%, and there is almost no loss compared to the original. Although the retention efficiency of 2^{ed} Generation and 3rd Generation slightly decreases, they are all above 70%, and the tensile strength is more than 60MPa. There are two reasons for the reduction in tensile strength. The first point is due to the accelerated aging of the cured epoxy resin under repeated high-temperature hot-pressing conditions. The second point is that although the powder milled by the vibration grinding machine is already very small, there are inevitable gaps between the small particles that may not be in contact with each other, resulting in a slight decrease in the degree of cross-linking of the reshaped sample, cause the loss of tensile strength.

The thermo-mechanical properties of the original and reprocessed specimens are shown in Fig. 8. The storage modulus and T_g of the reshaped specimens did not decrease, but rather increased. This is because the Reprocessing EPI is completed under the condition of high temperature hot pressing. The more the Reprocessing times, the more the hot pressing times. Under the re-

peated high temperature, T_g will increase slightly.

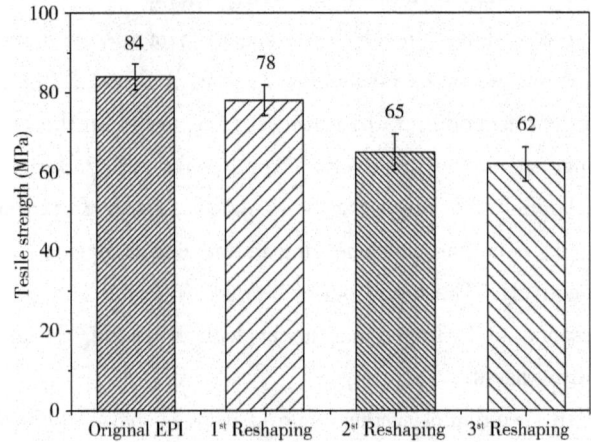

Fig. 7　The tensile strengths of the original and reprocessed samples

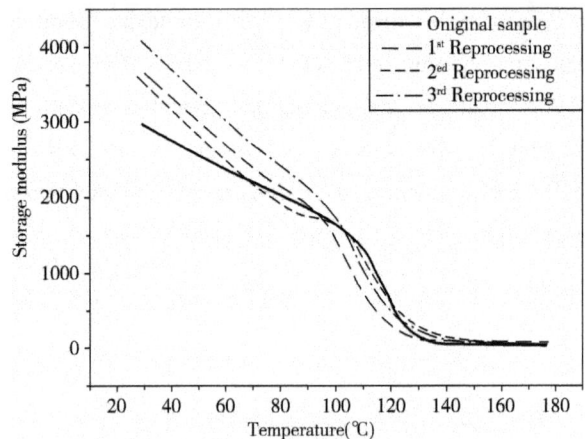

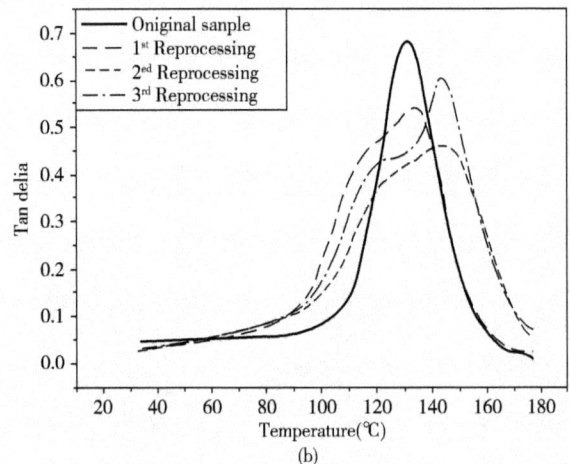

Fig. 8　(a) The storage modulus and (b) tan delta of the original and reprocessed samples

Tab. 1 Experimental parameters and properties of EPI after reprocessing

	Reprocessing temperature (℃)	Reprocessing time (min)	Reprocessing pressure (MPa)	T_g (℃)	Tensile strength (MPa)	Retention efficiency (%)
Original Sample	—	—	—	132	84	—
1st Reprocessing	180	40	5	133	78	93
2ed Reprocessing	180	40	5	143	65	77
3rd Reprocessing	180	40	5	144	62	74

3.4 Degradation and reprocessing

One of the most important challenges in recycling CFRPs is to degrade the resin matrix. The EPI can be reprocessed by exchange reaction of the dynamic covalent imine bond. Similarly, it can be degraded in EDA through the exchange reaction as shown in Fig. 9(a). And because this reaction is a reversible reaction, the high degree of cross-linked epoxy resin can be acquired by evaporate the EDA to reverse the reaction direction. Thus, the EPI can reach near 100% recyclability. As shown in Fig. 9(b), 0.5g EPI can be completely degraded into a viscous liquid in 10g EDA when heated at 100℃ for 2 hours. After evaporating off EDA, EPI powder can be obtained again. The EPI powder can be reprocessed to solid EPI sample through hot press at 180℃ for 40min (5MPa).

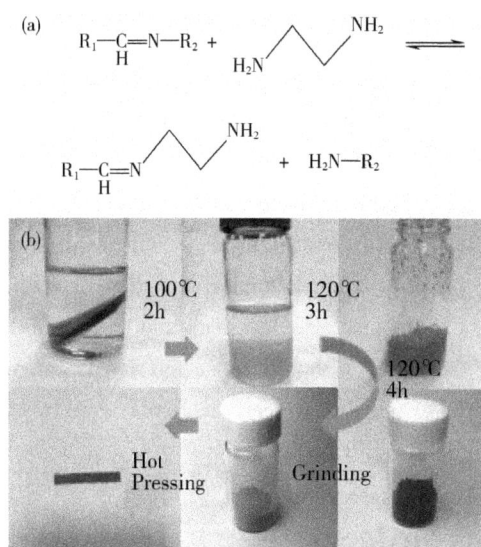

Fig. 9　The degradation and Reprocessing (a) principle and (b) flow chart of the EPI

3.5 Application of EPI in CFRPs

As shown in Fig. 10, even the carbon fiber prepreg has been cured, it can still be hot pressed into CFRP-2 by the exchange reaction through dynamic covalent imine bonds in its EPI resin matrix. And the CFRP-2 maintain certain mechanical properties. So, the carbon fiber prepreg with EPI resin matrix can be stored at room temperature for a long time. It should be noted that the mechanical properties of CFRP-2 is much inferior than CFRP-1 in both flexural strength and flexural modulus. This is mainly due to the fact that the surface of the prepreg which is directly cured without pressurization is not smooth, so that different prepreg surface cannot be completely contacted when hot pressing into the plate, causes many unhealed voids, seriously affected the mechanical properties of CFRP.

Fully recycling CFRPs involves recycling both the polymer matrix and the carbon fibers. Carbon fiber is the most expensive part of CFRPs, so we hope to achieve the recycling of carbon fiber by completely degrading the resin matrix in CFRP.

As shown in Fig. 11(a), a small piece of eight-layered CFRP was put into EDA. The resin matrix in CFRP can be completely degraded by heating at 100℃ for 6h. The obtained carbon fibers were then cleaned in the ethanol and dried in the oven. The microscale morphologies of both fresh and recycling fibers were observed by using a scanning electron microscope (SEM), and the images are shown in Fig. 11(b) and (c). There is no visible damage or alternation in fiber dimension. It is also seen that only a tiny amount of residual polymer is attached on the carbon fiber surfaces.

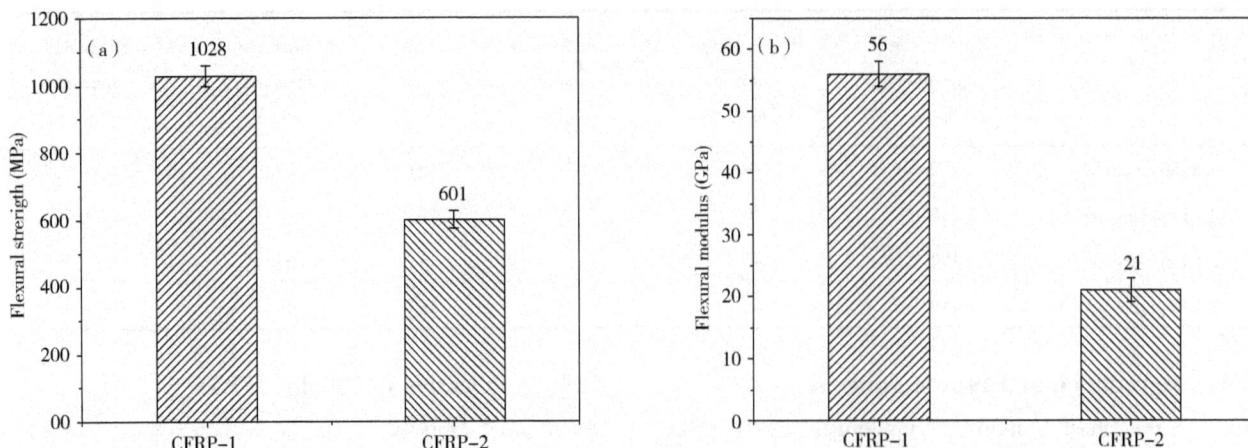

Fig. 10 (a) The flexural strength and (b) flexural modulus of CFRP-1 and CFRP-2

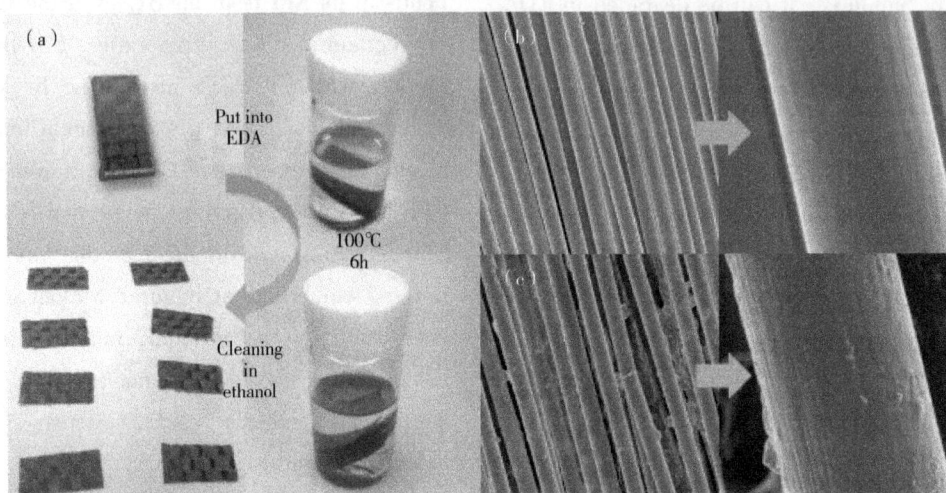

Fig. 11 (a) Recycling process of CFRPs; (b) SEM images of the fresh and (c) recycling carbon fibers

4 Conclusions

Abio-based curing agent containing dynamic covalent imine bond was synthesized. After curing with an epoxy resin monomer, a recyclable EPI was obtained. The tensile strength of EPI is 87MPa and its T_g is 132℃, which is similar to the conventional epoxy resins. Even if it is ground into a powder, it can still be reprocessed by hot pressing at a high temperature of 180℃ through the exchange of imine bonds on its surface, the tensile strength recovery efficiency is above 70%, and the T_g is even higher. EPI can also be degraded in EDA, and the degradation products can be cross-linked and polymerized into macromolecule epoxy polymers by evaporation of ethylenediamine, achieving 100% recycling. EPI can be used as a resin matrix for carbon fiber prepreg either, and even if the prepreg has been cured, it can still be bonded together into CFRP through the exchange of surface imine bonds, so this kind of prepreg can be stored at room temperature for a long period of time. However, due to the unsmooth surface of the prepreg, the mechanical properties of CFRP will have a certain loss. As an environmentally friendly material, the CFRP with EPI as a resin matrix can achieve recycling of expensive carbon fibers therein through degradation of EPI.

Acknowledgements

This work was supported by Shanghai Science and Technology Committee (No. 16DZ112140)

References

[1] Chung D. Carbon Fiber Composites, Butterworth Heinemann, Waltham, MA, USA 2012.

[2] Morgan P, Carbon Fibers and Their Composites [M]. CRC Press, Boca Raton, FL, USA 2005.

[3] 王新波, 黄龙男. 降解型环氧树脂[J]. 化学进展, 2009, 21 (12), 2704 −2711.

[4] Scott T F, Schneider A D, Cook W D, et al. Photo induced plasticity in cross-linked polymers [J]. Science, 2005, 308 (5728):1615.

[5] Montarnal D, Leibler L. Silica-like malleable materials from permanent organic networks[J]. Science, 2011, 334 (6058): 965 −968.

[6] Montarnal D, Tournilhac F, Hidalgo M, et al. Versatile one-pot synthesis of supramolecular plastics and self-healing rubbers[J]. Journal of the American Chemical Society, 2009, 131(23):7966 −7967.

[7] Yu K, Taynton P, Zhang W, et al. Reprocessing and recycling of thermosetting polymers based on bond exchange reactions [J]. Rsc Advances, 2014, 4(20):10108 −10117.

[8] Park H Y, Kloxin C J, Scott T F, et al. Stress relaxation by addition-fragmentation chain transfer in highly cross-linked thiol-yne networks [J]. Macromolecules, 2012, 43 (24): 10188 −10190.

[9] Kloxin C J, Scott T F, Adzima B J, et al. Covalent adaptable networks (CANs): A unique paradigm in cross-linked polymers[J]. Macromolecules, 2010, 43(6):2643 −2653.

[10] Bowman C N, Kloxin C J. Covalent adaptable networks: Reversible bond structures incorporated in polymer networks [J]. Angew Chem Int Ed Engl, 2012, 51(18)4272 −4274.

[11] Yu K, Taynton P, Zhang W, et al. Influence of stoichiometry on the glass transition and bond exchange reactions in epoxy thermoset polymers[J]. Rsc Advances, 2014, 4(89):48682 −48690.

[12] Bai N, Simon G P, Saito K. characterization of the thermal self-healing of a high crosslink density epoxy thermoset[J]. New J Chem, 2015 (39):3497 −3506.

[13] Lei Z Q, Xiang H P, Yuan Y J, et al. Room-temperature self-healable and remoldable cross-linked polymer based on the dynamic exchange of disulfide bonds[J]. Chem Mater, 2014 (26):2038 −2046.

Properties of Discarded Fiber/Polyurethane Flame Retardant Insulation Board

Lihua Lyu[1]*, Yingjie Liu[1], Congtan Li[1]

[1]*School of Textile and Material Engineering, Dalian Polytechnic University, Dalian 116034, China*

Corresponding author's email: lvlh@ dlpu. edu. cn

Abstract: In order to solve the recycling problem of discarded fibers, discarded fiber/polyurethane flame retardant insulation board was prepared by blending- hot pressing method with discarded fiber, discarded polyurethane, AC (azodimethylamide) foaming agent and APP (ammonium polyphosphate) flame retardant as raw materials. The necessary conditions to the optimized technology was mass fraction of discarded fibers 10%, mass fraction of AC foaming agent 3%, mass fraction of APP flame retardant 15%, hot pressing pressure 7MPa, hot pressing temperature 180℃, length of discarded fibers 20mm, mixing temperature 175-180℃, hot pressing time 8min, cool-down time 2h, which were optimized by thermal conductivity coefficient, limit oxygen index and mechanical properties. And, under the optimized technological conditions, the thermal conductivity coefficient was $0.06W/(m \cdot K)$, the limit oxygen index was 35.82%, the tensile strength was 2.642MPa, and the bending strength was 5.314MPa. The flame retardant mechanism and effect of the discarded fiber/polyurethane flame retardant insulation board were analyzed by TGA (thermogravimetric analysis) and residual carbon ratio. The average diameter of bubble pore was 350μm and the thermal insulation mechanism of the discarded fiber/polyurethane flame retardant insulation board was researched by SEM(scanning electron microscope). Finally, the abaqus finite element simulation software was used to simulate the thermal conduction process and verify the correctness of model.

Keywords: Discarded fiber; Flame retardant insulation board; Flame retardant mechanism; Thermal insulation mechanism; Finite element simulation

1 Introduction

Now there were more than 26 million tons of discarded textiles in China, but the recycling ratio was less than 10%. It is showed that more than 100 million tons of discarded textiles will be produced by the end of 2020 in China[1-2]. If the average period of clothes was 3 – 4 years, the discarded ratio of textiles was 70%[3]. These discarded textiles not only caused horrendous waste, but also got a worse influence on the environment. So, it was imminent to how to recycle these discarded textiles and manufacture high value-added products. Testore and Petri[4] studied the technique for recycling the so-called hard textile wastes, which came from fabric cuttings in making-up or from used clothing and were composed of cotton or man-made fibers or both. Sun et

al. [5] investigated the feasibility of using glass fibers, a recycled material from waste printed circuit boards (WPCB), as sound absorption and thermal insulation material. Glass fibers were obtained through a fluidized-bed recycling process. All the results showed that the reuse of RGF for sound and thermal insulation material provided a promising way for recycling WPCB and obtaining high beneficial products. Long et al. [6] fabricated natural fibers reinforced high density polyethylene (PE-HD) composites with ramie noil from textile industry and bamboo scrap fibers from paper-making industry as reinforcements, so the discarded fibers could be used reasonably. Chen et al. [7] used discarded flax fibers as raw material for pyrolysis treatment to study the oil absorption performance. It can be seen that, with the efforts of scholars, many discarded fibers have become valuable, but there is still a lot of space for the study of discarded fibers.

It was showed from the statistics that nearly 30% of the world's energy consumption was used on constructions. The ratio of China's building energy consumption was more than 27. 45% of the total energy consumption. The emissions ratio of greenhouse gas CO_2 caused by the building energy consumption run up to 25% of China's total greenhouse gas emissions[8-10]. China's new building areas reached 2 billion m^2 each year, and there were more than 95% of them were the high energy consumption buildings[11]. In the building enclosure, the thermal insulation wall occupied the largest proportion in the heating energy consumption, which accounted for 32%–36% of the total energy consumption[12]. Now, the ratio of good thermal insulation building wall materials used to reduce energy consumption was 25%–51%[13]. At present, the insulation materials used in building enclosure structure are mainly insulation mortar and insulation board. Panyakaew and Fotios[14] used cocoanut shell and bagasse to prepare the lightweight insulation board by hot pressing method and studied the mechanical properties and thermal insulation properties of insulation boards with different density. Then, the thermal conductivity coefficient was 0. 046 – 0. 068W/(m · K) under the densities of 250 – 350kg/m^2. Cai et al.[15] prepared sisal fiber/phenolic resin insulation board and studied the compressive strength, impact strength and thermal conductivity. Zhao[16] proposed the "phonon eutectic" theory to reduce the thermal conduction of materials and form a green and efficient thermal insulation board-SIB (Smart Insulation Board). Zhu[17] prepared SiO_2 aerogel core / polystyrene flame retardant insulation board with excellent thermal insulation properties, the thermal conductivity coefficient was 0. 026W/(m · K) and good mechanical properties. Polyurethane, known as the "fifth largest plastic", it was widely used in architectural, automotive, petrochemical, textile, electronic, mechanical, medical and other fields[18]. In the aspect of polyurethane composites, Ding et al.[19] prepared the wood fiber/polyurethane foam reinforced composites and the thermal conductivity coefficient was 0. 017W/(m · K). Yu et al.[20] used discarded polyes-

ter fiber to enhance thermoplastic polyurethane, and developed the sound absorption composites.

The purpose of this study is to reduce the harm of discarded fibers and improve the performance of thermal insulation composites. In this paper, discarded fibers were used as reinforced material and discarded polyurethane was used as matrix material. Then, discarded fiber/polyurethane flame retardant insulation board was prepared by blending-hot pressing method. The optimized technological conditions were obtained according to the thermal conductivity coefficient, limit oxygen index and mechanical properties. The flame retardant mechanism and thermal insulation mechanism of the discarded fiber/polyurethane flame retardant insulation board were analyzed by TGA, residual carbon ratio, average diameter of bubble pore were observed by SEM. Finally, the abaqus finite element simulation software was used to simulate the thermal conduction process.

2 Experiments

2.1 Materials

Discarded fibers which were obtained from Dalian Ganjingzi Huicheng Cotton Product Factory were employed as reinforced material. Discarded polyurethane which was obtained from Bayer Co. , Ltd. was employed as matrix material. Azodimethylamide which was obtained from Yuyao Tong Yong Plastic Dyeing Co. , Ltd. was employed as foaming agent. Ammonium polyphosphate which was obtained from Jinan Taixing Fine Chemical Co. , Ltd. was employed as flame retardant.

2.2 Instrument

QJK1000A Leftover Material Opening Machine which was from Qingdao Jingmengke Machinery Manufacturing Co, Ltd. was used for opening; SJK-180 Double Roll Plasticizer which was from Wuhan Yiyang Plastic Machinery Co. , Ltd. was used for mixing and plasticizing; QLB-50D/QMN Pressure Molding Machine which was from Jiangsu Wuxi Zhongkai Plastic Machinery Co. , Ltd. was used for forming; ZHY-W Universal Prototype which was from Hebei Chengde Testing Machine Factory was used for the preparation of testing samples; RGY-5 Microcomputer Control Electronic Universal Testing Machine which was from Shenzhen Regal Instrument Co. ,

Ltd. was used for testing mechanical properties; KES-F7 Tester which was from Hunan Zhenhua Analysis Instrument Co., Ltd. was used for measuring thermal properties; LFY-606B Digital Display Limit Oxygen Index Measuring Instrument which was from Shandong Textile Science Research Institute was used for measuring limit oxygen index; JSM-6460LV Scanning Electron Microscope which was from Japan was used for observing surface morphology; STAPT1600 Thermogravimetric Analyzer which was from Germany Lineis was used for testing the relationship between material temperature and quality; Muffle which was from Beijing Original Technology Co., Ltd. was used for hot processing.

2.3 Preparation process

The discarded fiber/polyurethane flameretardant insulation board was prepared by blending-hot pressing method with discarded fibers, discarded polyurethane particles, AC foaming agent and APP flame retardant as raw materials. The blending temperature was 175 – 180℃, hot pressing time was 8min and cool-down time was 2h. The specific preparation process of discarded fiber/polyurethane flame retardant insulation board was shown in Fig. 1.

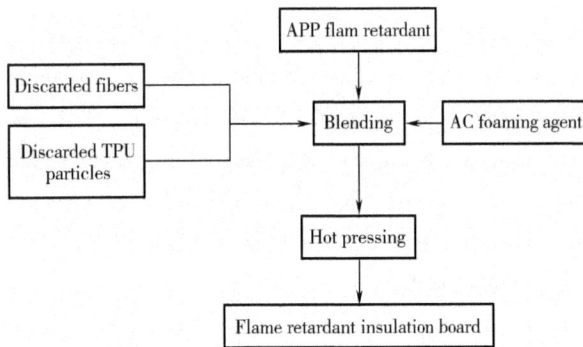

Fig. 1   Specific preparation process

2.4 Detection indexes

2.4.1 Thermal conductivity coefficient

The thermal conductivity coefficient was test according to GB/T 10295—2008. The thermal conductivity coefficient equation 1 is:

$$K = \frac{(Q \times D)}{A \times \Delta T} \quad (1)$$

In the equation: K is the thermal conductivity coefficient, the unit is W/(m · K); Q is the heat loss, the unit is W; D is the thickness of specimen, the unit is m; A is the area of specimen, the unit is m^2; ΔT is the temperature difference, the unit is ℃.

Substances with high thermal conductivity coefficient had excellent thermal conductivity. For thermal insulation materials, the thermal conductivity coefficient was lower and the insulation performance was better. Generally, materials with a thermal conductivity coefficient of less than 0.2W/(m · K) were called thermal insulation materials.

2.4.2 Limit oxygen index

The Limit oxygen index was test according to GB/T 8924—2005. The limit oxygen index was higher and the flame retardant perform was better. When the limit oxygen index was 22% – 25%, the material had the property of self-extinguishment; when the limit oxygen index was 26%, the material was flame retardant and the flame retardant property was well when the limit oxygen index reached 30%.

2.4.3 Mechanical properties

The testing standard and method of tensile properties were according to GB/T 1447—2005 *Test method for tensile properties of fiber-reinforced plastics*. And the testing standard and method of bending properties were according to GB/T 1449—2005 *Test method for bending properties of fiber-reinforced plastics*.

2.4.4 Thermogravimetric curve and residual carbon ratio

Thermogravimetric curve was according to GB/T 27761—2011 *Standard test method of mass loss and residue measurement validation of thermogravimetric analyzers*. The testing standard and method for testing residual carbon rate were according to GB/T 27761—2011. The details were as follows: a certain amount of sample was taken into the crucible and dried for 2h. And then, they were taken out and weighed m_0. The dried samples and crucible were put into the muffle, and the temperature of the muffle was set at 600℃. When the heating was finished, the weight of the samples and the crucible were m_1, the quality ratios of m_0 and m_1 were the residual carbon ratio. The residual carbon ratio was the higher and the produced gas was the lower when the materials were in high temperature. Also, the formed carbon layer covered the surface of the polymer and improved the heat and corrosion resistance.

2.4.5 Diameter of bubble pore

Diameter of bubble pore was measured by the average chord length method. Then, the average diameter of bubble pore D was obtained by equation (2), during this process, the bubble pore could be regarded as homogeneous sphere.

$$d = \frac{L}{0.7852} = \frac{L}{0.616} \tag{2}$$

In the equation: d is the average diameter of the bubble pore, the unit is μm; L is the average chord length of the bubble pore, the unit is μm.

3 Results and Discussion

3.1 Optimized technological conditions of discarded fiber/polyurethane flame retardant insulation board

3.1.1 Effect of mass fraction of discarded fibers on thermal conductivity coefficient K and limit oxygen index LOI

The mass fraction of discarded fibers was 10%, 20%, 30% and other technological parameters were as follows: hot pressing temperature 180℃, hot pressing pressure 5MPa, mass fraction of flame retardant 20%, mass fraction of foaming agent 2%, length of discarded fibers 20mm, mixing temperature 175 – 180℃, hot pressing time 8min, cool-down time 2h. The effect of the mass fraction of discarded fibers on the thermal conductivity coefficient $K = 10^{-2} W/(m \cdot K)$ and the limit oxygen index LOI were shown in Fig. 2.

It was seen from Fig. 2 that the mass fraction of discarded fibers had significant effect on thermal conductivity coefficient and limit oxygen index. The mass fraction of discarded fibers was higher, the thermal conductivity coefficient became greater and the limit oxygen index was smaller. That was to say, with the increasing of the mass fraction of discarded fibers, the thermal insulation properties and the flame retardant properties of the thermal insulation board got worse. The reasons might be as follows: With the increasing of the mass fraction of discarded fibers, there were more difficulties in blending and the viscosity was increased. So, the resistance of

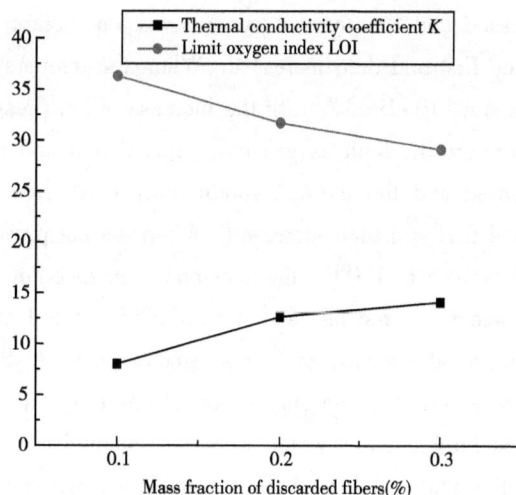

Fig. 2 Effect of mass fraction of discarded fibers on thermal conductivity coefficient K and limit oxygen index LOI

bubble pores was increased and it was easy to damage the structure of bubble pores, which the formation of bubble pores were affected. Therefore, the thermal insulation properties of the thermal insulation board were decreased. For the flame retardant properties, the sealing of carbon layer in the process of APP flame retardants was destroyed for excessive discarded fibers and oxygen could not be completely isolated, so the flame retardant properties of the thermal insulation board were affected. Therefore, the mass fractions was sure of discarded fibers were 10%.

3.1.2 Effect of hot pressing temperature on thermal conductivity coefficient K and limit oxygen index LOI.

The hot pressing temperature was 170℃, 180℃, 190℃ and other technological parameters were as follows: mass fraction of discarded fibers 10%, hot pressing pressure 5MPa, mass fraction of flame retardant 10%, mass fraction of foaming agent 2%, length of discarded fibers 20mm, mixing temperature 175 – 180℃, hot pressing time 8min, cool-down time 2h. The effect of hot pressing temperature on the thermal conductivity coefficient $K = 10^{-2} W/(m \cdot K)$ and the limit oxygen index LOI were shown in Fig. 3.

It was seen from Fig. 3 that hot pressing temperature had significant influence on thermal conductivity coefficient and limit oxygen index. With the increase of hot pressing temperature when the temperature was about 170℃ to 190℃, the limit oxygen index raised first and then decreased and the thermal conductivity coefficient decreased first and then increased. When the temperature was about 170-190℃, with the increase of hot pressing temperature the limit oxygen index raised first and then decreased and the thermal conductivity coefficient decreased first and then increased. When the hot pressing temperature was 190℃, the decomposition speed of foaming agent was too fast and it resulted in partial overheating for the release of a large amount of heat. So it was easy to destroy the bubble pore structure or form the opened bubble pores which were not conducive to the formation and stability of closed bubble pores, and the thermal insulation properties would also decrease. When the hot pressing temperature was 180℃, the thermal insulation properties and the flame retardant properties of the thermal insulation board were best, so the hot pressing temperature could be determined to 180℃.

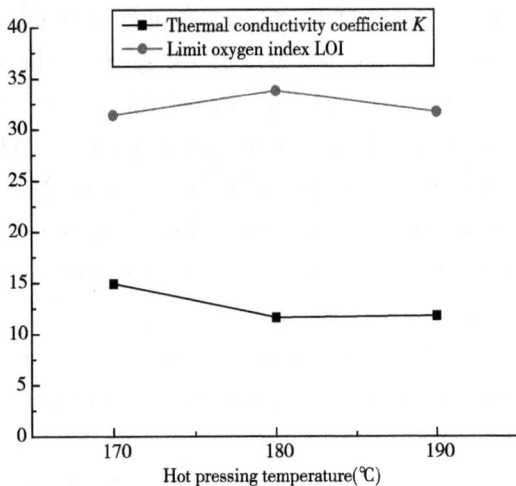

Fig. 3　Effect of hot pressing temperature on thermal conductivity K and limit oxygen index LOI

3.1.3　Effect of mass fraction of flame retardant on thermal conductivity coefficient K and limit oxygen index LOI

The mass fraction of flame retardant was 10%, 15%, 20% (the mass fraction related to the mass fraction of discarded TPU), and the other technological parameters were as follows: mass fraction of discarded fibers 10%, hot pressing temperature 180℃, hot pressing pressure 5MPa, mass fraction of foaming agent 2%, length of discarded fibers 20mm, mixing temperature 175-180℃, hot pressing time 8min, cool-down time 2h. Effect of mass fraction of flame retardant on thermal conductivity coefficient $K = 10^{-2} W/(m \cdot K)$ and limit oxygen index LOI were shown in Fig. 4.

It was seen from Fig. 4 that mass fraction of the flame retardant had little influence on the thermal conductivity coefficient, but it had obvious effect on the limit oxygen index. When the mass fraction of the flame retardant was in the range of 10% to 20%, with the increased of the mass fraction of the flame retardant, the limit oxygen index was increased. However, when the mass fraction of flame retardants was greater than 15%, the increasing trend of the limit oxygen index could reduce. So the mass fraction of flame retardant was 15%.

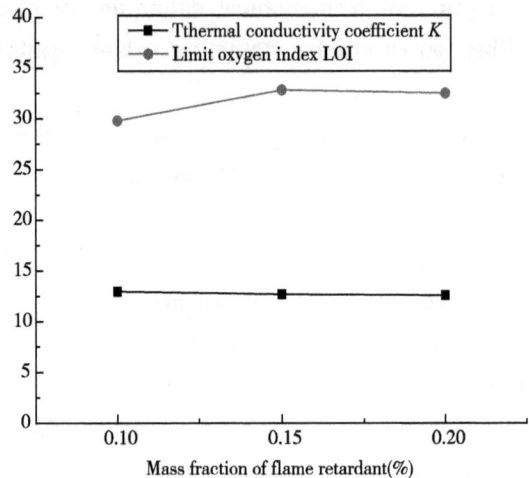

Fig. 4　Effect of mass fraction of flame retardant on thermal conductivity coefficient K and limit oxygen index LOI

3.1.4　Effect of mass fraction of foaming agent on thermal conductivity coefficient K and limit oxygen index LOI

The mass fraction of the AC foaming agent was 1%, 2%, 3% (the mass fraction related to the mass fraction of discarded TPU), and the other technological parameters were as follows: mass fraction of discarded fibers 10%, hot pressing temperature 180℃, hot pressing pressure 10MPa, mass fraction of flame retardant 15%, length of discarded fibers 20mm, mixing temperature 175-180℃, hot pressing time 8min, cool-down time 2h. Effect of mass fraction of foaming agent on thermal conductivity coefficient $K = 10^{-2} W/(m \cdot K)$ and limit oxygen index LOI were shown in Fig. 5.

It was seen from Fig. 5 that the mass fraction of the foaming agent had little effect on the limit oxygen index, but it had great influence on the thermal conductivity coefficient. With the increase of the mass fraction of the foaming agent, the thermal conductivity coefficient decreased and the thermal insulation properties were good. The reasons were as follows: The mass fraction of the foaming agent was low, the produced gas by decomposition was less, and the bubble pores were less. With the increased of the mass fraction of the foaming agent, the nucleation rate of the bubble pores increased and the more bubble pores were formed, so the thermal conductivity coefficient decreased and the thermal insulation properties was good. Then, the mass fraction of the foaming agent was 3%.

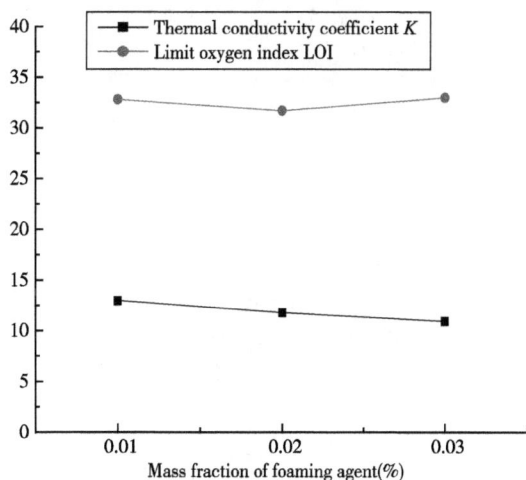

Fig. 5   Effect of mass fraction of foaming agent on thermal conductivity coefficient Kand limit oxygen index LOI

3.1.5   Effect of hot pressing pressure on thermal conductivity coefficient K and limit oxygen index LOI

The hot pressing pressure was 4,7,10MPa, and the other technological parameters were as follows: mass fraction of discarded fibers 10%, hot pressing temperature 180℃, mass fraction of flame retardant 15%, mass fraction of foaming agent 3%, length of discarded fibers 20mm, mixing temperature 175-180℃, hot pressing time 8min, cool-down time 2h. Effect of hot pressing pressure on thermal conductivity coefficient $K = 10^{-2}$W/(m·K) and limit oxygen index LOI were shown in Fig. 6.

It was seen from Fig. 6 that the hot pressing pressure had no effect on the limit oxygen index, but had a great influence on the thermal conductivity coefficient. When hot pressing pressure was too high or too low, the thermal conductivity coefficient was large and the thermal insulation properties were bad. Therefore, the hot pressing pressure was suitable for 7 MPa. When the hot pressing pressure was smaller, it was easy to cause the smaller solubility of gas, the wall of bubble pores was thick and the distribution of bubble pores was not uniform. So, the thermal conductivity coefficient was larger. When the hot pressure was too high, the gas diffusion ratio was so large and the escaped gas was too much, and it could not form the homogeneous structure of bubble pores. So, the thermal conductivity coefficient was larger. Meanwhile, the unloading pressure could also cause the excessive gas to gush out of the molten body and it caused the failure of fabrication of the flame retardant insulation board. Then, the hot pressing pressure was suitable for 7 MPa.

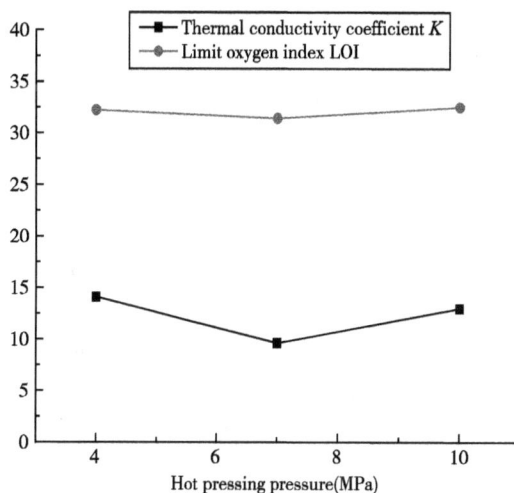

Fig. 6   Effect of hot pressing pressure on thermal conductivity coefficient K and limit oxygen index LOI

The necessary conditions to the optimized technology was mass fraction of discarded fibers 10%, mass fraction of AC foaming agent 3%, mass fraction of APP flame retardant 15%, hot pressing pressure 7MPa, hot pressing temperature 180℃, length of discarded fibers 20mm, mixing temperature 175-180℃, hot pressing time 8min, cool-down time 2h. And, under the optimized technological conditions, the discarded fiber/polyurethane flame retardant insulation board has good thermal insulation properties, flame retardation and mechanical properties. The thermal conductivity coefficient was 0.06W/(m · K), the limit oxygen index was 35.82%, the tensile strength was 2.642MPa, and the bending strength was 5.314MPa.

3.2 Flame retardant and thermal insulation mechanism analysis of flame retardant insulation board

3.2.1 Flame retardant mechanism analysis

(1) Analysis of thermogravimetric curve

The thermogravimetric curve of the thermal insulation board under the optimized technological conditions was shown in Fig.7.

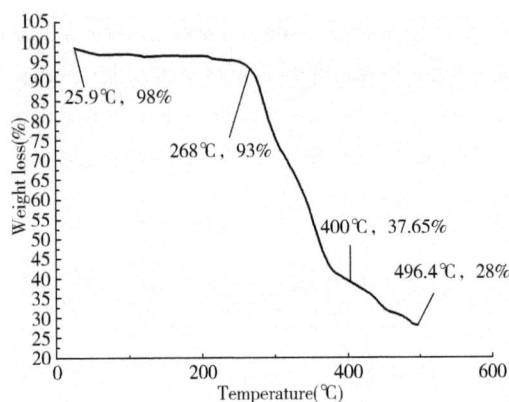

Fig.7　Thermal weightlessness curve

From Fig.7, it could be seen that the initial degradation temperature was about 268℃ and the end degradation temperature was about 500℃. The degradation ratio decreased obviously in 400℃. The initial degradation temperature of TPU was about 261℃, by contrast, the initial degradation temperature(268℃) of the discarded fiber/polyurethane flame retardant insulation board was improved. So, the effect of APP on flame retardation was obvious. The role of APP flame retardant was divided into three stages: release of ammonia, catalytic carbonization and decomposition of polyphosphoric acid chain. The APP flame retardant first decomposed into the ammonia, which diluted the concentration of oxygen and then produced the strong dehydration of the polyphosphoric acid, which made the polymer carbonization to form the protective and isolating carbon layer.

It promoted the formation of carbon layer, prevented the further decomposition, slowed down the degradation ratio and improved the total degradation temperature of the flame retardant insulation board.

(2) Analysis of residual carbon ratio

The pictures of residual carbon were shown in Fig.8, in which I was the residual carbon picture with none flame retardant, and II was the residual carbon picture under the optimized technological conditions.

Fig.8　Pictures of residual carbon ratio(I)

Fig.8　Pictures of residual carbon ratio(II)

The residual carbon ratio of I was 24.5%, II was 39.2%. It could be clearly seen from Fig.8 that the carbonized layer of the discarded fiber/polyurethane flame retardant insulation board prepared by the optimized technological conditions was better than the sample without flame retardant, which indicated that the APP flame retardant obtained good flame retardant effect on the flame retardant insulation board.

3.2.2 Thermal insulation mechanism analysis

The scanning electron microscope of the discarded fiber/

polyurethane flame retardant insulation board under the optimized technological conditions was shown in Fig. 9. Fig. 9 showed the bubble pores structure inside the flame retardant insulation board, the magnification of I was 50 times, and the magnification of II was 100 times. Calculated by the equation (2) in 1.4, the average diameter of bubble pores in the discarded fiber/polyurethane flame retardant insulation board under the optimized technological conditions was 350μm. It could be seen from Fig. 9 that the discarded fiber/polyurethane flame retardant insulation board had good and uniform bubble pores, mostly closed bubble pores, thin walls of the bubble pores, rounded shape of the bubble pores, so it has the excellent thermal insulation properties.

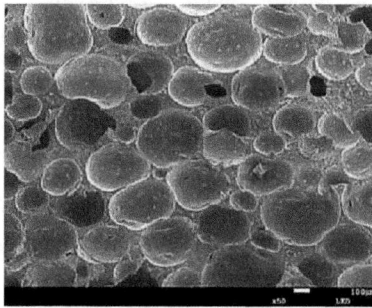

Fig. 9 (a) Scanning electron microscope scanning morphology of bubble pore(I)

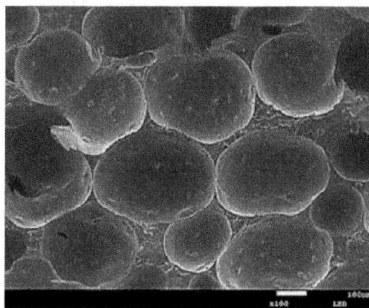

Fig. 9 (b) Scanning electron microscope scanning morphology of bubble pore(II)

3.4 Finite element analysis of thermal conduction of discarded fiber/polyurethane flame retardant insulation board

3.4.1 Create geometry

According to the measured sample specification (100mm × 100mm × 10mm), the geometry of the discarded fiber/polyurethane flame retardant insulation board was established.

3.4.2 Material properties

The material properties of the discarded fiber/polyurethane flame retardant insulation board were determined by the measured performances and homogenization theories of equivalent elastic modulus and equivalent thermal conductivity coefficient. The material properties of the discarded fiber/polyurethane flame retardant insulation board were shown in Tab. 1.

Tab. 1 Material properties of thermal insulation board

Density $(g \cdot cm^{-3})$	Poisson ratio	Young modulus (MPA)	Specific heat $(J \cdot g^{-1} \cdot ℃^{-1})$	Thermal conductivity $(W \cdot m^{-1} \cdot K^{-1})$
0.484	0.4	21.6	2800	0.06

3.4.3 Establish analytical steps, contact, load and meshing

The type of analysis was steady state thermal conduction analysis. According to measured conditions, the ambient temperatures on both sides of the discarded fiber/polyurethane flame retardant insulation board were 30℃ and 20℃. And the mesh unit type was DC3D8 in ABAQUS software. The meshing model was shown in Fig. 10.

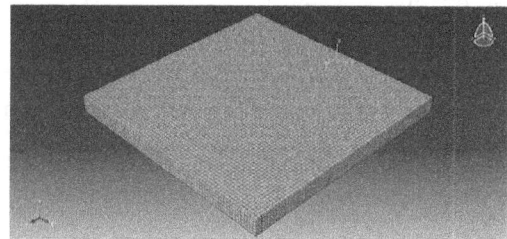

Fig. 10 Gridding model

3.4.4 Temperature distribution nephogram

The job was submitted for monitoring and analysis, and entered the visualization after the job was completed. The temperature distribution nephogram of the discarded fiber/polyurethane flame retardant insulation board was shown in Fig. 11 and the side temperature distribution nephogram was shown in Fig. 12.

From the temperature distribution nephogram of the model, it could be seen that the heat transfer process

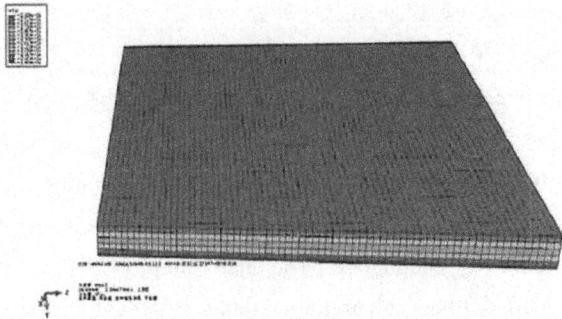

Fig. 11 Temperature distribution nephogram thermal of insulation board

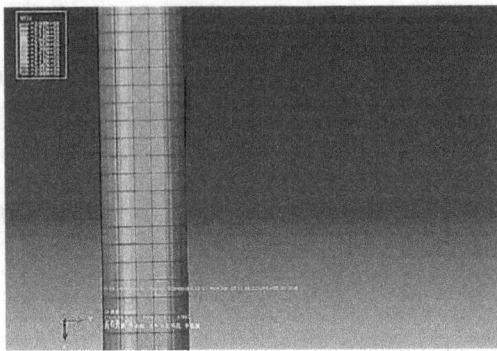

Fig. 12 Side temperature nephogram

was uniform. After the thermal conduction process was over, the temperatures of the two sides were 27.5℃ and 22.9℃. According to the calculation equation (3), the thermal loss was calculated:

$$Q = \frac{K \times A(T-t)}{D} \qquad (3)$$

In the equation: Q is thermal loss; K is thermal conductivity coefficient; A is the surface area of sample; D is thickness of the sample; T, t is the temperature on both sides of the sample;

The thermal loss of the material was 0.276W when the simulated data was taken in equation (3).

Through KES-F7, the thermal loss of the discarded fiber/polyurethane flame retardant insulation board was 0.27W. And the simulated thermal loss was basically the same as the measured thermal loss. It could be inferred that the actual and simulated thermal conduction processes of the discarded fiber/polyurethane flame retardant insulation board were consistent. Under the actual test conditions, it was very difficult to test the actual temperature distribution nephogram of the material.

And through the simulation of ABAQUS finite element software, we could not only get the temperature distribution nephogram, but also solve the temperature change under different ambient temperature conditions. It was helpful for designing the technological parameters of the thermal insulation board to analyze the temperature change in the simulation process.

4 Conclusions

The discarded fiber/polyurethane flame retardant insulation board had been prepared by blending-hot pressing method with discarded fibers, discarded polyurethane, AC foamingagent and APP flame retardant as raw materials. And the following conclusions were drawn:

(1) Through single factor experiments, the results showed that the optimized technological conditions were as follows: massfraction of discarded fibers 10%, mass fraction of AC foaming agent 3%, mass fraction of APP flame retardant 15%, hot pressing pressure 7MPa, hot pressing temperature 180℃, length of discarded fibers 20mm, mixing temperature 175 – 180℃, hot pressing time 8min, cool-down time 2h. And, under the optimized technological conditions, the thermal conductivity coefficient was 0.06W/(m·K), the limit oxygen index was 35.82%, the tensile strength was 2.642MPa, and the bending strength was 5.314MPa.

(2) The flame retardant mechanism and effect of the discarded fiber/polyurethane flame retardant insulation board was analyzed by TGA and residual carbon ratio and the APP flame retardant achieved good flame retardant effect on the flame retardant insulation board. The average diameter of bubble pores was 350μm by SEM and the discarded fiber/polyurethane flame retardant insulation board had good and uniform bubble pores, mostly closed bubble pores, thin walls of the bubble pores, round shape of the bubble pores, so it had the excellent thermal insulation properties.

(3) The ABAQUS finite element software was used to establish the model of two-dimensional steady-state thermal conduction and the steady temperature distribution nephogram was obtained. The simulated thermal loss was calculated and compared with the measured thermal loss of the sample. The calculated thermal loss of the

simulation results was basically the same with the measured thermal loss, which was to say, the thermal insulation properties of the thermal insulation board were feasible by the finite element simulation.

Acknowledgements

The authors of this paper gratefully acknowledge financial supports from of major projects of Industrial Technology Research Institute in Liaoning Province (2018003).

References

[1] Li P, Ye H W, Chen Y, et al. Waste and recycling textiles at home and abroad [J]. Synthetic Fiber in China, 2014, 43: 41-45.

[2] Ma L. The joy and worry of recycling waste textiles [J]. China Fiber Inspection, 2013; 33: 56-57.

[3] Qiu Y H. The comprehensive utilization of waste textiles [J]. Jiangsu Textile, 2007, 26: 68-70.

[4] Testore F, Petri A. An experimental study of the recovery of hard textile Wastes [J]. Journal of the Textile Institute, 1990, 81:69-78.

[5] Sun Z X, Shen Z G, Ma S L, et al. Novel application of glass fibers recovered from waste printed circuit boards as sound and thermal insulation material [J]. Journal of Materials Engineering and Performance, 2013, 22: 3140-3146.

[6] Long H S, Xue P, Ding Y, et al. Study on properties of waste natural fiber reinforced high density polyethylene composites [J]. China Plastics, 2014, 28: 95-99.

[7] Chen L, Zou L, Sun W G. Preparation and adsorption performance of oil absorbing material from waste flax pyrolysis treatment [J]. Journal of Textile Research, 2017, 38: 17-22.

[8] Zhao G. Building energy saving and energy saving design [J]. Science-Technology Information Development and Economy, 2005, 15: 147-148.

[9] Zhang Z P, Li Z, Dong Y L. The development status and prospect of building thermal insulation wall in buildings [J]. Engineering Mechanics, 2007, 24: 121-127.

[10] Qian B Z, Zhu Z F. Technological progress of building energy-saving thermal insulation materials [J]. Building Energy Efficiency, 2009, 37: 56-60.

[11] Chen X. To analyze the insulation and energy saving of the building perimeter [J]. Resource Economization and Environmental Protection, 2015, 33: 71.

[12] Li J. Preparation, application of fiber reinforced composite insulation board [J]. Master thesis, Yangzhou University, China, 2013.

[13] Zhu Q W, Wu F D, Zhao J P. Research status and progress of external wall insulation materials [J]. New Building Materials, 2012; 39: 12-15.

[14] Panyakaew S, Fotios S. New thermal insulation boards made from coconut husk and bagasse [J]. Energy and Buildings, 2011; 43: 1732-1739.

[15] Cai J P, Liu L, Chen X T, et al. Sisal fiber reinforced expanded glass beads / phenolic resin composite insulation board [J]. 2012, 39:19-22.

[16] Zhao R H, Sun J J, Cao J H, et al. Research on green and efficient insulation board [J]. Building Energy Efficiency, 2017; 45: 37-41.

[17] Zhu Y, Liu B, Gao H, et al. Experimental study on SiO2 aerogel core / polystyrene shell composite flame retardant insulation board [J]. Guangzhou Chemical Industry, 2015; 43: 78-80,104.

[18] Qin Y, Wang Q Q. The development of polyurethane materials [J]. China Building Materials Science & Technology, 2017, 26: 39-41.

[19] Ding Y J, Zhu Z, An S Y, et al. Preparation and properties of polyurethane foam / wood fiber composite material [J]. Building Energy Efficiency, 2010, 38: 62-64.

[20] Yu X, Lv L H, Wei C Y, et al. Research on sound absorption properties of multilayer structural material based on discarded polyester fiber [J]. Journal of the Textile Institute, 2014, 105: 1009-1013.

Recyclable Carbon Fiber Reinforced Polyimine Resin Composites

Qidi Zhu[1,2], **Yi Wei**[1,2], **Yiping Qiu**[2], **Wanshuang Liu**[1,2]*

[1] *Donghua University Center for Civil Aviation Composites, Donghua University, Shanghai 201620, China*

[2] *College of Textiles, Donghua University, Shanghai 201620, China*

* *Corresponding author's email*: wsliu@ dhu. edu. cn

Abstract: Covalent polymeric networks composed of imine cross-linkages have been prepared by condensation polymerization of polyethyleneimine and terephthalaldehyde. The crosslinked polyimine exhibits malleability and degradable characteristics. The polyimine could be remolded at 180℃ under hot pressure and the remolded samples showed high retention of mechanical properties. Finally, carbon fiber reinforced polymer composites were fabricated using the polyimine as matrix. Recoveries of carbon fibers could be realized through gentle depolymerization of the polyamine matrix in ethanediamine solution.

Keywords: Polyimine; Recyclable thermoset; Dynamic covalent bonds; Carbon fiber composites

1　Introduction

Carbon fibers (CFs) are lightweight graphitic material with higher mechanical strength than that of steel and lower density than aluminum[1]. Woven and nonwoven CFs can be combined with polymeric binder materials to form high-performance carbon fiber reinforced composites (CFRCs). Although the current cost of CFRCs is comparatively higher than metals, due to their excellent strength-to-weight ratios and durability, they have seen explosive growth in a large number of applications ranging from aerospace to ground transportation to sporting goods[2].

With increasing production of CFRCs, the environmental impact of these traditionally nonrecyclable materials and reduction in their material and manufacturing cost are of great concern. Typically epoxy thermosets are used as binders to produce high-performance CFRCs with superior mechanical properties (high strength and stiffness). However, the resulting CFRCs cannot generally be repaired or recycled[3]. Recycling of CFRCs (polymer matrix as well as CFs) has been the focus of a growing body of research over the last two decades in order to make them more cost effective and sustainable[4-6]. Many mechanical and thermochemical methods have been applied, mostly with the aim of recovering the valuable CFs with preservation of fiber length as a key objective. So far, researchers have managed to recover epoxy resins as fine powders[4-5,7], down graded chemical feedstocks or downgraded thermoplastic materials[8]. However, these processes either involve the use of novel synthetic monomers[8] or energy-intensive processes (such as use of supercritical solvents), which would be difficult to economically scale up[9]. The recycling difficulty come from the irreversible nature of the thermoset resins in CFRCs.

It can be envisioned that repairability and recyclability of CFRCs could be enabled by introduction of dynamic covalent bonds in the polymer matrix. Dynamic covalent chemistry has been demonstrated as a promising route to recyclable covalent network materials[10-15]. We describe the preparation of fully recyclable CFRCs from woven carbon fiber fabric and malleable polyiminenetworks. Terephthalaldehyde (TPAL) and polyethyleneimine (PEI) were used to build a cross-linked polyimine (PI) via Schiff base chemistry. The PI could be easily reprocessed by hot press and showed high retention of mechanical strength. In addition, CF could be recycled by degradation of CFRCs in anhydrous ethylene diamine (EDA). The process reported herein involves minimal energy input and could be easily scaled up.

2 Experiments

2.1 Materials

Carbon fibers SYT 45 (12k) which area density is 400g/m^2 were provided by Zhongfu Shenying Carbon Fiber Co. Ltd. PEI was purchased from Aladdin with purity of 99% and molecular weight of 10000. TPAL was purchased from J&K with purity of 99%. Other chemicals and reagents were purchased from Sinopharm Group.

2.2 Preparation of PI

According to the primary amine equivalent of PEI, PEI (10g) was dissolved in anhydrous ethanol (20mL), and TPAL (4.2g) was dissolved well in the dichloromethane (10mL). After mixing these two solutions, the blend of two solutions was poured into a polytetrafluoroethylene mold, and then the solvents were volatilized in an oven at 80℃ for one hour. After the solvent evaporation, the temperature of the oven is increased to 150℃ for post cure for another one hour. The prepared PI condensed into small pieces so that they need to be grounded into powders and hot-pressed in a mold before they can be used for various tests and characterizations.

2.3 Remolding of PI

The prepared PI spline was first crushed by a multifunctional crusher, and the powder was further pulverized with a vibration mill to obtain a yellow fine PI powder as shown in Fig. 1(a). Morphology of the PI powders under an optical microscope was shown in Fig. 1 (b). Then, the PI powder was poured into a special mental mold as showed in Fig. 1(c) and hot pressed under a pressure of 1MPa at 180℃ for 60 minutes to obtain dumb bell-shaped samples as shown in Fig. 1 (d).

2.4 Fabrication of CFRCs

TPAL (6.45g) was added to a 500mL Erlenmeyer flask followed by the addition of ethanol (400mL) and the solution was stirred for 10 minutes. Then, PEI (15.35g) was added to a tray prepared from a silicone coated release paper (approximate size: 43cm × 25.5cm ×

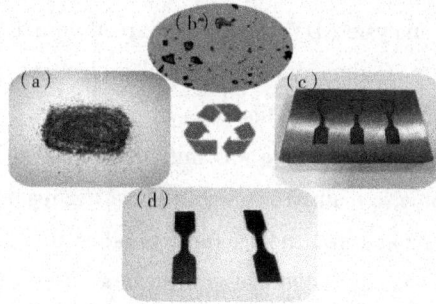

Fig.1 (a) PI powder; (b) Morphology of PI powders under an optical microscope (200 X); (c) PI powders in the hot press mould; (d) Dumbbell-shaped PI samples

2cm) followed by the addition of methylene chloride (~150mL, or enough to cover most of the surface area at the bottom of the tray). The TPAL solution was gently poured into the tray. A single piece of carbon fabric was put into the tray, and the solution was allowed to evaporate in a fume hood for 24h. The resulting uncured composite film was first heat pressed for 3h at 78℃, followed by 1h at 95℃, and finally 1h at 105℃ using a hot press machine. The obtained prepreg [Fig. 2(a)] was cut into 4 pieces of 10cm × 10cm in size, as shown in Fig. 2(b), and put them together in the hot press machine under the condition of 180℃ with a pressure of 0.5MPa for one hour, then, CFRC was obtained as shown in Fig. 2(c) and (d).

Fig. 2 (a) Carbon fiber prepreg; (b) 4 pieces of prepreg for hot pressing; (c) and (d) Cured CFRC panel

2.5 Characterization

Fourier transform infrared (FTIR) spectra were recorded on a Nicolet 6700 FTIR spectrometer using attenuated total reflection (ATR) mode. Thermal gravimetric analysis (TGA) was performed on a TA instruments

TGA Q 500 under a nitrogen atmosphere. Dynamic mechanical analysis (DMA) was performed on a TA DMA Q800 at a frequency of 1Hz and a heating rate of 3℃/min. Stress relaxation was also conducted on TA DMA Q800. The sample was initially preloaded by 1 × 10^{-3}N force to maintain straightness. After reaching the testing temperature, the sample was allowed to stabilize for 30min to reach thermal equilibrium. The specimen was stretched by 1% on the DMA machine and the deformation was maintained throughout the test. The GT200 Vibration Grinding Machine (Gelideman Instrument) was used to make PI powders. Hot press was conducted on a HY-10TK automatic hot press testing machine (Henghan Instrument). Tensile properties of PI were tested on a 203B-TS Wance electronic universal testing machine, following ASTM D638 (sample type V). Flexural properties of CFRC were tested according to the ASTMD 790. All composite samples were conditioned at 20℃ and 65% relatively humidity for 24h before testing. Scanning electron microscope (SEM) was conducted on a Quanta 250 Scanning Electron Microscope.

3 Results and Discussion

3.1 Structure of PI

The success in preparation of PI was confirmed by FTIR. The FTIR spectrum of PEI, TPAL and PI were showed in Fig. 3. The band at 3278cm^{-1} for PEI was from the stretching vibration of the N—H. The C =O stretch band at 1684cm^{-1}observed in the TPAL was nearly

dis-appeared in the spectrum of PI. The appearance of prominent C =N stretch at 1642cm^{-1} in the spectrum of PI confirmed the presence of imine bonds, indicating that the aldehyde group and the amino group in the two raw materials reacted and imine bonds were formed.

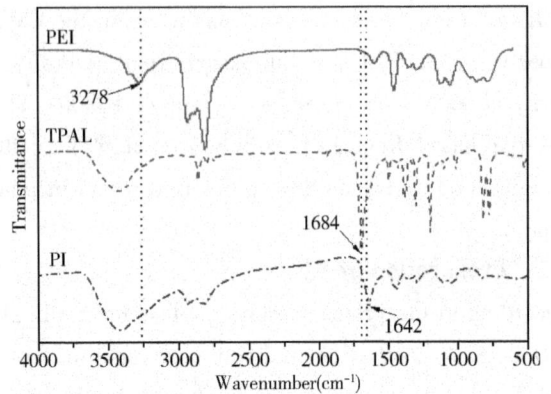

Fig. 3   FTIR spectra of PEI, TPAL and PI

3.2 Thermal properties of PI

In order to verify the variation of thermal properties for the reprocessed PI, the original polymer was reground into a powder and hot press under the same conditions. DMA was used to test the glass transition temperature (T_g) of the original and reprocessed PI. Fig. 4 shows the T_g of the first-generation polymer is 55℃ and the T_g of the reprocessed PI is 58℃. The storage modulus of two PI polymers are both about 2000MPa at room temperature. This indicates the thermal-mechanical properties of PI are well maintained after the reprocessing.

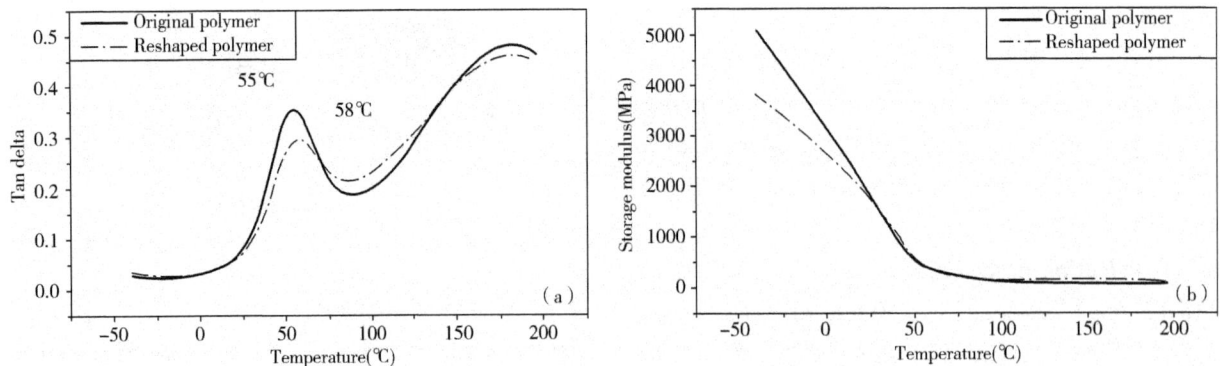

Fig. 4   (a) Tan Delta and (b) storage modulus *versus* temperature curves of original and reprocessed PI

TGA was used to investigate the thermal degradation of PI. Fig. 5 shows the nonisothermal degradation curves of PI under nitrogen atmospheres, and the initial degradation temperatures (the temperature for 5% weight loss, $T_d 5\%$) is about 250℃. This degradation temperatures of PI are much higher than the processing temperature, so that it can be ensured that the materials were not decomposed during the preparation process.

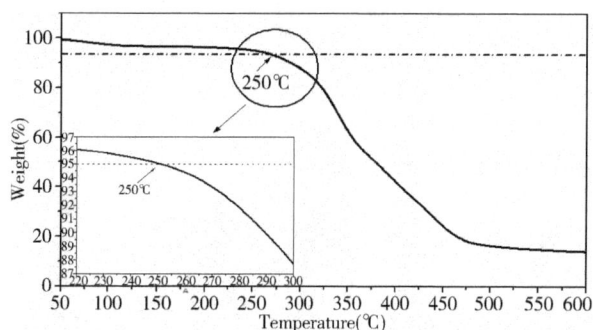

Fig. 5 TGA curve of PI

The stress relaxation test of PI was conducted by tensile mode. The stress relaxation curves of PI at 7 different temperatures are shown in Fig. 6. It can be seen that there is no stress relaxation below 30℃, and stress relaxation begins after 40℃, and the stress can only relax to the equilibrium value and cannot relax to zero. This further proves that PI is a cross-linked polymer. The stress relaxation phenomenon is due to the exchange reactions between dynamic imine bonds in PI.

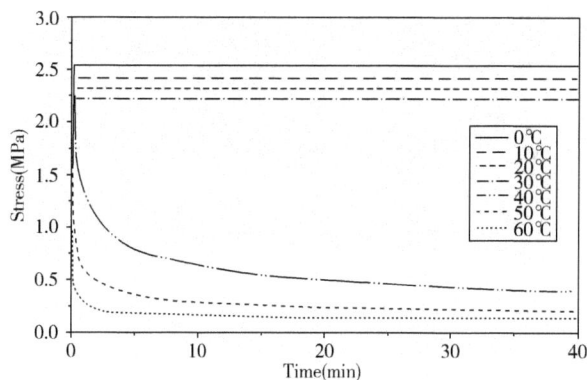

Fig. 6 The stress relaxation curves of PI at different temperature

3.3 Mechanical properties of PI and CFRCs

In order to verify the retention of mechanical properties of reprocessed PI, the tensile properties of original, 1st generation and 2nd generation PI were tested. As shown in Fig. 7, the Young's modulus of PI increases with the number of reprocessing times, and the tensile strength of the material keeps at around 30MPa. This indicates that there was almost no loss of the mechanical strength for there processed PI and the increase in Young's modulus with the reprocessing times. This may be because the reprocessing treatment (hot press) can lead to the increase in crosslinking degree of PI.

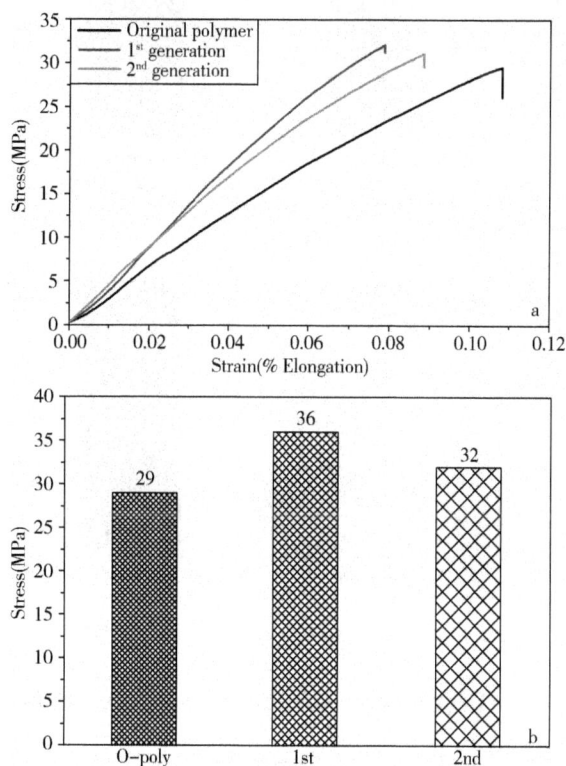

Fig. 7 (a) The tensile stress-strain curves of original and Reprocessed PI; (b) The tensile strength of original and Reprocessed PI

Imine polymer can be remolded after being damaged due to the dynamic covalent bond. Therefore, in this test, after the flexural test on the carbon fiber composite, the damaged sample was put into the hot press machine for 1 hour under the same conditions mentioned above, then, the healing sample was again subjected to a flexural test. We called the original composite CFRC-1, and the repressed composite CFRC-2. From the Fig. 8, we found that by repeating the heat pressing of the broken test samples, greater than 100% recovery of mechanical performance can be achieved. This Depending on the initial welding and subsequent healing conditions, the recovery of both flexural strength and modulus ranged from 85% to 107%.

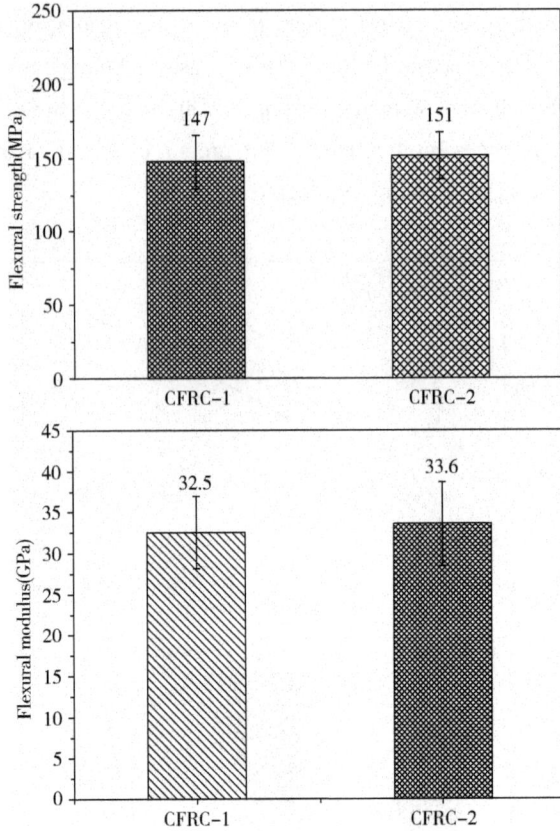

Fig. 8　Flexural strength and modulus of CFRCs

3. 4　Degradation of the PI and recyclability of CFRCs

The PI can be degraded by exchange reaction of the dynamic covalent imine bond. So, it can be degraded through the exchange reaction between imine bonds in PI and the primary amines in the EDA which is shown in Fig. 9 (a). And because this reaction is a reversible reaction, the high degree of cross-linked epoxy resin can be acquired by evaporate EDA to reverse the reaction direction. So that the PI can reach near 100% recycle. Fig. 10 (b) shows the PI spline was immersed in EDA for degradation and the state after placed at room temperature for 24 hours is showed in Fig. 9 (c). Considering that the T_g of PI is 55℃, the solution was transferred to a round bottom flask for a rapid degradation of the material. After 48h in the oil bath with the

temperature was 60℃, the material can be degraded completely. Then, the solution is poured into a beaker, EDA is volatilized in a vacuum oven, the oven temperature is set to 120℃, and the PI is recovered, as it is showed in Fig. 10 (e). Finally, the powder is placed in a mold and hot-pressed under the same conditions as above to obtain a hot-pressed sample of recycled PI showed in Fig. 9 (f).

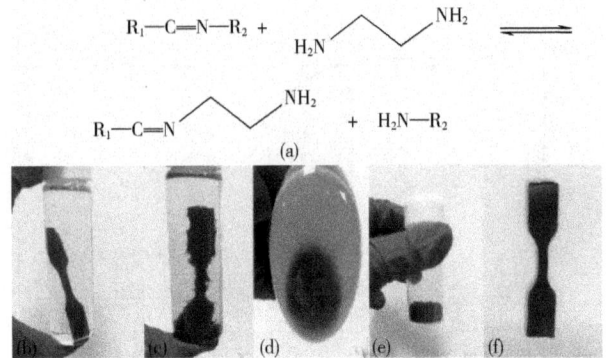

Fig. 9　(a) The degradation principle of the PI; (b) PI in EDA; (c) PI in EDA after 24h at room temperature; (d) Degraded PI after heating at 60℃ for 48h. (e) PI powder after evaporating excess EDA; (f) Reprocessed PI sample

Using the degradability of PI in EDA, CFRC can be placed in EDA, binder(PI) can be degraded in EDA, and carbon fiber can be complete recovered. The recycling process is shown in Fig. 10.

Fig. 10　(a) The surface of CFRC; (b) CFRC in the EDA; (c) Carbon fiber recovered from EDA

The surface morphology of both carbon fiber in CFRC and recycling fiber from EDA was observed by using a scanning electron microscope (SEM), and the images are shown in Fig. 11. There is no visible damage or alternation in fiber dimension. As shown in Fig. 11 (a), each carbon fiber was completely covered with PI; the surface morphology of recovered carbon fiber in EDA is shown in Fig. 11 (b). It can be observed that the PI was completely degraded and the fiber surface was smooth.

Fig. 11 (a), (b) SEM images of carbon fiber in CFRC; (c) The surface morphology of the recycling fiber

4 Conclusions

In this work, we have demonstrated that the use of malleable polyimine networks as the binder component of woven carbon fiber composites enables an efficient closed-loop recycling process, in which all of the fiber and binder materials are recovered and can be directly reused. Further, the malleable nature of the binder enables moldability and weldability of woven carbon fiber composite materials. Delamination damage can be perfectly repaired through simple heat-pressing. The use of malleable polyamines as binders in CFRCs is possibly the greenest potential approach to truly recyclable composites. Further, malleable PI composites enable easy repair, and can remove the time-consuming curing step from manufacture of discrete parts.

Acknowledgements

This work was supported by Shanghai Science and Technology Committee (No. 17511102800)

References

[1] American Chemical Society National Historic Chemical Landmarks. High performance carbon fibers, carbon fiber; accessed: January 2016.

[2] Holmes M. Carbon fibre reinforced plastics market continues growth path[J]. Reinforced Plastics, 2013, 57(6):24 -29.

[3] Mallick P K. Fiber-reinforced composites: Materials, manufacturing, and design[M]. 3rd ed., CRC Press, BocaRaton, FL, USA 2008.

[4] Pimenta S, Pinho S T. Recycling carbon fibre reinforced polymers for structural applications: Technology review and market outlook[J]. Waste Management, 2011, 31(2):378 -92.

[5] Pickering S J. Recycling technologies for thermoset composite materials—current status [J]. Composites Part A: Applied Science & Manufacturing, 2006, 37(8):1206 -1215.

[6] Oliveux G, Dandy L O, Leeke G A. Degradation of a model epoxy resin by solvolysis routes[J]. Polymer Degradation & Stability, 2015, 118:96 -103.

[7] Palmer J, Ghita O R, Savage L, et al. Successful closed-loop recycling of thermoset composites [J]. Composites Part A: Applied Science & Manufacturing, 2009, 40(4):490 -498.

[8] Pastine S. Can epoxy composites be made 100% recyclable? [J]. Reinforced Plastics, 2012, 56(5):26 -28.

[9] Morin C, Loppinet-Serani A, Cansell F, et al. Near-and super-critical solvolysis of carbon fibre reinforced polymers (CFRPs) for recycling carbon fibers as a valuable resource: State of the art[J]. Journal of Supercritical Fluids, 2012, 66(6):232 -240.

[10] Jin Y, Yu C, Denman R J, et al. Recent advances in dynamic covalent chemistry[J]. Chemical Society Reviews, 2013, 42(16):6634 -6654.

[11] Rowan S J, Cantrill S J, Cousins G R L, et al. Erratum: Angewandte chemie. Chem. Int. Ed. 2002, 41:898.

[12] Park J S, Darlington T, Starr A F, et al. Multiple healing effect of thermally activated self-healing composites based on Diels-Alder reaction[J]. Composites Science & Technology, 2010, 70(15):2154 -2159.

[13] Wojtecki R J, Meador M A, Rowan S J. Using the dynamic bond to access macroscopically responsive structurally dynamic polymers[J]. Nature Materials, 2011, 10(1):14 -27.

[14] Long T E. Toward Recyclable Thermosets [J]. Science, 2014, 344(6185):706 -707.

[15] García J M, Jones G O, Virwani K, et al. Recyclable, strong thermosets and organogels via paraformaldehyde condensation with diamines[J]. Science, 2014, 344(6185):732 -735.

Stable Gold Nanoparticle Modified Fabric Was Prepared by PDA In-Situ Reduction

Bingxue Huang[1,2], Bo Lu[1,2], Panpan Liu[1,2], Min Guo[1,2], Ying ma[1,2]*, Yiping Qiu[1,2]

[1] *Key Laboratory of Textile Science & Technology, Ministry of Education, Shanghai 201620, China*

[2] *Department of Technical Textiles, College of Textiles, Donghua University, Shanghai 201620, China*

* *Corresponding author's email*：yingma@ dhu. edu. cn

Abstract：Nanoparticles add to textile industry can achieve multi-functional applications. Therefore, the stable combination of nanoparticles and fabrics is very important. In our work, we use PDA as reducing agent and binder to in-situ reduce Auions into Au nanoparticles. And also Au nanoparticles can firmly adhere to the cellulose fabric' surface. After shaking in water for 24h, the AuNPs modified fabric has a good stability and its color has no change.

Keywords：Au nanoparticles; Polydopamine; Cellulose fabric; Stability

1 Introduction

Nanotechnology is currently in the forefront of high-tech research focus and the interest for textile nanocomposite materials in the research and development area is continually growing. The application of nanotechnology to the textile industry can achieve multi-functional applications and promote its transformation from traditional clothing to high-tech multi-functional direction. Compared with general materials, nanomaterials have many excellent properties. The modification of nanomaterials to the fiber surface can increase the fiber's functionality[1-2]. As one of the most stable metal materials, Au NPs have attracted much attention due to their unique physical and chemical properties. Au NPs can be used in many fields such as materials, medical tests, foods, chemicals, dyes, and ceramics. There are many preparation methods for Au NPs, which can be roughly divided into physical methods, chemical methods, green environmental methods, and some special methods[1,3-6]. Although widely implemented in research, many available methods have limitations for widespread practical use. In some conditions, the AuNPs has no strong interaction with the substrate resulting in a bad durability of the functional textile materials. Development of simple and versatile strategies for surface modification to get a stable textile AuNPs nanocomposite is necessary. Dopamine (DA) has been found to be an effective reductant in the synthesis AuNPs. It undergoes an oxidative cross-linking reaction in the presence of dissolved oxygen to form polydopamine (PDA) under water-soluble conditions[7-8]. The phenolic hydroxyl group and hydrazine functional group in PDA have a good chelating effect on cations and can deposit metal and metal oxides on the surface of substrate material in situ. At the same time, the active functional groups of PDA can also be used for surface grafting and molecular self-assembly of materials. PDA also has good hydrophilicity and can be well dispersed in water. Modifying it on the surface of substrate material can improve its hydrophilicity. In view of the strong adhesion of PDA to various substrates and the hydrophilicity, reducibility and other good characteristics of PDA, and it is possible to use PDA to reduce the absorbed gold ions into gold nanoparticles and at the same time bind gold nanoparticles tightly to fabrics.

The cellulose fabric as one of the most important biomass materials, is an attractive and promising supporter for nanoparticle due to its environmental friendliness, abundant functional groups for stable immobilization and simple separation process. In our work, we use DA to self-polymerization into PDA film on the fabric under alkali condition. Then obtained fabric was immersion in chloroauric acid solution (1mg/mL) for 30 minutes. The AuNPs was formed and stably anchored on the fabric surface with the assistant of the adhesive and reducing group of PDA.

2　Experiments

2.1　Materials and chemicals

Chloroauric acidtrihydrate (HAuCl$_4$ · 3H$_2$O), Dopamine hydrochloride, Tris (hydroxymethyl) aminomethane were purchased from Sigma-Aldrich. Hydrochloric acid (HCl) and sodium hydroxide (NaOH) were obtained from Sinopharm Chemical Reagent Co., Ltd. These materials were used without further purification. Milli-Q water (18.2MΩ/cm) was used throughout all experiments

2.2　Preparation of Au NPs modified fabric

Firstly, the cellulose fabric fiber was treated with 50mg/mL boiling NaOH solution for 1h to remove the impurities and put the fabric in a 60degree oven to dry. Then put the dried fabrics into 2mg/mL dopamine-tris solution (pH=8.5) with stirring at room temperature for 12h to obtained PDA-coatedfabric. The resulting PDA coated fabric (PDA @ fabric) was ultrasonically cleaned for 20 minutes, then washed with water until the water was colorless, and the water was blotted with filter paper. The dried PDA-coated fabrics were soaked in a 1mg/mL chloroauric acid solution at room temperature for 30 mi-nutes and washed with water to obtain the Au NPS modified fabric (PDA/Au NPs @ fabric). At last the PDA/Au @ fabric was dried in a vacuum oven at room temperature. 12 hours later the sample was made.

2.3　Characterization

UV-visible spectra of allthe fabrics were obtained by a UV-visible-near infra-red (UV-VIS-NIR) spectrophotometer (U-4100, Hitach Japan). The surface morphologies of metal NP platforms were captured by a scanning electron microscope (Hitachi S-4800). The nanoparticle size was analyzed by Nano Measurer software.

3　Results and Discussion

The chemical structure of dopamine (DA) Fig. 1 (a) used for coating the fabric and the two-step route employed for the construction of PDA/Au NPs @ fabric were shown in Fig.1 (a). Firstly, upon simple immersion of the fabric into dopamine solution (2mg/m, tris buffer, pH=8.5), a thin adherent PDA coating was spontaneously deposited on the substrate due to the self-polymerization property of DA. The resulting PDA coated fabric (PDA @ fabric) was then soaked in 1mg/mL chloroauric acid solution at room temperature for 30 minutes. Since PDA has a phenolic hydroxyl group and a functional group indol good chelation of cations, that can in-situ reduce gold ions into gold nanoparticles, at the same time, PDA have a good adhesive capacity that can adhere gold nanoparticles firmly to the fabric surface. At last, we get the Au NPs modified fabric PDA (PDA /Au NPs @ fabric).

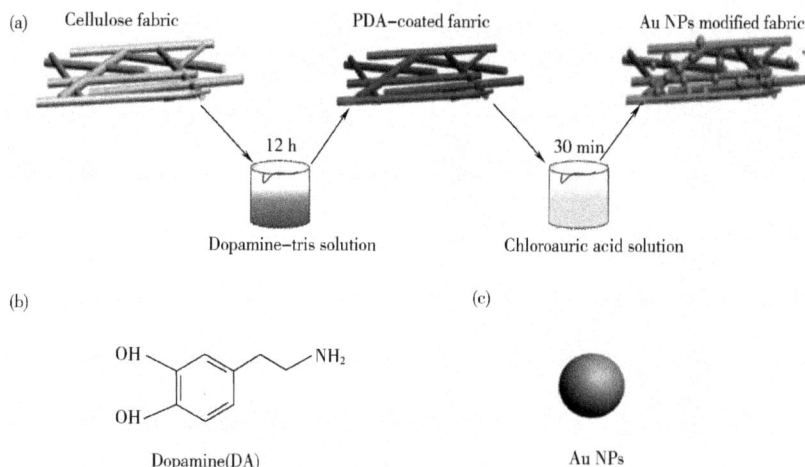

Fig. 1　(a) Fabrication of PDA/Au NPs @ fabric; (b) Chemical structure of dopamine(DA); (c) The scheme of Au NPs

Ascan be seen from Fig. 2 (a), the pure cellulose fabric is pure white in color and uniform in texture, the UV-vis spectra of the pure cellulose fabric is low and flat. There is no absorbance peak can be observed. But the surface color of the PDA @ fabric from Fig. 2 (b) is dark green. According to the change of the fabric color, it can be preliminarily judged that the dopamine buffer is in alkaline conditions. A certain amount of chemical reaction occurred in the solution. The color of the product after reaction was dark green and had a certain degree of adhesiveness and could adhere to the surface of the fabric. Meanwhile, after dopamine treatment, the color of the surface of the fabric was relatively uniform and preliminary. It could be judged that the PDA buffer solution reacted mildly, and slowly adhered to the surface of the cotton fabric after the reaction. The UV-vis spectra of the PDA @ fabric are much higher than the UV-vis spectra of pure cellulose in wavelength of 300 – 800nm that also verified the formation of the PDA. After modified Au NPs, the PDA/Au NPs@ fabric, shows the red wine color and the color is uniform Fig. 2 (c). The UV-vis spectra exhibit an absorption peak around 530 – 580nm. These peaks are related to the collective oscillations of the surface electrons, which is known as Surface Plasmon Resonance[1], indicating the clear formation of Au NPs.

It can be seen from Fig. 3 (a) that the surface of the pure cellulose fabric is smooth and has only a few wrinkles and roughness. However, after the PDA coated

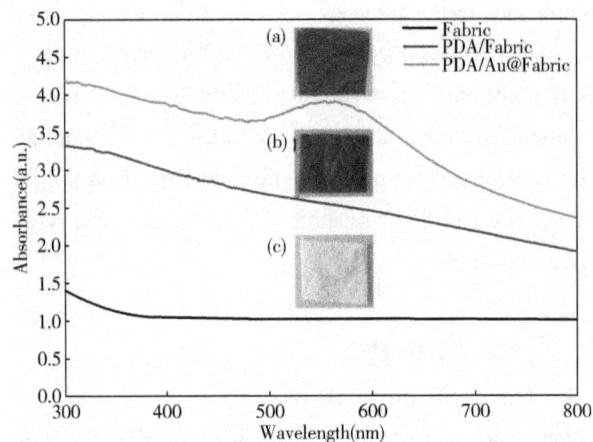

Fig. 2　Digital photo of (a) cotton fabric, (b) PDA coated fabric (PDA @ fabric), (c) Au NPs modified fabric PDA/Au NPs @ fabric and the UV-Vis absorbance spectra for them relatively

and the Au NPs modified the fabric Fig. 3 (b), the smooth surface disappears and is replaced with a roughness film with multiple regular tiny spheroids on the surface. In order to clearly observe the character of the nanoparticles, the magnifying SEM was shown in Fig. 2 (c). The Au NPs cover almost the entire surface of the cellulose fiber and that the aggregation of the Au NPs is obvious. That maybe caused by the excessive amount of the PDA on the surface. Most of the Au NPs have nearly uniform size distribution and size distribution shown in Fig. 3 (d). Their average diameter was about to be 40nm.

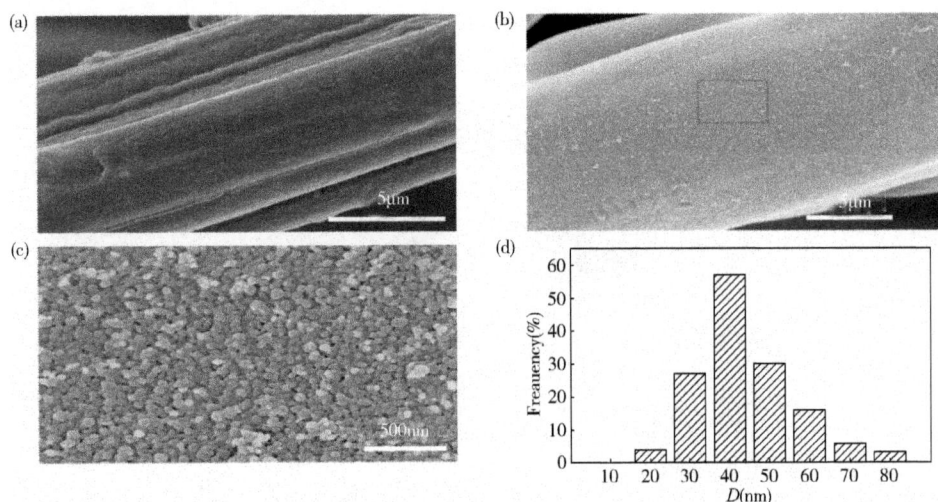

Fig. 3　SEM images of (a) pure cellulose fabric; (b) PDA/Au NPs @ fabric; (c) the magnifying SEM image of the Au NPS; (d) the diameter distribution histogram of the Au NPs

The stability of fabric and nanoparticle binding plays an important role in achieving the multifunctionality of the fabric. In our work, the stability of the PDA/Au NPs@ fabric was evaluated in water bath. As is shown in Fig. 4 (a), the color of the PDA/Au NPs@ fabric has no change after being treated in water bath for 24 hours under shaking. The washing solution is still transparent and colorless. The color of the PDA/Au NPs@ fabric after shaking for 24h is the same to the color before shaking. It suggests the strong adhesion of AuNPs on the PDA-coated fabric.

Fig. 4　(a) The optical image of the PDA/Au NPs @ fabric in water bath after 24h; (b) Photo of the PDA/Au NPs @ fabric after shaking in water for 24h

4　Conclusions

This work uses a simple two-step route to get Au modified cellulose fabric, where PDA was used as agent and binder to in-situ reduce Au ions into Au NPs and at the same time, Au NPs can firmly adhere to the surface of the fabric. After shaking in water bath for 24h, the PDA/Au NPs @ fabric has the same winered color as before. We also show PDA/Au NPs @ fabric has an absorption peak around 530–580nm and the average diameter of the Au nanoparticle was about to be 40nm.

References

[1] Emam H E, El-Hawary N S, Ahmed H B. Green technology for durable finishing of viscose fibers via self-formation of AuNPs [J]. International Journal of Biological Macromolecules, 2016, 96.

[2] Rehan M, Mowafi S, Aly S A, et al. Microwave-heating for in-situ Ag NPs preparation into viscose fibers [J]. European Polymer Journal, 2017, 86: 68–84.

[3] Mitrano D M, Limpiteeprakan P, Babel S, et al. Durability of nano-enhanced textiles through the life cycle: Releases from landfilling after washing [J]. Environmental Science Nano, 2016, 3(2): 375–387.

[4] Ahmed H B, Zahran M K, Emam H E. Heatless synthesis of well dispersible Au nanoparticles using pectin biopolymer [J]. International Journal of Biological Macromolecules, 2016, 91: 208–219.

[5] Sawada K, Sakai S, Taya M. Polyacrylonitrile-based electrospun nanofibers carrying gold nanoparticles in situ formed by photochemical assembly [J]. Journal of Materials Science, 2014, 49(13): 4595–4600.

[6] Velmurugan P, Shim J, Bang K S, et al. Gold nanoparticles mediated coloring of fabrics and leather for antibacterial activity [J]. J Photochem Photobiol B, 2016, 160: 102–109.

[7] Du S, Luo Y, Liao Z, et al. New insights into the formation mechanism of Au nanoparticles using dopamine as a reducing agent [J]. Journal of Colloid & Interface Science, 2018, 523: 27–34.

[8] Lee H, Dellatore S M, Miller W M, et al. Mussel-inspired surface chemistry for multifunctional coatings [J]. Science, 2007, 318(5849): 426–430.

Through-Thickness Properties of 3D Orthogonal Woven Carbon Fabric Reinforced Composites

Qiaole Hu[1,2], Hafeezullah Memon[1,2], Wanshuang Liu[2], Yiping Qiu[1,*], Yi Wei[2,*]

[1] Key Laboratory of Textile Science & Technology, Ministry of Education, Shanghai 201620, China

[2] Donghua University Center for Civil Aviation Composites, Donghua University, Shanghai 201620, China

* Corresponding author's email: ypqiu@dhu.edu.cn; weiy@dhu.edu.cn

Abstract: This paper reports tensile, compressive and shear test data directly measured in the Z-direction of 3D orthogonal woven fabric composite, which is rarely found in the published literature. The Vacuum-Assisted Resin Infusion process (VARI) was used to fabricate carbon fiber-epoxy composites and a comprehensive study on the tensile, compressive and shear properties in through-thickness direction was conducted. The results indicate that the Z-weft directional tensile and shear strength in 3D orthogonal woven composite (3DOW) is finer than that in Z-weft direction, due to the quantity of Z yarns in Z-weft direction was higher than that in Z-weft direction. In addition, the compressive strength in 3DOW was very low(i.e. 230MPa) for the reason that the Z yarns in the thickness direction even had a certain inclination.

Keywords: Through-thickness; 3D fabric; 3D woven composites; Out-plane; Z-direction

1 Introduction

Three-dimensional fabric reinforced composites have been applied in many fields, such as aerospace, automobiles, military, building in frastructures and so on due to their excellent through-thickness mechanical properties[1-2]. Meanwhile, the structure integrity, continuity, and designability can be achieved by special interweaving ways of yarns in the 3D woven structures, which in turn reduce the labor cost, preparation periods and easier performance optimization. The other distinct advantage of 3D fabrics reflected in manufacturing thick composites, when multiple layers of 2D fabric plies can be replaced by a single 3D fabric[1]. These excellent characteristics allow 3D fabrics to be used in some structural composites where the 2D laminates might not be suitable.

However, the abilities of 3D fabric reinforced composites are failed to replace 2D laminates in many structural applications. These unsuccessful replacements can be explained in two main aspects. First, the design of 3D fabric structures resulting in a large number of different weave architectures creates the difficulty for the establishment of the model in predicting their complex mechanical behavior, analytically or numerically. Second, the absence of national or international standards on testing through-thickness properties causes the difficulty for experimental characterization in out-plane properties. So, the available experimental data for 3D composites in thickness directions is really rare. The majority of experiments on 3D composites are mainly focused on in-plane properties, such as tension[3-5], compression[6-7], and so on. That is because the difficulty of gaining the out-plane properties directly through experiment, and testing of full-scale components is a time-consuming and costly task; especially uneasy to manufacture such thick composites with high fiber volume by VARI process. The existing literature addressing through-thickness properties of thick composites deals with tension and compression is mainly related to 2D laminates[8-11], which are manufactured by prepreg slay-up and cured in an autoclave. The test geometries available for through-thickness testing under tensile and compressive load are mainly more than 20mm or even to 150mm[12], which is really difficult for weaving 3D fabrics with such high thickness under the condition of high fiber volume. However, the 3D composites without the data of through-thickness properties can be questionable for replacing 2D laminates. Therefore, the data of out-plane properties gained from 3D composites experimentally is of particular interest for the composite scientists.

In this study, the typical 3D fabrics (i. e. 3D orthogo-nal) was woven on a modified loom and 3D composites were manufactured by VARI process. In order to observe the properties of 3D orthogonal woven fabric reinforced composites (i. e. 3DOW) in the thickness direction, a comprehensive comparison of out-plane properties under tensile and compressive load was investigated. Through this study, a data set addressing out-plane properties possibility would serve as a guide for the application of 3D composites and the selection of their structures.

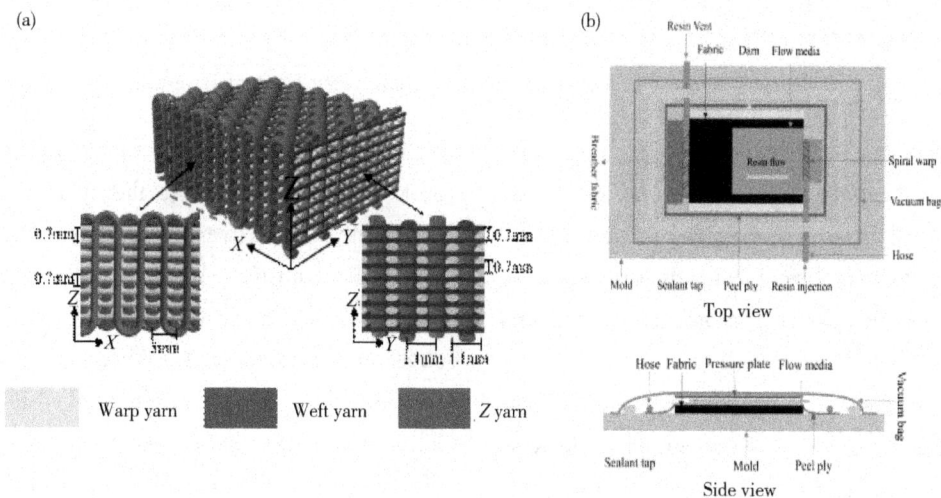

Fig. 1　(a) Schematic diagram of 3DO; (b) Illustration of VARI process for making 3DO

2　Experiment

2.1　Materials

The carbon fibers used in this study were a T800 grade 12K (SYT55S−12K) carbon fibers provided by Zhong-fu Shenying Carbon Fiber Co. , Ltd. The woven fabrics were manufactured by Huaheng High-Performance Fiber Textile Co. , Ltd. and the matrix was an epoxy resin, BAC 172, supplied by Zhejiang Baihe Advanced Co. , Ltd. The designed geometric parameters of 3D orthogonal woven fabric in this study are given here. The warp and weft densities were 9 picks/cm and 2 picks/cm, respectively, with 21 layers of fabric making the thickness of 16.5mm with 44.3% fiber volume.

2.2　Sample preparation

The VARI process was applied to manufacture the 3DOW. In order to control the fiber volume and the flow pattern of the 3D fabric, convex shape flow media and dams were used. The illustration of lay-up in VARI process are shown in Fig. 1 (b) and the final thickness of 3DOW and the fiber volume were 14.5mm and 45%, respectively.

In this study, the samples used for the compressive and shear test were parallel sided short blocks and short beam, respectively. Whereas, the I-section were applied in the Z-directional tensile test, which has been used for testing the 2D laminates[13]. The samples preparation are shown in Fig. 2 for a better intuitionistic expression.

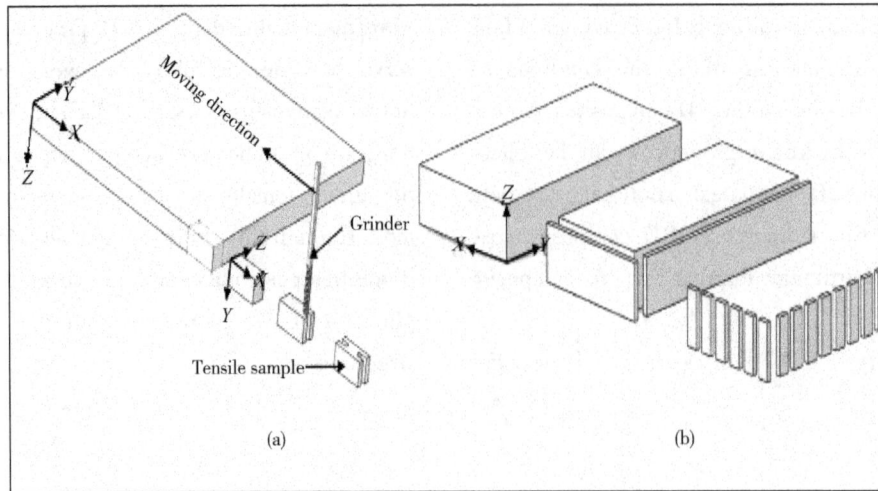

Fig. 2 Sample dimensions for (a) tensile test and (b) compressive test

2.3 Mechanical characterization

All the mechanical properties were tested by a PC-Controlled Electronic Universal Testing Bench provided by Labsans (LD26-5105). Five specimens were prepared and all testing was completed at room temperature and 55% RH, for each test.

The I-sectioned geometry was used to measure the out-plane tensile strength of 3D woven composites. Because the other shape samples mentioned in[12-13] were suitable for very thick materials and can't be reached by 3D woven fabrics under high fiber volume. On the other hand, considering the difficulties associated with forming a strong enough bond between aluminum block and specimen, the I-section parameters were particularly crucial to ensure the failure occurred within the gauge length, especially the thickness of mid-section and the filled radius.

The testing sample dimension was shown in Fig. 3 (a). The tensile strength was measured by applying the load via adhesively bonded aluminum bars at the speed of 2mm/min. A strain gauge was placed on one side of the specimen to measwre strains.

The parallel sided with square cross-section samples were used to carry out the compression tests, due to the thickness limitation and simplicity of specimen preparation. The compressive load was directly applied to the specimen by two flat and parallel stainless-steel platens, with the specimens located at the center of the platens, as shown in Fig. 3 (b). For the through-thickness compression testing, the specimen geometry and load configuration were absolutely critical to the final failure mechanisms. A length-width ratio between 2 : 1 and 3 : 1 was applied to ensure a relatively uniform stress at the center of specimens and prevent compressive buckling. A preload was applied to ensure the stability of specimen before testing and a strain gauge was placed on one side of the specimen in the center.

The short bean shear method was used to measure the shear strength in the Z direction. The through-thickness dimension was defined as the length of the specimen and the sample width and thickness were also decided according to the ASTM D 2344D-2344M. The loading span-to-measured thickness ratio is 4.0. Tests are conducted at the displacement rate of 1mm/min. Fig. 3 (c) shows the schematic diagram of sample dimension.

3 Results and Discussion

3.1 Tensile test

The I-sectioned samples were used to determine all tensile strength and the failure occurred within the gauge length, as expected. Fig. 4 showed the failure mode and the results of tensile strength. It can be seen that the strength in Z-weft direction was higher than that in Z-warp direction. Almost certainly it is due to lower Z yarn content in Z-warp direction than the Z-weft direction of the coupon.

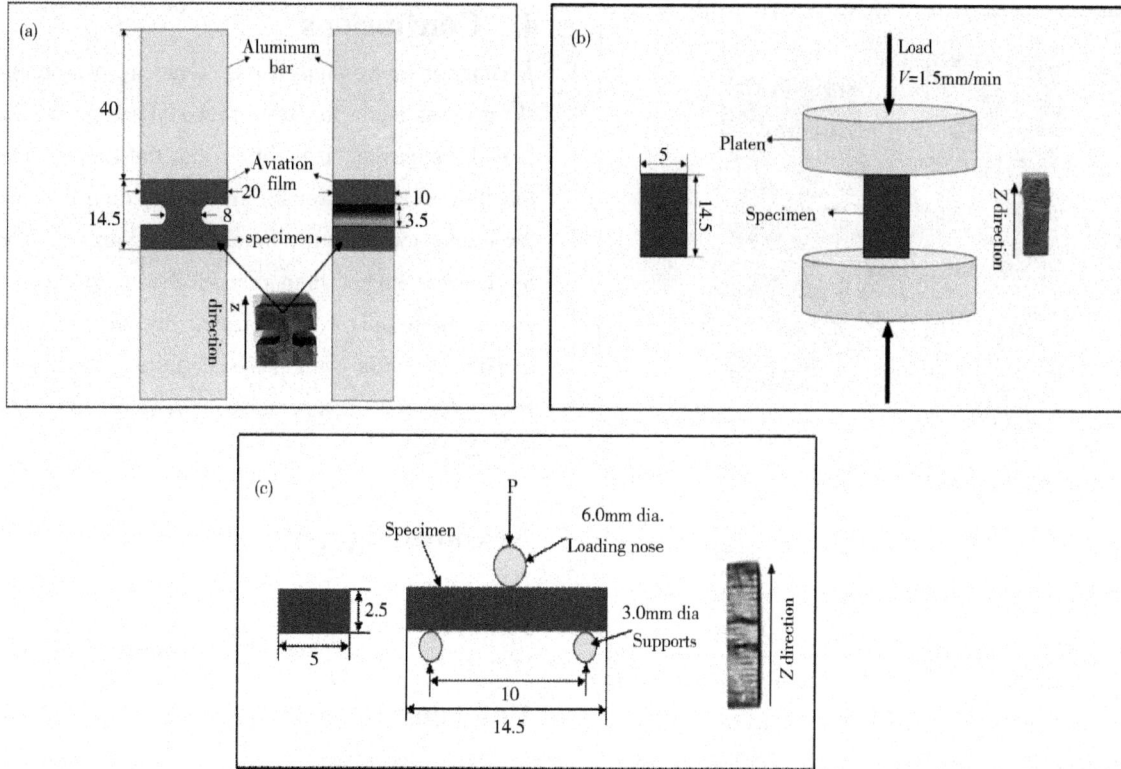

Fig. 3 Sample preparation for (a) tension (b) compression and (c) shear test

Failure modes analysis provides a clear picture of yarns quantity in the Z-direction that could bear the loads under tension. The main failure breaking Z yarns was seen in 3DOW and the number of bear load yarns (i. e. Z yarn) in the Z-weft direction was higher than that in Z-warp, as shown in Fig. 4. Therefore, the Z-weft directional tensile strength was higher than the Z-warp direction.

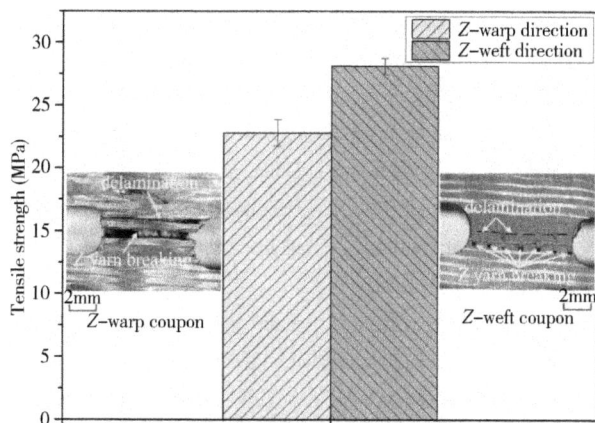

Fig. 4 Z-directional tensile strength and failure mode in Z-warp direction and Z-weft direction

3.2 Compression

The compressive failure mode and the bar graph depicting value of 3DOW are shown in Fig. 5. It is found that the compressive strength in 3DOW is too low, only 230MPa, despite there are additional Z yarns for 3DOW as the load bearing in the through-thickness direction. Nevertheless, there are only 4.5 Z yarns in the Z-direction and the Z yarns even has a certain inclination, thus the Z-directional compressive strength is lower.

In addition, the failure mode in 3DOW also provides a valid evidence. It can be seen that in 3DOW, the crack is preferentially expanded along the Z yarn, which means the inclined Z yarns can hardly prevent the crack propagation, resulting in the low Z-directional compressive strength.

3.3 Shear test

Considering the different yarn patterns in Z-warp directional and Z-weft directional flexural test coupon, it's necessary to divide the out-plane flexural test into Z-warp and Z-weft direction.

The out-plane shear strengths of 3DOW are shown in Fig. 6. The large discrepancy in shear strength between

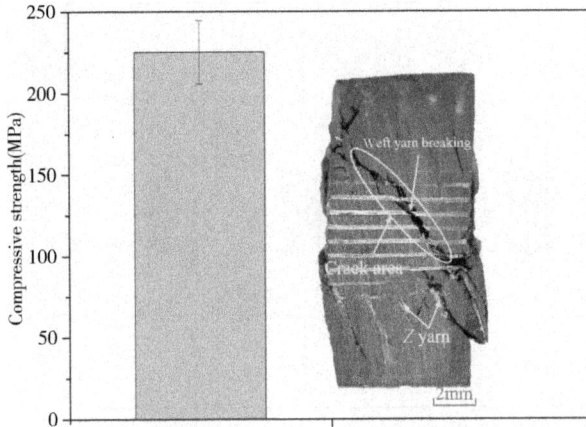

Fig. 5　Compression strength and failure mode in Z-direction

Z-warp and Z-weft direction is seen in 3DOW. This is attributed to the Z yarn content in a Z-warp direction (i. e. 3picks) was lower than Z-weft direction (i. e. 4.5picks), as shown in Fig. 6. Therefore, the Z-weft shear strength is higher than Z-warp.

The observation of out-plane shear failure mode is equally important and intuitive. As shown in Fig. 6, the failure modes is almost tension failure and crack propagation is along the yarn in the load direction in 3DOW. For example, in 3DOW, the crack is straight along the warp or weft yarns and the higher Z yarn content in Z-weft direction, shown in Fig. 6, is higher than that in Z-warp direction.

In summary, the above-shown failure modes agreed well with the obtained out-plane shear strengths, confirming that the Z-weft directional shear strength is higher than that in Z-warp direction, which is controlled by the number of Z yarns in the test direction, respectively.

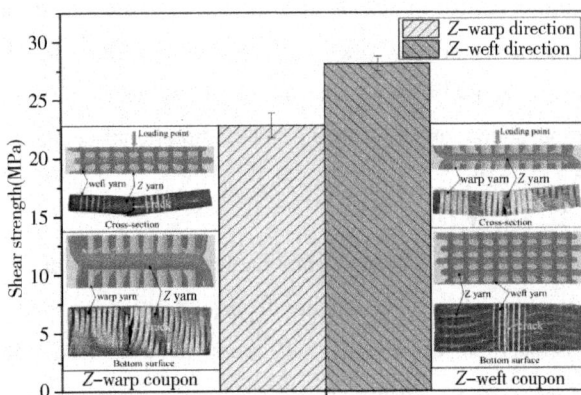

Fig. 6　Z-directional shear strength and failure mode in Z-warp direction and Z-weft direction

4　Conclusions

A comprehensive study (i. e. tension, compression and shear) was made for 3D orthogonal woven fabrics reinforced composite. It is found that the Z-weft directional tensile and shear strength are higher than that in Z-weft direction, owing to the number of Z yarns in Z-weft direction was higher than that in Z-weft direction. However, due to only 4.5 Z yarns in the thickness direction and the Z yarns even has a certain inclination, which leads to the compressive strength in 3DOW is only 230MPa.

Acknowledgments

This work was supported by Shanghai Science and Technology Committee (No. 15JC1400302)

References

[1]Hu J. Applications of three-dimensional textiles [M]. 3D Fibrous Assemblies, 2008: 33-69.

[2]Bogdanovich A E. Multi-scale modeling, stress and failure analyses of 3D woven composites [J]. Journal of Materials Science, 2006, 41(20): 6547-6590.

[3]Ivanov D S, Lomov S V, Bogdanovich A E, et al. A comparative study of tensile properties of non-crimp 3D orthogonal weave and multi-layer plain weave E-glass composites. Part 2: Comprehensive experimental results [J]. Composites Part A: Applied Science & Manufacturing, 2009, 40(8): 1144-1157.

[4]Dai S, Cunningham P R, Marshall S, et al. Open hole quasi-static and fatigue characterization of 3D woven composites [J]. Composite Structures, 2015, 131: 765-774.

[5]Tan P, Tong L, Steven G P, et al. Behavior of 3D orthogonal woven CFRP composites. Part I. Experimental investigation [J]. Composites Part A, 2000, 31(3): 259-271.

[6]Mahadik Y, Hallett S R. Effect of fabric compaction and yarn waviness on 3D woven composite compressive properties [J]. Composites Part A: Applied Science & Manufacturing, 2011, 42(11): 1592-1600.

[7]Ma P, Jiang G, Zhang F, et al. Experimental investigation on the compression behaviours of 3D angleinterlock woven composites with carbons nanotube under high strain rates [J]. Fibres & Textiles in Eastern Europe, 2015, 23(2): 44-50.

[8]Abot J L, Daniel I M. Through-thickness mechanical characterization of woven fabric composites [J]. J Compos Mater,

2004, 38(7): 543-53.

[9] Kim B C, Dong C P, Kim B J, et al. Through-thickness compressive strength of a carbon/epoxy composite laminate [J]. Composite Structures, 2010, 9 2(2): 480-487.

[10] Chen D, Lu F, Jiang B. Tensile properties of a carbon fiber 2D woven reinforced polymer matrix composite in through-thickness direction [J]. J Compos Mater, 2012, 46(26): 3297-3309.

[11] Mespoulet S, Hodgkinson J M, Matthews F L, et al. Design, development, and implementation of test methods for determination of through thickness properties of laminated composites [J]. Plastics Rubber & Composites, 2000, 29 (9): 496-502.

[12] Lodeiro M J, Broughton W R, Sims G D. Understanding limitations of through thickness test methods [J]. Plastics Rubber & Composites, 1999, 28(9): 416-24.

[13] Broughton W R. 8-Through-thickness testing[J]. Mechanical Testing of Advanced Fibre Composites, 2000, 39(3): 143-169.

Torsion Deformation and Damage of Bi-Axial Warp Knitted Composite Tubes

Bing He[1], Shuwei Huang[1], Chunlei Ren[1], Baozhong Sun[1], Bohong Gu[1]*

[1] *College of Textiles, Donghua University, Shanghai 201620, China*

* *Corresponding author's email*: gubh@ dhu. edu. cn

Abstract: Torsion deformation and damage of a bi-axial warp knitted (BWK) composite tube have been tested on CRIMS NWS500 torsion test system and simulated with finite element analyses (FEA) model. The testing angular velocity was 5°/min. The torque vs. torsion angle curves were obtained and the average failure torque is 328. 78 N · m at the average torsion angle of 12. 06°. The fracture region took place along the 45° direction to the longitudinal axis. We developed a FEA model at continuum level to simulate the torsion behaviors. There are good agreements of the failure torque, torsion angle and damage region between tests and FEA results. The continuum model of the bi-axial warp knitted composite could also be used for designing other engineering structures.

Keywords: Bi-axial warp knitted composite tubes; Torsion be haviors; Torque-torsion angle curves; Finite elemen tanalysis (FEA)

1   Introduction

Three-dimensional (3D) textile structure composites exhibit excellent damage tolerance and delamination resistance. It is suitable for designing high impact damage tolerance structures[1-2]. Composite tubes are quite popular structures for vehicle, liquid and gas transportations. The torsion behaviors of such kind of tube are important for life-long time service. The trade-off of the torsion behaviors and material's cost could be obtained from the optimum of the tube manufacturing.

The investigations on composite tubes mainly focus on dynamic crushing, quasi-static compression and energy absorption[3-8]. Furthermore, Sevkat et al. [9] explored the effect of loading rate and stacking sequence on torsion behaviors of laminated composite shaft. They found that the torsional speed has no significant influence on strength, while stacking sequence of the hybrid layers is critical for the torsional behavior. And Tarn et al. [12] presented an analytical approach to research the torsional properties of laminated composite tubes. Wang et al. [10] tested the effects of braided structures on torsion

properties. Potluri et al. [11] investigated the torsional behaviors of biaxial and triaxial braided composite shafts with different braid angles. The maximum torsion strength, modulus and failure modes are significantly influenced by the fabric architecture.

Here we presented a new kind of closed-form integrated tube, of which structure is bi-axial warp-knitted. Its tensile behaviors and ballistic impact damage tolerance were studied by Gu and his colleagues[13-14]. However, the torsional behaviors remain unclear. Therefore, we investigated the torsional behaviors of this carbon fiber multilayered bi-axial warp knitted fabric reinforced composite tubes with tests and numerical analyses to reveal its capabilities for structural application.

2   Experiments

2.1   Materials

Fig. 1 is a diagram of the BWK preform's structure. This bi-axial warp knitted fabric consists of seven cross-plied layers ($[+45/ -45/ +45/ \overline{-45}]_s$) of straight fiber tows and eighteen sets of knitted loop yarns. And the type of

FTA40-E13-3K type of carbon fiber tows was used.

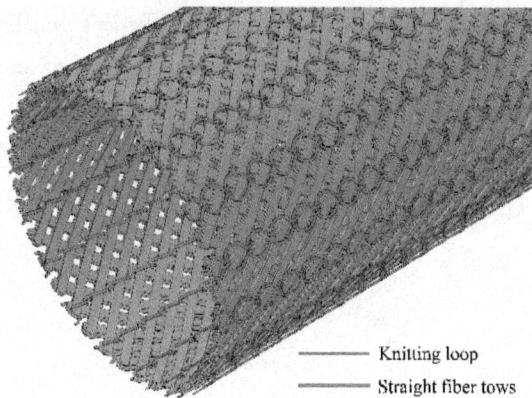

Fig. 1   Architecture of the BWK preform

2.2   Specimen preparation

We mixed JC-02A epoxy resin and JC-02B modified an hydride together with a mass ratio of 20 : 17 as the matrix material. Vacuum Assisted Resin Transfer Molding (VARTM) process (Fig. 2) was employed to prepare the composite tubes, as a schematic depicted in Fig. 2. We cured it at 90℃ for 2h, 110℃ for 1h, and 130℃ for 4h sequentially. Fig. 3 (a) shows a cured sample of 200mm long. And its inner diameter and the outer diameter of are 30.5mm and 34mm respectively. Fig. 3 (b) is a photograph of the clamped specimen, where the span is 100mm. We use this clamp to ensure torque transfer effectively without any slippage.

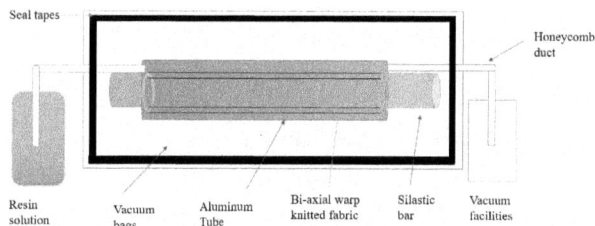

Fig. 2   VARTM device diagram

Quasi-statictorsion tests were operated using CRIMS NWS500 static torsion test machine as shown in Fig. 4 (a). The tests were repeated five times under the torsional speed of 5°/min.

3   Numerical Simulation

We introduced a finite element analysis model at contin-

Fig. 3   (a) Cured specimen

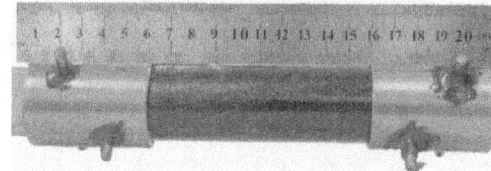

Fig. 3   (b) Clamped specimen

Fig. 4   (a) CRIMS NWS500 experimental apparatus

Fig. 4   (b) SEM photograph of the axial interface

uum level to simulate the torsional deformation and damage of this structural tubes. The continuum is composed of representative unit cells. The transversely isotropic fiber tows and isotropic epoxy resin region were homogenized in this unit cell.

3.1   Mechanical properties of fiber tows

Scan electron microscopy was employed todepict the cross-sectional structure of a single fiber tow. Fig. 4(b) is a SEM photograph after processing through the software called Image Pro Plus to distinguish fiber (black) from resin (white). The proportion of the shadow area to the total area was 60.2%, generally called filling factor.

Further, the fiber volume fraction of the whole composite tube was measured with combustion method. The obtained fiber volume fraction is approximately 26.64%.
The compliance matrix of the fiber and resin can be calculated from their material constants using the formula (1) and (2), respectively.

$$[S^f] = \begin{bmatrix} S_{11}^f & S_{12}^f & S_{12}^f & 0 & 0 & 0 \\ S_{12}^f & S_{22}^f & S_{23}^f & 0 & 0 & 0 \\ S_{12}^f & S_{23}^f & S_{22}^f & 0 & 0 & 0 \\ 0 & 0 & 0 & S_{44}^f & 0 & 0 \\ 0 & 0 & 0 & 0 & S_{55}^f & 0 \\ 0 & 0 & 0 & 0 & 0 & S_{55}^f \end{bmatrix} \quad (1)$$

where $S_{11}^f = \dfrac{1}{E_{11}^f}$, $S_{12}^f = -\dfrac{v_{12}^f}{E_{11}^f}$, $S_{22}^f = \dfrac{1}{E_{22}^f}$,

$S_{23}^f = -\dfrac{v_{23}^f}{E_{22}^f}$, $S_{44}^f = \dfrac{1}{G_{23}^f}$, $S_{55}^f = \dfrac{1}{G_{12}^f}$

where $[S^f]$ is the compliance matrix, E_{11}^f and E_{22}^f are the elastic modulus in axial and transverse direction, respectively. G_{12}^f and G_{23}^f are shear modulus. v_{12}^f and v_{23}^f are the axial and lateral poisson ratios, respectively. Carbon fiber material parameters are shown in the Tab. 1.

$$[S^r] = \begin{bmatrix} S_{11}^r & S_{12}^r & S_{12}^r & 0 & 0 & 0 \\ S_{12}^r & S_{11}^r & S_{12}^r & 0 & 0 & 0 \\ S_{12}^r & S_{12}^r & S_{11}^r & 0 & 0 & 0 \\ 0 & 0 & 0 & S_{44}^r & 0 & 0 \\ 0 & 0 & 0 & 0 & S_{44}^r & 0 \\ 0 & 0 & 0 & 0 & 0 & S_{44}^r \end{bmatrix} \quad (2)$$

$$S_{11}^r = \dfrac{1}{E^r}, S_{12}^r = -\dfrac{v^r}{E^r}, S_{44}^r = \dfrac{1}{G^r},$$

Where $[S^r]$ is the compliance matrix. E^r and G^r are elastic modulus and shear modulus of resin respectively. v^r is the poisson ratio. Elastic parameters of resin are also shown in Tab. 1.

Tab. 1 Mechanics properties of fiber and matrix

Material	Carbonfiber	Epoxyresin
E_1(GPa)	238	2.4
$E_2 = E_3$(GPa)	15	
G_{23}(GPa)	5.8	0.89
$G_{12} = G_{13}$(GPa)	9	
v_{23}	0.3	0.35
$v_{12} = v_{13}$	0.25	

Impregnated fiber tows are assumed as transversely isotropic materials, and resin is isotropic material. The mechanical properties were calculated using the bridge model. The relationship between the increase of internal stress of fiber and resin in unidirectional composites is as follows:

$$\{d\sigma^r\} = [A]\{d\sigma^f\} \quad (3)$$
$$\{d\varepsilon^f\} = [S^f]\{d\sigma^f\} \quad (4)$$
$$\{d\varepsilon^r\} = [S^m]\{d\sigma^r\} \quad (5)$$
$$\{d\sigma\} = V_f\{d\sigma^f\} + V_r\{d\sigma^r\} \quad (6)$$
$$\{d\sigma_i\} = \{d\sigma_{11}, d\sigma_{22}, d\sigma_{33}, d\sigma_{23}, d\sigma_{13}, d\sigma_{12}\}^T \quad (7)$$
$$\{d\varepsilon_i\} = \{d\varepsilon_{11}, d\varepsilon_{22}, d\varepsilon_{33}, d\varepsilon_{23}, d\varepsilon_{13}, d\varepsilon_{12}\}^T \quad (8)$$

The subscript f and r represent the fiber and resin, and V_f is the fiber filling coefficient of the yarn, V_r is the volume fraction of resin immersed in the yarn ($V_r = 1 - V_f$). The compliance matrix of yarn can be deduced from the following formulas.

$$[S^y] = (V_f[S^f] + V_r[S^r][A])(V_f[I] + V_r[A])^{-1} \quad (9)$$

Where $[A]$ is called bridging matrix.

$$[A] = \begin{bmatrix} a_{11} & a_{12} & a_{13} & 0 & 0 & 0 \\ 0 & a_{22} & 0 & 0 & 0 & 0 \\ 0 & 0 & a_{33} & 0 & 0 & 0 \\ 0 & 0 & 0 & a_{44} & 0 & 0 \\ 0 & 0 & 0 & 0 & a_{55} & 0 \\ 0 & 0 & 0 & 0 & 0 & a_{66} \end{bmatrix} \quad (10)$$

$$a_{11} = \frac{E^r}{E_{11}^f}, a_{12} = a_{13} = \frac{(S_{12}^f - S_{12}^r) \cdot (a_{11} - a_{22})}{(S_{11}^f - S_{11}^r)}$$

$$a_{22} = a_{33} = a_{44} = \frac{1}{2} \cdot \left(1 + \frac{E^r}{E_{22}^f}\right)$$

$$a_{55} = a_{66} = \frac{1}{2} \cdot \left(1 + \frac{G^r}{G_{12}^f}\right)$$

3.2 Unit cell homogenization

Unit cell model was established in the software CATIA, as shown in Fig. 5. The stiffness of yarns in the global coordinate system can be given in terms of the local coordinate system, as shown in formula (11). The stiffness matrix of the unit cell can be gained by formula (12).

$$[S]_g = [T_{ij}]_s [S]_l [T_{ij}]_s^T \quad (11)$$

$[S]_l$ and $[S]_g$ are the compliance matrix of composite materials in local coordinate system and global coordinate system, respectively. $[T_{ij}]_s$ is the transfer matrix. The compliance matrix of unit cell $[S]_{Cell}$ is derived

using homogenization method as follows

$$[S]_{\text{Cell}} = \frac{1}{V} \cdot (\int_{V_i}[S^i]dV + \int_{V_{i+1}}[S^{i+1}]dV + \cdots$$

$$+ \int_{V_k}[S^k]dV + \int_{V_r}[S^r]dV) \qquad (12)$$

Where $[S^i]$ represents the compliance matrix of a unidirectional composite material. k is the number of unidirectional composites in unit cell, V is the total unit cell volume.

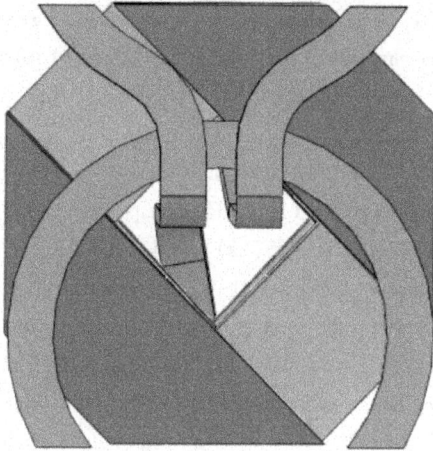

Fig. 6   Homogeneous model   (a) The loading and (b) fixed boundary conditions

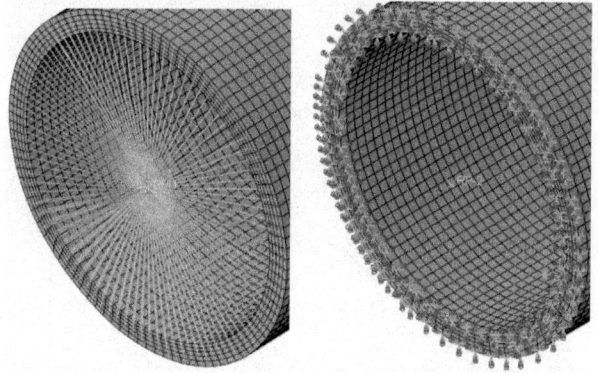

Fig. 5   Unit cell model

3.3   Finite element implementation

The homogenized model has been implemented into the commercial finite element code Abaqus/Standard (6.14) to simulate torsion behaviors and damage characteristics. Fig. 6 displays the set of boundary conditions of this finite element model. The degree of freedom (DoF) of nodes in one end is fixed ($U_x = U_y = U_z = 0$), while the DoF of nodes on the other end are coupled with a reference point. The specimen was meshed with 8−noded linear brick solid elements using a structural meshing technique. The mesh numbers in axial and circumferential directions are both 100, and in radial direction is 5. The torsion loading was applied on the reference point at the speed of 5°/min.

4   Results and Discussion

The Fig. 7 demonstrates the torque-torsion angle behavior of BWK composite tubes. The torque increases linearly as the torsion angle increases. The average failure torque is 328.78N · m at average torsion angle of

12.06°. Repeatability and consistency of all samples are very good. Since the torsional performances of each specimen in the same configuration fluctuate slightly, we selected one specimen to demonstrate and compare with the simulated result in Fig. 8 (a). The curve shows that the deviation of failure torque and torsion angle between the FEA results and tests is 5.6% and 5.1%, respectively. This difference can be attributed to the imperfections (void and fiber bundle undulation) in the specimen. The fractography of BWK composite under torsional load obtained from both experiment and numerical analysis are shown in Fig. 8 (b). The fracture region in FEA model shows an axial crack, which has a 45° angle to the axial direction, similar to those of experimental results. FEA results have good agreements on the torque-torsion angle curve and fractography. These results validate the proposed numerical unit-cell model.

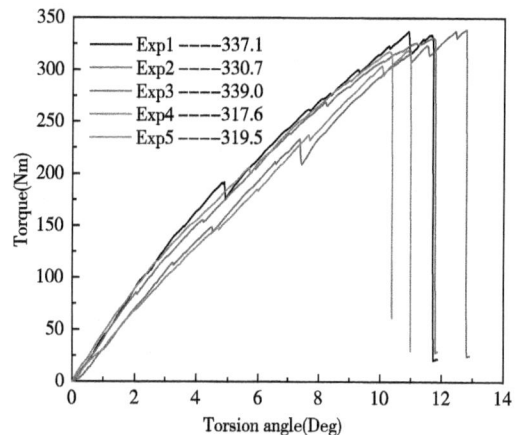

Fig. 7   Experimental torque-torsion angle curves

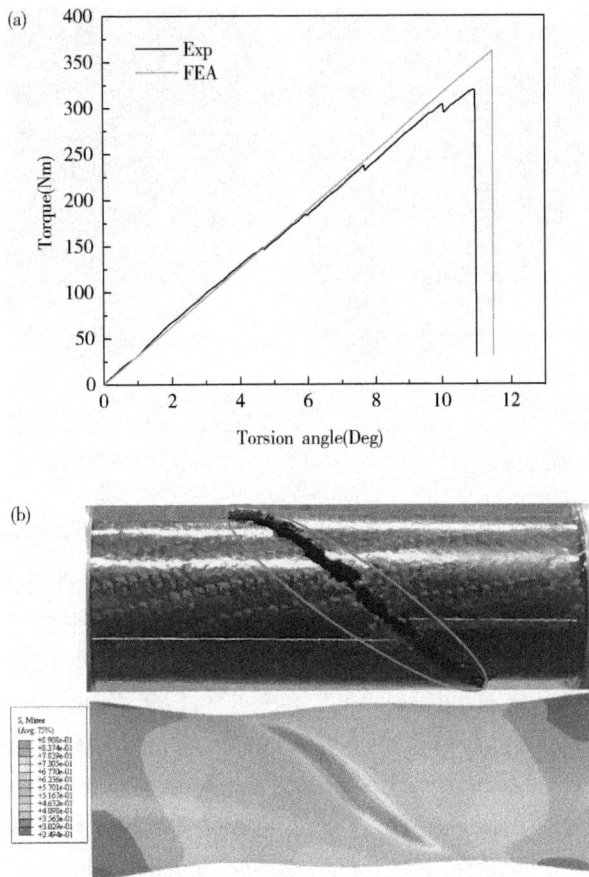

Fig. 8 (a) Torque-torsion angle curve compared with experimental test and FEA; (b) Fractography compared with experimental test and FEA

5 Conclusions

The quasi-static torsional behavior of BWK composite tubes has been investigated both experimentally and numerically. Experiment results reveal that the average failure torque is 328. 78N · m at the average 12. 06° torsion angle. We developed a unit-cell model at continuum level to simulate the torsional behaviors. The torque-torsional angle curve and fractography obtained from this FEA model and test results show reasonable agreements. This finite element method can be used to design and optimize the microstructure of the BWK composite tubes.

References

[1] Xiao X, Mcgregor C, Vaziri R, et al. Progress in braided composite tube crush simulation [J]. International Journal of Impact Engineering, 2009, 36(5): 711-719.

[2] Aly-Hassan M S, Hatta H, Wakayama S, et al. Comparison of 2D and 3D carbon/carbon composites with respect to damage and fracture resistance [J]. Carbon, 2003, 41 (5): 1069-1078.

[3] Mamalis A G, Manolakos D E, Ioannidis M B, et al. The static and dynamic axial collapse of CFRP square tubes: Finite element modeling [J]. Composite Structures, 2006, 74 (2): 213-225.

[4] Tang G, Yan Y, Chen X, et al. Dynamic damage and fracture mechanism of three-dimensional braided carbon fiber/epoxy resin composites [J]. Materials & Design, 2001, 22 (1): 21-25.

[5] Zeng T, Fang D N, Lu T J. Dynamic crashing and impact energy absorption of 3D braided composite tubes [J]. Materials Letters, 2005, 59(12): 1491-1496.

[6] Sancaktar E, Schauber D A. Failure behavior of filament-wound carbon fiber/epoxy composite tubes under axial compression[C]// ASME 2003 International Mechanical Engineering Congress and Exposition. 2003: 441-452.

[7] Wu F, Xiao X, Dong Y, et al. Quasi-static axial crush response and energy absorption of layered composite structure formed from novel crochet-sintered mesh tube and thin-walled tube [J]. Composite Structures, 2018.

[8] Gu B, Chang F K. Energy absorption features of 3D braided rectangular composite under different strain rates compressive loading [J]. Aerospace Science & Technology, 2007, 11 (7): 535-545.

[9] Sevkat E, Tumer H, Kelestemur M H, et al. Effect of torsional strain-rate and lay-up sequences on the performance of hybrid composite shafts [J]. Materials & Design, 2014, 60 (8): 310-319.

[10] Wang X, Cai D, Li C, et al. Failure analysis of three-dimensional braided composite tubes under torsional load: Experimental study [J]. Journal of Reinforced Plastics & Composites, 2017, 36(12):073168441769425.

[11] Potluri P, Manan A, Francke M, et al. Flexural and torsional behavior of biaxial and triaxial braided composite structures [J]. Composite Structures, 2006, 75 (1): 377-386.

[12] Tarn J Q, Wang Y M. Laminated composite tubes under extension, torsion, bending, shearing and pressuring: a state space approach [J]. International Journal of Solids & Structures, 2001, 38(50-51): 9053-9075.

[13] Jin L, Hu H, Sun B, et al. A simplified microstructure model of bi-axial warp-knitted composite for ballistic impact

simulation [J]. Composites Part B, 2010, 41 (5):
337-353.

[14] Dong K, Peng X, Nishonov A, et al. In-plane tensile behavior of bi-axial warp-knitted composites under quasi-static
and high strain rate loading [J]. Journal of Donghua University (English Edition), 2017, 34(4): 487-491.

A Novel Cord-Shaped Supercapacitor with High Stretchability

Shu Zhang[1], Wenqi Nie[1], Xin Ding[1,2]*, Jiyong Hu[1,2], Xudong Yang[1], Qiao Li[1]

[1] *College of Textiles, Donghua University, Shanghai 201620, China*

[2] *Key Laboratory of Textile Science and Technology (Donghua University), Ministry of Education, Shanghai 201620, China*

* *Corresponding author's email*: xding@ dhu. edu. cn

Abstract: Wire-shaped stretchable supercapacitors have received great attention because of high stretchability and three-dimensional flexibility. For coaxial supercapacitors, lower capacitive performance and the inextensibility of the separation layer are important factors restricting their development. In this work, we have achieved the integration of multiple yarn-electrodes by braiding method along elastic yarns to make a stretchable coaxial cord-shaped supercapacitor. The stretchable separator can be fabricated by braiding multiple spandex yarns, which can achieve high tensile deformation and high porosity. The cord-shaped supercapacitor possesses an excellent capacitive performance of 422. 14mF/cm³ and an extremely high capacitance retention rate of 99. 8% can be achieved under the stretching strain of 100% demonstrating the application value of this stretchable energy storage device.

Keywords: Stretchability; Cord-shaped; Wire-shaped; Braiding; Integration; Supercapacitor

1 Introduction

Stretchable electronics is an emerging field in large-area electronics wherein circuits can be built or embedded in stretchable substrates, which have the capacity to accommodate large strains without significant degradation in their electronic performance[1]. It has burgeoning potential in biomedical devices, wearable electronics, artificial skin incorporating sensor abilities, and so on[2-4]. Currently, some devices, such as light-emitting diodes (LED) and display panels, have remained their function when stained up to 100%[5-6]. As essential components of the stretchable electronics, energy storage units (such as batteries, supercapacitors) should be capable of accommodating large strain while retaining the performance to match these highly stretchable devices.

Recently, plenty of attentions were attracted to the wire-shaped stretchable supercapacitors (SSCs). For example, Yang et al.[7] demonstrated a fiber-shaped SSC by wrapping aligned CNT sheets on an elastic fiber. The high stretchability and specific capacitance (19. 2F/g at 0. 1A/g) was achieved simultaneously by designing a coaxial structure. As a special configuration, the fiber shape SSCs can achieve a high level of strain and three-dimensional flexibility, which enables them to weave into a cloth, or be integrated into microelectronics realizing the value of energy supply.

However, the capacitance of a single fiber or yarn electrode is not enough to achieve the energy supply. The high internal resistance[8] and low flexibility[9] brought by integration of the yarn electrode from the length and width direction also greatly limit the development of the wire-shaped SSCs. In the meanwhile, it is critical for stretchable coaxial SCs to achieve high stretchability while avoiding contact short circuit between inner and outer electrodes, which is easy to happen because of the non-stretchability of the separation layer. So far, less research focused on stretchable separation membrane has limited the development of stretchable coaxial wire-like SCs.

In this study, we fabricated a stretchable coaxial cord-shaped SC by means of a layer-by-layer braiding process. The inner and outer electrodes were coaxially braided with multiple electrically conductive energy storage yarns along an elastic core yarn, to form an integration of multiple yarn-electrodes in the circumferential direction. The stretchable separation layer was fabricated by braiding multiple spandex yarns between the inner and outer electrode. The fabricated cord-shaped SC can achieve more than 100% tensile deformation while maintaining more than 99.8% capacitive performance of $421\,mF/cm^3$, demonstrating an excellent application value.

2 Experiments

2.1 Material

Commercial PLA filament with a linear density of 150D/72F was purchased from Benhui Textile Co., Ltd. Pyrrole monomer, anthraquinone-2-sulfonic acid (AQSA), $FeCl_3 \cdot 6H_2O$, were purchased from Sinopharm Chemical Reagent Co., Ltd. Lycra-yarn and spandex covered yarn with linear densities of 1220D and 420D/40D/20D respectively were purchased from INVISTA Fiber Co., Ltd.

2.2 Preparation of PLA filament yarn-electrode

The preparation of the PLA yarn-electrode is briefly described: PLA filament was rinsed with acetone to remove impurities. Mixture solution of $FeCl_3/GO$ was adsorbed on PLA filament by dipping and coating process. After repeating dipping and drying, GO_{FeCl_3}/PLA (GO @ PLA) filament was obtained. The GO @ PLA filament was immersed into 20mL aqueous solution containing pyrrole (0.02mol/L) and AQSA (0.01mol/L). Then, 20mL $FeCl_3$ (0.18mol/L) was dropwise added to initiate the polymerization. After a chemical in-situ polymerization in an ice bath for 8h, the $GO_{FeCl_3}/PPy/PLA$ (GO/PPy @ PLA) filament electrode was obtained.

2.3 Preparation of stretchable cord-shaped electrode

The preparation of a stretchable cord-shaped electrode was shown in Fig.1 (a). Multiple PLA filament yarn-electrodes were braided along the core axis of a lycra-yarn, which was pre-stretched by 200% before braiding. After stretching recovery, a stretchable cord-shaped electrode was obtained with more than 100%

stretchability.

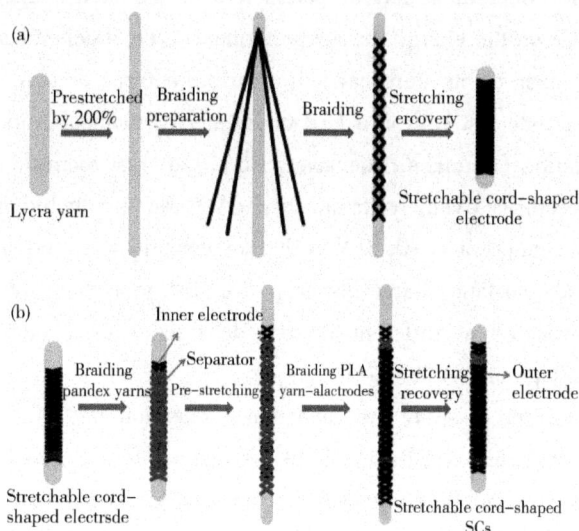

Fig. 1 (a) Preparation process of the stretchable cord-shaped electrode; (b) Preparation process of the stretchable cord-shaped SC

2.4 Preparation of stretchable separation layer

The stretchable separator was fabricated by braiding 12 spandex yarns along the inner electrode, which could achieve a full coverage for the inner electrode to avoid contact short circuit with the outer electrode. The braided separator provided a higher stretchability than the inner electrode and a porous structure that facilitated the impregnation of the electrolyte on the inner electrode.

2.5 Preparation of stretchable cord-shaped SCs

The preparation of stretchable cord-shaped SCs was shown in Fig.1 (b). The inner electrode was fabricated by braiding multiple PLA yarn-electrodes along a pre-strained elastic yarn. After stretching recovery, 12 spandex yarns were braided along the inner electrode acting as a separator. Finally, multiple PLA yarn-electrodes, which had the same number with the inner electrode, were braided along the circumference of the pre-stretched separator acting as the outer electrode, so that we got a stretchable cord-shaped SC with more than 100% stretchability.

2.6 Characterization

To characterize the capacitive properties of the stretchable cord-shaped electrodes which were braided with different number of PLA yarn-electrodes, and to clarify the effect of structural parameters of the cord-shaped SCs on the energy storage performance, electrochemical measurements were carried out using a three or two-electrode test cell on a CHI 660D electrochemical workstation (Shanghai Chenguang Co., Ltd.) at room temperature. Cyclic voltammetry (CV) was conducted in the range of 0-0.8 V with incremental sweep rates. Galvanostatic charge-discharge (GCD) properties were measured at different current densities with a cutoff voltage of 0-0.8 V.

In order to study the capacitance retention rate of the stretchable cord-shaped SC under different tensile strains and different cycles of stretching. The dynamic stretching and releasing could be realized by a JF-9003 computer tensile testing machine (Dongguan Jianfeng Instrument Co., Ltd.) with the tensile speed of 100mm/min and the maximum tensile deformation of 100%.

3 Results and Discussion

3.1 Electrochemical properties of the stretchable rope-shaped electrode

The stretchable cord-shaped electrode could be prepared by braiding multiple PLA yarn-electrodes along a pre-strained elastic yarn. The PLA filament yarn-electrode possessed an excellent capacitance performance of 158.8mF/cm^2 and a high GO/PPy weight loading of 36%, which was a prerequisite for a high-performance cord-shaped electrode. Fig.2 (a) showed the CV curves of the cord-shaped electrodes which were braided with different number of yarn-electrodes. The area enclosed by the CV curves increased with the number of braided yarns increasing, which demonstrated that more braided yarn-electrodes could provide more capacitive performance.

In order to determine the optimal number of braided yarns, Fig.2 (b) studied the capacitance and tensile properties of the cord-shaped electrodes braided with different number of yarn-electrodes. With the number of braided yarns increased gradually, the maximum tensile deformation of the cord-shaped electrode decreased rapidly, and even dropped to less than 100% when the

braiding number was higher than six. Considering the stretchability and the capacitive performance comprehensively, we concluded that the optimal number of braided yarn-electrodes should be six.

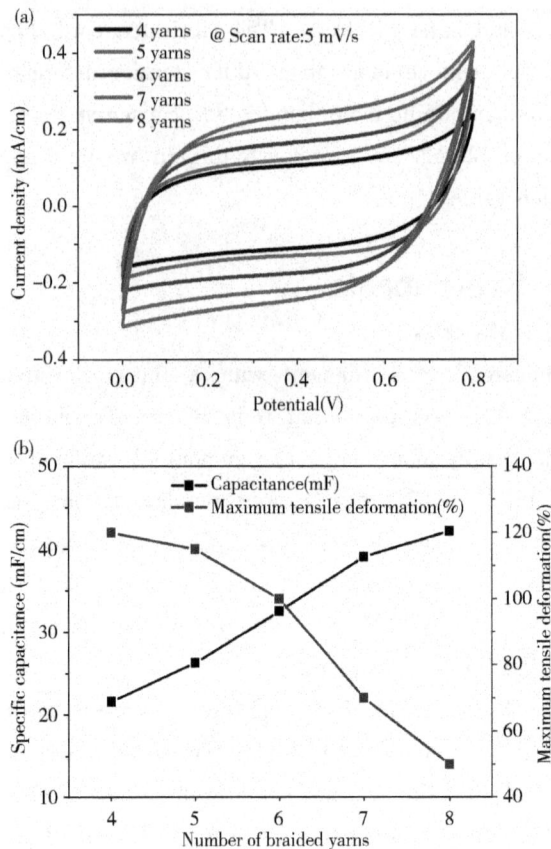

Fig.2　(a) CV curves of the cord-shaped electrodes with different number of braided yarns; (b) Effects of the braided number on specific capacitance and the maximum tensile deformation of the cord-shaped electrodes

3.2 Electrochemical properties of the cord-shaped SCs

The CV curves of the stretchable cord-shaped SCs with different structural parameters were shown in Fig.3 (a) and (b). The electrode was obviously polarized according to the CV curves of cord-shaped SCs, which could be attributed to two reasons. Firstly, long length of the cord-shaped electrode led to greater electrode resistance. Fig.3 (a) showed that the capacitive performance was effectively improved by reducing the electrode length. Secondly, the elastic separation layer made the electrolyte impregnate the inner electrode more difficult. So, Fig.3 (b) showed that the energy storage performance could be improved by reducing the diameter of spandex yarns to achieve more porosity after braiding. According to the comparison of the area enclosed by the CV curves, which represented energy storage performance, the optimal length of the stretchable cord-shaped SC was 2cm, and the optimal diameter of the spandex yarn in separation layer was 0.1mm.

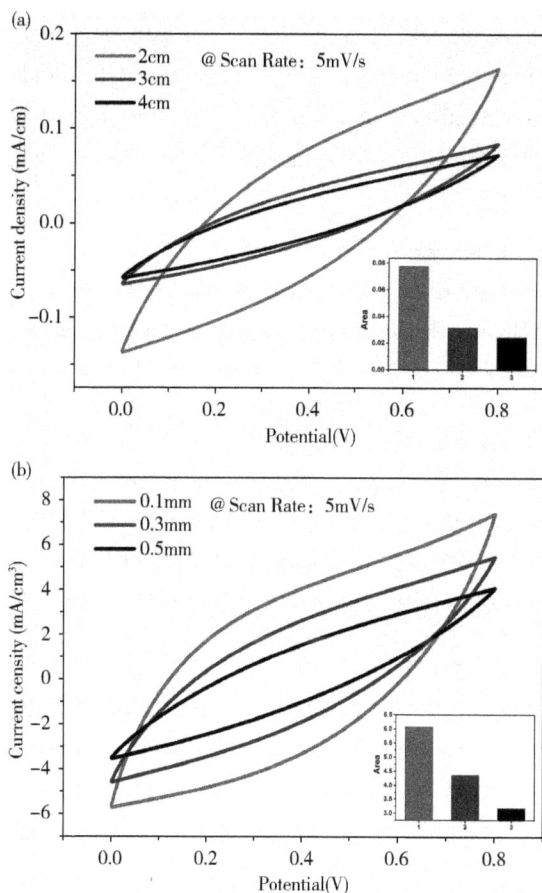

Fig. 3 CV curves and the bar charts of the area enclosed by CV curves for the stretchable cord-shaped SCs (a) with different lengths and (b) with different diameters of spandex yarns in separation layer

The CV curves at different scanning rates and Charging-discharging curves at different current densities of a cord-shaped SC with optimal structural parameters (2cm, 0.1mm) were shown in Fig. 4 (a) and (b). The CV curve formed a completely closed pattern implying that this structure has a reversible charge-discharge capacitance performance. The Galvano-static charge-discharge curves maintained an approximately symmetrical triangle at different current densities, indicating that

this structure has a great coulombic efficiency, which was as high as 87% with the charge-discharge current density of $2.5mA/cm^3$. The volume capacitance of the coaxial cord-shaped SC was $422.14mF/cm^3$ at the scanning rate of $5mV/s$, with the energy density of $0.0375mW/cm^3$ and the power density of $0.54mW/cm^3$. Therefore, it is possible to use this braiding structure to prepare a coaxial cord-shaped SC, which can achieve the integration of multiple energy-storage yarns to gain an excellent capacitive performance.

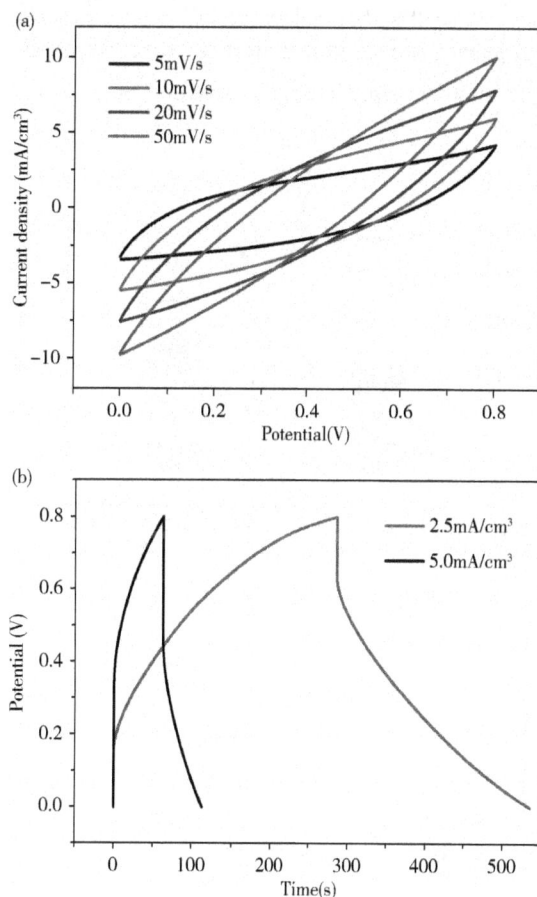

Fig. 4 (a) CV curves at different scan rates and (b) Charging-discharging curves at different current densities of a cord-shaped SC with optimal structural parameters

3.3 Capacitance retention after stretching and cyclic stretching

Fig. 5 (a) showed the capacitance retention of a stretchable cord-shaped SC under 0–500 cycles of dynamic stretching and releasing (DSR) with the tensile deformation of 100% and the tensile speed of 100mm/min. The capacitance retention rate kept declining when the DSR cyclic number increasing. A capacitance retention rate of 88.5% could be achieved after stretching by 100% for 500 cycles. Fig. 5 (b) showed that the stretchable cord-shaped SCs possessed excellent capacitance retention under different tensile strains. A high capacitance retention rate of 99.8% could be achieved under the stretching strain of 100%. When the cord-shaped SC was stretched, the deformation of the inner and outer electrodes could be realized by changing the braiding angles of energy storage yarns without stretching the active material on PLA yarns, which guaranteed an extremely high capacitance retention rate for the stretchable cord-shaped SC.

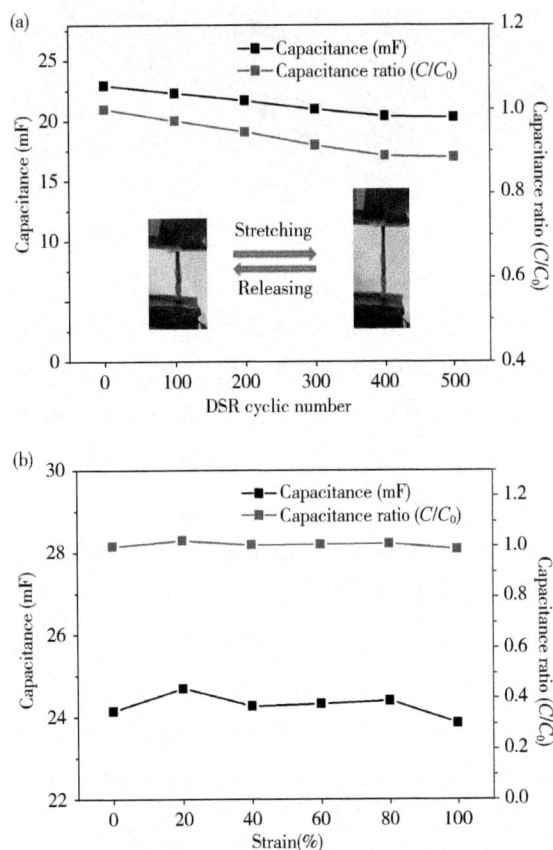

Fig. 5 Capacitance retention line charts under (a) 0-500 DSR cycles and (b) different tensile strains

4 Conclusions

In this study, we prepared a stretchable coaxial cord-shaped SC by means of a layer-by-layer braiding process. The inner electrode was braided with 6 PLA

yarn-electrodes along a pre-strained lycra-yarn, which could achieve a tensile strain of 100% and a relatively high capacitive performance. The stretchable separation membrane was fabricated by braiding 12 spandex yarns along the inner electrode core, which possessed high stretchability and porosity structure. Multiple yarn-electrodes could be integrated by braiding process, which endowed the cord-shaped SC an excellent capacitive performance of 422.14 mF/cm^3. An extremely high capacitance retention rate of 99.8% could be achieved under the stretching strain of 100%, demonstrating the application value of this stretchable cord-shaped SC.

References

[1] Kettlgruber G, Kaltenbrunner M, Siket C M, et al. Intrinsically stretchable and rechargeable batteries for self-powered stretchable electronics [J]. Journal of Materials Chemistry A, 2013, 1(18): 5505-5508.

[2] Khang D Y, Jiang H, Huang Y, et al. A stretchable form of single-crystal silicon for high-performance electronics on rubber substrates[J]. Science, 2006, 311(5758): 208-12.

[3] Yu C, Masarapu C, Rong J, et al. Stretchable supercapacitors based on buckled single-walled carbon-nanotube macrofilms [J]. Advanced Materials, 2010, 21 (47): 4793-4797.

[4] Zhu Y, Xu F. Buckling of aligned carbon nanotubes as stretchable conductors: A new manufacturing strategy [J]. Advanced Materials, 2012, 24(8): 1073.

[5] Hu X, Krull P, De Graff B, et al. Stretchable inorganic semiconductor electronic systems [J]. Advanced Materials, 2011, 23(26): 2933-2936.

[6] Yun S, Niu X, Yu Z, et al. Compliant silver nanowire-polymer composite electrodes for bistable large strain actuation [J]. Advanced Materials, 2012, 24(10): 1321-7.

[7] Yang Z, Deng J, Chen X, et al. A highly stretchable, fiber-shaped supercapacitor[J]. Angewandte Chemie, 2013, 125 (50): 13695-13699.

[8] Huang Q, Wang D, Zheng Z. Textile-based electrochemical energy storage devices [J]. Advanced Energy Materials, 2016, 6(22): 1600783.

[9] Liu W, Song M S, Kong B, et al. Flexible and stretchable energy storage: Recent advances and future perspectives[J]. Advanced Materials, 2017, 29(1).

Adsorption of Cationic Contaminants in Water by MXene Nanosheets/Alginate Composite Fibers

Bo Lu[1,2], Bingxue Huang[1,2], Chuntao Lan[1,2], Peng Wang[1,2], Yingrui Chen[1], Ying Ma[1,2]*, Yiping Qiu[1,2]

[1] *College of Textiles, Donghua University, Shanghai 201620, China*

[2] *Key Laboratory of Textile Science & Technology, Ministry of Education, Shanghai 201620, China*

* *Corresponding author's email*: yingma@ dhu. edu. cn

Abstract: Two-dimensional (2D) $Ti_3C_2T_x$ MXene nanosheets were mixed with sodium alginate, then composite fibers were prepared by wet spinning, researching the adsorption in aqueous media and the removal performance of copper ions and methylene blue (MB). By studying the morphology of the composite fibers, the content of Delaminated layered-$Ti_3C_2T_x$ (DL-$Ti_3C_2T_x$), the concentration of MB and Cu^{2+}, and the effect of adsorption time on the adsorption performance, giving the isothermal adsorption model. Due to its special surface area, hydrophilicity and unique surface functional properties, the DL-$Ti_3C_2T_x$ composite fiber has improved adsorption properties of cationic contaminants. Compared with pure alginate fibers, DL-$Ti_3C_2T_x$ composite fibers exhibited higher absorption capacity. The maximum experimental adsorption capacity (Q_{max}) of Cu^{2+} was 89. 75mg/g, MB was 91.6mg/g. 93% of the total metal ion content was adsorbed within 5min. By comparing the fit of Langmuir and Freundlich adsorption isotherms, it is proved that there are multiple adsorption modes for different contaminant composite fibers and the adsorption mechanism is explained. The current results indicate that DL-$Ti_3C_2T_x$/ CA composite fibers are the promising potential material for the removal cationic contaminants in water.

Keywords: $Ti_3C_2T_x$; MXene; Adsorption; Isotherms; Heavy metal

1 Introduction

Water pollution has become a serious problem, which will not only severely damage the environment but also endanger human health. Sewage treatment has always been considered as an important measure of environmental protection, and various methods of biological treatment, adsorption, chemical oxidation, membrane separation, electrodialysis and ion exchange have been developed[1-7]. In the adsorption technology, the bio-adsorption method has been rapidly developed due to its rich material sources, low cost and easy operation of the method, and easy degradation of the adsorbent material without causing secondary pollution to the environment. So in recent years, bio-adsorption technology has been rapidly developed in the treatment of industrial wastewater. Research on new-type adsorption materials

is the focus of current adsorption technology research. Seaweed is a rich source of marine. The economic algae is one of the pillar industries of marine agriculture. The alginic acid molecule chain has a large number of shuttle and light-group functional groups, and therefore it easily loses protons in aqueous solution and has a negative charge, and has strong binding ability with positively charged substance. Algae and its products have been widely used in the treatment of water pollution in recent years, such as alginate fibers, calcium alginate microspheres and so on. In these methods, sodium alginate was used as a raw material, calcium chloride was used as a coagulation bath, and calcium alginate fibers were prepared through a wet spinning process. Calcium alginate fibers were treated with hydrochloric acid to obtain alginate fibers. Alginate fiber has increased specific surface area, fast adsorption, easy operation, simple processing and bio-degradation of fiber into small molecules, and will not cause secondary pollution to the environment.

MXenes is a novel two-dimensional (2D) transition-metal carbide material with properties and structure similar to grapheme[8-9]. Preparations of MXenes are performed by aqueous and non-aqueous solutions of transition metal carbides that selectively etch certain elements in the hexagonal MAX phase. MAX phase ($M_{n+1}AX_n$; $n = 1$, 2 or 3)[10], by early transition metal (M), IIIA and IVA elements (A) and carbon and/or nitrogen component (X) composition[11]. Due to their unique structure and excellent electrical and chemical properties, they have been used for energy storage, chemical sensors, catalysts and super capacitors[12-14]. And its application in heavy metal adsorption and other environmental pollution repair applications has recently been explored[15]. Adsorption / photo degradation of dyes and adsorption of heavy metals on MXene have been reported[16-18]. However, no Delaminated – $Ti_3C_2T_x$ ($DL–Ti_3C_2T_x$)/calcium alginate (CA) composite fibers have been prepared by wet spinning and have been used as adsorbents to remove dyes in wastewater, and they have been used for the removal of dyestuffs from sewage by adsorption materials. In this paper, $DL–Ti_3C_2T_x$ nanosheets were prepared and mixed with sodium alginate solution. $DL–Ti_3C_2T_x$/CA composite fibers were prepared by wet spinning method. The effects of experimental parameters such as $DL–Ti_3C_2T_x$ content on the adsorption of cationic water contaminants Cu^{2+} and MB on $DL–Ti_3C_2T_x$/CA composite fibers were studied. The adsorption of cationic water contaminants Cu^{2+} and MB on $DL–Ti_3C_2T_x$/CA composite fibers was mechanistically fitted to better understand the removal mechanism. The $DL–Ti_3C_2T_x$/CA composite fibers samples produced in this work showed excellent performance in adsorbing cationic contaminants from aqueous solutions.

2 Experiments

2.1 Synthesis of delaminated–$Ti_3C_2T_x$

The $DL–Ti_3C_2T_x$ was prepared according to a reported method[19-20]. Specifically, 1g of LiF (Alfa Aesar) was added to 20 mL of HCl solution ($w = 37\%$, Sinopharm Group, China) to prepare a selective etching solution. Next, 1g of Ti_3AlC_2 (Forsman, China) as shownin Fig. 1(c) was added to the selective etching solution, and Al was etched away by constant stirring at 35℃ for 24 hours [Fig. 1(a), Fig. 1(b)]. The resulting black suspension was washed several times with deionized water to pH6 and centrifuged to obtain a multi-layered–$Ti_3C_2T_x$ [m-$Ti_3C_2T_x$, Fig. 1(d)] clay-like precipitate. Then, the m-$Ti_3C_2T_x$ sediment was mixed with 300mL of deionized water under vigorous shaking for 5mins. After centrifugation, the dark-green supernatant containing delaminated-$Ti_3C_2T_x$ ($DL-Ti_3C_2T_x$) as shown in Fig. 1(e) nanosheets was collected and freeze-dried.

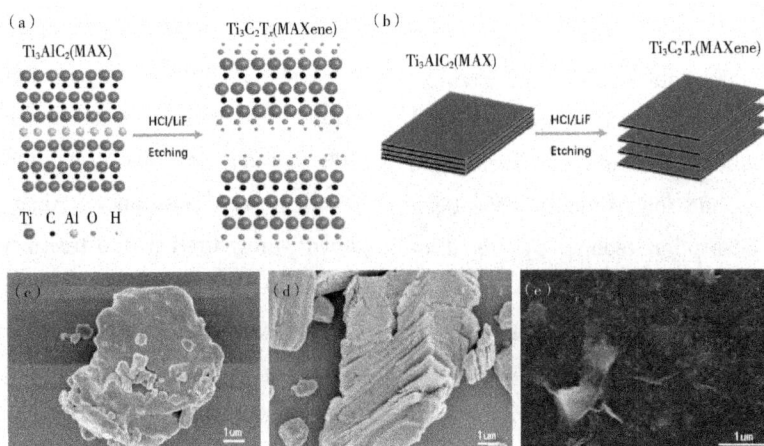

Fig. 1 The process of Ti_3AlC_2 etching into m-$Ti_3C_2T_x$ in (a) Atomic structure and in (b) micro structure; (c) SEM image of Ti_3AlC_2 Particles; (d) SEM image of m-$Ti_3C_2T_x$; (e) SEM image of $DL-Ti_3C_2T_x$ nanosheets

2.2 Preparation of DL-Ti$_3$C$_2$T$_x$/CA composite fibers

In this project, DL-Ti$_3$C$_2$T$_x$/ CA composite fiber was prepared by wet spinning. In its production process, an aqueous solution of calcium chloride (General-Reagent) was used as a coagulation bath, and DL-Ti$_3$C$_2$T$_x$/sodium alginate spinning dope was prepared using distilled water as a solvent. DL-Ti$_3$C$_2$T$_x$/CA composite fibers were then prepared by solidification. The specific process is: After the DL-Ti$_3$C$_2$T$_x$ prepared in the above Synthesis of Delaminated-Ti$_3$C$_2$T$_x$ is released to (3%, 5%, 7%, 10%), it is dispersed by ultrasonic and a certain amount is added to a certain amount of sodium alginate (J&K Scientific) solution. Stirring for 2h at high speed, configure a series of DL-Ti$_3$C$_2$T$_x$/sodium alginate and mixed spinning dope, extruding the spinning dope through a needle into a calcium chloride coagulation bath at a certain temperature, collecting and winding the prepared primary fibers. Soaked in distilled water for 10min, washed several times, fully washed calcium chloride solvent left in the silk, and dried to obtain DL-Ti$_3$C$_2$T$_x$/ CA composite fibers.

2.3 Characterization of concentration

The MB absorption performance of pure alginate fiber and DL-Ti$_3$C$_2$T$_x$/ CA composite fibers was tested by measuring the absorption rate of MB (Methylene blue, AR, ShangHai) in aqueous solution. 200mL (5–100) mg/L MB of aqueous solution was placed in the environment (pH = 7, RT) and 100mg of DL-Ti$_3$C$_2$T$_x$/ CA composite fiber was added and placed in a shaker (150r/min, 25℃). The supernatant was tested to measure the maximum absorbance by UV-vis spectroscopy (Shimadzu-UV2550) and to evaluate the residual concentration of MB. The concentration of residual MB was calculated by comparing the absorbance peak of MB at 662nm. Cu^{2+} solution (1–25mg/L) reacted with copper reagent (sodium diethyldithiocarbamate, DDTC-Na, Chemical-Reagent) to produce different concentrations of yellow-brown colloidal complexes in aqueous solution. The maximum absorption wavelength of the pure alginate fiber and the DL-Ti$_3$C$_2$T$_x$/ CA composite fiber was 452nm, which was determined by measuring the light absorption value and drawing a standard curve to quantitatively determine the copper ion concentration. Cu$_2$SO$_4$ · 5H$_2$O (Sinopharm Group, China) Configure 200 mL (20–100mg/L) Cu^{2+} aqueous solution in the environment (pH = 7, RT), add 100mg DL-Ti$_3$C$_2$T$_x$/ CA composite fiber, place it in shaker (150 r/min, 25℃). Take the adsorbed solution and add DDTC-Na (400mg/L). Q_e is the adsorption amount, which is the mass of alginate adsorbed by the unit mass after adsorption reaches the equilibrium state, formula is as (1):

$$Q_e = \frac{(C_e - C_0) \times V}{m} \qquad (1)$$

The removal rate (R%) refers to the percentage of the mass of contaminants adsorbed by the alginate fibers after the adsorption reaches an equilibrium state to the mass of the initial contaminants in the solution. The calculation formula is shown as (2):

$$R\% = \frac{(C_e - C_0)}{C_0} \times 100\% \qquad (2)$$

The initial concentration is C_0 (mg/L). C_e (mg/L) is the equilibrium concentration. V (L) is the volume of the solution and m (g) is the weight of the DL-Ti$_3$C$_2$T$_x$/CA composite fiber.

2.4 Characterization of DL-Ti$_3$C$_2$T$_x$/CA composite fibers

The CA fiber [Fig. 2 (a)] has a high transmittance, but DL-Ti$_3$C$_2$T$_x$/CA composite fiber as shown in Fig. 2 (b) prepared with DL-Ti$_3$C$_2$T$_x$ with a mass fraction of 7% becomes black opaque. Both fibers are relatively uniform in size. Field emission scanning electron microscope (FESEM) (S–4800, HITACHI, Japan) observed the microstructure of the sample. Observation by scanning electron microscopy revealed that the surface roughness of the DL-Ti$_3$C$_2$T$_x$/CA composite fiber [Fig. 2 (c)] was greater than that of the CA fiber [Fig. 2 (d)], and it was observed that this roughness was formed by a combination of block-like projections and groove. This is due to the fact that the DL-Ti$_3$C$_2$T$_x$ sheets increase the degree of difference in the shrinkage in different directions inside the fibers during fiber solidification molding. The rougher surface of DL-Ti$_3$C$_2$T$_x$/ CA composite fiber is beneficial to the enhancement of the adsorption performance of DL-Ti$_3$C$_2$T$_x$/ CA composite fiber.

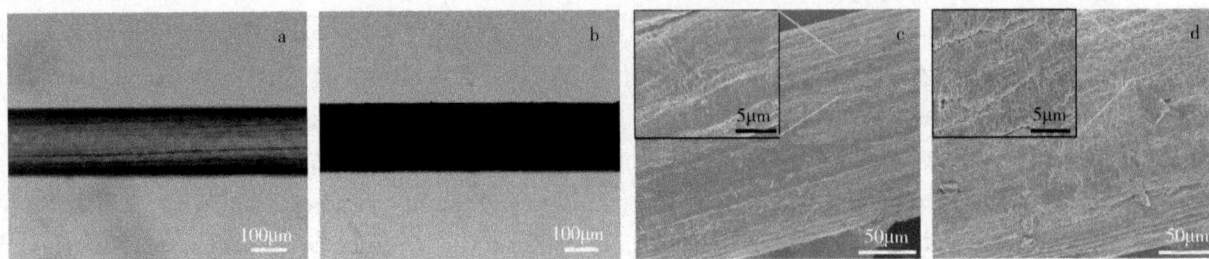

Fig. 2 (a) Optical microscope image of the pure CA fiber; (b) Optical microscope image of DL-Ti$_3$C$_2$T$_x$/ CA composite fiber; (c) SEM image of the pure CA fiber; (d) SEM image of m-Ti$_3$C$_2$T$_x$

3 Results and Discussion

3.1 Influence of the content of DL-Ti$_3$C$_2$T$_x$ on the adsorption

As shown in Fig. 3 (a) – (c), different proportions of DL-Ti$_3$C$_2$T$_x$/ CA composite fibers were absorbed at equilibrium UV absorption curves at initial concentrations of 100mg/L MB, initial concentrations of 50mg/L and 100mg/L Cu^{2+} (temperature = 298K, pH = 7.0). It can be clearly seen from Fig. 3 (d) and (e) that with the increase of DL-Ti$_3$C$_2$T$_x$ content, the removal rate first increases and then drops, peaks when the DL-Ti$_3$C$_2$T$_x$ content is 7%, and Cu^{2+} (50mg/L) is 89.4%, Cu^{2+} (100mg/L) is 94.9%, MB(100mg/L) is 91.6%. As shown in Fig. 3 (f), the effect of MB and Cu^{2+} concentration on the adsorption amount and removal rate was studied at a mass fraction of DL-Ti$_3$C$_2$T$_x$ of 7% (pH = 7, RT). Adsorption capacity of Cu^{2+} and MB increased with the increase of MB and Cu^{2+} concentrations. When the initial Cu^{2+} concentration ranged from 20mg/L to 100mg/L, the removal rate of Cu^{2+} gradually decreased with the increase of Cu^{2+} concentration from 96.8% (Cu^{2+} 20mg/L) to 89.7% (Cu^{2+} 100mg/L). When the mass fraction of DL-Ti$_3$C$_2$T$_x$ is 7% and the initial MB concentration is in the range of 5 – 100mg/L, the MB removal rate gradually increases with MB concentration, from 79.4% (MB 5mg/L) to 91.6% (MB 100mg/L). As the initial concentration of MB and Cu^{2+} increased, the adsorption capacity and equilibrium concentration increased. This may be because when the concentration of MB and Cu^{2+} are low, the DL-Ti$_3$C$_2$T$_x$/CA composite fiber is accompanied

with the increase in concentration as the solution is constantly oscillated and easily contacts with the adsorption point of the DL-Ti$_3$C$_2$T$_x$/CA composite fiber. The chance of contact with the adsorption spot increases. Therefore, there is more adsorption, that is, an increase in adsorption capacity. However, the removal rate of Cu^{2+} decreased with the increase of the concentration, because the adsorption capacity of DL-Ti$_3$C$_2$T$_x$/CA composite fibers became saturated gradually. Instead, the equilibrium concentration became larger and the removal rate became smaller and smaller. On the contrary, the removal rate of MB increased with the increase of the concentration because the adsorption capacity of DL-Ti$_3$C$_2$T$_x$/CA composite fibers to MB had not reached the maximum value when MB concentration was 100mg/L, so it was an upward trend from 79.4% (MB 5mg/L) to 91.6% (MB 100mg/L). As the initial concentration of MB and Cu^{2+} increased, the adsorption capacity and equilibrium concentration increased. This may be because when the concentration of MB and Cu^{2+} are low, the DL-Ti$_3$C$_2$T$_x$/CA composite fiber is accompanied with the increase in concentration as the solution is constantly oscillated and easily contacts with the adsorption point of the DL-Ti$_3$C$_2$T$_x$/CA composite fiber. The chance of contact with the adsorption spot increases. Therefore, there is more adsorption, that is, an increase in adsorption capacity. However, the removal rate of Cu^{2+} decreased with the increase of the concentration, because the adsorption capacity of DL-Ti$_3$C$_2$T$_x$/CA composite fibers became saturated gradually. Instead, the equilibrium concentration became larger and the removal rate became smaller and smaller. On the contrary, the removal rate of MB increased with the increase of the concentration because the adsorption capacity of DL-Ti$_3$C$_2$T$_x$/CA composite fibers to MB had not reached the maximum value when MB concentration was 100mg/L, so it was an upward trend.

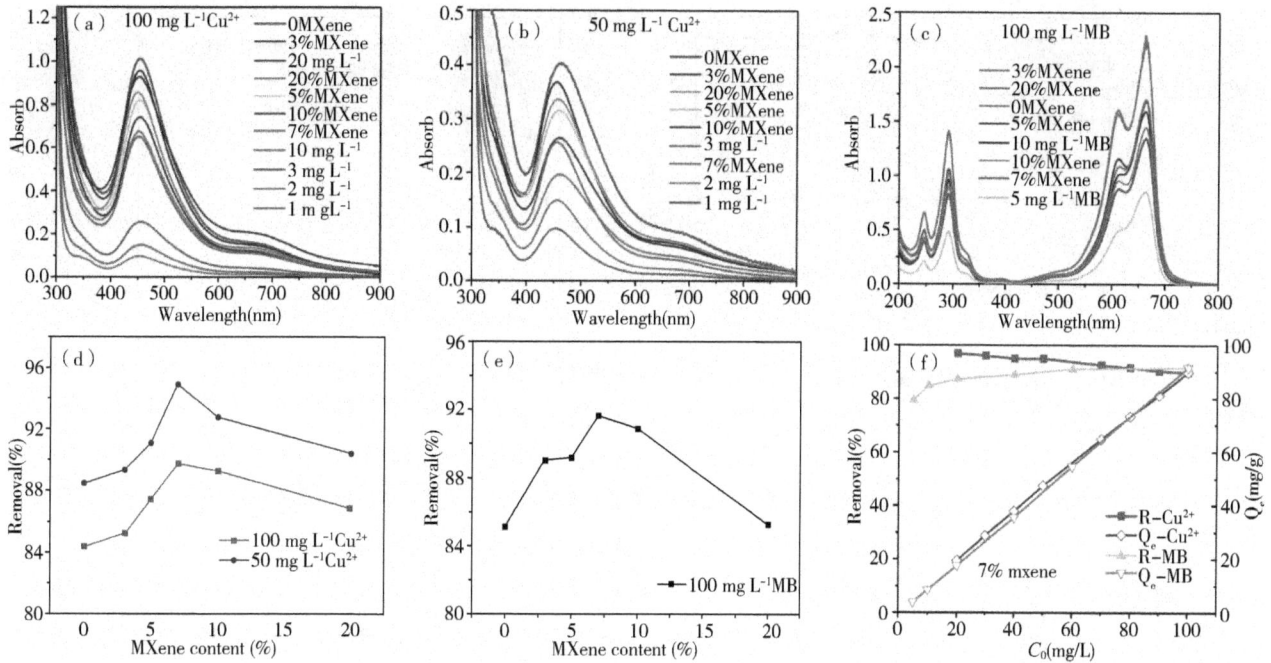

Fig. 3　Different concentrations of Cu^{2+} adsorption curves (1–20mg/L) and concentrations of Cu^{2+} adsorption curves after adsorption of Cu^{2+} solution (100mg/L) by different ratios of DL-Ti$_3$C$_2$T$_x$/CA composite fibers (100mg) after adsorption of 200mL Cu^{2+} solution (100mg/L) (a) and Cu^{2+} solution (50mg/L) (b); And the MB adsorption curves (c); The removal of different ratios of DL-Ti$_3$C$_2$T$_x$/CA composite fibers to (d) Cu^{2+} solution and to (e) MB solution; (f) Removal rate and adsorption amount at different initial concentrations

3. 2　Adsorption time and isothermal adsorption model

As shown in Fig. 4(a), (b), adsorption equilibrium has been reached when Cu^{2+} (50mg/L) is adsorbed for 5 mins, and adsorption equilibrium is reached when MB (100mg/L) is adsorbed for 20min. DL-Ti$_3$C$_2$T$_x$ is a nano-material with the characteristics of hydrophilicity, large specific surface area and high density of surface functional groups (O, OH, and F). Its surface adsorption site can rapidly contact with MB molecules and Cu^{2+} ions. And generate adsorption. After DL-Ti$_3$C$_2$T$_x$ is compounded with CA, a rough cracked surface is formed. This facilitates the rapid diffusion of MB and Cu^{2+} into the fibers through cracks, thereby increasing the adsorption rate of DL-Ti$_3$C$_2$T$_x$/CA composite fibers. The initial high removal rate may be attributed to the large number of vacancy binding sites available on DL-Ti$_3$C$_2$T$_x$ to adsorb molecules and ions. When the surface of DL-Ti$_3$C$_2$T$_x$ is saturated, the adsorption rate of mole Cu^{2+} les and ions begins to decline, eventually reaching an apparent equilibrium. Adsorption of MB and Cu^{2+} takes place in more than one adsorption mode, defining three and two linear portions, respectively. The initial linear portion may be due to external surface adsorption and noticed higher absorption. The middle linear portion refers to a gradual adsorption due to diffusion within the particles. Thereafter, as the adsorption approaches equilibrium, the final linear portion corresponds to a very stable and relatively slow absorption. It can be seen that the influence of time on the adsorption capacity and the adsorption rate is very small. That is, the DL-Ti$_3$C$_2$T$_x$/CA composite fiber reaches the adsorption equilibrium within a very short period of time when immersed in the solution, and desorption does not increase significantly with time. This shows that there is a strong interaction between the adsorption site and adsorption, which is not easy to desorb.

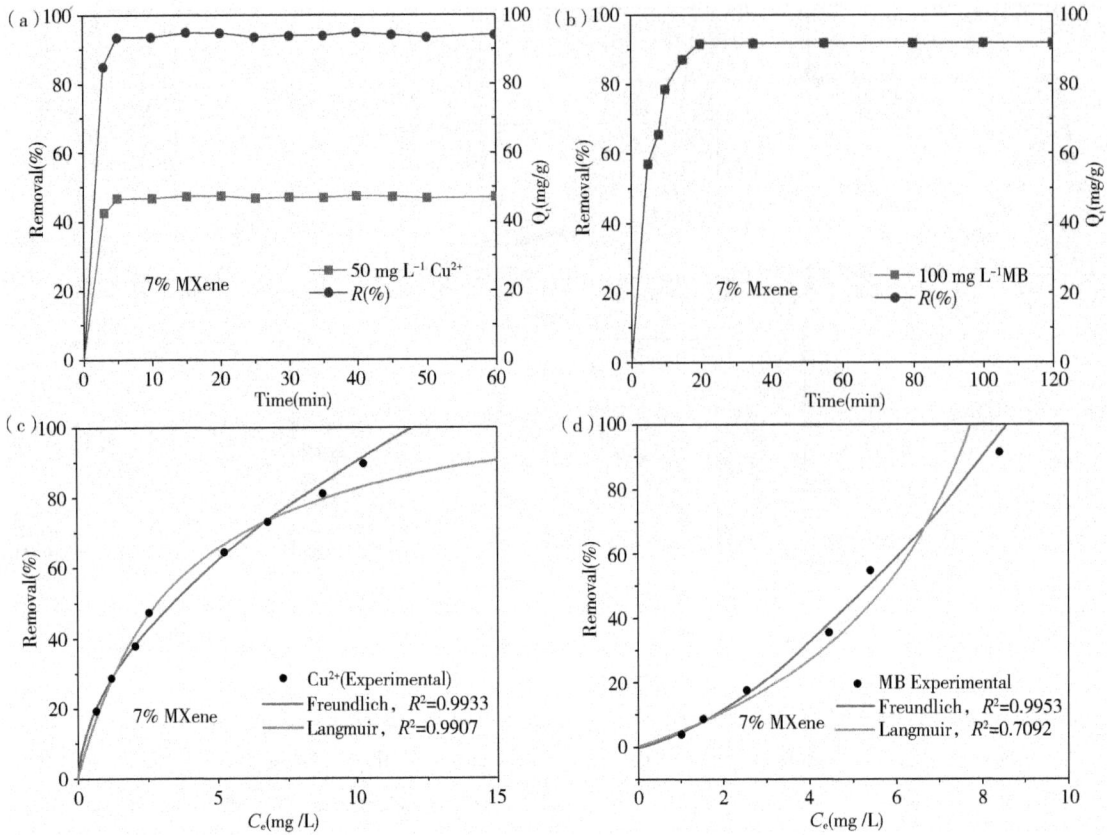

Fig. 4　At 7% DL-Ti$_3$C$_2$T$_x$/CA composite fibers, the relationship between adsorption capacity and removal of time, Cu^{2+} (a) and MB (b); Adsorption isotherms of Cu^{2+} (c) and MB (d)

Langmuir model theory is based on monolayer adsorption. The model assumes that the surface of the adsorbent is uniform and that only one molecule is adsorbed at one adsorption site on the adsorbent surface, and there is no interaction between the adsorbed molecules. The adsorption energy of the adsorbent surface is the same everywhere. When the absorption reaches the saturation state on the surface of the adsorbent, the adsorption amount of the adsorbent reaches a maximum value. When the saturated state reaches the saturated state, there is no transfer movement to the dynamic equilibrium between the adsorption sites on the surface of the adsorbent, and the adsorption and desorption rates of the adsorbent on the adsorbent surface are the same. The relationship between the equilibrium adsorption capacity and the solution equilibrium concentration in the Langmuir equation (4):

$$Q_e = \frac{Q_{max}KC_e}{1 + KC_e} \qquad (4)$$

Where C_e(mg/L) is the equilibrium concentration, Q_e (mg/g) is the equilibrium adsorption capability; Q_{max} (mg/g) is the adsorption capability. K(L/mg) characterizes the constant of affinity with the binding site, and Q_{max}(mg/g) denotes the maximum adsorption capacity of monolayer on the surface of the unit adsorbent when the adsorption reaches saturation. Unlike the Langmuir model, the Freundlich model is not limited to monolayer adsorption. The model can be used to absorb the adsorbent on the surface of the adsorbent. In addition, this model is also suitable for adsorptive adsorption of high concentrations of adsorption, but for low concentrations of adsorption does not meet the actual adsorption phenomenon. Freundlich equation is as follow (5):

$$Q_e = K_F C_e^{1/n} \qquad (5)$$

Freundlich empirical formula, constants K_F and n, can be used to reflect the properties of the adsorbent and adsorbed material. The basic rule is that K_F and n values are large, indicating that the adsorption capacity is strong over the entire concentration range studied. Low values of K_F and n have poor adsorption capacity at low concentrations and strong adsorption at high concentrations. It is generally believed that the K_F value is large and the adsorption capacity is strong. When $1/n = 0.1$–0.5, it is easy to adsorb, and $1/n > 2$ is difficult to adsorb.

Tab. 1

Adsorption isotherm	Langmuir			Freundlich		
Parameter	$Q_{max}(\text{mg} \cdot \text{g}^{-1})$	$K(\text{L} \cdot \text{mg}^{-1})$	R^2	$K_F(\text{mg} \cdot \text{g}^{-1})$	$1/n$	R^2
Cu^{2+}	0.2884	111.1111	0.9907	25.9537	0.5424	0.9933
MB	-52.9101	-0.0845	0.7092	4.1908	1.4760	0.9953

The simulation results of the adsorption of Cu^{2+} and MB by composite fibers and their correlation coefficients are shown in Tab. 1. In Fig. 4c, the adsorption of Cu^{2+} on DL-$Ti_3C_2T_x$/ CA composite fibers, the adsorption of Cu^{2+} on DL-$Ti_3C_2T_x$/ CA composite fibers, and the R^2 values of the Langmuir and Freundlich models are all greater than 0.99, which is consistent with Langmuir adsorption isotherms. Freundlich adsorption isotherm, there is uniform adsorption and non-uniform adsorption. The Freundlich model corresponds to the empirical relationship of non-uniform surface adsorption and is not limited by the number of surface adsorption layers. The adsorption experiment of MB on DL-$Ti_3C_2T_x$/ CA composite fiber is shown in Fig. 4 (d), the corresponding isotherm curve closely reproduced the experimental data, with an R^2 value of 0.9953, which is higher than that of the Langmuir ($R^2 = 0.7092$). Compared with Langmuir, the Freundlich isotherm has a higher correlation coefficient, indicating that the adsorption of methylene blue by alginate fibers does not conform to the Langmuir isotherm model. It can be seen from the table that the fitting degree with the Freundlich model is better; indicating that the process of the adsorption of methylene blue dye by the alginate fibers conforms to the Freundlich model. The methylene blue dye and the cationic blue dye have a positive charge in the aqueous solution and are easily adsorbed by the negatively charged alginate fibers due to the attraction of the heterogeneous charges to each other, and the adsorption amount and the removal rate of the methylene blue dye and the cationic blue dye at different concentrations are comparable high. In accordance with the Freundlich model, which does not conform to the Langmuir model, the adsorption of methylene blue dye and cationic blue dye by the alginate fiber is not a single molecule adsorption, and the adsorption point on the fiber surface is not uniform.

3.3 Adsorption mechanism

The possible explanation for the mechanism of Cu^{2+} adsorption on the surface of DL-$Ti_3C_2T_x$ nanosheets may involve the contribution of surface functional groups. The surface of DL-$Ti_3C_2T_x$ nanosheets contains terminal groups, such as O, OH and F, which can serve as the available sites for trapping cationic metal ions[21]. The adsorption of Cu^{2+} may also be affected by the hydrophilicity of DL-$Ti_3C_2T_x$ and its negative surface function influences. GO is another member of the two-dimensional material family and has the same nanosheets structure as DL-$Ti_3C_2T_x$ · Cu^{2+} adsorption on 2D GO nanosheets is explained by a layer mechanism in which Cu^{2+} undergoes an ion exchange reaction with carboxylic acid (—COOH) and hydroxyl (—OH) surface functional groups[22]. Similarly, Cu^{2+} adsorption on DL-$Ti_3C_2T_x$ can pass the ion exchange reaction between positively charged Cu^{2+} ions and negatively charged terminal groups (—O and —OH) on the surface of $Ti_3C_2T_x$ · Ti—O and Ti—OH have a strong adsorption capacity for metal ions. Spinning solution solidification takes place in $CaCl_2$ solution. Na^+ ions in the sodium alginate molecule exchange with Ca^{2+} ions in the solution to form an eggshell structure of calcium alginate. At the same time, Na^+ is an alkali metal, and it is known that the presence of F content together with the presence of alkali metal ions confirms that the alkalization process is beneficial for the conversion of the —F group to the —OH group[23].

This functional group transformation can be written as the following chemical equation (7):

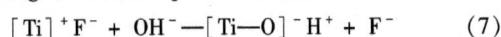

$$[Ti]^+F^- + OH^- —[Ti—O]^-H^+ + F^- \quad (7)$$

Cations can be adsorbed on the surface and between layers of DL-$Ti_3C_2T_x$ to reduce energy[24].

This ion exchange process, which can be expressed as the following equation (8):

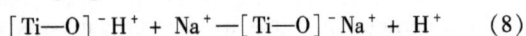

$$[Ti—O]^-H^+ + Na^+ —[Ti—O]^-Na^+ + H^+ \quad (8)$$

It has been shown that —OH groups easily adsorb small molecules or ions in aqueous solutions, whereas —F may worsen this process[25-26]. It is reasonable to have more —OH groups on the surface of DL-$Ti_3C_2T_x$ so that the DL-$Ti_3C_2T_x$/ CA composite fiber has better adsorption performance. Since the terminal group of —OH (or —ONa) on the surface of DL-$Ti_3C_2T_x$ tends to adsorb cationic contaminants, the DL-$Ti_3C_2T_x$/ CA composite fiber has a higher removal rate than pure alginate fiber. The expression is as follows:

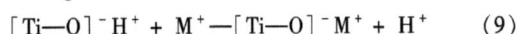

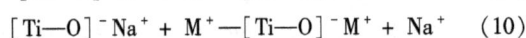

$$[Ti—O]^-H^+ + M^+ —[Ti—O]^-M^+ + H^+ \quad (9)$$

$$[Ti—O]^-Na^+ + M^+ —[Ti—O]^-M^+ + Na^+ \quad (10)$$

M^+ represents the cationic contaminants MB^+ and Cu^{2+}.

4　Conclusions

DL-$Ti_3C_2T_x$/CA composite fibers were successfully prepared by wet spinning. The surface morphology of the fiber was observed by SEM, and it was proved that the addition of DL-$Ti_3C_2T_x$ changed the fiber morphology. The adsorption properties of cationic dyes (MB) and Cu^{2+} were studied. The results of adsorption experiments show that DL-$Ti_3C_2T_x$/CA composite fibers can effectively remove methylene blue from aqueous solution, and the introduction of DL-$Ti_3C_2T_x$ is effectively enhanced compared to pure alginate fibers. Isothermal adsorption studies show that the difference between the fit of the Freundlich model and the Langmuir model reflects the difference in adsorption mechanism when adsorbing different contaminants. The adsorption of Cu^{2+} on DL-$Ti_3C_2T_x$/CA composite fibers was higher than 0. 99 for both Langmuir and Freundlich models. The Langmuir adsorption isotherm and the Freundlich adsorption isotherm also existed. The adsorption was uniform and heterogeneous. The adsorption of MB on DL-$Ti_3C_2T_x$/CA composite fiber does not conform to the Langmuir model, but it is in accordance with the Freundlich model. The process of adsorbing methylene blue dye is not a single molecular layer adsorption, and the adsorption point on the fiber surface is not uniform. Electrostatic attraction negatively charged DL-$Ti_3C_2T_x$/CA composite fibers and positively charged MB and Cu^{2+} particles. Due to the strong mutual attraction of positive and negative charges, the MB molecules and Cu^{2+} rapidly adsorb to the surface of the alginate fibers. Then through the particle diffusion, it gradually diffuses into the interior of the fiber, and the ion exchange process occurs in contact with DL-$Ti_3C_2T_x$, thereby enhancing the adsorption capacity. These findings may lead to the development of a promising candidate for wastewater treatment.

References

[1] Buntiä‡ A V, Pavloviä‡ M D, Å iler-Marinkoviä‡ S S, et al. Biological treatment of colored wastewater by streptomyces fulvissimus CKS 7[J]. Water Science & Technology, 2016, 73(9): 2231-2236.

[2] Suba V, Rathika G. Novel adsorbents for the removal of dyes and metals from aqueous solution—A review[J]. Journal of Advanced Physics, 2016, 5(4): 277-294.

[3] Mounir B, Pons M N, Zahraa O, et al. Discoloration of a red cationic dye by supported TiO_2, photocatalysis [J]. Journal of Hazardous Materials, 2007, 148(3): 513-520.

[4] Fane A G, Wang R, Hu M X. Synthetic membranes for water purification: status and future[J]. Angewandte Chemie International Edition, 2015, 54(11): 3368-3386.

[5] Mohammadi T, Razmi A, Sadrzadeh M. Effect of operating parameters on Pb^{2+}, separation from wastewater using electrodialysis[J]. Desalination, 2004, 167(1): 379-385.

[6] Fu F, Wang Q. Removal of heavy metal ions from wastewaters: A review[J]. Journal of Environmental Man-

agement, 2011, 92(3): 407-418.

[7] Zhang Q, Li Y, Phanlavong P, et al. Highly efficient and rapid fluoride scavenger using an acid/base tolerant zirconium phosphate nanoflake: Behavior and mechanism [J]. Journal of Cleaner Production, 2017, 161: 317-326.

[8] Come J, Naguib M, Rozier P, et al. A non-aqueous asymmetric cell with a Ti_2C-based two-dimensional negative electrode[J]. Journal of the Electrochemical Society, 2012, 159 (8): A1368-A1373.

[9] Lei J C, Zhang X, Zhou Z. Recent advances in MXene: Preparation, properties, and applications [J]. Frontiers of Physics in China, 2015, 10(3): 276-286.

[10] Wang H W, Naguib M, Page K, et al. Resolving the structure of $Ti_3C_2T_x$ MXenes through multilevel structural modeling of the atomic pair distribution function[J]. Chemistry of Materials, 2016, 28(1).

[11] Naguib M, Gogotsi Y. Synthesis of two-dimensional materials by selective extraction[J]. Accounts of Chemical Research, 2015, 48(1): 128-135.

[12] Ling Z, Ren C E, Zhao M Q, et al. Flexible and conductive MXene films and nanocomposites with high capacitance [J]. Proceedings of the National Academy of Science, 2014, 111(47): 16676-16681.

[13] Dall'Agnese Y, Lukatskaya M R, Cook K M, et al. High capacitance of surface-modified 2D titanium carbide in acidic electrolyte[J]. Electrochemistry Communications, 2014, 48 (48): 118-122.

[14] Yang E, Ji H, Kim J, et al. Exploring the possibilities of two-dimensional transition metal carbides as anode materials for sodium batteries[J]. Physical Chemistry Chemical Physics, 2015, 17(7): 5000-5005.

[15] Ghidiu M, Halim J, Kota S, et al. Ion-exchange and cation solvation reactions in Ti_3C_2 MXene[J]. Chemistry of Materials, 2016, 28 (10): 3507-3514.

[16] Mashtalir O, Cook K M, Mochalin V N, et al. Dye adsorption and decomposition on two-dimensional titanium carbide in aqueous media [J]. Journal of Materials Chemistry A, 2014, 2(35): 14334-14338.

[17] Peng Q, Guo J, Zhang Q, et al. Unique lead adsorption behavior of activated hydroxyl group in two-dimensional titanium carbide[J]. Journal of the American Chemical Society, 2014, 136(11): 4113-4116.

[18] Guo J, Peng Q, Fu H, et al. Heavy-metal adsorption behavior of two-dimensional alkalization-intercalated MXene by first-principles calculations[J]. Journal of Physical Chemistry C, 2015, 119(36): 20923-20930.

[19] Zhang C J, Anasori B, Seralascaso A, et al. Transparent, flexible, and conductive 2D titanium carbide (MXene) films with high volumetric capacitance[J]. Advanced Materials, 2017, 29(36).

[20] Alhabeb M, Maleski K, Anasori B, et al. Guidelines for synthesis and processing of two-dimensional titanium carbide ($Ti_3C_2T_x$ MXene) [J]. Chem. Mater, 2017, 29: 7633-7644.

[21] Halim J, Cook K M, Naguib M, et al. X-ray photoelectron spectroscopy of select multi-layered transition metal carbides (MXenes)[J]. Appl. Surf. Sci, 2016, 362: 406-417.

[22] Yusuf M, Elfghi F M, Zaidi S A, et al. Cheminform abstract: Applications of graphene and its derivatives as an adsorbent for heavy metal and dye removal: A systematic and comprehensive overview[J]. Cheminform, 2015, 46(31): 50392-50420.

[23] Peng Q, Guo J, Zhang Q, et al. Unique lead adsorption behavior of activated hydroxyl group in two-dimensional titanium carbide[J]. Journal of the American Chemical Society, 2014, 136(11): 4113-4116.

[24] Luo J, Tao X, Zhang J, et al. Sn^{4+} ions decorated highly conductive Ti_3C_2 MXene: Promising lithium-ion anodes with enhanced volumetric capacity and cyclic performance [J]. Acs Nano, 2016, 10(2): 2491.

[25] Li Z, Wang L, Sun D, et al. Synthesis and thermal stability of two-dimensional carbide MXene Ti_3C_2 [J]. Materials Science & Engineering B, 2015, 191: 33-40.

[26] Guo X, Zhang X, Zhao S, et al. High adsorption capacity of heavy metals on two-dimensional MXenes: an ab initio study with molecular dynamics simulation [J]. Physical Chemistry Chemical Physics, 2015, 18(1): 228.

Bending Properties of Zigzag Shaped 3D Woven Spacer Composites: Experiment and FEM Simulation

Xue fei Zhang[1], Li hua Lyu[1]*, Li ming Zhu[1], Jing jing Wang[1], Xiao qing Xiong[1]*

[1] *Department of Textile Engineering, Dalian Polytechnic University, Dalian, China*

* *Corresponding author's email*: lvlh@ dlpu. edu. cn; xiongxq@ dlpu. edu. cn

Abstract: In order to solve the problems of poor impact resistance, low interlaminar strength, easy peeling or cracking, and poor integrity of conventional laminated spacer composites, the zigzag shaped 3D woven spacer fabrics with the basalt fiber filaments tows 400tex used as warp and weft yarns were fabricated on common loom by reasonable design with low cost processing. And the zigzag shaped 3D woven spacer composites were obtained by VARTM (vacuum assisted resin transfer molding) process. Then, the bending properties of zigzag shaped 3D woven spacer composites with different directions, different numbers of weaving cycle and different heights were tested throughout the universal testing machine with the velocity of 10mm/min. And, the load-displacement curves and bending failure modes were obtained. The results showed that the weft direction sample was better than the wrap direction one to be the researched material. Moreover, the bending perform of materials were related to the zigzag structure's numbers which were the more support parts under the bending stress, the bending performance was more excellent and an increase in spacer heights of 3D woven spacer composites slightly increased the bending properties. Finally, the ABAQUS software was employed to yield the bending load-displacement curves and failure modes for foreseeing the bending properties of 3D woven spacer composites. The good agreements of comparisons proved the validity of the FEM models.

Keywords: 3D woven spacer composites; Bending properties; FEM simulation; Basalt fiber; VARTM process

1　Introduction

At present market, the general spacer composites could be fabricated via this way that the preprocessing planar materials were adhered, then it was pressed and finalized the structure. Specifically, a space frame was formed by the layered and stacked two-dimensional planar materials, then the relevant junctions of the material's interlamination were cohered by some special adhesive, finally, the common spacer composite could be gained by the process of finalization[1]. Above operated process was simple and available, but there will be a great numbers of uncontrollable structure flaws which was contribute to lower integrity of composite. The junctions of adhered layers will be cracked and damaged simply, when it is in the hot and humid environment or the interaction of the external forces repeatedly[2-3]. The junctions would become a fatal shortcoming.

The features of higher fracture toughness and inter-layer shear strength of 3D textile composites lead to the wide application of the composites in mechanical areas[4-5]. The 3D woven spacer composites have been recognized as more competitive than other 3D textile structural composites because of its light weight, simple microstructure, highest stiffness and strength, low fabrication cost and high manufacturing efficiency. The 3D woven spacer composites have been extended to aerospace, vehicle, and civil engineering, etc. Mountasir et al. [6-7] researched the woven process of the 3D spacer textile, and introduced the technological process and relative work theory of common and special loom. Gu et al. [8] studied the weaving principles and conditions of 3D spacer woven fabrics, and recommended the 3D integral structure of the junction type of round, rectangle and honeycomb in detail. Zigzag shaped and X-shaped 3D spacer woven fabrics were regarded as examples to state the weaving principles and conditions on common loom. But they only researched the woven process of 3D spacer fabric, and didn't explore the properties of 3D woven spacer composite. Liu et al. [9-11] explored the mechanical properties of the 8-shapeed 3D woven composites with glass fiber, such as bending property, tensile property, low velocity impact characteristics, and the deformation and failure mechanism. The author[12-14] researched the mechanical properties and employed the rational FEM simulated models to predict the tensile and bending properties of the 3D woven basalt fiber composite, these works laid a certain foundation for this paper. In this article, the zigzag shaped 3D woven spacer fabrics with the basalt fiber filaments tows 400 tex as warp and weft yarns were fabricated on common loom by reasonable design with low cost processing. And the zigzag shaped 3D woven spacer composites were obtained by VARTM process. Then, the bending properties of zigzag shaped 3D woven spacer composites with different heights, different directions, and different numbers of weaving cycle were tested throughout the universal testing machine with the velocity of 10mm/min. Finally, the ABAQUS software was employed to yield the bending load-displacement curves and failure modes for foreseeing the bending properties of 3D woven spacer composites.

2 Experiments

2.1 Design and weaving of zigzag shaped 3D woven spacer fabrics

The zigzag shaped 3D woven spacer composite shown in Fig. 1, was the target subject. The warp section diagram of the zigzag shaped 3D woven spacer fabric was shown in Fig. 2 (The small circle indicated the weft yarn, and the line indicated the warp yarn).
The 400tex basalt fiber filaments tows (Zhejiang stone basalt fiber Limited by Share Co., Ltd.) were employed as warp and weft yarns. Loom (SGA 598 from Jiangyin Tong Yuan spinning machine Co., Ltd.) for weaving was used. The zigzag shaped 3D woven spacer fabric was composed of two surfaces and a connect layer

which linked top and bottom surfaces as well as made a steady structure and they were constructed by plain woven fabric, respectively.

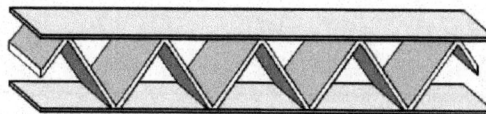

Fig. 1　Diagrammatic drawing of zigzag shaped 3D woven spacer composite

Fig. 2　Warp section diagram of the zigzag shaped 3D woven spacer fabric

The parameters of the zigzag shaped 3D woven spacer fabrics with three different heights were shown in Tab. 1. The pictures of the zigzag shaped 3D woven spacer fabrics were shown in Fig. 3.

Fig. 3　Pictures of the zigzag shaped 3D woven spacer fabric

2.2 Fabrication of zigzag shaped 3D woven spacer composites

Vinyl ester resin was used as matrix. Methyl ethyl ketone peroxide was used as solidification reagent, and cobalt was used as promoter. VARTM molding system was used for molding. The resin, relative solidification reagent and promoter were provided by Wuxi Qian Guang chemical raw material Co., Ltd.

Tab. 1　3D fabric three different heights

Cross-sectional shapes	Space-height (cm)	Warp density (yarn/10cm)	Weft density (yarn/10cm)	Reed counts (reed dent/10cm)	Yarn counts (reed)	Total number of warp yarns
	1					
Zigzag	1.7	60	1181	30	6	360
	2.4					

2. 3　Testing of zigzag shaped 3D woven spacer composites

The testing of bending properties was according to GB/T 1456—2005 and universal system prototype (NHY-W) was utilized for cutting samples which were obtained from composite materials in warp and weft direction. Then, microcomputer control electronic universal testing machine was applied for three-point bending test and the bending test schematic was shown in Fig. 4. The test speed was 10mm/min, spacing was 100mm, and sample length was 140mm.

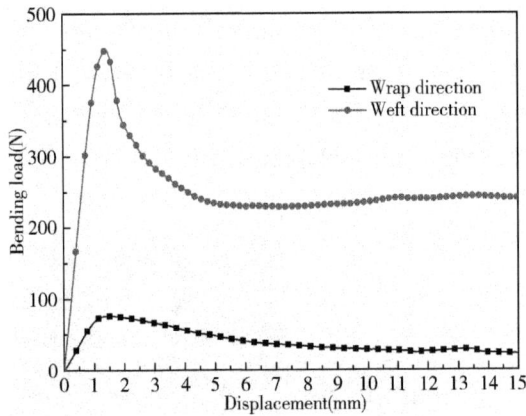

Fig. 4　Bending test schematic

3　Results and Discussion

Bending load-displacement curves of zigzag shaped 3D woven spacer composites with different directions. The bending load-displacement curves of zigzag shaped 3D woven spacer composites with warp and weft directions were shown in Fig. 5. It was obvious that the top point of the warp and weft direction were different in above curves. The different max load value showed that the structures of the warp and weft direction samples had different damaged performance in the same testing condition.

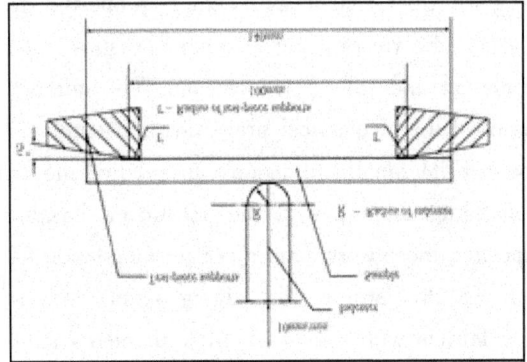

Fig. 5　Bending load-displacement curves of zigzag shaped 3D woven spacer composites with different directions

The wrap direction sample was consisted of continued zigzag structures with limited wide and thin walls and it was shown in Fig. 6. When this sample was going to test on the device, it was observed that when the indenter of the universal testing machine touched the sample surface, as the surface was very thin, so the zigzag structure couldn't support the surface against the load. With the growing load, the warp direction sample as a whole became bent, and then occurred destruction quickly. The typical bending failure modes were the compression failure in touched surface and the tensile failure in untouched surface.

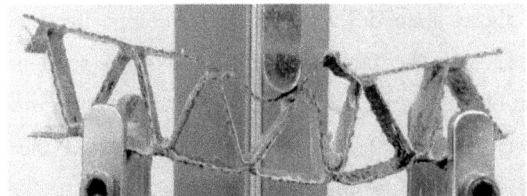

Fig. 6　Warp direction sample on testing

The weft direction sample was shown in Fig. 7. But it was different from the warp sample, it had only a zigzag structure through the whole material and there were junctions to connect bottom or surface and middle layer. So, the three layers became a integrity. In bending testing, the surface of weft direction sample didn't fail quickly. when the loads worked on the sample, the whole sample was bended gradually, until the zigzag structure began to be broken. During this process, it could be found that zigzag structure of 3D woven spacer composites shouldered the main bending stress. So the zigzag structure could enhance the capability against the stress obviously from comparing the warp and weft load-displacement curves. From the comparing analysis of bending load- displacement curves with warp and weft directions in Fig. 5, the bending performance of the weft direction material was relevant to the connect layer's structure closely, so the weft direction material was applied as the sample of the subsequent experiment.

Fig. 7　Weft direction sample on testing

3. 1　Bending load-displacement curves of zigzag shaped 3D woven spacer composites with different numbers of weaving cycle

There was a roughly similar tendency on the curves of single and double weaving cycles in Fig. 8, which indicated that the zigzag shaped 3D woven spacer composites had the same failure mold. Of course, the zigzag shaped 3D woven spacer composite with double weaving cycles had more support parts and could be distributed more small loads on per wall, so it had bigger bending load than the single one. It also hold that the bending load was interrelated to the numbers of weaving cycle, so the number of weaving cycle was more, the bending load was bigger and the bending performance was more excellent.

3. 2　Bending load-displacement curves of zigzag shaped 3D woven spacer composites with different heights

The bending load-displacement curves of zigzag shaped

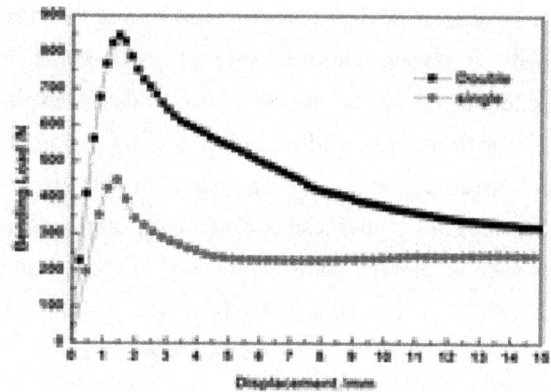

Fig. 8　Bending load-displacement curves of zigzag shaped 3D woven spacer composites with different numbers of weaving cycle

3D woven spacer composites with three different heights were shown in the Fig. 9. The three curves had similar tends, that's to say their failure models were same. The 2.4cm sample had the biggest bending load value among the three spacer heights of samples, which exhibited its bending property was best. The bending load value of sample with 1.7cm was second, and the 1cm sample's bending load value was lowest. Thus, the higher zigzag structure had the bigger bending load.

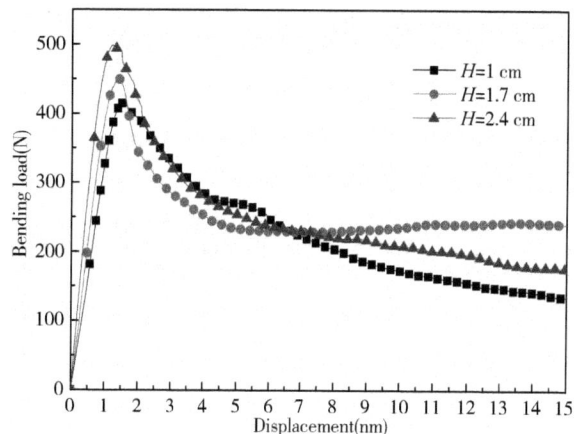

Fig. 9　Bending load-displacement curves of zigzag shaped 3D woven spacer composites with different heights

3. 3　Bending properties of zigzag shaped 3D woven spacer composites: Experiment and FEM simulation

To exhibit the failure mode and mechanism of the zigzag shaped 3D woven spacer composites exactly, the ABAQUS software was adopted to simulate the three-point bending test. The geometrical models of the zigzag shaped 3D woven spacer composites were established according to the actual specimen in Standard/ Explicit module with dynamic and explicit way. The geometrical model of sample with 1cm was shown in Fig. 10. For approaching the actual testing conditions, more touched parts were employed, shown in the Fig. 11. The material properties of the zigzag shaped 3D woven composites were shown in Tab. 2. The C3D8R solid element was utilized for the geometrical model, so total number of elements of mesh model with 1cm was 5600, mesh model with 1.7cm was 11200 and mesh model with 2.4cm was 15680.

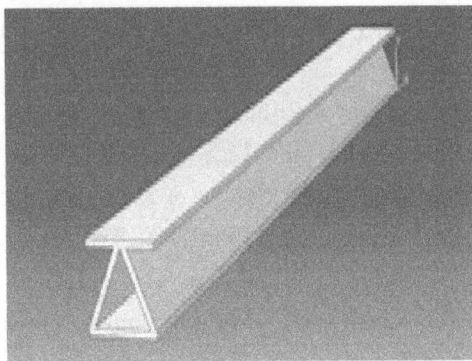

Fig. 10　Geometrical model of the zigzag shaped 3D woven spacer composite

The bending load-displacement curves of the zigzag shaped 3D woven spacer composites: Experiment and

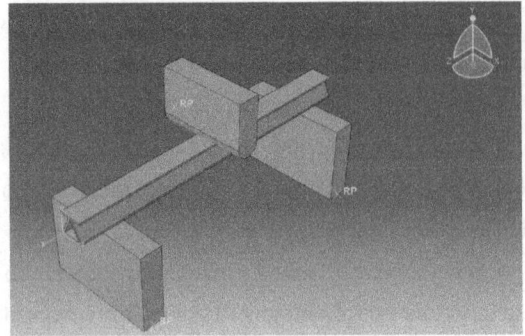

Fig. 11　Assembly model of the zigzag shaped 3D woven spacer composite

FEM simulation was shown in Fig. 12. It was obvious that the simulated curves had the similar tendency to the experimental results, which indicated that the good agreement of the comparisons proved the validity of the FEM models. Of course, two kinds of curves had many differences, especially in some certain location, such as yield point, destruction point and the like. These differences existed which was attributed to the self-defect of the zigzag shaped 3D woven spacer composites. In the fabricated process of 3D woven spacer composites, because the misoperation and limit of environment condition caused the difference of curves, and the simulated models were the ideal condition, simulated results was higher. To sum up, the simulated curves could approach and forecast the experimental results, but they never be same.

Tab. 2　Material properties of the three kinds 3D woven spacer composite bending load-displacement curves

Spacer heights	E11 (Gpa)	E22 (GPa)	E33 (GPa)	$\nu 12$	$\nu 23$	$\nu 13$	G12 (GPa)	G13 (GPa)	G23 (GPa)
$H = 1$cm	32	9.79	9.79	0.21	0.21	0.3	9.56	9.56	21
$H = 1.7$cm	149.9	44.5	44.5	0.22	0.22	0.3	43.45	43.45	95.6
$H = 2.4$cm	158.9	47.1	47.1	0.25	0.25	0.3	46.06	46.06	101.34

3.4　Failure mode and mechanism

The bending FEM simulation equivalent stress nephograms were shown in Fig. 13. As the bending load increased gradually, the model became bent. From Fig. 13(a), it was evident that the top and bottom surface of model generated some changes. On the top surface, from Fig. 13(b), the major bending stress cen-

tred around the touched areas of the indenter of universal testing machine and the sample, and the bending stress extended along the top surface unevenly, and the max bending stress occurred in the top surface's centre that was the junction of walls of the zigzag structure, which indicated that the zigzag structure could bear the main bending stress, and the stress extended along the

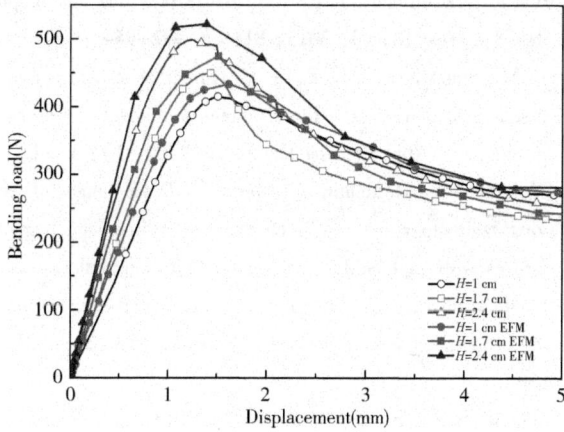

Fig. 12 Bending load-displacement curves of the zigzag shaped 3D woven spacer composites: Experiment and FEM simulation

direction of junction. From Fig. 13(c), it observed that the distribution of bending stress of bottom surface differed from the top surface. Its characteristics were that the distribution of stresses narrowed gradually from edge to center, which amounted to a hourglass. Because the bending stress of top surface spread to the bottom surface by the walls, then the stress spread to other place, so that the distribution of bending stress of edges will be wider than the centre. Fig. 14 was the compared results of the bending FEM simulation equiva-lent stress nephograms and experimental samples of 3D woven spacer composite. It was clear that the bending FEM simulation equivalent stress nephograms were similar to the experimental results of 3D woven spacer composite, which revealed that the simulated process could display the experimental process in some extent. Specifically, the top surface bore the compression to make itself downward indentation and it was shown in the Fig. 14 (a). According to the compared pictures, their indentation differed and the indentation of simulated model were displayed on the overall, but the indentation of experimental sample was centered around the touched regions of the indenter of machine and the sample, what caused the difference was in that the model was set up as homogeneous material, while the experimental sample was heterogeneous material. Then, the connect layers were compressed and generated the outward convex shape, shown in the Fig. 14(b), the simulated model and the experimental sample had the same change. The bottom surface shouldered the tension, so the bottom surface had a slight bending, and the bending stress concentrated upon the middle of sample, shown in the Fig. 14(c), the simulated model and the experimental sample had a similar condition.

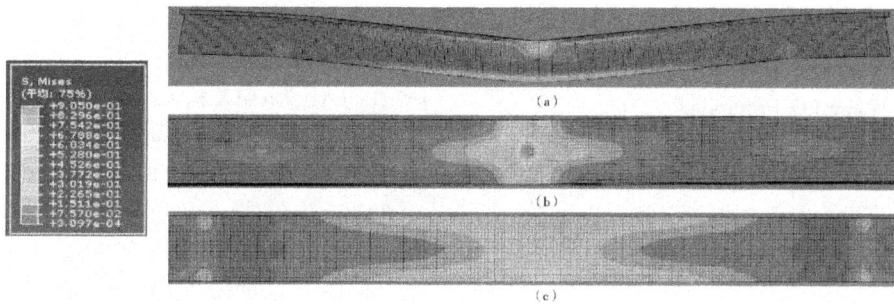

Fig. 13 Bending FEM simulation equivalent stress nephograms (a) Profile; (b) Top surface; (c) Bottom surface

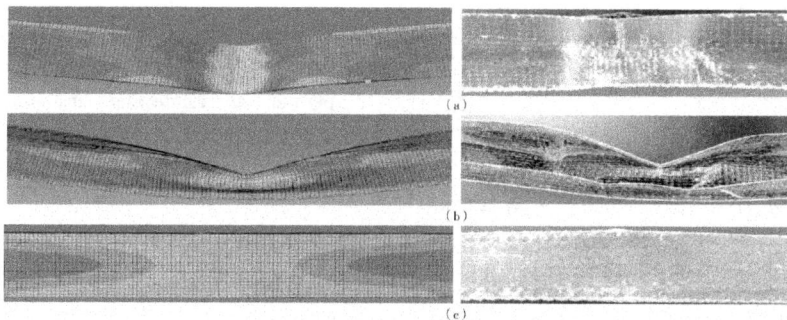

Fig. 14 Bending FEM simulation equivalent stress nephograms and experimental samples of 3D woven spacer composite (a) Top surface; (b) Profile; (c) Bottom surface

To sum up, the simulated model and the experimental sample had a similar failure model, which indicated that the good agreement of the comparisons proved the feasible of the FEM models.

4 Conclusions

The three-point bending performance of the zigzag shaped 3D woven spacer basalt fiber composites with different directions, different numbers of weaving cycle and different heights were studied. The results indicated that the weft materials were fit to be used as the bending test sample, because of its bending load formed by the zigzag structure, which bore the main load. Moreover, the more numbers of weaving cycle would make samples steady, and could enhance the bending properties of spacer composite effectively. In addition, in some extent, the higher zigzag sample had better bending properties. Finally, foreseeing the bending condition and the failure model of experimental sample was done via adopting the FEM simulated model, the similar results of comparisons proved the feasible of the FEM simulated model.

5 Acknowledgements

The authors gratefully acknowledge financial support from the major projects of Industrial Technology Research Institute in Liaoning Province.

References

[1] Cui J R. Mechanical property and finite element analysis of 3D honeycomb woven composites [M]. Master Thesis, Dalian Polytechnic University, China, 2015.

[2] Huang G. Structure and weaving process of 3Dimensional honeycomb fabric[J]. Dept text Eng,1998, 14(2): 15-18.

[3] Menta V G K, Vuppalapati R R, Chandrashekhara K, et al. Manufacturing and mechanical performance evaluation of resin-infused honeycomb composites[J]. J Rein Plas Comp, 2012, 31(6): 415-423.

[4] Chen X G, Taylor L W, Tsai L J. An overview on fabrication of three-dimensional woven textile preforms for composites[J]. Text Rese J, 2011, 81(9): 932-944

[5] Li M, Wang S, Zhang Z, et al. Effect of structure on the mechanical behaviors of three-dimensional spacer fabric composites[J]. Appl Compos Mater, 2009, 16(1): 1-14

[6] Mountasir A, Hoffmann G, Cherif C. Development of weaving technology for manufacturing three-dimensional spacer fabrics with high-performance yarns for thermoplastic composite applications: An analysis of two-dimensional mechanical properties[J]. Text Rese J, 2011, 81(13): 1354-1366.

[7] Badawi M S S S. Development of the weaving machine and 3D woven spacer fabric structures for lightweight composites materials[M]. VDM Verlag Dr. MŸller Aktiengesellschaft & Co. KG, 2008.

[8] Gu P. The weaving principle and upper machine condition of the spacer 3D woven fabric[J]. J Nantong Text Vocational Tech Colle 2007, 7(4): 1-3.

[9] Liu J, Jiang H. Bending property of glass-fiber composite reinforced by 8-shape 3D woven fabric pretreated with hypo-atmospheric-pressure plasma[J]. J Ind Text, 2011, 41(2): 174-182.

[10] Karahan M, Gül H, Ivens J, et al. Low velocity impact characteristics of 3D integrated core sandwich composites [J]. Text Rese J, 2012, 82(9): 945-962.

[11] Li D S, Zhao C Q, Jiang L, et al. Experimental study on the bending properties and failure mechanism of 3D integrated woven spacer composites at room and cryogenic temperature[J]. Compos Struct, 2014, 111(1): 56-65.

[12] Lv L H, Zhang X F, Liu G B, et al. Mechanical properties of 3D woven basalt fiber composite materials: Experiment and fem simulation[J]. J Fiber Sci Technol, 2016, 72: 33-39.

[13] Lv L, Zhang X, Yan S, et al. Bending properties of T-shaped 3D integrated woven composites: experiment and FEM simulation[J]. J Fiber Sci Technol, 2017, 73(7): 170-176.

[14] Lv L, Huang Y, Cui J, et al. Bending properties of three-dimensional honeycomb sandwich structure composites: experiment and Finite Element Method simulation[J]. Text Re J,2017.

Fast-Curing Halogen-Free Flame-Retardant Epoxy Resins and Their Application in Glass Fiber Reinforced Composites

Bo Yang[1,2], Yi Wei[2]*, Wangshuang Liu[2]*, Yiping Qiu[1]

[1] *College of Textiles, Donghua University, Shanghai 201620, China*

[2] *Center for Civil Aviation Composites, Donghua University, Shanghai 201620, China*

* *Corresponding author's email*：weiy@ dhu. edu. cn; wsliu@ dhu. edu. cn

Abstract：A series of novel fast-curing halogen-free flame-retardantepoxy resins were developed and applied in glass fiber reinforced composites. The results of dynamic mechanical analysis showed that optimized epoxy system could be completely cured in 1. 5h at 150℃ and had a glass transition temperature (T_g) of above 130℃. The optimized epoxy system was also used as matrix to make glass fiber prepregs and composite panels. The flame-retardant properties of the glass fiber reinforced composites were investigated, including limiting oxygen index (LOI), burning level, smoke density and toxic gas release. The glass fiber reinforced composite had excellent flame retardancy with UL−94 V−1 rating and high LOI of −36%. More significantly, the composite based on the flame-retardant epoxy resin showed lower smoke density compared with those based on the phenolic resins. Finally, the glass fiber prepregs were used to fabricated honeycomb sandwich composites. The peel strength of the epoxy-based composites was almost twice in comparison to the composites based on phenolic resin.

Keywords：Epoxy resins; Glass fiber reinforced composites; Halogen-free flame retardancy; Fast cure; Prepregs

1 Introduction

With the increasing popularity of the concept of lightweight, energy conservation and environmental protection, the trends of material selecting have changed from the metal materials to the lightweight high-strength composite materials in the rail transit and automotive industries. However, due to the cost and efficiency concerns, the additional functional requirements are also highly desired. Continuous fiber reinforced thermosetting resin composites, which possess flame retardant, lightweight, high strength and fast curing properties, have become an available choice for the load-carrying structure and interior decorating materials[1,3].

Flame retardancy is one of the most important requirements for interior decorating material in the commercial aircraft and rail transit fields. The premier requirements for the typical resins are flame retardant or noncombustible. The introduction of halogen-containing compounds are staple methods, together with aluminum hydroxide, melamine, antimony trioxide (Sb_2O_3) and other auxiliary flame retardants[2,6−7]. Although the effects of the halogen-containing flame retardants are very good, the halogen-containing materials in the combustion will produce a lot of thick toxic smoke, which can greatly reduce the chance of escape in the fire accidents. It has been verified that the smoke and gas in the combustion are the direct causes of death. Therefore, low smoke and toxicity are the important requirements for flame retardant materials. At present, the development trends of flame retardants are halogen-free, low smoke, low toxicity and multi-functions[4−5,8−12].

In this work, a series of novel fast-curing halogen-free flame-retardant epoxy resins were studied and applied in glass fiber reinforced composites. Thermo-mechanical properties, the flame-retardant properties and the peel strength of the epoxy-based composites were investigated in comparison to the composites based on phenolic resin.

2　Experiments

2.1　Materials

Diglycidyl ether of bisphenol A (DGEBA) with an epoxide equivalent of 182–192 was purchased from Sanmu Group, China. Dicyandiamide (DICY, cas: 461–58–5) with the purity of 99% obtained from Sinopharm Chemical Reagent Co., Ltd. was used as the curing agent. Modified imidazole (Hubei YCSC Technology Co., Ltd) and modified urea (Hubei YKY Chemical Co., Ltd) were used as accelerators in the epoxy system. Polyphosphamide (APP) was purchased from Shenzhen Jingcai Chemical Co., Ltd. PX–200 is a phosphate ester flame retardant and obtained from Shanghai Chempal Trade Co., Ltd. Nitrogen-and phos-

phorus-containing flame retardant DJ 701 was purchased from Shenzhen Ruihong Chemical Co., Ltd. Phosphorus flame retardant 6200 was purchased from Dongguan Doher Chemical Co., Ltd. Novel halogen-free and fast cure epoxy resins BAC 130EL and its prepreg BAC 430EL, the phenolic resin (PF) reinforced glass fabric composites BAC 400 are produced by Zhejiang Baihe Advanced Composites Co., Ltd.

2.2　Sample preparation

Dicyandiamide and urea were firstly dissolved in DMF solvent, and then flame retardant, epoxy resin and modified imidazole were added. The formulas are shown in Tab. 1.

Tab. 1　The formulas of different epoxy systems

Resin system	DICY(%)	Modified urea(%)	Modified imidazole(%)	APP(%)	PX-200(%)	DJ 701(%)	6200(%)
A1	5	5	0	30	0	0	0
A2	5	5	0.5	30	0	0	0
A3	5	5	2.5	30	0	0	0
B1	5	0	0.5	30	0	0	0
B2	5	0	1	30	0	0	0
B3	5	0	1.25	30	0	0	0
B4	5	0	2.5	30	0	0	0
C1	0	5	0.5	30	0	0	0
C2	0	5	1	30	0	0	0
C3	0	5	1.25	30	0	0	0
C4	0	5	2.5	30	0	0	0
D1	2.5	2.5	0.5	30	0	0	0
D2	2.5	2.5	1	30	0	0	0
D3	2.5	2.5	1.25	30	0	0	0
D4	2.5	2.5	2.5	30	0	0	0
D4-1	2.5	2.5	2.5	0	30	0	0
D4-2	2.5	2.5	2.5	0	0	30	0
D4-3	2.5	2.5	2.5	0	0	0	30

2.3　Measurements

The gel time of different epoxy systems was tested using wire click method. The glass transition temperature was measured by dynamic mechanical analysis (TA Q800) at a heating rate of 2℃/min. Combustion grade test in accordance with UL94 (IEC60695–11–20) standards for testing. Oxygen index test in accordance with GB/T

2406—2008 standard test. Flame diffusion level was tested in accordance with BS476–7 standard. Density and toxicity of gas detection was tested according to BS6853 standard. The peel strength of the sandwich-composites was tested followed the standard of GB/T 1457—2005.

3 Results and Discussion

3.1 Curing activity and thermo-mechanical properties

Gel time can reflect the required time to form sufficiently large molecular with the addition of the catalyst at a specific temperature. The gel time of the system A–D was summarized in Fig. 1. With the increase of the modified imidazole compound, the reaction rate of the resin system can be greatly accelerated. The minimum gel time of B4, C4 and D4 systems at 130℃ was about 6 minutes, which can meet the requirements on the curing rate.

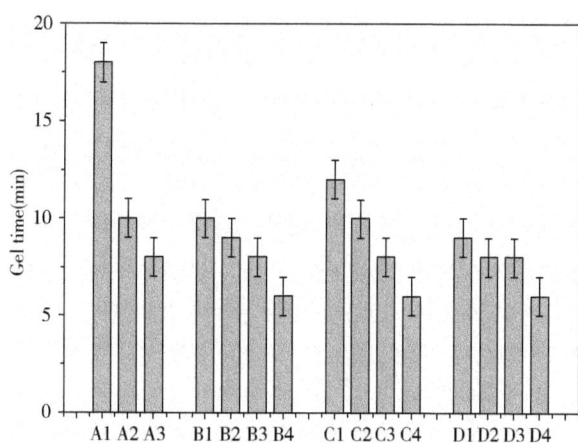

Fig. 1 Gel time of different resin systems

After cured for two hours at 130℃, the specimens of B4, C4 and D4 resin systems were used to conduct DMA test to get their storage modulus, loss modulus and tan delta, as shown in Fig. 2. From the peak of tan delta curve of Fig. 2, the glass transition temperature (T_g) values of the B4, C4 and D4 systems are 185℃, 155℃ and 179℃, respectively.

All these T_g values meet the requirements for the practical application. However, the content of dicyandiamide in the B4 system is high, and a large amount of high boiling point solvent DMF is required to dissolve it. Therefore, the D4 system has better performance with regard to fast curing epoxy resins.

The curing degree of D4 system at specific temperature with different curing time was studied by the analysis of loss modulus. After curing for 60 minutes at 130℃, the loss modulus showed double peaks, and the first peak is around 100℃. When further cured for another 30 mi-

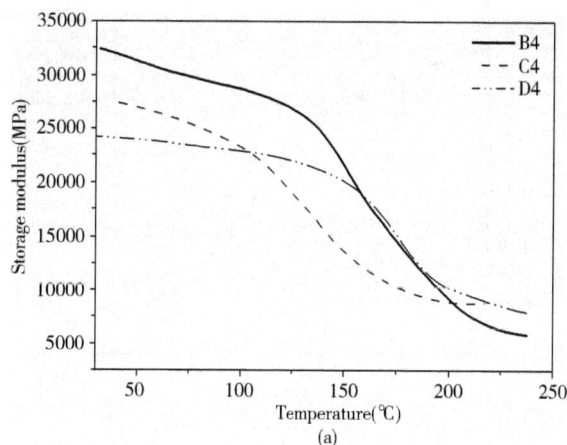

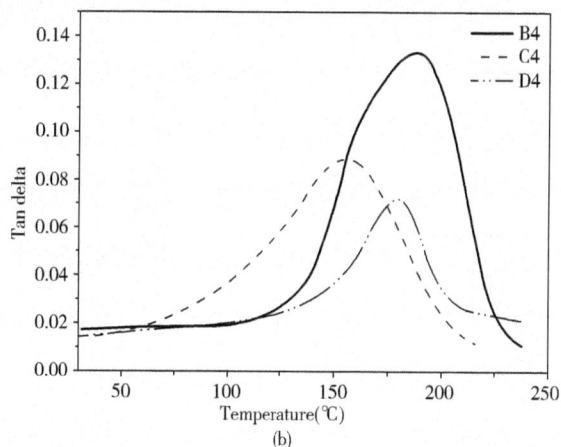

Fig. 2 Storage modulus (a) and tan delta (b) versus temperature for the epoxy resin systems

nutes, the first peak almost disappeared, but still there will be a slight hump, which indicates that curing does still not complete. To continue curing for 30 minutes, the first peak completely disappeared, leaving only the second peak at 150℃. After curing at 150℃ for 15 minutes, the loss modulus had only one peak, but the peak value of the tan delta was only 94℃. After curing for 60 minutes at 150℃, the peak value of the tan delta is up to 139℃. It can be concluded that the system can be fully cured at 130℃ for one and half an hours or at 150℃ for half an hour. Their T_g values (above 130℃) meet the requirements of rapid curing and practical application herein(Fig. 3).

3.2 Flame retardancy of the composites

The results of vertical combustion tests for D4, D4-1, D4-2 and D4-3 systems are shown in Tab. 2. D4 and D4 – 2 systems can be self-extinguishing. From the spread length of the flame at the same time, distance of

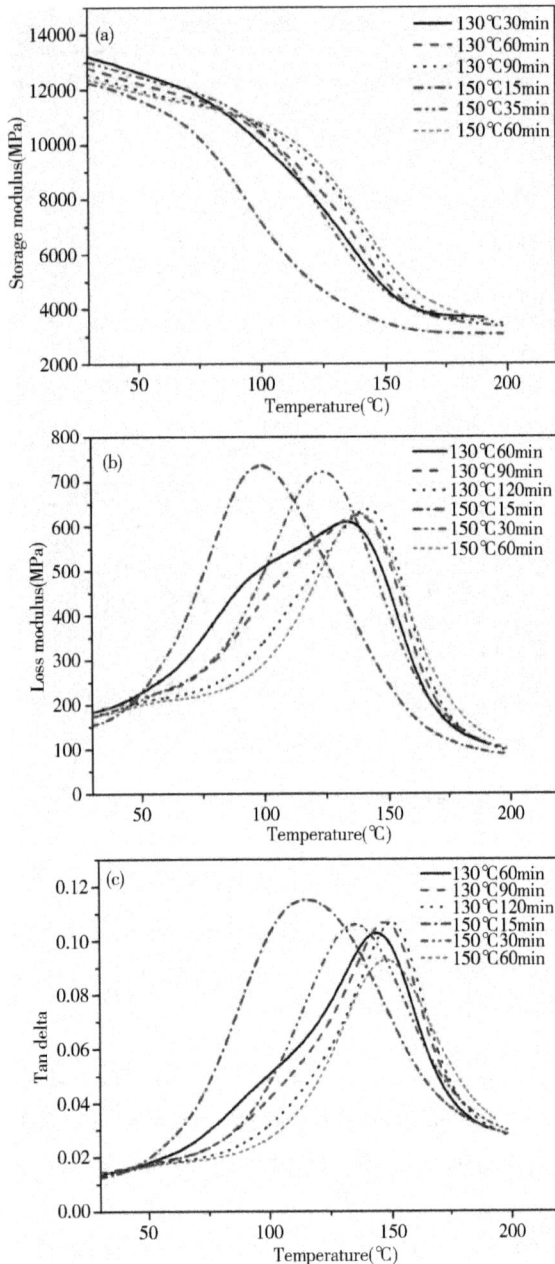

Fig. 3 Storage modulus (a), loss modulus (b) and tan δ (c) versus temperature for the D4 epoxy resin system at different curing conditions

D4 system is the shortest, while D4-1 system spread the furthest distance. The flame spread length can reflect the performance of the flame retardancy. So the D4 system was chosen and identified as BAC 130EL, a new halogen-free flame retardant fast curing epoxy resin system. The glass fiber prepregs based on BAC 130EL were named as BAC 430EL. The combustion level and flame propagation level of PF, BAC 430EL and BAC 400 are V-1 level and class 1.

Tab. 2 Results of vertical combustion tests

Resin systems	Flame spread length at one minute(mm)	Whether the laminates can be self-extinguished after the flame removing
D4	25	Yes
D4-1	55	No
D4-2	30	Yes
D4-3	50	No

V-1 level refers to the second burning time is less than 30 seconds for one sample after removal of the flame. The total burning time of 10 samples does not exceed 250 seconds and no drop to ignite the cotton.

The range of class 1 of flame propagation is defined as the flame propagation distance at 1.5 minutes and the final flame propagation distance is below 165mm, and the distance of a single specimen is limited to 190mm. Halogen-free epoxy resin system can also achieve the same flame retardant indicators as the phenolic resin.

The limit oxygen index (LOI) is the minimum volume percentage of oxygen concentration required to maintain balanced combustion of the sample under specified conditions such as nitrogen and oxygen mixed gases. The LOI value of polymer material is related to the factors such as the charring rate, the combustion enthalpy and the element composition during combustion. In general, the LOI value for a flammable material is below 22. The LOI value for combustible material is between 22 and 27, and LOI value for flame retardant material is over 27.

With regard to the interior decorating material, the oxygen index should be more than or equal to 32. The measured LOI values of various composites are summarized in Tab. 3.

Tab. 3 Comparison of flammability indexes of various composites

Resin system	LOI(%)	Combustion level	Flame diffusion level	Density of smoke
BAC 430EL	36.5	V-1	Class 1	0.063
BAC 400	40.5	V-1	Class 1	0.800
PF	43.6	V-1	Class 1	0.880

As can be seen, the LOI values of composites based on phenolic resin PF, BAC 400 and BAC 430EL glass fiber prepregs are 43.6, 40.5 and 36.5, respectively. As expected, phenolic resin has the highest LOI values and superior flame retardancy. While the LOI value of BAC 430EL is still greater than 32, belonging to the category of flame retardant materials, and meeting the standards of flame retardant on the interior materials.

Density of smoke indicates the degree of thermal decomposition or combustion of materials. Values of Smoke density of composites based on PF and BAC 430EL are 0.063 and 0.800, respectively. It is clear that smoke density of BAC 430EL system is much smaller. It shows that halogen-free flame retardant epoxy resin system BAC 430EL shows better suppression effects for smoke release.

Toxic gas release test is the most critical part for flame retardant materials, which greatly affects the speed of relief operations in the fire. According to the procedure of BS 6853: 1999, B.4.2, the toxic gas was quantitatively tested and the weighted value of toxicity index of BAC 430EL was calculated.

$$R_x = C_x / f_x \qquad (1)$$

$$R = \sum r_x \qquad (2)$$

Where C_x is the measured value of the x-th gas; f_x is the reference value for the x-th gas; r_x is the weight of the x-th gas; and R is the weight index of the toxicity index. The toxicity index R of the BAC 430 EL system can be calculated to be 0.63. The maximum cigarette toxicity index of the material on the Ia type vehicle is 5.0, which is much more than that of the BAC 430EL materials (Tab.4).

Tab.4　The toxicity index of the BAC430 EL system

Toxic gas	Reference value (g/m²)	Measurements (g/m²)
CO_2	14000	1589.7
CO	280	31.49
HF	4.9	0
HCl	15	0
HBr	20	0
NO_2	11	3
SO_2	7.6	1.1

3.3　Climbing drum peel strength of the sandwich structure

The BAC 430EL and BAC 400 prepregs and the aramid paper honeycomb core are used to fabricate sandwich composite panels by co-curing process without the usage of traditional adhesive film. This not only further reduces the weight of the sandwich composites, but also saves the cost of production. The resulting sandwich composite panel was subjected to a roller peeling test. As a result, the peel strength of the sandwich composite based on BAC 430EL was 53.3 N as shown in Fig.4. While the peel strength of the phenolic prepreg BAC 400 was only 20 N. It indicates that the developed epoxy resin system BAC 430EL has the good bonding properties with aramid paper honeycomb core material, and its strength is almost twice of the value of phenolic resin.

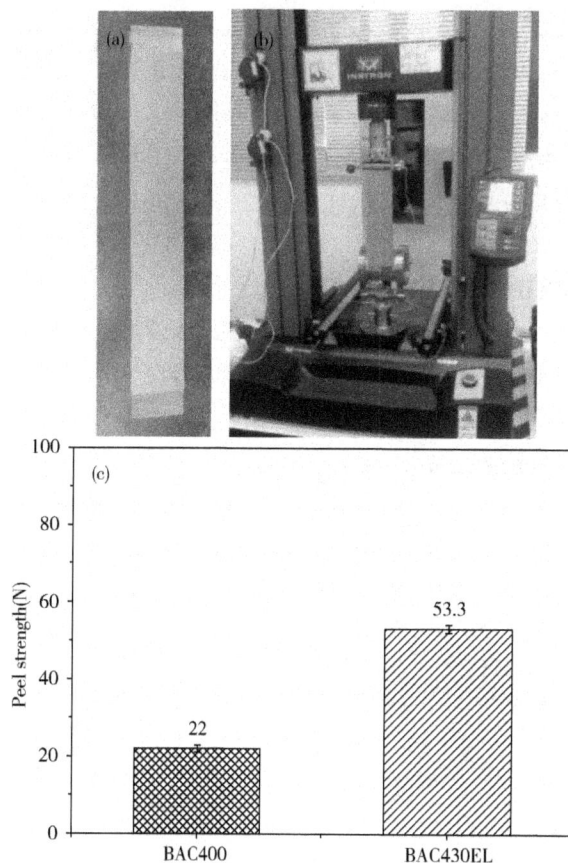

Fig.4　Peel strength of two sandwich composite panels

4　Conclusions

In this work, a series of novel fast-curing, halogen-free

and flame-retardant epoxy resins were developed and their properties, including gel time and thermal-mechanical properties were characterized. In the curing reactivity of the resin system, the BAC 430EL system is fully cured at 130℃ for one and half an hour or 150℃ for half an hour, and the glass transition temperature is above 130℃. BAC 430EL, a fast curing system at the medium temperature, and has a high glass transition temperature. It can wider the range of the operating temperature and improve the processing efficiency greatly. The LOI value of the BAC 430EL system is 36.5. The combustion level is V-1. The flame diffusion level is the class 1. The density of smoke is 0.063. The gas toxicity index is 0.63. These properties meet the requirements of the halogen-free, low smoke, low toxicity and flame retardant on rail transportation and interior decorating materials. In the mechanical properties of sandwich composites, the peel strength of the BAC 430EL is 53.3 N, which is almost twice of thepeel strength of the phenolic resin. Without the use of reinforcement film, sandwich composite has still a good bonding strength by co-curing with BAC 430EL and honeycomb core.

Acknowledgements

This work was supported by Shanghai Science and Technology Committee (No. 15JC1400302)

References

[1] Martin Rogers, Lisa Sterner, Thomas Amos, et al. A novel non-halogenated flame retardant for composite materials[J]. Composites Research Journal, 2007, 1: 12-18.

[2] Almaamori M, Almosawi A, Hashim A. Flame retardancy enhancement of hybrid composite material by using inorganic retardants[J]. Materials Sciences & Applications, 2011, 2 (8).

[3] Bar M, Alagirusamy R, Das A. Flame retardant polymer composites[J]. Fibers & Polymers, 2015, 16 (4): 705-717.

[4] Kicko-Walczak, Grazyna, Rymarz. Flame retardants nanocomposites-synergistic effect of combination conventional retardants with nanofillers of the flammability of thermoset resins[J]. Techniques and Methods, 2015, 60(9): 510-518.

[5] Gérard C, Fontaine G, Bourbigot S. New trends in reaction and resistance to fire of fire-retardant epoxies[J]. Materials, 2010, 3(8): 4476-4499.

[6] Yang S, Wang J, Huo S, et al. Synergistic flameretardant effect of expandable graphite and phosphorus-containing compounds for epoxy resin: Strong bonding of different carbon residues[J]. Polym. Degrad. Stab. 2016(128): 89-98.

[7] Xu M, Xu G, Leng Y, et al. Synthesis of a novel flame retardant based on cyclotriphosphazene and DOPO groups and its application in epoxy resins[J]. Polym. Degrad. Stab. 2016(123): 105-114.

[8] Wang J, Qian L, Huang Z, et al. Synergistic flame-retardant behavior and mechanisms of aluminum poly-hexamethylenephosphinate and phosphaphenanthrene in epoxy resin[J]. Polym. Degrad. Stab. 2016(130): 173-181.

[9] Schartel B, Braun U, Balabanovich A I, et al. Pyrolysis and fire behaviour of epoxy systems containing a novel 9,10-dihydro-9-oxa-10-phosphaphenanthrene-10-oxide-(DOPO)-based diamino hardener[J]. Eur. Polym. J. 2008 (44): 704-715.

[10] Müller P, Morys M, Sut A, et al. Melaminepoly (zinc phosphate) as flame retardant in epoxy resin: Decomposition pathways, molecular mechanisms and morphology of fire residues[J]. Polym. Degrad. Stab. 2016(130) 307-319.

[11] Zhang T, Liu W, Wang M, et al. Synergistic effect of an aromatic boronic acid derivative and magnesium hydroxide on the flame retardancy of epoxy resin[J]. Polym. Degrad. Stab. 2016(130): 257-263.

[12] Zhao X, Babu H, Llorca J, et al. Impact of halogen-free flame retardant with varied phosphorus chemical surrounding on the properties of diglycidyl ether of bisphenol-A type epoxy resin: Synthesis, fire behaviour, flameretardant mechanism and mechanical properties[J]. RSC Adv, 2016 (6): 59226-59236.

Development of Multi-Functional Cotton Using Fluorocarbon Resin

Anil Kumar Jain[1]* , Addisu Ferede Tesema[1] , Adane Haile[1]

[1] *Ethiopian Institute of Textile and Fashion Technology, Bahir Dar University, Bahir Dar, P. O. Box: 1037, Ethiopia*

* *Corresponding author's email:* anilkumarjain220561@ gmail. com

Abstract: An attempt has been made to develop multi-functional cotton fabric having water repellent, stain repellent, shrink resistance and quick dry properties using fluorocarbon resin. The hydrophobicity of cotton fabric was determined by carrying out water repellency test, taking SEM photographs and measuring water contact angle. The durability of hydrophobicity of cotton was tested till 20 washes and found satisfactory. The oil repellency was determined employing hydrocarbons resistance test. The air permeability of cotton fabric was also determined keeping in view the impact on breathability of treated cotton and was found quite good. The untreated & treated cotton fabric was subjected to repeated domestic laundry condition and shrinkage was measured which indicated excellent shrink resistance behaviour because of its water repelling characteristic. This hydrophobicity of cotton also added to its quick dry behaviour even at low temperature and high relative humidity. The physical properties of treated dyed cotton fabric samples were compared with untreated and no significant changes were observed in colour fastness to washing, rubbing, perspiration & light. The tensile and tear strength showed good retention even at higher concentration of fluorocarbon resin. This work is of great industrial importance for textile products used in home textiles. The textile industry can fetch more export earnings by doing multiple value addition using same chemical. The work reported in the literature was about using fluorocarbon and developing water and oil repellent fabrics. In the present work, apart from water and oil repellency, shrink resistance and quick dry behaviour of cotton textile has also been established using same fluorocarbon because of hydrophobicity imparted to cotton.

Keywords: Hydrophobic; Water repellency; Oil repellency; Shrink resistance; Quick dry cotton

1 Introduction

Various methods have been reported in the literature to get water repellent cotton[1-4]. Among these, the most common method is to use fluorocarbon which impart both water and oil repellency to cotton because of its ease of application. Apart from this, the fluorine has got unique characteristics of lowering down the surface energy and making cotton fabric both water and oil repellent[5-6].

Any liquid drop on the fibre surface will have two types of interaction namely, the internal cohesive interaction within the liquid and the adhesive interaction between the liquid and the fibre surface. The liquid will spread only when the interaction with fibre surface will be more than cohesive interaction within the liquid. The internal cohesive interaction or surface tension of water is 73 mNm^{-1}. Any finish which will reduce the surface energy of a cotton surface below the surface tension of water will make it water repellent. Similarly, the surface tension of oil is in the range of $10-20$mNm^{-1}. To make cotton oil repellent, its surface energy must be lower than that of oil. The major advantage of fluorocarbon is that both water and oil repellency can be attained, because of providing surface energy of cotton lower than the surface tension of oil. A fluorocarbon polymer sheath formed around the cotton fibres reduces the surface energy of cotton. This is accompanied by the increase of the contact angle of liquids on cotton surface[7]. Fluorocarbon surfactants based on perfluoro alkyl hydroxyl alkyl siloxane compounds are capable of withstanding numerous washing and dry cleaning cycles[8].

The water contact angle (WCA) at the liquid/solid interface on any solid surface determines its hydrophilic and hydrophobic characteristics. If WCA at the liquid/solid interface, becomes lower than 90°, the surface becomes hydrophilic (water loving). On the other hand, if WCA becomes higher than 90°, the solid surface becomes hydrophobic (water hating). However, any solid surface will attain super hydrophobic characteristics, if WCA is greater than 150°[9].

There are many examples of super-hydrophobic surfaces in nature. The wings of butterflies[10-11], the feet of water striders[12] and the leaves of plants[10,13] are few examples. The development of techniques like, scanning electron microscopy (SEM) have made it possible to study the surface morphology at ultra-micro scale and find out the possible explanations for super-hydrophobicity. The conclusion drawn is that both low surface energy and nano-roughness contribute directly to attain super- hydrophobic character. Any solid surface will exhibit wettability and repellency behaviour, depending upon the surface energy and roughness of material[11,14-18].

The cotton absorbs moisture in the amorphous region and water molecules then act as lubricant and helps in movement of internal polymer chains. The existing hydrogen bonds are disrupted and new hydrogen bonds are formed in the swollen state of cellulose in new configuration and are locked after drying. Therefore the wrinkled appearance of the cellulose fabric persists even after drying, in contrast to non-swelling synthetic fibres[19] and also the fabric shrinks[20].

To produce non-swelling, durable press or shrink resistance cellulose fabrics, the following two different chemical approaches have been used. The first approach is to block the pores of the fibres by incorporating polymeric finish. It inhibits the penetration of water. The second approach is using multifunctional cross linking agents. The multifunctional cross linking agents reacts with the hydroxyl groups of nearby cellulose molecules thereby hindering the swelling of the cellulose fi-

bre[21-22].

The work reported in the literature was about using fluorocarbon and developing water and oil repellent fabrics. In the present work, apart from water and oil repellency, shrink resistance and quick dry behaviour of cotton textile has also been established objectively using same fluorocarbon because of hydrophobicity imparted to cotton.

The cellulose has been made hydrophobic using fluorocarbon polymer. The hydrophobic cellulose repels water and inhibits its penetration even in amorphous region. This will result in development of shrink resistance cotton textiles. Since the water repellent property has been imparted to cotton and penetration of water is inhibited, it enables cotton textiles to dry quickly even at low temperature and at high relative humidity.

The micro-roughness on cotton surface has been studied taking pictures from SEM. The hydrophobicity, water repelling and oil repelling characteristics of cotton have been established by determining WCA and carrying out water repellency and oil repellency tests respectively. The anti-shrinkage behaviour and quick dry characteristics have also been established by carrying out repeated washings and measuring shrinkage and drying time in comparison to untreated fabric.

2　Experiments

2.1　Materials

The plain weave fabric used for experimentation was of two types; 100% bleached cotton and 100% dyed cotton with reactive dyes, having weight $140g/m^2$, without any finishing agent.

The water repellent chemical used was fluorocarbon resin emulsion with C8 chemistry, supplied under the trade name of Bioguard 581X by Biotex Co., Ltd., Malaysia along with Biocat M as universal catalyst.

2.2　Application of water repellent chemical

100% bleached cotton fabric was padded with solutions of 10, 20, 30, 40, 50 & 60 grams/litre, Bioguard 581X along with catalyst Biocat M, with concentrations varying from 2, 4, 6, 8, 10 & 12 grams/litre respectively, at pH 5 to 6 using acetic acid. The following padding conditions were used to get 80% pick up:

Mangle Pressure: 4.5 bar

Speed: 2.50 metres/minute

After padding, the treated fabric samples were dried in Shirley Development Limited (SDL), Mini dryer at 150°C for 2 minutes followed by curing at 185°C for 1 minute.

The 100% dyed cotton fabric sample was treated with 60g/L, Bioguard 581X along with 12g/L Biocat M catalyst at pH 5 to 6 maintained using 0.5g/L acetic acid. The padding conditions like mangle pressure, speed and wet pick up were same as above.

2.3 Determination of wet pick up

The wet pick up of 100% cotton fabric was determined, at different pressure readings (2, 3, 4 & 5 bar) at constant mangle speed of 2.50m/min, using two bowls laboratory vertical padding mangle, manufactured by Mathis, Switzerland.

The wet pick up was calculated by calculating the weight difference of wet and dry fabric and expressed in percentage on the basis of weight of dry fabric. The padding mangle pressure of 4.5 bar was used to get 80% pick up in the application of water repellent chemical.

2.4 Determination of water repellency (WR)

The WR of treated bleached cotton fabric samples were determined employing SDL water spray tester using AATCC Test Method 22—2001.

2.5 Determination of oil repellency (OR)

The oil repellency of treated bleached cotton fabric samples were determined using hydrocarbon resistance test, AATCC Test Method 118—2002.

2.6 Determination of durability of WR effect

The durability of WR effect of bleached cotton fabric samples treated with various concentrations of fluorocarbon were determined by subjecting to 10 & 20 washing cycles employing DIN EN ISO 6330 standard for domestic laundry using launder-meter supplied by Mesdan Lab, Italy.

After completing 10 & 20 washing cycles, the water repellent efficacy test was done employing SDL water spray tester using AATCC Test Method 22—2001.

2.7 SEM photographs

The SEM photographs were taken using SEM supplied by Carl Ziess, model–EVO 18 and at voltage of 20kV. The photographs were taken at 1000 × & 10000 × magnification of untreated and treated cotton samples.

2.8 Determination of WCA

The WCA of water repellent cotton fabric samples were determined by spreading cotton samples on flat table. One fine drop of water was placed on fabric samples using medical syringe of 0.5mL capacity. The pictures were taken using Kodak 15 × Zoom camera. Horizontal and tangential lines were drawn on pictures and water contact angles were measured using protractor.

2.9 Determination of shrinkage of untreated & treated cotton samples

The shrinkage of untreated and treated bleached cotton samples were determined employing DIN EN ISO 6330 standard for domestic laundry using launder-meter made by Mesdan Lab, Italy.

2.10 Determination of quick drying behaviour of hydrophobic cotton

The drying behaviour of untreated and treated cotton samples were studied by washing the samples as per DIN EN ISO 6330 method followed by uniform hydro extraction. The excess water was extracted by padding the samples at 3.5 bar at a speed of 2.5 metres/min followed by drying at 65% relative humidity and at 30°C using mesdan spa, Type M250–RH conditioning chamber.

2.11 Determination of air permeability

The air permeability of various untreated and treated samples were determined using FX 3300 type calibrated air permeability tester supplied by Textest AG, Switzerland employing ASTM D737–96 method.

2.12 Determination of colour fastness to washing

The colour fastness to washing of both untreated and treated dyed cotton fabric samples were tested using ISO–2 test in launder-meter supplied by Mesdan Lab, Italy.

2.13 Determination of colour fastness to crocking

The colour fastness to crocking of both untreated and treated cotton fabric dyed samples were tested employing AATCC Test Method–8—2004 using crock meter supplied by Mesdan Lab, Italy.

2.14 Determination of colour fastness to perspiration

The colour fastness to perspiration of both untreated and treated cotton fabric dyed samples were tested employing ISO 105-EO4 1994 (Acid and Alkaline perspiration) using perspirometer supplied by Mesdan Lab, electrical Heat Thermostatic Culture Box. , Model DH-4000B, Italy.

2.15 Determination of colour fastness to light

The natural sunlight source was used for determining the colour fastness towards light of both untreated and treated cotton fabric dyed samples.

The light fastness rating system was based on the rate of fading of eight blue-dyed wool standard samples which were rated from 1 (poor) to 8 (excellent). All the eight blue wool standard samples were exposed to natural sunlight source along with untreated and treated cotton fabric. The light fastness rating was given comparing the fading of blue wool standard number and tested samples placed parallel to blue wool standard.

2.16 Determination of tear strength

The tear strength of both untreated and treated cotton dyed fabric samples were determined employing ASTM D 1424 method, using SDL Atlas M008E Digital Elmendorf Tester.

2.17 Determination of tensile strength

The tensile strength of both untreated and treated cotton dyed fabric samples were determined employing ISO 13934/1 - EN 13534/1, using fabric traction strip method with Tenso Lab Strength Tester, Mesdan Lab, Italy.

3 Results and Discussion

3.1 Effect of fluorocarbon concentration on water repellency of cotton

In order to make cotton hydrophobic, the bleached cotton samples were treated with various concentration of fluorocarbon emulsion along with catalyst. The water repellency of treated fabric samples were tested before and after 10 & 20 washes respectively using SDL water spray tester. The results are given in Tab. 1.

Tab. 1 Water repellency of cotton fabric before and after domestic laundry

Concentration of fluorocarbon (g/L)	Water spray rating		
	Before wash	After 10 washes	After 20 washes
10	100	90	80
20	100	90	80
30	100	100	90
40	100	100	90
50	100	100	90
60	100	100	100

The spray test rating of 100 before wash, indicates that there was no sticking or wetting of upper surface by water even at lowest concentration of 10g/L fluorocarbon. However, after 10 & 20 washes, a rating of 90 & 80 respectively was obtained showing that there was slight random wetting of upper surface with water at spray point only. This clearly indicates that hydrophobicity of cotton fabric was maintained even after 20 washes at almost all concentrations of fluorocarbon.

3.2 Effect of fluorocarbon concentration on oil repellency of cotton

The oil repellency of treated fabric samples were tested before and after 10 & 20 washes employing hydrocarbon resistance test. The results are given in Tab. 2.

Tab. 2 Oil repellency of cotton fabric before and after domestic laundry

Concentration of fluorocarbon (g/L)	Oil Repellency Grade		
	Before wash	After 10 washes	After 20 washes
10	5	4	3
20	5	5	4
30	5	5	5
40	5	5	5
50	5	5	5
60	5	5	5

The oil repellency grade of 5 before wash indicates very good oil repellent properties even at a concentration of 10 to 20g/L fluorocarbon. The same performance was maintained even after 10 washes at 20g/L and above.

After 20 washes, a grade of 4 at 20g/L fluorocarbon indicates slight deterioration of performance. However, 30 to 60g/L fluorocarbon treated cotton showed a very good rating of 5. This clearly indicates that the durability of oil repellency of hydrophobic cotton fabric was maintained even after 20 washes at above 20g/L fluorocarbon concentration.

SEM photographs of untreated and treated cotton fabrics were taken at 100 × & 10000 × magnification as shown in Fig. 1. The pictures clearly show that micro-roughness was developed on fluorocarbon treated cotton in comparison to untreated cotton fabric having smooth surface. This micro-roughness on treated cotton fabric is making cotton hydrophobic.

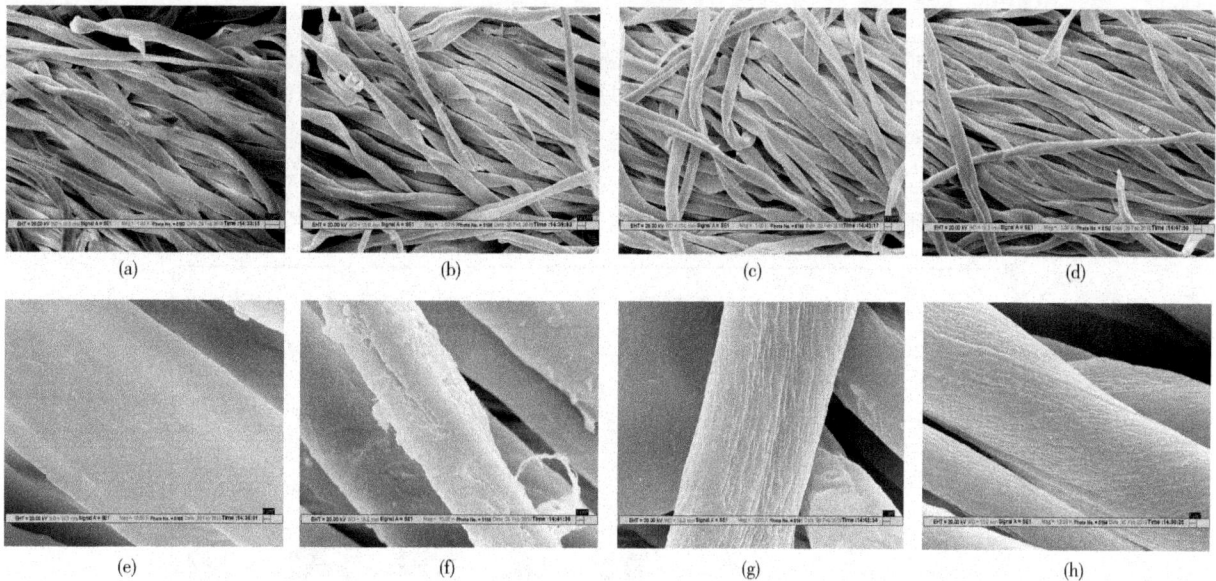

Fig. 1 SEM photographs of untreated and treated cotton with fluorocarbon at 100 × & 10000 × magnification （a）Untreated cotton at 100 × ; （b）20g/L treated cotton at 100 × ; （c）40g/L treated cotton at 100 × ; （d）60g/L treated cotton at 100 × ; （e）Untreated cotton at 10000 × ; （f）20g/L treated cotton at 10000 × ; （g）40g/L treated cotton at 10000 × ; （h）60g/L treated cotton at 10000 × with fluorocarbon resin

3. 3 WCA of fluorocarbon treated cotton before and after 20 washes

The WCA of treated cotton at various concentrations of fluorocarbon （20, 40 & 60g/L） were measured before and after 20 washes.

It can be seen from Fig. 2 that WCA of treated cotton fabrics were above 90° both before and after 20 washes, indicating that cotton fabric has become hydrophobic. Another observation is that WCA are almost constant between 123° to 127° before washes. It shows increase in concentration of fluorocarbon from 20g/L to 60g/L have minimal impact on hydrophobicity of cotton. After 20 washes, although there was reduction in water contact angle but in all cases, it was above 90° indicating that hydrophobicity of cotton was maintained.

3. 4 Shrinkage behaviour of hydrophobic cotton

It can be seen from Fig. 3 that the shrinkage in warp di-

rection increased with increase in number of washes. The shrinkage became almost constant after 7 washes. The untreated cotton showed shrinkage of 9. 5% after 8 washes. However, the fluorocarbon treated cotton showed shrinkage varying from lowest 3. 5% （at 60g/L） to maximum 5% shrinkage （at 10g/L） treatment. The fluorocarbon treated cotton samples from 20 to 50g/L showed shrinkage varying from 4. 0% to 4. 5%. About 58% to 53% reduction in shrinkage has been observed in treated cotton samples at varying concentration of fluorocarbon （20 to 50g/L） because of hydrophobicity imparted to cotton as shown in water repellency rating and WCA before and after washes. This hydrophobicity prevents the penetration of water in cotton thereby imbibing the swelling of cotton and making it shrink resistance.

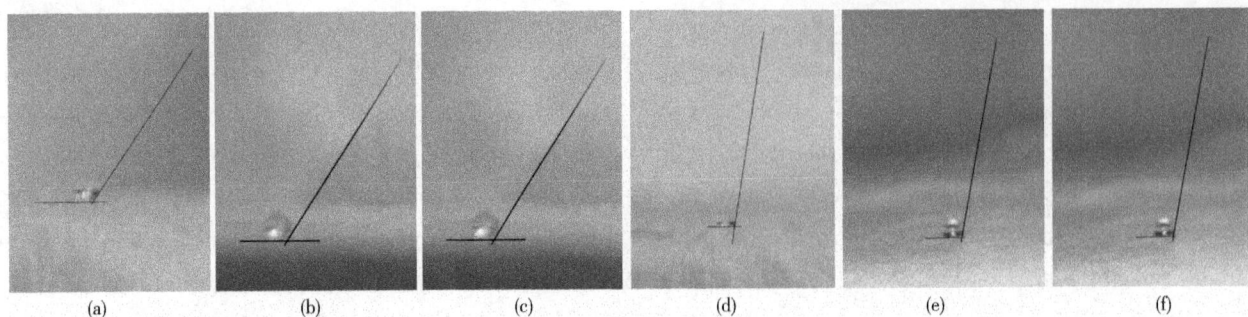

Fig. 2　WCA of treated cotton with fluorocarbon before and after 20 washes　(a) 20g/L-unwashed-WCA (123°); (b) 40g/L-unwashed-WCA (123°); (c) 60g/L-unwashed-WCA (127°); (d) 20g/L-20 washes-WCA(98°); (e) 40g/L-20 washes-WCA (101°); (f) 60g/L-20 washes-WCA (101°)

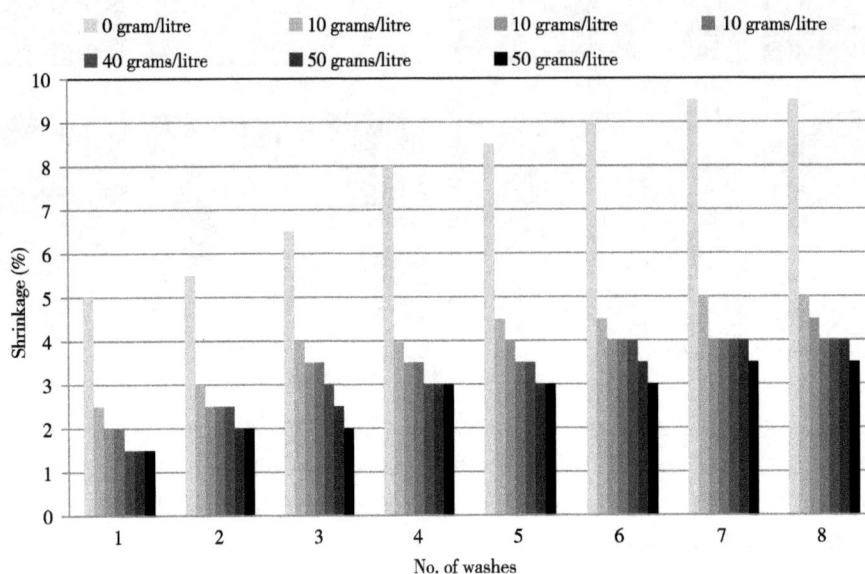

Fig. 3　Warp-wise shrinkage of untreated and treated cotton with fluorocarbon

The weft direction shrinkage is shown in Fig. 4. The weft direction shrinkage became almost constant after 2 washes. The untreated cotton showed maximum shrinkage of 2.5% after 2 washes. However, the fluorocarbon treated cotton showed shrinkage varying from 0.5% to 1.0% at various concentrations of fluorocarbons. About 60% to 80% reduction in shrinkage has been observed in treated cotton fabric samples at varying concentration of fluorocarbons in weft direction because of cotton becoming hydrophobic.

3.5　Quick dry behaviour of hydrophobic cotton

In Fig. 5, drying behaviour of treated cotton samples have been studied against untreated at 65% relative humidity and 30℃. The initial moisture of untreated cotton sample (0g/L) after washing and hydro-extraction through padding mangle was 90%. In case of treated cotton samples after hydro extraction, the initial moisture was around 50% irrespective of concentration of fluorocarbon used because of hydrophobicity imparted to cotton with fluorocarbon.

After 10 minutes drying at 65% relative humidity and 30℃, the untreated cotton showed moisture content around 50% and all treated samples were almost dried having moisture content between 13% and 15%. The reason for quick drying even after 10 minutes was because the initial water picked up by treated cotton was lower due to their hydrophobic nature. It showed reduction in drying time of treated cotton samples by more than 50%.

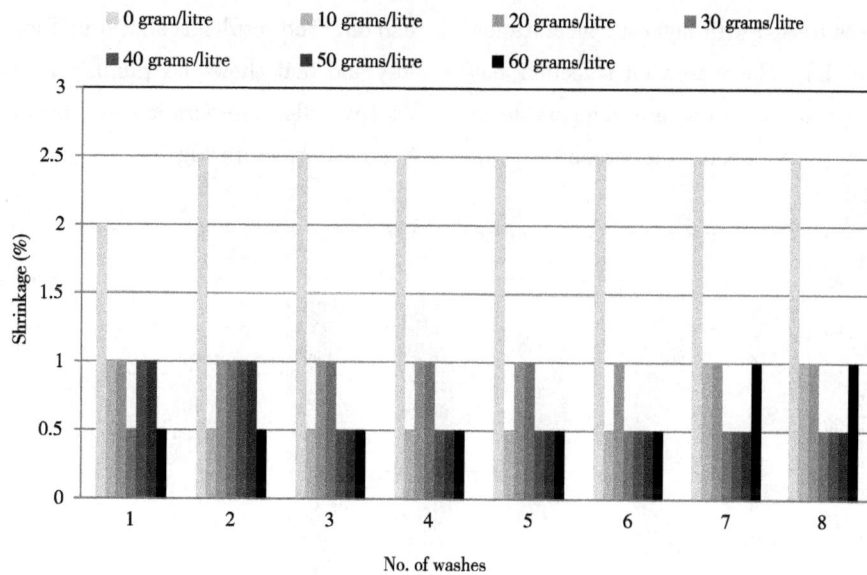

Fig. 4   Weft-wise shrinkage of untreated and treated cotton with fluorocarbon

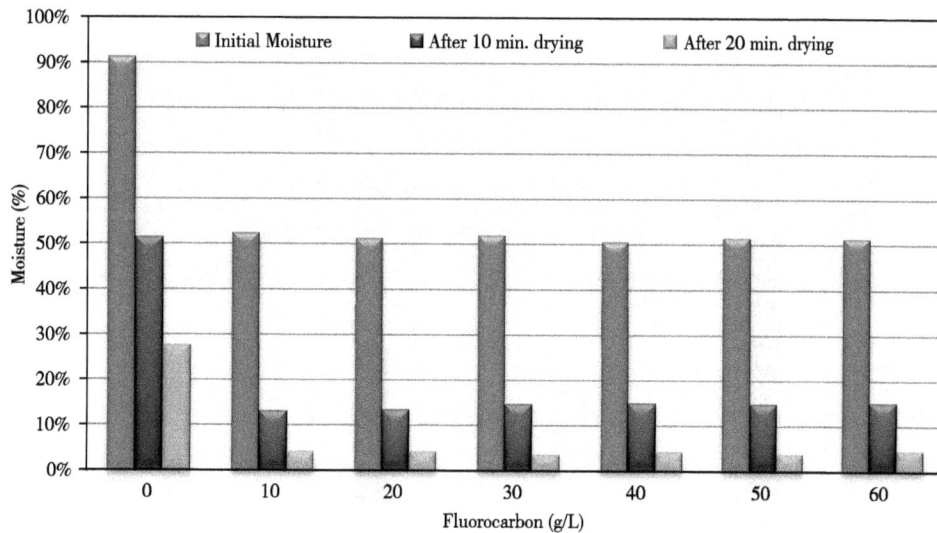

Fig. 5   Drying graph of hydrophobic cotton

3.6 Air permeability of untreated and treated cotton with fluorocarbons

The air permeability of untreated and treated cotton with varying concentration of fluorocarbon was determined. The results are shown in Fig. 6.

It can be seen in Fig. 6 that untreated cotton (shown as 0gram/litre fluorocarbon concentration) showed air permeability of $42kg \cdot m^{-1}s^{-2}$. The air permeability values of treated cotton with 10g/L to 40g/L fluorocarbon varied between 40 and $44kg \cdot m^{-1}s^{-2}$. It indicates that air

permeability/ breathability of treated cotton fabric was closer to untreated cotton upto 40g/L. However, at 50 to 60g/L of fluorocarbon little deterioration was observed. This further shows that no continuous film of fluorocarbon polymer was formed and porosity of fabric was sustained below 50g/L fluorocarbon.

3.7 Comparison of colour fastness and physical properties of untreated and treated dyed cotton fabric

In order to compare, various colour fastness and physical properties of untreated and treated cotton fabric, the dyed cotton fabric was treated with highest concentration of fluorocarbon (60g/L). The reason for selection was that if the tested physical properties are comparable at this concentration of fluorocarbon, the properties will also remain comparable at lower concentration of fluorocarbon. The results as shown in Tab. 3 are self-explanatory and that shows no significant change in properties except little deterioration in tensile strength (below 8%) as shown in Fig. 7.

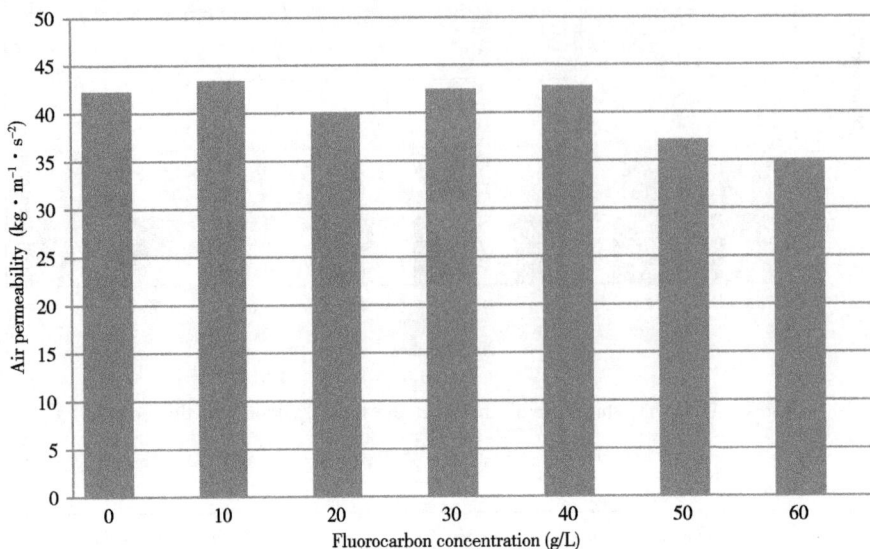

Fig. 6   Air permeability of untreated and treated cotton with fluorocarbon at varying concentrations

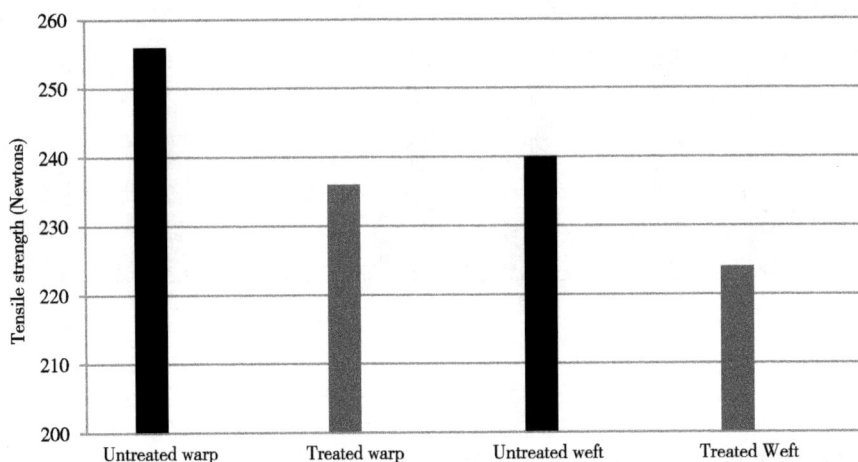

Fig. 7   Tensile strength of untreated and treated cotton with 60g/L fluorocarbon

Tab. 3   Comparison of fabric properties between untreated and treated dyed cotton

S. No.	Parameters	Untreated Dyed Fabric	Treated Dyed Fabric
	Colour Fastness to Washing		
1	Change in Colour	4 to 5	4 to 5
	Staining on Adjacent Fabric	4 to 5	4 to 5

Continued

S. No.	Parameters	Untreated Dyed Fabric	Treated Dyed Fabric
2	Colour Fastness to Rubbing		
	Staining on Adjacent Fabric		
	Wet Rubbing	4 to 5	4 to 5
	Dry Rubbing	4 to 5	4 to 5
3	Colour Fastness to Perspiration		
	Acidic		
	Change in Colour	4 to 5	4
	Staining on Adjacent Fabric	4 to 5	4 to 5
	Alkaline		
	Change in Colour	4 to 5	4 to 5
	Staining on Adjacent Fabric	4 to 5	4 to 5
4	Colour Fastness to Light	>3	>3
	Change in Colour		
5	Tensile Strength (Newtons)		
	Warp	256	236
	Weft	240	224
6	Tear Strength (Newtons)		
	Warp	37.85	35.10
	Weft	37.52	34.34

Although the decrease in tensile strength is minimal, the probable reason for decrease may be due to the reaction of fluorocarbon resin with cellulose which decreases little elasticity & flexibility of cellulose fibres. The durability of finish towards domestic laundry also confirms the reaction of fluorocarbon resin with cellulose.

4 Conclusions

It has become possible to produce multi-functional cotton textiles by making it hydrophobic using fluorocarbon polymer. The desired water repellency, oil repellency, shrinkage resistance, quick dry properties can be achieved even at lower concentration of 20g/L of fluorocarbon. SEM photographs and WCA clearly established the generation of micro surface roughness and hydrophobicity of cotton. The finishes imparted are durable and can withstand 20 domestic laundry cycles.

The air permeability test indicated that breathability of untreated and treated cotton fabric was sustained indicating no continuous film formation.

The fabric properties of untreated and treated dyed cotton fabrics at 60g/L fluorocarbon were found similar in terms of various colour fastness and tear and tensile strength indicating no deterioration of fabric performance even at high concentration of fluorocarbons.

References

[1] Xue C H, Jia S T, Zhang J, et al. Preparation of super hydrophobic surface on cotton textile [J]. Sci Tech of Adv Mat, 2008, 9:1-7.

[2] Shosha M H, Hilw Z H, Aly A A, et al. Paraffin wax emulsion as water repellent for cotton/polyester blended fabric [J]. J Ind Text, 2008, 37: 315-325.

[3] Przybylak M, Maciejewicz H, Dutkiewicz A, et al. Fabricationof superhydrophobic cotton fabric by a simple chemical modification[J]. Cellulose, 2016, 23: 2185-2197.

[4] Li Y, Zheng X, Xia Z, et al. Synthesis of fluorinated block copolymer and superhydrophobic cotton fabric preparation [J]. Prog Org Coat, 2016, 97: 122-132.

[5] Holmquist H, Schellenberger S I, Vander V, et al. Properties performance and associated hazards of state of the art durable water repellent (DWR) chemistry for textile finishing [J]. Environment International, 2016, 91: 251-264.

[6] Mckeen L W. Fluorinated coatings and finishes handbook [M]. 2006.

[7] Schindler W D, Hauser P J. Chemical finishing of textiles [M]. 2004.

[8] Lal R. Water and oil repellent finishes [J]. Colourage, 2007, 54(10): 67

[9] Song J, Rojas O J. Approaching super-hydrophobicity from cellulosic materials: A Review [J]. Nordic Pulp & Paper Research Journal, 2013, 28(2): 216-238.

[10] Cheng Y T, Rodak D E, Wong C A, et al. Effects of micro-andnano-structures on the self-cleaning behaviour of lotus leaves [J]. Nano Technology, 2006, 17(5): 1359-1362.

[11] Genzer J, Efimenko K. Recent developments in superhydrophobic surfaces and their relevance to marine fouling: A review [J]. Biofouling, 2006, 22(5): 339-360.

[12] Gao X F, Jiang L. Biophysics: Water-repellent legs of water striders [J]. Nature, 2004, 432:36.

[13] Koch K, Bhushan B, Barthlott W. Multifunctional surface structures of plants: An inspiration for biomimetics [J]. Progr Mater Science, 2009, 54(2):137-178.

[14] Cassie A B D, Baxter S. Wettability of porous surfaces [J]. T Faraday Soc, 1944, 40:546-550.

[15] Koch K, Barthlott W. Superhydrophobic and superhydrophilic plant surfaces: An inspiration for biomimetic materials [J]. Phil Trans R Soc A, 2009, 367:1487-1509.

[16] Nakajima A, Hashimoto K, Watanabe T. Recent studies on super-hydrophobic films [J]. Monatsh Chem: 2001, 132 (1):31-41.

[17] Sun T L, Feng L, Gao X F, et al. Bio-inspired surfaces with special wettability [J]. Acc Chem Res, 2005, 38(8): 644-652.

[18] Wenzel R N. Resistance of solid surfaces to wetting by water [J]. Ind Eng Chem, 1936, 28:988-994.

[19] Lam Y, Kan C and Yuen C, Wrinkle-resistant finishing of cotton fabric with BTCA- the effect of co-catalyst [J]. Textile Res J, 2011, 81: 482-493.

[20] Schindler W D, Hauser P J. Easy-care and durable press finishes of cellulosic. In: Chemical finishing of textiles [M]. Cambridge, Woodhead, 2004;51-72.

[21] Shahin U, Gursoy N, Hauser P J, et al. Optimization of ionic crosslinking process: An alternative to conventional durable press finishing [J]. Textile Res J, 2009, 79: 744-752.

[22] Lacasse K and Baumann W, Textile chemicals: Environmental data and facts [M]. Berlin: Springer, 2004.

Optimal Scheduling for Mobile Device with Heterogeneous Energy Management Units

S. M. Abis Naqvi[1,2]* , **S. Ikram Shahzad**[1,2] , **Sadia Batool**[3] , **Habiba Halepoto**[1,2] , **Guanglin Zhang**[1,2]

[1] *College of Information Science and Technology, Donghua University, China*

[2] *Engineering Research Center of Digitized Textile and Apparel Technology, Ministry of Education, China*

[3] *College of Control Science and Engineering, Zhejiang University, China*

* *Corresponding author's email*: glzhang@ dhu. edu. cn

Abstract: Energy storage unit is a key component for durable functionality in a mobile device. A solar energy resource with a commercial electricity source has been considered for multiple timescale batteries in the mobile device. Charging and discharging storage capacity and response time are dissimilar for different storage technologies. Two different timescale approaches for batteries conceivably considered in a mobile device to reduce the charging cost of energy storage units. In a mobile device, slow and fast timescale batteries for energy management were studied here. A fast battery was charged by a solar panel, at the same time the slow battery has been charged on an hourly basis, and one cannot change the decision over mutual fast time slots. These batteries have been charged using Lyapunov optimization approach with significant sub-optimality bounds. Hence, a stochastic approximation problem has been formulated. An online algorithm is formulated by using Lyapunov optimization approach for establishing virtual queues of energy storage unitsina mobile device. Simulations and results have been shown the advantage of using dual timescale batteries in the mobile device.

Keywords: Lyapunov optimization; Two timescale approach; Stochastic approximation; Mobile device

1 Introduction

Due to the rapid technological advancement, the demand for the mobile device has been enhanced considerably because mobile devices have fortified the computational power of communication devices. A Lyapunov approach was first used to mount up price differentials in the smart grid context and energy storage in data-centers[1-2]. A multiple timescale Lyapunov energy management scheme to reduce the smart grid cost is considered[3]. With real-time solutions, the Lyapunov optimization approach is proposed, which relaxes time coupling constraints with suboptimality bound[4]. Solutions for storage scheduling can be divided into three categories. The first group consists of model predictive control (MPC)-schemes, where battery charging has been undertaken in a stochastic or deterministic fashion without performance guarantees[5-6]. The second

group approximate dynamic programming solvers sustain high-level computational complexity and oblige the joint probability distribution function (pdf) of random processes must be known[7-8]. The third group engages real-time solutions from Lyapunov optimization technique using relatively mild assumptions. The increased degradation cost of batteries may be minimized by slower control rules[9]. A dual timescale Lyapunov optimization technique was introduced to decreased power in data centers[10]. Furthermore, a real-time control technique was developed for batteries controlled at different timescales using stochastic approximation and Lyapunov optimization for feasible results with bounded suboptimality gap[11].

In this motivational approach, the mobile device electricity scheduling problem using Lyapunov optimization technique has been formulated, which is a useful approach for the solution of stochastic optimization with stability problems[12-13]. Moreover, this scheme was applied to tackle down energy management problems[1] and present online solutions with performance bounds. The concept of dual timescale batteries in the mobile device has introduced to improve the energy capacity of a mobile device for minimizing the energy cost. We considered the approach of virtual queues and proposed two virtual queues: the virtual queues of two timescale batteries to transform management problems of slow-fast timescale batteries to queue stability problems. Furthermore, performance bonds for proposed algorithm have been proved using Lyapunov optimization technique. Due to the Lyapunov stability approach, this algorithm converges[14]. Numerical analysis of real-time data shows the benefit of heterogeneous storage units in a mobile device. The format of this research paper is as follows. The system model is described in section 2, the problem formulation is introduced in section 3. In section 4, an adaptive mobile device energy scheduling algorithm is designed. In section 5, simulation figures are shown. The numerical results are shown in section 6. Finally, Section 7 concludes the paper.

2 System Model

The categorization of energy storage units could be organized on the basis of their appearance which they use to forage the power. For example, energy storage units are piezoelectric harvesting devices forage mechanical energy and then convert it into utilizable electrical energy. The numerous sources for energy storage units are wind turbines, thermoelectric generators, mechanical vibration devices such as electromagnetic devices, piezoelectric devices and photovoltaic cells i. e. solar panel[15]. Tab. 1 shows power generation capability on the basis of their harvesting methods[16].

Tab. 1 Energy Storage Units[16]

Storage method	Density
Solar panel cells	$15\mu W/cm^3$
Thermoelectric generators	$40\mu W/cm^3$
Mechanical vibration	$116\mu W/cm^3$
Piezoelectric device	$330\mu W/cm^3$

Consider a mobile device consisting of a photovoltaic cell i. e. solar panel, a change able load and energy storage units which are synchronized by a controller as shown in Fig. 1. By the heterogeneous energy storage approach and the energy has exchanged between the real-time market and the mobile device, organize operations evolve in dual timescales. The controlling perspective at the fast timescale has distributed into fast time slots for equal duration which has indicated by f. A series of F successive fast-timescale slots comprises a control parameter for slow timescale which has been indicated by $s = [f/F]$, then time f could be expressed by $f = sF + \omega$ which specify the slow control parameter and it relates to and the interconnected offset ω.

For the slow timescale, the real-time market has exchanged energy with mobile device throughout a time-ahead energy and then it operated the slow timescale battery. The control parameters have been taken for slow time period s remains unchanged over the upcoming F fast control timeslots. If R_s signify the state of charge (SoC) of slow timescale battery at the start of slow time period s, and P_s is the amount from which the same energy unit has charged over s parameter then it shows as,

$$R_{s+1} = R_s + P_s \qquad (1)$$

$$\underline{R} \leqslant R_s + \overline{R} \qquad (2)$$

$$\underline{P} \leqslant P_s \leqslant \overline{P} \qquad (3)$$

Now (1) captures battery charging for next times lot (2) conserve the (SoC) within the capacity ($\underline{R}, \overline{R}$) and (3) impose charging rates of a slow battery ($\underline{P}, \overline{P}$). The mobile device has bought energy B_s from the real-time market to charge the slow timescale battery by charging rate P_s, in the meanwhile the leftover energy as follow,

$$G_s = B_s - P_s \qquad (4)$$

Where G_s is the total energy that remains from the real-time market. It's bounded as $G_s \in [\underline{G}, \overline{G}]$ and it also provides the load over fast time slot for the next F. The controller gathers the information on renewable solar energy generation and a load demand, it operates on the fast timescale battery and it exchanges the energy with the mobile device through a real-time market at the fast time slots. Thus, k_f denotes the dissimilarity between demand energy and solar generation energy over fast period time slot f. Likewise to (1-3), the (SoC) r_f and the charging rate p_f for the fast battery at time slot f it satisfies as follow,

$$r_{f+1} = r_f + p_f \quad (5)$$

$$\underline{r} \leqslant r_f + \bar{r} \quad (6)$$

$$\underline{p} \leqslant p_f \leqslant \bar{p} \quad (7)$$

If b_f is the renewable energy from the photo voltaic cell i. e. solar panel at period f and the total energy G_s is distributed uniformly over the next F fast times slots then renewable energy involves,

$$b_f = k_f + p_f - \frac{G_s}{F} \quad (8)$$

Charging cost is modeled at two timescales, a slow battery has charged by the real-time market has convex rising function $C_s(B_s)$ and a fast battery has charged by renewable solar energy so it has no charging cost.

3 Problem Formulation

It is enviable to minimize energy operational cost in order to optimize the overall system cost. Having the time-ahead cost $C_s(B_s)$ from the real-time market occurs once every F control parameter, the energy scheduling management task into the Lyapunov optimization technique could be used as follow,

$$P_1 = \min \lim_{s \to \infty} \frac{1}{SF} \sum_{s=0}^{S-1} \sum_{f=0}^{F-1} \left[\frac{C_s(B_s)}{F} \right] \quad (9)$$

Over $\{B_s, P_s, R_s, G_s\}$, $\{r_f, p_f\}$

$$\lim_{s \to \infty} \frac{1}{S} \sum_{s=0}^{S-1} P_s = 0$$

$$\lim_{s \to \infty} \frac{1}{SF} \sum_{s=0}^{S-1} \sum_{f=0}^{F-1} p_f = 0$$

Solving (9) is confronted by the randomness and the combination across successive parameter in (1) and (5). In joint probability distribution function (pdf) that the conventional solutions are based on estimate dynamic programming which could be suffering from the curse of presuming and dimensionality[17]. Furthermore, Lyapunov optimization technique can approximately manage infinite-horizon problems of exacting structure which can be solved by a series of relatively uncomplicated problems as time slots proceeds[18].

The Lyapunov optimization technique introduces two virtual queues Y_s and y_f and it minimizes the drift plus penalty cost function for all s [17].

$$\min: Y_s P_s + VC_s(B_s) + \sum_{f=0}^{F-1} [y_f p_f] \quad (10)$$

Where these virtual queues linked to SoCs as follows:

$$Y_s = R_s + \sigma \quad (11)$$

$$y_f = r_f + \varphi \quad (12)$$

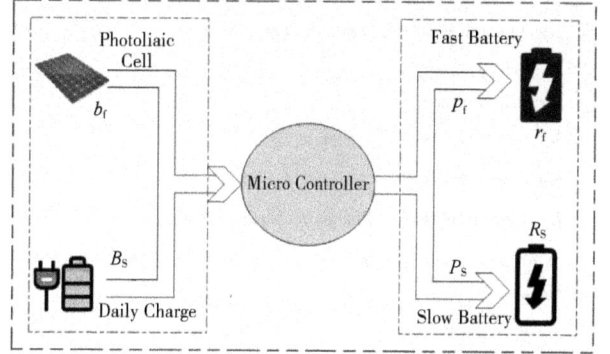

Fig. 1 Charging batteries at dual timescale

Thus, σ and φ are the constants and explained later. Notice that the probability in the cost of (10) is now only with respect to (k_f). Nevertheless, equation (10) is still challenging for us since it involves many expectations over the values of the future in the queue constraint y_f. To conquer this difficulty, the values of virtual queue $\{y_f\}_{f=0}^{F-1}$ are substituted by Y_s and the final problem is optimized using a technique of stochastic approximation.

4 Algorithm Design

In this section, we will propose the online energy management algorithm for two timescale batteries based on Lyapunov optimization approach. It is significant mentioning that the conventional Lyapunov optimization approach, where the decisions of i. i. d. , cannot directly be applied to two timescale batteries. Thus, first we provide the conditions where these solutions are possible under the charging and discharging decisions of Alg. 1 are more feasible for the problem (9) [2-10].

Using Lyapunov penalty and drift technique, for every time slot, we have transform problem (9) to the problem (10) for the desired solution. This online algorithm has subsequent properties for the optimal energy scheduling.

The given real-time algorithm used the Lyapunov optimization technique to dynamically balance the cost minimization. It is an online real-time algorithm and vigorous to non-ergodic method and non-i. i. d. [1-19].

Alg. 1 Dual Timescale Energy Management Unit

1. At the start of each time slot acquire the energy virtual queue state Y_s, slow timescale y_f, fast timescale
2. for $f = 0, 1, 2, \cdots$ do
3. if f/F is integer then
4. Set $s = f/F$ and also observe cost C_s
5. Set $Y_s = R_s + \sigma$
6. Buys energy $B_s = G_s + P_s$ from real-time market
7. end if
8. Observe k_f
9. Set $y_f = r_f + \varphi$
10. Get energy from the solar panel
11. end for

Theorem 1:

The constraint for slow timescale battery energy level $E_s(t)$, $E_s(\min) \leqslant E_s(t) \leqslant E_s(\max)$, it must be satisfied the constraints for all s and t. E_s, E_f energy levels for slow and fast timescale battery.

Likewise, the constraint for fast timescale battery energy level $E_f(t)$, $E_f(\min) \leqslant E_f(t) \leqslant E_f(\max)$, it must be satisfied the constraints for all f and t. The detailed proof of Theorem1 is not here for brevity (see, e. g. [3]).

5 Simulations

In this section, we will confirm the conjectural results consequent in section 3 and also evaluate the performance of the proposed online algorithm through the results of simulations in MATLAB. We show the performance of proposed mobile device energy scheduling online algorithm by simulations.

Two timescale batteries have been charged by electricity that is bought by the real-time market and the renewable energy source i. e. photovoltaic cells solar energy. In our system model, mobile device consists of two batteries, first one is considered as the slow timescale and

the second one is considered as the fast timescale battery. 8 watt-hour is the maximum charged capacity of a slow timescale Li-ion battery and the 0 watt-hour is the minimum energy capacity, 0.8 kilo-watt-hour is the maximum capacity of the fast timescale Li-ion battery and zero watt-hour is the minimum energy. Within 8 hours, these batteries can be fully charged and discharged[20]. For the mobile device, the service prices are obtained from[21] which are very time-varying. We used MATLAB Linprog solver technique to solve the final problem (10).

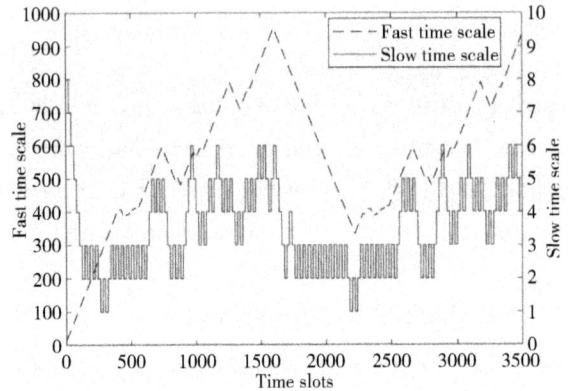

Fig. 2 Energy levels for two timescale approach

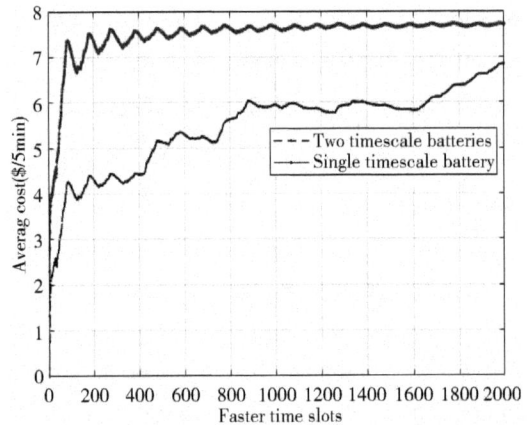

Fig. 3 Time-average mobile device operational cost

Now, we have examined the battery energy levels for single timescale and it has one watt-hour charging and discharging capacity in single time-slot. Then, we have examined the battery energy levels for two timescale technique. For the two timescale approaches, the fast battery has charged and discharged in the range between 0 to 0.8 kilo-watt-hours, it has fallen strictly within range of capacity limit of the battery. Similarly, the slow battery has charged and discharged in the range between 0 to 8 watt-hours.

The distinction for battery energy level in Fig. 2 should be higher. By Theorem1, the feasibility of battery energy management constraints have always been ensured, if the control horizon V satisfied the $0 < V \leqslant V_{\max}$. The energy level for the slow timescale battery has charged and discharged of single time-slot is restricted by one watt-hour and likewise, the energy level for fast timescale battery is 2 watt-hours approximately. Finally, Energy levels of dual timescale approach are compared. We have also plotted the mobile device operational cost in Fig. 3. It has observed that cost for single timescale battery has converged to $\$7.5$ approximately which has little higher as compared to dual timescale battery. The operational cost for the proposed energy online algorithm policy drops significantly with dual timescale battery approach.

6 Numerical Test

Algorithm 1 was examined using 5-min demand energy load data from Home Smart Project[22], ranges up by a factor of 10 to 20 weeks of load[22]. Cost for C_s was modeled as piecewise, linear with dissimilar buying and selling prices. Buying price for C_s was taken as an hourly day-ahead price for Michigan hub in MISO market in April, 2015.

The fast timescale battery has $F = 20$ fast timescale battery intervals. The charging and discharging rate of the battery were set to $R = 10$ watt-hour, $r = 1$ kilo-watt-hour, $\underline{R} = \underline{r} = 0$ watt-hour, and $\overline{P} = -\underline{P} = 1$ watt-hour, $\overline{p} = -\underline{p} = 2$ watt-hour, and $\overline{G} = -\underline{G} = 30$ watt-hour.

7 Conclusions

In this research approach, an online energy management scheduling algorithm has developed for the energy storage of mobile device with the help of renewable energy source (photovoltaic cells i. e. a solar panel), and utility market price participation. We transformed the energy storage problem into the queue stability problem by introducing battery virtual queues. The technique we used to solve this problem is Lyapunov optimization method with the help of an efficient online energy scheduling online algorithm, while ensuring the performance bounds.

In this work, we have only focused on mobile device operational cost on market energy and energy scheduling but not focus on the daily basis of the energy future prices and also demand. Our simulation study authenticated the superior performance of the proposed algorithm. It could be interesting to utilize such daily pattern to pull out the proposed online algorithm by the interaction between future prices and delayed requests and also under the supply-demand response strategy for the future work.

References

[1] Neely M J, Tehrani A S, Dimakis A G. Efficient algorithms for renewable energy allocation to delay tolerant consumers [C]. 2010 First IEEE International Conference on Smart Grid Communications, 2010.

[2] Urgaonkar R, et al. Optimal power cost management using stored energy in data centers [C]. in Proceedings of the ACM SIGMETRICS joint international conference on Measurement and modeling of computer systems. 2011, ACM.

[3] Huang Y, Mao S, Nelms R M. Adaptive electricity scheduling in microgrids [C]. in INFOCOM, 2013 Proceedings IEEE. 2013, IEEE.

[4] Gupta S. Kekatos V. Real-time operation of heterogeneous energy storage units in Signal and Information Processing (GlobalSIP) [C]. 2016 IEEE Global Conference on. 2016, IEEE.

[5] Xie L. et al. Fast MPC-based coordination of wind power and battery energy storage systems [J]. Journal of Energy Engineering, 2012, 138(2): 43-53.

[6] Fortenbacher P, Mathieu JL, Andersson G. Modeling and optimal operation of distributed battery storage in low voltage grids [C]. IEEE Transactions on Power Systems, 2017, 32 (6): 4340-4350.

[7] Faghih A, Roozbehani M, Dahleh M A. On the value and price-responsiveness of ramp-constrained storage[C]. Energy Conversion and Management, 2013, 76: 472-482.

[8] Qin J, Su H I, Rajagopal R. Storage in risk limiting dispatch: Control and approximation [C]. American Control Conference (ACC), 2013, IEEE.

[9] Castillo A, Gayme D F. Grid-scale energy storage applications in renewable energy integration: A survey[J]. Energy Conversion and Management, 2014, 87: 885–894.

[10] Yao Y, et al. Data centers power reduction: A two time scale approach for delay tolerant workloads[C]. in INFOCOM, 2012 Proceedings IEEE. 2012, IEEE.

[11] Fumagalli E, et al. Quality of service provision in electric power distribution systems through reliability insurance[C]. IEEE Transactions on Power Systems, 2004, 19(3): 1286–1293.

[12] Tassiulas L, Ephremides A. Stability properties of constrained queueing systems and scheduling policies for maximum throughput in multihop radio networks[C]. IEEE Transactions on Automatic Control, 1992, 37(12): 1936–1948.

[13] Neely M J, Modiano E, Rohrs C E. Dynamic power allocation and routing for time-varying wireless networks [C]. IEEE Journal on Selected Areas in Communications, 2005, 23(1): 89–103.

[14] Slotine J J E, Li W. Applied nonlinear control[J]. Prentice hall englewood cliffs, NJ:199,1991.

[15] Park G, et al. Energy harvesting for structural health monitoring sensor networks[J]. Journal of Infrastructure Systems, 2008, 14(1): 64–79.

[16] Warneke B, Atwood B, Pister K S. Smart dust mote forerunners. in Micro Electro Mechanical Systems, 2001. MEMS 2001[C]. The 14th IEEE International Conference. 2001, IEEE.

[17] Powell W B. Approximate Dynamic Programming: Solving the Curses of Dimensionality[M]. Wiley, 2009.

[18] Neely M J. Stochastic network optimization with application to communication and queueing systems[J]. Synthesis Lectures on Communication Networks, 2010, 3(1): 1–211.

[19] Neely M J. Stock market trading via stochastic network optimization[C]. Decision and Control (CDC), 2010 49th IEEE Conference on. 2010, IEEE.

[20] Peterson S B, Whitacre J, Apt J. The economics of using plug-in hybrid electric vehicle battery packs for grid storage [J]. Journal of Power Sources, 2010, 195(8): 2377–2384.

[21] Ela E, Kirby B, ERCOT event on February 26, 2008: lessons learned. National Renewable Energy Lab. (NREL), Golden, CO (United States), 2008.

[22] Barker S, et al. Smart *: An open data set and tools for enabling research in sustainable homes. SustKDD, August, 2012, 111(112): 108.

Optimization of Microwave Extraction Process for Pigment from Walnut Husk by Using Response Surface Methodology

Gulisitan Yigemu[1], Reheman Aila[2], Yiping Qiu[1]*

[1]*College of Textile, Donghua University, Shanghai 201620, China*

[2]*College of Food Science, Xinjiang Agriculture University, Urumqi 830052, China*

* Corresponding author's email：ypqiu@ dhu. edu. cn

Abstract：The article is about optimization of microwave extraction process and dyeing effect for fresh Walnut pigment. Based on single factor experiments, it was selected of fresh walnut peel extraction and by use of response surface methodology the extraction process parameters were optimized. By establishing mathematical model of solid-liquid ratio, extraction time and microwave frequency it can be found the optimum process conditions for extraction of walnut peel pigment. That was the solid-liquid ratio：1 : 60；Microwave time：30s；Extraction times：2. In a result, under this condition, colour difference b was 12.5198.

Keywords：Walnut outer peel；Natural pigment；Microwave-assisted extraction；Response surface methodology

1 Introduction

Walnut husk covers the wrinkly walnut shell and is a typical agriculture waste in the process of walnuts. The worldwide production of walnuts in shell was 3. 46 million ton, among which China alone contributes 46% , in 2014 (Production quantities of Walnuts, with shell by country, Food and Agriculture Organization of United Nations, Statistics Division, February 13, 2017). Therefore, the annual production of walnut busk should be in millions of tons worldwide. Extracting useful substances from waste walnut husk not only makes full use of the walnut fruits but also solves the problem of potential environmental pollution[1-2]. Of all plants, only the husk juice, after the oxidation of yellow-green peel juice could be used as a black plant based dye. In ancient times it was recorded that walnut husk dye was used to dye fibers and fabrics. Using walnut husk dye to dye hair may not damage the hair[3]. Extracting the pigment from walnut is a time-consuming, energy-consuming, solvent consumption work. The traditional extraction method has many disadvantages such as low extraction efficiency, long cycle extraction, and solvent

and energy consumption[4]. With the development of science and technology, a number of new technologies such as supercritical fluid extraction in the extraction of natural products began to be worked out[5]. Because of the complex equipment, higher operating costs, it is restricted in the application. Therefore microwave extraction overcomes the above-described method disadvantages[6-10].

In order to make the development and utilization of resources from Walnutpeel, Walnut pigment was extracted with water as the extraction agent by the use of microwave-assisted extraction method to dye wool that is close to human hair. The response surface test was based on single factor experiment and sensory analysis test and it was established to define the optimum conditions to extract dye from walnut green husk.

2 Experiments

2.1 Materials and equipment

2.1.1 Raw materials

Leatheroid walnut greenpeel in Hotan, Xinjiang

Unskimmed wool.

2.1.2　Reagent

Distilled water

Antioxidants: 1g ascorbic acid dissolved in a little water and dilute to 100mL in brown dropper

2.1.3　Equipment

PL203 Electronics Mettler Tory instrument Co., Ltd.;

HH-54 Digital temperature water bath Jintan Medical Instrument Factory;

WD900B Galanz microwave ovens, Shunde City Electric Industrial Co., Ltd.;

SHZ-D (Ⅲ) Circulating water pump The YUHUA instrument in Henan Province;

DZKW-D-2 electric heated water bath Guangming Medical Instrument Factory in Beijing;

EYELA rotary evaporator Airo Instrument Co., Ltd., Shanghai;

TGL-10C centrifuge Shanghai Anting Scientific Instrument Factory;

Hunter Lab D-25 colorimeter US Hunter Lab company.

2.2　Test method[11-15]

2.2.1　Technological process

Fresh walnut outer peel→ crush→ water soak→ microwave-assisted extract → extracted solution filtration → evaporation and concentration→ dye in water bath

2.2.2　Operation point

2.2.2.1　Pre-treatment

Crush the fresh walnut outer peel with mortar.

2.2.2.2　Dissolve and soak

Weigh 5 parts of crushed walnut peel; Each part is of same weight; Put it in triangular flask of 250mL; The solid to liquid ratio (g/mL) is 1 : 10, 1 : 25, 1 : 40, 1 : 55, 1 : 70; Soak in water temperature of 60℃ for 5min; Extract 25 s under 20% microwave power; Extract liquid with vacuum filtration and concentrate liquid by rotary evaporation for about 30min; Analyze color difference after soaking in a water bath for 30min.

2.2.2.3　Soak and extraction with water bath

A. Time for water bath

Weigh 5 parts of crushed walnut peel, each part is of same weight; Put it in triangular flask of 250mL; The solid to liquid ratio (g/mL) is 1 : 10, 1 : 25, 1 : 40, 1 : 55, 1 : 70; Under 60℃ water bath each part is soaked 5min, 20min, 35min, 50min, 65min; Extract

25s under 20% microwave power; Extract liquid with vacuum filtration and concentrate liquid by rotary evaporation for about 30min; Analyze color difference and do sensory test after soaking in wool water bath for 30min.

B. Temperature for water bath

Weigh 5 parts of crushed walnut peel; Each part is of same weight; Put it in triangular flask of 250mL; The solid to liquid ratio (g/mL) is 1 : 55, and soak for 5min under 0℃, 20℃, 40℃, 60℃, 80℃; Extract 25 s under 20% microwave power; Extract liquid with vacuum filtration and concentrate liquid by rotary evaporation for about 30min; Analyze color difference and do sensory test after soaking in wool water bath for 30min.

2.2.2.4　Micro-assisted extract

A. Microwave extract time

Weigh 5 parts of crushed walnut peel; Each part is of same weight; Put it in triangular flask of 250mL. The solid to liquid ratio (g/mL) is 1 : 55, and soak for 5min under 60℃; Extract 10s, 25s, 40s, 55s, 70s under 20% microwave power; Extract liquid with vacuum filtration and concentrate liquid by rotary evaporation for about 30min; Analyze color difference and do sensory test after soaking in wool water bath for 30min.

B. Microwave extract heat power

Weigh 5 parts of crushed walnut peel; Each part is of same weight; Put it in triangular flask of 250mL; The liquid to solid ratio (g/mL) is 1 : 55, and soak for 5min under 60℃, Extract 25s under 20%, 40%, 60%, 80% microwave; Extract liquid with vacuum filtration and concentrate liquid by rotary evaporation for about 30min; Analyze color difference and do sensory test after soaking in wool water bath for 30min.

2.2.2.5　Response surface methodology to optimize the extraction conditions

On the base of single factor, use Design-Expert 8.0.4 software to design principles of Box-Behnken central combination experiment and choose three factors which have a significant impact on the Walnut pigment extraction: solid-liquid ratio X_1, microwave time X_2, extraction times X_3, design 3 factors and then design 3 levels of 3 factors to do response surface experiments, each factor and level is shown in Tab.1, the center has three repeats.

Tab. 1 Factors and levels of the experiment

Level	Facto		
	Solid-liquid ratio X_1	Microwave time X_2 (s)	Extraction times X_3
-1	1:50	30	3
0	1:55	25	2
1	1:60	20	1

2.3 Measurement method

2.3.1 Precipitate measurement method

Choose 3 levels for each sample of pigment after water bath, put proper amount of them into empty centrifuge tube that is weighed as m_1 and then weigh the total mass as m_2; centrifuge them in centrifugal machine of 4000 turn/min for 15min and then weigh mass as m_3, calculate precipitation by the formula as A. After concentrated by distillation measure the amount of precipitation B in the same way.

Precipitation amount:

$$A = \frac{(m_3 - m_1)}{(m_2 - m_1)} \qquad B = \frac{(m_3 - m_1)}{(m_2 - m_1)}$$

Precipitation amount $C = B/A$.

In the formula: m_1 is centrifuge tube (g);

m_2 is centrifuge tube and extracted solution (g);

m_3 is centrifuge tube and precipitation (g).

2.3.2 Color difference analysis method

Measure walnut pigment reflected color and color difference, measure Hunter system Lab and Hunter Lab whiteness, yellowness, ΔL + represents whiter, ΔL− represents blacker, Δb + represents yellower, Δb− represents bluer. Pay attention to covering sample plates during the process of measuring and no light leaking. Measure dyed wool volume: length 5cm, width 5cm, height 3cm.

2.3.3 Sensory analysis and evaluation

Make a color evaluation table, divide three groups of people: under 25 years old as a group, between the age of 25−55 as a group and above 55 years old as a group. Based on age's division, divide them as gender of men and women. The amount of each group is 10 people. According to the degree of color, the degree of sensory pleasure, smell, durability, uniformity, each factor is marked as full marks as 10 and tested dyed wool samples were evaluated and analyzed by health people randomly in public places. The result is converted hundred marks and data is analyzed by histogram (Tab. 2).

Tab. 2 Sensory evaluation table

No.	Age group	Gentle	Number	Degree of yellow	Degree of black	Degree of joviality	Odor	Durability	Uniformity
1	Under 25 years old	Male	10	(Each item is scored by 10 points as full marks)					
2		Female	10						
3	25−55 years old	Male	10						
4		Female	10						
5	Above 5 years old	Male	10						
6		Female	10						

3 Results and Discussion

3.1 Single factor test analysis[16]

3.1.1 Effect of solid-liquid ratio on the dyeing degree of Walnut pigment

It can be found out that when the solid-liquid ratio is 1:55, dyeing degree had higher level and then although with the increase of solid-liquid ratio dyeing degree of walnut peel pigment did not increase much and precipitation amount was in high level, which indicated that dissolved out pigment particles were enough and easy to dye. Also people preferred this ratio when they did sensory analysis. As a result, the best solid to liquid ratio was 1:55.

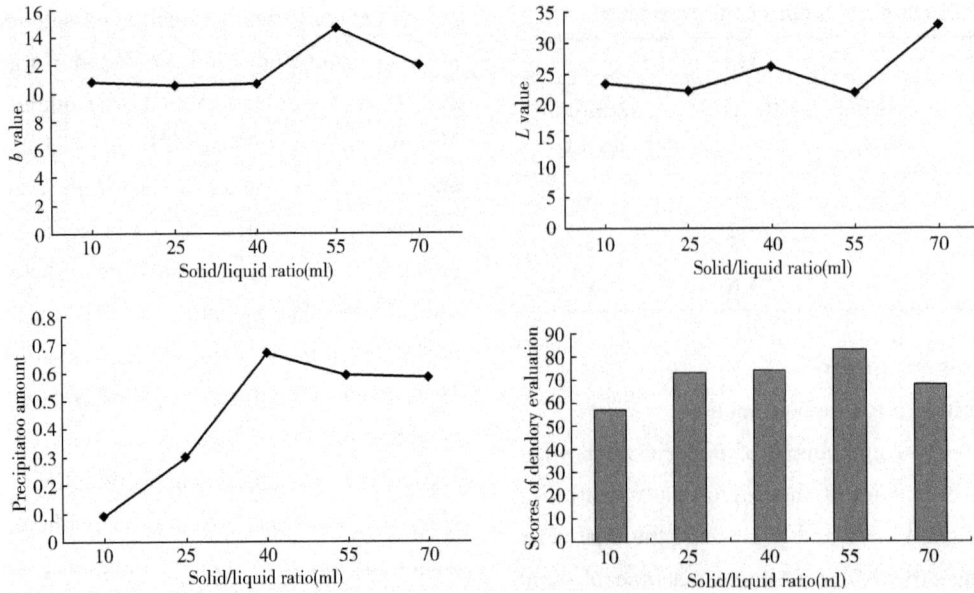

Fig. 1　Effect of solid/liquid ratio on dyeing degree by walnut peel pigment

3.1.2　Effect of extraction time on dyeing degree by walnut peel pigment

A sit can be seen from Fig. 2, in the range of 10 -70s, Walnut pigment extraction efficiency increased with the increase of irradiation time, but extraction efficiency declined with irradiation time extending. This may be-cause that by prolonged radiation walnut pigment oxida-tion rate was accelerated and the amount of precipitation was in the high level. However, the groups of sensory evaluation were tended to 55s. Hence according to the comprehensive analysis, optimum extraction time was 25s.

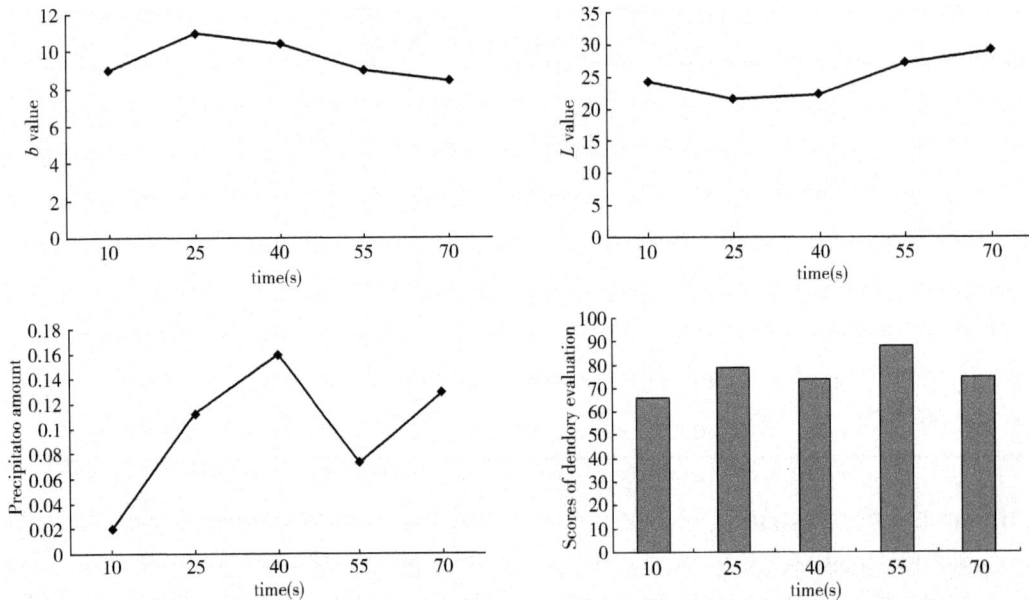

Fig. 2　Effect of extraction time on dyeing degree by walnut peel pigment

3.1.3　Effect of microwave power on dyeing degree by walnut peel pigment

It can be found out that when power was more than 20%, the dyeing degree didn't improve obviously and also precipitation amount declined with increase of mi-crowave power which was not good for dyeing. And groups' sensory evaluation declined too. Therefore the best microwave power was 20%. Overall, its effect was relatively low.

3.1.4 Effect of water bath temperature on dyeing degree by walnut peel pigment

Asit can be seen from Fig. 4, between 0–60℃ dyeing degree increased with temperature increasing, however the degree declined when the temperature was more than 60℃. Also the trend in the amount of precipitation maintained a state of equilibrium at 60℃, which had little influence on the dyeing. The sensory evaluation was almost the same. And in general the effect was not so much. Therefore, the best water bath temperature was selected as 60℃.

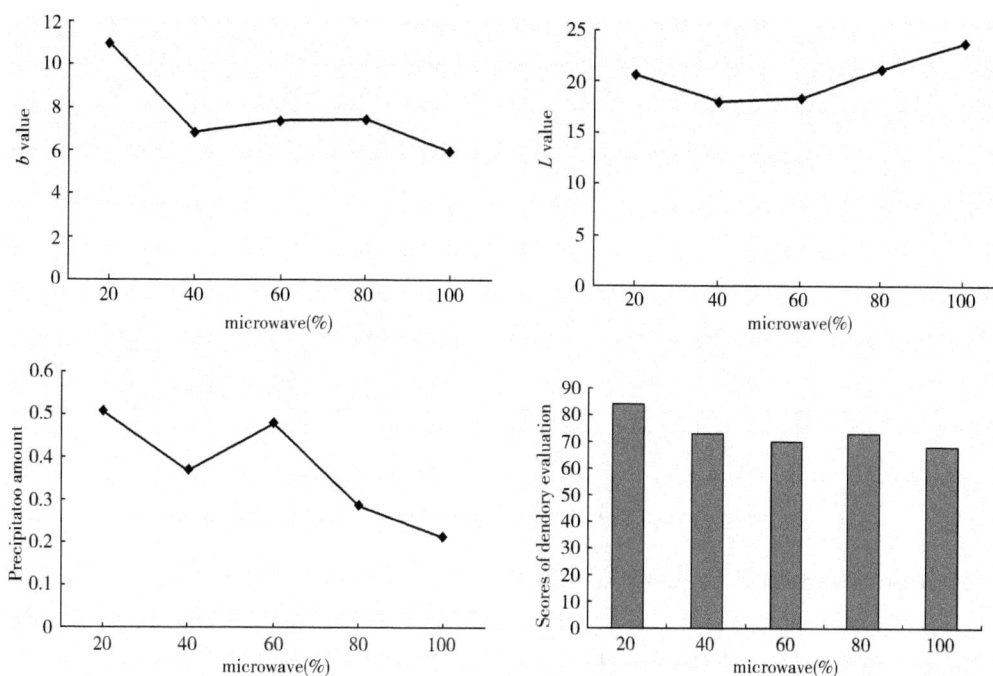

Fig. 3　Effect of microwave power on dyeing degree by walnut peel pigment

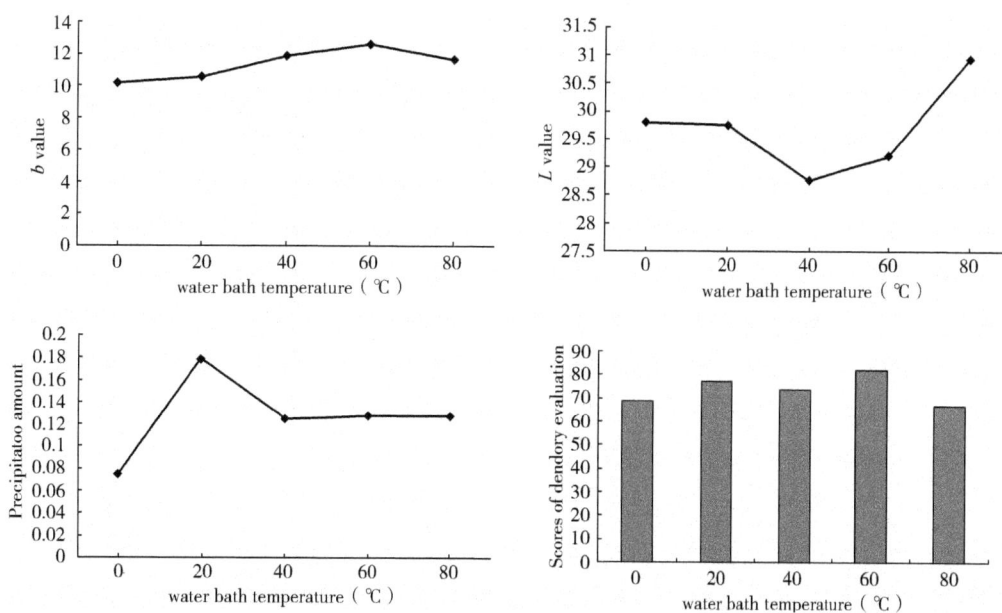

Fig. 4　Effect of water bath temperature on dyeing degree by walnut peel pigment

3.1.5 Effect of water bath time on dyeing degree by walnut peel pigment

As it can be seen in Fig. 5, dyeing degree continued to decline as time increased and precipitation amount was in middle level after 5min. There were the highest scores of sensory evaluation for the time of 5min. And in general impact was the minimum. That indicated that the best water bath time was 5min.

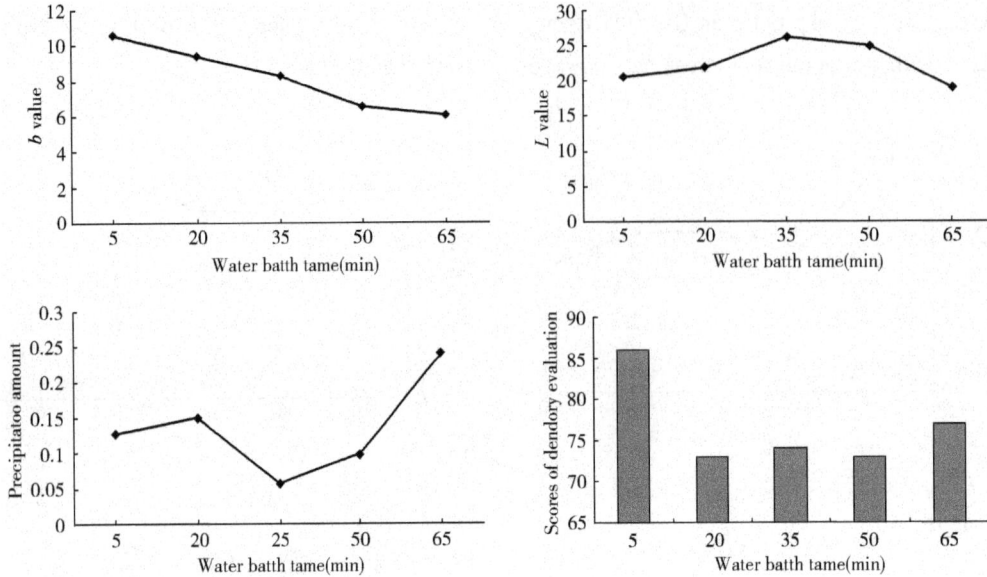

Fig. 5　Effect of water bath time on dyeing degree by walnut peel pigment

3.2　Result analysis of optimized response surface method

According to single factor range analysis it canbe figured out the significant factor and using Design-Expert 8.0.4 software Box-behnken test was launched. The result was listed in Tab. 3.

Tab. 3　Box-behnken design and results of response surface analysis

Test number	X_1 solid/liquid ratio	X_2 microwave time	X_3 extraction time	Y_1	Y_2	$Y_{average}$	$Y_{0\ prediction}$
1	0	1	1	11.4517	11.1017	11.2767	11.2900
2	1	0	-1	11.4200	11.6200	11.5900	11.5700
3	1	0	1	10.9356	10.8444	10.8900	10.7900
4	-1	1	0	10.7730	10.8470	10.8100	10.8200
5	-1	0	1	11.2369	10.5897	10.9133	10.9200
6	0	-1	-1	11.5222	11.5312	11.5267	11.5600
7	-1	0	-1	11.5140	11.0326	11.2733	11.2600
8	0	0	0	12.5780	12.2886	12.4333	12.4200
9	-1	-1	0	11.4460	11.5140	11.4800	11.4700
10	0	0	0	12.8864	12.9270	12.9067	12.9000
11	1	1	0	11.2947	11.5919	11.4433	11.4500
12	0	0	0	12.3272	11.7462	12.0367	12.0300
13	0	-1	1	9.8871	9.9263	9.9067	9.9000
14	0	1	-1	11.4152	11.2648	11.3400	11.3200
15	1	-1	0	10.4142	10.1192	10.2667	10.2600

3.2.1 Establishment of mathematic model

According to the experimental data from Tab. 4, response surface statistical method fit the experimental data to establish the three-factor quadratic regression mathematical equation of color difference value b to solid-liquid ratio, microwave extraction time and the extraction times:

$$Y = 12.45891 - 0.035833X_1 + 0.21125X_2 - 0.34292X_3 + 0.46167X_1X_2 - 0.085000X_1X_3 + 0.38917X_2X_3 - 0.65237X_1^2 - 0.80654X_2^2 - 0.63987X_3^2$$

Variance analysis of Regression model can be seen in Tab. 4. The regression model for the color difference b was significant, $P < 0.05$ which was significant, lack of fit $P = 0.7961 > 0.05$ which was not significant, correlation coefficient $R^2 = 0.9287$ which meant that the model fit well and the experimental error is small. To sum up, meanwhile, the first-degree X_3, quadratic terms X_1^2, X_2^2, X_3^2, and the interaction term X_1X_2 had a significant impact on a significant value. As a result, the regression equation provided an appropriate model that can be used to analyze and predict microwave extraction process conditions from fresh walnut pigment[17]. The results are shown in Tab. 4.

Tab. 4　Statistical results of regression analysis

Variation source	Square of deviance	Variance	Mean-square deviation	Value F	Value P
Model	7.56	9	0.84	7.24	0.0211 (<0.05)
Residual	0.58	5	0.12		
Lack of fit	0.20	3	0.067	0.35	0.7961
Error	0.38	2	0.19		
Sum	8.14	14			

3.2.2 Response surface interaction

3.2.2.1 Interaction between solid/liquid ratio and microwave time

Fig. 6 showed the response surface figure of X_1 (solid to liquid ratio) and X_2 (microwave time) to Y (wool b), make $X_3 = 0$, regression equation was established:

$$Y = 12.45891 - 0.035833X_1 + 0.21125X_2 + 0.46167X_1X_2 - 0.65237X_1^2 - 0.80654X_2^2$$

When X_1 was in the range of 53.85–55.9, and X_2 was in the range of 24.5–26.5, Y had extreme value. With the increase of X_1 and X_2, Y reached the maximum value and then declined whose trend was obvious. It could be easily seen in Fig. 6 that contour lines were elliptical[18], which proved that solid-liquid ratio interacted with the microwave time significantly because pigment particles were dissolved better under the proper solid-liquid ratio. Consequently it interacted with microwave to increase the destruction of walnut tissue cells and also made the pigment particles diffusion movement speed up; thereby it can make a better dyeing effect for wool.

3.2.2.2 Interaction between solid/liquid ratio and extraction times

Fig. 7 showed the response surface figure of X_1 (solid to liquid ratio) and X_3 (microwave times) to Y (wool b), make $X_2 = 0$, regression equation was established:

$$Y = 12.45891 - 0.035833X_1 - 0.34292X_3 - 0.085000X_1X_3 - 0.65237X_1^2 - 0.63987X_3^2$$

When X_1 was in the range of 53.9–55.115, and X_3 was in the range of 1 to 3, Y had extreme value. With the increase of X_1 and X_3, Y reached the maximum value and then declined, but the trend is not obvious. If extraction times did not change, the dyeing degree increased as solid/liquid ratio increase, and the increase is quite obvious. Therefore if enhance the solid/liquid ratio properly, it is benefit for pigment extraction and can shorten extraction time. As we can see from Fig. 7 obviously, contour line was round, and there was a certain interaction between solid-liquid ratio and extraction times, but not significant[18].

3.2.2.3 Interaction between microwave time and extraction times

Fig. 8 showed the response surface figure of X_2 (microwave time) and X_3 (microwave times) to Y (wool b), make $X_1 = 0$, regression equation was established:

$$Y = 12.45891 + 0.21125X_2 - 0.34292X_3 + 0.38917X_2X_3 - 0.80654X_2^2 - 0.63987X_3^2$$

When X_2 was in range of 24.8 – 25.5 and X_3 was in range of 1–3, Y had extreme value. With the increase of X_1 and X_3, Y reached the maximum value and then declined, but the trend is not obvious. It was shown that gradient was larger than solid/liquid ratio; however, the slope of surface was smaller which indicated that the interaction between microwave and extraction times was not significant.

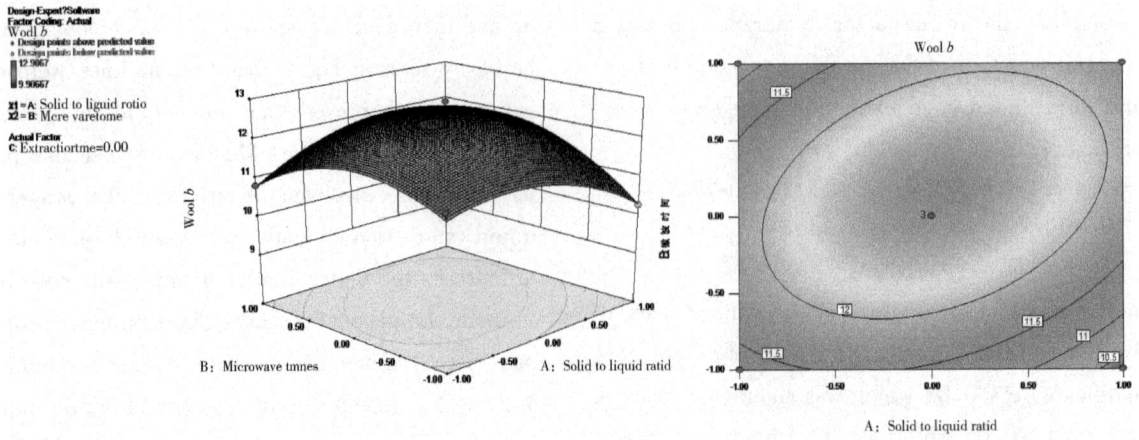

Fig. 6　Response surface and contour analysis of $Y = f(X_1, X_2)$

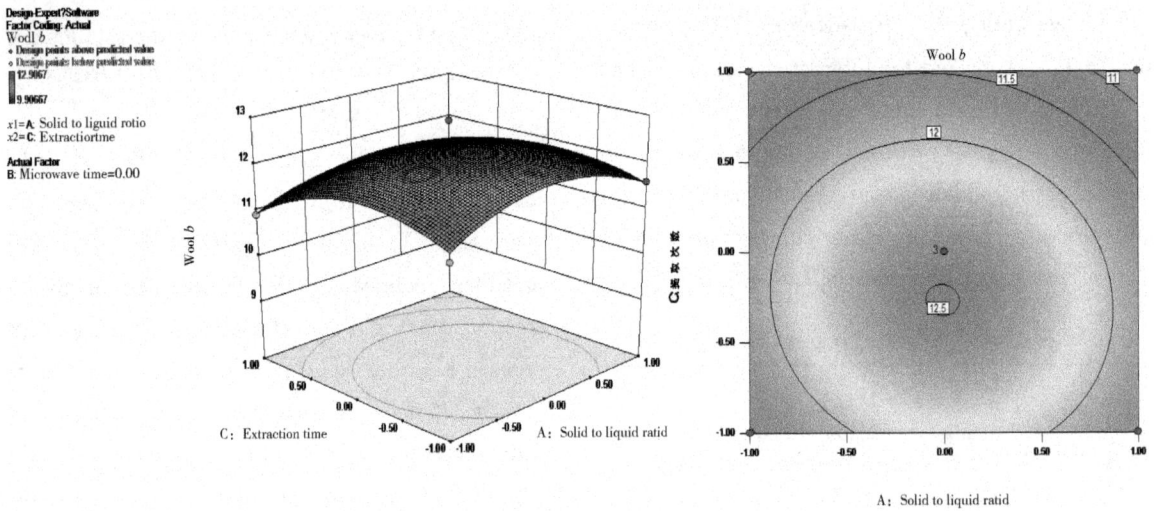

Fig. 7　Response surface and contour analysis of $Y = f(X_1, X_3)$

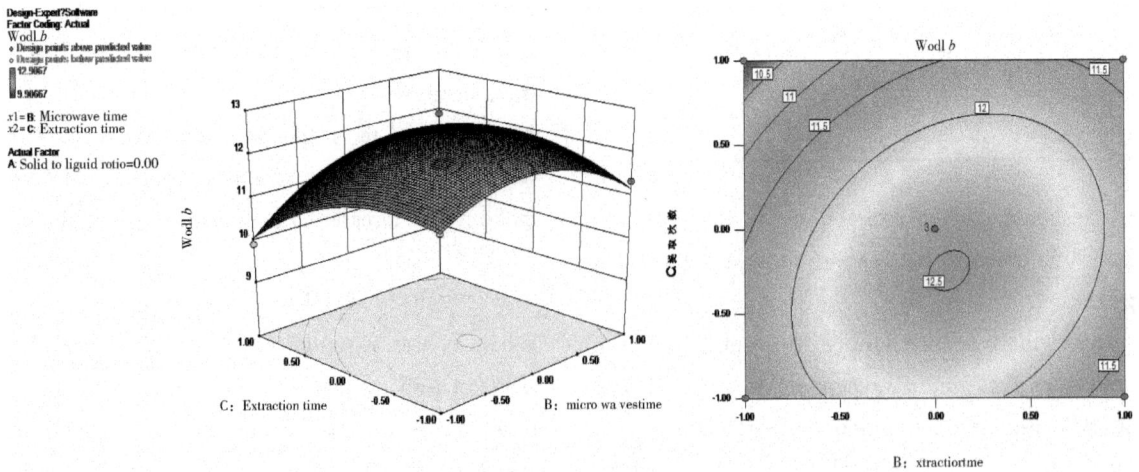

Fig. 8　Response surface and contour analysis of $Y = f(X_2, X_3)$

3.2.2.4　Interaction of solid/liquid ratio, microwave time, extraction times

Primary and secondary relationship of three factors' impact on the experimental results were as follows: solid-liquid ratio > extraction times > microwave time, and interaction between solid-liquid ratio and microwave time had a significant impact, and interaction between solid-liquid ratio and extraction times was not significant which represented relatively steep surface, but whose contour was circular. Interaction impact between extraction times and microwave was not significant, and the surface was relatively smooth, contours were round.

In order to verify the precision of model, three parallel tests were done under thebest-optimized conditions. It was found out that colour difference was respectively 12.3606, 12.6262, and 12.5226 and the average value was 12.5043. In the meanwhile, the sensory analysis was carried out. The result was 87, 95, 92 and average value was 91.3333.

Verification and predicted values were very close, which indicated that the regression equation could relatively truly reflect the influence of each selected factor. And also the established model was consistent with the actual situation, which meant that the regression model had its feasibility[19].

4　Conclusions

The public accepted the extraction method of fresh walnut outer peel through single factor experiment and dyeing effect of tan color that extracted from walnut peel by this method. In the same time, solid/liquid ratio, microwave time and extraction times were defined as important factors for extraction and dye process. With the response surface methodology optimum conditions were analyzed. With color difference b as response value, by Box-Behnken design and Design-Expert 8.0.4 software analysis the optimum process parameters were determined: solid-liquid ratio 1 : 60 microwave time 30 s, extraction times 2. As a result, in this condition, the color difference b value was 12.5198.

The natural pigment extracted from walnut outer crust has strong adhesion and is of rich resource through recycling the waste. The production process is simple and the productivity is high. Also it is of low cost, safe and nontoxic. However the test method is effected by raw materials and if crust is not crushed completely the pigment particle mass is not easy to control. Moreover, if soaked in hot water for too long, the collagen will enter pigment solution leading to turbid solution and difficult vacuum filtering and the dyeing effect will be impacted. If there are methods that can crush crust evenly and control temperature properly, the pigment as a hair dye will have a good development and application value.

In this experiment, with fresh green husk as raw material, hot distilled water as the extraction agent, it has better extraction effect compared to the traditional organic solvent, and also distilled water as the extraction agent can meet health requirements for printing, dyeing or food colorants. Thus, hot pure water is chosen as the extraction agent. Penetration of microwave-assisted extraction for walnut peel is much stronger and it can penetrate into raw materials immediately and hot them evenly which is easy to control. Therefore microwave-assisted distilled water will be more convenient to produce. But due to the complex equipment, expensive operating cost and other defects, the method is mostly for laboratory research. Therefore it needs to be further studied.

References

[1] Fang L J, Liu Q R, Chen X L, et al. Walnut cuticle brown pigment stability test by different dry methods[J]. Yan'an University: Natural Science Edition, 2003, 22 (1): 52-55.

[2] Fang L J, Chen X L, High G Z, et al. Research on development and utilization of walnut epicarp (I)[J]. Chinese Agricultural Science Bulletin, 2004, 20 (2): 52-55.

[3] Zhao Y, Liu S P, Xia L Z. Chemical composition and utilization of Walnut[J]. Processing of agricultural products, 2008, 11: 66-68.

[4] Xue X L, Jiang C H. New method of a natural product extraction method from the chemical composition-microwave extraction method[J]. North China University of Technology, 2006, 7 (3): 37-39.

[5] Shao Wei, Tang Ming, Xiong Ze. Supercritical CO_2 extraction of monascus pigment[J]. China Brewing, 2005, (7): 22-24.

[6] Sporring S, Bowadt S, Svensmark B, et al. Comprehensive

comparison of classic Soxhlet extraction with Sovtec extraction, ultrasonication extraction, supercritical fluid extraction, microwave assisted extraction and accelerated solvent extraction for the determination of polychlorinated biphenyls in soil [J]. J Chromatogr A, 2005, 1090 (122): 1291.

[7] Barbarum L, Elton W, Wang Y J. Comparative study about wolfberry flavonoids extraction methods[J]. Ningxia University: Natural Science Edition, 2007, 28 (1): 602-621.

[8] Elton W, Cai Y J, Rao G F. Research of comparison of flavonoids extraction method [J]. Accumulator Progress in Modern Biomedicine, 2008, 8 (6): 10782-10811.

[9] Zhang F, Chen B, Xiao S, et al. Optimization and comparison of different extraction techniques for sanguinarine and chelerythrine in fruits of Macleay a cordata (Willd) R1 Br. [J]. Separ Puri f Technol, 2005, 42 (3): 2832-2901.

[10] Fulzele D P, Satdive R K. Comparison of techniques for the extraction of the anticancer drug camptothecin from Nothapodytes foetida [J]. J Chromatogr A, 2005, 1063 (122): 92-131.

[11] Xu Z H, Tan J H, Zhang X, et al. Study on the extraction of natural food coloring matter from walnut outer peel and its physical-chemical properties[J]. Journal of Sichuan Normal University, 2006, 29(4): 488-490.

[12] Zhang S H. Food analysis experiments [M]. Beijing: Chemical Industry Press, 2006: 34.

[13] Liu C H. Food analysis experiments[M]. Beijing: Chemical Industry Press, 2006: 93.

[14] Li Guihua. Fuel oil testing and analysis [M]. Beijing: Chemical Industry Press, 2006: 111-115.

[15] Xu Mudan, Mao Gennian. Food safety detection and analysis[M]. Beijing: Chemical Industry Press, 2003: 196.

[16] Lv jun fang, Zhang Meili, Liu Qirui, et al. Walnut cuticle brown pigment extraction and characterization testing [J]. Chemical Research and Application, 2001, 13 (4): 388-390.

[17] Bai Yunfeng, Yuan Hui, Xue Shengxia. Central composite design and response surface analysis and optimization of naringin in citrus peel extraction process [J]. Chinese Medicine, 2010, 29 (4): 372-375.

[18] Zhang Kai, Huang Guolin, Huang Xiaolan, et al. Response surface optimization study on lemon peel pectin extraction[J]. Fine Chemicals, 2010, (27) 1: 52-56.

[19] Yu Hao, Ruan Meijuan, Zhao Long, et al. Research of response surface method on extraction conditions optimization from lotus leaf ultrasound[J]. Food Research and Development, 2010, 31 (1): 55-60.

Separation Model of Dual-Beard Cotton Sample for Short Fiber Contents Measurement

Jingye Jin[1]* , Fumei Wang[2], Bugao Xu[3], Yiping Qiu[1,2]

[1] *College of Textiles and Apparel, Quanzhou Normal University, Quanzhou, Fujian 362000, China*

[2] *College of Textiles, Donghua University, Shanghai 201620, China*

[3] *Department of Merchandising and Digital Retailing, University of North Texas, Denton, TX, U. S.*

* *Corresponding author's email*: jin_jingye@ 163. com

Abstract: Dual-beard cotton sample can be made via clamping a cotton sliver and combing it in the two opposite ends, which can be wholly scanned for cotton fiber length measurement and provide more detailed length information, compared with HVI® beard. This paper introduced a novel modelon iteratively separating fibers shorter than a certain threshold from the dual-beard sample. Based on this model, the formulae of the weight-based short fiber content (SFC) in cotton bale were deduced out. Eight cotton samples were tested, and the bias of results between these SFC formulae and manual single fiber measurements was proved statistically indistinctive. In contrast to costly dedicated devices, dual-beard method with these formulae can be capable of providing accurate measurements of short fiber content in an economical way.

Keywords: Short fiber content; Cotton; Dual-beard sample; Image measurement

1 Introduction

Short fibers are acknowledged as a negative role in yarns manufacture and cost reduction, leading to obvious increases of breakage rates, yarn unevenness and yarn hairiness. Thus, measuring and controlling short fiber contents in raw cotton continues to be a big concern for the textile manufacturing industry[1-3].

Short fiber content (SFC) is a common parameter for quantifying the weight-based or number-based proportion of fibers shorter than a certain threshold; that is 12.7mm (0.5 inch) in the USA and 16mm in China. Methods for testing SFC are usually applied to measure other length parameters simultaneously. In the High Volume Instrument® (HVI®), an efficient device for evaluating the integrated quality of raw cotton, fibers are randomly grabbed by a row of needles and combed to form a tapered beard which can be scanned by a light slit to generate a fibrogram. Parameters are extracted from the fibrogram except SFC, which is because the fiber segments nearby the needles are too tangled to be

meaningfully measured. Instead, HVI® provides Short Fiber Index (SFI) which is calculated by a prediction algorithm on the basis of some other available HVI parameters[4-5]. The Advanced Fiber Information System® (AFIS®) is another widely employed instrument which separates cotton sliver into individual fibers and measures them by a photoelectric sensor, fiber by fiber. AFIS® outputs length histogram and parameters on the basis of a mass of directly measured data, which makes it becoming a prevalent SFC measuring instrument. However, many studies have testified that possible fiber breakages in the opening process may bring a bias into the measurement[2,6]. It is obvious that, the shorter an individual fiber is, the more difficult it can be easily felicitously controlled, arranged and identified. Hence, the accurate and practical determination of SFC remains a challenge to be beaten.

As a new type of sample for length determination, dual-beard has two tapered ends in the opposite directions, which is made via clamping a cotton sliver and combing it in the two opposite ends. The dual-beard sample can be scanned to generate a transmission grayscale image. As the gray values of pixels reflect the intensity of transmission light, the image can be transformed into the dual-beard's relative fiber number (R. F. N.) curve, showing the change of fiber numbers from dual-beard's one end to the other[7-8].

Dual-beard has an inherent potential for accurately testing short fibers because it effectively eliminates the fiber entanglements that severely harm the SFC measurement. In this paper, we present a novel theory model on how to separate short fibers from dual-beard sample and how to calculate their contents based on the R. F. N. curve.

2　Theoretical Analysis

2.1　Separating short fibers from dual-beard

The separating operations demonstrated as follow are fictitious, however, which are extremely critical for explaining the principle of SFC formulae.

The first step of operation is shown by Fig. 1 (a), where α is the length threshold of short fibers, L represents the protruding distance of fibers. Imaginarily,

clamping the original dual-beard at $L = \frac{1}{2}\alpha$, moving the hold fibers (Beard 1) away without influencing others, then clamping the remainder dual-beard at $L = -\frac{1}{2}\alpha$, moving the hold fibers (Beard 2) again. Now the fibers left (Beard 3) are definitely shorter than α, however, Beards 1 and 2 still include short fibers and need further separations.

In the second step, as shown in Fig. 1 (b) and (c), imaginarily clamping Beard 1 at $L = \frac{3}{4}\alpha$ and $L = -\frac{1}{4}\alpha$ successively, moving away the clamped fibers to generate Beards 4 and 5 with Beard 6 left. Beard 2 is successively clamped at $L = \frac{1}{4}\alpha$ and $L = -\frac{3}{4}\alpha$, divided into three parts including one completely consisting of short fibers (Beard 9). Fibers in Beards 4, 5, 7 and 8 are all longer than $\frac{3}{4}\alpha$, so there is still a need for separating the fibers shorter than α. Note that the distance between the two virtual clamping lines when dividing beards should be α, to ensure the remainder fibers are all short fibers.

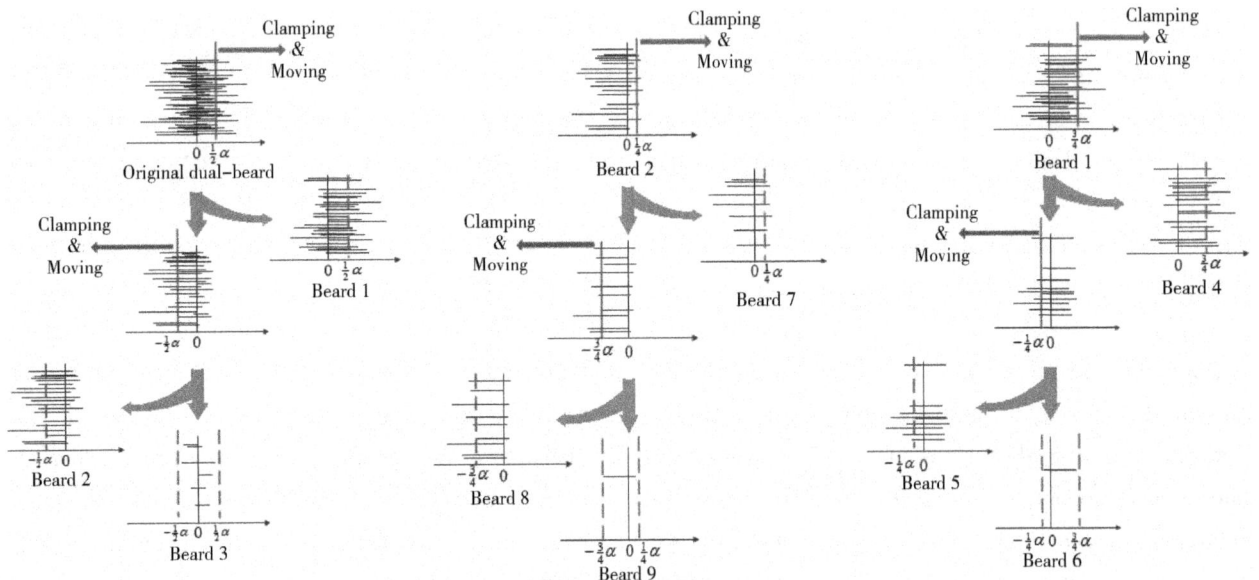

Fig. 1　Diagram of separating short fibers

Further, Beards 4, 5, 7 and 8 are divided into more sub-beards. As the iterative separation process continues, the aggregate number of fibers in beards such as

Beards 3, 6, 9, ⋯, which totally consist of short fibers, gets closer and closer to the real number of short fibers in the original dual-beard, until the difference can be ignored. According to previous literatures, the weight-based SFC of raw cotton equals the number-based SFC of its dual-beard sample[7-8]. In this paper, we obtain the weight-based SFC of raw cotton (expressed as SFW) by calculating the number-based SFC of dual-beard (expressed as SFN) which is the summation of relative fiber numbers of Beards 3, 6, 9 ⋯

2.2 Deducing SFC calculation formulae

It's obvious that the number of fibers in Beard 3 can be calculated via subtracting the fiber number of Beards 1 and 2 from that of the original dual-beard. Fig. 2 shows the R. F. N. curves corresponding to the first separation step. The R. F. N. of the original dual-beard is $F(0)$, and that of Beard 1 (red curve) is $F(\frac{1}{2}\alpha)$. The R. F. N. of Beard 2 is $F(-\frac{1}{2}\alpha)-F_1(-\frac{1}{2}\alpha)$, where $F_1(-\frac{1}{2}\alpha)$ is the R. F. N. of fibers extending beyond both $L = \frac{1}{2}\alpha$ and $L = -\frac{1}{2}\alpha$, which will be clamped at $L = \frac{1}{2}\alpha$ to constitute Beard 1 and can't be hold into Beard 2. Fibers extending beyond both $L = \frac{1}{2}\alpha$ and $L = -\frac{1}{2}\alpha$ are represented by the shadow area in Fig. 2.

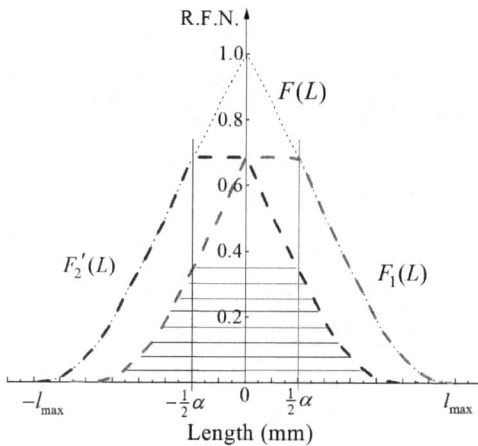

Fig. 2   R. F. N. curves in separating the original dual-beard

Plotted by dash red curvein Fig. 2, the R. F. N. function of Beard 1 can be written as:

$$F_1(L) = \begin{cases} F(L-\frac{1}{2}\alpha) & L \in [-l_{max}+\frac{1}{2}\alpha,0) \\ F(\frac{1}{2}\alpha) & L \in [0,\frac{1}{2}\alpha] \\ F(L & L \in (\frac{1}{2}\alpha,l_{max}] \end{cases} \quad (1)$$

Combined with $F(-L) = F(L)$ and Equation(1), the relative number of fibers in Beard 3 can be figured out by

$$\begin{aligned} SFN_3 &= F(0)-F(\frac{1}{2}\alpha)-[F(-\frac{1}{2}\alpha)-F_1(-\frac{1}{2}\alpha)] \\ &= F(0)-2F(\frac{1}{2}\alpha)+F(\alpha) \end{aligned} \quad (2)$$

Note that the difference between Beards 1 and 2 only involves the fibers extending beyond $L = \frac{1}{2}\alpha$ and $L = -\frac{1}{2}\alpha$ which are definitely longer than α, in other words, they have the same amount of short fibers, i. e. $SFN_1 = SFN_2$. Thus, the calculation formula of SFN could be

$$SFN = SFN_1 + SFN_2 + SFN_3 = 2SFN_1 + SFN_3 \quad (3)$$

Now the focus turns to how to calculate SFN_1. The calculation of SFN_1 is analogous to the afore mentioned analysis on SFN. The corresponding R. F. N. curves are plotted in Fig. 3, and equations can be deduced as

$$\begin{aligned} SFN_1 &= SFN_4 + SFN_5 + SFN_6 \\ &= 2SFN_4 + SFN_6 \end{aligned} \quad (4)$$

$$\begin{aligned} SFN_6 &= F_1(\frac{1}{2}\alpha)-F_4(\frac{3}{4}\alpha)-[F_1(-\frac{1}{4}\alpha)-F_4(-\frac{1}{4}\alpha)] \\ &= F(\frac{1}{2}\alpha)-2F(\frac{3}{4}\alpha)+F(\alpha) \end{aligned}$$

$$(5)$$

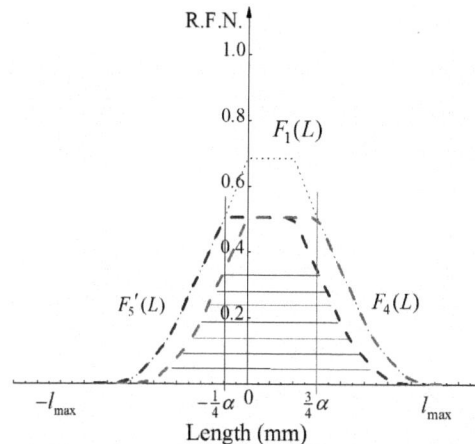

Fig. 3   R. F. N. curves in separating Beard 1

According to the iterative separation process, the relative numbers of short fibers in sub-beards have relations as Equations (6) and (7), where m is the sequence number of the separation step.

$$\left\{\begin{array}{l} SFN = 2SFN_1 + SFN_3 \\ SFN_1 = 2SFN_4 + SFN_6 \\ SFN_4 = 2SFN_{10} + SFN_{12} \\ SFN_{10} = 2SFN_{22} + SFN_{24} \\ \cdots \\ SFN_{3 \times 2m-1-2} = 2SFN_{3 \times 2m-2} + SFN_{3 \times 2m} \end{array}\right. \quad (6)$$

$$\left\{\begin{array}{l} SFN_3 = F(0) - 2F(\frac{1}{2}\alpha) + F(\alpha) \\[2mm] SFN_6 = F(\frac{1}{2}\alpha) - 2F(\frac{3}{4}\alpha) + F(\alpha) \\[2mm] SFN_{12} = F(\frac{3}{4}\alpha) - 2F(\frac{7}{8}\alpha) + F(\alpha) \\[2mm] SFN_{24} = F(\frac{7}{8}\alpha) - 2F(\frac{15}{16}\alpha) + F(\alpha) \\[2mm] \cdots \\[2mm] SFN_{3 \times 2m} = F(\frac{2^m-1}{2^m}\alpha) - 2F(\frac{2^{m+1}-1}{2^{m+1}}\alpha) + F(\alpha) \end{array}\right. \quad (7)$$

Merging Equations (6) and (7), it comes

$$SFN = F(0) + (2^{m+1}-1)F(\alpha) \\ -2^{m+1}F(\frac{2^{m+1}-1}{2^{m+1}}\alpha) + 2^{m+1}SFN_{3 \times 2m-2} \quad (8)$$

Actually the last term of Equation (8) represents the short fibers that have not been filtered out after the step of $m + 1$, which is so little when $m \to +\infty$ that it can be ignored. If m is large enough, Equation (8) can be simplified to

$$SFN = F(0) + (2^{m+1}-1)F(\alpha) - 2^{m+1}F(\frac{2^{m+1}-1}{2^{m+1}}\alpha) \quad (9)$$

In practical application, however, the factor 2^{m+1} will sharply increase when the value of m gets bigger, and the last two items of Equation (9) will become unstable because of the existence of measurement errors in R. F. N. curve. In this paper, we set $m = 4$ and transform Equation (9) into

$$SFN = F(0) + 31F(\alpha) - 32F(\frac{31}{32}\alpha) \quad (10)$$

As the R. F. N. curve of dual-beard is theoretically symmetrical, we can apply

$$SFN = F(0) + 31F(-\alpha) - 32F(-\frac{31}{32}\alpha) \quad (11)$$

to provide the other SFN estimate based on the left side data of the curve, and consider the average of Equations (10) and (11) as the final SFN, which is

$$SFN = F(0) + 15.5[F(\alpha) + F(-\alpha)] \\ -16[F(\frac{31}{32}\alpha) + F(-\frac{31}{32}\alpha)] \quad (12)$$

As mentioned above, the number proportion of short fibers in dual-beard sample is equal to the weight proportion of them in raw cotton, the weight-based short fiber content in cotton bales or semi-finished slivers (SFW) can be calculated by

$$SFW_{12.7} = F(0) + 15.5[F(12.7) + F(-12.7)] \\ -16[F(12.3) + F(-12.3)] \quad (13)$$

and

$$SFW_{16} = F(0) + 15.5[F(16) + F(-16)] \\ -16[F(15.5) + F(-15.5)] \quad (14)$$

respectively according to the American and the Chinese standard.

3　Results and Discussion

Eight types of cotton samples were tested according to the described image processing procedures, then the proportions of short fibers were calculated using Equations (13) and (14). The reference SFWs of cotton samples were also obtained by manually measuring the lengths of over 1000 single fibers per sample.

Fig. 4 and Fig. 5 display the results comparisons of $SFW_{12.7}$ and SFW_{16} by dual-beard method and single fiber method. It can be seen that spots locate closely near the 45° lines, and the correlation coefficients provided by SPSS between the results by the two methods are 0.963 and 0.992.

T-test was applied to test the significance of differences between SFW measurements by the two methods. The T-test statistics of $SFW_{12.7}$ and SFW_{16} are 0.816 and 0.166, obviously smaller than $t_{+0.05/2}(8-1) = t_{0.975}(7) = 2.3646$ (the confidence degree is 95%). Thus, the differences are deemed to be not significant, and it can be considered that these short fiber content calculating formulae based on dual-beard are capable of accurately testing the SFCs of raw cotton.

4　Conclusions

The theory on how to separate short fibers from dual-beard cotton sample and how to quantify them is the ba-

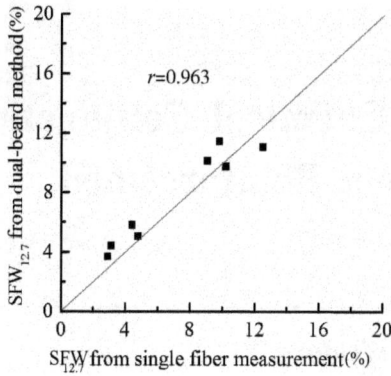

Fig. 4　Comparison of $SFW_{12.7}$ results by dual-beard and reference methods

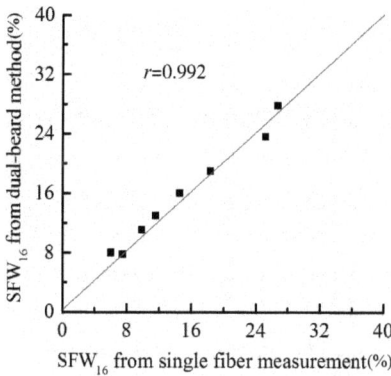

Fig. 5　Comparison of SFW_{16} results by dual-beard and reference methods

sis of the SFC calculation formulae of dual-beard method. In this study, eight cotton samples were tested to examine the trueness of SFC measurements from dual-beard method with our formulae. It was found that there was statistically no difference between the results from dual-beard formulae and single fiber measurements. As only a set of imaging device are needed, dual-beard method with the use of our SFC formulae could be a cheap approach for accurately determining the short fiber content of cotton fibers.

References

[1] Cai Y, Cui X, Rodgers J, et al. An investigation on different parameters used for characterizing short cotton fibers[J]. The Journal of the Textile Institute, 2010, 101(11): 958 -966.

[2] Cui X, Cai Y, Rodgers J, et al. The advantage of lower half mean length in characterizing short fibers[C]. Proceedings of the 2009 Beltwide Cotton Conference, 1227-1228.

[3] Thibodeaux D, Senter H, Knowlton J, et al. A comparison of methods for measuring the Short Fiber Content of cotton [J]. Journal of Cotton Science, 2008, 12: 298-305.

[4] Gibson L. HVI Short Fiber Content measurement[C]. Proceedings of the 1999 Beltwide Cotton Conference, 1406-1407.

[5] Knowlton J L. HVI short fiber measurements[C]. Proceedings of the 2001 Beltwide Cotton Conference, 1372-1374.

[6] Krifa M. Fiber length distribution in cotton processing: a finite mixture distribution model[J]. Textile Research Journal, 2006; 76(5): 426-435.

[7] Wu H, Wang F. Dual-beard sampling method for fiber length measurements[J]. Indian Journal of Fiber and Textiles, 2014, 39: 72-78.

[8] Wu M, Wang F. Optical algorithm for calculating the quantity distribution of fiber assembly[J]. Applied Optics, 2016, 55: 71.

Silk Fabric Protection Obtained via Chemical Conjugation Transglutaminase and Silk Fibroin Reinforcement

Suhua Zhao[1,2], Hongling Liu[1,2]*, Weidong Yu[1,2]

[1] *Key Laboratory of Textile Science & Technology, Ministry of Education, Shanghai 201620, China*

[2] *Department of Technical Textiles, College of Textiles, Donghua University, Shanghai 201620, China*

* *Corresponding author's email*: hlliu@ dhu. edu. cn

Abstract: Historic silk fabric is an important part of Chinese precious cultural heritage and its protection has always been a major problem. Transglutaminase (TGase) and sodium caseinate (SC), composed of protein, were used to reinforce silk fabrics. The reinforcement mechanism is that TGase catalyzes SC form macromolecular polymers by self-assembly in the pores of silk fabrics, resulting in cross-linking between silk fibers. Thereafter, silk fibroin (SF) was sprayed on the surface of silk fabric and reinforced the cross-linking structure. Compared to untreated fabrics, the weight gain rate of treated fabrics was remarkably improved. Meanwhile, the breaking stress and strain of the treated silk fabric were increased by 16.7% and 7.14%, respectively, when the SF concentration is 1%. Within the range of acceptable color difference for cultural protection, the results indicated that the method does not affect the color of the silk fabric. The treated silk fabric showed enhanced ultraviolet (UV) absorption, better heat aging resistance and UV resistance. Enzymatic reactions and film adhesion are considered to reasonable for the reinforcement of silk fabrics.

Keywords: Silk fabric; Silk fibroin; Reinforcement; Sodium casein; TGase

1 Introduction

Exquisite and luxurious silk is a treasure in the long river of chinese history. It is a witness to human civilization and a symbol of ancient culture in China. However, it is easily destroyed when silk fabric is exposed to heat or light[1-3]. Moreover, water and microorganism also accelerate aging of silk fabrics[4-5] so that it is difficult to preserve and research. Various methods applied to the protection and reinforcement of ancient silk fabrics including dipping[6], film[7-8], spraying[9] and enzymatic[10], etc.

Huang[11] proposed a new consolidation system that silk fibroin and ethylene glycol diglycidyl ether (EGDE) for the reinforcement of fragile silk fabrics. This method has been shown to improve the mechanical properties of artificially aged silk fabrics, but the cross-linking agent (EGDE) needs to be considered for its degradation products. Zhu[10] explored the condition of TGase-mediated thermal aging silk reinforcement, and the results showed that the recovery effect was significant. However, it is inconvenient to store considering that the solid powder TGase enzyme is easily inactivated in inappropriate conditions. Flanagan and Myllarinen et al.[12-13] researched cross-links between protein molecules induced by TGase catalyze SC. The enzymatic reaction applied to the reinforcement of silk fabrics needs further investigation and research. In this paper, the liquid TGase, which is conveniently stored at room temperature, was chosen to reinforce silk fabrics. Macromolecular biopolymers were generated in the crosslinked state between silk fibers by infiltrating the TGase and SC. SF solution were sprayed on the surface of fabrics treated with TGase and SC forming a film by the physical combination to protect cross-linking structure. Mechanical properties, color difference and UV absorbance of treated fabrics were researched. In addition, heat and UV aging properties of treated fabrics were demonstrated. This method, which is harmless to silk fabrics, is considered to provide a reference for the reinforcement of historic silk fabrics and has potential applications for the protection of historical silk.

2 Experiments

2.1 Materials

Silk fabric (130g/m²) was purchased from Hangzhou Mengjin Silk Co., Ltd. (Hangzhou, China). Silkworm cocoon was obtained from a Sericulture farmhouse. TGase (120 units/mL) was kindly supplied by Shanghai Qingrui Food Technology Co., Ltd. (Shanghai, China). Sodium caseinate was purchased from Luancheng County Farming Trading Co., Ltd. (Shangqiu, China). PBS phosphate buffer was provided by Rui Chu Biological Technology Co., Ltd. (Shanghai, China).

2.2 Fabric treatment

Silk worm cocoon was dissolved in 9.3 M LiBr solutions at 60℃ with a bath ratio of 1:6 for 4h. After dissolved completely, the solution was filled in a dialysis bag (molecular weight 3500) immersed in deionized water (replace every 4h) for 3 days. The extracted silk fibroin solution was obtained.

Silk fabrics were immersed in PBS buffer solution containing 5% TGase and 2% SC with a bath ratio of 1:25 at a water bath of 50℃ for 2 h. The fabric was then placed in deionized water (1:25) for 10min to remove raffinate, which called reinforcement sample and recorded as 0. After 10min at room temperature, the reinforcement sample was evenly sprayed with the SF solution at 0.5%, 1.0%, 1.5%, 2.0% on the silk surface at a distance of 20cm from the silk, respectively, which recorded as 0.5%, 1.0%, 1.5%, 2.0%, respectively. All specimens were conditioned at 20℃ and 65% relatively humidity for 2 days.

2.3 Thermal and UV aging of the treated fabrics

The treated silk fabrics were exposed to 125℃ heating for 24h in an oven and 365 nm UV irradiating for 24h in an Ultraviolet aging box.

2.4 Measurement of the treated fabrics

The mechanical properties of treated silk fabrics (100mm × 30mm) was measured by the electronic fabric strength tester (HD026N +, Nantong Hongda Experimental Instrument Co., Ltd., China) with 50mm of gauge length and 100mm/min of stretching speed at 20℃ and 65% RH.

Bending length of treated silk fabrics (100mm × 25mm) was tested using an electronic stiffness tester (LLY-01, Laizhou Electronic Instrument Co., Ltd., China) with 4mm/s of platen pushing speed and 41.5° of test angle at 20℃ and 65% RH. Fabric stiffness is calculated according to equation.

$$G = m \times C^3 \times 10^{-3} \tag{1}$$

In the formula, G is the bending stiffness per unit width, mN·cm; m is the mass per unit area, g/m²; C is the average bending length, cm.

Color differences caused by reinforcing material were characterized using a computer color measurement colorimeter (Datacolor 650, Datacolor, USA). The average value was measured four times with an accuracy of 0.1. The calculation formula of total color difference as equation.

$$\Delta E^* = \sqrt{(\Delta L^*)^2 + (\Delta a^*)^2 + (\Delta b^*)^2} \tag{2}$$

Where L^* indicates bight and dark ($+\Delta L^*$, bright; $-\Delta L^*$, dark); a^* indicates red and green ($+\Delta a^*$, redder; $-\Delta a^*$, Greener); b^* is yellowish blue ($+\Delta b^*$, yellower; $-\Delta b^*$, bluer).

UV absorbance of the treated silk fabric was tested by UV-Vis near-infrared spectrophotometer (U-4100, Hitachi, Japan) in the wavelength range of 200-400nm, analyzed the effect of the SF concentration to UV light absorption of treated silk fabrics.

3 Results and Discussion

3.1 Weight gain rate of treated fabrics

For the sake of characterization of the attachment of reinforced materials to the fabric, the weight of treated fabric was tested and the weight gain rate was calculated as shown in Fig. 1. The weight gain rate of TGase catalyze SC reinforced silk fabrics without SF was 4.38%, indicating that the amount of material attached to the silk fabric is considerable. After spraying SF with different concentrations on the sample surface treated by TGase and SC, the weight gain rate increases as the SF concentration increases, appeared a good linear correlation, as shown in Fig. 1.

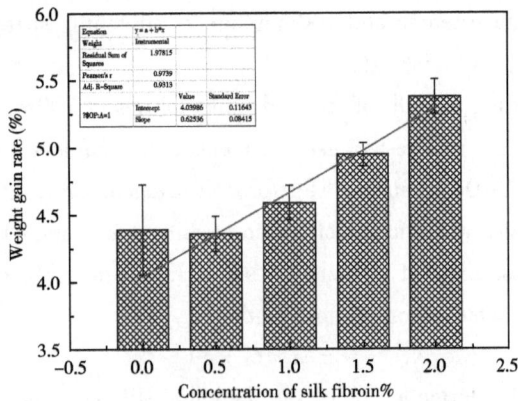

Fig. 1　Weight gain rate of the silk fabrics treated by TGase + SC and sprayed SF with different concentration

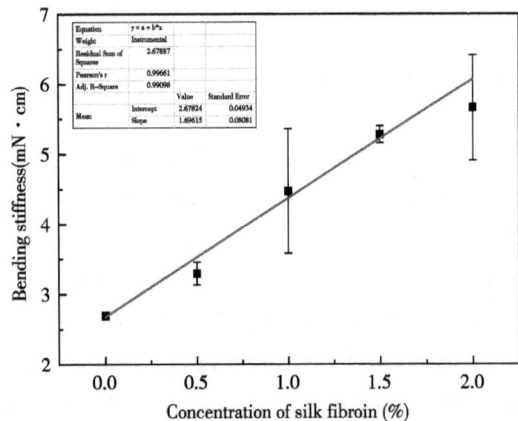

3.2　Mechanical properties of treated fabrics

In order to study the mechanical properties of the treated silk fabric, the stress-strain curves of the fabric were given, as shown as Fig. 2 (a). The breaking stress and strain of TGase catalyzed SC strength silk fabrics were significantly higher than untreated samples due to cross-linking between protein molecules. When SF was sprayed on the surface of silk fabrics treated by TGase and SC, the breaking stress and strain decreased with the increase of SF concentration while the initial modulus increased, indicating that SF was not conducive to the reinforcement of silk fabrics, as shown in Fig. 2 (b). The reason may be that the interweaving points of the warp and weft yarns were adhered by SF, resulting in being constrained during stretching process. Furthermore, when the SF concentration is 1%, the breaking stress and strain of the treated silk fabric are increased by 16.7% and 7.14%, respectively, compared to untreated fabrics according to Fig. 2 (b).

3.3　Bending stiffness of treated fabrics

The softness of silk fabrics is also another indicator of the protection of ancient silk fabrics. The untreated sample has a bending stiffness of 0.92 after measuring and calculating. Bending stiffness is used to characterize the softness of the fabric, which are opposite indicators. Bending stiffness increases with the increase of SF concentration, showing a good linear correlation, as shown in Fig. 3, indicating that SF adheres to the silk

fibers and the sliding tangential resistance of the fabric increases.

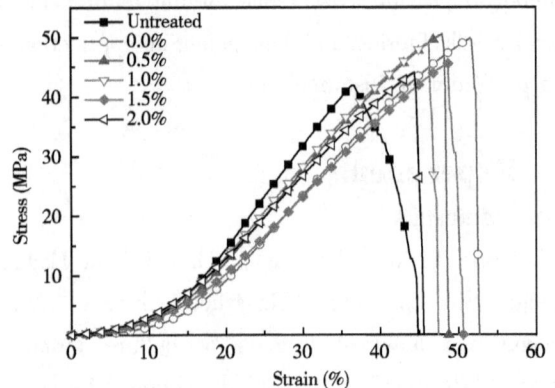

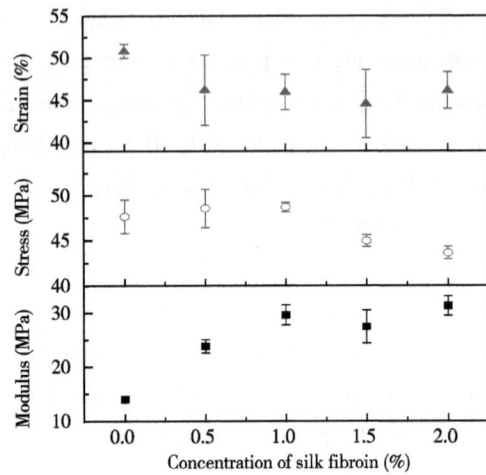

Fig. 2　(a) Stress-strain curves; (b) Mechanical properties of the silk fabrics treated by TGase + SC and sprayed SF with different concentration

Fig. 3　Stiffness of silk fabric of the silk fabrics treated by TGase + SC and sprayed SF with different concentration

largest, indicating that the change is most obvious here. It shows that the increase of SF concentration will reduce the softness of the fabric

3.4 Color difference of treated fabrics

In order to determine the color change of the silk fabric after reinforcement, we tested the color difference between the treated and the untreated samples. According to Tab. 1, total color difference (ΔE^*) increases with the increase of SF concentration. When the SF concentration is 1%, ΔE^* is 0.99, which satisfies the acceptable range of color difference in the field of conservation of cultural heritage (< 1.00). Meanwhile, there was no significant change in the color of the treated fabric photos, indicating that this method does not affect the visual effect.

Tab. 1 $L^*a^*b^*$ value of silk fabric of the silk fabrics treated by TG + SC and sprayed SF with different concentration

Concentration of SF (%)	ΔL^*	Δa^*	Δb^*	ΔE^*	Fabric pictures
Untreated fabric	0	0	0	0	
0.0	−0.17	−0.30	0.83	0.90	
0.5	−0.42	−0.30	0.70	0.86	
1.0	−0.56	−0.29	0.76	0.99	
1.5	−0.67	−0.31	0.78	1.07	
2.0	−0.73	−0.32	0.85	1.17	

3.5 UV absorbance of treated fabrics

The UV absorbance can characterize ability of fabrics to absorb UV light in a range of wavelengths. It can be seen the UV absorbance curves of treated silk fabrics are higher than untreated fabric, as shown in Fig. 4 (a).

The ratio of the curve integral of the silk fabrics treated by TGase and SC and sprayed SF with different concentration to the untreated sample in the range of 200–400 nm, as shown in Fig. 4 (b), is calculated according to equation (1).

$$S_{Abs} = \frac{\int_{200}^{400} A_c \, dx}{\int_{200}^{400} A_0 \, dx} \qquad (1)$$

In the formula, A_c is the UV absorbance of the silk fabric treated with TGase + SC and different SF concentrations; A_0 is the UV absorbance of the untreated silk fabric.

We notice that the ratio of UV absorbance curve integral increases with increasing SF concentration at 0.5%–2.0% according to Fig. 4 (b), indicating that higher concentrations of SF have strong UV absorption. Moreover, when SF concentration is less than 1.5%, UV absorption of treated fabric is lower than treated fabric without SF. However, when SF concentration is 2.0%, UV absorption is higher than treated fabric without SF. It can be explained that the SF film blocks a large number of UV-absorbing groups such as tryptophan and tyrosine residues inside the silk fabric. When the SF concentration is large enough, SF contains ultraviolet absorbing groups more than the inside of the silk fibers.

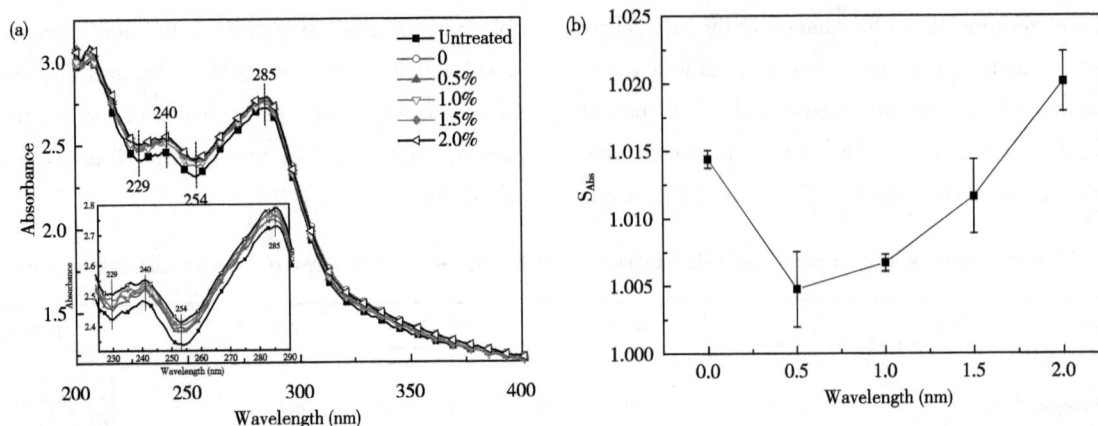

Fig. 4 (a) UV absorbance curve; (b) The ratio of the curve integral of the silk fabrics treated by TGase + SC and sprayed SF with different concentration to the untreated sample in the range of 200–400 nm

3.6 Thermal and UV aging properties of treated fabrics

In order to evaluate the anti-aging properties of the reinforced silk fabrics, heat aging and UV aging tests were performed on untreated fabric and treated samples including TGase catalyze SC reinforced samples and 1% SF sprayed samples after treating by TGase and SC. The breaking stress and strain of the fabric after heat aging and UV aging are given as shown in the Fig. 5, demonstrating that the reinforced silk fabric has better UV resistance and higher strain. On the one hand, the heat aging effect is relatively mild and has less damage to the mechanical properties of fabrics compared to UV aging. Compared with the original silk fabric, the stress and strain of the untreated sample after heat aging decreased by 14.73% and 10.18%, respectively, and the stress of 1% SF sprayed samples treated by TGase and SC was reduced by 31.75% and the strain increased by 2.71%. Compared with the original silk fabric, the stress and strain of the untreated sample after UV aging decreased by 68.27% and 41.38%, respectively, and 1% SF sprayed samples treated by TGase and SC was decreased by 67.61% and 35.54%. On the other hand, the strain of treated fabrics after heat aging is significantly higher than the original silk fabric, and stress of treated fabrics after UV aging is better than untreated. This phenomenon may be due to the fact that the tryptophan and tyrosine inside the fabric are sensitive to UV radiation, resulting in greater internal structural damage. In addition, we characterize the anti-aging properties of the reinforced silk fabric by calculating the breaking strength retention rate of the fabric. Calculation formula of breaking strength retention rate R (%) of fabrics is shown in equation (2).

$$R(\%) = \frac{F_{after}}{F_{before}} \times 100\% \qquad (2)$$

In the formula, F_{after} indicates the breaking strength after aging 24h, and F_{before} indicates the breaking strength before aging.

The breaking strength retention rate of the reinforced silk fabrics after heat treatment for 24h is more than 85%, while the same time for the UV aging is only about 36% according to Tab. 2. It can be concluded that the reinforced silk fabrics have better anti-aging properties.

Tab. 2 Breaking strength retention rate after fabric aging

	Heat aging (%)	UV aging (%)
Untreated	84.39 ± 2.03	31.40 ± 1.02
TG + SC	93.13 ± 3.25	41.85 ± 2.21
TG + SC + SF	85.16 ± 1.41	36.24 ± 1.18

4 Conclusions

This work has demonstrated that the SF solution is sprayed on TGase and SC treated samples to effectively

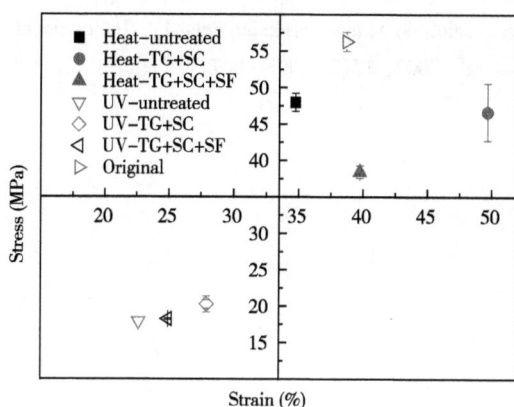

Fig. 5 The breaking stress and strain of the fabric after heat aging and UV aging

protect and strengthen silk fabrics. The selected materials are safe and harmless, which have good biocompatibility with silk fabrics because of protein composition of TGase and SC. Furthermore, the method of chemical cross-linking inside the fabric and the physical combination of the fabric surface is meaningful for the protection of silk fabrics. Compared with the original fabric, the weight of the fabric treated by this method was significantly increased above 4%, indicating that the materials were grafted on the fabric. The breaking stress and strain of the reinforced silk fabric were increased by 16.7% and 7.14%, respectively, when the SF concentration was 1.0%. Moreover, the bending stiffness of the treated fabric was linearly related to the SF concentration and the color difference results indicated that this method did not affect the aesthetic appearance of the silk fabric. Due to the presence of UV-sensitive groups such as tryptophan and tyrosine, the UV absorbance of the reinforcing silk fabric was changed. The reinforced fabric after heat and UV irradiation for 24h, respectively, showed that the UV aging had greater damage strength to the fabric by analyzing of breaking stress and strain. In addition, the retention rate of reinforced fabrics after heat aging was above 85%, but it was about 36% after UV aging, resulting good anti-aging properties compared with unreinforced samples. This method is expected to be applied to the protection and restoration of historical silk fabrics.

Acknowledgements

This work was supported by the National Key R&D Program of China (No. 2016YFC0802802).

References

[1] Zhang X, Berghe I V, Wyeth P. Heat and moisture promoted deterioration of raw silk estimated by amino acid analysis [J]. Journal of Cultural Heritage, 2011; 12 (4): 408-411.

[2] Paul W. Performance measurement of sericin-coated silks during aging[J]. Science China Chemistry, 2011, 54(6): 1011-1016.

[3] Vilaplana F, Nilsson J, Sommer D V P, et al. Analytical markers for silk degradation: Comparing historic silk and silk artificially aged in different environments[J]. Analytical and Bioanalytical Chemistry, 2015, 407(5): 1433-1449.

[4] Li M Y, Zhao Y, Tong T, et al. Study of the degradation mechanism of Chinese historic silk (Bombyx mori) for the purpose of conservation[J]. Polymer Degradation & Stability, 2013; 98(3): 727-735.

[5] Moini M, Klauenberg K, Ballard M. Dating silk by capillary electrophoresis mass spectrometry[J]. Analytical Chemistry, 2011; 83(19): 7577-7581.

[6] Hansen E F. The conservation of silk with parylene-C[J]. Historic Textile & Paper Materials II, 1989.

[7] Wu S Q, Li M Y, Fang B S, et al. Reinforcement of vulnerable historic silk fabrics with bacterial cellulose film and its light aging behavior[J]. Carbohydrate Polymers, 2012; 88 (2): 496-501.

[8] Ragauskiene D, Makuška R. Consolidation and ageing features of vinylneodecanoate containing in adhesive films used as a support for museum textiles[J]. Chemija, 2006, 17 (2): 52-59.

[9] Wu Z, Huang D, Hu Z, et al. A new consolidation system for aged silk fabrics: Interaction between ethylene glycol diglycidyl ether, silk fibroin and artificial aged silk fabrics[J]. Fibers & Polymers, 2014; 15(6): 1146-1152.

[10] Zhu Z, Gong D. Determination of the experimental conditions of the transglutaminase-mediated restoration of thermal aged silk by orthogonal experiment[J]. Journal of Cultural Heritage, 2014; 15(1): 18-25.

[11] Huang D, Peng Z, Hu Z, et al. A new consolidation system for aged silk fabrics: Effect of reactive epoxide-ethylene glycol diglycidyl ether[J]. Reactive & Functional Polymers, 2013; 73(1): 168-174.

[12] Flanagan J, Gunning Y, Fitzgerald R J. Effect of cross-

linking with transglutaminase on the heat stability and some functional characteristics of sodium caseinate[J]. Food Research International, 2003; 36(3): 267-274.

[13] Myllarinen P, Buchert J, Autio K. Effect of transglutaminase on rheological properties and microstructure of chemically acidified sodium caseinate gels[J]. International Dairy Journal, 2007; 17(7): 800-807.

Structural and Mechanical Properties of Silk Biomaterials Plasticized by Glycerol

Yifan Zhang[1,2], Ronghui Wu[1,2], Liyun Ma[1], WeidongYu[1,2] *

[1] *Department of Technical Textiles, College of Textiles, Donghua University, Shanghai 201620, China*

[2] *Key Laboratory of Textile Material & Technology, Ministry of Education, Donghua University, Shanghai 201620, China*

* *Corresponding author's email*: wdyu@ dhu. edu. cn

Abstract: Much attention has been paid to the structure and properties of silk fibroin material for an extension of application in biomedical field, in which secondary structure regulation is one of the most important works. We blended the glycerol into SF films and the structural change of silk fibroin/glycerol blend films with different concentrations was investigated by fourier transform infrared spectroscopy (FTIR) and X-ray diffraction (XRD). The results indicated that addition of glycerol exhibited complex impacts on the secondary structure of SF film. With increasing glycerol content, the β-sheet content of the films untreated increased, while that the mechanical strength of films decreased and ductility increased. The molecular interactions of silk materials plasticized using glycerol were studied, as these materials provide options for biodegradable and flexible protein-based textile materials.

Keywords: Silk fibroin; Glycerol; Film; Mechanical properties

1 Introduction

Protein-based polymer has been used for an alternative to petroleum-based plastics in the medical industries because of their green origins and biocompatibility. Silk fibroin, a high molecular weight amphiphilic protein (upto 390 kDa) and has excellent film-forming capabilities, has been widely used in biomedical and tissue engineering[1-2].

However, the structural of the silk fibroin materials can be transformed from random coil to β-sheet form by film-formation process. This process ultimately yields materials which may be susceptible to tearing and cracking, thus less useful for biomedical and other applications such as sensor platforms[3]. Therefore, there remains a need to modify the physical and mechanical properties of silk films to control properties, mainly toward more flexible systems.

Generally speaking, the outstanding performance of materials can be attributed to the secondary structures of protein materials[4]. Much attention has been paid to the structure and properties of silk fibroin material for an extension of application in biomedical field, in which secondary structure regulation is one of the most important works. In many cases, improved blends to control mechanical properties of silk fibroin remain a challenge.

Glycerol has previously been used to improve silk film properties, including the use of 10% glycerol solutions during film formation[5]. These plasticizers can induce structural changes, resulting in increased crystallinity and β-sheet content, yet the resulting materials are generally softer and highly flexible[6].

In the present study, we blended the glycerol into SF films and the structural change of silk fibroin/glycerol blend films with different concentrations was investigated by fourier transform infrared spectroscopy (FTIR) and X-ray diffraction (XRD). The results indicated that addition of glycerol exhibited complex impacts on the secondary structure of SF film. With increasing glycerol content, the β-sheet content of the films untreated increased, while that the mechanical strength of films decreased and ductility increased.

2 Experiments

2.1 Materials

Preparation of silk fibroin solution was showing in Fig. 1: Silk fibers were obtained from Bombyx mori silkworm silk (Guangxi Sericulture Technology Co., Ltd., China). The silkworm silk was degummed in boiling aqueous solution of 0.5% (w/v) NaHCO$_3$ for 30 minutes twice with frequent stir, then rinsed thoroughly using DI water. The regenerated silk fibroin was obtained by dissolving the degummed silk into a 9.3 M LiBr solution for 4 hours at 60 ℃, and then extracting LiBr molecules from silk fibroin solution via a dialysis tube (MWCO 3500 Da, Spectra/Por, USA) for 2 days with frequent change of DI water. The solution would be diluted into 5% (w/v) in concentration for following experiments.

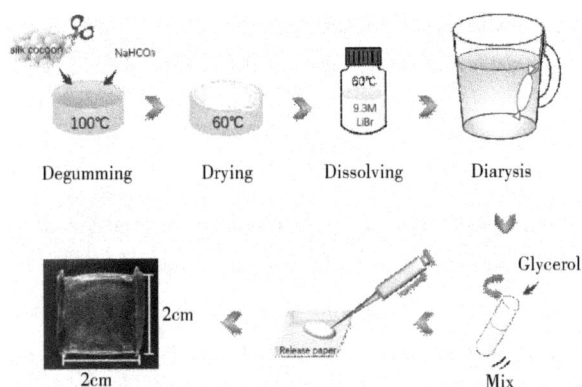

Fig.1　Schematic illustration for the fabrication process of Silk/Glycerol hybrid films

2.2 Preparation of silk/glycerol blend films

Preparation of SF/glycerol composite films: SF composite films were fabricated by a solution casting method. A glycerol was blended with an SF solution (5‰) at weight of 0mg/mL, 10mg/mL, and 20mg/mL. Then, 1mL of mixture solutions were cast in an uncovered release paper (2cm × 2cm) and dried at a temperature of 25 ℃ and a relative humidity of 50% for 48h.

2.3 Structural analysis of the films

The secondary structures of above composite films were measured by the FTIR with a Nicolet IN10 spectrometer (Thermo Fisher, USA). For each measurement, 64 scans were dealt with a resolution of 4cm^{-1} and a scope of 500 – 4000cm^{-1}. Fourier self-deconvolution (FSD) of the infrared spectra covering the amide I region (1600–1700cm^{-1}) was analyzed by Peak fit software to identify secondary structures. The XRD (Bruker D8 ADVANCE) patterns of composite films were collected with a beam size of 0.5mm in the range of 0° – 60° and a scanning rate of 2°min^{-1}.

2.4 Morphological characterization of SF/glycerol films

The morphologies of the two kinds of composite films were observed using SEM (Hitachi SU70, Tokyo, Japan).

2.5 Mechanical properties of the films

The tensile and bursting properties of keratin/SF films were measured by Instron 5948 microtester (Instron, UK) with a 100 N load cell. For the uniaxial tensile test, the composite film samples were cut into strips (3mm in width and 40mm in length) and then tested with a tensile speed of 5mm min^{-1} and a tensile gap of 10mm. The overall evaluation of 10 measurements was reported for each sample.

3 Results and Discussion

3.1 Secondary structural of SF/glycerol composite films

In previous studies, various conformations for silk fibroins were identified by FTIR and X-ray diffraction: random coils, α-form (α-helix and β-turn, Silk I), and β-form (anti-parallel β-pleated sheet, Silk II)[7]. To address the concern of the effect of glycerol on the structure of SF films, a series of experiments were carried out. The structures of the blended silk films of different glycerol ratios, were examined by fourier transform infrared spectroscopy (FTIR) and X-ray diffraction (XRD). Fig.2 (a) presents the FTIR spectra of SF films at different ratios Glycerol. Neat silk films show a strong band around 1646cm^{-1}, indicating the dominant α-helical and amorphous forms in untreated silk films. It follows that a red shift to 1627cm^{-1} occurred once glycerol was added to the silk fibroin. This is subject to the occurrence of β-conformations in the protein materials.

The wide dispersion peak of untreated silk films around 20.8° reveals the silk I structure as shownin Fig. 2

(b). As the ratio of glycerol increases in the films, the XRD patterns of the composite films exhibit gradually a sharper and stronger diffraction peak at $2\theta = 20.2°$, which is a typical characteristic pattern of the β-crystallite structure. As glycerol increases in the composite films, another weak peak $2\theta = 24.8°$ attributed to the silk II shows up either, representing increasing β-crystallites are formed in the composites.

tallites gauged by XRD from the total percentage β-conformations measured by FTIR as shownin Fig. 3 (a) and (b). It is worth noting that with increasing glycerol content, the β-structure of silk fibroin was increased and the α-helix was declined. This indicates that the interactions between silk fibroin molecules and glycerol promote the formation of extra β-conformations, which to a large extent are in the form of β-crystallites.

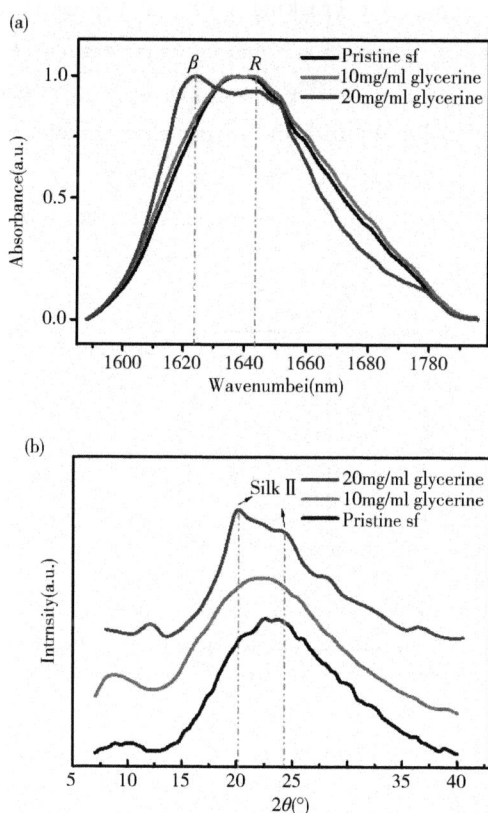

Fig. 2 (a) FTIR spectra of SF/Glycerol dense films in amide I region, which red shift due to the transition of random coils (R) to β-sheets (B) with the SF content; (b) XRD results of dense films indicate the transformation to the crystalline structures (Silk II) by the sharping the crystalline peak around $2\theta = 20.2°$ and the emergence of a new one at $2\theta = 24.8°$. As SF becomes a predominant component in the composite films, the peak at $2\theta = 20.2°$ grows sharper and stronger

To compare the various secondary structural components in the blended films, the percentage of the secondary structural components at different glycerol ratios of silk films acquired from FTIR and XRD are showing in Fig. 3 (c)[8-9]. The contents of intramolecular β-sheets were obtained by subtracting the percentage of β-crys-

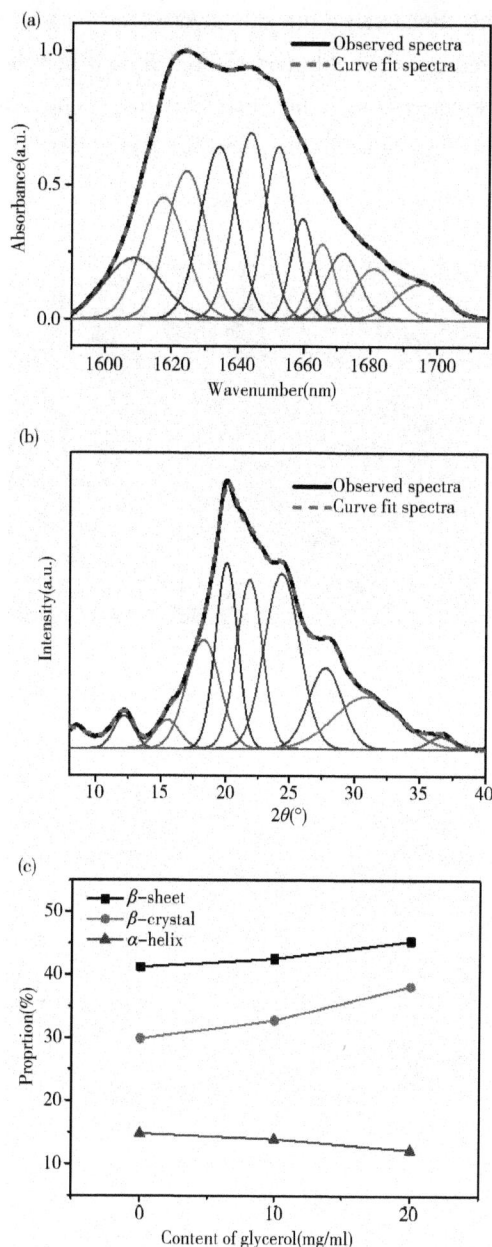

Fig. 3 Peak-fit processing on (a) FTIR analysis and (b) XRD analysis of the secondary structure and crystallinity for SF film sample prepared by casting 5% SF solution & 20mg/mL glycerol with Gaussian and Pearson distribution; (c) The secondary structures of composite films

3.2 Interior morphologies of SF/glycerol composites films

For a better view on the guiding phenomenon of SF/glycerol dense films, SEM cross-section images (Fig. 4) were performed based on two randomly selected regions. The cross-section of silk film without glycerol was exhibited in Fig. 4 (a). It can be observed that the solid of untreated silk was smooth and close-grained. Relatively, the silk/glycerol composites films appeared more roughly and showed fibroid morphological characteristics, which indicates the strong interactions between silk fibroin molecules with glycerol participation.

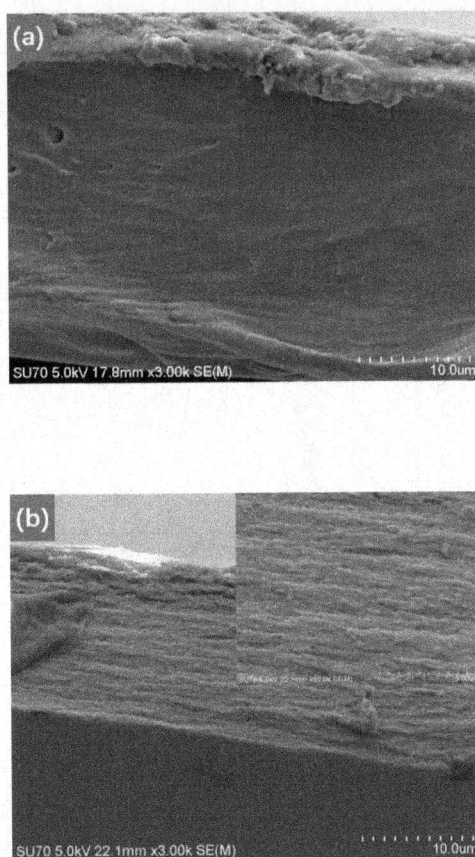

Fig. 4   SEM of cross-section diagram SF dense films
(a) the untreated silk film showed compact over layer;
(b) the silk film with 20mg/mL glycerol exhibit flexibility

3.3 Mechanical properties of SF/glycerol composites films

Fig. 5 shows the yield strength, breaking strength, and breaking strain of SF films of various glycerol ratios. It follows that the ratio of glycerol in the composites increases from 0mg/mL to 20mg/mL, the breaking strain increase from 65.25% to 250.32%, respectively, on the contrary, the break strength decreases from and 8.23 to 16.05MPa. In past studies, the extendibility of the β-crystallite molecular networks is to a large extent subject to by α-helices or the intramolecular β-sheets. In this sense, the breaking stress, and breaking strain of blended films in Fig. 5 can be explained by the component data given by Fig. 3 and Fig. 4: As illustrated by Fig. 3 and Fig. 4, with increasing glycerol content, the β-structure content of the films untreated increased, and the intermolecular interactions of silk fibroin enhanced.

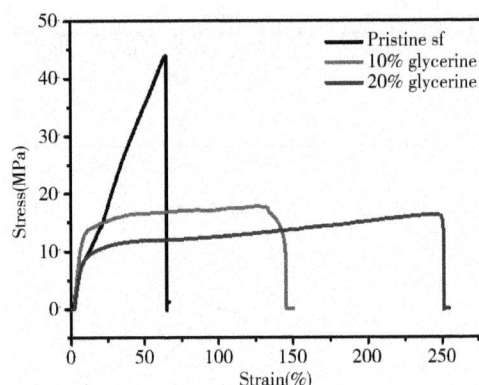

Fig. 5   Stress-strain curves of the composite films of various ratios of glycerol

4   Conclusions

This study has focused on the secondly structure and mechanical properties of silk fibroin with glycerol composites. We have reported that glycerol is able to change the secondary structures of SF to some extent. Silk fibroin films blended with a high concentration of glycerol induce β-sheet and β-crystallinity structure and reduce α-helix structure. Therefore, the addition of glycerol increases the ductility of the film, but the strength of the membrane declines. This suggests that silk fibroin composite films with tunable performance by mesoscopic structural engineering, based on the secondary structural synergy between glycerol and silk fibroin. The results obtained will inspire us to fabricate protein materials with tunable and remarkable property for widely applications.

References

[1] Vepari C, Kaplan D L. Silk as a biomaterial[J]. Progress in Polymer Science, 2007, 32(8-9): 991.

[2] Rockwood D N, Preda R C, Yücel T, et al. Materials fabricated from bombyx mori silk fibroin[J]. Nature Protocol, 2011, 6(10): 1612-1631.

[3 Athamneh A I, Griffin M, Whaley M, et al. Conformational changes and molecular mobility in plasticized proteins[J]. Biomacromolecules, 2008, 9(11): 3181.

[4] Lin N, Liu X Y. Correction: Correlation between hierarchical structure of crystal networks and macroscopic performance of mesoscopic soft materials and engineering principles[J]. Chemical Society Reviews, 2015, 44(21): 7881-915.

[5] Brown J E, Davidowski S K, Xu D, et al. Thermal and structural properties of silk biomaterials plasticized by glycerol[J]. Biomacromolecules, 2016, 17(12): 3911-3921.

[6] Lu S, Wang X, Lu Q, et al. Insoluble and flexible silk films containing glycerol [J]. Biomacromolecules, 2010, 11(1): 143.

[7] Tu H, Yu R, Lin Z, et al. Programing performance of wool keratin and silk fibroin composite materials by mesoscopic molecular network reconstruction[J]. Advanced Functional Materials, 2016, 26(48).

[8] Xu G, Gong L, Yang Z, et al. What makes spider silk fibers so strong? From molecular-crystallite network to hierarchical network structures[J]. Soft Matter, 2014, 10(13): 2116-2123.

[9] Li A B, Kluge J A, Zhi M, et al. Enhanced stabilization in dried silk fibroin matrices[J]. Biomacromolecules, 2017, 18(9): 2900-2905.

Textile-Based Passive RFID Tag with Text-Meandered Structure

Shuo Tan[1], Shenghai Yu[1], Lan Yao[1]*, Kuang Ye[1]

[1] *Department of Technical Textiles, College of Textiles, Donghua University, Shanghai 201620, China*

* *Corresponding author's email:* yaolan@ dhu. edu. cn

Abstract:RFID (radio frequency identification) technology is an automatic identification method, transferring object data wirelessly, and can be used in security, healthcare and biomedical applications. Wearable RFID tag gives the object a unique ID card so that they can be read and traced. In this paper, a design of textile-based RFID tag with text-meandered structure is presented. The tag comprised three alphabet texts with a small size of 64mm × 35mm × 0.78mm and was optimized to provide a conjugate match to the RFID chip impedance at the operation frequency, 915MHz. The single-ended probe method was used to test the input impedance of the tag antenna by the vector network analyzer. In addition, the measured maximum read range results of the tag achieved up to 15.5m in free space, which was measured by the ultra-high frequency reader.

Keywords: Impedance matching; Ultra-high frequency; Passive RFID tag; Wearable electronics; Read range

1　Introduction

The radio frequency identification (RFID) tag has been widely used in supply chain and entrance guard system due to the function of data storage. Take the advantage of RFID tag, and it can also be applied in the field of smart textile industry as network terminal.

In the previous research, wearable RFID tag has been studied by many researchers. Those studies were mainly focus on the design, properties and applications of RFID tag. J. Virkki et al.[1] put forward a T-matching structure dipole antenna which has been most widely used in the study of RFID tag based on textile substrate. Then, the reduce of material, manufactory technology, interconnector with chip were studied[2-5]. Properties like durability and moisture effect were also discussed[6-7]. As for the application, wearable RFID tags can be applied in Body-worn communication, human monitoring and senor and so on[8-10].

With the use of T-matching structure, RFID antenna can be modified easily to match the impedance of RFID chip[11-12]. In this paper, a text-meandered RFID tag was designed based on the principle of T-matching structure and simulated under ultra-high frequency (UHF) band(840-960MHz). The tag consists of three letters "DHU", which stands for Donghua University. The impedance of the antenna was first simulated in the HFSS software and then measured by the vector network analyzer (VNA). Besides, the tags were tested by the UHF RFID reader to obtain its read range property. The proposed UHF RFID tag was designed to be applied in the wearable application for entrance guard system, especially for students' security.

2　Experiments

2.1　Materials

Plain woven cotton fabric was used as the substrate which has the thickness of 0.78mm. The relative dielectric constant of the substrate is 1.7 (*T* 25℃, *RH* 75%) and tan δ is 0.018. For the radiation part of the tag antenna, copper foil was used. It was provided by Dongguan Xinshi Package Materials Co., Ltd. The thickness of the copper is 0.05mm. In addition, the IC (Integrated Circuit) is the NXP UCODE G2XM Series (item code #SL3ICS1002) with the input impedance of

$22-j195\,\Omega$ at 915MHz.

2.2 Antenna design

Based on the input impedance of UHF chip under 915MHz, the antenna was designed and simulated through HFSS software. And Fig. 1 shows the geometry of the proposed antenna.

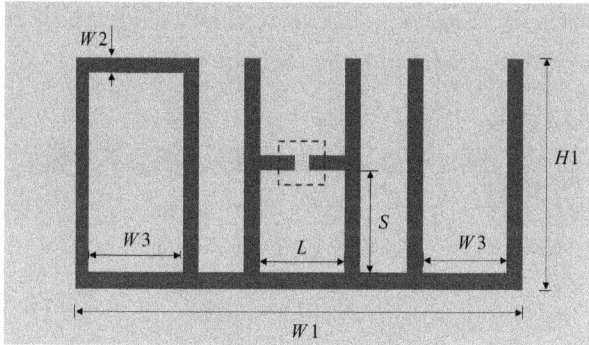

Fig. 1 The geometry of thetag antenna

For the RFID tag design, the impedance matching is the vital factor to consider. The tag was optimized to provide a conjugate match with the RFID chip impedance at the operation frequency with the center frequency of 915MHz. For the chosen UHF IC, the input capacitance is 0.88pF and the quality factor [Im(Zic)/Re(Zic)] is 9. The input impedance of the chip can be calculated from

$$Zic = \frac{1}{\dfrac{1}{Z_{req}} + \dfrac{1}{Z_{ceq}}} \qquad (1)$$

$$\frac{1}{Z_{req}} = -j \cdot (2\pi f C) \qquad (2)$$

Where Z_{req} is the input parallel resistance and Z_{ceq} is the input parallel capacitance of the RFID IC. So, the aimed impedance of the RFID antenna was $22 + j195\,\Omega$. As shown in the Fig. 1, the red part is the conductive part of the antenna and the grey part means the substrate, cotton woven fabric. The square with dotted line is the place for RFID chip to be mounted on.

The initial parameters are illustrated in Tab. 1. In order to optimize the structure, $H1$, $W1$, $W3$, L and S were adjusted in HFSS software. The antenna can be seen as the heteromorphic T-matching which is parasitic loading structure so that L and S are mainly responsible for the imaginary part of the impedance. The other parameters

like $H1$, $W1$ and $W3$ were modified mainly to adjust the real part. The thickness of the substrate is 0.78mm, just the same with the fabric. The optimized progress and the result of antenna's impedance will be discussed in the following part.

Tab. 1 Initial parameters of the RFID antenna

Parameters	$W1$	$H1$	$W2$	$W3$	L	S
Value(mm)	65.0	35.0	2.0	15.0	15.0	10.0

Fig. 2 Prototype of copper RFID tag

2.3 Impedance testing on RFID antenna

After the optimization of RFID antenna's parameters in simulation, the impedance of the tag antenna was tested by VNA PNA3766 machine. As for the frequency set in the VNA, it covered UHF band with the step size of 1.00MHz. Since the tag had the balanced feed structure, a SMA connector was used in the measurement as Fig. 3 shows.

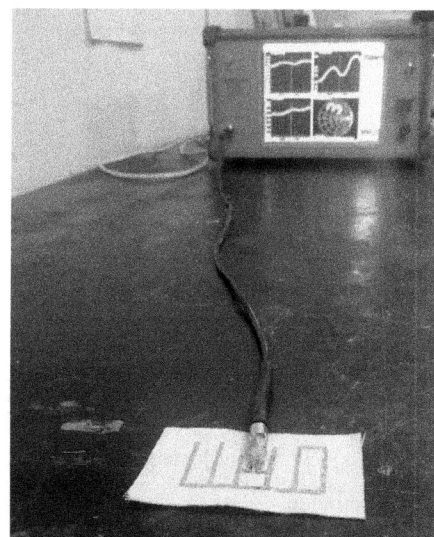

Fig. 3 Impedance measurement

2.4 Read range testing on RFID tags

For UHF RFID tags, read range is an important property to evaluate their performances. Generally, read range is the maximum distance that the information stored in the IC of the tag can be read by the reader antenna. The free-space read range can be obtained from

$$d_{tag} = \frac{\lambda}{4\pi} \qquad (2\text{-}3)$$

$$\tau = \frac{4 R_{IC} R_{ant}}{|Z_{ant} + Z_{IC}|^2} \qquad (2\text{-}4)$$

Where λ is the wavelength, τ is the tag antenna to IC power transfer efficiency, G_{tag} is the tag antenna gain, EIRP is the maximum equivalent isotropically radiated power allowed by local regulations (3.28W in Europe), and pic 0 is the sensitivity of the IC.

The IC we used was NXP UCODE G2XM series RFID IC with the wake-up power of −15dBm. As shown in Fig.4, the chip was provided by the manufacturer in a fixture patterned from copper on a plastic film. The copper pads of the UHF RFID chip were connected to the two ports of antenna with conductive sliver glue respectively. Additionally, the UHF reader was set at the US band with the power of 30W.

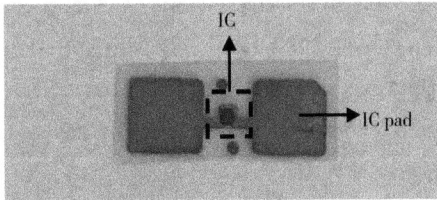

Fig.4　UHF RFID chip structure

3　Results and Discussion

3.1 Impedance of RFID antenna

In the simulation, the optimized process can be concluded into three steps. Firstly, the values $W1$, $H1$ and $W3$ were optimized mainly to adjust the real part of input impedance of the proposed antenna. Then L and S were modified to meet the demand of the imaginary part. In the last, $H1$ was adjusted slightly to obtain the final ideal impedance.

In the first step, $H1$ was set from 30 to 35mm, $W1$ was set from 60 to 65mm, $W3$ was set from 10 to 15mm and

step size for all the values mentioned above was 1mm. Then we got the optimized parameters as Tab.2 shows. And the result of the RFID antenna's impedance is demonstrated in Fig.6. As seen in Fig.7, the impedance is 23.2 + j231.3Ω which still had a gap between the aimed impedance of 22 + j195Ω. The imaginary part especially needed to be reduced to realize impedance matching. Secondly, the value L and S were both set from 10 to 15mm with the step size of 1mm.

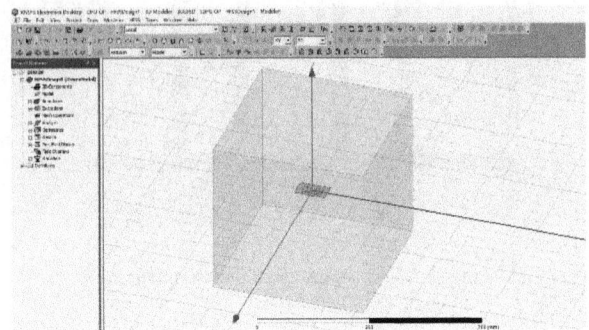

Fig.6　UHF RFID antenna model in the simulation

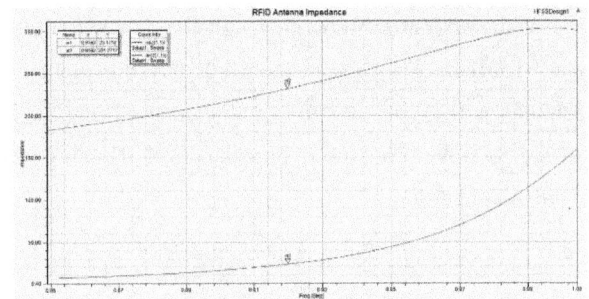

Fig.7　Optimized impedance of the RFID antenna

Tab.2　The first optimized parameters of RFID antenna

Parameters	$W1$	$H1$	$W2$	$W3$	L	S
Value(mm)	64.0	33.0	2.0	10.0	15.0	10.0

However, the parameters we got from the previous adjustment happened to be the best one among all the results. So, the value $H1$ was added into the consideration for the third times optimization. The settings of optimization were set as below: L from 10 to 12mm, S from 10 to 13mm and $H1$ from 33 to 35mm.

In the last, the optimized parameters are shown in Tab.3 and the result of impedance was 22.7 + j208.5Ω (as seen in Fig.8) which was close to the ideal input impedance $(22 + j195\Omega)$.

Tab. 3　The final optimized parameters of RFID antenna

Parameters	W1	H1	W2	W3	L	S
Value(mm)	64.0	35.0	2.0	10.0	12.0	10.0

The measured impedance of RFID antenna is displayed in Fig. 8. The measured impedance of RFID antenna is $22.5 + j117.1\Omega$ at 915 MHz. From the testing results, it is found out that the imaginary part of the RFID antenna's impedance was affected more than the real part in the real application environment. The differences between simulated tag antenna and fabricated prototypes may due to the fabrication process and use of SMA connector which caused unexpected parasitic impedance. Besides, the measurement environment may also have side effect on the property of tags.

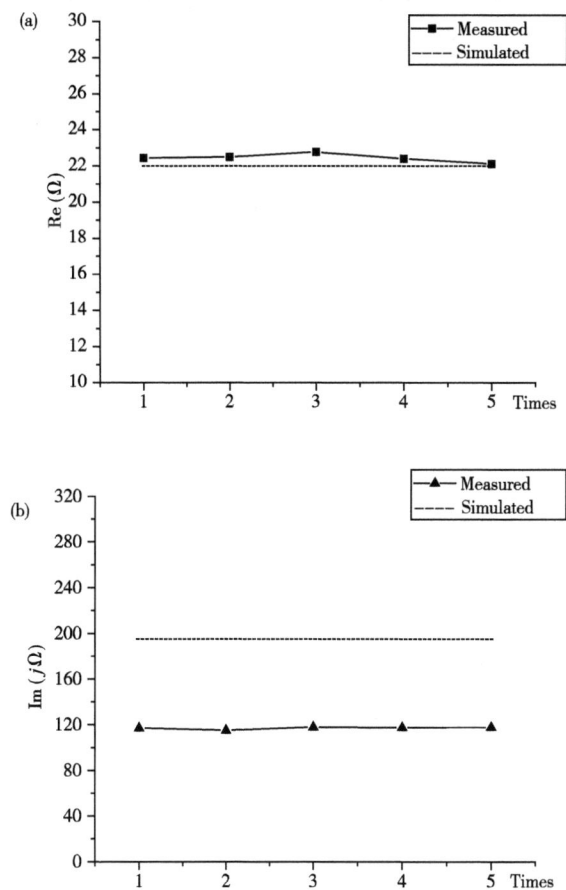

Fig. 8　Measured RFID antenna impedance at 915 MHz
(a) The real part of impedance; (b) The imaginary part of impedance

3.2　Read range of the copper RFID tags

The existence of breakpoint is the result of multiple factors such as the construction of RFID system, properties of RFID reader and RFID tag and so on[13]. The measured read range of copper UHF RFID tags are presented in Tab. 4, which shows the good performances of the designed RFID tag. Both of the maximum continuous read range and the maximum range with breakpoint included were measured under UHF band. The copper tag achieved a peak read range of 15.50m and the maximum continuous read range was 11.90m.

Tab. 4　Read range of copper RFID tag

Tag	Read range(m)	
	Continuous length	Length with breakpoint
1	11.18	15.50
2	11.90	15.31
3	11.75	15.45

4　Conclusions

In this paper, we put forward a text-meandered copper UHF RFID tag which was based on the textile substrate. The impedance optimization process and read range test of the proposed antenna were discussed. The text-meandered UHF RFID tag can be attached to clothing for human monitoring since it had a small size of 64mm × 35mm × 0.78mm. And the measured data showed its good performance in the far field. The design of RFID tag is full of possibilities for the RF designers to develop. In the future work, we will use embroidery technology to realize the textile conformal RFID tag.

References

[1] Virkki J, Björninen T, Merilampi S, et al. The effects of recurrent stretching on the performance of electro-textile and screen-printed ultra-high-frequency radio-frequency identification tags [J]. Textile Research Journal, 2015, 85(3): 294-301.

[2] Moradi E, Bjorninen T, Ukkonen L, et al. Effects of sewing pattern on the performance of embroidered dipole-type RFID tag antennas [J]. IEEE Antennas & Wireless Propagation Letters, 2012, 11(5): 1482-1485.

[3] Brechet N, Ginestet G, Torres J, et al. Cost- and time-ef-

fective sewing patterns for embroidered passive UHF RFID tags[C]// International Workshop on Antenna Technology: Small Antennas, Innovative Structures, and Applications. IEEE, 2017.

[4]Ginestet G, Brechet N, Torres J, et al. Embroidered antenna-microchip interconnections and contour antennas in passive UHF RFID textile tags[J]. IEEE Antennas & Wireless Propagation Letters, 2017, 16(99): 1205-1208.

[5]Chen X, Ukkonen L, Björninen T. Passive e-textile UHF RFID-based wireless strain sensors with integrated References [J]. IEEE Sensors Journal, 2016, 16 (22): 7835-7836.

[6]Koski K, Moradi E, Babar A A, et al. Durability of embroidered antennas in wireless body-centric healthcare applications[C]// European Conference on Antennas and Propagation. IEEE, 2013: 565-569.

[7]Toivonen M, Bjorninen T, et al. Impact of moisture and washing on the performance of embroidered UHF RFID tags [J]. IEEE Antennas & Wireless Propagation Letters, 2013, 12(12): 1590-1593.

[8]Zhang J, Tian G Y, et al. A review of passive RFID tag antenna-based sensors and systems for structural health monitoring applications[J]. Sensors, 2017, 17(2): 265.

[9]Shuaib D, Ukkonen L, Virkki J, et al. The possibilities of embroidered passive UHF RFID textile tags as wearable moisture sensors[C]. IEEE International Conference on Serious Games & Applications for Health, 2017: 1-5.

[10]Wang Z, Lee L Z, Psychoudakis D, et al. Embroidered multiband body-worn antenna for GSM/PCS/WLAN Communications[C]. IEEE Transactions on Antennas & Propagation, 2014, 62(6): 3321-3329.

[11]Gaetano Marrocco. The art of UHF RFID antenna design: Impedance-matching and size-reduction techniques [C]. IEEE Antennas & Propagation Magazine, 2008, 50 (1): 66-79.

[12]G Zamora, S Zuffanelli, et al. Design and synthesis methodology for UHF-RFID tags based on the T-match network [C]. IEEE Transactions on Microwave Theory & Techniques, 2013, 61(12): 4090-4098.

[13]Deng X Y, Wang Y, He Y J. Antenna theory and engineering for passive RFID tag [M]. Tsinghua University Press, 2016.

The Development of High-Performance Natural Ramie Fibers Reinforced Polylactic Acid Composite via Surface Modification of Fibers and Composite Thermal Annealing

Dereje Kebebew Debeli[1], Jiansheng Guo[1]*, Zhi Zhang[1], Senay Yacob Baraki[1]

[1]*Key Laboratory of Textile Science and Technology, Ministry of Education, Shanghai 201620, China*

* *Corresponding author's email*: jsguo@ dhu. edu. cn

Abstract: In this study, the surface of ramie fibers was treated with various techniques before compressed to ramie fibers/PLA biocomposite. The produced biocomposite was then followed by composite post thermal annealing. The properties of fabricated composite were evaluated using SEM (scanning electron microscopy) for morphological analysis, XRD (X-ray diffraction) for the degree of crystallization changes, DSC (differential scanning calorimetry) and TGA (thermogravimetric analysis) for thermal analysis. The XRD test results illustrated that the crystallinity of PLA was improved by 50% whereas the thermal resistance properties was tuned by 20% due to the application of thermal annealing. The consecutive mechanical test results were also consistent with the improved surface compositions observed from DSC and TGA curve results in the composite. In conclusion, the produced biocomposites were possibly visible to apply in electronics and packaging industries.

Keywords: Ramie fibers; PLA polymer; Surface modification; Thermal annealing; Composite

1 Introduction

Composite material is a strong, light and a low-density product obtained by embedding fibers in the polymer matrix[1]. The fibers contribute to the strength and stiffness of the composite while the polymer matrix helps to bind the embedded fibers in place. In a composite material, a larger portion of the composite is mainly a matrix which bonded with high strength and modulus fibers. The matrix as well as the reinforced fibers retain their physical and chemical identities, however, exhibiting a combined property that cannot be achieved with either of the two constituents alone[2-4]. The matrix used to distribute forces among reinforced fibers and protect fibers from the external environment. It also dominates in shape and surface appearance which likely determines the tolerance and durability of the composite life. It is expected to have good stiffness as well as strength, moreover, reinforced fibers are expected to share, carry the load distributed by the matrix during in the entire composite life.

Biopolymers made from renewable agricultural products are purely biodegradable, environment friendly and recently showed the promising result to replace the carbon footprint (conventional composites). The reinforcement of natural plant fibers with biodegradable polymers are eco-materials exclusively used in the application of automobile, packaging, electronics, biomedical engineering, and construction industries[5].

Studies have indicated that natural plant fibers reinforcement with PLA is one of the most effective approach to enhance the overall properties of PLA composites[6]. However, the physical (mechanical) and chemical (thermal) properties obtained from bio-plastic composites are generally inferior to the corresponding thermoplastic composites derived from oil[7]. The low interfacial adhesion between bio-plastic PLA resin and reinforcing fillers are responsible for the over deteriorating properties of reinforced composites. It was also reported by B. Priya et al. [8] that the tensile and flexural moduli of treated fiber biocomposite was remarkably enhanced as compared with the untreated matrix of PLA and flax. This improvement was also analyzed with varying fiber volume contents from 5%–30%. The values of tensile and flexural moduli observed at 5% were 1.47GPa and 3.07GPa, respectively. In contrast to treated fibers, the untreated biofibers showed slightly lower tensile and flexural moduli. This was better explained by N. Le Moigne et al. [9] as state of adhesion between fibers and matrix. Similarly, after conducting sizing and desizing, hemp fibers were reinforced to unsaturated polyester from which the desized hemp reinforced composite characterized with high tensile strength and high bending strength[10]. The sized hemp fiber has showed smoother surface which was seen from the SEM graph (image) taken, and at the same time seen exhibited excellent adhesion at fibers-matrix interface.

Therefore, it is required to design and achieve an appropriate interfacial adhesion that would contribute to an overall mechanical and chemical behavior of the composite materials. The introduction of natural fibers into PLA (polylactic acid) polymer system has obtained great research attention in various applications due to its biodegradability, renewability and lightweight options. However, up to this date, the low thermal resistance and poor mechanical performances of ramie fibers reinforced PLA composite limited the industrial application. Herein, we present an approach to solve the shortcomings by the surface modification of ramie fibers using different techniques followed by post composite thermal annealing.

2 Experiments

2.1 Materials

Ramie fiber with the following parameters (diameter of 0.31mm, density 1.3g/m³, length of 60–250mm) and thermoplastic polylactic acid fiber (length of 38–40mm, melting point of 165–175℃, the density of 1.25g/cm³ and melt flow index of 4–10m/min) were purchased from Tianjin Glory Tang Technology Co., Ltd., China. Sodium hydroxide (NaO), 3–Aminopropyl triethoxysilane (KH550) and acetone were purchased from Sinopharm Chemical Reagent Co., Ltd., Shanghai, China.

2.2 Methods

The surface of ramie fibers was modified using alkali and silane treatment techniques (alone or in combinations). Ramie fibers were manually chopped to an average length of 30–40mm. Then, it was soaked in a solution of sodium hydroxide (NaOH) and silane coupling agents (5g/100mL of water) for 3h. Later, the alkali and silane treated ramie fibers were rinsed with tap water several times with a drop of acetic acid until excess sodium hydroxides and silane on fibers were removed. Detail information of used materials and combination can be seen in Tab. 1. The fibers were exposed to open air for three days and later heated to 80℃ for 6h. The prepared combination of blends was opened to ramie fiber/PLA fiber mat on opening machine.

Tab. 1 The molding composition of ramie fiber and PLA polymer reinforced composite

Samples	Ram (%)	PLA (%)	Alkali (5g)	Silane (g)	Combined Alk-Silane (g)	Annealing (℃)
PLA	30	70	—	—	—	130
Ram/PLA	30	70	5	5	5	130
Ram-Alk/PLA	30	70	5	5	5	130
Ram-Sil/PLA	30	70	5	5	5	130
Ram-Alk-Sil/PLA	30	70	5	5	5	130

Finally, the prepared ramie fiber/PLA fiber mat was molded on heat compression machine (Platen vulcanizing press, Shanghai Light Industry Machinery Co., Ltd., China), with the 170℃ working temperature, 8MPa molding pressure and 6min of pressing time.

2.3 Characterization

The surface morphologies of ramie fibers PLA composites were observed by a scanning electron microscopy

(SEM) TM3000, (Interphase morphology analysis). DSC was done on using DSC 4000 thermal analyzer under a nitrogen flow of 20mL/min at a heating rate of 20℃/min, while, TGA was performed on a TGA4000 thermogravimetric analyzer at a heating rate of 10℃/min, pressure bar of 2 bars. The tensile and flexural properties of ramie fibers reinforced PLA composites were measured on Instron 5967 (testing solution, USA) based on ASTM D638 standard.

3　Results and Discussion

3.1　Mechanical property

The performances of composite materials are always presented in terms of their mechanical strength such as tensile, flexural, impact, thermal stability and wear behavior properties. These properties are very decisive in measuring the reliability of fabricated material especially under extreme conditions that directly measures and tells us the engineering performances[3-4, 11]. The use of ramie fibers in reinforced composite has been studied and presented to characterize the potential of this fiber in a composite application. The tensile strength of ramie fiber reinforced PLA composite is shown in Fig. 1 (a) and Fig. 1 (b). From the graph, the tensile load of untreated composite exhibited lower breaking strength than the untreated asshown in Fig. 1 (b). Similarly, the application of thermal annealing reduced the ductility of molded materials. This attributed to the increase in degree of crystallinity of materials that have a tendency to present brittle properties[12].

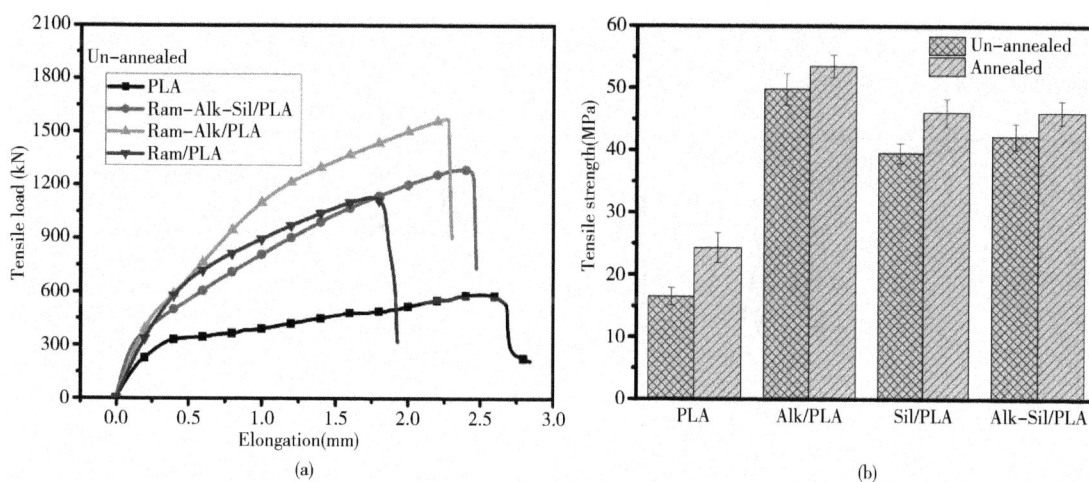

Fig. 1　Ramie fiber/PLA composite (a) elongation at break and (b) tensile strength

3.2　Increase in the crystallinity of composite

A controlled addition of fibers in PLA composite can enhanced overall performance of PLA polymer. PLA has exhibited a low crystallization growth during melt crystallization process molding stage. Fig. 2 demonstrates the crystallization and crystal grow of PLA polymer during molding process measured by XRD. From the graph, thermal annealing, it can be seen from the comparison of annealed and un-annealed PLA that annealed PLA showed some remarkable improvements in crystallinity growth. The introduction of different surface treatments techniques remarkably encouraged the percentage of crystalline level. This was attributed to the removal of unwanted impurities and dirt which reduced the hydrophilic behavior of ramie fibers in the consecutive treatments[13-14]. As a result, alkali treated ramie fibers exhibited maximum crystalline growth, in fact, alkali is a standard surface treatment in industries in washing impurities.

3.3　Thermal analysis

Fig. 3 is the thermogravimetric analysis (TGA) of ramie fibers/PLA composite analysis at temperature range of 30-450℃. The application of ramie fibers in PLA as a reinforcement has considerably improved the rate of decomposition. In particular, the effect of composite annealing tremendously imparted the thermal resistance behavior of ramie fibers/PLA biocomposites[15-16]. This property was due to a higher temperature exposure experience tuned a freedom of movement in PLA molecules that was trapped in the molding process. Moreover, ramie has good thermal resistance behavior due to its higher percentage of cellulosic components when compared with other natural fibers[17-18].

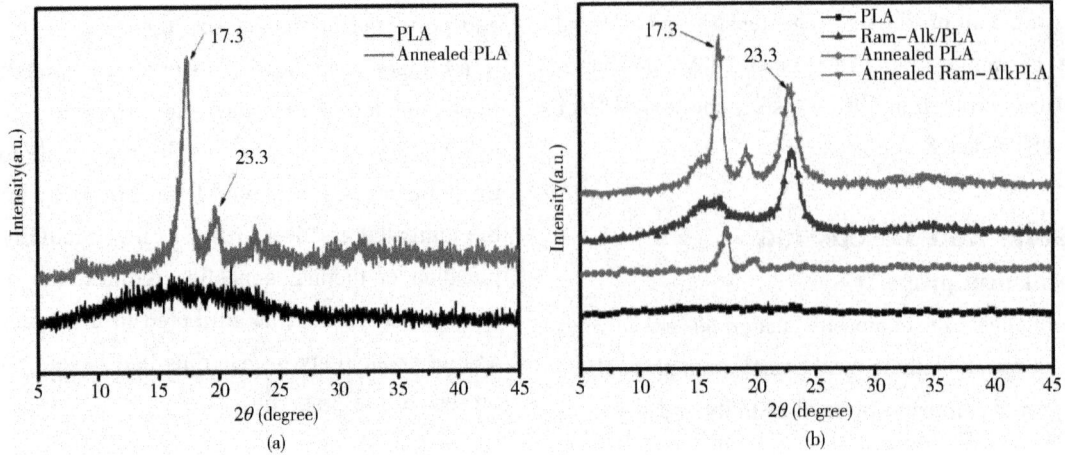

Fig. 2 The XRD graphs of ramie fibers/PLA composite (a) crystalline peaks (b) surface modification on crystallite growth

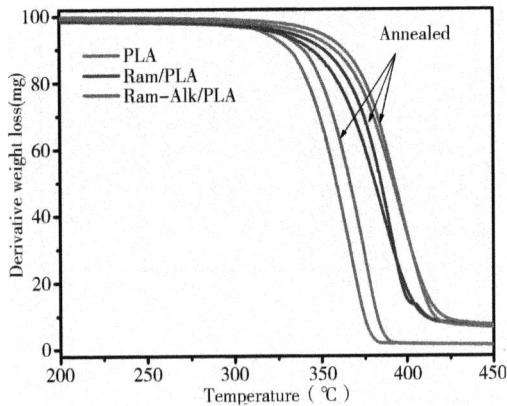

Fig. 3 The effect ofthermal annealing onramie fiber/PLA composites

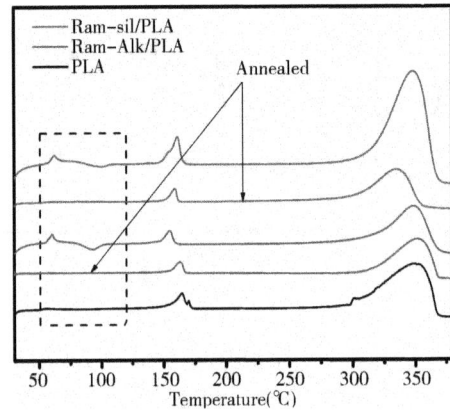

Fig. 4 The DSC heating scan showing effect of thermalannealing on ramiefibers/PLAcomposites

3.5 DSC analysis results

The effect of composite post thermal annealing is presented in Fig. 4. As it can be referred from Fig. 4, the introduction of ramie fibers as reinforcement in PLA polymer has improved the crystallinity value of PLA, which was acted as a nucleating agent. This can be seen from un-annealed composites samples that have exhibited crystallization peaks at around 90℃ except neat PLA. However, these peaks were disappeared in thermally annealed biocomposites samples. This is ascribed to the growth of crystals in PLA polymer composites due to annealing (crystal perfection)[12, 16].

3.6 Dynamic mechanical property results

Fig. 5 represents the thermomechanical behavior of bio composite exposed to elevated temperature. All composite samples demonstrated similar pattern at a temperature below glass transition temperature (T_g) as shown in Fig. 5(a). The un-annealed PLA polymer has exhibited a sharp decrease in storage modulus at T_g temperature (60℃), whereas thermally annealed reinforced composite was superior than the untreated samples. The increased phenomenon in storage modulus corresponding to the formation of crystal after the treatment that was not observed in the untreated neat PLA[1, 14]. Similar to the storage modulus, the loss modulus exhibits the maximum heat release of composite material at glass transition temperature. The maximum heat dissipation was occurred at the value where loss modulus was highest, as seen from Fig. 5(b)[15].

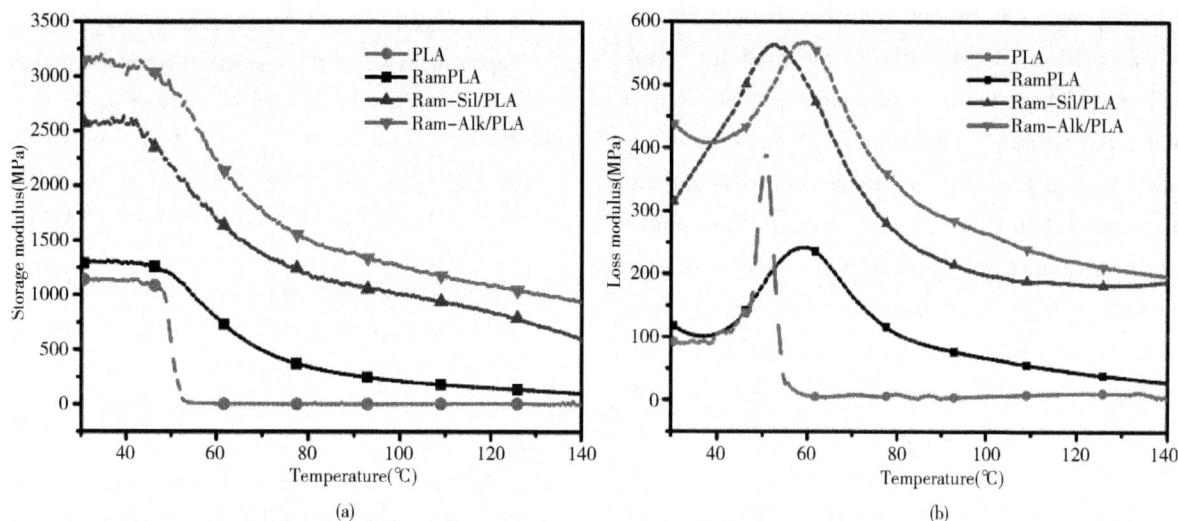

Fig. 5 The DMA curves (a) storage modulus and (b) loss modulus

3.7 Morphological analysis results

The morphological analysis results of ramie fibers/PLA composites are shown in Fig. 6. As it can be observed from Fig. 6(a), the morphological surface of PLA polymer was uneven, with more visible crack portion on the surface. With the thermal annealing treatment, these uneven surface portions were melted away and through time changed to a smooth uniform part of surface as shown in Fig. 6(c). The introduction of ramie fiber surface treatments techniques has helped in removing unwanted part of substances from the surface of the fibers, hence improve surface compatibility between the polymer and fiber[17]. Alkali surface treatment method was contributed for cleaning ramie fiber surface with improved and mechanical properties[14].

Fig. 6 The SEM micrographs of (a) & (b) untreated and (c) & (d) thermally annealed ramie fiber/PLA composite

4 Conclusions

In summary, different surface modification techniques were applied on ramie fibers before consolidated to ramie fibers/PLA composite. Such surface modified reinforced composite was further annealed to optimize the overall properties. Alkali surfaced modified fibers exhibited the highest thermo-mechanical properties over the untreated samples. Furthermore, thermal annealing was also applied following the molding process and the results showed that it was also one of the method similar to surface treatment in improving ramie fiber reinforced composite. This type of biocomposite obtained from ramie fibers and PLA polymer composite with superior properties can easily find application in emerging technologies and high-performance application.

References

[1] Debeli D K, Qin Z, Guo J. Study on the pre-treatment, physical and chemical properties of ramie fibers reinforced poly (lactic acid) (PLA) [J]. Biocomposite. J Nat Fiber, 2017, 15(4): 596-610.

[2] Delgado-Aguilar M, Julian F, Tarres Q, et al. Bio composite from bleached pine fibers reinforced polylactic acid as a replacement of glass fiber reinforced polypropylene, macro and micro-mechanics of the Young's modulus [J]. Compos Part B-Eng, 2017, 125: 203-210.

[3] Erpek C E Y, Ozkoc G, Yilmazer U. Comparison of natural halloysite with synthetic carbon nanotubes in poly (lactic acid) based composites [J]. Polym Compos, 2017, 38 (11): 2337-2346.

[4] Huda M S, Drzal L T, Mohanty A K, et al. Effect of fiber surface-treatments on the properties of laminated biocomposites from poly (lactic acid) (PLA) and kenaf fibers [J]. Compos Sci Techn, 2008, 68(2): 424-432.

[5] Terzopoulou Z N, Papageorgiou G Z, Papadopoulou E, et al. Green composites prepared from aliphatic polyesters and bast fibers [J]. Ind Crop Prod, 2015, 68(Supplement C): 60-79.

[6] Zhang Q, Shi L, Nie J, et al. Study on poly(lactic acid)/natural fibers composites [J]. J App Polym Sc, 2012, 125: E526-E533.

[7] Fujiura T, Sakamoto K, Tanaka T, et al. A study on preparation and mechanical properties of long jute fiber reinforced polylactic acid by the injection molding process [J]. In: DeWilde WP, Brebbia CA, eds. High Perf Struct Mater, 2008, 97: 231.

[8] Bajpai P K, Singh I, Madaan J. Joining of natural fiber reinforced composites using microwave energy: Experimental and finite element study [J]. Mater Design, 2012, 35: 596-602.

[9] Le Moigne N, Longerey M, Taulemesse J M, et al. Study of the interface in natural fibres reinforced poly (lactic acid) biocomposites modified by optimized organosilane treatments [J]. Indus Crop Prod, 2014, 52: 481-494.

[10] Pickering K L, Efendy M G A, Le T M. A review of recent developments in natural fibre composites and their mechanical performance[J]. Compos Part a-Appl Sci Manuf, 2016, 83: 98-112.

[11] Chuayjuljit S, Wongwaiwattanakul C, Chaiwutthinan P, et al. Biodegradable poly (lactic acid)/poly (butylene succinate)/wood flour composites: Physical and morphological properties [J]. Polym Compos, 2017, 38 (12): 2841-2851.

[12] Takayama T, Todo M, Tsuji H. Effect of annealing on the mechanical properties of PLA/PCL and PLA/PCL/LTI polymer blends[J]. J Mech Behav Biomed Mater, 2011, 4(3): 255-260.

[13] Baley C, Busnel F, Grohens Y, et al. Influence of chemical treatments on surface properties and adhesion of flax fibre-polyester resin [J]. Compos Part a-App Sci Manuf, 2006, 37(10): 1626-1637.

[14] Guo J H, Qiao J X, Zhang X. Effect of an alkalized-modified halloysite on PLA crystallization, morphology, mechanical, and thermal properties of PLA/halloysite nanocomposites[J]. J App Polym Sc, 2016, 133(48): 9.

[15] Kebebew D D, Mike T, Jia H, et al. Improved thermal and mechanical performance of ramie fibers reinforced poly(lactic acid) biocomposites via fiber surface modifications and composites thermal annealing[J]. Poly Compos, 2018.

[16] Lai S M, Wu W L, Wang Y J. Annealing effect on the shape memory properties of polylactic acid (PLA)/thermoplastic polyurethane (TPU) bio-based blends[J]. J Polym Res, 2016, 23(5).

[17] Debeli D K, Guo J, Li Z, et al. Treatment of ramie fiber with different techniques: the influence of diammonium phosphate on interfacial adhesion properties of ramie fiber-reinforced polylactic acid composite[J]. Iran Polym J, 2017, 26(5): 341-354.

[18] Debeli D K, Zhang Z, Jiao F, et al. Diammonium phosphate-modified ramie fiber reinforced polylactic acid composite and its performances on interfacial, thermal, and mechanical properties[J]. J Nat Fiber, 2018: 1-15.

The Effect of Alkali Treatment on the Characterization of Apocynum Venetum Bast Fibers and It's Weibull Distribution Prediction

Lantao Wu[1], Ahsan Ali[1], Lan Yao[1]*, Yiping Qiu[1], Meiling Zong[1]

[1]*Department of Technical Textiles, College of Textiles, Donghua University, Shanghai 201620, China*

* *Corresponding author's email*: yaolan@ dhu. edu. cn

Abstract: Apocynum venetum(AV), which is famous as the "King of wild fibers" in Xinjiang Province in China due to its excellent properties. Herein, the AV bast fibers were treated with 2%, 5% and 7% NaOH solution, and the properties of the AV bast fibers before and after treatment were characterized by the mechanical test, scanning electron micrographs (SEM), fourier transform infrared spectroscopy (FTIR), and X-ray diffraction (XRD). It was found that the tensile strength of the treated AV bast fibers was significantly improved in comparison with the untreated fibers. The average tensile strength of the untreated group was 1.03 cN/dtex, while the average tensile strengths of the treated groups were 1.70cN/dtex, 1.73cN/dtex, and 1.42cN/dtex, respectively. Especially, the failure probability of the AV bast fibers agreed well with two parameter Weibull distribution model through the statistical analysis. The X-ray diffraction results showed that the degree of crystallinity was changed due to the alkali treatment. In addition, the SEM pictures showed that most of the impurities on the surface of the AV bast fibers can be removed in the 5% group, which was consistent with the results of the FTIR test.

Keywords: AV bast fiber, Alkali treatment, Mechanical properties

1 Introduction

Apocynum venetum (AV) is a kind of herb perennial plant, which grows along the banks of the Peacock River and the Tarim River in Xinjiang Province, China, and it was discovered initially on the Loblin Plain[1]. The fineness and strength of the AV fibers can be comparable to ramie fibers, and the elongation of the fibers is very less, in this case, the AV fibers were hailed as the "King of wild fibers" by the expert Yunhe Bian. However, the AV plants have different heights and shapes, and the qualities of the AV fibers are varied extremely, which has a direct effect on the spinning behavior[2]. In addition, due to its excellent anti-bacterial and deodorant performance, it has been widely applied to fabrics and household accessories.

Alkali treatment is one of the most used chemical treatments to improve the composite properties[3-4], which is a low-cost method and can be easily conducted. Alkali treatment can effectively remove the non-cellulosic components such as lignin, hemicellulose, pectin, wax, etc. existing on the surface of bast fibers, thereby improve the mechanical properties of fibers. Li et al. [5] found that alkali treatment can remove impurities, which led to the content of the cellulose increased, and the strength of single fibers was improved. Yang et al. [6] found that the alkali treatment can not only made the surface of the fibers got roughed through removing the impurities on the surface, but also led to the fiber fibrillation, which meant that the fiber bundles split into smaller diameter fibers. Liu et al. [7] found that the grooves on the surface of the ramie fiber would be exposed after the alkali treatment, which led to the roughness of the surface increased.

The Weibull distribution is based on the"defect theory" to predict the strength dispersion of the bundle fibers. Wu et al. [8] designed the Weibull program using VB program to analyze the intensity distribution of carbon fibers and it was proved that the Weibull model is suitable by the strength probability simulating curves of carbon fibers under different oxidative stretching conditions. Dieter Loidl et al. [9] conducted single fiber tensile tests on Tenax HTA5131 fibers, then used a double Weibull distribution to statistically analyze the tensile strengths of single PAN-based carbon fiber under the different temperatures. Naik DL et al. [10] studied the tensile strength and Young's modulus of kenaf fibers at different gage length by the two-parameter and three-parameter Weibull distributions, respectively, and found that the two-parameter Weibull distribution can be better followed by the data.

In this paper, the properties before and after alkali treatment of AV bast fibers were compared to study the effect of alkali treatment, and the Weibull distribution model was used to predict the tensile strength dispersion of bast fibers.

2 Experiments

2.1 The obtaining of the AV bast fibers

The apocynum venetum (AV) plants were collected from Xinjiang Province without any treatment. After the preliminary experimental, the optimum process of getting the AV bast fibers was immersing the AV stalks into the boiled water for 1.5 hours, and then the AV bast fibers can be got by manual peeling in wet condition, afterwards, the AV bast fibers were dried in the normal condition for about 24h.

2.2 The alkali treatment

In this study, in order to analyze the effect of alkali treatment on AV bast fibers, the concentrations of NaOH solution used for alkali treatment were 2%, 5%, and 7%, respectively.

To avoid the bast fibers entangled together in the solutions, a fiber board was prepared by fixed the both ends of fibers on the plastic board, and then treated in the alkali solution for an hour, after that the acetic acid (2%) was used to neutralize the alkali residue on the surface, besides the fibers should be washed with distilled water more than three times until pH = 7. Finally, the treated bast fibers were dried for about 24h in the normal condition.

2.3 The tensile strength test

The tensile strength test of AV bast fibers was conducted on the YG026 MB-250 electronic textile strength machine in accordance with ASTM D1294. The test was carried out with a fiber gage length of 25.4mm at the crosshead speed of 20mm/min. Four groups of treated and untreated AV bast fibers samples were tested and the results were analyzed statistically by the two parameter Weibull distribution. The schematic diagram of the samples is shown in Fig. 1, and the tensile strength of bast fibers was calculated by the following equation:

$$\sigma = 76.2 \times 10^{-5} \times (B/m)$$

Where σ is the stress of the AV bast fiber, B is the strength which obtained during the stretching processing, m is the weight of fiber bundle.

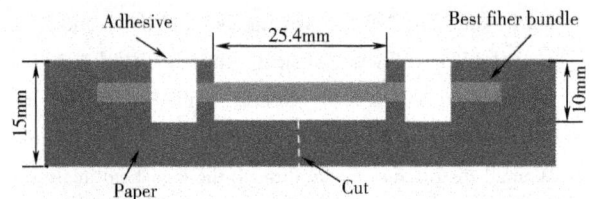

Fig. 1 Schematic diagram of samples for tensile test

2.4 The surface morphology of AV bast fibers

The surface morphology of AV bast fibers before and after alkali treatment was obtained by Scanning Electron Microscope TM3000. The AV bast fibers in the length of 10mm were prepared to observe the longitudinal and the cross section surfaces respectively by adjusting the scanning magnification.

2.5 Fourier transform infrared spectroscopy (FT-IR) analysis

FTIR analysis of AV bast fibers before and after alkali treatment was conducted by Perkin Elmer UATR Two. The bast fibers in the length of 1cm were prepared and detected with the range 4000-400cm^{-1}.

2.6 X-ray diffraction analysis

To detect the effect of the alkali treatment, four groups' powder of AV bast fibers, the untreated one included, were prepared to measure the crystallinity degree using a D/MAX2500PC X-ray diffractometer.

3 Results and Discussion

3.1 The effect of alkali treatment on AV bast fibers

The results of the tensile test were shown in Fig. 2, the average tensile strength of the untreated group was 1.03cN/dtex, and the strengths of the treated groups all were increased significantly, as 1.70cN/dtex, 1.73cN/dtex, and 1.42cN/dtex, respectively. The tensile strength of the alkali-treated AV bast fibers under the concentration of 5% was increased by 67% compared with the untreated ones.

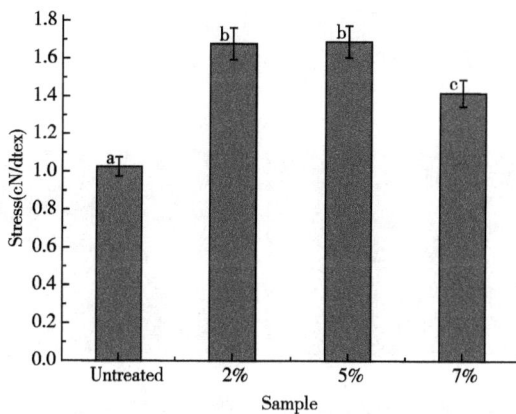

Fig. 2　Tensile strength of AV bast fibers under different conditions

This was mainly due to the hydrolytic degradation of impurities like hemicellulose, lignin, pectin, etc. in the fibers by the OH$^-$ in the alkali solution. In the comparison with the 2% group, there were more OH$^-$ in the 5% alkali solution, which could have reaction with more impurities, while under the concentration of 7%, most of the impurities were removed, then the cellulose in the fibers were also reacted by the OH$^-$, which led to the decrease of the tensile strength.

3.2 The Weibull distribution of tensile strength of AV bast fibers

Weibull distribution analysis can effectively analyze the strength and dispersibility of brittle materials[11]. The key point of the Weibull distribution theory is that the fracture is often happened at the weakest place, and the cracks in the brittle material do not interfere each other when the break happens.

The Weibull cumulative distribution functionis:

$$F = 1 - \exp[-(\sigma/\sigma_0)^m]$$

Herein, the AV bast fiber is a kind of brittle material, so the Weibull distribution can be used to statistically analyze its strength and dispersion. After removing some abnormal data, the statistical analysis was conducted to see whether the remaining data got from the tensile test can have a good consistence with the Weibull distribution.

As is shown in Fig. 3 that the distribution of the tensile strength of the untreated and treated AV bast fibers were almost linear, and the fitting coefficient all were over 0.95. Therefore, the strengths of the AV bast fibers can have a good consistence with the Weibull distribution.

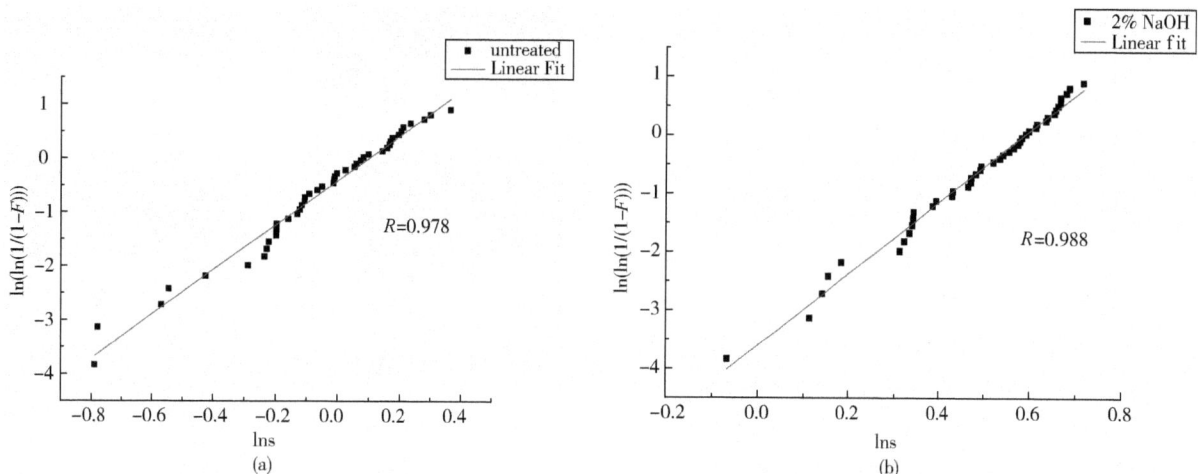

Fig. 3

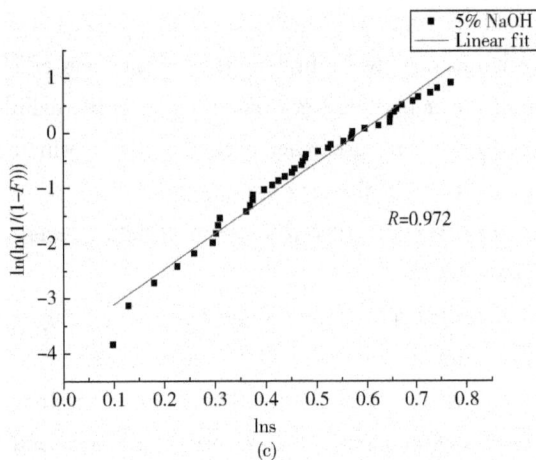

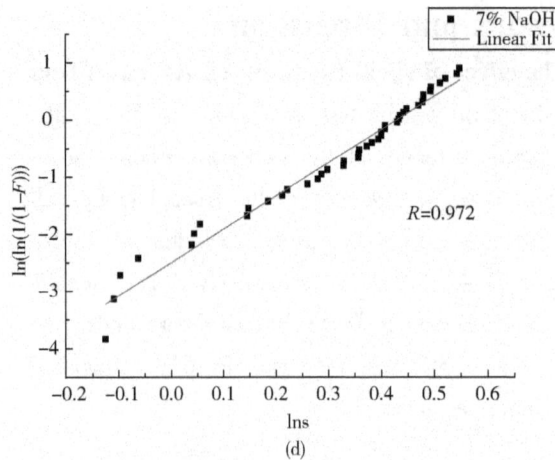

Fig. 3　Weibull distribution of AV bast fibers under different conditions（a）untreated（b）2% NaOH（c）5% NaOH（d）7% NaOH

3.3　The surface morphology of AV bast fibers

As shown in Fig. 4（a）–（d）, along the longitudinal direction, the surface of the untreated AV bast fiber was covered with small white particles, which were pectin, wax, and other impurities. The impurities on the surface of treated AV bast fibers were partially removed in the 2% NaOH group, while in 5% NaOH group, the pectin and hemicellulose on the AV bast fibers surface were almost removed, but there were more grooves along the fiber axis in 7% NaOH group due to the wax, pectin and other impurities were partially removed between the fibers.

As for the cross section shown in Fig. 4（e）–（h）, the shapes were not uniform and curved naturally when they were dried, which due to the large differences in the diameter of the AV stalks, and the manually peeling procession. Besides, due to the outer layer of the AV bast fiber was covered with hemicellulose, pectin, lignin, wax, etc. as the protection, which prevented the bundle fibers from destruction, the shape of cross section depended on the stem to which it stuck.

3.4　The FTIR analysis

As is shown above in Fig. 5, the peak at $1030cm^{-1}$ referred to the cellulose structure, there was not much change, which indicated that the alkali treatment just had an effect on the surface. The peak at $1240cm^{-1}$ was associated with the stretching vibration of group C—O in hemicellulose, compared with the untreated fibers, this peak disappeared in the alkali-treated groups, indicating

Fig. 4　Longitudinal and cross section surface morphology（SEM）of AV bast fibers Longitudinal: （a）untreated; （b）2% NaOH; （c）5% NaOH; （d）7% NaOH; Cross section: （e）untreated; （f）2% NaOH; （g）5% NaOH; （h）7% NaOH

that the hemicellulose on the surface of the AV bast fibers were removed. The peak at 1614cm^{-1} was attributed to the ester group[12], compared with the untreated ones, the content of the ester group was significantly reduced after alkali treatment, which meant that the lignin and gum were removed. The peak at 2916cm^{-1} was referred to the wax, and its value decreased with the alkali concentration increased, indicating that the wax on the surface of the AV bast fiber was removed gradually. The peak at 3280cm^{-1} was related to the vibrational absorption peak of hydroxyl groups, compared with the alkali-treated AV bast fibers, the peak of untreated fibers was stronger, indicating the hydroxyl group reduced by the reaction with the alkali.

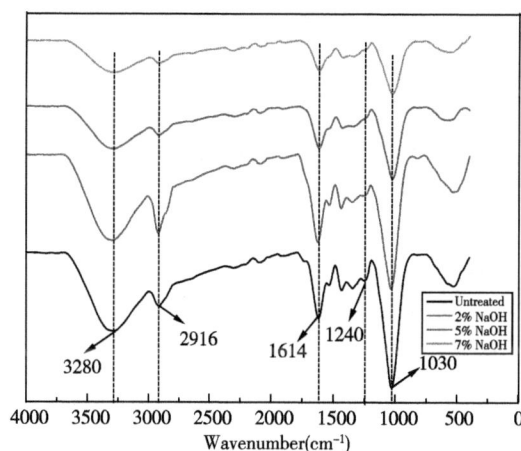

Fig. 5　Infrared spectra of AV bast fibers before and after alkali treatment

3.5　The X-ray diffraction analysis

According to the results of X-ray diffraction analysis, the crystallinity degree of AV bast fibers is shown in Tab. 1.

Tab. 1　Crystallinity of AV bast fibers before and after alkali treatment

The concentration	Crystallinity(%)
Untreated	34.92
2%	39.85
5%	44.30
7%	42.11

It showed that the crystallinity of the AV bast fibers in the untreated group was 34.92%, while in 2%, 5%, and 7% NaOH group, the crystallinity was 39.85%, 44.30%, and 42.11%, respectively. It can be explained that during the alkali treatment, water in the alkali solution entered the amorphous region of the AV bast fibers, which led to the fiber orientation changed, but when it came to the 7% NaOH group, the alkali affected the crystal area for its reaction with the cellulose, resulting in a decrease in crystallinity.

4　Conclusions

In this work, the properties of treated and untreated AV bast fibers were tested, and the effects of alkali treatment were analyzed. The conclusions are as follows:

1. The results of strength tests showed that the 5% NaOH group got the highest tensile property with 1.73 cN/dtex, which was 67% higher than that of the untreated group. In addition, it was found that the tensile strength and dispersibility of AV bast fibers followed the two-parameter Weibull distribution.

2. The SEM pictures showed that the alkali treatment can remove the impurities such as wax, pectin and other impurities on the surface. Among the different concentration, the effect of the 5% NaOH group got the best.

3. The FTIR analysis showed that the alkali treatment can make the lignin, pectin and other impurities significantly reduced. Besides, as the XRD results showed that the alkali treatment will have an effect on the crystallinity degree of the AV bast fibers, which can have a good consistence with the tensile test.

References

[1] Chao Wei. Study on the growth characteristics and physical and chemical properties of ApocynumVenetum [J]. China Fiber Inspection, 2013(11): 85-87.

[2] Hao Ma, et al. Research status and development and utilization of apocynum venetum[J]. China Chiwa Science, 2017, 39(03): 146-152.

[3] Li X, Lope G, Panigrahi S, et al. Chemical treatments of natural fiber for use in natural fiber-reinforced composites: a review[J]. J of Polymers and the Environment, 2007, 15(1): 25-33

[4] Hu Q X. Study on flame retardancy and moisture absorption properties of hemp/polypropylene composites [D]. Changchun University of Technology, 2017.

[5] Li X, Tabil L G. Panigrahi S. Chemical treatments of natural fiber for use in natural fiber-reinforced composite [J]. A Review Polym Environ, 2007 (15) : 25-33

[6] Yang Yazhou, et al. Mechanical properties of modified jute fiber reinforced phenolic resin composites [J]. J of Jilin Agr University, 2009, 31 (06) : 788-792.

[7] Liu Xuan, Cheng Ling. The effect of alkali treatment and cold plasma treatment on the properties of ramie fibers [J]. Shanghai Textile Sci and Tech, 2017, 45 (06) : 23 - 25 + 52.

[8] Wu Q L. Study on strength distribution of viscose-based carbon fibers based on Weibull model under different tensile conditions [J]. Synthetic Fiber Industry, 2002 (02) : 25-28.

[9] Dieter L, Oskar P, Rennhofer H. et al. Skin-core structure and bimodal Weibull distribution of the strength of carbon fibers [J]. Carbon, 2007, 45 : 2801-2805

[10] Naik D L, Fronk T H. Weibull distribution analysis of the tensile strength of the kenaf bast fiber [J]. Fibers & Polymers, 2016, 17 (10) : 1696-1701.

[11] Wu Q. Study on strength distribution based on Weibull model for rayon-based carbon fibers at various draft ratios [J]. China Synthetic Fiber Industry, 2002, 25 (2) : 25-28.

[12] Tang D, Zhao Y P, Zhang J. Effect of surface modification of jute fiber on mechanical properties of thecomposites [J]. J of Anhui Agricultural Sciences, 2011, 39 (05) : 3052 - 3054.

The Effect of Chemical Degumming on Component, Structure and Properities of Apocynum Venetum

Jianting Lou[1], Sihao Qi[1], Lan Yao[1,2]*, Yiping Qiu[1,2]

[1] *Key Laboratory of Textile Science & Technology, Ministry of Education, Shanghai 201620, China*

[2] *Department of Technical Textiles, College of Textiles, Donghua University, Shanghai 201620, China*

* *Corresponding author's email*: yaolan@ dhu. edu. cn

Abstract: Apocynum venetum (AV) is a member of the oleander family, which is widely spread throughout mid and northwestern China. With the unique advantages of apocynum venetum fiber (AV fiber) in medicine, clothing and ecological rehabilitation, it has attracted increasing interest, which is also named as "the king of wild fiber". However, AV fiber has not been systematically studied yet. In this paper, the existing degumming technology of bast fiber was improved. What's more, the composition, structure, hydroscopicity and mechanical properties before and after degumming were tested and analyzed. The chemical composition analysis showed the cellulose content of AV fibers was 87.1%. Compared to apocynum venetum bast fibe (AV bast fiber), the weight percentage of wax, pectin, hemicellulose, lignin and water soluble dropped significantly. Thus, the effect of degumming process was obvious and confirmed by the results of XRD and FT-IR. As seen from the SEM images, it was found that the outer layer of AV bast fiber was composed of lipid wax, pectin, etc. But after degumming process, the surface of AV fiber was smooth, and the fiber had a middle cavity, which was usually parallel to the fiber longitudinal. The moisture regain of AV bast fibers and AV fibers were 11.56% and 8%, respectively, indicating the strong water absorbance. After the tensile properties test, the tenacity of AV fiber was 4.16cN/dtex, and higher than AV bast fiber.

Keywords: Apocynum venetum; Degumming; Chemical component; Mechanical properties

1 Introduction

Apocynum venetum (AV) is a kind of rare wild plant with strong resistance in the world, which is widely distributed in saline-alkali soil, river banks, fluvial plains, and sandy soil[1-2]. Apocynum venetum fiber (AV fiber) is abundant in the phloem of plants and has attracted increasing interest due to its excellent physical and mechanical properties[3], which is also named as "the king of wild fiber"[4]. In recent studies, the cellulose and hemicellulose contents of AV fiber were not different from those of flax and ramie fibers. But the contents of pectin and lignin were much higher than flax and ramie fibers, affecting its spinnability, dyeing properties. Therefore, the fiber must be degummed to remove gummy composition such as pectin and lignin[5-6]. Then the most commonly used method was chemical degumming[6]. In this paper, the existing chemical degumming technology of bast fiber was improved and the physical and chemical properties of AV bast fiber and AV fiber were tested and analyzed, including the chemical composition, crystalline, structure, hydroscopicity fiber morphology, and breaking tenacity to observe the degumming effect.

2 Experiments

2.1 Materials

All the samples of Apocynum venetum were collected from Xinjiang province, China. Apocynum venetum bast fibers were obtained by manual peeling after water boiling process at 100℃ for 1.5h. Then the each batch of 20g of dried AV bast fiber was prepared as an original sample. The main chemicals used in this study were sulfuricacid (98% H_2SO_4), sodium hydroxide (NaOH), sodium metasilicate ($NaSiO_3$), sodium sulfite(Na_2SO_3), sodium tripolyphosphate, glacial acetic acid, acetone solution, sodium chlorite and ethanol, which were purchased from China National Medicines Co. , Ltd.

2.2 Chemical degumming

The chemical dugumming process[7] was shown as below:

pre-acid treatment →washing → first-cooking → washing → second-cooking → washing → acid rinsing → washing → dewatering → shaking → drying

The weight of AV bast fibers used for each degumming process was around 20. 0g and the dosages of chemicals were the weight percentage on AV bast fibers.

Pre-acid treatment: H_2SO_4 solution (2g/L), temperature 60℃ and normal pressure, liquor ratio 1:15, time 1h.

First cooking: NaOH solution (5g/L), Na_2SiO_3 solution(3%), Na_2SO_3 (2. 5%), normal pressure, temperature 100℃, liquor ratio 1:10, time 2. 5h.

second cooking: NaOH solution (15g/L), Na_2SiO_3 solution (3%), sodium tripolyphosphate (2%), normal pressure, temperature 100℃, liquor ratio 1:10, time 2. 5h.

Acid rinsing: H_2SO_4 solution (1g/L), normal pressure and temperature, liquor ratio 1:15, time 10min.

Washing: washing by hand and spray rinsing with tap, normal pressure and temperature.

2.3 Test methods

2.3.1 Fiber morphology

In this experiment, the surfaces of AV bast fiber and AV fiber were characterized by TM 3000 scanning electron microscope. Before the test, to ensure good electrical conductivity of samples, they needed to be fixed on the circular iron platform with conductive adhesive, and the samples were coated with a thin layer of gold[8]. Then the samples could be observed and pictured.

2.3.2 Moisture regain and moisture content

The experiment referred to GB 5883—1986 standard test method for moisture regain and moisture content of ramie[9] to test moisture regain and moisture content of

AV bast fiber and AV fiber, which were made by using Y802 ventilated fast 8-basket oven. The moisture regains and moisture contents were calculated using equation (1) and (2):

$$W_1 = \frac{G - G_0}{G_0} \times 100\% \qquad (1)$$

$$W_2 = \frac{G - G_0}{G} \times 100\% \qquad (2)$$

Where W_1 is the moisture regain, W_2 is the moisture content, G is the weight of wet fibers, G_0 is the weight of dried fibers.

2.3.3 Chemical component analysis

This experiment referred to GB 5889—1986 quantitative analysis method of chemical composition of ramie[10] for the determination of components of AV bast fiber and AV fiber. The whole process was shown in the Fig. 1. The weight percentages of wax, water soluble, pectin, hemicellulose were obtained[11], the fibers (1g) were burned by an alcohol lamp until the ashes turned pale gray, and the content of ash was got, then the weight percentage of cellulose content was calculated using equation(3):

$$W = 1 - (W_1 + W_2 + W_3 + W_4 + W_5) \qquad (3)$$

where W is the weight percentage of cellulose content; W_1 is that of wax, W_2 is that water soluble; W_3 is that of pectin; W_4 is that of hemicellulose; W_5 is that of lignin.

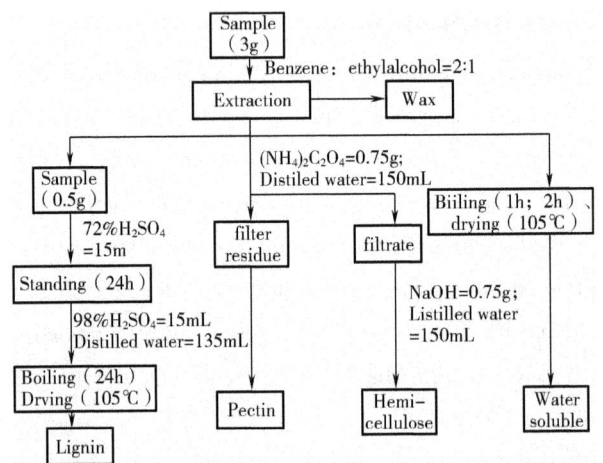

Fig. 1 The process of chemical component analysis

2.3.4 FT-IR spectroscopy

Infrared spectroscopy (IR), as one of the common methods for molecular structure analysis, is widely used for qualitative analysis of molecular structure. The information of the corresponding group is found by analyzing the absorption peak in the infrared spectrogram. In this experiment, the fourier transform infrared spectrometer of Bruker company in Germany was used to conduct infrared spectrum analysis of AV bast fibers and AV fibers.

2.3.5 Crystalline structures

In this experiment, in order to study the differences of the fiber crystal structure of AV bast fiber and AV fiber, 18kW target X-ray diffractometer was used. Crystallinity of cellulose in fibers was calculated from diffraction intensity data using the crystallinity index.

2.3.6 Tensile properties test

Fiber samples were conditioned in standard atmospheric condition (temperature 20℃ ±2℃; RH 65% ±2%) for 24 hours prior to test. For AV bast fibers, 0.045 – 0.075g of fibers, a total of 20groups were weighed, the ends of each bundle of bast fibers with double-sided tape were attached to the board that had been prepared in accordance with ASTM 1290[12] as shown in Fig. 2. Fabric tester was used to obtain the tenacity of AV bast fibers and the standard selection was GB/T 3923 sample method[13], the standard distance was 25.4mm, the rising speed was 20mm/min, and the descending speed was 30mm/min. For AV fibers, the strength of fibers was tested by XQ–2 electronic single fiber strength meter. The stretching velocity was 10mm/min and the clamping distance was 10mm.

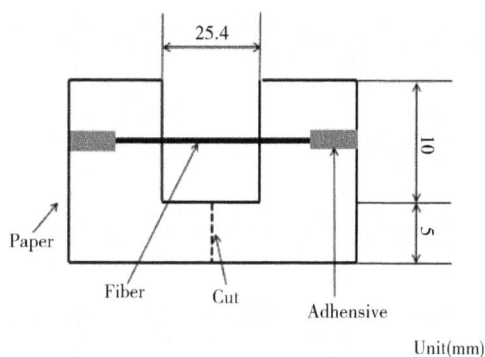

Fig. 2　Sample preparation according to ASTM 1290 standard

3　Results and Discussion

3.1　The morphology of the samples

AV bast fibers were covered with a layer, consisting of hemicellulose, pectin, lignin, and wax as shown in Fig. 3, which could help to bind the single fiber and form optimum organizations to protect the AV fibers from being damaged by the ambient environment. After the degumming process, it was found that the longitudinal surface of AV fiber was smooth, had cracks, no torsion. As a whole, the single fiber was similar to spindle-shaped shuttle with a certain number of nodes distributed randomly on the surface. There was a middle cavity in the fiber, which was usually parallel to the fiber longitudinal.

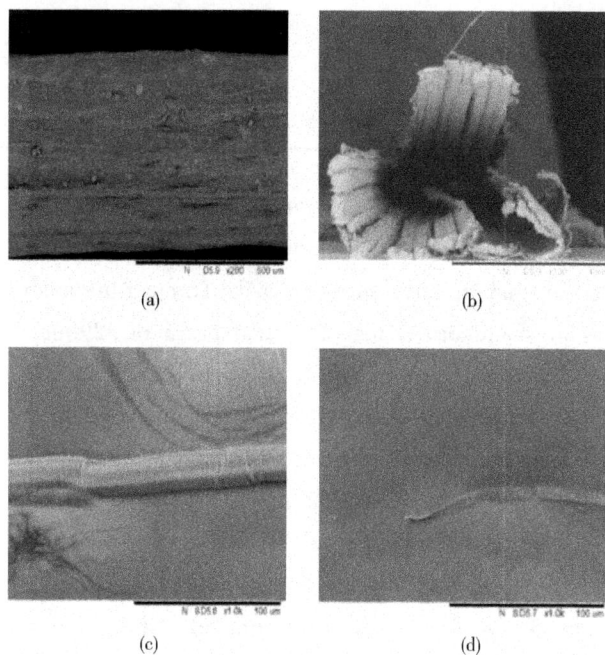

(a)　(b)

(c)　(d)

Fig. 3　SEM micrographs of AV bast fibers and AV fibers (a) The longitudinal section of AV bast fibers(200 ×); (b) The cross section of AV bast fibers(100 ×); (c) The longitudinal section of AV fiber(1000 ×); (d) The cross section of AV fiber(1000 ×)

3.2　Moisture regain and moisture content results

According to the formula, the moisture regain of AV bast fibers and AV fibers were obtained, about 11.56%, 8.70%, respectively. It could be seen that the moisture regain of bast fiber was higher than that of AV fiber. That was because the bast fiber had more pectin and nitrogen-containing compounds absorbing water easily, which made AV bast fiber had better hygroscopicity. The moisture regain and moisture content of AV bast fibers and AV fibers are shown in Tab. 1.

Tab. 1 The moisture regain and moisture content results in AV bast fibers and AV fibers

	Moisture regain	Moisture content
AV bast fiber	11.56%	10.04%
AV fiber	8.7%	8%

3.3 Chemical component analysis

Through component analysis steps, the content of the main components of AV bast fibers and AV fibers were measured, as shown in Tab. 2. Before the degumming, the cellulose content of AV bast fibers was less, the proportion of which is only 27.5%. After chemical degumming, the cellulose content of AV fibers was improved greatly, the proportion of which is 87.1%. The contents of pectin, wax, and water soluble and hemicellulose, reduced significantly. For instance, the content of water soluble dropped to 0.8%, and pectin decreased to 0.2%. This indicated that chemical degumming had achieved a more thorough degumming effect, removing the majority of the gum in the bast fiber of apocynum venetum effectively.

Tab. 2 Chemical composition in AV bast fibers and AV fibers

Composition	Cellulose	Hemi-cellulose	Lignin	Wax	Ash	Pectin	Water-soluble
AV bast fiber	27.5%	25.4%	19.3%	5.7%	2.5%	8%	14%
AV fiber	87.1%	4.1%	6.4%	1.4%	1.1%	0.2%	0.8%

3.4 FT-IR spectroscopy analysis

The FT-IR spectra of apocynum venetum before and after degumming are shown in Fig. 3. Through the analysis we could draw, the absorption peaks of $3296cm^{-1}$ and $1026cm^{-1}$, which ascribed to O—H group and C—O vibration of cellulose, respectively, did not change for two samples. In addition, the $897cm^{-1}$ absorption peak was due to β-glycosidic linkages between the monosaccharides of cellulose, which suggested chemical degumming did not cause greater damage to the molecular structure of fibers. After degumming, the peaks at $2855.5cm^{-1}$, $1719cm^{-1}$, $1613.5cm^{-1}$, $1530.5cm^{-1}$, and $1173cm^{-1}$ became unobvious, even disappeared, indicating chemical reagents treatment removed lots of pectin, hemicellulose, and lignin[14-16].

3.5 Crystalline structures analysis

The X-ray diffraction (XRD) test results of fibers were analyzed, as shown in Fig. 4. The peaks at 15.16°, 16.68°, 22.88° and 34.52° were observed in XRD curves of fibers, and were the same diffraction peaks of the 2θ angles at the XRD spectra of two samples. The four major diffraction peaks represented the cellulose I, which verified that the chemical degumming process

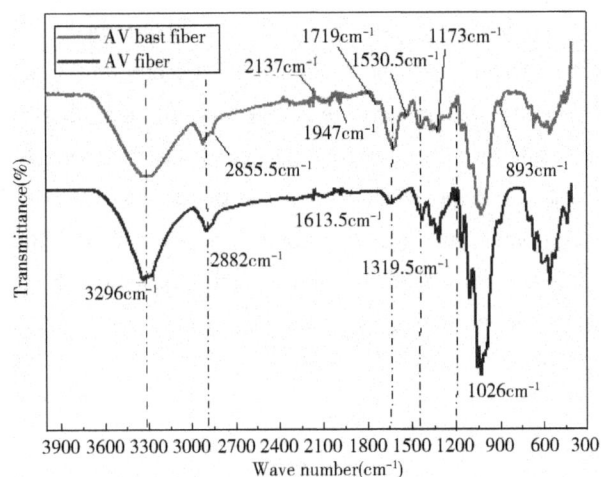

Fig. 3 FT-IR spectra of Apocynum Venetum fibers (a) AV bast fiber; (b) AV fiber

could not change the crystal structure of AV bast fiber. However, the crystalline index was changed. After chemical degumming, AV fibers contained more crystalline cellulose and the crystallinity index increased from 34.92% to 70.36%. This was because lignin and hemicelluloses etc. had been removed, the macromolecule chain of fibers rearranged and the molecules were more organized.

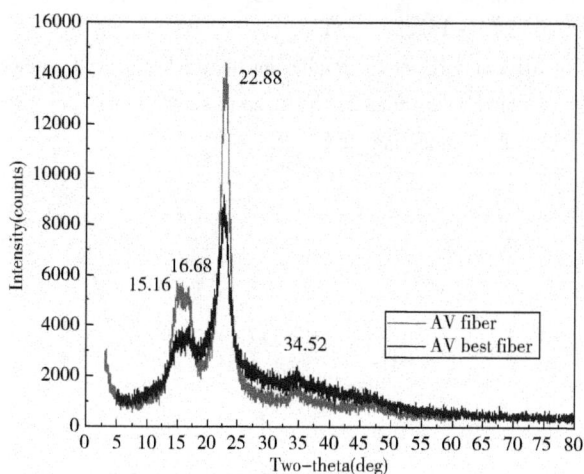

Fig. 4 XRD spectra of Apocynum Venetum fibers (a) AV bast fiber; (b) AV fiber

3.6 Tensile properties test

The results of tensile properties test can be observed from Tab. 3. The results showed that AV fibers had good breaking strength, which were higher than AV bast fiber. This was because AV bast fibers contained more gum and less fibers, resulting in low tenacity. Moreover, the effectiveness of degumming could be further confirmed.

Tab. 3 The mechanical properties of AV bast fibers and AV fibers

Properties	Tenacity (CN/dtex)	Elongation (%)
AV bast fiber	1.09	5.2
AV fiber	4.16	3.15

4 Conclusions

AV fibers were obtained from chemical degumming and were characterized by various techniques. SEM and FT-IR results showed that chemical degumming has no significant influence on the main components and molecular structure of the fiber. Then the gum could also be removed effectively, and the chemical component analysis confirmed the results. XRD indicated that the crystal structure of the degummed fibers was better than the bast. What's more, AV bast fibers and AV fibers had a strong ability to absorb moisture, and compared to AV bast fibers, the mechanical strength of AV fibers was preferable. These results may help to provide basic properties of AV bast fibers and AV fibers, which can prepare to get high quality raw materials for subsequent processing and make better use of apocynum venetum in the industry, and further work is ongoing.

References

[1] Han G, Wang L, Liu M, et al. Component analysis and microfiber arrangement of apocynum venetum fibers: The MS and AFM study[J]. Carbohydrate Polymers, 2008, 72(4): 652-656.

[2] Xie W Y, Zhang X Y, Tian W G, et al. Botany, traditional uses, phytochemistry and pharmacology of apocynum venetum L. (Luobuma): A review [J]. J Ethnopharmacol, 2012; 141: 1-8.

[3] Wei C. Study on growth characteristics of apocynum venetum and properties[J]. China Fiber Inspection,2013(11): 85-87.

[4] Gu Q, Xie C, Wang G, et al. Study on fiber structure and properties of ramie fiber[J]. Silk, 2017, 54(2): 11-15.

[5] Kunlin W. Study on the wearability of apocynum fabric[D]. Wuhu:Anhui Polytechnic University, 2014: 11-14.

[6] Li M H, Han G T and Yu J Y. Microstructure and mechanical properties of apocynum venetum fibers extracted by alkali-assisted ultrasound with different frequencies [J]. Fiber Polym 2010; 11: 48-53.

[7] Wang L, Han G, Zhang Y. Comparative study of composition, structure and properties of apocynum venetum, fibers under different pretreatments[J]. Carbohydrate Polymers, 2007, 69(2): 391-397.

[8] Zhou J, Li Z, Yu C. Property of ramie fiber degummed with Fenton reagent[J]. Fibers & Polymers, 2017, 18(10): 1891-1897.

[9] GB 5883—1986. Test method for moisture regain and moisture content of ramie[S].

[10] GB 5889—1986. Ramie chemical composition quantitative analysis method[S].

[11] Song Y, Han G, Jiang W. Comparison of the performance of kenaf fiber using different reagents presoak combined with steam explosion treatment[J]. Journal of the Textile Institute, 2017, 108(10): 1-6.

[12] Tagawa T, Kayamori Y, Ohata M, et al. Comparison of CTOD standards: BS 7448-Part 1 and revised ASTM E1290 [J]. Engineering Fracture Mechanics, 2010, 77(2): 327-336.

[13] GB/T 3923. 1—1997. Determination of strength and elongation at break of fabric[S].

[14] Cerhard Stock, et al. Upgrading rycycled pulps using enzymatic treatment[J]. 1995, 78(2): 9.

[15] Marx-Figini M, Finetti M, Ellenrieder G V. Enzymatic degradation of cotton cellulose by separated endo-and exocellulase[J]. Cellulose Chemistry & Technology, 1997, 31 (3): 155–162.

[16] Krishna S H, et al. Studies on the production and application of cellulose from Trichoderma reesei QM-9414[J]. Bioprocess Engineering. 2000, 22, 4.

The Influence of Woven Fabric Structure on the Characteristics of Capillary Action

Qingqing Zhou[1], Xiaocai Li[1]*, Qinliang Zhuang[1]

[1] College of Textiles, Donghua University, Shanghai 201620, China

* Corresponding author's email: 15202155708@163. com

Abstract: This study was to explore the effect of woven fabric structure on the liquid movement in the fabric. And the characteristics of the liquid transfer across fabric plane as well as liquid movement along the fabric plane were discussed. It is found that the fabric with bi-component configuration can effectively enhance the property of capillary action for quicker liquid transfer. The bi-component configuration can be either a combination of hydrophilic natural fiber and hydrophobic wicking synthetic fiber or a combination of different capillary equivalent radii for both sides of the fabric. In addition, the application of wicking synthetic yarn employed to a certain proportion in the single layer cotton fabric can significantly increase the rate of in-plane liquid spreading. Also, the results show there are anisotropic feature of liquid spreading. The liquid moved faster along the direction the wicking yarn distribution. The fabric formed by interlaced synthetic wicking yarn to cotton yarn can provide comfort for wearers in a wider range of climate changes.

Keywords: Woven structure; Capillary action; Bi-component configuration; Wicking

1 Introduction

Textiles with excellent wicking behavior have been caught attention for quite many years. According to statistics, in the western developed countries, people who regularly participate in physical training account for more than 60% of the total population, which require a great number of apparels with good comfort performance, and in China it also reaches 35%[1]. With the development of high performance fibers such as Coolmax by Dopont as well as other similar fibers, numerous fabrics with good wicking property have been constructed for sportswear or apparels with particular comfort performance. Most fabrics with wicking property are knitted fabrics due to its relatively short processing line for producing the fabrics. The knitted fabrics can be directly made of fibers with good wicking property, which can spread the liquid in the fabric effectively to the larger area for quick drying. The fabric can also be composed of bi-component configuration for both surfaces of the fabric respectively, either using hydrophilic natural fiber/hydrophobic wicking fiber or using smaller/larger capillary radii of yarns[2]. Compared to the developed knitted wicking fabrics with a success in the area of professional sportswear, woven fabrics with wicking property are rarely within consideration. This is because functional fibers for wicking contain very fine filaments with profiled cross-section, which can be fully filled with size during slashing process so that the wicking properties of fabrics have significant loss. Even after desizing, the wicking property of fabric still cannot completely recover.

Since woven fabrics are widely used in all fields, its wicking property has become a rising concern in most applications and systems today. For example, wearing comfort of fine cotton, silk fabrics etc. can be enhanced when they are combined with wicking fibers because the clinging of fabric to the skin due to perspiration can be avoided. Ramie or linen fabrics combined with wicking fibers can also provide much better comfort performance while maintaining its own natural look and unique "green" property. In addition, development of cotton fabric with wicking performance has come into consideration for researchers for more wide use rather than only professional sportswear[3]. However, limited research on mechanism of capillary action in woven construction has been found in the literature. The aim of this research was to investigate the effect of structural factors of woven construction on transport of liquid moisture in the fabric so as to bring about positive impact for designing and engineering functional woven fabrics for wider applications.

2 Principles for Construction of Woven Structures with Effective Capillary Action

Previous study shows that the transmission of sweat in the fabric is mainly in three ways[4]: (1) Fiber itself hygroscopic, which means the fiber has a certain moisture absorption capacity and can absorb part of the sweat; (2) The vaporous perspiration diffuses through the tiny aperture in the fabric; (3) Liquid water passes the capillary tube and is discharged from the body surface under the effect of additional pressure.

Although the liquid water in the fabric is not affected by the potential energy difference in the external force field, it can flow in the capillary under the action of the interfacial tension of the liquid and gas in the capillary. This is called the capillary action[5]. Capillary action is the main driving force to transport the liquid within the fabric. It is closely related to the surface tension of liquid to gas, the contact angle between solid and liquid, and particularly the diameter and length of capillaries.

The liquid transportation in woven fabric can be divided into the liquid transfer perpendicular to the fabric plane and the liquid transfer along the fabric plane. The liquid transfer perpendicular to the fabric plane is the ability to transfer the liquid from one side of the fabric to the other side of the fabric. It can be achieved by two approaches. One is using a hydrophilic fiber / hydrophobic fiber to form two surfaces of the fabric (as shown in Fig. 1). After the sweat is discharged from the skin, the liquid is wicked by hydrophobic inner layer followed

by absorbing by hydrophilic outer layer. The hydrophobic fibers with profiled cross-section absorb little moisture. They form many capillary tubes and drain the liquid to the hydrophilic outer layer. The hydrophilic fibers, usually natural fibers, are characterized by a large number of hydrophilic groups on the macromolecular chain, which is easy to combine with water molecules. Its moisture absorption capacity is much larger than that of ordinary chemical synthetic fibers. Spreading of liquid on the larger area of outer layer of fabric increases the evaporation rate of moisture to the environment so as to keep the body dry and comfortable. Another approach is that the two surfaces of the fabric are made up of capillary tubes with different diameters (as shown in Fig. 2). The inner layer is formed with coarser capillary while the outer layer is formed with finer capillary. The pressure difference produced by different capillary diameters drives the liquid from inner layer to the outer layer of the fabric.

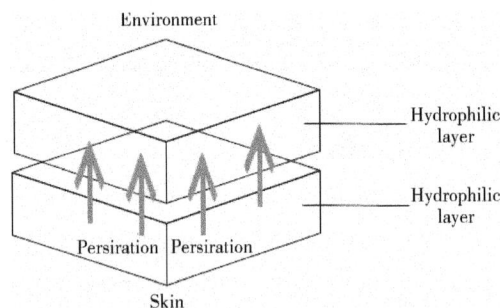

Fig. 1 Hydrophobic/Hydrophilic model

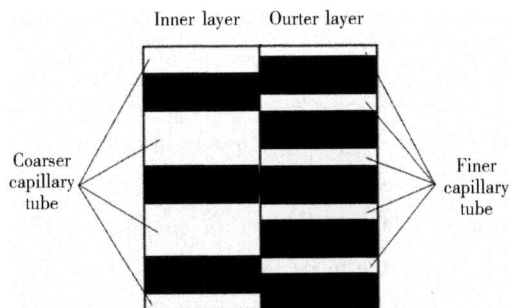

Fig. 2 Smaller/Larger capillary radius model

For the liquid transfer along the fabric plane, numerous synthetic wicking fibers[2,6-15] can perform to provide desired wicking property. These synthetic fibers can be directly used to produce woven fabrics. However, as mentioned previously, the slashing process hinders wicking function of fabric. In order to make the single layer woven fabric has excellent wicking performance, wicking fiber can be selected to be served only as weft yarns which do not require slashing process. The combination of this wicking weft yarns with either natural fiber or synthetic fiber as warp yarns reduces the moisture conductivity of the fabric as a whole, compared to pure cotton fabric. But it has been found that the combination of wicking yarn with natural fiber such as cotton can exhibit promising application because it can provide good comfort to the wearer in a wider range of temperature changes or between mild exercise and intense exercise. Therefore, its application will be much wider than the fabrics constructed from 100% synthetic wicking fibers.

3 Experiments

3.1 Specifications of woven fabrics

According to the principles of constructing woven fabrics for better wicking performance, 14 fabrics have been designed and engineered in this study. For producing fabrics with bi-component configuration, PP (polypropylene, 300 D/72F) was employed for warp yarns, the fabric warp count and weft count were 225 ends/cm and 410 picks/cm respectively. Cotton yarn is $40^{s/2}$ and Coolest yarn is 100 D/36F. The fabric constructions are shown in Fig. 3 – Fig. 6. The specifications of fabrics with bi-component configuration are seen in Tab. 1.

Tab. 1 Specifications of fabrics with bi-component effect

Sample No.	Face weft	Back weft	Ratio	Weave features
1#	Cotton	Coolbst*	1:1	Same weaves on both sides
2#	Cotton	Coolbst*	1:1	Different weaves on both sides
3#	Cotton	PP	1:1	Same weaves on both sides
4#	Cotton	PP	1:1	Different weaves on both sides
5#	Cotton	PP	1:2	Different weaves on both sides
6#	Cotton	PP	1:3	Different weaves on both sides
7#	PP	PP	1:1	Same weaves on both sides
8#	PP	PP	1:2	Different weaves on both sides
9#	PP	PP	1:3	Different weaves on both sides

* Coolbst is brand name of polyester fiber with profiled cross-section developed by Chinese Yi-Zheng Chemical Co., Ltd.

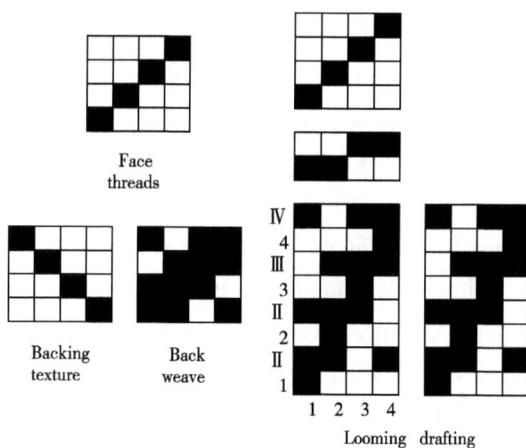

Fig. 3   Weft-backed weave & loom program for sample 1#, 3#, 7#

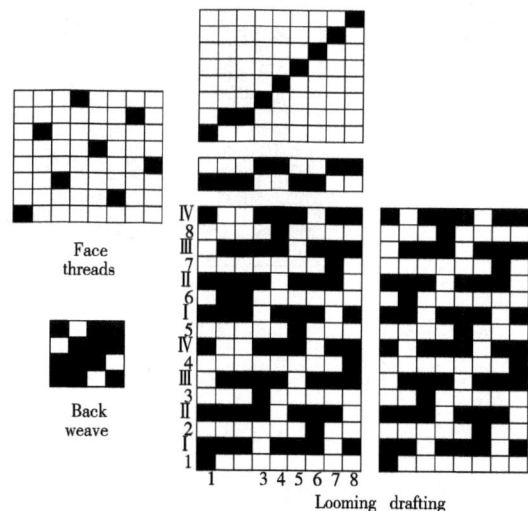

Fig. 4   Weft-backed weave & loom program for sample 2#, 4#

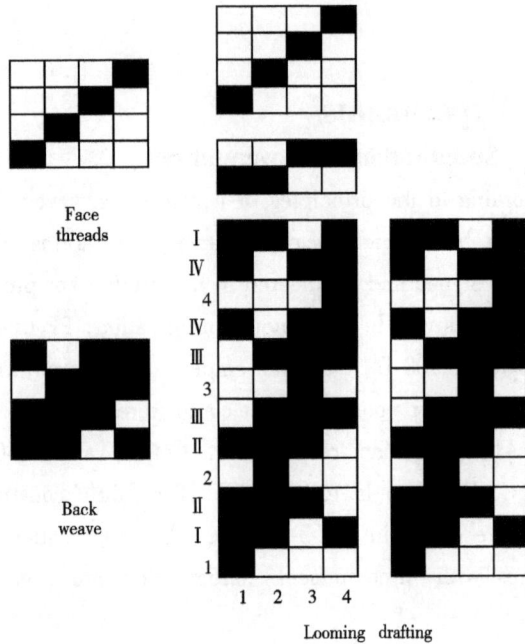

Fig. 5 Weft-backed weave & loom program for sample 5#, 8#

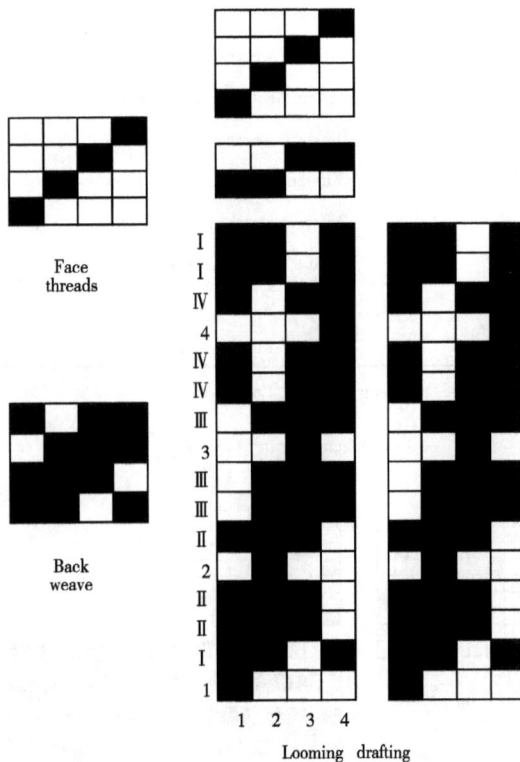

Fig. 6 Weft-backed weave & loom program for sample 6#, 9#

The constructions of single layer fabric for in-plane quick liquid spreading are shown in Tab. 2. Cotton

yarns are interlaced with synthetic wicking yarns with five different ratios.

Tab. 2 Specifications of fabrics constructed with single layered plain weave

Sample No.	Warp	Weft (Cotton: coolbst)	Warp count (ends/10cm)	Weft count (picks/10cm)
10#		1:0		
11#		3:1		
12#	Cotton	1:1	225	210
13#		1:3		
14#		0:1		

3.2 Experimental measurement

Several experiments were undertaken for this investigation.

1. Strip Test[16]: One end of the fabric sample was vertically immersed in water. The height of liquid rising along the fabric at a certain time was recorded. The YG871-II capillary action tester was used for the measurement.

2. Liquid Retention[17]: The liquid retention was to evaluate the water absorption capacity of fabrics. The fabric sample with standard size was weighed as W_0 after been placed in oven at 60℃ for 10 hours. Then the fabric was weighed again as W_1 after been immersed in distilled water for 3 hours followed by water extracting for 2 minutes. Finally, the liquid retention was calculated by the following equation.

$$\text{Liquid Retention Rate}(\%) = (W_1 - W_0)/W_0 \times 100\% \quad (1)$$

3. Liquid Drying[18]: it is one of the most important values to evaluate the fabrics property of quick drying. The fabric sample was weighed as W_0 after been placed in oven at 60℃ for 10 hours. Then the fabric was weighed again as W_1 after been immersed in distilled water for 3 hours followed by water extracting for 2 minutes. The fabric sample was put back to the oven at 37℃ for 5 minutes. The fabric weight was measured again as W_2. Finally the liquid drying was calculated by the following equation.

$$\text{Liquid Drying}(\%) = (W_1 - W_2)/(W_1 - W_0) \times 100\% \quad (2)$$

4. Drop Test[19]: the fabric sample was conditioned in

the environment of (20 ± 2) ℃ and $(65 \pm 2)\%$ RH for 24 hours. A drop of liquid with 1 milliliter was dropped onto the fabric from the position of 1cm above the fabric. A time period of 30 seconds later, the length of liquid movement along the warp direction "a" and along the weft direction "b" are measured and the liquid spreading area was estimated.

4　Results and Discussion

The results from strip test, liquid retention rate and drying rate for weft-backed fabrics are shown in Tab. 3 and Tab. 4. Application of synthetic wicking yarn in cotton blend fabric constructed with plain weave provides unique wicking performance. The experiment results for the wicking measurement are shown in Tab. 5.

Tab. 3　Wicking property of fabrics with hydrophilic/hydrophobic model

Fabric sample No.	Liquid rising length in 30 mins(cm)	Liquid retention (%)	Liquid drying (%)
1#	16.7	96.4	83.5
2#	16.6	95.0	84.7
3#	12.3	83.5	66.2
4#	12.4	84.3	63.3
5#	9.7	79.2	73.9
6#	8.1	72.9	79.6

Tab. 4　Wicking property of fabrics with different capillary radius model

Fabric sample No.	Face weft: back weft	Liquid rising length in 30 mins(cm)	Liquid retention (%)	Liquid drying (%)
7#	1:1	9.5	64.9	88.5
8#	1:2	11.3	66.8	92.7
9#	1:3	13.2	70.1	92.9

Tab. 5　Wicking property of fabrics with different amount of coolbst

Fabric Sample No.	Coolbst amount (%)	Liquid rising length in 30 mins(cm)	Liquid Drying (%)	Liquid movement in warp direction$a$ (cm)	Liquid movement in weft direction$b$ (cm)	Spreading Area (cm²)
10#	0	10.5	51.3	2.42	2.33	4.42
11#	25	11.2	55.2	2.78	3.74	8.16
12#	50	12.7	58.9	2.83	5.26	11.69
13#	75	14.1	65.6	3.17	7.35	18.29
14#	100	14.2	69.2	3.30	9.86	25.54

4.1　Effect of construction of bi-component configuration with hydrophilic absorbing fiber and hydrophilic wicking fiber on liquid transfer

The bi-component configuration with hydrophilic absorbing fiber and hydrophilic wicking fiber is effective for liquid transfer across the plane of fabric. Fig. 7 and Fig. 8 show that compared with Fabric 7# made of entirely synthetic fiber, Fabric 1#-4# have higher wicking height and amount of liquid retention. Moreover, the use of synthetic wicking fiber (Coolbst) in Fabric $1^{\#}$ and $2^{\#}$ increases the liquid movement than ordinary synthetic fiber (PP) used in Fabric $3^{\#}$ and $4^{\#}$. Coolbst provides higher capillary pressure due to its built-in finer capillary tubes so that it drives liquid faster than those made of PP with conventional round cross-section. Therefore, combination of hydrophilic absorbing fiber and hydrophilic wicking fiber enhance the liquid transfer significantly. Faster liquid transferring rate and existence of hydrophilic absorbing fiber make it hold more liquid as shown in Fig. 8. For fabric drying rate, as shown in Fig. 9, liquid evaporation is faster from Fabric $7^{\#}$ because it does not contain any absorbing fiber. And Fabric $1^{\#}$ and $2^{\#}$ show quicker drying rate than Fabric $3^{\#}$ and $4^{\#}$ since the wicking fiber in Fabric $1^{\#}$ and $2^{\#}$ spread the liquid in larger area.

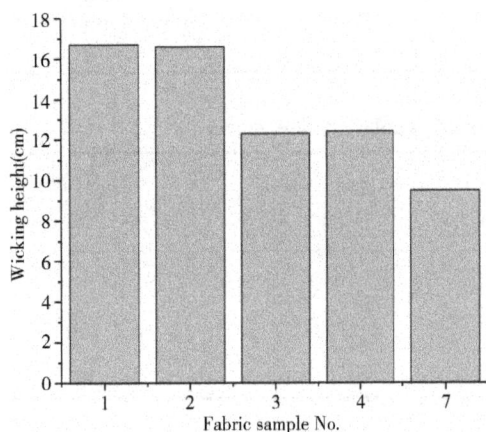

Fig. 7　Effect of construction of bi-component configuration on wicking height

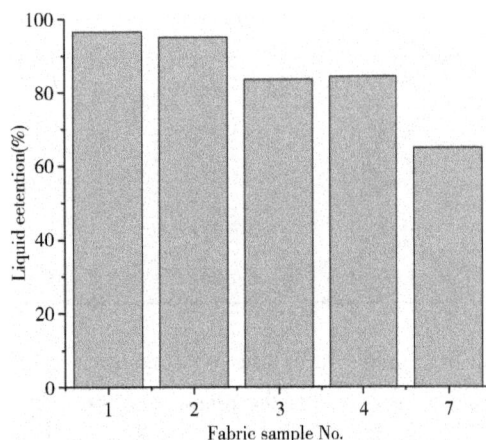

Fig. 8　Effect of construction of bi-component configuration on liquid retention

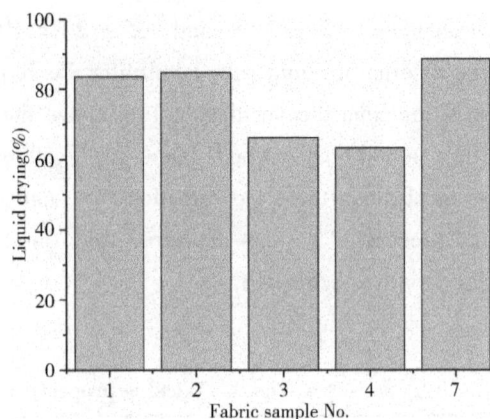

Fig. 9　Effect of construction of bi-component configuration on fabric drying rate

4.2　Effect of construction of bi-component with fibers containing different capillary radii on liquid transfer

When the capillary diameters of the two sides of the fabric are different from each other, the additional pressure difference due to capillary action will drive the liquid to move. Assume that σ is liquid-gas surface tension (Nm^{-1}); θ_1 is contact angle of fiber to the inner layer of fabric; θ_2 is contact angle of fiber to the outer layer of fabric; r_1 is the equivalent capillary radius of inner layer; r_2 is the equivalent capillary radius of outer layer. The capillary action can be triggered only when the pressure difference ΔP does not equal to zero. The pressure difference can be expressed as following equation.

$$\Delta P = 2\sigma \left(\frac{\cos \theta_2}{r_2} - \frac{\cos \theta_1}{r_1} \right) \tag{3}$$

When the fibers for inner layer and outer are the same, then $\theta_1 = \theta_2 = \theta$, thus

$$\Delta P = 2\sigma \cos\theta \left(\frac{1}{r_2} - \frac{1}{r_1} \right) \tag{4}$$

When the capillary radius of the inner layer is larger than that of the outer capillary equivalent radius, i. e. $r_1 > r_2$, then $\Delta P > 0$.

The existence of pressure difference due to different capillary radii for both sides of fabric drives the liquid transferring from inner layer to the outer layer of fabric. The results of strip test for Fabric $7^{\#}$-$9^{\#}$ are shown in Fig. 10. The liquid moving rate increases as the equivalent capillary radius of outer layer of fabric decreases.

According to the construction of Fabric $7^{\#}$–$9^{\#}$, Fabric $9^{\#}$ contains the finest capillary tubes, namely r_2 is much smaller than r_1 so as to trigger the liquid transfer more quickly.

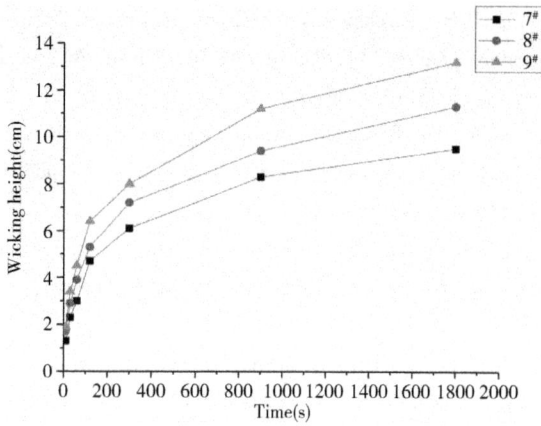

Fig. 10   Liquid rising height with time for fabric $7^{\#}$, $8^{\#}$ and $9^{\#}$

4.3   Effect of blend of synthetic wicking yarn to cotton yarn in plain weave fabric on its liquid spreading property

The results from drop test show that liquid spreading area increases with an increase of the amount of wicking yarn (Coolbst) used, as shown in Fig. 12. Liquid spreading to a larger area can impel water evaporation more quickly. Meanwhile, liquid spreads much faster along the weft direction where Coolbst yarns are distributed than warp direction where there was cotton yarns only (as shown in Fig. 11). This anisotropic feature of liquid spreading depends on the distribution of synthetic wicking yarn in the fabric.

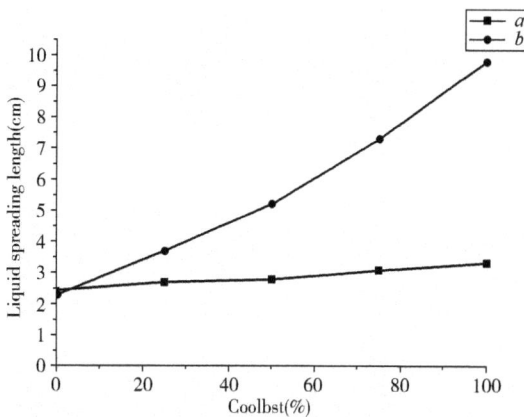

Fig. 11   Effect of Coolbst amount on liquid moving rate

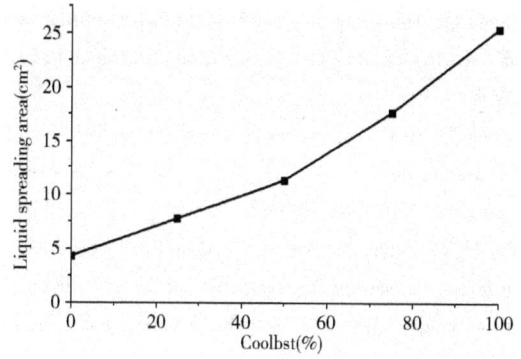

Fig. 12   Effect of Coolbst amount on liquid spreading area

5   Conclusions

This study was to explore the effect of woven fabric structure on the liquid movement in the fabric. And the characteristics of the liquid transfer across fabric plane as well as liquid movement along the fabric plane were discussed. It is found that the fabric with bi-component configuration can effectively enhance the property of capillary action for quicker liquid transfer. The bi-component configuration can be either a combination of hydrophilic natural fiber and hydrophobic wicking synthetic fiber or a combination of different capillary equivalent radii for both sides of the fabric.

In addition, the application of wicking synthetic yarn employed to a certain proportion in the single layer cotton fabric can significantly increase the rate of in-plane liquid spreading. Also, the results show there are anisotropic feature of liquid spreading. The liquid moved faster along the direction the wicking yarn distribution. The fabric formed by interlaced synthetic wicking yarn to cotton yarn can provide comfort for wearers in a wider range of temperature changes.

References

[1] Zhou L B. Development and study of knitted fabrics with moisture-transfer and cooling properties [D]. Shanghai: Donghua University, 2011.

[2] Zhao H Y. The study on wet permeability and vapor transmission of Coolbst fiber and fabrics[D]. Shanghai: Donghua University, 2004.

[3] Chen W. Research on properties and ecological processing technology of silk fabrics[D]. Jiangsu: Soochow University, 2014.

[4] Zhang Q. The study on comfort and function of fabrics made of sea-island filament [D]. Shanghai: Donghua University, 2004.

[5] Zhang J, Gu P. An overview of coolmax and coolplus fibers for wicking and quick drying [J], Silk Textile Technology Overseas, 2007 (4): 38-40.

[6] Wu H Y, Zhang Y, Xie H. Study on the moisture transfer principle of waterproof breathable fabric by different treatments using MMT [J]. Shanghai University of Engineering Science, 2010: 1225-121.

[7] Zhang Y P, Xu R C, Chen L. The status quo of research and development of moisture-transfer and fast drying fiber &yarn [J]. Shandong Textile & Technology, 2006(1): 42-45.

[8] Tang S J, Yu S J, Latest highly absorbent HYGRA fiber and its applications [J], Beijing Textile Journal, 2000, 21(5): 37-38.

[9] Wang J B, Li Y P, Zhang G C. Dyeing and finishing of polyester and wool dri-release ponte-de-roma with property of hydroscopic and fast dry [J]. Knitting Industry, 2016(4) 44-46.

[10] Guo L Q. Study on thermal-wet comfort of table tennis apparels [D]. Beijing: Beijing Institute of Fashion Technology, 2010.

[11] Wu J S, Xiao J, Ling W Y. Moisture absorbency and sweat transport of Cooldry filament [J]. Journal of Textile Research, 2006, 27(10): 74-76.

[12] Cui P, Dai L C, Huang L G. The inquiry into wet functional and moisture sorption of Coolbst profiled polyester fiber [J]. Journal of Xi'an University of Engineering Science and Technology, 2006, 20(3): 266-269.

[13] Zhu B H. Development of coolnice-lycra denim fabric with cooling property [J], Shanghai Textile Science & Technology, 2003, 31(3): 56-57.

[14] Yan Y. The Research status and structure analysis of coolplus fiber [J]. Synthetic Materials Aging and Application, 2016, 45 (2): 77-82.

[15] Li C Y, Luo Y W, Yang X. Experimental study of fabric moisture conductivity [J]. Cotton Textile Technology, 2015, 43(1): 25-28.

[16] Wang Y W, Yang J Z, Zhang J C. Study on vapor and liquid transportability of coolmax fabric [J]. Journal of Xi'an University of Engineering Science and Technology, 2003, 17 (4): 304-307.

[17] Yu S Y, Zhang H P, Yan X. Testing technology progress of liquid transportability of fabrics [J]. Progress in Textile Science & Technology, 2008 (1): 35-36.

[18] Zhang H X, Liu F R, Wang J. Effects of fabric weave and cover factor on moisture ability of moisture absorbent and fast drying fabric [J]. Journal of Textile Research, 2008, 29 (5): 31-33.

The Study of Omnidirectional Stretchable CNT/PDMS Electro-Heating Composite

Shan Xiao[1], Dongsheng Ge[2], Fujun Xu[1,2]*, Yiping Qiu[1,2]*

[1]*College of Textiles, Donghua University, Shanghai 201620, China*

[2]*Shanghai Key Laboratory of Advanced Micro & Nano Textile Materials, shanghai 201620, China*

* *Corresponding author's email*: fjxu@ dhu. edu. cn;ypqiu@ dhu. cn

Abstract:In this paper the omnidirectional stretchable CNT/PDMS electro-heating composite was prepared by inflating-combining-degassing method with carbon nanotube (CNT) film as the heating material, polydimethylsiloxane (PDMS) as the protective layer and the elastic substrate. The results show that the mechanical properties in the orientation direction of the composite are similar to those in the vertical orientation direction. The resistance change rates in the orientation direction and the vertical orientation direction are 3.39% and 2.01% respectively when the strain is 40%, which mean the composite has resistance stability during the tensile process. And, due to Joule law, the composite has electric-heating stability under 40% strain. The research is of great significance in promoting the applications of electro-heating composites in the field of flexible electronics and intelligent wearable.

Keywords:Omnidirectional stretchable; CNT film; PDMS; Electric-heating stability

1 Introduction

Electric-heating material is such one that converts electric energy into heat energy through the conductive material in it. Conductive polymer composites (CPCs) have become a hot topic in recent years. CPCs are made of polymer materials which mixed with a certain amount of conductive material. The conductive material forms a continuous conductive network in the polymer matrix to realize the electrical function[1]. The common filler in CPCs is metal, carbon and metal oxides. Carbon filler is the most widely used filler, including carbon black, carbon fiber, graphite, carbon nanotube (CNT) and graphite. Because of the large aspect ratio, carbon nanotube has excellent electrical, thermal, mechanical and optical properties along the axial direction[2-4]. Carbon nanotubes (CNTs), as new conductive and electric-heating filler, have made some progress in the electric-heating properties of composites. At present, the polymers used in electric-heating materials are epoxy resin[5], polydimethylsiloxane

(PDMS)[6] and polyurethane (PU)[7]. The CNT composites based epoxy resin lack good flexibility. PDMS is in the hottest study at present.

They are mostly CNT powders when carbon nanotubes used in electric-heating materials. Jing Yan[8] found that the higher the content of CNT powder, the stronger the conductivity of the composites. The conductive properties of CNT powder filled CPCs are better than other kinds of filler, but the content of the CNT powder is low, less than 1%, and the electrical and tensile deformation properties are poor. Qiang Bu[9] and others deposited carbon nanotubes (CNTs), mechanical peeling graphene (GE) and original graphene oxide (rGO) on PDMS films by spraying. They found that the CNT/PDMS composite has the best conductivity and the temperature can reach 200℃ under 110V. The prepared CNT/PDMS composite has certain stretchability, but the resistance becomes larger during the tensile process and the resistance change rate is 2% when the tensile strain is 10%.

Since there is no one kind of electric-heating material with high thermal conductivity, light flexibility, high elasticity, wearable and omnidirectional stretchable characteristics, this paper used CNT film and PDMS to prepare a kind of omnidirectional stretchable electric-heating composite with microcosmic omnidirectional fold structure by inflating-combining-degassing method. The electricial, mechanical and the electric-heating properties of static and tensile states of the composite in different directions were studied. It is of great significance to promote the applications of electric-heating composites in the field of flexible electronics and intelligent wearable.

2 Experiments

2.1 Materials

CNT film, prepared by an optimum floating chemical vapor deposition technique, was provided by Suzhou Institute of Nano-Tech and Nano-Bionics (SINANO), Chinese Academy of Sciences. CNT film contained both SWNT and MWNT, particularly, the main part is MWNT. PDMS and curing agent are analytical AR, were produced by the ELO Trading Co., Ltd. Silver paste, purity > 99.9%, was produced by Hong Kong

maintenance man. Copper wire was used as electrode, and the diameter is 0.1mm.

2.2 Specimen preparation

Preparation of the elastic basement membrane: PDMS solution and curing agent were mixed evenly, whose mass ratio was 4 : 1, and poured into a round culture dish, then put into the oven to solidify. The curing temperature was 100℃ and the time was 35min.

Pretreatment of CNT film: slicing method was used to cut a certain size (20mm × 5mm) of CNT film, copper wire electrodes were assembly on both ends of the orientation and vertical orientation direction of the CNT film, and the distance between copper wires was 10mm.

Preparation of omnidirectional stretchable electro-heating composite: as shown in Fig. 1, by inflating, the PDMS elastic basement membrane fixed on the hollow cylinder was prestretched to a certain strain, and it was combined with the pretreated CNT film by PDMS binder, then the stress of the PDMS elastic basement membrane was removed by degassing after the composite completion. The combining temperature is 100℃, time is 20min.

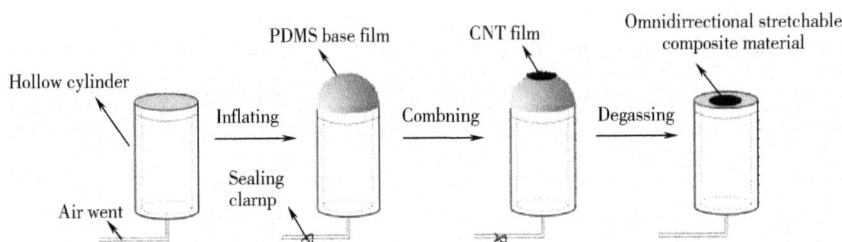

Fig. 1　Preparation process of omnidirectional stretchable CNT/PDMS electro-heating composite

2.3 Performance testing

Micro-morphologies of CNT film and omnidirectional stretchable electro-heating composite including surface and cross- section were investigated using a scanning electron microscope(SEM, Hitachi TM 3000) operated at an accelerating voltage of 15 kV. The thickness of CNT film can also be obtained by analyzing the SEM images, using an image analysis program (Image-Pro Plus). Samples were sputtered with gold before ima-

ging.

Electrical properties of omni-directional stretchable electro-heating composite was obtained using method of two point probe testing[10]. Test parameters: stretching speed: 1mm/min.

Electro-heating properties of omni-directional stretchable electro-heating composite, including temperature, reaction rate, consistency, were measured using a digital thermometer.

3 Results and Discussion

3.1 Morphological observations

The morphology of CNT film in Fig. 2 (a) depicts that the CNTs are entangled together by a number of micrometer to dozens of microns of unequal CNT bundles in length, so that the CNT film has a self-supporting structure and forms a clear orientation. The section of the CNT film is shown in Fig. 2 (b). The thickness of the CNT film is (8.56 ± 0.74) μm and the volume density is $0.342 \mathrm{g/cm^3}$, so the CNT film is thin and soft. Fig. 2 (c) shows the surface of the omnidirectional stretchable electro-heating composite, with fold structure in different directions which stores a certain length of CNT film to ensure that CNT film is not destroyed when the composite is stretched. The cross section of the composite in Fig. 2 (d) shows the composite is made up of PDMS protection layer, CNT film and PDMS elastic basement membrane. Fig. 2 (e) and (f) show the static and tensile state of the omnidirectional stretchable electro-heating composite.

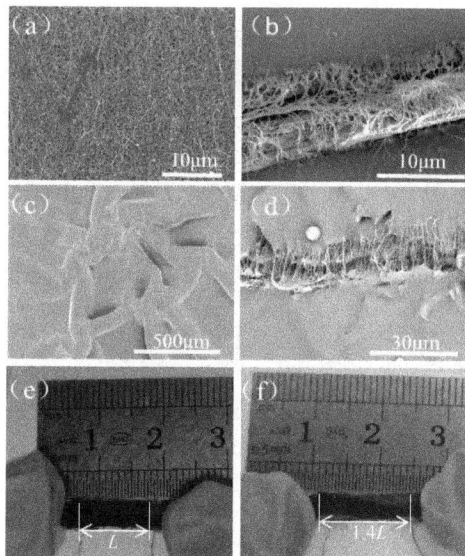

Fig. 2 SEM image and macroscopical optical photographs (a) (b) Surface and cross section of CNT film; (c) (d) Surface and cross section of omnidirectional stretchable electro-heating composite; (e) (f) Macroscopical optical photographs

3.2 Electrical and mechanical properties

Fig. 3 (a) (c) and (b) (d) show the electrical and mechanical properties of the composite. It shows that the resistance change rate of the composite is basically unchanged under a certain tensile strain, and then the resistance change rate increases linearly. This is due to the wrinkle structure in different directions in the surface of the electro-heating composite, which stores a certain length of CNT film in different directions. The CNT film is stretched to plane at the initial stretch, and is not destroyed, then the CNT tow in the CNT film gradually stretches and slids, so the resistance increase gradually.

In addition, Fig. 3 (a) and (b) show that the mechanical properties in orientation direction are slightly higher than the vertical orientation direction. As the composite is composed of PDMS protective layer, CNT film and PDMS elastic basement membrane, the external force on the tensile direction is shared, so the mechanical properties in different directions are basically similar.

3.3 Electric-heating stability

Fig. 4 shows the temperature-time curves of the electro-heating composites under static and tensile conditions. When electrified at 10s, the temperature of the composite rises rapidly to steady state and when the power is cut off at 3min, it rapidly drops to room temperature, showing fast temperature response. The electro-heating stability is better when the composite is continuously electrified in the static (tensile 0) and 40% tensile deformation range.

Fig. 4 (a) and (b) show that the temperature in orientation direction is obviously higher than that in the vertical orientation at the same voltage, because the orientation resistance of the CNT film is less than the vertical orientation, which is in accordance with the Joule law of the heating principle. In the CNT film, the CNT tow entanglement, when electrified, electrons along the CNT tow in orientation direction, and the electrons in vertical orientation direction need to overcome the gap between the CNT tow and jump, thus the orientation resistance is smaller.

Fig. 4 (c) and (d), the infrared images show the composites have certain elasticity and can maintain the stability of the electro-heating performance in the case of tension. The properties of the composite depend on the special structure, with a fold structure in different directions in the surface. The resistance only changes a slight when 40% strain. It is the stability of the resistance that ensures the CNT film cannot be affected when the composite is subjected to a certain tension, so that the electro-heating stability of the composite is maintained when it is stretched in full directions.

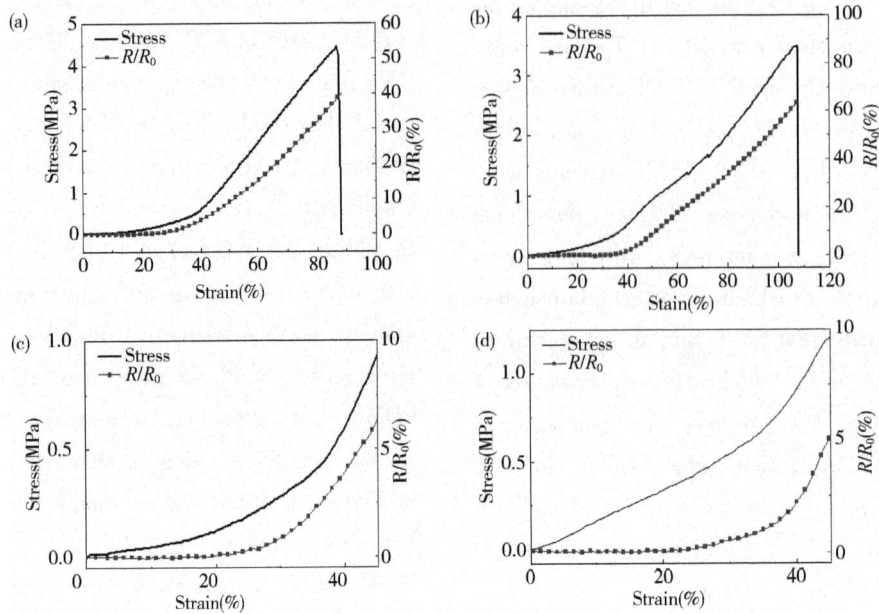

Fig. 3 Stress-strain-resistance change rate curves of omnidirectional stretchable electro-heating composite (a) (c) In orientation direction; (b) (d) In vertical orientation direction

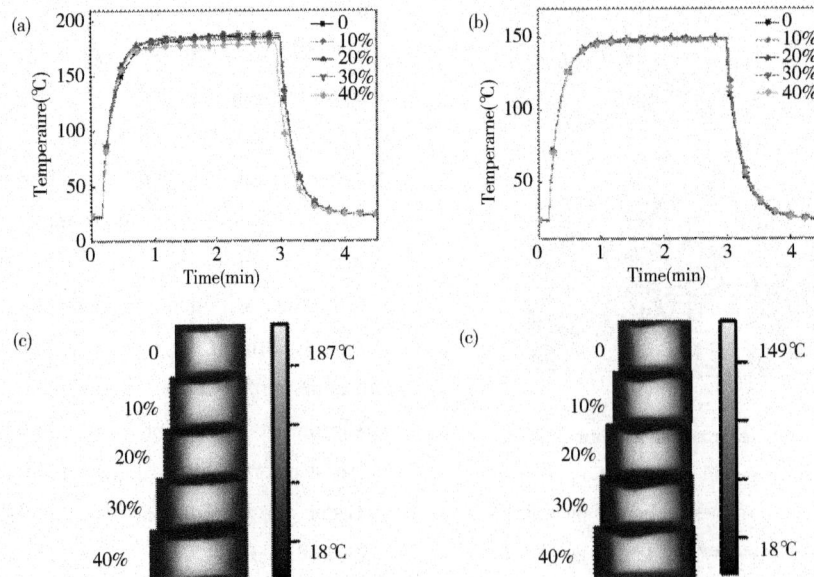

Fig. 4 Temperature-time curves and infrared images of electric-heating composites under static and tensile conditions (a) (c) In orientation direction; (b) (d) In vertical orientation direction

3.4 Application of electro-heating composite

Fig. 5 shows the physical and infrared images of the electro-heating composite used as electro-heating wrister. It shows that the electro-heating properties of the composite are stable when the wrist moves up, down, left and right under the bending state. This kind of wrister is more suitable for movement. Omnidirectional stretchable CNT/PDMS electro-heating composite has great potential in the application of intelligent wearable fields, such as electrothermal kneecap, electrothermal gloves, electro-heating clothing and so on.

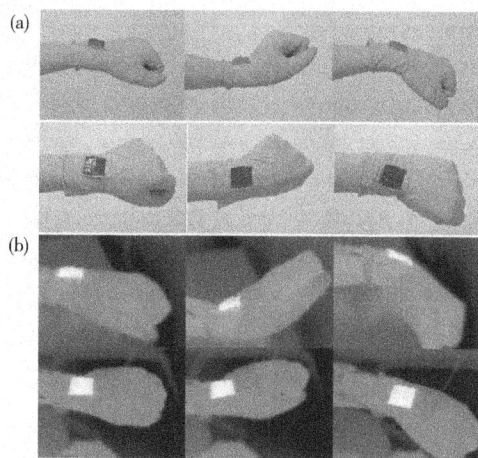

Fig. 5 Application of electro-heating composite and infrared images

4 Conclusions

(1) Using CNT film with excellent mechanics, high conductivity, flexibility, high orientation structure and good viscoelastic PDMS prepared omnidirectional stretchable electro-heating composite through inflating-combining-degassing method, which surface with microcosmic omnidirectional fold structure. The composites made up the defects of the non omnidirectional electro-heating composites. The composite has great potential in the application of intelligent wearable fields, such as electrothermal kneecap, electrothermal gloves, electro-heating clothing and so on.

(2) The mechanical properties in orientation direction of the composite are basically the same as those in vertical orientation direction, while the composites have certain resistance stability during the tensile process. When the tensile strain is 40%, the resistance change rate is 3.39% and 2.01% in orientation direction and vertical orientation direction.

(3) The omnidirectional stretchable electro-heating composites have better electro-heating stability. The temperatures in vertical orientation direction and orientation direction under 40% strain are equal to that at the static, showing electro-heating stability during the tensile process.

References

[1] Zhang R. Research on conductive mechanism and electro-thermal properties of polyethylene based composites [D]. Dalian University of Technology, 2014.

[2] Yu Z Z, Wang B, Niu T T. Research progress in thermal conductivity of carbon nanotubes/rubber composites[J]. J of Mat Sci and Engg, 2016 (4).

[3] Kenji H, Don N F, Kohel M, et al. Water-assisted highly efficient synthesis of impurity-free single-walled carbon nanotubes[J]. Science, 2004, 11(5700): 1362-1364

[4] Oliva A A, FSosa L V. Electrical and piezoresitive properties of multi-walled carbon nanotube/polymer composite films aligned by an electric field[J]. Carbon, 2011, 49(9): 2989-2997.

[5] Jeong Y G, An J E. Effects of mixed carbon filler composition on electric heating behavior of thermally-cured epoxy-based composite films[J]. Composites Part A Applied Science & Manufacturing, 2014, 56(1): 1-7.

[6] Yu J. Omnidirectionally stretchable high-performance supercapacitor based on isotropic buckled carbon nanotube films [J]. ACS Nano, 2016, 10(5): 5204-5211.

[7] Zhang T. PU/AgNWs/PDMS elastic conductive composites: preparation and properties [J]. New Chemical Materials, 2016 (5).

[8] Yan J, Jeong Y G. Multiwalled carbon nanotube/polydimethylsiloxane composite films as high performance flexible electric heating elements[J]. App Phys Letters, 2014. 105(5): 19051907.

[9] Bu Q. Stretchable conductive films based on carbon nanomaterials prepared by spray coating[J]. J of App Poly Sci, 2016, 133(15).

[10] Jing Y, Jeong Y G. Highly elastic and transparent multi-walled carbon nanotube/polydimethylsiloxane bilayer films as electric heating materials[J]. Materials & Design, 2015, 86: 72-79.

A Wearable Pressure Sensor Based on Facilely Prepared Carbonized Woven Cotton Fabric

Ronghui Wu[1,2], Liyun Ma[1], Yifan Zhang[1,2], Weidong Yu[1,2]*

[1] *Department of Technical Textiles, College of Textiles, Donghua University, Shanghai 201620, China*

[2] *Key Laboratory of Textile Material & Technology, Ministry of Education, Shanghai 201620, China*

* *Corresponding author's email*: wdyu@ dhu. edu. cn

Abstract: With the recent booming development of wearable electronics, flexible pressure sensors were urgently called for. To date, it is still a challenge to manufacture flexible pressure sensors with good performance. In this work, we reported a sandwiched pressure sensor based on carbonized cotton fabric with RGO on the surface through a low-cost, green, and scalable process, and demonstrated its superior performance in pressure sensor. The carbonized fabric has electricity conductivity of $50\Omega \cdot sq^{-1}$. The sandwiched pressure sensor exhibits high sensitivity of $1.992kPa^{-1}$, and a wide test range from 0 to 80kPa. The sensor has a quick response to the outside pressure. The superior performance can be ascribed to the plain weave network structure of the carbonized cotton fabric. The present work offers an effective strategy to rapidly prepare low-cost flexible pressure sensors with potential applications in the fields of wearable electronics, artificial intelligence devices, and so forth.

Keywords: Wearable pressure sensor; Reduced graphene oxide; Carbonized cotton fabric

1　Introduction

Electric components based on fibers or textiles have been increasingly investigated owing to their potential applications in wearable devices. Flexible sensor has a widely potential application in electronic skin and intelligent medicine for the years to come[1]. Recently, various nano-materials, including nanowires[2-3], carbon nanotubes[4], polymer nanofibers, metal nanoparticles[5] and graphene[6] have been used for the design of flexible pressure sensors. Usually, there are three types of sensing mechanisms for flexible sensors, piezo-resistivity[7-8], piezo-capacity[5, 9-10], and piezo-electricity[11]. For the resistive sensors, a change in the electrical resistance occurs when the geometry of the textile deforms upon the application of strain and stress. Some researchers make carbonized cotton fabric[12] or cotton fabric coated with RGO[13] into stretchable strain sensor. In this study, we reported a sandwiched pressure sensor based on carbonized cotton fabric with RGO on the surface through a low-cost, green, and scalable process, and demonstrated its superior performance in pressure sensor. We coated graphene oxide on the surface of cotton fabric and carbonized in tube furnace under the temperature of 800℃ for 30 minutes. Under this condition, the cellulose was transferred into amorphous carbon with the graphene oxide being reduced simultaneously. After assembling and encapulation, a sandwiched pressure sensor based on carbonized carbon fabric was obtained. The sensing properties of the textile based pressure sensor were measured. The flexible sensor could be used as wearable electronics to detect human motions.

2　Experiments

2.1　Materials

Plain woven cotton fabrics were obtained from Wujiang Shunye textile limited company (Suzhou). Two-component material Ecoflex was provided by Zhonghua Suhua

Co. , Ltd. (Guangdong). Sulfuric acid, Potassium permanganate, hydrogen peroxide, graphite, hydrazine hydrate, Sodium nitrate, and analytical purity, were supplied by Xilong chemical incorporated company (Guangdong).

2.2 Preparation of graphene oxide (GO)

The graphene oxide was prepared by modified Hummers method[14], including several steps: putting 120mL of 98% sulfuric acid (H_2SO_4) and 2. 000g of sodium nitrate ($NaNO_3$) powder in an open glass beaker, followed by placing the beaker in a basin of ice water for the purpose of cooling the beaker 0℃; adding 4. 000 g of graphite, followed by magnetic stirring for 30min, while the beaker remain cooled, slowly added 20. 000 g potassium permanganate ($KMnO_4$), while the beaker remained cooled, allowing the beaker to be heated naturally (due to the exothermic reaction) to 35℃, which was kept for 12h while magnetic stirring took place; slowly added 90mL of ice de-ionized water, while stirred occured, maintained the temperature at 45℃ and stirred for 1.5h; added 700mL de-ionized water inside; added 20mL of 30% hydrogen peroxide (H_2O_2) drop by drop until the liquid turned into yellow in order to reduce the residual potassium per manganate and manganese dioxide (MnO_2) to form soluble manganese sulfate ($MnSO_4$); dried the dispersion to obtain the solid (GO), which was dark brown.

2.3 Fabric treatment

Before coating with GO, the cotton fabric was washed in the solution of acetone for 10mins under the temperature of 60℃, and then followed by washing with deionized water for 3 times. Treated fabrics were dried at 60℃ in an oven for 2h to remove all absorbed moisture before carbonization. The pre-treated cotton fabric was dipped in the solution of 10mg/mL GO for 30mins and dried in the oven under 60℃, the dip-coating process was repeated for 3 times.

2.4 Carbonization of the cotton fabric

Fig. 1 illustrates the fabrication process of the carbonized cotton fabric-based pressure sensor. Pristine plain weave cotton fabric contains twisted cotton yarns composed of dozens of cellulose fibers, which are composed of millions of cellulose molecules, and release small

molecules, such as H_2O, CO_2, and CO, and transform into carbon with distorted graphited structure under high temperature treatment. The pristine cotton fabric was thermal treated at 800℃ under the argon atmosphere, with the GO on the surface being reduced into graphene meanwhile. The composite carbonized cotton fabric could be further fabricated into flexible pressure sensors by overlapping two layers together and encapsulating it into an elastic matrix (Ecoflex).

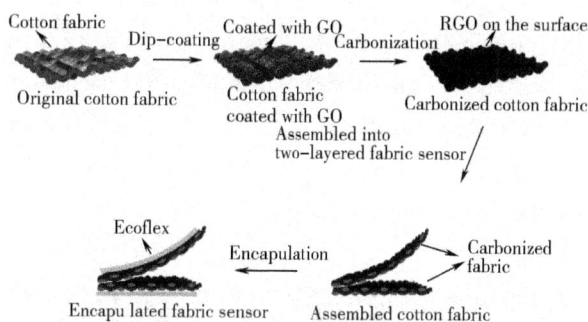

Fig. 1 Fabrication process of carbonized cotton fabric coated with graphene

2.5 Preparation of fabric based pressure sensor

An enameled Cu wire was attached on the side of carbonized fabric by conductive silver paste (Dupont 4929N) and conducting resin stabilizing the linkage segment. Two carbonized carton fabric with RGO (CCF @ RGO) was touched and sewed together and then encapsulated by Ecoflex. The double components of Ecoflex were mixed up compeletely before being poured into the self-made template with the size of 5mm × 20mm × 20mm. The flexible sensor after encapulation was stabilized under the room temperature.

2.6 Structure characterization of cotton fabric before and after several treatments

SEM, XRD and Raman shift was used to measure the structural variation of materials before and after carbonization.

2.7 Property testing of the fabric based pressure sensor

The square resistance of the carbonized fabric was measured by RTS - 8 four-probe resistance tester. Mechanical property and electricity response of the corresponding pressure sensor were measured through compression test of composites using a micro force tension meter Instron 5565A with a load cell capacity of 100N. The capacitance of the pressure sensor was measured by Keithley 2400.

3 Results and Discussion

3.1 SEM measurement and square resistance of the CCF@RGO

The plain weave structure of the cotton fabric retained very well after carbonization, as shown in the scanning electron microscope (SEM) image (Fig. 2). The carbonized cotton fabric showed good electrical conductivity with a sheet resistance of $50\Omega \cdot sq^{-1}$, which could be attributed to the formation of graphite-like carbon and the enhancement of RGO.

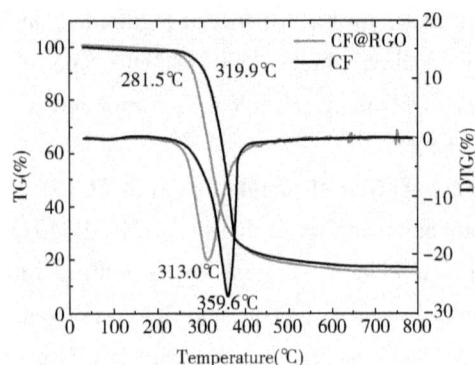

Fig. 3 TG and DTG of the cotton fabric with or without reduced graphene oxide

Fig. 2 SEM image of the carbonized fabric

As shown in Fig. 3, cotton cellulose degrades at a temperature of 200 – 400℃, during this period, cellulose cracked into small molecular gases and left carbon and ash, during which the carbon recombines to form new products. After coating with graphene oxide, the degradation temperature varied from 359.6℃ to 313.0℃, which shows that graphene coating on the surface of cotton fabrics will promote the thermal decomposition process of cotton fabrics and have a catalytic effect on the carbonization of cotton fabrics.

Fig. 4 shows that the characteristic peaks of the XRD spectrum appearing at 2 θ at 14.36°, 16.36°, 22.60°, and 33.98° are the characteristic peaks of cellulose I.

The characteristic peaks at 9.74° is the characteristic peaks of graphene oxide for CF@GO, which disappeared for CF@RGO because of the reduction of the graphene oxide. After carbonization, the characteristic peaks of cellulose disappeared and an abvious peak at 23.58° of amorphous carbon, which shows that the cellulose was carbonized under the temperature of 800℃, with graphene oxide been reduced simultaneously. The Raman spectrum in Fig. 5 further ascertained that graphite-like carbon formed after the thermal treatment, and the 2D band showed the GO was successfully reduced into graphene. The theory of percolation threshold can be used to explain the carbonization and electricity conductivity of the carbon fabric[15].

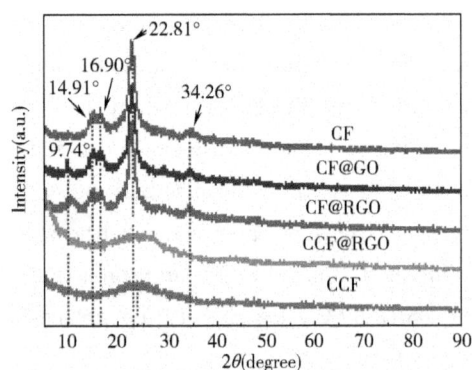

Fig. 4 XRD spectrum of the cotton fabric(CF), cotton fabric coated with graphene oxide(CF@GO), cotton fabric coated with reduced graphene oxide(CF@RGO), carbonized cotton fabric coated with reduced graphene oxide(CCF@RGO), carbonized cotton fabric

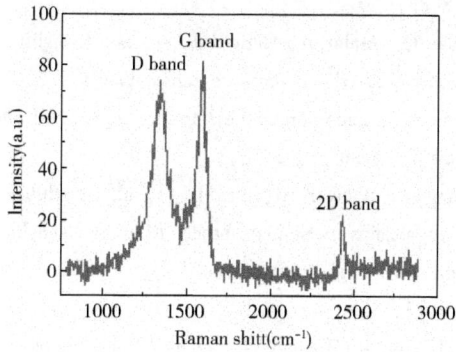

Fig. 5 Raman spectrum of the carbonized cotton fabric coated with reduced graphene oxide(CCF@RGO)

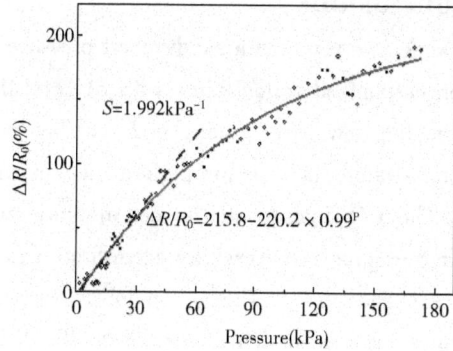

Fig. 6 Relative change in sensors resistance under pressure from 0kPa to 180kPa

3.2 Property measurement of the fabric based sandwiched pressure sensor

The sandwiched pressure sensor was composed of Ecoflex sheet and two-layer CCF sheet coated with RGO, the fabricated devices are wearable and bendable due to the flexible nature of both textile and Ecoflex. The sensing mechanism is due to pressing force-dependent contact between the cross point between two-layer plain cotton fabric. The plain weave fabric has the biggest yarn crimp height among woven fabric, so that more spaces was existed between the touched two layers of carbonized fabric. When applying an external pressure, a small compressive deformation of the carbonized fabric enabled more cross point in contact with two electrodes, leading to more conductive pathways. This caused an increase in current when a fixed voltage of 1V was applied. On unloading, both Ecoflex and cotton fabric recovered to their original shapes, leading to the decrease of the current.

Fig. 6 shows the electrical response of the fabric based sensors. Measured sensitivities were 1.992kPa^{-1} for the sensor, with a good linearity of 0.98(R^2), in the area of 0 to 30kPa. With pressure increasing, the resistance variation shows a relation of exponential function. The equation of the fitting curve is

$$\frac{\Delta R}{R_0} = 215.8 - 220.2 \times 0.99^P \qquad (3-1)$$

This is because with the distance between two electrodes decreasing when pressing, more forces are needed to change the same quantity of resistance.

The pressure sensor showed a stable response to the different pressure, respectively, which is shown in Fig. 7 and Fig. 8. Five pressure distances of 0.15mm, 0.2mm, 0.25mm, 0.3mm, 0.35mm, 4mm were applied on the pressure sensor for 4 times, the result shows that the sandwiched conductive fabric based sensor can response to different pressure stably and validly.

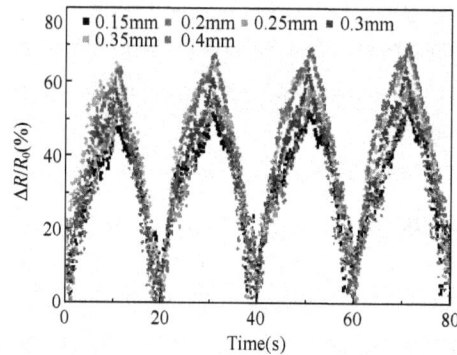

Fig. 7 The resistance response for 4 times under the pressure distances of 0.15mm, 0.2mm, 0.25mm, 0.3mm, 0.35mm and 4mm, respectively

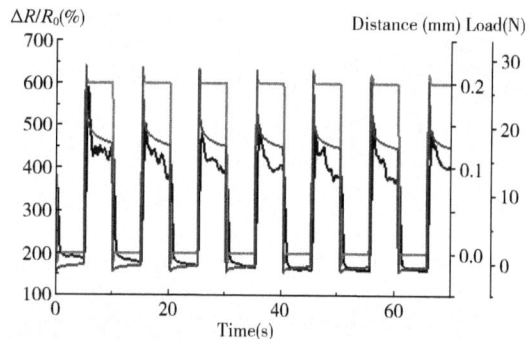

Fig. 8 The resistance, distance, load variation when press the sandwiched fabric, holding and releasing for 5 s

4 Conclusions

In this work, we reported a sandwiched pressure sensor based on carbonized cotton fabric with RGO on the surface through a low-cost, green, and scalable process, and demonstrated its superior performance in pressure sensor. The GO coating on the cotton fabric was reduced into graphene successfully according to the XRD and Raman spectrums. The cotton fabric was carbonized into amorphous carbon according to the XRD and FTIR spectrums. The carbonized fabric has electricity conductivity of $50\Omega sq^{-1}$. The sandwiched pressure sensor exhibits high sensitivity of $1.992kPa^{-1}$, and a wide test range from 0 to 80kPa. The sensor has a quick response to the outside pressure. The superior performance can be ascribed to the hierarchal network structure of the carbonized cotton fabric. The strain-induced reversible contact and separation of tentacle like cotton fibers enable its excellent sensing performance in monitoring both large and subtle deformation. We foresee that the high performance pressure sensors, which can be fabricated from abundant natural cotton fiber sources through a green, cost-effective, and simple process, will find great potential for applications in wearable electronics.

References

[1] L H M, Alex C, C K T B, B H T J, et al. 25th Anniversary Article: The evolution of electronic skin (e-skin): A brief history, design considerations, and recent progress [J]. Advanced Materials, 2013;25:5997-6038.

[2] Sang S, Liu L, Jian A, et al. Highly sensitive wearable strain sensor based on silver nanowires and nanoparticles [J]. Nanotechnology, 2018;29.

[3] Eom J, Lee W, Kim Y H, Kim Y H. Textile-based wearable sensors using metal-nanowire embedded conductive fibers[J]. Sensors, 2017: 1-3.

[4] Pan J, Liu S, Yang Y, et, al. A highly sensitive resistive pressure sensor based on a carbon nanotube-liquid crystal-PDMS composite[J]. Nanomaterials (Basel, Switzerland), 2018,8.

[5] Atalay O, Atalay A, Gafford J, et, al. A highly sensitive capacitive-based soft pressure sensor based on a conductive fabric and a microporous dielectric layer[J]. Advanced Materials Technologies, 2018,3.

[6] Cheng Y, Wang R R, Sun J, et, al. A stretchable and highly sensitive graphene-based fiber for sensing tensile strain, bending, and torsion [J]. Advanced Materials 2015;27,7365.

[7] Ge J, Sun L, Zhang F R, et al. A stretchable electronic fabric artificial skin with pressure, lateral strain, and flexion sensitive properties [J]. Advanced Materials, 2016, 28: 722-728.

[8] Wang Q, Jian M Q, Wang C Y, et, al. Carbonized silk nanofiber membrane for transparent and sensitive electronic skin[J]. Advanced Functional Materials, 2017;27.

[9] Lee J, Kwon H, Seo J, et al. Conductive fiber-based ultrasensitive textile pressure sensor for wearable electronics[J]. Advanced Materials, 2015,27;2433-2439.

[10] Li J F, Xu B G. Novel highly sensitive and wearable pressure sensors from conductive three-dimensional fabric structures[J]. Smart Materials and Structures, 2015, 24.

[11] Pu X, Li L, Liu M, et al. Wearable self-charging power textile based on flexible yarn supercapacitors and fabric nanogenerators[J]. Advanced Materials, 2016, 28;98-105.

[12] Zhang M, Wang C, Wang H, et, al. Carbonized cotton fabric for high-performance wearable strain sensors[J]. Advanced Functional Materials, 2017, 27.

[13] Yin B, Wen Y, Hong T, et al. Highly stretchable, ultrasensitive, and wearable strain sensors based on facilely prepared reduced graphene oxide woven fabrics in an ethanol flame[J]. ACS Applied Materials & Interfaces, 2017, 9: 32054-32064.

[14] Hong X, Yu W, Chung D D L. Electric permittivity of reduced graphite oxide[J]. Carbon, 2017,111;182-190.

[15] Rhim YR, Zhang D, Fairbrother D H, et al. Changes in electrical and microstructural properties of microcrystalline cellulose as function of carbonization temperature[J]. Carbon, 2010,48;1012-1024.

A Graphene-Based Yarn Strain Sensor with Low Electrical Hysteresis

Shen Jiang[1,2], Qiao Li[1,2]*, Xin Ding[1,2]

[1] *Key Laboratory of Textile Science & Technology, Ministry of Education, Shanghai 201620, China*

[2] *College of Textiles, Donghua University, Shanghai 201620, China*

* *Corresponding author's email:* qiaoli@ dhu. edu. cn

Abstract: Soft strain sensor has attracted more and more attention in recent years because of its outstanding advantages in human conditions detecting. However, the wide application is limited by their large hysteresis. In this paper, a new yarn strain sensor based on elastic double-covered yarn is developed. By combining dip coating with in-situ polymerization, a conductive layer of graphene oxide/polypyrrole is formed, fabricating a sensor with enhanced performance. The electrical hysteresis reaches as low as 7.01% with good sensitivity at an average of 6.61.

Keywords: Strain sensor; Graphene; Polypyrrole; Hysteresis

1 Introduction

In recent decades, a number of wearable sensing devices and systems have been developed[1-5]. Many investigators have made great efforts in flexible strain sensors which are able to detect human physiological conditions such as running[3], finger-bending[4] and breathing[6]. Among them, fiber-based strain sensors are very promising because of their easy fabrication, wide work range, high sensitive property and most importantly, superior ability in integrating with clothes.

Various conductive materials have been frequently employed in flexible strain sensor, including polypyrrole[5,7], carbon nanotubes[8-9] (CNTs), grapheme[2-3,10] and metallic nanowires[11]. Despite of high performance of these devices, there still exists one shortcoming which restricts the widespread application, which is their large hysteresis error. To date, there has been a lack of reported work on the coating of graphene oxide/polypyrrole (GO/PPy) layers onto a double-covered yarn (DCY) substrate which is composed of a highly elastic Spandex core multifilament and Polyamide yarns winding around helically to fabricate yarn strain sensors. Here, we develop a facile, low-cost and scalable strategy for fiber-based composite sensors, which exhibits a low electric hysteresis error (7.01%) as well as good sensitivity (8.20).

2 Experiments

2.1 Materials

Spandex/Polyamide/Polyamide double-covered yarn (420D/40D/20D) was obtained from INVISTA. Sodium hydroxide, analytical grade, was supplied by Pinghu Chemical Reagent Factory (Zhejiang, China). Pyrrole monomer, Anthraquinone-2-sulfonic acid sodium salt (AQSA) and Iron (III) chloride hexahydrate ($FeCl_3 \cdot 6H_2O$) were purchased from Sinopharm Chemical Reagent Co. , Ltd. (Shanghai, China). The pyrrole monomer was purified by distilling before use.

2.2 Sensor fabrication

Alkaline treatment: DCY was immersed in NaOH solution (1mol/L) for 40min to remove impurities on the surface. Then it was washed with deionized water for 6-7 times until the pH of the liquid was around 7. The yarn was dried in a hot air oven at 60℃.

GO yarn preparation: a GO solution with a concentration of 3mg/mL was prepared by diluting original GO solution (10mg/mL) with deionized water and dispersed ultrasonically for 40min. The dried yarn was dipped into the GO solution for about 3mins, accompanied with color changing from white to yellowish. Then it was dried in an oven for 2mins. Repeated the coating process for 13 times to get a uniform layer.

GO/PPy yarn preparation: an in-situ polymerization method was adopted on the basis of GO yarn. Firstly, the yarn was soaked in a beaker which contained a mixed solution of pyrrole (0.12mol/L) and AQSA (0.008mol/L) for 2 hours in a low-temperature environment (0–4℃). Secondly, a FeCl₃ aqueous solution was added dropwise through a burette to initiate polymerization. The reaction was kept for 3 hours at 0℃. Finally, a yarn coated with GO/PPy was obtained, washed with deionized water to remove impurities and residual PPy particles, and afterwards dried in an oven at 60℃.

2.3 Characterization

The morphological structure of the sensor was examined by using scanning electron microscopy (Hitachi TM3000, Japan). Before electromechanical behaviors were tested, both ends of the sensor were connected to copper wires as external electrodes with the help of conductive copper tapes.

The dynamic electrical resistance was measured with Agilent 34970A data logger system (Agilent Technologies, America) based on two-wire channel. The load and deformation were recorded using a fiber tension tester (XQ–2, Shanghai New Fiber Instrument). As Fig. 1 shows, these two testing apparatus worked together to collect the mechanical and electrical changes simultaneously. Besides, they were both interfaced with a computer respectively. The sensor was pre-treated for 10 tensile cycles with a maximum extension up to 100% at a speed of 40mm/min in order to reorient the Polyamide filaments to get a more stable structure. Then it was stretched and recovered under a gauge length of 20mm at a crosshead speed of 5mm/min. At least 5 samples were tested from the yarn and then mean value was determined. Consequently, load-strain and resistance-strain curves were generated to evaluate the sensor performance. Based on these curves, the primary char-

acteristics of the strain sensor especially electrical hysteresis error were calculated.

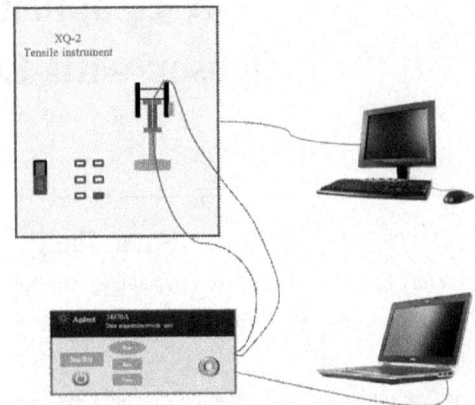

Fig. 1   Schematic illustration of sample testing system

The hysteresis error[10] is defined as a deviation of the sensor's output at a certain point of the input signal when it is approached from opposite directions. The hysteresis error can be obtained with:

$$\Delta H = \frac{\Delta R_{\text{maxdifference}}}{\Delta R} \times 100\% \qquad (1)$$

Where $\Delta R_{\text{maxdifference}}$ and ΔR are the maximum difference between resistances and the changes in resistances respectively when the sensor is stretched or released.

The sensitivity is represented as the gauge factor (GF), which is the ratio of relative resistance changes to the applied tensile strain, shown as the following:

$$GF = \frac{\Delta R / R_0}{\varepsilon} \qquad (2)$$

Where R_0 is the initial resistance and ε is the applied strain.

3   Results and Discussion

3.1   Morphology of DCY with different treatments

The morphological structure of the spandex/polyamide/polyamide DCY has substantial impacts on the sensor properties and was examined in an experiment with yarns mentioned above. Besides, conductive yarns using the spandex/polyamide/polyamide DCY as substrates were also tested to see what the surface changes are like under different treatments. As shown in Fig. 2 (a), the polyamide filaments covering around the pristine DCY are much smooth and fairly clean. After immersed in GO solution, SEM image Fig. 2 (b) shows the polyamide filaments were completely coated with GO film along with a little twinkle, which was beneficial for the formation of PPy layer because of the interaction[12] between GO and PPy. There existed hydrogen bonding of residual oxygen functional groups on graphene or maybe π—π stacking between graphene backbone and polypyrrole. It can be observed from Fig.2 (c) that the poly

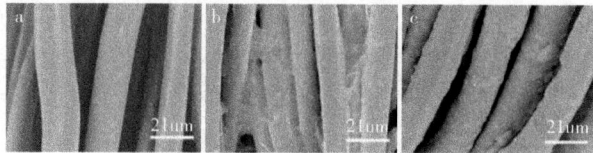

Fig.2 SEM images of different double-covered yarns
(a) DCY; (b) GO DCY; (3) PPy/GO DCY

pyrrole coatings are dense and evenly adhere on the surface of GO layer, with particles assembled tightly instead of loose and club-shaped.

3.2 Mechanical properties of DCY

As Fig.3 shows, both yarns exhibit relatively low mechanical hysteresis error with an average of 6.69% for pristine yarn and 7.08% for PPy/GO sensor respectively. It seems the thin conductive layer on the sensor makes little difference in the mechanical hysteresis. Further, what can be inferred from Fig.3 is the sensor has a higher Young's Modulus compared with the pristine yarn due to the rigidity and brittleness of the PPy/GO coating.

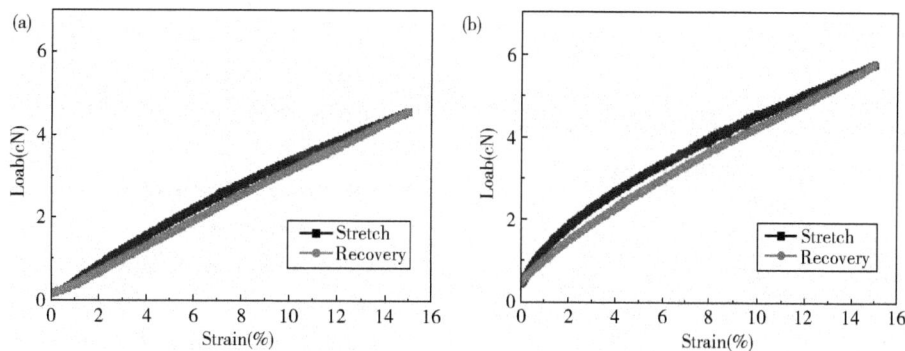

Fig.3   Mechanical hysteresis of pristine DCY (a) and PPy/GO DCY (b)

3.3   Electromechanical behaviors of GO/PPy DCY

3.3.1   Hysteresis and sensitivity

Fig.4 (a) and (b) show the electrical hysteresis and sensitivity of the DCY sensor at the sensitivity of the DCY sensor at the strain of 15%. As is shown in Fig.4 (a), the small gap between the upper stretch curve and recovery curve below indicates a very low electrical hysteresis error which is 7.01%. Of these samples tested, the average value is 9.22%. A main reason is possibly

the existence of GO layer contributes to the formation of continuous thick conductive coating, which is necessary for reducing resistance variations at a specific point during the stretch and recovery process, thus leading to a low electrical hysteresis. Fig.4 (b) illustrates sensitivity changes of the DCY sensor under tensile strain. For all the samples, there is a highest GF value appearing at a small strain level with the tensile strain up to 15%. The average is 6.61 and the highest is 8.20.

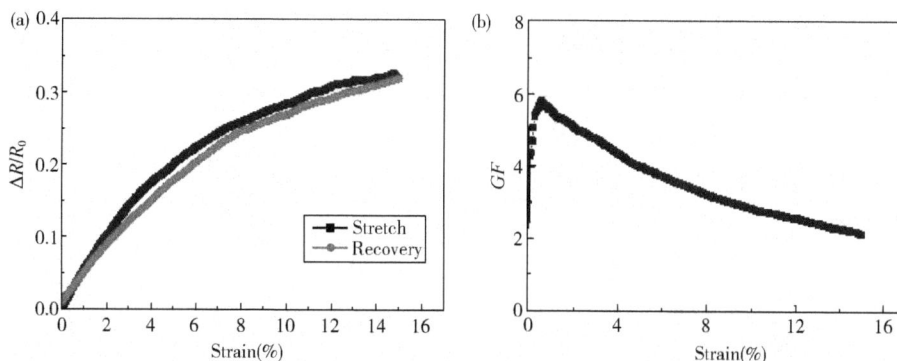

Fig.4   Electrical properties of the strain sensor   (a) Electrical hysteresis; (b) Sensitivity

3.3.2 Threshold

To realize the detection limit of the DCY sensor, gradually diminishing step strain with 20 continuous cycles is applied in the experiment. Fig. 5 shows the detection limit could be as tiny as 0.5% strain and the output signal still remains highly reproducible even at minimal strains.

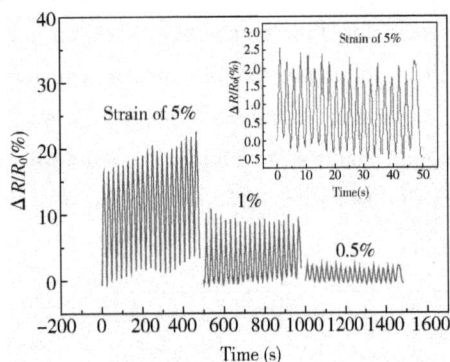

Fig. 5 Resistance variation under minimum strain of 5%, 1%, 0.5% during circular stretching and recovering

4 Conclusions

In this study, we have presented a graphene-based DCY strain sensor which has both good sensitivity and low hysteresis in cyclical stretching process. The yarn strain sensor samples are fabricated by combining dip coating with in-situ polymerization which is low-cost, scalable and simple. The results show that continuous thick conductive coating may be the main reason for the improved electromechanical properties.

Acknowledgements

The authors acknowledge funding support from the National Science Foundation of China (Grant No. 51603039), the Fundamental Research Funds for the Central Universities, the Key Laboratory of Textile Science and Technology (Donghua University), Ministry of Education (Grant No. KLTST201623), and the Initial Research Funds for Young Teachers of Donghua University for this research.

References

[1] Schwartz G, Tee B C, Mei J, et al. Flexible polymer transistors with high pressure sensitivity for application in electronic skin and health monitoring [J]. Nat Commun, 2013, 4: 1859.

[2] Li X, Zhang R, Yu W, et al. Stretchable and highly sensitive graphene-on-polymer strain sensors [J]. Sci Rep, 2012, 2: 870.

[3] Cheng Y, Wang R, Sun J, et al. A stretchable and highly sensitive graphene-based fiber for sensing tensile strain, bending, and torsion [J]. Adv Mater, 2015, 27(45): 7365-7371.

[4] Frutiger A, Muth J T, Vogt D M, et al. Capacitive soft strain sensors via multicore-shell fiber printing [J]. Advanced Materials, 2015, 27(15): 2440-2446.

[5] Xue P, Wang J, Tao X. Flexible textile strain sensors from polypyrrole-coated XLA elastic fibers [J]. High Performance Polymers, 2013, 26(3): 364-370.

[6] Wu X, Han Y, Zhang X, et al. Highly sensitive, stretchable, and wash-durable strain sensor based on ultrathin conductive layer @ spandex yarn for tiny motion monitoring [J]. ACS Appl Mater Interfaces, 2016, 8(15): 9936-9945.

[7] Xue P, Tao X M, Tsang H Y. In situ SEM studies on strain sensing mechanisms of PPy-coated electrically conducting fabrics [J]. Applied Surface Science, 2007, 253(7): 3387-3392.

[8] Wang Z, Huang Y, Sun J, et al. Spandex/cotton/carbon nanotubes core-spun yarn as high reliability stretchable strain sensor for human motion detection [J]. ACS Appl Mater Interfaces, 2016, 8(37): 24837-43.

[9] Zhao H, Zhang Y, Bradford P D, et al. Carbon nanotube yarn strain sensors [J]. Nanotechnology, 2010, 21(30): 305502.

[10] Li X, Hua T, Xu B. Electromechanical properties of a yarn strain sensor with graphene-sheath/spandex-core [J]. Carbon, 2017, 118: 686-698.

[11] Lee T, Lee W, Kim S W, et al. Flexible textile strain wireless sensor functionalized with hybrid carbon nanomaterials supported ZnO nanowires with controlled aspect ratio [J]. Advanced Functional Materials, 2016, 26(34): 6206-6214.

[12] Zhang D, Zhang X, Chen Y, et al. Enhanced capacitance and rate capability of graphene/polypyrrole composite as electrode material for supercapacitors [J]. Journal of Power Sources, 2011, 196(14): 5990-5996.

A Novel Method to Test Moisture Dissipation of Woven Fabrics

Yue Hu[1], Yanxue Ma[1,2]*, Yuling Li[1,2], Longdi Cheng[1,2]

[1]Key Laboratory of Textile Science & Technology, Ministry of Education, Shangha 201620, China

[2]College of Textiles, Donghua University, Shanghai 201620, China

* Corresponding author's email: yxma@ dhu. edu. cn

Abstract: Water in the fabric was transferred in a process of moisture absorption—moisture conduction—moisture dissipation. These three stages are always interrupted with each other, so it is difficult to measure fabric moisture dissipation accurately. The research proposed a new method to test moisture dissipation of fabrics. The traditional method is to test fabrics' evaporation rate, which is hard to control the "moisture-conductivity" process. The novel testing method proposed in this paper could greatly reduce the impact of the moisture absorption and moisture conduction on moisture dissipation, and could characterize water loss of fabrics in the moisture dissipation process.

Keywords: Moisture dissipation; Testing method; Fabric surface evenness; Water transfer

1 Introduction

With increasing requirements of fabric comfort, lots of researches were carried out to develop a good moisture-absorbing and quick-drying functional product, that is, the fabric has a rapid evaporation of sweat at a high temperature and is not stuffy, as well as the heat can be quickly conducted and the human body does not feel wet and cold at a low temperature. This demand has become one of the research hotspots in the textile industry.

In most existing research, fiber modification and finishing methods were applied to achieve improved moisture absorption and quick drying. In the view of fiber, physical or chemical modification treatments were used, such as polymers with hydrophilic groups, surface modification or uneven cross-sections, to increase moisture absorption and moisture transfer capacity of fibers[1]. In the view of fabric, on one hand, a moisture-absorbing and fast-drying gradient structure is constructed by changing fabric structure, yarn arrangement ratio or yarn linear density[2-3]. On the other hand, the fabric is designed as a tree-like branch structure with a simulated plant shape inside to improve fabric water transport per-formance[4]. In the view of finishing, chemical finishing[5], plasma treatment[6], electro-spinning[7] and photocatalytic treatment[8] were adopted to modify fabric surface with different hydrophilic properties on both sides, thereby improving fabric moisture with directional conduction. Most of these studies improve the hygroscopicity and fast-drying performance of fabrics by increasing their moisture absorption and moisture conduction. Actually, comfort of fabrics on human body was affected with interaction of moisture absorption, moisture conduction and moisture dissipation. Dissipation of water as the process of moisture leaving the fabric surface has great significance on fabrics' moisture absorption and quick drying function. However, studies of water dissipation in fabrics are very rare.

Since water transferring in fabrics requires a "moisture absorption, moisture conduction, moisture dissipation" process, it is often difficult to characterize water dissipation separately in the traditional testing method. To address the problem on individually measuring fabric moisture dissipation, this paper proposes a new testing method. In the study, different woven structures were designed to explore their effects on fabric moisture dissipation.

2　Experiments

2.1　Sample preparation

Surface evenness of fabrics is represented by interlacing frequency of weft and warp yarns, which means the ratio of interlacing points and weave points in one repeat[9]. Usually, bigger interlacing frequency indicates tighter fabric and shorter average floats, and smaller interlacing frequency means looser fabric and longer floats also, varied fabric tightness and average floats in the fabric could create uneven fabric surfaces. Therefore, six woven structures shown in Fig. 1 were designed. Tightness was decreasing from structure A to structure F. Plain weave Fig. 1 (a) had the best evenness. Surface of matt weave Fig. 1 (b) was even, but it had two kinds of floats. Evenness of stripe weave as shown in Fig. 1 (c) and plaid weave as shown in Fig. 1 (d) is reducing compared to plain and matt weave, but they have partially uniform area in a repeat. Crepe weave as shown in Fig. 1 (e) has the most uneven surface and

its floats are most chaotic. Loose weave as shown in Fig. 1 (f) contains even but longer floats compared to other weave structures, so it is very loose.

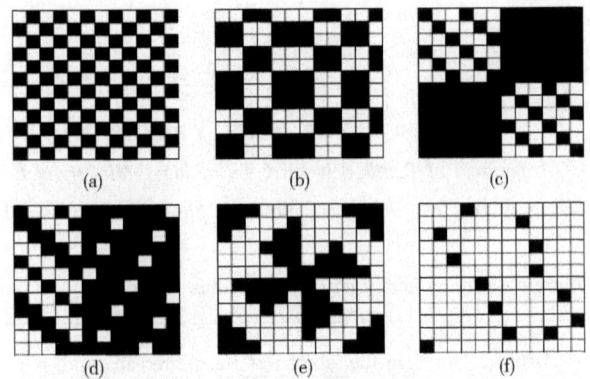

Fig. 1　Weave structure

In the study, all samples were woven with $40^{s/2}$ 100% cotton yarns on the TNY501C-20 automatic rapier machine. Weaving specifications are shown in Tab. 1.

Tab. 1　Specifications of weave structures

Sample	Fabric weave	Density(p/10cm) Warp weft		Weight (g · m²)	Thickness (mm)	Interleaving frequency
A	Plain weave	260	240	168.73	0.55	0.50
B	Matt weave	260	240	160.47	0.65	0.25
C	Plaid weave	260	240	163.03	0.92	0.21
D	Strip weave	260	240	163.03	0.88	0.20
E	Crepe weave	260	240	165.20	0.97	0.14
F	Loose weave	260	240	161.27	0.99	0.08

Samples are subjected to an alkali treatment process with a bath ratio of 1:50, a concentration of 0.8% NaOH solution at 95–100℃ for 60 minutes. Treated samples was washed five times in warm water and then dried.

2.2　Testing methods

Samples were tested at a temperature (20 ± 2)℃ and humidity (65 ± 2)%. Before being tested, all samples were subjected in a condition of constant temperature and humidity for 16 hours.

2.2.1　Traditional testing

Referring to GB/T 21655. 1—2008 *Test Method for*

Moisture Evaporation Rate in Evaluation of Moisture absorption and Quick-Drying Properties of Textiles Part 1: Individual Combination Test Method, five samples were taken from the same fabric with one structure and each sample has a size of 10cm × 10cm. Totally, 30 samples were tested. First, original samples were weighed. Then, 0.2mL of tertiary water was dropped onto the sample. After fully absorbing moisture, the sample were again weighed immediately and hanged naturally. Mass of the sample was weighed every (5 ± 0.5)min, the test was terminated until the mass was changed within 1%. Fabric mass was tested on an electronic balance (Mode: HANGPING FA1004 with an accuracy of 0.0001 g and a measuring range of 100 g). According to the testing data, time-evaporation curves of samples with varied structures could be created.

2.2.2 Novel testing method

A new device was developed in the study, as shown in Fig. 2. The device was installed in a semi-sealed test box. An electronic balance (Model: HBK-503H electronic balance with accuracy of 0.001 g and measuring range of 500g) was used to test fabric weight changes. As shown in Fig. 2, a spring clamp was used to hold one end of the tested sample. The other end of the sample was immersed to water in a container, which has an opening with 5 mm × 60 mm on the top to avoid water evaporation. The immersion level of samples could be adjusted based on the position of spring clamp.

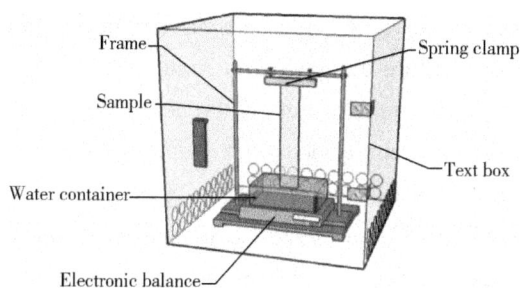

Fig. 2　Sketch of the new testing device

Based on preliminary research, the sample size was specified as 8cm × 5cm, and the length of immersed sample was 3cm. Three samples were achieved on one fabric with one weave structure. Totally, 18 samples were measured.

When the sample was immersed into the water, data on the electronic balance was collected immediately. Then, data was recorded every 10 minutes till 2 hours. At beginning, reduction of data on the balance meant water quality absorbed by the fabric. With decreasing area in the fabric for water conduction, reduction of water quality was slower and slower. When water quality is almost constant, effects of water absorption and conduction is far less than effects of water dissipation. Finally, a time-quality curve was generated to test the moisture dissipation of each sample.

3　Results and Discussion

3.1　Results of traditional testing

As shown in Fig. 3, the water evaporation rate of tight structures, such as plain weave and matt weave, is faster than loose structures. However, only one drop of water was placed on the sample in each test. For a 10cm × 10cm sample, one drop of water had an infinite moisture transferring area, which meant the method cannot control the moisture conductivity. In this experiment, results could only show that fabrics with tight structure had a faster process of moisture absorption, moisture conduction and moisture dissipation than that with loose structures. The traditional evaporation testing method could not characterize the moisture dissipation ability of fabrics.

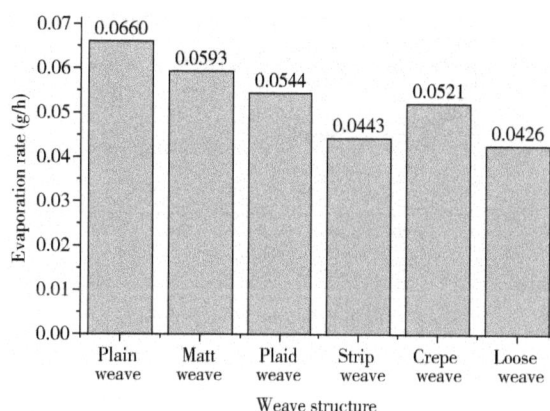

Fig. 3　Traditional evaporation rate test results

In addition, human operation and air flow during the test process increased the error of testing results that were hard to be avoided.

3.2　Results of novel testing

As shown in Fig. 4 and Fig. 5, in first 30 minutes, water absorption and water conduction mainly dominated the quality changes. After 30 minutes, the time-quality curve was going to be straight. At that time, it was regarded that the entire sample was filled with moisture. Thus, changes in water quality could be used to characterize moisture dissipation rate.

In the novel testing method, environmental effects were eliminated as far as possible. All data were collected without human operation, so that to avoid personal in-

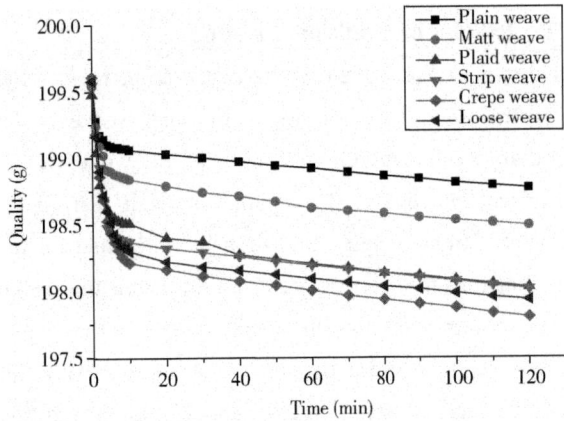

Fig. 4　Testing results in warp direction

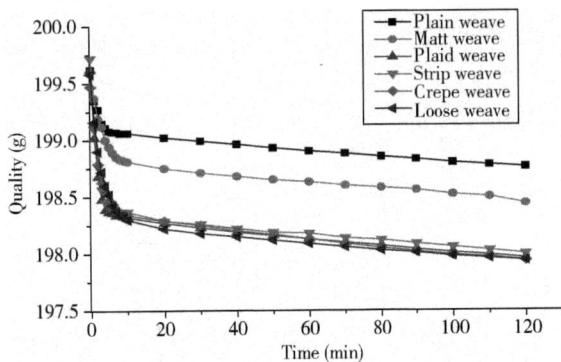

Fig. 5　Testing results in weft direction

terference.

A fitting analysis was performed based on data collected in the period of 30－120min, and moisture dissipation rates of each sample are presented in Fig. 6.

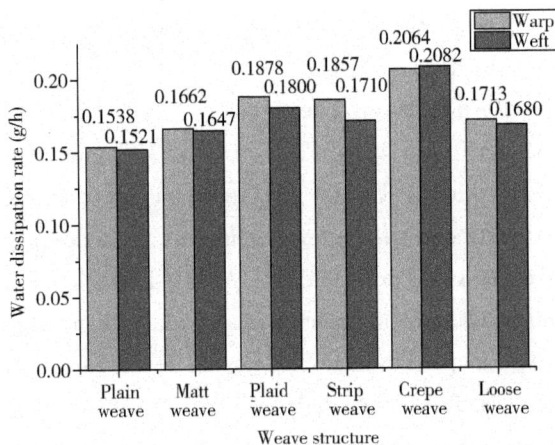

Fig. 6　Water dissipation rate testing results

According to statistical analysis, weave structures have a significant effect on fabric moisture dissipation. In this experiment, plain weave, matt weave and loose weave indicate lower moisture dissipation rate in comparison to plaid weave, strip weave and crepe weave structures. This is because the later three structures have relatively uneven surface, which also influence fabric moisture dissipation. The way to express fabric surface evenness and its effects on moisture dissipation will be further explored in depth.

4　Conclusions

This paper introduced an innovative method to test moisture dissipation of woven fabrics with different structures, to eliminate testing errors caused by human operation and environmental influences. In the new method, the moisture absorption and conductivity process in the fabric could be controlled so that to characterize moisture dissipation individually.

According to testing results in the new method, the water dissipation ability of fabrics is highly related woven structures. When raw materials, yarn fineness, and warp and weft density were maintained in the same, interlacing frequency and fabric surface evenness affected the fabric moisture dissipation.

Although the study has proved possibility of the new method to characterize fabric moisture dissipation, results are still influenced by the dynamic moisture absorption and conduction. Improvements of the device are needed, and impact of woven structures on moisture dissipation will be investigated in future research.

Acknowledgements

The research was supported by National Key R&D Program of China (Grant No. 2017YFB0309102) and National Natural Science Foundation of China (Grant No. 71704021).

References

[1] Ma Lei. Status and development of moisture absorbent and quick drying textiles [J]. China Textile Leader, 2017, 09: 22-24.

[2] Tan Dongyi, Wan Nanfang, Fan Yanping. Single-side mois-

ture transported fabric and Its property study [J]. Cotton Textile Technology, 2015, 43(2): 69-72.

[3]Zhang Huimin, Shen Lanping, Huang Heliu. The development of unidirectional water transport 3D woven fabrics [J]. Synthetic Fiber in China, 2016(8): 28-31.

[4]Fan J,He J. Biomimic design of multi-scale fabric with efficient heat transfer property [J]. Thetmal Science, 2012, 16 (5): 1349-1352.

[5] Carran R S, Ghosh A, Dyer J M. Modification of surface properties of wool fabric with linde type a nano-zeolite [J]. Journal of Applied Polymer Science,2015, 132(2): 92-97.

[6]Wang Weiling, YU Weidong. Influence of low temperature plasma on chitosan/waterborne polyurethane finishing on cotton fabric [J]. Advanced Materials Research, 2014, 1051: 117-120.

[7]Li Yang, Yaue Fangfang, Yu Jiangyong, et al. Hydrophobic fibrous membranes with tunable porous structure for equilibrium of and waterproof performance [J]. Advanced Materials Interfaces, 2016,3(19): 516-524.

[8]Wang Hongxia, Wang Xungai, Lin Tong. Unidirectional water transfer effect from fabrics having a super hydrophobic to hydrophilic gradient [J]. Nanoscience and Nanotechnology, 2013,13(2): 839-842.

[9]Zhang Hongxia, Liu Furong, Wang Jing. Effects of fabric weave and cover factor on moisture transfer ability of moisture absorbent and fast drying fabric [J]. Journal of Textile Research. 2008, 05: 31-38.

A Stretchable Woven Fabric Circuit: Fabrication and Application

Ziyuan Ran[1,2], Qiao Li[1,2 *], Xin Ding[1,2]

[1] *Key Laboratory of Textile Science & Technology, Ministry of Education, Donghua University, Shanghai 201620, China*

[2] *College of Textiles, Donghua University, Shanghai 201620, China*

* *Corresponding author's email*: qiaoli@ dhu. edu. cn

Abstract: Flexible circuit which has good sensitivity and conductive stability under large deformation is one of the most important conditions to achieve widely acceptance of wearable electronic devices. This study presents a way of manufacturing flexible woven circuit by embedding elastic yarns and silver coated conductive yarns into fabrics. Due to large-deformation capability of the fabric circuit, the packaged fabric sensing network could remain electrical integrity with a maximum strain of 37%, and withstand a fatigue life of at least 10,000 cycles under 30% strain. The fabric circuit also shows a good applicability that a smart garment integrated the assembly can be quite sensitive in detection of skin temperature, without error caused by the conductive tracks and circuit joint.

Keywords: Flexible woven circuit; Fabric sensing network; Large-deformation; Conductive stability

1 Introduction

Wearable comfort and functional stability required for wearable electronic products can be achieved by integrating electronics into textiles with the excellent characteristic of flexibility, deformation and breathability[1-4], in order to adapt to the complex postures of the human body. The advantages of textiles are due to their unique structure which is porous, warp and weft crimps, soft. Electronic textiles which can be the developing trend in electronics, are of great importance in medical detection, electronic skin[5-6], flexible displays[7], soft robots[8-9] and energy harvesting[7]. The sensors and other electronic components need to be connected by a circuit[6] in which many efforts concentrate on flexible circuit design, as the traditional circuit with poor flexibility can no longer meet the requirements. Flexible circuit which has good conductive stability under large deformation is also one of the most important conditions to achieve widely acceptance of wearable electronic devices[10].

In the previous studies of flexible circuit, the conductive stability of circuit prepared by using a knitted fabric structure is not very good, compared with the woven fabric circuit because of the unstable looped structure[11]. Meanwhile, the fabric circuit obtained by printing has distinctive changes in contact resistance under tensile state, due to the damage of the coating, as well the electrical integrity is affected.

In this study, we have developed a woven fabric circuit with electrical stability under large strain, which was accomplished by embedding elastic yarns and silver coated conductive yarns into woven fabrics. To study the impacts and performance of woven fabric circuit to the whole electronic applications, we further demonstrated a fabric sensing network by connecting the temperature sensors to the elastic fabric circuit in simple processes with the advantage of a high level integration and low-cost. The tensile and electrical properties were evaluated for the fabric sensing network.

2 Experiments

2.1 Materials

Silver coated polyamide yarns(100D × 4, 1.05Ohm per cm) were provided by Xiamen Unibest Import and Export Co., Ltd. Double covered yarns made of spandex yarns and two layers of nylon yarns (140D/70D/70D)

were obtained from Shanghai Qingxi Chemical Fiber Technology Co. , Ltd. The conductive silver paste was supplied by Guangzhou Youte New Material Co. , Ltd.

2.2 Design and fabrication of woven fabric circuit

Woven fabrics usually contain three structures, i. e. , plain, twill, and satin. The plain weave has more interlacing points, harder sense of touch, and shorter float lines; the satin has poor wear resistance; twill weave has less crossing points and longer float lines, good flexibility, which was selected to fabricate highly elastic conductive fabrics. In the work, we choose 1/3 ↗ twill weaves to weave fabric circuits, the Fig. 1 (a) shows the structure of stretchable fabric circuit, and Fig. 1 (b) shows the manufacture process of it. The warp yarns are made of polyamide yarns, and the weft yarns are made of elastic warp yarns and silver-coated polyamide yarns.

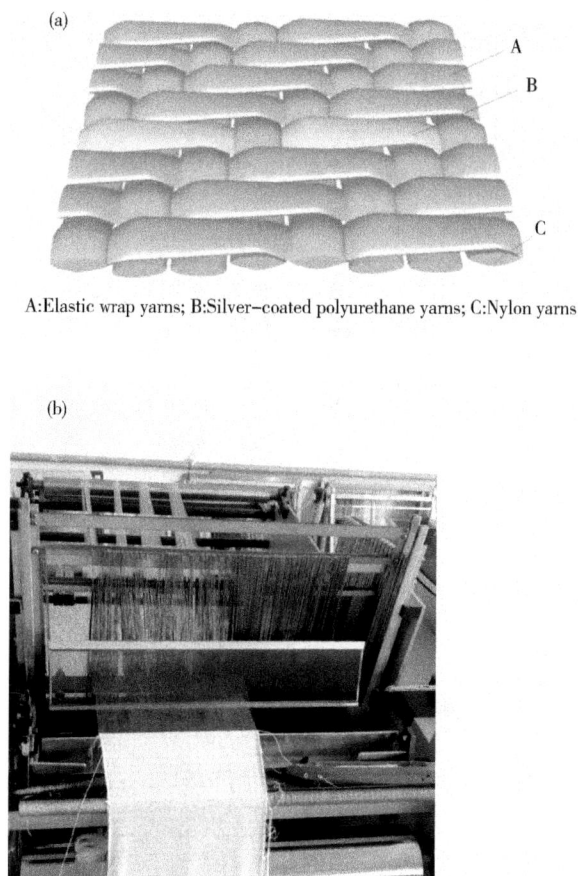

A:Elastic wrap yarns; B:Silver-coated polyurethane yarns; C:Nylon yarns

Fig. 1 (a) The structure design of stretchable fabric circuit; (b) The fabrication scheme based woven fabric on the weaving machine

2.3 Electro-mechanical test of the woven fabric circuit

In order to study the maximum stretch rate under which electrical stability of the fabric circuit maintains, and the electrical stability under 20%–30% strain which means an average stretch of various parts of the human body under dynamics, the experiment was performed on a computer controlled multifunctional strength tester YG (B) 026G-500 with a strain rate of 400mm/min. Tensile tests were accomplished according to ASTM D638 standard test method. Every sample had a gauge length of 50mm and an effective width of 30mm. Meanwhile, contact resistance was measured with Agilent 34970A. Before test, fabrics were conditioned at 20℃ and 65% relatively humidity for 24h. Five fabric specimens were stretched in weft direction.

2.4 Fabrication of temperature sensing network

As illustrated in Fig. 2, a fabric sensing network comprised of temperature sensors by fabric circuit was fabricated. The first step was to weave a jacquard pattern on weaving machine which describes the distribution of the conductive tracks. Secondly, seven temperature sensor elements weres set at predetermined positions. Third, those sensors were connected to the conductive tracks at predetermined positions with conductive silver paste, while the obtained electrical signals from sensors was transmitted to the external circuit through conductive tracks. The fourth procedure was to link the other side of conductive tracks in the fabric sensing network with the outer circuit by means of bonding selected interposers to the conductive tracks.

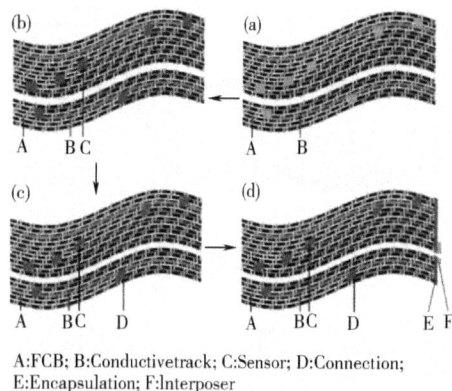

A:FCB; B:Conductivetrack; C:Sensor; D:Connection; E:Encapsulation; F:Interposer

Fig. 2 The whole fabrication process of stretchable fabric sensing network

2.5 Fatigue test of the fabric sensing network

The fabric sensor network was cyclically stretched 10000 times at 30% strain, and the changes of initial resistance were used to evaluate the effect of repeated mechanical deformation on the electrical properties of the fabric sensor network. The tensile test was performed on a multifunctional strength tester YG(B)026G-500. The stretching test was at an elongation speed of 600mm/min, with the measurement length of 50 mm, the influence width of 30 mm, and it was performed at a room temperature of 25℃. The resistance was tested with Agilent 34970A.

3 Results and Discussion

3.1 Electrical response to in-plane tensile strain

Fig. 3 (a) shows the tensile load-strain curve in the weft direction of a stretchable fabric circuit. The conductive path maintains its electrical integrity under 37% strain. The average elongation rate of the human body is 20%–30%. As shown in Fig. 2 (b), the fabric sensor network maintains stable conductive performance during the strain range of 0 to 30%. The elastic yarn is elongated as the strain increases, while the silver coated conductive yarn changes from the curved state to the original length. Hence, as the length of the silver wire does not change, the resistance remained stable.

3.2 Durability

From Fig. 4 (a) we can see that in the 10000 cycle stretching test, there are low resistance fluctuations with good stability for fabric sensor network. Fig. 4 (b) shows that in the 10000 cycle test, the initial resistance value has a tendency to increase, but it still maintains a small fluctuation range, indicating that the stretchable fabric sensor network has so excellent stretch-ability and cycle durability, that it is suitable for long-term monitoring of human skin.

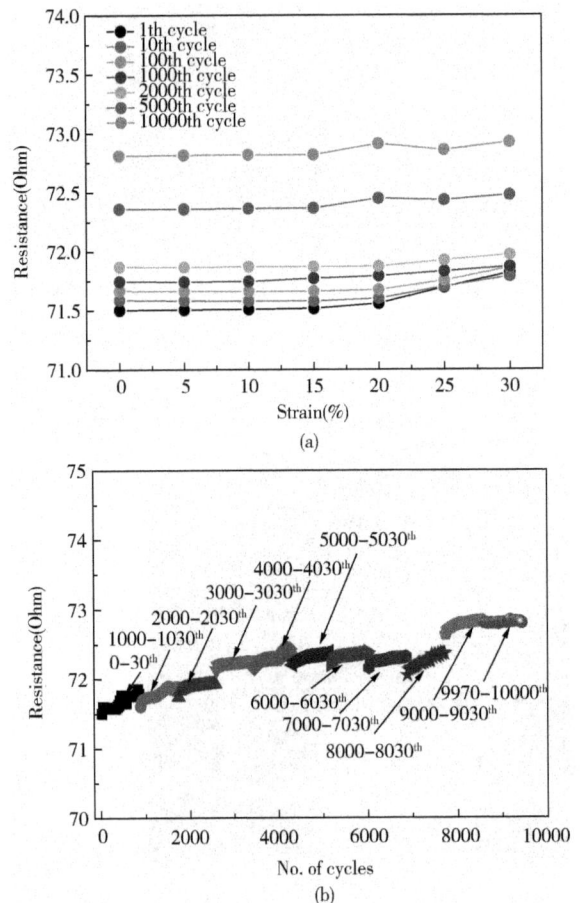

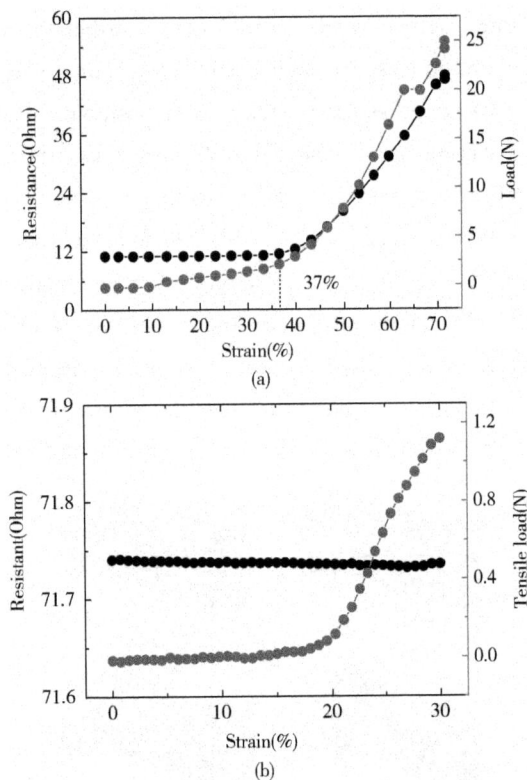

Fig. 3   (a) Typical resistance-strain curves of fabric circuit under large deformation; (b) Resistance-strain curves of fabric circuit under 30% strain

Fig. 4   (a) Resistance-strain curves of 10000 cycles of tensile for the fabric sensing network; (b) Resistance of the fabric sensing network under cyclic tests

4 Conclusions

This study has developed a conductive fabric circuit and its application in fabric sensing network. Due to large-deformation capability of the fabric circuit, the packaged fabric sensing network could remain electrical integrity with a maximum strain of 37%, and withstand a fatigue life of at least 10,000 cycles under 30% strain, suggesting prospects for next skin friendly electronics.

Acknowledgements

The authors acknowledge funding support from the National Science Foundation of China (Grant No. 51603039), the Fundamental Research Funds for the Central Universities, the Key Laboratory of Textile Science and Technology (Donghua University), Ministry of Education (Grant No. KLTST201623), and the Initial Research Funds for Young Teachers of Donghua University for this research.

References

[1] Lee J W, Xu R X, Lee S, et al. Soft, thin skin-mounted power management systems and their use in wireless thermography [C]. Proceedings of the National Academy of Sciences of the United States of America, 2016 (113): 6131-6136.

[2] Ma Y J, Pharr M, Wang L, et al. Soft elastomers with ionic liquid-filled cavities as strain isolating substrates for wearable electronics [J]. Small, 2017 (13).

[3] Lee S, Reuveny A, Reeder J, et al. A transparent bending-insensitive pressure sensor [J]. Nature Nanotechnology, 2016 (11): 472.

[4] Cherenack K, Zysset C, Kinkeldei T, et al. Wearable electronics: Woven electronic fibers with sensing and display functions for smart textiles [J]. Advanced Materials, 2010 (22): 5178-82.

[5] Shin S, Kumar R, Roh J W, et al. High-performance screen-printed thermoelectric films on fabrics[J]. Scientific Reports, 2017 (7).

[6] Lee C J, Park K H, Han C J, et al. Crack-induced Ag nanowire networks for transparent, stretchable, and highly sensitive strain sensors [J]. Scientific Reports, 2017 (7).

[7] Gong S, Schwalb W, Wang Y, et al. A wearable and highly sensitive pressure sensor with ultrathin gold nanowires [J]. Nature Communications, 2014, 5(2): 3132.

[8] Valentine A D, Busbee T A, Boley J W, et al. Hybrid 3D printing of soft electronics [J]. Advanced Materials, 1703817-n/a.

[9] Zhao S, Zhu R. Electronic skin with multifunction sensors based on thermosensation [J]. Advanced Materials, 2017 (29).

[10] Stoppa M, Chiolerioa. Wearable electronics and smart textiles: A critical review [J]. Sensors, 2014, 14 (7): 11957.

[11] Bogan K M, Marie K. Formation and integrity evaluation of woven electrically conductive [J]. Textiles. 2016.

Quasi-Static and Tensile Impact Properties of 3D Angle-Interlock Carbon/Epoxy Woven Composites

Anvarjon Nishonov[1]†, Kai Dong[1]†, Chunlei Ren[1],
Amna Siddique[1], Baozhong Sun[1], Bohong Gu[1]*

[1] College of Textiles, Donghua University, Shanghai 201620, China

† These authors contribute equally to this work

* Corresponding author's email: gubh@ dhu. edu. cn

Abstract: The quasi-static and tensile impact behaviors of 3D angle-interlock woven composites (3DAWC) under various strain rates were tested along both warp and weft directions. The tensile tests under quasi-state and high strain rate loading were performed with MTS material tester and split Hopkinson tension bar (SHTB), respectively. We found the significant strain rate sensitivity from the stress-strain curves. The failure modes and fracture morphologies of the 3DAWC demonstrated that fiber debonding and resin crack mainly existed in the quasi-static condition, while fiber breakage and pull-out mainly occurred at high strain rates.

Keywords: Three-dimensional angle-interlock woven composites; Quasi-static; High strain rates; Tensile properties

1 Introduction

Carbon fiber reinforced composites possess high specific strength and outstanding impactresistance, it plays an important role in engineering industries, such as automotive and aeronautics fields. Among them, a new kind of 3D woven composite with layer to layer angle-interlock structure has been proposed. The developed 3D angle-interlock woven composites (3DAWC) consist of undulated warp yarns and non-crimp weft yarns impregnated with matrix, showing excellent delamination resistance, interlaminar fracture toughness and higher tensile strain-to-failure values compared with traditional 2D laminated composites[1-2]. The tensile properties of textile structural reinforced preforms as well as their corresponding composites have already been investigated by several researches. Hou et al. [3-4] investigated the quasi-static and tensile impact properties 3D orthogonal woven fabric and 3D angle-interlock woven fabric. It was found that both the tensile strength and the failure strain increased with the increases in the strain rate. Sun et al. [5-7] conducted researches on the tensile

impact behaviors of co-woven-knitted composites and 3D braided composites under high strain rates. It was shown that the two kinds of composites are strain rate-sensitive materials. Lomov et al. [8-9] presented a comprehensive experimental study of the comparison of in-plane tensile properties between non-crimp 3D orthogonal weave composites and multi-layer plain weave composites. The results demonstrated that the 3D composites have higher in-plane failure stresses and strains, as well as damage initiation strain thresholds than their 2D counterpart. Naik et al. [10] studied the high strain rate tensile behavior of a plain weave fabric E-glass/epoxy composite along thickness, warp and fill directions. The result showed that there was a significant increase in through the thickness tensile strength at high strain rate loading compared with that at quasi-static loading. Although these studies have already done some fundamental works on the tensile properties of textile structural fabrics or their reinforced composites, the quasi-static and dynamic tensile properties of 3DAWC are seldom simultaneously reported. In addition, its failure modes and fracture morphologies under the two loading conditions are also little-known. Therefore, the aim of the current work is to investigate the tensile behaviors of 3DAWC under various strain rates. The stress-strain curves and fracture morphologies obtained from the tensile experiments under different strain rates were also discussed in this paper[11-14].

2　Experiments

2.1　Materials

The 3D angle-interlock woven fabric (3DAWF) with layer to layer angle-interlock structure was fabricated by Torayca carbon fiber tows (T700-12k). Epoxy resin (JA-02C) from Jiafa Chemical Co. Ltd., was used to impregnate the 3DAWF with the assistant of vacuum assisted resin transfer molding (VARTM) technique. The photograph of vacuum insulation bags is shown in Fig. 1 (a). The epoxy resin was first vacuumed to remove the residual air bubbles before being injected into the textile preform. The curing temperature was 90℃ for 2h, 110℃ for 1h, and finally 130℃ for 4h. Fig. 1 (b) shows the surface photograph of the cured 3DAWC. The final specimens were removed from the oven after cooling for 12h, and then machined into flat dog bone shape as shown in Fig. 1 (c). The basic dimension parameters of the flat dog bone shaped specimen are shown in Fig. 1 (d) and Fig. 1 (e).

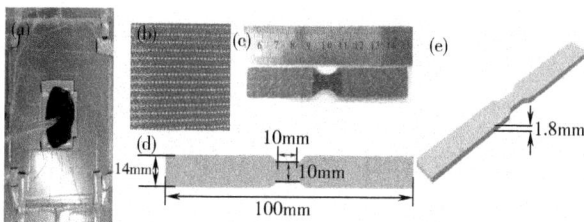

Fig. 1　Preparation of 3D angle-interlock carbon/epoxy woven composites (a) Photograph ofvacuum insulation bags for VARTM technique; (b) Surface photograph of the 3DAWC; (c) Photograph of the cutting 3DAWC specimen; (d), (e) Basic dimensions of the cutting 3DAWC specimen

As shown in Fig. 2 (a), the 3DAWC is composed of three parts, i. e., the resin matrix, warp and weft yarns. The warp yarns are undulated distributed and in-

terweave with the straight weft yarns along the thickness direction to form a stable and integrated woven construction. The optical microscope photographs of the cross section of the 3DAWC along the warp and weft directions are shown in Fig. 2 (b) and Fig. 2 (c), respectively. A more obvious distribution differences between warp and weft yarns can be observed.

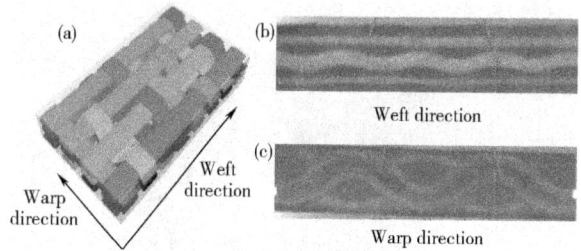

Fig. 2　(a) Schematic diagram of the basic structure of the 3DAWC; (b) Cross-section of 3DAWC along the weft direction; (c) Cross-section of 3DAWC along the warp direction

2.2　Quasi-static and dynamic tension

The tensile tests of 3DAWC along both the warp and weft directions were conducted under both quasi-static and high strain rates. The quasi-static tensile experiments were performed on an MTS 810.23 material testing system at a speed of 5mm/min. Fig. 3 (a) shows the photographs of quasi-static tensile testing. The approximate strain rate under quasi-static tension can be calculated as

$$\dot{\varepsilon} = \frac{v}{L} \qquad (1)$$

where $\dot{\varepsilon}$ is the approximate strain rate, v is the speed of tension, and L is the length of sample. When the gage length was selected as 10 mm, the approximate strain rate was 0.001 s^{-1}.

The tensile tests under high strain rates were performed on a split Hokinson tension bar (SHTB) apparatus. The SHTB apparatus was modified from the split Hopkinson pressure bar (SHPB). The photograph and sketch of the SHTB apparatus are shown in Fig. 3 (b) and Fig. 3 (c), respectively. The SHTB system mainly consists of a strike bar, a transmission bar, and an incident bar. All the bars are composed of the same material with the same diameter of 14.5mm. The length of the strike, transmission, and incident bar are 200mm, 1200 mm, and 800 mm, respectively. As shown in Fig. 3 (c), the strike bar with the same cross-sectional area and modulus as the incident and transmission bars is propelled with a gas gun. Velocity of the strike bar can be adjusted with the gas pressure. When the compress elastic wave passed through the stress transfer parts and reached the bottom surface of the incident

bar, it would be reflected by the pressure block at the bottom surface and propagated backwards. This backwards propagated elastic wave was a tensile wave, and would pass through the specimen and finally spread to the transmission bar. Then the movement of the transmission bar induced by the elastic wave resulted in the tensile failure of the composite specimens.

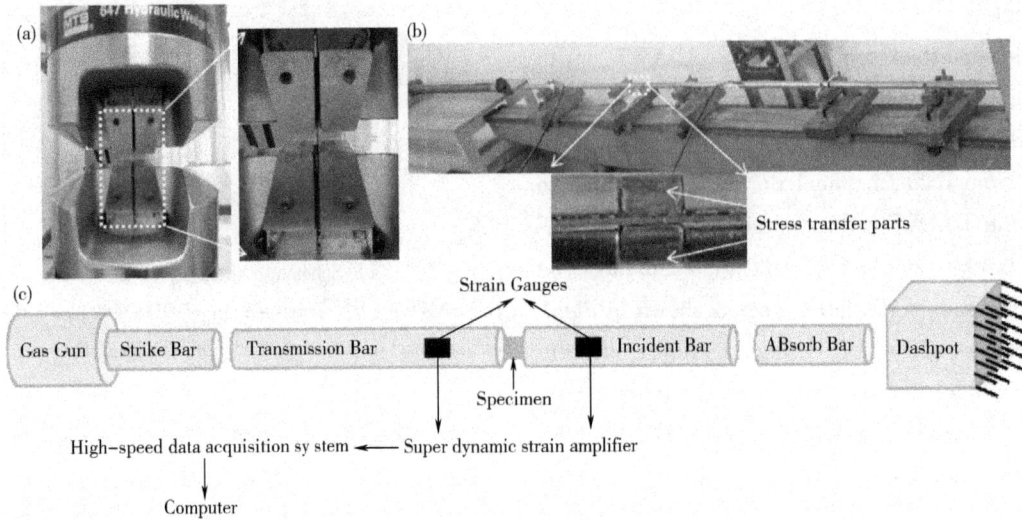

Fig. 3 Quasi-static and dynamic tensile tests (a) Photograph of quasi-static tensile tests in MTS; (b) Photograph of dynamic impact tensile tests by using SHTB apparatus; (c) Schematic diagram of dynamic impact tensile tests by using SHTB apparatus

Based on the SHTB testing system, the stress wave along the incident bar and transmission bar could be measured by strain gauges. If the modulus, cross-section area and density of the bar are denoted by E_b, A_b and ρ_b, and those of the specimen are E_s, A_s and ρ_s, respectively. The equations for strain-rate ($\dot{\varepsilon}$) , strain (ε) and stress (σ) of composite specimen are given as follows.

$$\dot{\varepsilon}(t) = -\frac{2C_0}{L_s}\varepsilon_R(t) \tag{2}$$

$$\varepsilon(t) = -\frac{2C_0}{L_s}\int_0^L \varepsilon_R(t)\,\mathrm{d}t \tag{3}$$

$$\sigma(t) = \frac{E_b A_b}{A_s}\varepsilon_T(t) \tag{4}$$

where $C_0 = \sqrt{E_b/\rho_b}$ is the longitudinal wave velocity in the bar, L_s is the specimen length, $\varepsilon_R(t)$ and $\varepsilon_T(t)$ are the strain gage signals of the reflected and the trans-

mitted pulses, respectively.

Equations (2)-(4) indicate that the average stress and strain are functions of time. The induced strain can be obtained by integrating the reflected pulse and the stress from the transmitted pulse.

3 Results and Discussion

3.1 Strain rate effect

Tensile tests were conducted at four strain rates along both warp and weft directions. The composite specimens were tested at least three times at each strain rate, including quasi-static state and high strain rates. There are three kinds of different air gas pressure used in the tensile testing, e.g., 0.5MPa, 0.7MPa and 0.9MPa, and their corresponding strain rate-time curves are presented in Fig. 4.

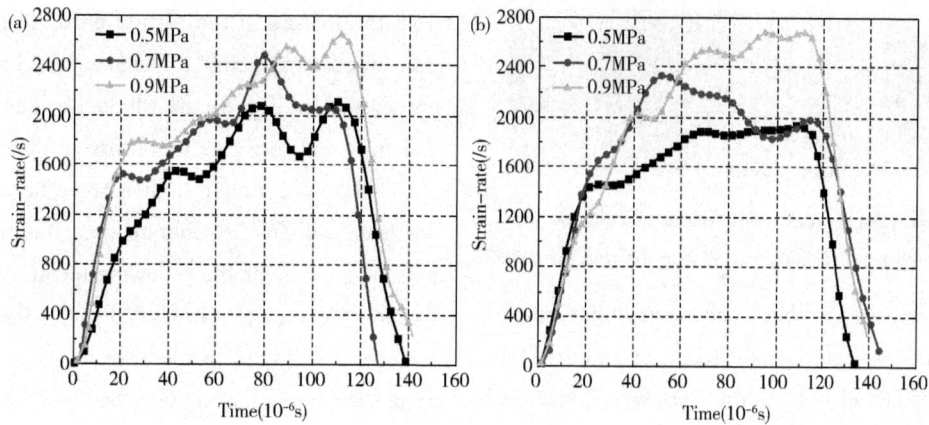

Fig. 4　Strain rate vs. time curves of 3DAWC under different gas pressure　(a) Along the warp direction; (b) Along the weft direction

According to the 1D stress wave propagation theory, the corresponding stress-strain curves are calculated and shown in Fig. 5. It can be found that the stress-strain curves are sensitive to strain rates. The stress-strain curves experienced initially linearly increase, and then gradually decrease after the stress reached a maximum value. As shown in Fig. 5, the failure stress, strain, and the initial modulus increased with the increase of strain rate.

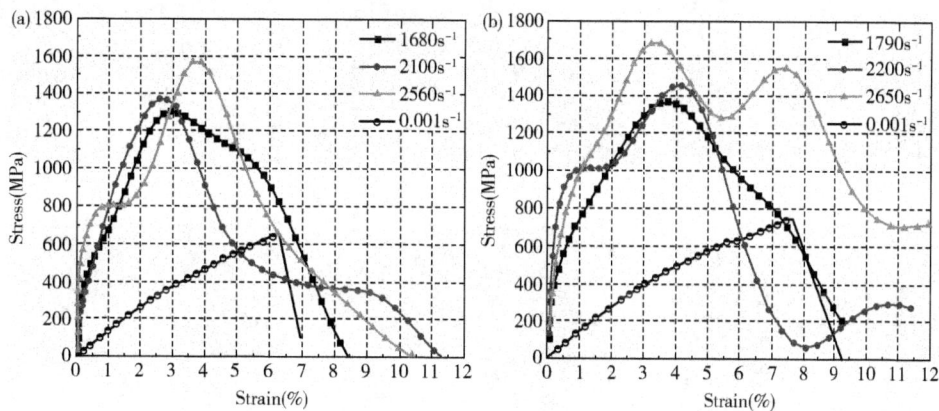

Fig. 5　Stress-strain curves of 3DAWC under different strain rates　(a) Along the warp direction; (b) Along the weft direction

Therefore, it can be concluded that the tensile properties of 3DAWC are significantly influenced by the strain rate. However, under the same impact pressure (or strain rate), the tensile stress-strain curves along the weft direction are a little higher than those along the warp direction. This phenomenon can be attributed to the special geometric structure of 3DAWC. According to the basic structure of 3DAWC, the warp yarns are undulated distribution, while the weft yarns present straight arrangement. The weft yarns absent of crimp will withstand more tensile loads than the undulated warp yarns. Therefore, the weft direction of 3DAWC will be more resistant to stretching. In addition, the stress-strain curves of 3DAWC under quasi-static loading are much lower than those under high strain rate loading. It can be

explained that the specimen will absorb more energy and there is no time for different components to reach stress equilibrium under high strain rate loading.

3.2　Failure mode and fracture morphology

The failure mode and fracture morphology of 3DAWC under quasi-static test are different from those under dynamic test. The damage photographs of 3DAWC under quasi-static tensile tests are shown in Fig. 6. There is no obvious fracture separation phenomenon occurring under quasi-static state. The main failure modes of 3DAWC under quasi-static loading are fiber debonding and matrix crack. Considering the loading time of quasi-static test is much longer than that of dynamic condition, there will be enough time for fibers and matrix to reach the stress equilibrium.

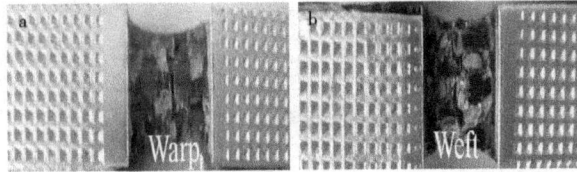

Fig. 6 Fracture photographs of 3DAWC under quasi-static loading. (a) Along the warp direction; (b) Along the weft direction

Therefore, the stresses in fibers and resin under quasi-static loading are the same before fracture, and no fiber is pulled out. However, when the 3DAWC specimens are subjected to high strain rate loading, the impact wave will lead to different stress distributions between fibers and resin. Fig. 7 shows the typical damage morphologies of 3DAWC under in-plane impact tensile tests. The specimens were fractured into two pieces

from the middle of the testing part. The scanning electron microscope (SEM) images of fracture morphologies are shown in Fig. 8, in which obvious fiber breakage and fiber pull-out can be observed. The failure processes of 3DAWC under high strain rate loading are that the resin will firstly generate shear failure, and then fibers begin to bear the following tensile loading until the specimen completely break. Because the fibers are non-uniform distributed in the yarn, a yarn will break at its weakest place based on the weak-links principle. Therefore, the main failure modes of 3DAWC under high strain rates are fiber pull-out and fiber breakage along the fibers' axial direction. The fibers under high strain rate tensing are totally fractured, while less fiber damage impart under quasi-static test.

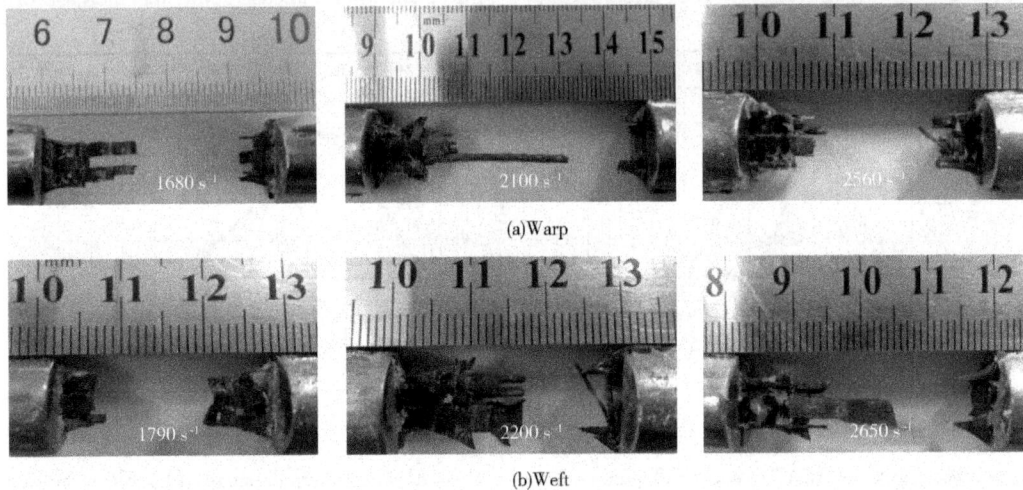

(a)Warp

(b)Weft

Fig. 7 Fracture morphologies of 3DAWC under high strain rates (a) Along the warp direction; (b) Along the weft direction

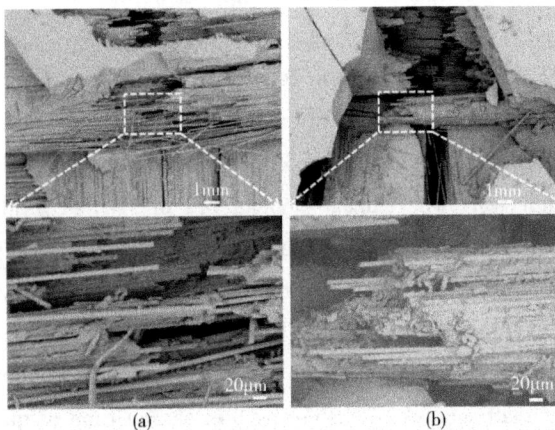

(a)　　　　　　　　(b)

Fig. 8 SEM images of fracture surface of 3DAWC subjected to high strain rate loading (a) along the warp direction; (b) along the weft direction

Although the distributions of warp and weft yarns in 3DAWC are different, the tensile failure morphologies of them are almost the same, which can be wellexplained by their similar mechanism properties. Under high strain rate loading, there is no distinct difference existing in the fracture morphologies at different strain rates. Therefore, the fracture morphologies appear to be insensitive to the varying strain rates.

4　Conclusions

The quasi-static and dynamic tensile behaviors of 3D angle-interlock woven composites (3DAWC) were studied along both warp and weft directions. The MTS material tester and the SHTB were used to measure the tensile properties under quasi-static and high strain rate loading condition, respectively. It was found that the tensile behaviors of 3DAWC were sensitive to the strain rate. The tensile strength and failure strain were both strain rate sensitive, which increased significantly with the increase of the strain rate. The failure modes and fracture morphologies showed a little difference between quasi-static and high strain rate loading. The failure modes were fiber debonding and matrix crack under quasi-static loading and obvious fiber breakage and pull-out under high strain rate loading. Due to the different distribution states of the warp and weft yarns in 3DAWC, the tensile stress-strain curves under the similar strain rate along the weft direction are a little higher than those along the warp direction. However, the fracture morphologies under high strain rate loading appeared to be insensitive to the varying strain rates.

Acknowledgements

Nishonov A and Dong K contributed equally to this work. All the authors acknowledge the financial supports from National Science Foundation of China (Grant Numbers 11272087 and 11572085).

References

[1] Dong K, Liu K, Pan L, et al. Experimental and numerical investigation on the thermal conduction properties of 2. 5D angle-interlock woven composites [J]. Composite Structures, 2016, 154: 319-333.

[2] Ansar M, Wang X, Zhou C. Modeling strategies of 3D woven composites: A review [J]. Composite Structures, 2011, 93: 1947-1963.

[3] Hou Y, Jiang L, Sun B, et al. Strain rate effects of tensile behaviors of 3D orthogonal woven fabric: Experimental and finite element analyses [J]. Textile Research Journal, 2013, 83: 337-354.

[4] Hou Y, Hu H, Sun B, et al. Strain rate effects on tensile failure of 3D angle-interlock woven carbon fabric [J]. Materials & Design, 2013, 46: 857-866.

[5] Sun B, Pan H, Gu B, Tensile impact damage behaviors of co-woven-knitted composite materials with a simplified microstructure model [J]. Textile Research Journal, 2014, 84: 1742-1760.

[6] Sun B, Liu F, Gu B. Influence of the strain rate on the uniaxial tensile behavior of 4-step 3D braided composites [J]. Composites Part A: Applied Science & Manufacturing, 2005, 36: 1477-1485.

[7] Ma P, Hu H, Zhu L, et al. Tensile behaviors of co-woven-knitted fabric reinforced composites under various strain rates [J]. Journal of Composite Materials, 2011, 45: 2495-2506.

[8] Lomov S V, Bogdanovich A E, Ivanov D S, et al. A comparative study of tensile properties of non-crimp 3D orthogonal weave and multi-layer plain weave E-glass composites. Part 1: Materials, methods and principal results [J]. Composites Part A: Applied Science & Manufacturing, 2009, 40: 1134-1143.

[9] Ivanov D S, Lomov S V, Bogdanovich A E, et al. A comparative study of tensile properties of non-crimp 3D orthogonal weave and multi-layer plain weave E-glass composites [J]. Part 2: Comprehensive experimental results. Composites Part A: Applied Science & Manufacturing, 2009, 40: 1144-1157.

[10] Naik N K, Yernamma P, Thoram N M, et al. High strain rate tensile behavior of woven fabric E-glass/epoxy composite [J]. Polymer Testing, 2010, 29: 14-22.

[11] Li X, Yan Y, Guo L, et al. Effect of strain rate on the mechanical properties of carbon/epoxy composites under quasi-static and dynamic loadings [J]. Polymer Testing, 2016, 52: 254-264.

[12] Zhang H, Yao Y, Zhu D, et al. Tensile mechanical properties of basalt fiber reinforced polymer composite under varying strain rates and temperatures [J]. Polymer Testing, 2016, 51: 29-39.

[13] Dong K, Peng X, Nishonov A, et al. In-plane tensile behaviors of bi-axial warp-knitted composites under quasi-static and high strain rate loading [J]. Journal of Donghua University (Eng. Ed.), 2017, 34: 487-491.

[14] Zhao J, Zhang L, Guo L, et al. Dynamic properties and strain rate effect of 3D angle-interlock carbon/epoxy woven composites [J]. Journal of Reinforced Plastics & Composites, 2017, 36: 073168441771571.

Design and Weaving of Three-Dimensional Woven Fabric with Rectangular Shape

Shina Wang[1], Yanxue Ma[1,2]*, Yuling Li[1,2], Weidong Gao[3]

[1] *Key Laboratory of Textile Science & Technology, Ministry of Education, Shanghai 201620, China*

[2] *College of Textiles, Donghua University, Shanghai 201620, China*

[3] *Jiangnan University, Wuxi 214000, China*

* *Corresponding author's email*: yxma@ dhu. edu. cn

Abstract: In the development of feather down products, fabrics are always cut and sewn into a rectangular shape form for feather filling. To improve comfort, shaping and down proof property of the down product used woven fabrics, an in-depth study was carried out on design of rectangular shape 3D fabrics. Structural diagram and looming draft were created. Proper machine settings for warp let-off motion and take-up mechanism were adopted, and a sample of rectangular shape 3D woven fabric was developed in the weaving process without further cutting and sewing. This study proved possibility of integral weaving of the rectangular shape 3D structures on the ordinary weaving machine.

Keywords: Rectangular shape; Integral weaving; 3D woven fabric; Ordinary loom

1 Introduction

Nowadays, feather-filled products such as down clothes or quilts are wildly used in daily life, and are favored by the vast number of consumers. Down fabrics are the basis of feather-filled products. In the development process of down fabrics, woven fabrics are needed to cut and sewn to form a multi-layer for feather filling, such as arectangular shape for feather filling. The cut and sewn method to form the rectangular shape fabric is flexible to change the shape and achieve varied thicknesses of down products. However, the cutting and sewing is very time-consuming. More seriously, sewing stitches on down products always cause the leakage of small feather that would reduce the quality. Therefore, the idea to form a rectangular shape woven fabric without cutting and sewing was proposed in some research. In some patents, two layers of woven fabrics could be linked together to form an oval shape[1] (Fig. 1), or a trapezoid shape[2] (Fig. 2) in the warp direction. These structures will increase the space of down activities and store more static air to improve the warmth of

the feather down fabric. However, it is so hard for the feather-filled products by using the oval and trapezoid shape to stick closely with the human body due to the lower and upper sides of these structures are not equal in length and warmth of the feather down products is reduced. In order to improve these disadvantages caused by the oval shape or trapezoid shape, a woven fabric with rectangle shape has developed (Fig. 3).

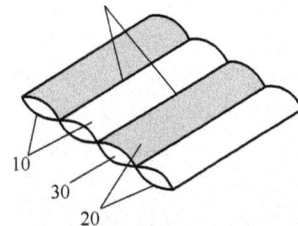

Fig. 1 Oval shape

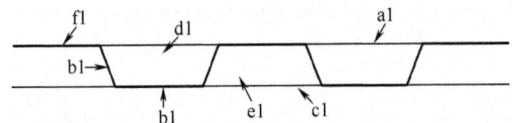

Fig. 2 Trapezoid shape

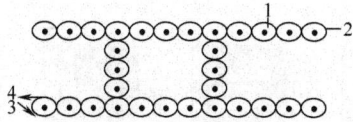

Fig. 3 Trapezoid shape

At present, the rectangular shape structure can be woven on a three-dimensional loom, and can also be woven on an ordinary two-dimensional loom. Binbin Han et al. [3] transformed an ordinary loom into a three-dimensional loom to weave carbon fiber rectangular cross-section woven fabrics. But the cost of the rectangular shape structure weaving on the three-dimensional looms is expensive and the equipment price is high and the possibility of large-scale production is small in this way [4]. Yan et al. [5] successfully weaved rectangular shape structural fabrics on ordinary loom by applying multiple heddle heals in conjunction. However, the heddle used in the weaving process was very complex and difficult to control. Haiwen Liu, Sainan Wei et al. [6] wove a three-dimensional fabric with rectangle shape on two-dimensional weaving machines by flattening-weaving-reduction method. This method can reduce the production cost, but it requires complicated design and has limited fabric width.

The fabric structure with rectangular shape designed in this paper not only can be formed on an ordinary weaving machine, but it is also easy to design and operate. The length of the vertical lining layer in weft direction could be varied from 0 to 2cm. At the same time, size of the rectangular shape was easy to change based on requirements in practice.

2 Structure Design

2.1 Structure sketch of 3D woven fabrics with rectangular shape

This article firstly drawed the rectangular shape structural warp-wise structure sketch of 3D woven fabric. Fig.4 shows the structure sketch with two repeats. The rectangular shape structural warp-wise structure sketch of three-dimensional woven fabric was divided into three parts: the upper layer fabric, the lower layer fabric and the intermediate lining in weft direction. The upper layer fabric or the lower layer fabric was woven with plain weave

structures or warp backed weave structures and the intermediate lining was interwoven with the upper and lower layer to form the rectangular shape in the weft direction.

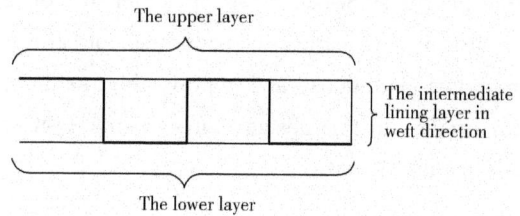

Fig. 4 Structure sketch of rectangular shape in weft direction

2.2 Weave diagram of 3D woven fabrics with rectangular shape

As shown in Fig.5, there are 6 warps and 216 wefts in total. ■ represents warp interlacing point, □ represents weft interlacing point, 1, 2 represent the upper layer warp, I and II represent the middle layer warp, and①, ②represent the lower layer warp. 1', 2', 3', 4', 5', 6' represent heddle frame.

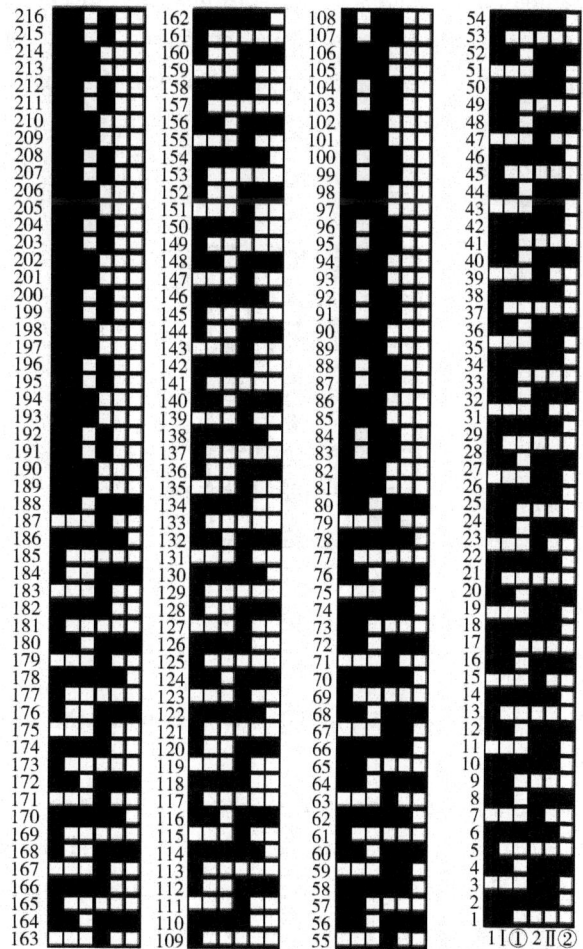

Fig. 5 The weave diagram of the rectangular shape structural 3D woven fabric

· 217 ·

2.3 Denting plan of 3D woven fabrics with rectangular shape

The rectangular shape structural 3D woven fabric of the denting plan is shown in Fig. 6. In order to reduce the occurrence of reed marks, the occurrence of appearance of grounding conditions, and improve the quality of the fabric surface, in this design, three-in-one wear of the reed-in method is used.

Fig. 6　The denting plan of the rectangular shape structural 3D woven fabric

2.4 Drafting plan of 3D woven fabrics with rectangular shape

The rectangular shape structural 3D woven fabric of the drafting plan is shown in Fig. 7. In this part, the woven fabric was a rectangular shape structure, which was equivalent to weaving three-layer fabrics. To ensure clear warp opening and easy to weave, grouped draw-in method was applied.

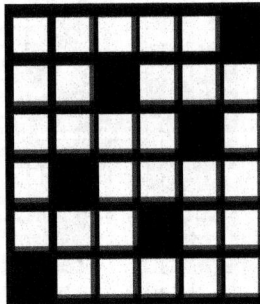

Fig. 7　The drafting plan of the Rectangular shape structural 3D Woven Fabric

2.5 Looming draft of 3D woven fabrics with rectangular shape

According to the organization chart, the denting plan and the drafting plan of the three-dimensional woven fabric, the looming draft of the rectangular shape structural 3D woven fabric is shown in Fig. 8.

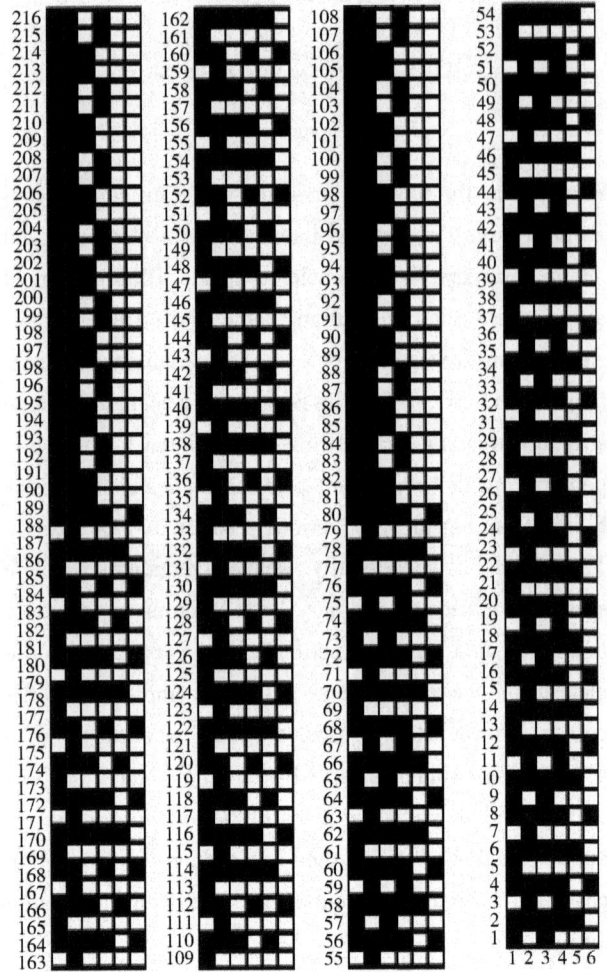

Fig. 8　The looming draft of the rectangular shape structural 3D woven fabric

3　Weaving Process

Warps for the upper layer were threaded into 1' and 2' heald frames, warps for the intermediate lining were threaded into 3' and 4' heald frame, and warps for the lower layer were threaded into 5' and 6' heald frames. Design of fabric repeat is properly matched with warp let-off and take-up mechanismin this study. For the sake of weaving the rectangular shape structural three-dimensional fabric, the weaving process was divided into four stages. When warps for the upper layer and the intermediate lining were woven together, they became the upper-middle layer. When warps for the lower layer and the intermediate lining were woven together, they became the lower-middle layer. The warp density of fabric was set as 200 ends /10cm. The weaving process is shown in Fig. 9.

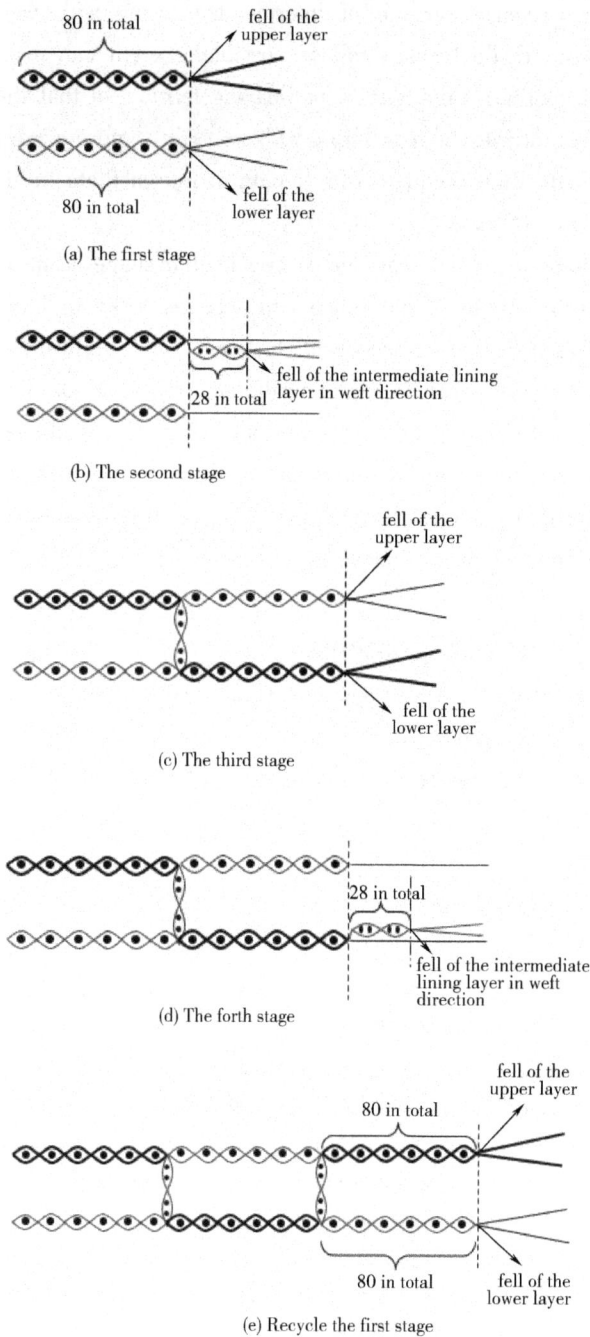

(a) The first stage

(b) The second stage

(c) The third stage

(d) The forth stage

(e) Recycle the first stage

Fig. 9　The weaving process of the rectangular shape structural 3D woven fabric

3.1　The first stage

The upper-middle and lower-middle layers were woven together. From the 1st to the 79th weft, the upper-middle and lower-middle layers were normally woven. The warp beam took off the warp normally and batch roller took up the fabric that was already woven normally. When picked the 80th weft, the upper-middle and lower-middle layer of the fabric had reached the given length. The upper-middle and lower-middle layers of the fabric stopped weaving. The warp beam stopped sending the warp and the batch roller stopped taking-up. The weaving of the first stage was completed (as shown in Fig. 9).

3.2　The second stage

Intermediate liningin weft direction was independently woven. From the 81st weft, the lower and middle layers were searated. Intermediate lining was woven independently. The warp beam did not send the warp and the batch roller did not roll. The fell of intermediate lining with weft was moving back towards the loom. Intermediate lining in weft direction weaving was not finished until it was given 28 wefts.

3.3　The third stage

The upper and lower-middle layers were woven meanwhile. From the 109th, the warp yarns of the intermediate lining with weft that we got in the second stage were connected with the warp yarns of the lower layer surface. The upper and the lower-middle layers began to be woven at the same time. The warp beam began to run-innormally and the reel began to roll normally. At the 188th weft, the fabrics of upper and lower-middle layers stopped weaving. Moreover, the warp axis stop sped feeding, and the roller stopped winding in the third stage as shown by (c) in Fig. 9.

3.4　The fourth stage

Intermediate liningin weft direction was woven independently. From the 189th weft, the lower and middle layers were separated and intermediate lining with weft was started to be woven. The warp beam shaft did not send the warp and the reel did not roll. The cloth-fell of intermediate lining with weft was moving back towards the weaving machine continually. We got the 216 weft yarns in this fabric finally as shown in Fig. 9 (d). After these four stages of weaving, a complete weaving cycle was got. After that, repeated the first process as shown by (e) in Fig. 10.

4 Results and Discussion

4.1 Results

Fig. 10 shows the physical map of the rectangular shape structural 3D woven fabric. The upper part is the upper layer, the lower part is the lower layer, and the middle part is intermediate lining in weft layer direction. The length of the intermediate lining in weft direction fabric is 1.5cm.

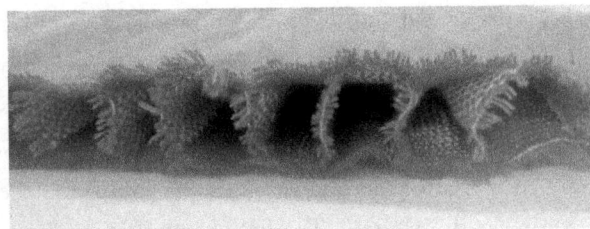

Fig. 10　The physical map of the rectangular shape structural 3D woven fabric

4.2 Key points in weaving

In the weaving cycle, when intermediate lining in weft layer was transited from the upper or lower layers to the upper or lower layers, the amount of warp run-in was larger than that of upper and lower layers. Thus the warp beam (at least two beams) should be used to let off the warp that the fabic needs. One or two of the warp beams is used to transport the upper and lower layers of warp yarns. And control their tension and for controlling the weft density of the fabric, a positive let-off system is needed. Intermediate lining in weft layer is using a passive let-off system.

In order to weaving easily, plain weave is adopted for the fabrics weave of upper and lower layers. The fabrics of upper-middle and lower-middle layers are composed of the warp backed weave. There is no need for intermediate lining with weft layer fabric to have much dense with the warp and weft and for the better connection between intermediate lining with weft layer. Intermediate lining with weft layer fabric structure adopts the warp rip.

In order to make intermediate lining with weft more suitable for bonding with the upper layer fabric or the lower layer fabric without a floating line, it is needed to stop the warp let-off system and the rolling of the batch roller, when the 1st–8th and 109th–116th weft yarns are woven. Tension of intermediate lining with weft warp should be as small as possible when it can meet the normal warp tension of weaving fabric, so that the warp of intermediate lining with weft can require a warp length that is equal to the length of intermediate lining with weft layer.

However, due to the current rectangular shape of fabric in the middle of the height can only be woven to 2cm. When the length received 1.5cm, the middle-layer warp yarn began to relax and the opening were not clear if continuing to weave the middle lining. The main research direction in the future is that how to increase length of intermediate lining to meet requirements of different down products.

Acknowledgements

The research was supported by National Key R&D Program of China (Grant No. 2017YFB0309200) and National Natural Science Foundation of China (Grant No. 71704021)

References

[1] Hu Feng, Huang Wei, Wei Feng. A seamlessly knotted and Intertwined down jacket fabric structure: China. 204519455 [P]. 2015-08-05.

[2] Zhou Yan, Cai Dongzhao, Qiu Yuejian. A three-dimensional fabric: China. 205115746 [P]. 2016-03-30.

[3] Han Binbin, Wang Yixuan. The design of three-dimensional spacer fabric and development of weaving machines [J]. Industrial Textiles. 2015; (06): 6-11.

[4] Li Gang, Guo Xingfeng, Liu Lanfang. Design and weaving methods of 3D woven fabrics [J]. Hebei Textiles. 2008 (01): 17-22.

[5] Yan Xining, Xie Guangyin. Structure and weaving of three-dimensional hollow core of three-dimensional woven fabrics [J]. China Textile Leader. 2010; (02): 53-55.

[6] Liu Haiwen, Wei Sainan, et al. A hollow double " I " type three-dimensional fabric: China. 204097658 [P]. 2015-01-04.

Dopamine Modified Wool Fabrics for Formaldehyde Removal

Shijiao Han[1,3] , Dong Jia[2] , Xuqing Yang[1,3] , Yao Du[1,3] , Quan Zhu[5] ,
Wanshuang Liu[4] , Yiping Qiu[1,3,4] , Qiuran Jiang[1,3] *

[1] *Key Laboratory of Textile Science & Technology , Ministry of Education , Shanghai 201620 , China*

[2] *The Fiber Inspection Bureau in Xingjiang Uygur Autonomous Region , Urumchi , Xinjiang 83000 , China*

[3] *Department of Technical Textiles , College of Textiles , Donghua University , Shanghai 201620 , China*

[4] *Donghua University Center for Civil Aviation Composites , Donghua University , Shanghai 201620 , China*

[5] *Department of Applied Chemistry , College of Chemistry , Chemical Engineering and Biotechnology , Donghua University , Shanghai 201620 , China*

* *Corresponding author's email : jj@ dhu. edu. cn*

Abstract : To reduce the indoor formaldehyde pollution , wool fabrics with natural affinity to formaldehyde were modified by dopamine (DOPA) to enhance their attraction to formaldehyde. After testing for 120min , the original wool fabric could reduce around 20. 1% of the initial formaldehyde , while the modified fabrics displayed substantial increments in formaldehyde removal efficiency. The fabric treated for 4h has a raised efficiency about 34. 0% , and a linearly increasing trend was kept after 120min. The abrasion and washing processes could reduce the formaldehyde removal efficiencies of fabrics , and the effect was more obvious for the fabrics modified for a longer time , but the maximum reduction was only 5. 3% , which indicated sufficient durability. The results proved the potential of the modified wool fabrics for the development of indoor formaldehyde removal products.

Keywords : Dopamine ; Wool fabrics ; Formaldehyde removal ; Abrasion resistance ; Washing resistance

1 Introduction

Formaldehyde is a widely used solvent in industry and can be released from the materials for construction and indoor decoration[1] . Since formaldehyde with a concentration above $0.08 mg/m^3$ is considered harmful and can elicits nasopharyngeal carcinoma , brain tumor and colon cancer[2] , it is recognized as one of the major indoor pollution. Wool is one of the major fibers used for fabrication indoor decoration textiles , such as carpets , rugs , tapestries and slipcovers. Wool molecules contain various hydrophilic groups , such as amino groups , carboxyl groups and hydroxyl groups , which have affinity to formaldehyde[3] . Besides , wool fibers from Xinjiang province possess a special hollow structure , which facilitates the attraction of formaldehyde. Thus , wool fibers can serve as a desire raw material for the development of indoor formaldehyde removal products[4] . However , the adsorption ability of wool fibers is limited and needs to be enhanced.

Dopamine (DOPA) possesses a structure similar to pyrocatechin , which endows mussel with strong adhesion to various surfaces , and can be polymerized into polydopamine (PDA) with controlled thickness in an alkaline condition[5] . PDA can adhere to a variety of materials , such as stone , metal , ceramics and so on. Therefore , DOPA has been used for surface modification for many applications[5] . Since PDA displays affinities to various materials , it has the potential to attract formaldehyde[6] .

In this research , wool fabrics were modified by DOPA aiming to produce wool products with enhanced formaldehyde elimination function. The effects of the modification time on the formaldehyde removal performances were investigated. The resistances of the modified fabrics to the washing and abrasion processes were also evaluated.

2 Experiments

2.1 Materials

The plain wool fabrics were supplied by the Fiber Inspection Bureau in Xinjiang Uygur Autonomous Region with a fabric weight of 210g/m². Dopamine hydrochloride (DOPA, 98%) was purchased from J&K Scientific Ltd. The Tris powders and the formaldehyde solution (37%) were purchased from Shanghai Sinopharm Chemical Reagent Co. , Ltd. Other chemicals were provided by Shanghai Sinopharm Chemical Reagent Co. , Ltd.

2.2 Dopamine modification of wool fabrics

Wool fabrics (30cm × 40cm) were washed in a detergent bath (2g/L, liquor ratio 50:1) at 50℃ for 10min and then rinsed by distilled water for three times. The untreated fabrics were served as control (W). The Tris buffer was prepared by dissolving the Tris powders in distilled water at 1.2g/L, and adjusted to pH 8.5 by hydrochloric acid. The DOPA modification bath was prepared at a concentration of 2.2g/L in the Tris solution. The wool fabrics were immersed in the DOPA modification bath and treated for designed durations (1–4h). After the treatment, fabrics were rinsed in distilled water for three times and then dried at 50℃. The treated fabrics were labeled as DW1 to DW4.

2.3 Evaluation of formaldehyde removal performance

The formaldehyde removal performances of the original and DOPA modified wool fabrics were evaluated by a self-built formaldehyde tester. The sample fabrics (30cm × 40cm) were hung vertically in the test chamber. The formaldehyde solution (1%, 4mg) was injected on the dispersion stage in the chamber, which could accelerate the evaporation by heating and evenly disperse formaldehyde by air blowing. The temperature and the relative humidity were maintained at (20 ± 2)℃ and (65 ± 3) RH%. The initial concentration of formaldehyde in the test chamber was set at (0.50 ± 0.03)mg/m³. The change of formaldehyde concentration was recorded by a formaldehyde detector (LB-HD,

Lianyungang Yubao Electronic Technology Co. , Ltd.). The formaldehyde removal efficiency was calculated using the following equation:

$$R = \frac{C_0 - C_t}{C_0} \times 100\% \qquad (1)$$

where R is the formaldehyde removal efficiency, C_0 is the initial formaldehyde concentration and C_t is the concentration recorded at the time point t.

2.4 Abrasion resistance test

The modified fabrics (30cm × 40cm) were first balanced under the standard condition (20 ± 2)℃ and (65 ± 3) RH% for 24h and then wore for 5000 times with a pressure of 12kPa and abrasion rate at (25 ± 2) r/min. Then, the formaldehyde removal efficiency was tested as described above.

2.5 Washing durability test

The modified fabrics were washed in the SW-12A soapfastness color fastness tester according to the standard of GB/T 3921—2008 at 40℃ with a liquor ratio of 50:1 and a rotation rate of (40 ± 2) r/min. The washing bath was the mixture of the standard detergent (5g/L) and sodium carbonate (2g/L). After washing, the change of formaldehyde removal efficiency was measured.

2.6 Statistical analysis

A one-way analysis of variance with fisher's pair wise multiple comparison was employed to analyze the data. The confidence interval was set at 95% and a p-value less than 0.05 was considered to be a statistically significant difference. Different characters were used to label the significant different data. The standard deviations were indicated by the error bars.

3 Results and Discussion

3.1 Effect of dopamine modification duration on the removal of formaldehyde

(W) and modified wool fabrics (DW1 to 4) along with time.

Fig.1 presents the change of the formaldehyde concentration within 120min by samples. In the first 90min, the concentration of formaldehyde was reduced almost linearly by the original wool fabric, and then leveled off. The result indicated that the maximum reduction in the formaldehyde concentration by the untreated wool fabric was around 0.10mg/m³.

All the modified fabrics could remove formaldehyde more efficiently, especially in the first 30min. During 30 to 120min, the formaldehyde concentrations were slightly reduced when the DW1 and DW2 samples were tested. However, the concentrations decreased obviously when the DW3 and DW4 samples were evaluated and the trend was almost linear. It indicates that the concentration would be further reduced, if the test duration was prolonged.

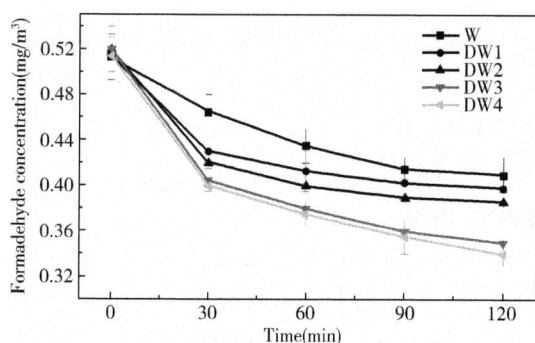

Fig. 1　Formaldehyde removal performances of the original

Fig. 2 shows the effects of the DOPA modification duration on the formaldehyde removal efficiency of fabrics. The original wool fabrics could remove 21.5% of formaldehyde in 120min. The original wool fabrics displayed a relatively high formaldehyde removal rate compared to other comment fibers. The samples modified by DOPA for less than 2h displayed a slight increase in formaldehyde removal efficiency, but the changes were

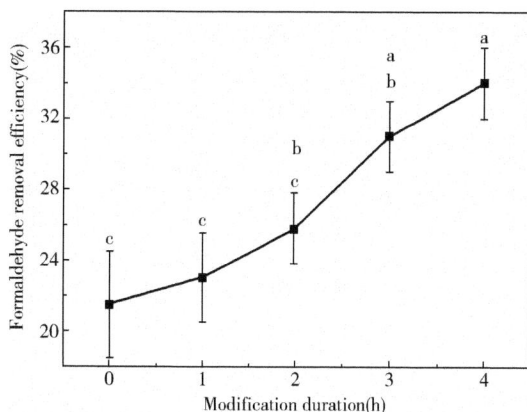

Fig. 2　Effect of dopamine modification duration on the formaldehyde removal efficiency of the DW fabrics

not significant. When the modification duration was prolonged to 3h and 4h, the formaldehyde removal efficiencies could achieve 31.0% and 34.0%. The difference between the efficiencies of samples modified for 3h and 4h was not significant. The results indicat that DOPA has a higher affinity to formaldehyde, but an obvious enhancement in the formaldehyde removal rate required for a sufficient accumulation of PDA on the fiber surface. Once the surface of fibers was fully covered, a further elongation of the modification duration did not introduce substantial enhancement of the formaldehyde removal performance.

3.2　Effect of dopamine modification time on the abrasion resistance

Fig. 3 delineates the effect of abrasion on the formaldehyde removal performances of the wool fabrics modified for different durations. After the abrasion process, the formaldehyde removal efficiencies of all samples were reduced. The efficiency of the sample DW1 decreased around 2.8%, similar to the decrement of the original wool fabric. By prolonging the modification time, the decrement in the formaldehyde removal efficiency increased almost linearly. During the abrasion process, some wool fibers were shed off from fabrics, and the PDA coating layers of a portion of fibers were worn down, which caused the reduction in formaldehyde removal. The thickness of the PDA layer increased along with the modification duration. A thicker PDA layer was easier to be peeled off from the fibers. Therefore, to select an optimum modification time needs to consider not

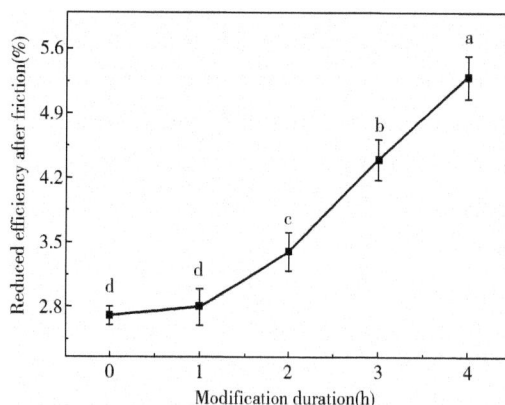

Fig. 3　Effect ofabrasion on the formaldehyde removal performance of the wool fabrics

only the formaldehyde removal efficiency but also the fixation fastness. However, the maximum decrement was merely 5.3% (DW4), which means the major portion of the modified fibers retained intact.

3.3 Effect of dopamine modification time on the washing fastness

The effect of the washing process on formaldehyde removal performance was shown in Fig.4.

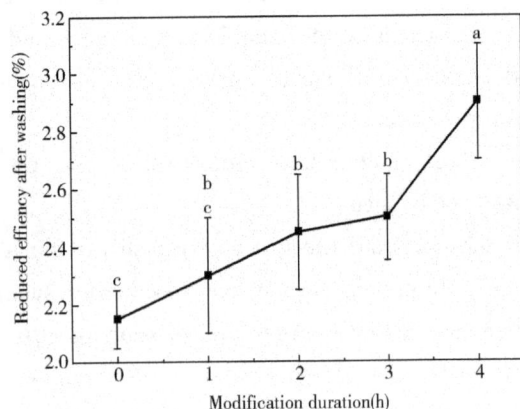

Fig.4   Effect of the laundry process on the formaldehyde removal performance of the wool fabrics

The formaldehyde removal efficiencies of all samples were reduced, and the efficiency of the sample modified for a longer duration was weakened more obviously. The trend was similar to the influence of the abrasion process, but the effect was moderate. The maximum reduction in the formaldehyde removal efficiencies was only 2.9%.

4   Conclusions

To eliminate indoor formaldehyde pollution, wool fabrics were modified with DOPA to enhance their formaldehyde removal performance. As the modification time increased, the formaldehyde removal efficiency of fabrics was enhanced. The highest formaldehyde removal efficiency could achieve 34% by the fabric treated for 4h after the test for 120min, and a higher efficiency would be reached by prolonging the test duration. The abrasion and the laundry processes could slightly reduce the formaldehyde removal performance, but the maximum reduction was merely 5.3%. Therefore, the modified wool fabrics have the potential to fabricate indoor textile products with the formaldehyde removal function.

Acknowledgements

The project was financially supported by the Xinjiang Uygur Autonomous Region Quality and Technical Supervision of Science and Technology Projects (2015NO7), the NSFC Project (51503031), the Scientific Research Foundation for the Returned Overseas Scholars from the Ministry of Education (15B10127), and the Fundamental Research Funds for the Central Universities (2232015D3-02).

References

[1] Zhu X, Gao X, Qin R, et al. Plasma-catalytic removal of formaldehyde over Cu-Ce catalysts in a dielectric barrier discharge reactor [J]. Applied Catalysis B-Environmental, 2015, 170:293-300.

[2] Lemus R, Abdelghani A A, Akers T G, et al. Potential health risks from exposure to indoor formaldehyde [J]. Reviews on Environmental Health, 1998, 13(1-2): 91-98.

[3] Hearle J W S. A critical review of the structural mechanics of wool and hair fibres [J]. International Journal of Biological Macromolecules, 2000, 27(2): 123-138.

[4] Gharehaghaji A A, Johnson N G, Wang X. Wool fibre microdamage caused by opening processes-Part IV: In-situ SEM studies on the compressive microdamage and failure of wool fibres looped around opening elements [J]. Journal of the Textile Institute, 1999, 90(1): 23-34.

[5] Liu Y, Ai K, Lu L. Polydopamine and its derivative materials: synthesis and promising applications in energy, environmental, and biomedical fields [J]. Chemical Reviews, 2014, 114(9): 5057-115.

[6] Pebg L, Guo R, Lan J, et al. Microwave-assisted deposition of silver nanoparticles on bamboo pulp fabric through dopamine functionalization [J]. Applied Surface Science, 2016, 386: 151-159.

Effect of Cryogenic Treatment on the Interfacial Properties of Carbon Nanotube Yarn / Epoxy Resin Composite

Yifan Wang[1], Fujun Xu[1,2][*]

[1] College of Textiles, Donghua University, Shanghai 201620, Shanghai 201620, China
[2] Shanghai Key Laboratory of Advanced Micro & Nano Textile Materials, Shanghai 201620, China

[*] Corresponding author's email: fjxu@ dhu. edu. cn

Abstract: The influence of cryogenic treatment (−196℃) on interfacial properties of the carbon nanotube (CNT) yarn/epoxy composite are investigated by using cryogenically conditioned in different cooling and heating rate. The interfacial shear strength (IFSS) of the composite materials is measured by the micro debonding experiment. The results shows that cryogenic treatment can improve the interface bonding properties of carbon nanotube yarn/epoxy composite, especially through the method of rapid cooling and slow heating treated, the interface shear strength increased by 24.697%. Cryogenic treatment is an effective method to improve the interfacial bonding properties of carbon nanotube yarn/epoxy resin composites.

Keywords: Cryogenic treatment; Carbon nanotube yarn; Epoxy resin; IFSS

1 Introduction

Now composite materials play a more and more important role in the fields of aerospace, electrical and electronic, structural material aspects. The carbon nanotube yarn as a continuous high-performance material is very promising, its superior strength and high modulus, excellent thermal conductivity properties have been fascinated for researchers, especially the application in composite materials[1-2]. However, how to make carbon nanotube composites be comparable to carbon fiber composites is still a challenge. The highly oriented carbon nanotube yarns prepared by the array spinning technique are composed of long aligned carbon nanotubes and it can be used to produce high-performance composite materials better than the most advanced carbon fiber composites at present[3]. However, because of the unique structure of the carbon nanotube yarns, the interfacial bonding ability between the yarns and the resin is weak[4], which greatly affects the overall properties of the carbon nanotube yarn composites. Liu[5] studied the influence of different kinds of resin on the interfacial properties of carbon nanotube yarn composites by single

filament fracture method. It was found that the interfacial shear strength could raise by 10 times. Lei[6] choosed micro debonding test to study how the generalized surface sizing method improved the interfacial properties of epoxy resin composites, when used diluted resin/acetone solutions to treat resin, the carbon nanotube yarn/epoxy resin composite material could improve the interface of 11MPa. However, there is no simple, easy and environmentally friendly method to improve the interfacial problems of carbon nanotube yarn composites.

Cryogenic treatment, also called ultralow temperature treatment, refers to the process that treat materials −130℃ Celsius by using liquid nitrogen as refrigerant to achieve the purpose of modification[7]. This method is often applied to improve the hardness and wear resistance of metal parts[8]. In recent years, studies have shown that a new spark is also emerging between Cryogenic treatment and composite materials. Cryogenic treatment not only can enhance the tensile properties of fiber reinforced composites and optimize the internal structure of the composites[9], but also can strengthen the interfacial bonding properties of the composites[10]. In this study, different coolingand heating conditions were used to treat the carbon nanotube yarn/epoxy resin micro composites, then tested the interfacial shear strength of composite materials and used the SEM method to analyze the causes of the results, tried to find the best way to improve the interfacial properties of carbon nanotube yarn/epoxy resin composite materials.

2 Experiments

2.1 Materials

The carbon nanotube yarns used in the experiment with the purity of the carbon nanotube yarn is more than 95% were provided by the Suzhou Institute of Nanotech and Nano-bionics. They were prepared by the array spinning technology, and had the advantages of high orientation and uniform diameter. The epoxy resin (JL–235) and curing agent (JH–242)were provided by Changshu Jia FA Chemical Co., Ltd. (Zhejiang, China)

2.2 Specimen preparation

Shown in Fig. 1, in order to reduce the error of the experimental results, first prepared all the samples of debonding test at the same time, and then randomly treated the samples under different conditions to ensure the consistency of the samples before treatment. Epoxy resin and curing agent mass ratio was 10∶3.3, dropped

the epoxy resin droplets in carbon nanotube yarns, then placed the specimens in the oven, dried at 50 degrees for 3 hours then raised the temperature to 70 degrees for seven hours to thoroughly cure epoxy resin. Took out the samples and put them in the constant temperature and humidity box for at least 12 hours, then carried out the follow-up treatment and test.

The cryogenic treatment was carried out using a temperature-programmable cryogenic chamber (SXL–30, Institute of physics and chemistry, Chinese Academy of Sciences). The composite samples were subjected to cryogenic temperature respectively by three different methods (shown in Fig. 1): the samples directly put into liquid nitrogen (77K) environment, which means the treated temperature suddenly decreased from room temperature to cryogenic temperature, and then maintained at 77K for 12 hours, finally directly put the sample out the 77K environment; Slow cooling-rapid heating: the cooling rate is 2℃ per minute when the treated temperature decrease from room temperature down to 77K, and then maintained at 77K for 12 hours, finally directly put the sample out to the room temperature; Rapid cooling-slow heating: the samples directly put into liquid nitrogen (77K) environment for 12 hours, then the rising temperature rate is 2℃ per minute when the treated temperature rise to room temperature.

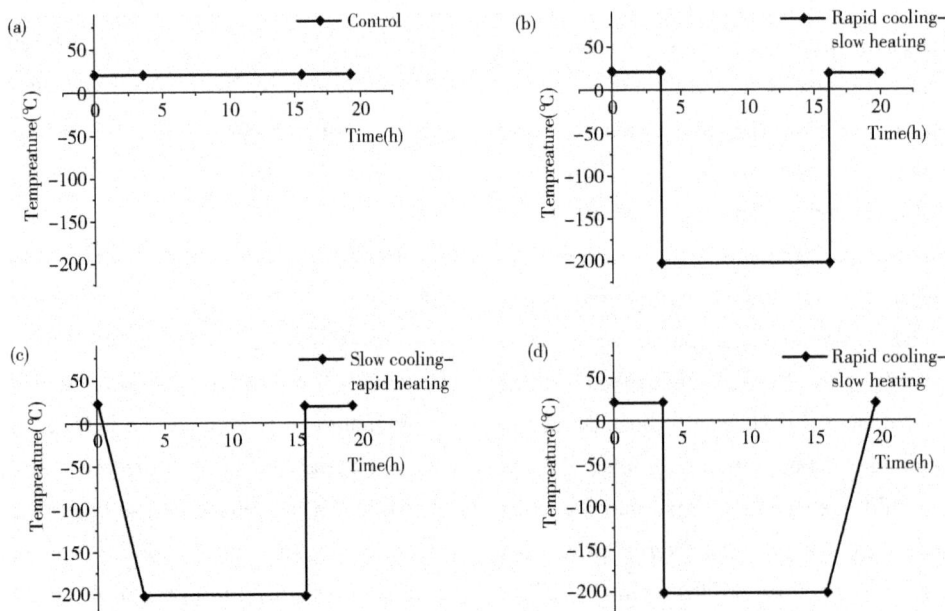

Fig. 1　Parameters of cryogenic treatment of different samples

2.3 Micro debonding experiment

In this experiment, the interfacial shear strength of the composites was measured by micro debonding test. The micro debonding experiment is to drop the liquid resin onto the fiber and then solidify the resin into an oval bead. The elliptical microsphere is loaded by the micro clamp so that the interface between fiber and the resin bead appears shear stress. When the load reaches a certain value, the resin bead and the fiber will be separated. Now the tension and the interfacial shear force reach equilibrium, the interfacial shear strength can be calculated. Since the resin and yarn in this paper are consistent and the properties don't affect the experimental results, this paper uses the simple formula for calculating the interfacial shear strength:

$$\text{IFSS} = \frac{F}{\pi DL} \qquad (1)$$

Where F is the peak load, L is the embedded length, D is the fiber radius.

First measured the diameter D of the carbon nanotube-yarn and bead embedded length L. The sample pictures were taken with a polarizing microscope, and the diameter of the sample was measured by the software, and the average diameter more than 10 data was used as the diameter of the yarn. Used XQ−2 single fiber tensile strength tester (Shanghai xusai instrument) to carry out micro debonding test, as shown in Fig. 2. Adjusting the jaw position and stopping it not far above the micro bead, using the downward force of the micro clamp, the adhesion between the epoxy micro bead and the carbon nanotube yarn were separated and the beads moved. The maximum strength F obtained in this process was the stress value when calculating the interfacial shear strength. The formula is used to calculate the interfacial shear strength of composite materials according to formula (1). Finally, using TM−3000 scanning electron microscope (Hitachi) analyzed the experimental results.

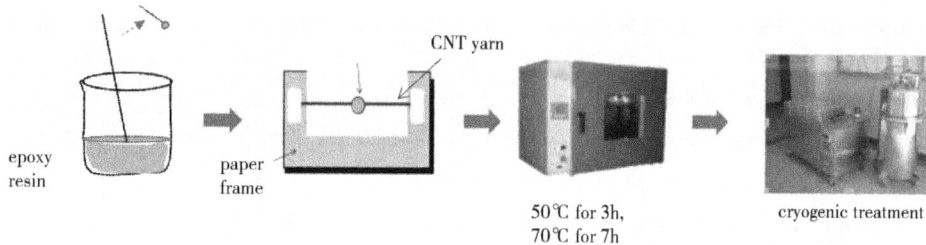

Fig. 2　Schematic diagram of samples preparation and cryogenic treatment

3　Results and Discussion

3.1　Interfacial shear strength (IFSS)

Fig. 3 (a), (b) was a position diagram of an epoxy resin droplet in the micro debonding experiment, under the action of a jaw, the interface between the carbon nanotube yarn and epoxy resin was debonding and the bead was sliding. Fig. 3 (c) was a graph of a typical force-displacement curve of four kinds of specimen, the changing trends of four samples' force value were consistent, however, it could be seen the sample A without cryogenic treatment may own more surface friction.

The IFSS values between carbon nanotube yarn / epoxy resin were shown in Fig. 3 (d). The statistic results analyzed by one-way anova showed the sample B (sharp cooling-sharp rising temperature treatment) increased by 7.250% over the interfacial shear strength of sample A; Sample C (slow cooling-sharp rising temperature treatment) increased by 7.533% over the interfacial shear strength of sample A; The interfacial shear strength of sample D(sharp cooling-slow rising temperature treatment) increased by 24.697% than sample A, which means that the cryogenic treatment was effective for enhancing the interface of carbon nanotube yarn/epoxy resin composite, especially the cryogenic treatment method of sharp cooling then slowly rising to room temperature, it could significantly improve the carbon nanotube yarn/epoxy resin composite interfacial properties.

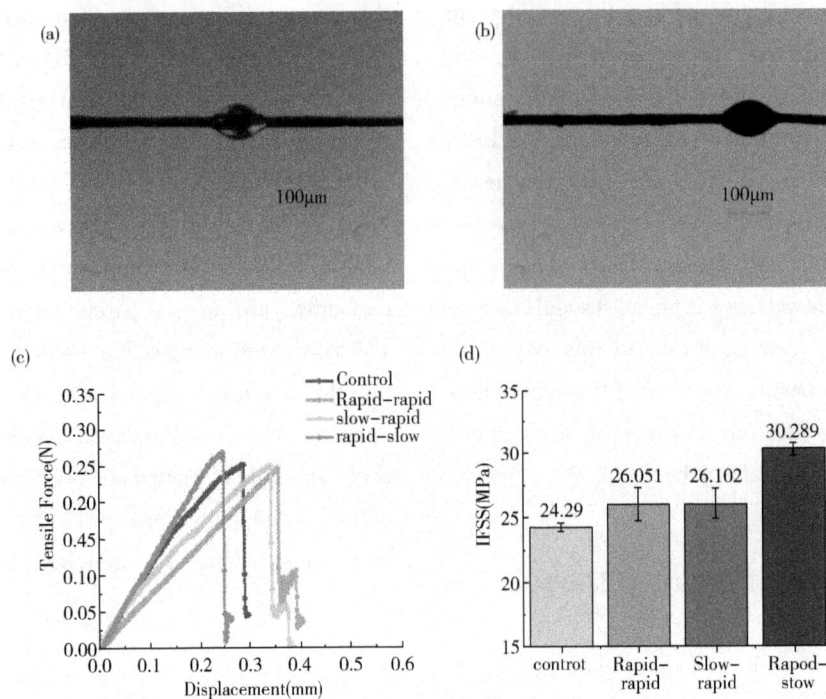

Fig. 3   The polarizing microscope images of the beads (a) before and (b) after the experiments; (c) the typical micro debonding curves of different samples; (d) IFSS results of the cryogenic treated carbon nanotube yarn / epoxy resin composites

3.2   Morphological analysis of interface

In the process of cryogenic treatment, the internal stress appeared with the temperature down to 77K, which made epoxy resin beads and carbon nanotube yarn contract. However, the thermal expansion coefficient of epoxy resin was far greater than the carbon nanotube yarn, its shrinkage rate was much higher than carbon nanotube yarns' shrinkage rate. In the result, there was a compact effect between carbon nanotubes yarn and epoxy resin after cryogenic treatment, and the interface enhanced. The rising temperature rate of the cryogenic treatment affected the keep of this compaction effect, when using the sharp rising temperature method to treat the sample, the two phases were instantaneous expansion at the same time and the interface was destroyed again; and when using the way of slow rising temperature treatment, it could ease the damage and reserve the interface enhancement effect by greater degree.

As shown in Fig. 4, the micro composite debonding sliding area after cryogenic treatment covered more epoxy resin. Meanwhile, fewer carbon nanotube bundles were drawn out. It directly proved that cryogenic treatment improved the interfacial properties of carbon nanotube yarn/epoxy resin composite materials. When using the cryogenic treatment method of sharp rising temperature rate, the interfacial debonding occurred between the epoxy resin and the yarn, while using the cryogenic treatment method of slow rising temperature rate, the interfacial debonding occurred in the epoxy resin beads interior. This showed that carbon nanotube yarn and epoxy resin interfacial performance by the slow rising temperature treatment was very good, before the destruction of the interface between two phase, the epoxy resin itself appeared broken, which was consistent with the conclusion of the Fig. 3(d).

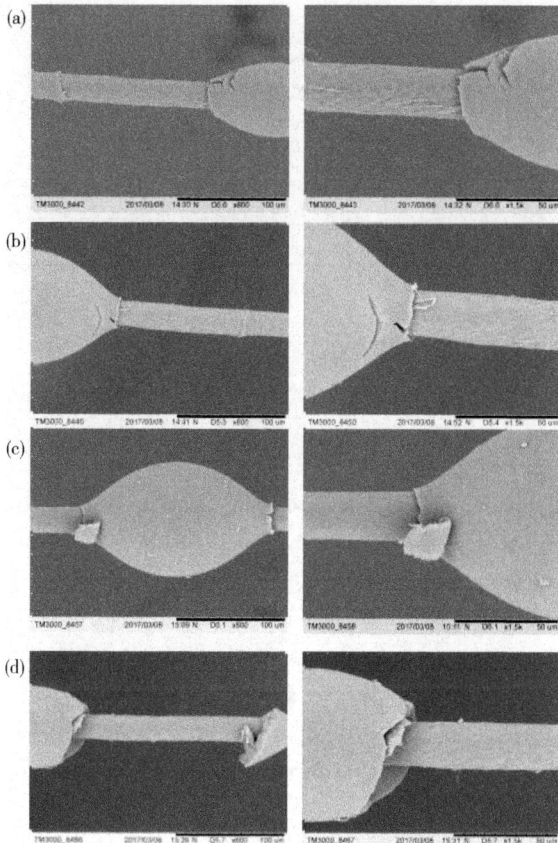

Fig. 4　SEM pictures of different specimens　(a) Sample A (original sample); (b) Sample B (sharp cooling-sharp rising temperature treatment); (c) Sample C (slow cooling-sharp rising temperature treatment); (d) Sample D (sharp cooling-slow rising temperature treatment)

4　Conclusions

In this paper, we studied the effect of cryogenic treatment on carbon nanotube yarn/epoxy resin composite material interfacial properties. We used three kinds of cryogenic treatment conditions to treat samples, which mean different cooling rate and rising temperature rate. The results showed that cryogenic treatment could improve the interfacial bonding ability of carbon nanotube yarn/epoxy resin composites. The method of sharp cooling-slow rising temperature treatment have the best modification effect, which means the samples were directly put into liquid nitrogen (77K) environment for 12 hours, then the rising temperature rate was 2℃ per minute to reach the room temperature, it could improve interfacial shear strength by 24%. The main reason was that the compaction effect caused by cryogenic treatment, as well as the way of slow rising temperature treatment which maintained more compression effect, so the IFSS improved more. Cryogenic treatment is undoubtedly a green, environmentally friendly, inexpensive and efficient method to improve the interfacial bonding properties of carbon nanotube yarn / epoxy resin composites.

References

[1]Liu L Q, Ma Q G, Zhang Z. Macroscopic carbon nanotube assemblies: preparation, properties and potential applications [J]. Small, 2011, 7(11):1504-20.

[2] Park J, Lee K H. Carbon nanotube yarns [J]. Korean Journal of Chemical Engineering, 2012, 29(29): 277-287.

[3] Zhang M, Atkinson K R, Baughman R H. Multifunctional carbon nanotu be yarns by down sizing ganancient technology [J]. Science, 2004, 306(5700):1358-1361.

[4] Monta Z. Visco elastic and mechanical properties of multi-walled carbon nanotube/epoxy composites with different nanotube/epoxy composites with different nanotube content [J]. Materials & Design, 2011, 32(4):2301-2307.

[5] Liu Y, Li M, Gu Y, et al. The interfacial strength and fracture characteristics of ethanol and polymer modified carbon nanotube fibers in their epoxy composites [J]. Carbon, 2014, 52:550-558.

[6] Lei C, Zhao J, Zou J, et al. Assembly-dependent interfacial property of carbon nanotube fibers with epoxy and its enhan cement via generalized surface sizing [J]. Advanced Engineering Materials, 2015.

[7] Kevin H, Anthony S. Method for measuring liquid cryogen level using a level probe[P]. US, 2011.

[8] Rezaeian A, Zhirafar S, Pugh M. Effect of cryogenic treatment on the mechanical properties of 4340 steel [J]. Journal of Materials Processing Technology, 2007, 186: 298-303.

[9] Kwon D J, Wang Z, Jin Yeung, et al. Interfacial evaluation of carbon fiber/epoxy composites using electrical resistance measurements at room and a cryogenic temperature [J]. Composites Part A Applied Science & Manufacturing, 2015, 72: 160-166.

[10]Disdier S, Rey J M, Pailler P, et al. Helium permeation in composite materials for cryogenic application [J]. Cryogenics, 1998, 38(38):135-142.

Effect of Garment Pressure from Running Compression Pants on Lower Limbs Muscles' Fatigue Threshold

Jianmei Sui[1]*

[1]*School of Fashion Technology, Shanghai University of Engineering Science, Shanghai 200444, China*

* Corresponding author's email: xiehongyyjs@ 163. com

Abstract: The pressure of the compression pants for muscle bound and support, not only wearing comfort, but also contributing soft tissue slow movement of tremor and delaying muscle fatigue. Compression pants getting the more and more favor of professional and amateur athletes, but its protective effect has not a clear indicators to evaluate. $iEMG_{FT}$ (muscle fatigue threshold) was selected in this article to evaluate the effect of the different tightness compression trousers to the lower limbs target muscle fatigue. Conclusion: the best protection state is 10 + 20 in the 1500m running (fabric tensile rate of thigh and calf were 10% and 20% respectively). Quantizing the influence of fatigue threshold from compression pants on running sports with fabric tensile rate, as reference data for functional compression garments' development.

Keywords: Running compression pants; Electromyographic fatigue threshold; Muscle fatigue; Garment pressure; Fabric stretch rate

1 Introduction

In recent years, more and more scholar began to study the effect of pressure used in the sport, including enhancing athletic performance, promoting the blood circulation, reducing fatigue and promoting the recovery of muscle fatigue. Wang P, Mclaren J, Leong K F[1] by muscle activity tests to assess the performance of the clothing pressure are defined that, sports compression clothing pressure to the elastic fabric, it can improve sports performance and reduce the sports injuries were often dressed on athletes. And functional exercise compression pants is one of the sports compression garment, its function mainly precipitates in: it can be decreased by the activation of muscle vibration amplitude and reduce unit number and adjust the time to slow down the activation of motor units of muscle fatigue, so as to improve sports performance; It is conducive to exercise fatigue recovery; It also has favorable comfort. Engel F, Sperlich B[2] summarized in the book the role of pressure clothing in sports: performance and recovery, compression garment was increasingly popular among professional athletes and amateur sports fans.

Li Ya-ning et al. investigated that the effect of pressure exerted by knee-high gradient compression socks (GCS) on the lower limb muscles, found that pressure exerted on the lower limb by GCS gradually decreased from ankle to below-knee; GCS pressure helped to reduce muscle oscillation; wearing GCS seemed to help to reduce muscle fatigue during running[3]. Frédérique HINTZY et al draw the conclusion that wearing compression shorts on the thigh was effective in reducing both vibration transmissibility along the thigh and muscle vibrations of the thigh during cycling. And the effect sizes at 6mmHg compression were substantial with commercially available competitive shorts. To verify compression stocking may thus influence the EMG signal, they concluded that attenuation of the muscle vibration with the mechanical advantage of the compression shorts should attenuate of the VL muscle during cycling[4]. Then on the base of these, in 2013, Beijing Institute of Fashion Technology has a master's degree paper by comparing the discharge duration of the lower limb muscles and the difficulty of fatigue, explained the structural design principle of compressed pants in the market from a biomechanical point of view, and on this basis, the school has also optimized the structure of the compressed pants in 2016. In 2015, by researching healthy people running 30min on a treadmill, Miyamoto and Kawakami found that the pressure on the calf was more effective than the gradient pressure from the ankle to the lower leg to reduce muscle pain and fatigue[5].

Most literature studied comparison of the effects of two pairs of compressed pants and no compression pants on Athletes' sports performance or fatigue time. For the specific compactness and specific compression parts, there are few in-depth studies. From the point of muscle fatigue protection, from fatigue protection mechanism to product development research aiming at fatigue protection, this paper aims to provide theoretical reference for independent research and development of functional clothing. The index used in this paper is the myoelectric fatigue threshold, in order to evaluate the effect of different sizes of compressed pants on fatigue protection. Therefore, the paper aims to analyze the myoelectric fatigue threshold of the measured muscles using the EMG signal, and to compare the fatigue threshold of the compression pants with different fabric tensile rates in 1500 meters running. Then finding out the best clothing pressure threshold that is not only comfortable, but also for fatigue protection, so providing a theoretical reference for the development of compression products pants.

2　Research Method

2.1　Subjects

15 students from Shanghai university of engineering science, height: (157.50 ± 5) cm, age: (22.00 ± 1.41) yr, weight: (50.20 ± 0.28) kg, they are all non-professional runner. These subjects haven't participated in professional running training, but they usually have the habit of running. They run two times a week on an average of 5000m, with an average speed of 9km/h, which can adapt to the speed of treadmill and complete the experiment.

One week before the experiment, the subjects were allowed to go to the laboratory to familiarize themselves with the experimental environment, mainly to adapt to the speed and operation of the treadmill, and to inform the subjects of the experimental plan, so that the subjects could be psychologically prepared to minimize psychological impact. 24h before the start of the experiment, the subjects were told not to do strenuous exercise and to clean up the hair of the body where the experiment needed to be attached to the electrode. Before the start of the experiment, the subjects were reconfirmed that all were prepared according to the requirements and had no physical injury and normal motor function. The basic information of the subject is shown in Tab. 1.

Tab. 1　Basic information of the subjects ($X \pm SD$)

Height(cm)	Weight(kg)	Age(yr)	Calf girth(cm)	Thigh girth(cm)	Waist girth(cm)	Hip girth(cm)	Length of lower limb(cm)
157.50 ±0.71	50.20 ±0.28	22.00 ±1.41	64.47 ±0.19	93.07 ±0.20	34.00 ±0.08	50.07 ±0.12	83.00 ±0.82

2.2　Experiments

2.2.1　Experimental materials

Donghua university institute of textile clothing pressure studied from the angle of fabric tensile rate mechanism, it was concluded that clothing comfort and the theoretical relation of elastic fabric tensile rate: $k + 1 = (x + 1)(y + 1)$, k is on the surface of human body skin elongation, x is the allowance for clothing, y for fabric elastic elongation. Ignoring the changes of skin dimension when moving down, then according to formula $(x + 1)(y + 1) = 1$, if fabric elastic elongation of y is known, the clothing sample quantity of x can calculate, so the relationship exploration between clothing pressure and ample quantity can be transformed into the relationship between the pressure and the fabric elastic elongation rate[6].

Elastic elongation refers to the percentage of the length of elastic fabric to its original length at a certain external force[7].

$$a = (\Delta L/L_0) \times 100\% \qquad (1)$$

Inside, a is the elongation of the fabric, ΔL refers to the length of the fabric elongation (unit: m), and L_0 indicates the original length of the fabric (unit: m).

According to the formula, the elastic elongation of the thigh and calf was 10%, 20% and 30% respectively, and 16 combinations were produced. The influence of clothing pressure on muscle fatigue threshold was compared one by one.

By testing the basic parameters and tensile properties of eight kinds of fabrics, the tensile properties of the eight fabrics are not very different. In the end, the fabric with a small elastic modulus, a large elastic recovery rate, a large poisson and a better pressure comfort was selected as the experimental fabric.

Custom-made sewing of experimental compressed pants: paste lines paste tape cut the tape along the line riot into version finished products (Fig. 1).

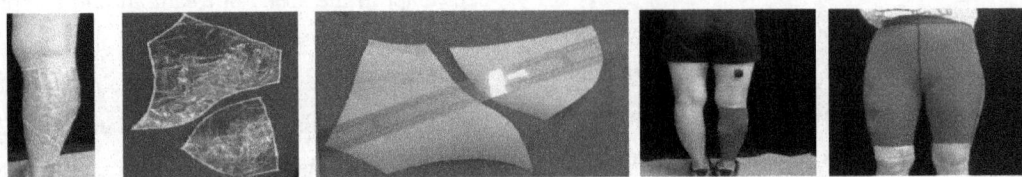

Fig. 1   Sketch of the production process of compression trousers

The various parts of the body when the person is moving the compression force is different, incremental gradient pressure can help venous blood circulation, accelerate the venous return, improve muscle oxygen, and thus effectively improve athletic performance. Therefore, the experimental products of this study adopt three kinds of tightness of thigh and calf to combine in pairs, so as to explore the best pressure combination that can delay fatigue.

2.2.2   Garment pressure test

The higher the tensile rate of the fabric, the greater the pressure. The purpose of the clothing pressure test is to explore the maximum comfort clothing pressure to constrain the maximum tightness of the compression pants (Tab. 2). Each subject wore a variety of combined states to test dynamic clothing pressure using the German clothing stress testing system, Novel pliance-x-32, and took the average value of each state for 3 times to record the data. The test site was the myoventral position of the eight major muscles of the lower limb, and the exercise program was that the subjects ran at a speed of 9km/h for 1min.

Tab. 2   The pressure of each muscle under different fabric stretching rate (unit: kPa)

Fabric stretching rate(%)	TA	GM	GL	VL	VM	RF	BF	Gluteus
10	1.05	0.68	0.18	1.16	0.34	1.74	1.62	0.59
20	1.39	1.03	0.58	1.58	0.64	1.78	1.14	0.84
30	5.56	2.05	3.02	8.25	6.74	7.21	7.28	3.45

In the range of 10% to 30% fabric stretch rate, the size range of clothing pressure is 0.18-8.25kPa. Under the condition of 10% and 20% fabric stretch rate, the difference of clothing pressure is not obvious, but when the fabric stretch rate reaches 30%, the clothing pressure increases significantly, but none of them exceeds 10kPa.

Combined with the comfort of clothing pressure, the stretch rate of fabric is 30%, which determines the boundary conditions for the subsequent experiment. On this basis, subjects wore experimental compression pants to perform the fatigue threshold test scheme.

The steps are as follow steps:

(1) Looking for the muscles to be tested and marking

the muscles in accordance with the anatomical position of the muscles.

(2) Alcohol was used to wipe the muscles of the subjects to be tested. After the alcohol volatilized, the sensor was placed on the target muscle. The sensor should be attached to the muscle belly of muscles (the most muscular part of muscles), the direction parallel to the muscle fiber and the sensor arrow upward.

(3) Turn on the switch of the sensor, first let the subjects walk 20s at the speed of 6km/h at the treadmill (Germany, h/p/cosmos), at the same time checking whether the location of the sensor is correct and whether the electromyography signal is regular or not. If the signal is too complex or the amplitude is large, it needs to be adjusted. Repeat the process until the EMG signal presents a clear, independent and regular signal segment, and then the data is recorded.

(4) Running scheme. Each experiment asked the subjects to have a different combination of the compressed pants, and the other clothing and equipment were the same. The running experiments were carried out at the same time every day in the constant temperature and constant humidity cabin to ensure that the factors of the other conditions of each experiment were reduced to the lowest. Before the test, the subjects were warm up for 5 minutes, then the test was conducted according to the running program, and the 24h was rested for second times. In order to reduce the measurement error, each subject was measured 5 times each, using the 5 iEMG mean of each person as the fatigue threshold[8]. The running plan of 1500 meters is shown in the Tab. 3.

Tab. 3 1500m running at a constant speed experimental scheme

Action	time(min)	speed(km/h)
Walking	2	6

Continued

Action	time(min)	speed(km/h)
Jogging	2	8
The test speed	1	9
A formal test	10	9
rest	30	0

3 Experimental Data Processing

The time section of EMG signal processing in the experiment of general increasing load power vehicle is 20s[10], 10s[9], 6s[15]. The time segments of EMG signal processing in running experiment were 30s[11], 15s[15], 10s[11-16], 5s[13] and 20s[9] respectively[9-16]. In this paper, the total time 600s of the test was divided into 5 segments, and the length of each section was 300m timing 120s, which was divided into 8 segments, and each segment was 15s. Then the iEMG value of each segment was calculated, and the linear fitting of iEMG value and time was done. Both of the obtained slope taken as the abscissa and the mileage as the ordinate were then linearly fitted, so the intercept value on the Y axis is the muscle EMG fatigue threshold (Tab. 4).

Firstly, the fatigue threshold of each muscle in each combination state was calculated, and the specific calculation method of fatigue threshold was as follows (taking in some combination of a subject's gluteus maximus as an example).

Step 1: divide the original electromyography into 40 segments, each time was 15s. Five experimental data were averaged to eliminate the measurement errors, and the EMG scores of the eight muscles of each subject were obtained respectively.

Step 2: according to the value of each of the electromyography above, the eight iEMG values in 300m miles were fitted linearly with the corresponding time, and the slope of the fitting line is obtained (Fig. 3).

Tab. 4 The EMG integral value of the lower limbs-the slope of the time fitting line

Running distance(m)	TA	GM	GL	VL	VM	RF	BF	Gluteus
0-300	0.00	-0.18	-1.25	0.91	0.18	1.44	0.24	0.30
300-600	0.36	1.70	1.51	-1.94	1.07	-0.53	0.63	1.78
600-900	0.02	-0.97	0.56	-0.83	0.32	-0.04	-0.48	-0.52

Running distance(m)	TA	GM	GL	VL	VM	RF	BF	Gluteus
900-1200	0.03	-0.04	-0.54	-0.32	0.19	-0.56	-0.57	-1.47
1200-1500	-0.02	-0.10	-0.14	-0.13	0.24	-0.17	-0.25	-0.46

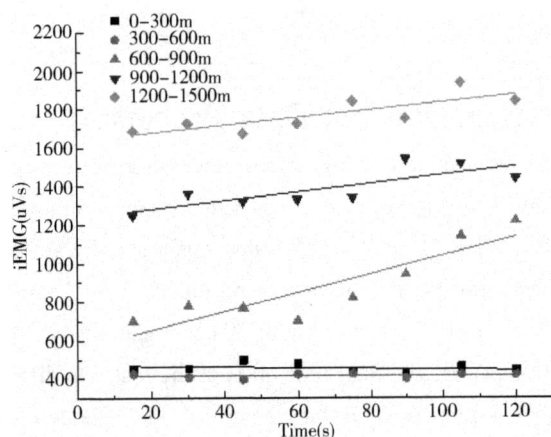

Fig. 3　The slope of the iEMG value and time linear fitting within 8 segments every 300m

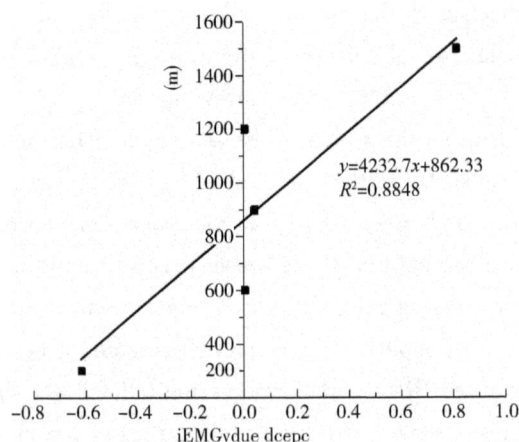

Fig. 5　Intercept of the slope of iEMG value and the running distance

Step 3: Calculation of fatigue threshold. The slope value in is used as a horizontal coordinate, and the mileage is used as an ordinate, both of them are linearly fitted, and the intercept value on the Y axis is the EMG fatigue threshold as Fig. 5. The electromyographic fatigue threshold of other subjects' tested muscles was calculated by the same method.

4　Results and Discussion

According to the same procedure, the electromyographic fatigue threshold of the lower limb target muscles of all the subjects was calculated. The results are as follows:

Tab. 7　iEMGFT of muscles under different protection conditions (m)

Thigh + calf fabric stretch rate(%)	TA	GM	GL	VL	VM	RF	BF	Gluteus
0 + 30	844.36	897.00	942.95	747.98	917.65	970.89	1011.20	923.21
0 + 20	984.82	833.37	975.57	941.24	675.17	812.50	902.78	968.07
0 + 10	1039.90	900.74	892.84	851.23	1020.60	950.25	1004.10	902.41
0 + 0	949.17	901.30	914.63	862.33	856.91	911.21	932.65	712.89
10 + 30	897.08	947.82	1074.10	1041.80	926.42	910.50	1069.80	1056.60
10 + 20	1066.50	904.49	900.50	1409.70	1000.78	1074.00	1055.80	1021.80
10 + 10	877.93	1351.50	908.60	933.71	896.64	991.57	918.53	932.90
10 + 0	1041.90	868.61	1111.70	1256.10	923.69	937.80	947.37	888.47
20 + 30	982.93	799.58	1089.30	932.90	1032.20	884.45	885.06	715.88
20 + 20	866.36	775.02	940.95	767.59	994.94	1082.30	910.71	899.28
20 + 10	877.48	1166.80	1153.20	1005.00	976.54	988.49	1014.10	899.05
20 + 0	973.84	899.06	915.57	1275.50	903.01	1105.40	1026.30	1005.90

Thigh + calf fabric stretch rate(%)	TA	GM	GL	VL	VM	RF	BF	Gluteus
30 + 30	972.75	982.75	1083.80	924.34	846.72	971.45	924.46	983.91
30 + 20	1143.20	1095.10	1133.00	1047.60	1009.80	808.59	945.59	1085.30
30 + 10	748.97	1259.80	1297.70	1229.10	884.40	1114.30	1234.60	887.99
30 + 0	906.31	1459.80	646.61	843.36	918.44	1025.00	1183.80	1162.50
Minimum protection status	30 + 10	20 + 20	30 + 0	0 + 30	0 + 20	30 + 20	20 + 30	20 + 30

The compensatory mechanism of muscle is that when the local motor muscle fiber unit of the body is fatigued, the nervous system will collect other sports muscle fiber units around the body instead of fatigue muscles to do the work. Therefore, the optimal protective condition can be obtained by comparing the minimum threshold of muscle fatigue in various states. The dark font in the tab. indicates that the fatigue threshold is the minimum under this protective condition, the initial fatigue of the muscle in this state is the least protective effect of all the combination. By comparison, the best pressure combination of 1500m running compression pants is 10 + 20.

It can be seen from the above tab. that compared with the unprotected state, applying a certain garment pressure to the muscle surface does not necessarily increase the fatigue threshold, instead, in some cases it may also reduce the fatigue threshold of the muscle, that is,

increasing the muscle fatigue rate. The dark font in the Tab. 8 indicates that the muscle has the smallest fatigue threshold in this protective state, which is the worst protective effect on muscle fatigue. The fatigue mileage of the dark font in the Tab. 8. indicates the earliest fatigue of the muscles in this state, and the protective state should be abandoned. The rejected protection states are: 30 + 10, 20 + 20, 30 + 0, 0 + 30, 0 + 20, 30 + 20, 20 + 30, 20 + 30. Of course, the best clothing pressure matching in 800m mileage is also likely to have a better protective effect on 1500m running. However, in the end, it needs to compare with other protective states to get the best protection. So there are eight cases left, 0 + 10, 10 + 30, 10 + 20, 10 + 10, 20 + 10, 10 + 0, 20 + 0, 30 + 30. The fatigue threshold corresponding to the remaining eight protection states was compared, and the results are as follows:

Tab. 8　iEMGFT of each muscle corresponding to the other eight protective states (m)

Thigh + calf fabric stretch rate(%)	TA	GM	GL	VL	VM	RF	BF	Gluteus
10 + 30	897.08	947.82	1074.10	1041.80	926.42	910.50	1069.80	1056.60
10 + 20	1066.50	904.49	900.50	1409.70	1000.78	1074.00	1055.80	1021.80
10 + 10	877.93	1351.50	908.60	933.710	896.64	991.57	918.53	932.90
10 + 0	1041.90	868.61	1111.70	1256.10	923.69	937.80	947.37	888.47
20 + 10	877.48	1166.80	1153.20	10050	976.54	988.49	1014.10	899.05
20 + 0	973.84	899.06	915.570	1275.50	903.01	1105.40	1026.30	1005.90
30 + 30	972.75	982.75	1083.80	924.34	846.72	971.45	924.46	983.910

Through the above-mentioned each muscle in eight different protection under the state of fatigue mileage comparative analysis found that the rest eight kinds of protection only 10 + 20 and 20 + 0 two kinds of protection

is not dark, namely, in a state of the eight kinds of protective first experienced muscle fatigue phenomenon did not happen in 10 + 20 and 20 + 0 state of the two lines. Therefore, the optimal state of protection should be selected from these two states. And by comparing the two conditions of each muscle fatigue mileage can be easily found that the lower limb muscle fatigue range in 10 + 20 state is generally higher than 20 + 0 state, therefore, the optimum pressure combination of 1500 m running compression pants is 10 + 20.

5 Conclusions

The best protection in the 1500m running movement is 10 + 20 (the stretch rate of the fabric on the thigh is 10%, the part of the calf is 20%), so it is not obvious that the greater the pressure, the better the protection effect will be. Clothing pressure over the assembly affects the coordination between muscles, causing premature fatigue in the local muscles, and then affecting the muscles around them to follow fatigue.

Acknowledgements

Thank you to all the volunteers who volunteered to participate in this experiment. Thanks for the suggestions made by the team members and tutor's hardworking guidance.

References

[1] Bringard A, Perrey S, Belluye N. Aerobic energy cost and sensation responses during submaximal running exercise-positive effects of wearing compression tights [J]. International Journal of Sports Medicine, 2006, 27(5): 373-378.

[2] Engel F, Sperlich B. Compression garments in sports: Athletic performance and recovery [M]. Springer International Publishing, 2016.

[3] Li Y N, Lu A M, Dai X Q, et al. Effect of garment pressure on lower limb muscle activity during running[J]. Advanced Materials Research, 2001, 175-176: 832-836.

[4] Hintzy F, Gregoire N, Samozino P, et al. Effect of thigh-compression shorts on muscle activity and soft tissue vibration during cycling [J]. Journal of Strength & Conditioning Research, 2017:1.

[5] Miyamoto N, Kawakami Y. No graduated pressure profile in compression stockings still reduces muscle fatigue [J]. Int J Sports Med, 2015, 36(3): 220-225.

[6] Li Q L, Xie M D. Relation between cloth pressure and stretch rate of elastic knitted fabric [J]. Progress in Textile Science & Technology, 2008.

[7] Bouissou P, Estrade P Y, Goubel F, et al. Surface EMG power spectrum and intramuscular pH in human vastus lateralis muscle during dynamic exercise [J]. Journal of Applied Physiology, 1989, 67(3): 1245-9.

[8] Matsumoto T, Ito K, Moritani T. The relationship between anaerobic threshold and electromyographic fatigue threshold in college women [J]. European Journal of Applied Physiology & Occupational Physiology, 1991, 63(1): 1.

[9] Galen S S, Guffey D R, Coburn J W, et al. Determining The electromyographic fatigue threshold following a single visit exercise test [J]. Journal of Visualized Experiments Jove, 2015, 101: 52729.

[10] Briscoe M J, Forgach M S, Trifan E, et al. Validating the EMG (FT) from a single incremental cycling test [J]. Int J Sports Med, 2014, 35(7): 566-570.

[11] Camic C L, Kovacs A J, Enquist E A, et al. An electromyographic-based test for estimating neuromuscular fatigue during incremental treadmill running [J]. Physiological Measurement, 2014, 35(12): 2401-2413.

[12] Lawrence D, Kakkar V V. Graduated, static, external compression of the lower limb: a physiological assessment [J]. British Journal of Surgery, 1980, 67(2): 119.

[13] Crozara L F, Castro A, Af D A N, et al. Utility of electromyographic fatigue threshold during treadmill running [J]. Muscle & Nerve, 2015, 52(6): 1030-1039.

[14] Matsumoto T, Ito K, Moritani T. The relationship between anaerobic threshold and electromyographic fatigue threshold in college women [J]. European Journal of Applied Physiology & Occupational Physiology, 1991, 63(1): 1.

[15] Ohya T, Yamanaka R, Hagiwara M, et al. The 400-and 800-m track running induces inspiratory muscle fatigue in trained female middle-distance runners [J]. Journal of Strength & Conditioning Research, 2016, 30 (5): 1433-1437.

[16] Guffey D R, Gervasi B J, Maes A A, et al. Estimating electromyographic and heart rate fatigue thresholds from a single treadmill test [J]. Muscle & Nerve, 2012, 46(4): 577-581.

Effect of Jute Fiber Modification on Mechanical Properties of Jute Fiber Composite

Md. Arshad Ali[1,2], Hua Wang[1,2]*, S. M. Kamrul Hasan[1,2]

[1]Department of Textile Engineering, College of Textiles, Donghua University, Shanghai 201620, China
[2]Key Laboratory of Textile Science & Technology, Ministry of Education, Shanghai 201620, China

* Corresponding author's email: huawang@ dhu. edu. cn

Abstract: In order to make jute fiber composite with optimum performance, fiber modification demands a special attention. Here, chemical treatments (alkaline, oxidation, scouring) were employed on the jute fibers to modify them first. Then, Jute fiber/epoxy composite was prepared with unidirectional jute fibers. The basic properties such as tensile strength, elongation at break of the composites were studied. Scanning electron microscope (SEM) images of treated and untreated jute fibers were analyzed to understand the influence of chemical modifications on the fiber. It was found that chemical treatment of jute fiber has significant impact on mechanical properties of jute fiber composites as well as the formation of voids in the composites.

Keywords: Jute fiber composite; Chemical treatment; Surface openness; Physical properties; Tensile properties

1 Introduction

Jute is the second most natural and biodegradable fiber[1]. Jute fiber is an excellent alternative when strength, thermal conductivity and cost are major concerns. On top of it, jute fibers are eco-friendly. Now days, jute fiber composite has become an important area of research[2]. Typically, jute fiber is used for basic and low-end textile products. If the properties of jute can be modified in favor of high value and technical textile, not only the cost but also the environment will enjoy a great deal.

Jute is composed of cellulose (45%–71.5%), Hemicelluloses (13.6%–21%), lignin (12%–26%)[3]. Lignin is responsible for mechanical support[3]. Any material besides cellulose content that hampers smoothness, pliability, fineness of jute is denoted as gum. Chemical treatment makes fiber smooth, easy to adhesion, strong and flexible by opening up cellulose content and removing unnecessary materials. Besides, It has a lasting effect on the mechanical behavior of natural fibers, especially on their strength and stiffness[4]. Alkaline treatment (or mercerization) is a widely used chemical treatment for natural fibers. It disrupts the hydrogen bonding in the network structure and reduces fiber diameter and thereby increases aspect ratio[1].

Thus, we treat the fibers chemically before making composite and compare the tensile properties of the produced composites with that of untreated jute fiber composites. Since, composite tensile properties are greatly influenced by voids, the volume fractions of voids of the treated jute fiber composites are also measured and compared with that of corresponding raw jute composites.

2 Experiments

2.1 Materials

The naturally grown straight & long raw jute fibers (Corchorus olitorius) were collected from Bangladesh. Epoxy resin (JC–02A) and the corresponding hardener (JC–02B) were supplied by Changshu Jiafa Chemical Co., Ltd., China.

2.2 Methods

Our experiment had been carried out in following steps as bellow. These steps were the combination of acids, oxidizing pretreatment and scouring. Firstly, the samples were cut into 7 inch and were frivolously combed. Then oven dry weights of the fibers were used for the following processes.

2.2.1 Chemical treatment

The fibers were treated in three steps according to the protocol found elsewhere[5]. Firstly, treated with H_2SO_4 in one bath and followed by treated with H_2O_2, Na_2SiO_3 and Na_3PO_4 in another bath. Both steps were carried out at 50℃ for 30 minutes in a 1∶20 bath. In the third step, we used NaOH along with Na_2SiO_3, Na_2SO_3, $MgSO_4$ to treat the fibers at 80℃ for 90 minutes at same liquor ratio used in the previous step and followed by washing three times with distilled water. The fibers were dried in an oven at 70℃ for 3 hours before composite fabrication.

2.2.3 Composite preparation

Unidirectional jute fiber composite was prepared by hand lay-up technique. Composite specimens with different fiber loading (0, 8%, 10%, 12%) were prepared where epoxy resin and hardener ration was 5∶4. The specimens were then subjected to curing (at 90℃ for 2 hours followed by 110℃ for 1 hour and 130℃ for 4 hours) and post curing (at room temperature for 24 hours). Composites from both treated and raw jute were prepared, where the later was considered as control.

2.2.3 Physical and mechanical characterization

The void fraction (V_{fr}) of the composites were calculated by using Eq. (1).

$$V_{fr} = \frac{\rho_t - \rho_{exp}}{\rho_t} \qquad (1)$$

Where, ρ_t and ρ_{exp} are theoretical and experimental densities of the composite respectively. The theoretical density of the composites were calculated using the Eq. (2).

$$\rho_t = \frac{1}{\dfrac{W_f}{\rho_f} + \dfrac{W_m}{\rho_m}} \qquad (2)$$

Where, ρ and W are the density and weight fraction respectively. The suffix, t, f and m correspond to the composites, fiber and matrix, respectively. Water immersion technique had been used to determine the actual density of the prepared composites experimentally.

Tensile test was performed as per ASTM D 3039 test standards using universal testing machine Instron 1195.

2.2.4 SEM observation

SEM (TM 3000, Hitachi, Japan) was used to observe the surface morphology of the raw jute fibers, pretreated jute fibers, scoured jute fibers and the cross-sections of the broken parts of both type of composites after tensile experiments. For surface examination 200 × magnifications was used. The samples were sputter coated with gold before observation.

2.2.5 Statistical analysis

In this research, the one-way analysis of variance with Tukey's pair wise multiple comparison was used to analyze data. With a confidence interval set at 95%, a P value smaller than 0.05 was considered to be a statistically significant difference. Significant differences among data were labeled by different characters on the figures. The error bars shown in Fig. 2 stood for standard deviations.

3 Results and Discussion

3.1 Physical properties of the treated fiber and the composites

Due to the chemical treatment process, significant changes were found in jute fiber surface & their physical properties with the elimination of gum (weight loss of around 25% after chemical treatment). Excellent changes were visible in every step till the scouring treatment. It was clear from the SEM images that key structure of jute became prominent after removal of impurities through chemical treatment (Fig. 1). This cleanliness was further evident from the void fraction of composites. The void content decreased with the increase of fiber content which was obvious as found previously by Mishra et al. [6]. But important fact was that the smaller volume fractions of voids were found in all the composites with treated jute fibers than the raw ones (Tab. 1). This finding suggested that the treated fibers allowed the epoxy resin to penetrate easily into the inter-fiber gaps of the unidirectional fibers and consequently yield fewer voids.

Tab. 1 The void fractions of the composites

Designation	Composite composition	Theoretical density (g/cm³) ρ_t	Experimental density (g/cm³) ρ_{ex}	Void fraction(%) V_{fr}
JC 0%	EPOXY + 0 jute fiber	1. 15	1. 147	0. 260869565
JC$_R$8%	EPOXY + 8% raw jute fiber	1. 157	1. 112	3. 889369058
JC$_R$10%	EPOXY + 10% raw jute fiber	1. 164	1. 121	3. 694158076
JC$_R$12%	EPOXY + 12% raw jute fiber	1. 17	1. 128	3. 58974359
JCc8%	EPOXY + 8% chemical treated jute fiber	1. 155	1. 1	4. 761904762
JCc10%	EPOXY + 10% chemical treated jute fiber	1. 161	1. 106	4. 737295435
JCc12%	EPOXY + 12% chemical treated jute fibet	1. 165	1. 11	4. 721030043

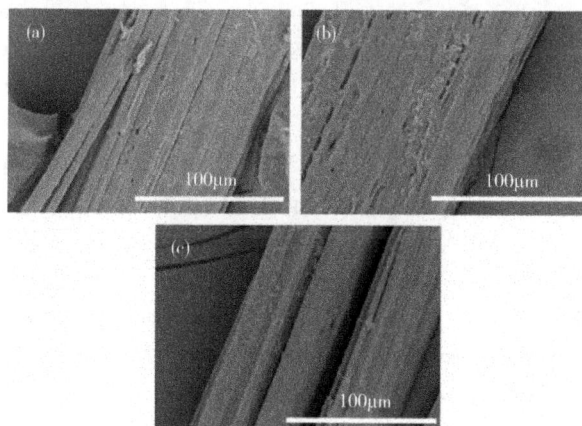

Fig. 1 SEM of raw (a), Alkali treated (b) and scoured (c) jute fiber under 1000 × magnification

3.2 Tensile properties of the composites

All the jute fiber composites had shown higher tensile strength (>43MPa) than the pure epoxy one. The tensile strength for both raw jute composite and treated jute composite seemed to increase with the fiber weight percentages.

However, the tensile strength of treated jute fiber composites was found higher than that of their corresponding raw jute fiber composites (Fig. 2). The lower void fraction might be responsible for the higher tensile strength of treated jute composites. But, since the composites contained unidirectional fibers, the variation in tensile strength might be attributed to another important aspect. This might be the adhesion of epoxy with the fibers. Removal of gum (through alkali treatment) might have resulted in higher surface area of treated jute fibers than the raw jute fibers and consequently created more opportunity for van der waals forces formation between

the treated fiber and epoxy. This could also be evidenced from Fig. 3 where the treated jute fiber composite showed lower elongation at break than the raw one at each fiber weight percentage.

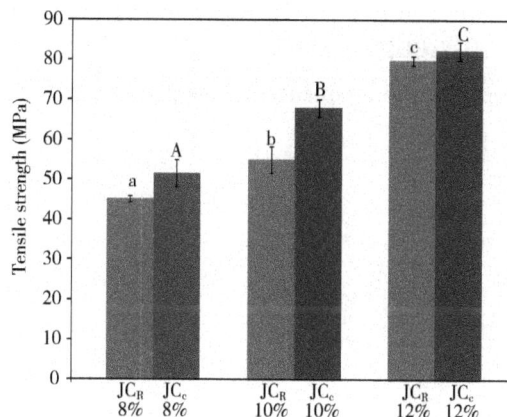

Fig. 2 Effect of fiber loading on tensile strength of composites. JC$_R$ and JC$_C$ represent the composites with raw and chemical treated jute fibers respectively

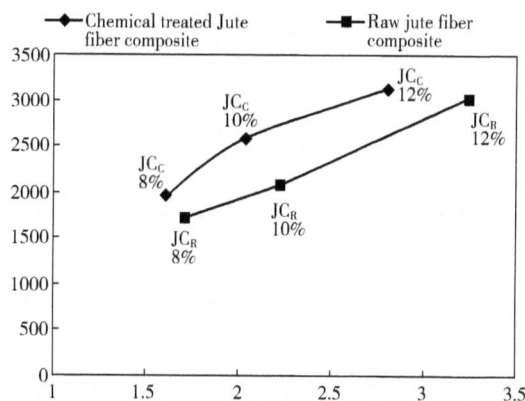

Fig. 3 Elongation at break of the jute fiber composites at different fiber contents

This behavior suggested poor bonding of epoxy resin with the weak spots of the raw jute fibers due to presence of impurities. Studies for example single fiber pull out test are needed to further validate this notion.

4   Conclusions

This work had focused on the influence of alkali treatment of jute fiber on the physical and mechanical properties of jute fiber composite. Composites prepared from chemical treated jute fibers were found superior to the raw jute composites in terms of tensile strength, elongation at break and void fraction. The findings of this work suggest that the chemical treatment of jute fiber could allow the matrix to have better adhesion with the fiber more efficiently than the untreated one.

Acknowledgements

This research was financially supported by Donghua University.

References

[1] Liu L, Wang Q, Xia Z, et al. Mechanical modification of degummed jute fibre for high value textile end uses [J]. Industrial Crops and Products, 2010, 31(1): 43–47.

[2] Basak R, Choudhury P L, Pandey K M. Effect of temperature variation on surface treatment of short jute fiber-reinforced epoxy composites [J]. Materials Today: Proceedings, 2018, 5(1, Part 1): 1271–1277.

[3] Khan J A, Khan M A. The use of jute fibers as reinforcements in composites [J]. Biofiber Reinforcements in Composite Materials: Woodhead Publishing, 2015: 3–34.

[4] Jabbar A, Militky J, Madhukar Kale B, et al. Modeling and analysis of the creep behavior of jute/green epoxy composites incorporated with chemically treated pulverized nano/micro jute fibers [J]. Industrial Crops and Products, 2016, 84: 230–240.

[5] Mwaikambo L Y, Ansell M P. Chemical modification of hemp, sisal, jute, and kapok fibers by alkalization [J]. Journal of Applied Polymer Science, 2002, 84(12): 2222–2234.

[6] Mishra V, Biswas S. Physical and mechanical properties of bi-directional jute fiber epoxy composites [J]. Procedia Engineering, 2013, 51: 561–566.

Effect of Plasma Modification on Carbon Fiber Surface

Shiting Hong[1, 2], Ziqi Liang[1, 2], Lan Yao[1, 2*], Yiping Qiu[1, 2]

[1] *Key Laboratory of Textile Science & Technology, Ministry of Education, Shanghai 201620, China*

[2] *Department of Technical Textiles, College of Textiles, Donghua University, Shanghai 201620, China*

* *Corresponding author's email*: yaolan@ dhu. edu. cn

Abstract: Carbon fiber is widely used in composite materials due to its excellent mechanical properties. However, the surface chemical activity of carbon fibers is inert. Therefore, the plasma modification on carbon fiber has become a frequent method to modify carbon fiber surface in order to improve the adhesion of fibers to resins. In order to investigate the effect of plasma modification on carbon fiber surface properties, carbon fibers T 300 were treated with air plasma for different durations. In this paper, tensile strength of untreated and plasma treated carbon fibers was studied. Scanning electron microscopy (SEM) and atomic force microscopy (AFM) determined that carbon fiber surfaces were roughened by the plasma treatment. X-ray photoelectron spectroscopy (XPS) showed that the relative concentration of oxygen increased after plasma treatment. The plasma treatment decreased the water contact angle of carbon fiber. It was proved that the oxygen containing functional groups and the roughness of the carbon fiber surface increased after plasma treatment.

Keywords: Carbon fiber; Plasma treatment; Surface properties

1 Introduction

Carbon fibers are characterized by high modulus, high strength, low density, fatigue resistance, high temperature resistance and corrosion resistance. With its excellent properties, carbon fiber is frequently added to the resins, metals, concretes, ceramics and other materials to form carbon fiber composites. The carbon fiber composites have good performance and are widely used in transportation, construction engineering, sports, aviation, national defense and military, navigation, medical machinery and other fields[1-2].

However, the surface of the carbon fiber has a large number of non-polar groups, and lacks functional groups with chemical activity. Therefore, the surface of carbon fiber is highly chemically inert and the wettability of carbon fiber is poor. The weak bonding property between carbon fiber and composite matrix leads to the weak performance of composite materials. Therefore, it is necessary to improve the surface activity of carbon fiber by surface treatment, so that it can be better combined with other materials in the preparation of carbon fiber composites[3-5].

Many kinds of surface treatment methods are used for composite materials, including gas phase oxidation, liquid phase oxidation and plasma treatment, among which plasma treatment is the most widely studied method at present[6]. It requires small amounts of chemical substances, low temperature and less time, and because of the general use of oxygen and air in plasma treatment, it do not cause pollution to the environment.

In this study, T 300 carbon fibers were treated by plasma for different durations. The single fiber tensile strength of carbon fibers before and after plasma treatments was investigated. SEM and AFM were used to observe the plasma etching of the carbon fiber. The wettability of carbon fiber surface was characterized by contact angle tests. Chemical element content of the carbon fiber surface was determined by XPS.

2 Experiments

2.1 Materials

Carbon fibers T 300 produced by Toray were observed in

this study. The average diameter of carbon fibers T 300 was about 7μm and tensile strength was approximately 3500MPa. Prior to Plasma treatment, acetone was used to clean the carbon fibers for 6 hours at 75℃ with the Soxhlet extractor in order to remove the size on the fiber surface. Then the desizing carbon fibers were dried for 2 hours at 100℃.

2.2 Plasma treatment

Vacuum plasma treatment equipment for textile materials was used to treat the carbon fiber. The power was set at 80W and the pressure was set at 50Pa. Samples were treated for different treatment durations of 60s, 120s, and 180s, respectively.

2.3 Single filament tensile tests

The single filament tensile strength of carbon fibers before and after the plasma treatment was test by single filament tensile tests according to XQ-2 single fiber tensile tester. In order to prepare monofilament tensile test samples, single fiber was separated from the carbon fiber bundles and taped on both sides of the paper frame. The size of the paper frame was showed in Fig. 1[7]. Then the paper frames were gripped in the fixture of the testing machine and were cut carefully before testing. The load was applied at a speed of 10mm/min with a gage length of 20mm.

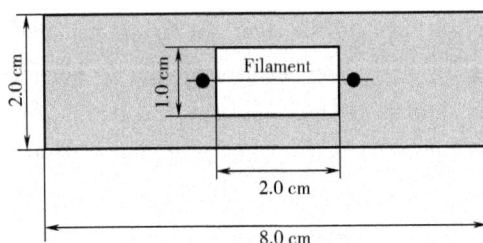

Fig. 1 The paper frame for single filament tensile tests

2.4 Contact angle tests

Contact angles tests of carbon fibers were measured by optial contact angle meter (OCAI5EC, Dataphysics, Germany). The preparation between the hydrophilic and hydrophobic samples was different. To prepare the hydrophilic specimens, the fibers were carded and finished into a layer with uniform and smooth surface. The carbon fiber layer with the size of 40mm × 6mm was stick in the middle of the glass slide. To prepare the hy-

drophobic specimens, the size of a carbon fiber layer changed to 45mm × 6mm and the axial direction of the fibers was perpendicular to the length of the glass slide.

2.5 Surface morphology of carbon fiber

The surface morphology of carbon fibers before and after the plasma treatment was observed by SEM (TM3000). The samples were stuck on a conductive double-sided tape and then sprayed with a layer of gold. The magnification of the single carbon images was set at 5000 ×.

The surface topology of carbon fibers before and after the plasma treatment was observed by AFM (NTEGRA, NT-MD) with a tapping mode. Specimens were straightened and stuck to thin cardboards with a size of 18mm × 18mm. The investigation of carbon fiber surface roughness was performed from the image of the area of 2μm × 2μm. The dark color of the images represented the concave portion, and the light color represented the convex portion[8].

2.6 X-ray photoelectron spectroscopy (XPS)

The chemical element content of the carbon fiber surfaces before and after the plasma treatment was determined by XPS (Thermo ESCALAB 250Xi, USA). A monochromatic Al Kα X-ray source (1486.6 eV) was used to collect the spectra. The power was set at 150W and the beam spot was 500μm. The energy analyzer had fixed transmission energy of 30eV. The data was calibrated and the binding energy of the main peak of sample C1s was set at 284.8eV. The surface chemical composition was calculated from the associated spectral peak areas.

3 Results and Discussion

3.1 The surface morphology of carbon fiber

The surface morphology of carbon fiber with different plasma treatment times determined by SEM was presented in Fig. 2. Due to the manufacturing process of carbon fiber, the surfaces of fibers had clear ridges and stripes parallel to the fiber axes. The difference of the carbon fibers before and after plasma treated was that the particulates of the untreated carbon fiber surface were almost eliminated after plasma treatment as the result of etching and cleansing actions of the plasma treatment. Removing the particles on the surface of the fiber could help reduce the potential weak adhesion between fibers and matrices.

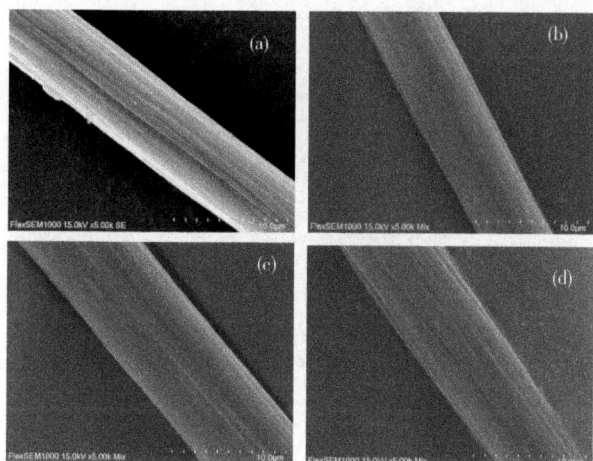

Fig. 2   SEM images of carbon fiber with different plasma treatment times   (a) 0s; (b) 60s; (c) 120s; and (d) 180s

The surface topographies of carbon fibers before and after plasma treatment investigated by AFM and were presented in Fig. 3.

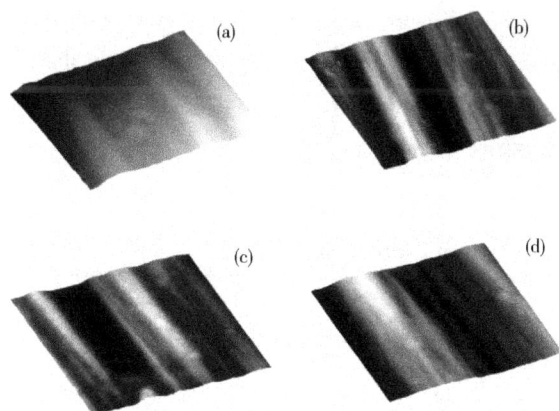

Fig. 3   AFM images of carbon fiber with different plasma treatment times   (a) 0s; (b) 60s; (c) 120s; and (d) 180s

It could be observed that the surface of the untreated carbon fiber was relatively smooth. With 60s and 120s plasma treatment, the roughness of the carbon fiber surface increased significantly. When the time of plasma treatment increased from 120s to 180s, the surface roughness of carbon fiber decreased. The results indicated that the surface roughness of the carbon fibers was enhanced via plasma modification due to etched effects and oxidative reactions. This could increase the contact

area between the fiber and the resin, thereby enhancing the interfacial bonding performance of the composite. While prolonging the treatment time could decrease the roughness of surface, which might be due to the excessive plasma etchings and oxidative reactions. This would give a negative impact to the bulk properties of the carbon fiber and reduce the mechanical properties of composites.

3.2   The tensile strength of carbon fiber

The tensile strength of carbon fibers for different times by air plasma treatment was listed in Tab. 1. From the table, it could be observed when the plasma treatment time was 60s and 120s; The tensile strength of the carbon fibers was close to the tensile strength of untreated carbon fibers. At this point, the air plasma treatment could be used to modify the surface properties of carbon fibers without altering its bulk properties. However, it could be observed that the tensile strength of carbon fiber decreased about 18% with 180s plasma treatment. Combining the analysis of AFM, it was found that the fibers were excessively etched at 180s plasma treatment and bulk properties of carbon fiber might be damaged at the time. The tensile strength of carbon fiber would be affected over a certain plasma treatment time.

Tab. 1   Single fiber tensile strength of carbon fiber treated for different times by plasma

Treatment times(s)	Single fiber tensile strength(MPa)	Standard deviation(MPa)
0	3513	602
60	3544	639
120	3355	553
180	2870	459

3.3   The surface chemical composition of carbon fiber

The chemical composition of carbon fiber surface was frequently determined by XPS. The C1s, O1s, N1s spectra of carbon fiber surface were showed in Fig. 4. And the relative concentration of elements for carbon, oxygen, and nitrogen was listed in Tab. 2. It was noted that the concentration of carbon decreased from 80.99% to 75.24% with 120s air plasma treatment, while the concentration of oxygen increased from 14.78% to 20.43% and the ratio of oxygen to carbon atoms increased from 0.18 to 0.27. When the time of plasma treatment increased from 120s to 180s, the oxygen con-

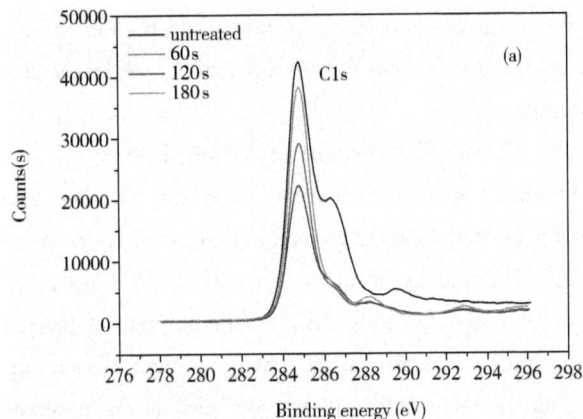

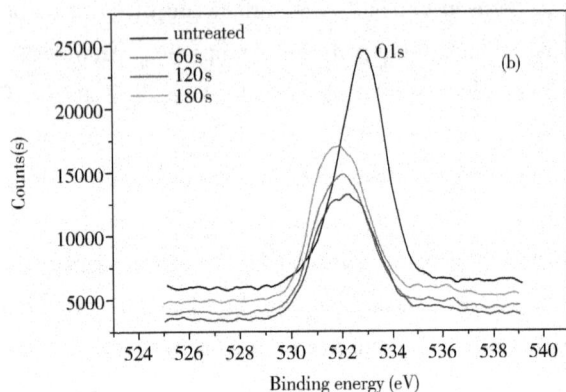

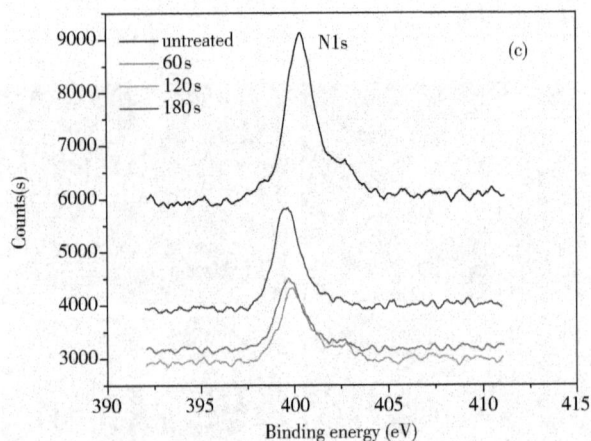

Fig.4 XPS spectra of carbon fiber surface (a) C1s; (b) O1S; (c) N1s

centration decreased from 20.43% to 16.81% and the ratio of oxygen to carbon atoms decreased from 0.27 to 0.21. The increase of oxygen concentration and ratio of oxygen to carbon atoms indicated that additional oxygen containing polar groups were introduced onto the surface of carbon fiber after air plasma treatment. However, prolonged exposure to plasma could decrease the oxygen concentration and nitrogen concentration on the fiber surface since the originally generated polar groups may be destroyed.

Tab.2 Surface compositions of carbon fibers treated for different times

Treatment times(s)	Relative concentration of elements (%)			Atomic ratio	
	C	O	N	O/C	N/C
0	80.99	14.78	4.23	0.18	0.05
60	78.07	18.81	3.12	0.24	0.04
120	75.24	20.43	4.33	0.27	0.06
180	79.81	16.81	3.39	0.21	0.04

3.4 The contact angle of carbon fibers

Good wettability was one of the prerequisites for the formation of composite materials between fibers and resins. The contact angles of untreated and plasma treated carbon fibers were presented in Fig.5. It was observed that the contact angle of the carbon fibers decreased significantly with plasma treatment. The carbon fibers changed from hydrophobic to hydrophilic after plasma treatment. To further increase the processing time, the contact angle of carbon fiber basically unchanged. These results indicated that the polar groups were introduced to the surface of carbon fibers, which had increased the surface activity of carbon fibers and improved their wettability.

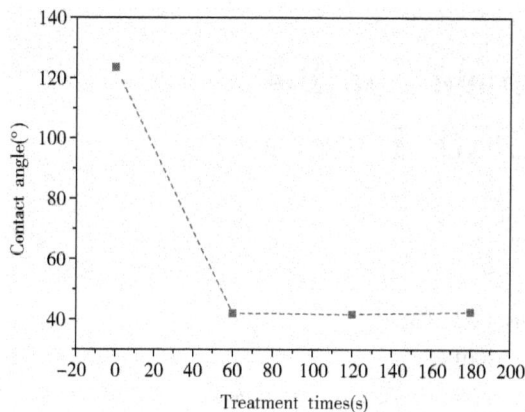

Fig. 5 The contact angle of untreated and plasma treated carbon fibers

4 Conclusions

The surface of carbon fiber was successfully modified by the air plasma treatment. SEM and AFM analyses indicated that plasma modification could clean carbon fiber surface and enhance the fiber surface roughness, so that the interfacial bonding of carbon fibers and matrixes increased in order to improve the composite performance. The single filament tensile strength of carbon fiber was not affected within a certain plasma treatment time, whereas it would decrease after excessive exposure to plasma treatment. XPS and contact angle analyses proved that additional oxygen containing groups were introduced to carbon fiber surface and the wettability of carbon fiber was significantly improved after plasma modification. This made it easier for the carbon fiber to bond with the resin.

References

[1] Lee H, Ohsawa I, Takahashi J. Effect of plasma surface treatment of recycled carbon fiber on carbon fiber-reinforced plastics (CFRP) interfacial properties [J]. Applied Surface Science, 2015, 328: 241-246.

[2] Hossain M K, Chowdhury M M R, Imran K A, et al. Effect of low velocity impact responses on durability of conventional and nanophased CFRP composites exposed to seawater [J]. Polymer Degradation & Stability, 2014, 99(1): 180-189

[3] Liu Z, Tang C, Chen P, et al. Modification of carbon fiber by air plasma and its adhesion with BMI resin [J]. Rsc Advances, 2014, 4(51): 26881-26887.

[4] Iris Käppler, Rolf Dieter Hund, ChokriCherif. Surface modification of carbon fibres using plasma technique [J]. Autex Research Journal, 2014, 14(1): 34-38.

[5] Park J M, Wang Z J, Kwon D J, et al. Optimum dispersion conditions and interfacial modification of carbon fiber and CNT - phenolic composites by atmospheric pressure plasma treatment [J]. Composites Part B Engineering, 2012, 43(5): 2272-2278.

[6] Xie J, Xin D, Cao H, et al. Improving carbon fiber adhesion to polyimide with atmospheric pressure plasma treatment [J]. Surface & Coatings Technology, 2011, 206(2-3): 191-201.

[7] Li W, Yao S Y, Ma K M, et al. Effect of plasma modification on the mechanical properties of carbon fiber/phenolphthalein polyaryletherketone composites [J]. Polymer Composites, 2013, 34(3): 368-375.

[8] Foray G, Descamps-Mandine A, R'Mili M, et al. Statistical flaw strength distributions for glass fibres: correlation between bundle test and AFM-derived flaw size density functions [J]. Acta Materialia, 2012, 60(9): 3711-3718.

Effect of Lay-Up Sequence on the Flexural Properties of CFRP Laminates

Lyutao Zhu[1,2]*, Chengyan Zhu[1]

[1] *College of Materials and Textiles, Zhejiang Sci-Tech University, Hangzhou, 310018, China*

[2] *Key Laboratory of Advanced Textile Materials and Manufacturing Technology, Ministry of Education, Hangzhou, 310018, China*

Corresponding author's email: zhult@ zstu. edu. cn

Abstract: In the current studies, the flexural behavior of carbon fiber reinforced polymer laminates was investigated experimentally. The CFRP laminates were fabricated using unidirectional prepreg molding process. Three-point bending test were performed using a material testing system. The present results showed that the flexural strength and modulus of laminates were strongly dependent on the lay-up sequence of the fiber reinforcement. The ply stacking sequence 0° exhibited best flexural properties than others. The flexural failure of CFRP was initiated that the upside of the CFRP suffers compression failure and the lower surface suffers tension failures.

Keywords: Lay-up sequence; Flexural behavior; Failure mode; Molding process; Prepreg

1 Introduction

Carbon fiber reinforced polymer (CFRP) laminates are widely used as light-weight materials in aerospace, marine, sport equipment, automotive and building materials due to their better properties[1-4]. The utilized of CFRP laminates as structural members often subject bending loading. Therefore, it is very important to understand the mechanical properties of the laminates when they are subjected to bending moments[5]. Although, more and more studies have been forced on the flexural behavior of CFRP laminates[6-8], only a limited number of literature focus on the effect of the lay-up sequence on flexural damage behavior of laminates[9-10]. Morioka et al.[11] studied the effect of the lay-up sequences on the mechanical properties and fracture behavior of the advanced CFRP laminate by tensile, slow bend and instrumented Charpy impact tests. Subagia et al.[12] investigated the effect of different stacking sequences of carbon and basalt fabrics on the flexural properties of hybrid composite laminates. The results showed that all the stacking sequences showed a positive hybridization effect and the flexural strength and modulus of hybrid composite laminates were strongly dependent on the sequence of fiber reinforcement. Caminero et al.[13] characterized the damage in CFRP composite laminates with different stacking sequences subjected to flexural loading. The result shows that the effect of the stacking sequences on the flexural response depicted similar trends than in the case of tensile response. Meng et al.[14] developed 3D FEA to investigate the effect of fibre lay-up on the flexural failure mechanisms in composite laminates and give some suggestions to improve the design of composite laminates.

Through these studies, we can clearly see that, there is a lack of knowledge about the relationship between the effect of the lay-up sequences and the complex failure mode, such as coupling effect or shear effects. The objective of this work is to experimentally investigate the flexural behavior of CFRP laminates. Different lay-up sequence was examined to understand how the fibre lay-up sequences affect the initiation of failure of laminates in bending loading.

2 Experimental

2.1 Materials and specimen

The material used inthe present article consists of carbon fiber/epoxy prepreg of CFS–1500 with high strength and modulus. The fiber area density was $150g/m^2$ and the nominal resin content was 32%. The material was supplied by Shandong Jiangshan Fiber Technology Co., Ltd. The carbon fiber prepreg properties are presented in Tab. 1.

Eight different lay-up sequences of laminates were designed and investigated for the flexural loading, the lay-up schemes are showed in Tab. 2.

Tab. 1   The parameter of the prepreg

Thickness (mm)	Carbon fiber	FAW WT (g/m^2)	Carbon fiber (%)	Resin	Resin WT (g/m^2)	Resincontent(%)
0.13	A45–12k	150	68	epoxy resin	71	32

Tab. 2   The lay-up schemes of the laminates

No	Thickness H (mm)	Test speed (m/min)	L (mm)	Layer count	Sample size (mm)	Lay-up scheme
1	1.26	0.63	20.16			$[90]_{10}$
2	1.3	0.65	20.8	10		$[0_2/\pm45/90]_S$
3	1.54	0.77	24.64			$[0]_{12}$
4	1.56	0.78	24.96	12		$[90_2/\pm45/90/0]_S$
5	1.82	0.91	29.12		40×15	$[90]_{14}$
6	1.82	0.91	29.12	14		$[90_3/\pm45/90/0]_S$
7	2.26	1.13	36.16			$[0]_{16}$
8	2.26	1.13	36.16	16		$[0_2/\pm45/0/\pm45/90]_S$

2.2 CFRP laminates fabrication

The CFRP laminates were manufacture dusing a prepreg pressure molding process in the MN semi-automatic equipment. The process consists of seven steps (Fig. 1). Fig. 2 is the hearting and curing process of laminates fabrication.

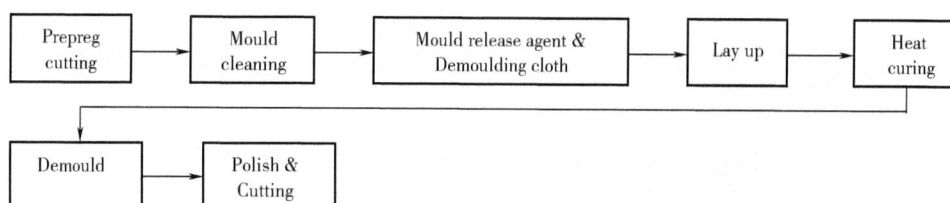

Fig. 1   The process flow of the laminates fabrication

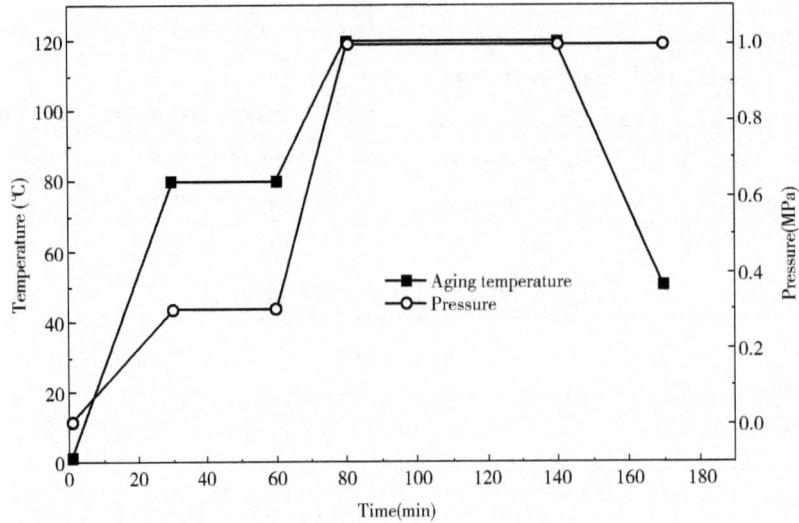

Fig. 2　The hearting and curing process of the laminates

2.3　Flexural test

The three-point bending tests for CFRP laminates were perform following the procedure GB 1449—2005 – T. The Material testing system (MTS 8801) was used for the bending test. In this process, a specimen of 40 mm length and 15 mm wide were carefully cut by a composite cutting machine and then it was loaded in the support with recommended span to depth ratio as shown in Fig. 3 and Fig. 4 respectively. Transverse load was applied gradually in the middle until the sample fails. The specific test scheme as shown in Tab. 2. According to the test criteria, calculate the span to depth ratio $l = (16 \pm 1)h$ and the test speed $V = \dfrac{h}{2}$.

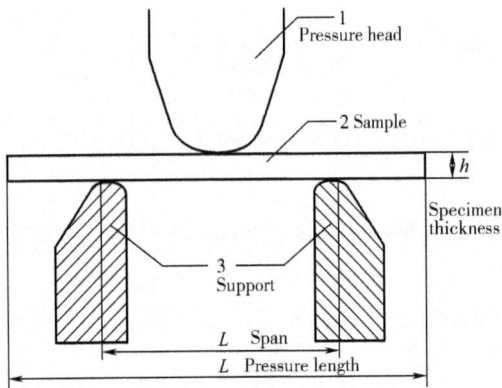

Fig. 3 Three-point bend test

Fig. 4　MTS testing machine

2　Results and Discussion

3.1　Flexural properties

In flexural test at least five specimens were taken. Fig. 5 is the time-deflection curves. It can be seen that, the deflection increases with the time. Sample 6 ($[90_3/ \pm45/90/0]_s$) shows the max deflection, however, sample 1, sample 4 and sample 5 shows shorter deflection due to poor bending resistance.

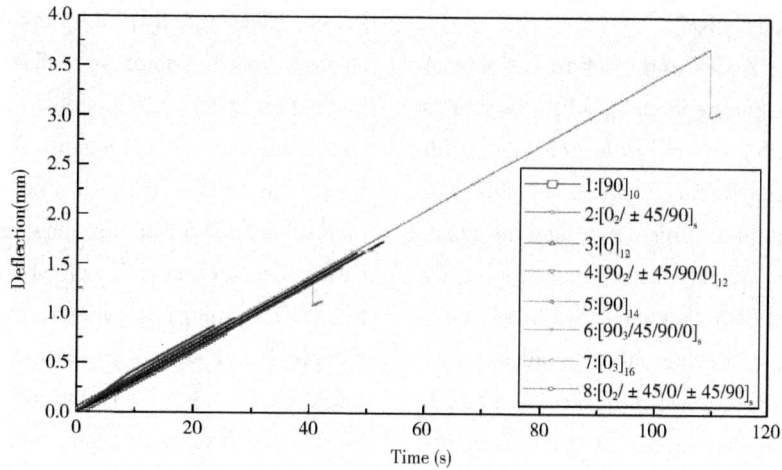

Fig. 5 The time vs. deflection curves

Fig. 6 is the typical load-deflection curves. It can be shown that, sample 2, sample 3, sample 7 and sample 8 exhibited best bending rigidity than others. We can infer that the outermost layer of 0° will improves the bending resistance effectively. Sample 4, sample 2, sample 5 and sample 6 exhibited poor bending rigidity due to the increase of 90° lay-up ratio.

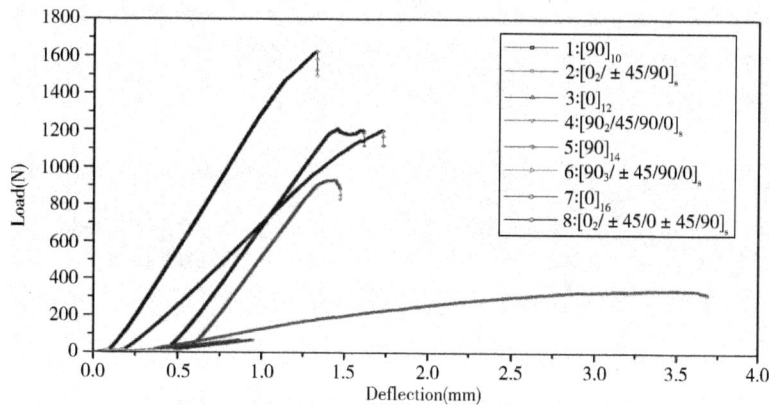

Fig. 6 The load vs. deflection curve

Fig. 7 depicts a comparison of flexural behavior of CFRP laminates with different lay-up in terms of flexural strength. As shown in this figure, unidirectional $[0]_{12}$ laminate exhibited best performance in terms of flexural strength. Unidirectional $[90]_{12}$ showed the lowest flexural strength due to their brittle behavior. It can be seen from the figure that the content of 90° lay-up sequences will decrease the flexural property.

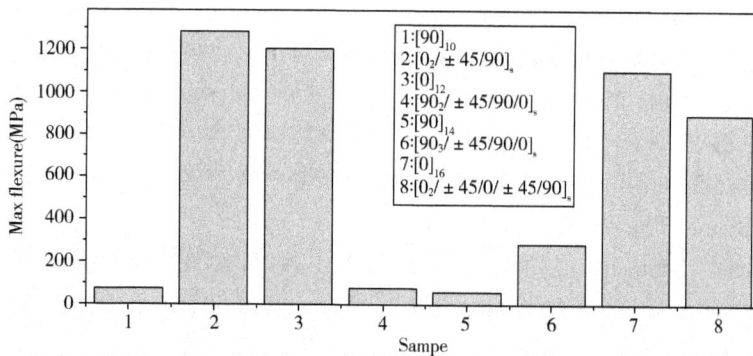

Fig. 7 The relationship of flexural properties with lay-up sequences

3.2 Fracture characteristics

Fig. 8 shows the failure modes and fracture surfaces of CFRP specimens. The unidirectional $[90]_{10}$ laminates (sample 1 and sample 5) shows brittle behavior, with matrix cracking initiation in the compressive side and the crack parallel to the fiber direction. Once the crack initiated, it spreads quickly and catastrophically through the specimen. Both laminates exhibited lower flexural strength and stiffness than other samples.

Sample 2 and sample 8 is quasi-isotropic laminate. It can be observed that the crack initiation at the compressive side of the specimen. With the increasing of pressure, fiber/matrix interfacial fracture and delamination occurred in the 90° and ±45° layers due to high shear stress. Consequently, fiber breakage of the 0° layers occurred on the compressive side at an early stage. Delamination at the tensile side was also observed.

Unidirectional $[0]_{16}$ (sample 3 and sample 7) laminates exhibited higher flexural strength and stiffness than others. The samples show matrix cracking at first, as the load increase, it will observed delamination and fiber failure due to quasi-static pressure.

Sample 4 and sample 6 observed resin cracking under initial load, as the load continues, it will appear delamination and fiber failure phenomenon, the contact point between the sample and the pressure head shows the indentation of the matrix, and the specimen showes a great degree of bending deformation.

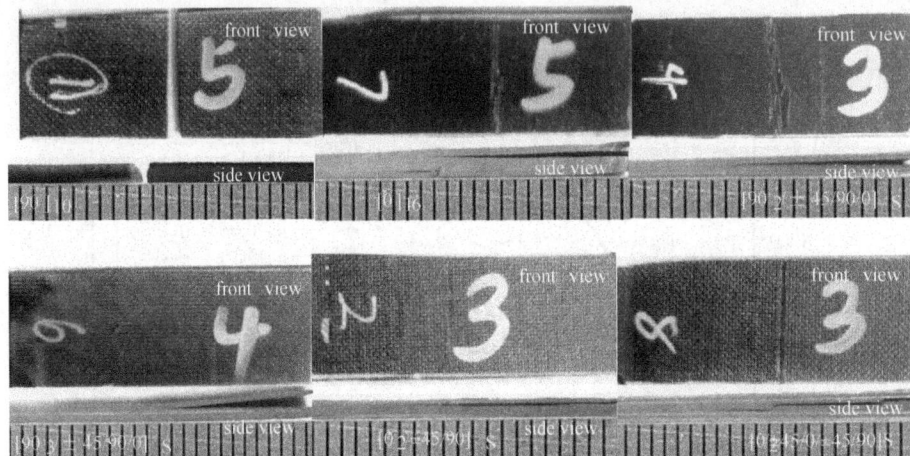

Fig. 8 The failure modes and fracture surfaces of multi-directional specimen

4 Conclusions

This study explored the flexural behavior of CFRP laminates under three-point bending loading. The present results showed that the flexural strength and modulus of CFRP laminates were strongly dependent on the lay-up sequence of the fiber reinforcement. The unidirectional laminates ($[0]_{12}$ and $[0]_{16}$) exhibited better performance in terms of flexural strength. The laminates show matrix cracking at first, then occurs delamination and fiber failure due to quasi-static pressure. The outermost layer of 0° will improve the bending resistance effectively. Another unidirectional laminates ($[90]_{10}$ and $[90]_{14}$) showed brittle behavior, the laminates had broken off in the middle of the sample parallel to the fiber direction, the laminates show poor flexural property. The quasi-isotropic laminate ($[0_2/\pm45/90]_s$ and $[0_2/\pm45/0/\pm45/90]_s$) showed multiple fracture modes, including resin crack, delamination and fiber breakage phenomenon. Sample 4 and sample 6 ($[90_2/\pm45/90/0]_s$ and $[90_3/\pm45/90/0]_s$) generated resin cracking under initial load, as the load continues, it will appear delamination and fiber failure phenomenon, the contact point between the sample and the pressure head shows the indentation of the matrix, and the specimen showed a great degree of bending deformation.

5 Acknowledgements

The authors acknowledge the financial supports from the Zhejiang Sci-Tech University Scientific Research Project (17012050 – Y), the financial supports from the Key

Laboratory of Advanced Textile Materials and Manufacturing Technology (Zhejiang Sci-Tech University), Ministry of Education (2017QN07).

References

[1] Soutis C. Fibre reinforced composites in aircraft construction [J]. Prog Aerosp Sci, 2005, 41(2):143-151.

[2] Hu F Z, Soutis C. Strength prediction of patch-repaired CFRP laminates loaded in compresion [J]. Compos Sci Technol, 2000, 60(7):1103-1114.

[3] Jumahat A, Soutis C, Hodzic A. A graphical method predicting the compressive strength of toughened unidirectional composite laminates [J]. Appl Compos Mater, 2011, 18 (1):65-83.

[4] Shi Y, Swait T, Soutis C. Modelling damage evolution in composite laminates subjected to low velocity impact [J]. Compos Struct, 2012, 94(9):2902-2913.

[5] Morozov E V, Morozov K E, Selvarakalu V. Progressive damage modelling of SMC composite materials [J]. Compos Struct, 2003, 62: 361-366.

[6] David-West O, Alexander N, Nash D,et al. Energy absorption and bending stiffness in CFRP laminates: The effect of 45 plies [J]. Thin-Walled Struct, 2008, 46 (7-9): 860-869.

[7] Wisnom M R. The relationship between tensile and flexural strength of unidirectional composites [J]. J Compos Mater, 1992, 26(8): 1173-1180.

[8] Whitney J M, Knight M. The relationship between tensile and flexure strength in fiber-reinforced composites [J]. Exp Mech, 1980, 20: 211-216.

[9] Morioka K, Tomita Y. Effect of lay-up sequences on mechanical properties and fracture behavior of CFRP laminate composites [J]. Mater Charact, 2000, 45(2): 125-136.

[10] Subagia I A, Kim Y, Tijing L,et al. Effect of stacking sequence on the flexural properties of hybrid composites reinforced with carbon and basalt fibers [J]. Compos B, 2014, 58(3): 251-258.

[11] Morioka K, Tomita Y. Effect of lay-up sequences on mechanical properties and fracture behavior of CFRP laminate composites [J]. Mater Charact, 2000, 45(2): 125-136.

[12] Subagia I A, Kim Y, Tijing L,et al. Effect of stacking sequence on the flexural properties of hybrid composites reinforced with carbon and basalt fibers [J]. Compos B, 2014, 58(3): 251-258.

[13] Caminero M A, Rodríguez G P, Muñoz V. Effect of stacking sequence on Charpy impact and flexural damage behavior of composite laminates [J]. Composite Structures 2016, 136: 345-357.

[14] Meng M, Le H, Rizvi M J,et al. 3D FEA modelling of laminated composites in bending and their failure mechanisms [J]. Composite Structures, 2015, 119: 693-708.

Effects of Nano-Silica Particle on the Properties of Phenolic Resin/Glass Fiber Composites

Yifei Wang[1,2], Wanshuang Liu[1,2], Yiping Qiu[1,2], Yi Wei[1,2] *

[1] *Donghua University Center for Civil Aviation Composites, Donghua University, Shanghai 201620, China.*

[2] *College of Textiles, Donghua University, Shanghai 201620, China.*

* Corresponding author's email: weiy@ dhu. edu. cn

Abstract: Glass fiber/phenolicresin composites (GFPCs) containing nano-silica were fabricated for improving their interlaminar fracture toughness. Mode I and II interlaminar fracture tests were conducted to evaluate the toughening effects of nano-silica on GFPCs. The results showed that all nano-silica-dispersed GFPCs laminates exhibited higher interlaminar fracture toughness without sacrificing their flexural and flame retardant properties. Notably, The addition of only 5% nano-silica could give 153% and 149% enhancement in Mode I and II interlaminar fracture toughness, respectively.

Keywords: Glass fiberreinforced composites; Phenolicresin; Nano-silica; Interlaminar fracture toughness

1 Introduction

Glass fiber/phenolic resin composites (GFPCs) are a class of fiber reinforced polymercomposites, which is increasingly being employed ina wide variety of structural applications ranging from general purpose parts in construction and civil infrastructures to high-performance structural components in aerospace, aircraft and track traffic industries[1]. GFPCs have a combination of good mechanical properties, low thermal conductivity and excellent flame retardancy[2]. However, it is well known that composite structures in the form of laminates are extremely susceptible to crack initiation and propagation along the laminar interfacesin various failure modes. Delamination is one of themost prevalent life-limiting crack growth modes in laminate composites as delamination may cause severe reductions inin-plane strength and stiffness, potentially leading to catastrophic failure of the whole structure[3].

So far, several techniques have been successfully developed to improve the interlaminar fracture toughness, namely designing 3D fabric architecture, transverse stitching or pinning the fabric, fiber hybridization, toughening the matrix resin, and placing interleaves made of tough resin materials in the interplayregions of the laminate[4-7]. Among them, toughening the matrix resin is a simple and efficient method. For phenolic resin (PR), internal and external toughening are two main methods to improve the toughness of PR. In the internal toughening method, flexible molecular chains are introduced into PR to change the molecular structure, such as epoxidized soybean oil[8], and cardanol[9]. In external toughening method, toughening agents are added to the synthesized PR, such as nitrile rubber[10], polyamides[11], nanoparticles[12]. Although the toughening effects of rubbers and thermoplastic polymers are significant, the high loadings (5%–20%) of these modifiers can distinctly reduce the other performances of PR, such as glass transition temperature, stiffness, strength, and solvent resistance. Unlike soft polymeric modifiers, the incorporation of inorganic nanoparticles can increase the fracture toughness of PR without any significant reduction in modulus, glasstransition temperature and flame retardancy.

In this study, glass fiber prepregs were prepared using nano-silica modified PR as polymer matrix. The glass fiber prepregs were used to fabricate GFPCs by hot press.

The effects of nano-silica on the flexural properties, interlaminar fracture toughness, and limit oxygen index of GFPCs were systematically investigated.

2　Experiments

2.1　Materials

The PR aqueous dispersion (solid content is 77%) was purchased from Huakai Co., Ltd. Colloidal silica (43%) was purchased by Qingdao Yijida Co., Ltd. Stain glass fabric (7581) (300g/m², 8 gold stain) was suppliedby Baihe Hangtai Co., Ltd.

2.2　Preparation of silica modified PR

A calculated amount of colloidal silica was added to PR aqueous dispersion (weight ratios between silica and PR are 5:95 and 10:90, respectively). After stirring for 4h, silica modified PR dispersion was obtained.

2.3　Preparation of glass fiber prepregs

The produce of glass fiber prepreg textile: the resin content can be controlled by the adjustment of the distance of press cudgel for the resin content is up to 40%. The B-stage resin is produced in 80 for 9min, as shown in Fig. 1.

Fig. 1　The prepreg of PR

2.4　Fabrication of GFPCs

According to the standard, eight or twenty pieces of glass fiber fabrics were stacked, then the whole assembly was then placed between two aluminum sheets coated with Polytetrafluoroethylene (PTFE) and compressed in hot press at 80℃ for 90min and 180℃ for 60min in the press of 0.15MPa.

2.5　Characterization

The gel time was carried out in 135℃ and 150℃ (Gel time determination method). The hydrodynamic radius of silica in aqueous dispersions was obtained by dynamic light scattering measurement using a Malvern Nano-ZS analyzer. The mechanical performances of composite panel including flexural properties, Mode I and Mode II interlaminar fracture toughness are measured using universal testing machine according to ASTM D7264/D7264M-07[13], ASTM D5528-01[14], D7905M-14[15] and ASTM D1781-98[16]. The fracture surface of GFPCs was observed on a scanning electron microscope (SEM). Limited oxygen index measurements were performed on the Oxygen Index Flammability Gauge based on ASTM D2863-00[11].

3　Results and Discussion

3.1　Properties of the glass fiber prepregs

Gel time is an important parameter for the practical application, because it greatly affects the manufacturing efficiency. The gel time of PR used in this study is 104s and 68s at 135℃ and 150℃, respectively, which meets the requirements of fast-curie resin matrix. The particle size of silica was measured by dynamic light scattering technology. The average hydrodynamic radius of silica is 22nm. The resin content and the surface density in the prepreg is 41% and 510g/m².

3.2　In-plane mechanical properties of the GFPCs

It shows that use of nano-silica particles in Phenolic matrix increases flexural strength. For example, specimens having 5% nano-silica (PF-5) and 10% nano-silica (PF-10) show 16% and 25% increase in flexural strength than the unmodified specimen that can be considered as the physical or chemical combination between nanoparticle and the matrix enhance the interfacial action, thus the nano-particle bear partial load in Fig. 2 (a). Fig. 2 (b) indicates that flexural modulus thevalues decrease when phenolic matrix was modified with nano-silica particles.

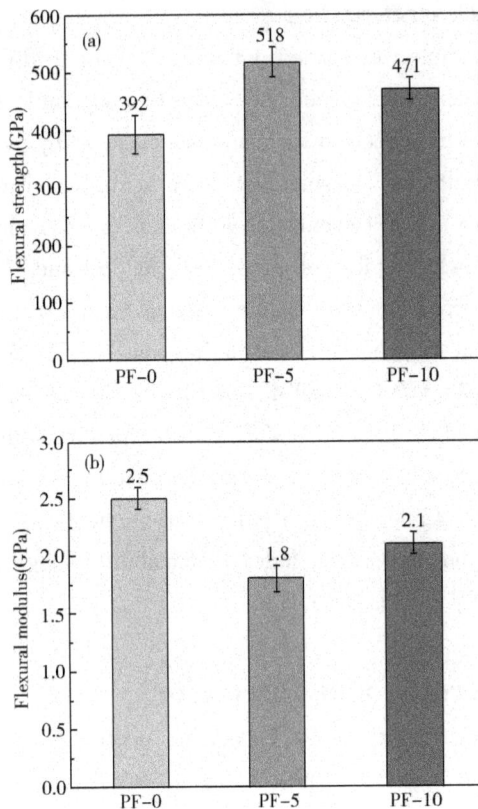

Fig. 2 Flexural strength (a), flexuralmodulus (b) of fabricated GFPCs

Fig. 3 The test setup (a), Mode I interlaminar fracture toughness of GFPCs based on unmodified PR and nano-silica modified PR (b)

3.3 Mode I interlaminar fracture toughness

It shows the testing process of mode I interlaminar fracture toughness in Fig. 3 (a). Fig. 3 (b) shows that mode I interlaminar fracture toughness of neat phenolic specimen (PF-0) was improved when modified with nano-silica particles. For instance, the increases being 153% and 110% in the specimens PF-5 and PF-10, respectively. This is reasonable due to which delay or decrease the growth rate of main and secondary cracks propagating in the stiff but brittle phenolic matrix. Thus, phenolic resin gains some toughening by several energy absorption mechanisms. Some of these mechanisms could be silicastretching, multilevel fracture path, crack deflection, crack pinning, and the shear deformation, which is themain toughening mechanism for thermosets. However, increasing nano-silica content decreases the improvement maybe because of the agglomeration of nano-particle.

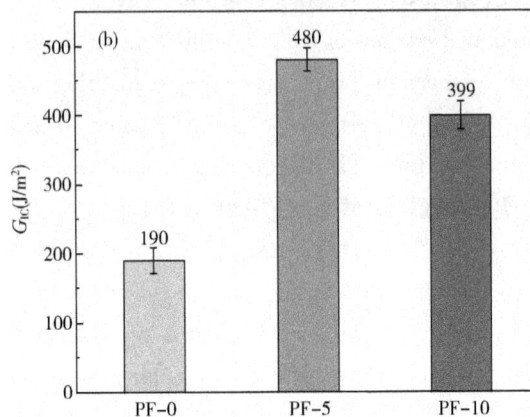

3.4 Mode II interlaminar fracture toughness

It show the test process and the test result respectively in Fig. 4 (a). Fig. 4 (b) indicates that mode II interlaminar fracture toughness test results are very well correlated with the mode I interlaminar fracture toughness results. When the neat phenolic specimen is modified with nano-silica particles, its mode II fracture toughness increases 149%, and 74% in the specimens PF-5, PF-10 respectively. Again, increasing particle content decreases the improvement due to the agglomeration of particle.

3.5 Morphology of fracture surfaces

Fig. 5 (a) - (c) indicate that there is the stripping of large area in the split between resin matrix and glass fiber in the unmodified PR, and the surface of the glass

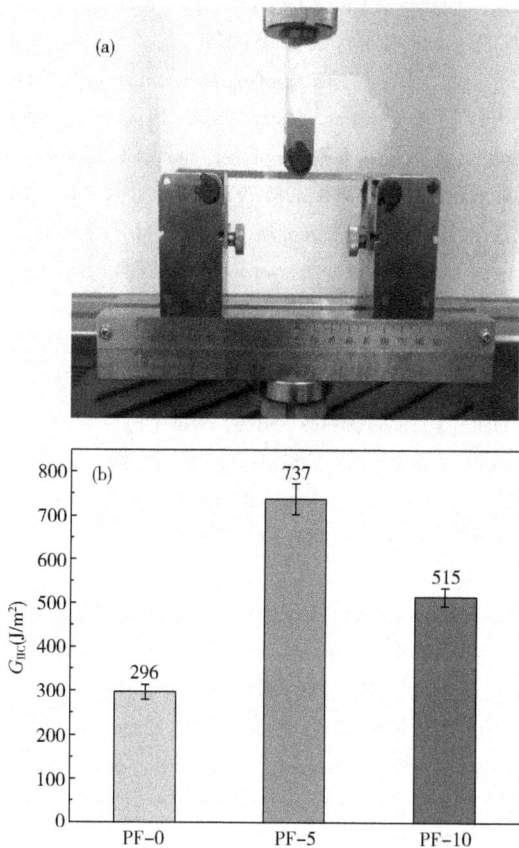

Fig. 4 (a) The test setup; (b) Mode II interlaminar fracture toughness of composites of GFPCs based on unmodified PR and nano-silica modified PR

fiber is smooth, which show there is weak interface in the resin matrix and glass fiber. However, as Fig. 5 (d) – (f) show, the adhesive part of large area can be found in the fracture surface of resin and glass fiber in phenolic resin/glass fiber composite material modified by nano-silica. Meanwhile, the resin layer internal damage is also the major failure mode besides the interface damage between resin and glass fiber.

The above phenomenon indicates that The interlamellar fracture behavior glass fiber/phenolic resin composites was changed after the addition of nano-silica in the resin matrix, and the interface effect of the resin matrix and glass fiber was enhanced. This may be due to the fact that the nano-silica in the resin matrix prevents the crack propagation to some extent and shares part of the load when the glass fiber/phenolic resin composite is damaged.

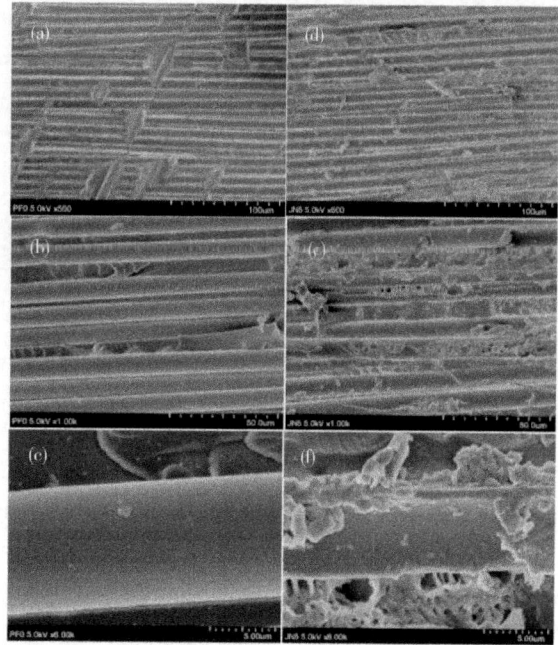

Fig. 5 SEM images of fracture surfaces of phenolic resin/glass fiber with pure phenolic resin [(a) – (c)] and nano-silica modified phenolic resin [(d) – (f)]

3.6 Flame retardant of the GFPCs

LOI measurements were employed to investigate the flame retardant of the cured PR, and the corresponding data was summarized in Tab. 1. As we can see, the adding of nano-silica do not decrease. That can be considered as the reason that nano-silica is a kind of flame resistant material, so the LOI of PR modified by nano-silica do not decrease. Fig. 6 shows that the morphologic

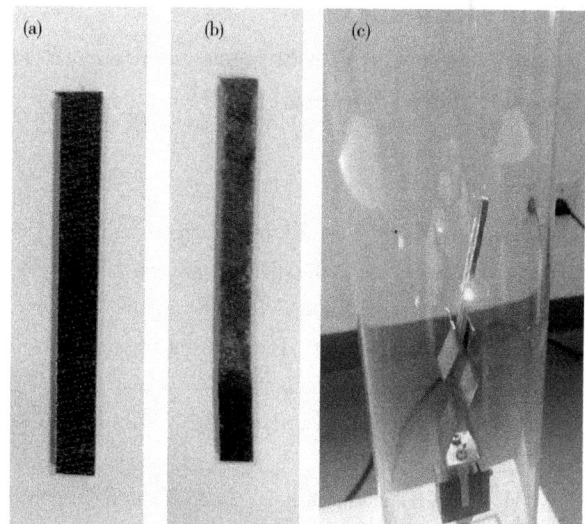

Fig. 6 (a) Unburned composite panel; (b) Tested composite panel; (c) Combustion process

change between unburned composite panel (a) and tested composite panel (b). Fig. 6 (c) show the burning process of composite panel, in which there are no smoke.

**Tab. 1 LOI of PR composite panel
with different content nano-silica**

	PR-0	PR-5	PR-10
LOI	>90%	>90%	>90%

4　Conclusions

This study has focused on the effect of nano-silica particle on the properties ofphenolic resin/glass fiber composites. After modified by nano-silica, flexural strength of GFPCs modified by nano-silica have improved significantly by 16% and 25%. the result of Mode I and II interlaminar fracture tests showed that all nano-silica-dispersed GFPCs laminates exhibited higher interlaminar fracture toughness, in which the addition of only 5% nano-silica could give 153% and 149% enhancement in Mode I and II interlaminar fracture toughness, respectively. Meanwhile, the LOI measurements show that the LOI of all GFPCs is more than 90%, which mean the adding of nano-silica do not sacrifice their flame retardant properties.

Acknowledgements

This work was supported by Shanghai Science and Technology Committee (No. 16DZ112140)

References

[1] Gardziella A, Pilato L A, KnopA. Phenolic resins: chemistry, applications, standardization, safety and ecology[M]. 2nd, Berlin: Springer Verlag, 2000: 12.

[2] Chen Y, Hong C, Chen P. The effects of zirconium diboride particles on the ablation performance of carbonphenolic composites under an oxyacetyleneflame [J], RSC Adv, 2013, 3 (33): 13734-13739.

[3] Ku H, Wang H, Pattarach A N, Trada M. A review on the tensile properties of natural fiber reinforced polymer composites [J]. Composites Part B, 2011 (4):856-873.

[4] Dransfield K, Baillie C, Mai Y W. Improving the delamination resistance of CFRP by stitching a review [J]. Compos. Sci. Technol, 1994, 50: 305-317.

[5] Kim J K. Methods for improving impact damage resistance of CFRPs [J]. Key Eng. Mater, 1998; 141(143): 149-68.

[6] Mouritz A P. Review of z-pinned composite laminates[J]. Compos. A, 2007, 38:2383-97.

[7] Hojo M, Matsuda S, Tanaka M, et al. Mode I delamination fatigue properties of interlayer-toughened CF/epoxy laminates [J]. Compos. Sci. Technol, 2006, 66:665-675.

[8] Ku H, Wang H, Pattarac-haiyakoop N, et al. A review on the tensile properties of natural fiber reinforced polymer composites [J], Composites Part B, 2011 (4).

[9] Cardona F, Kin-Tak A L, Fedrigo J. Novel phenolic resins with improved mechanical and toughness properties [J]. Journal of Applied Polymer Science, 2012, 123 (4): 2131-2139.

[10] Kaynak C, Cagatay O. Rubber toughening of phenolic resin by using nitrile rubber and amino silane [J]. Polymer Testing, 2006, 25(3): 296-305.

[11] Yang T P, Kwei T K, Pearce E M. Blends and interpenetrating networks of phenolic resins and polyamides [J]. Journal of Applied Polymer Science, 1990, 41 (5 - 6): 1327-1332.

[12] Mechanical and thermal properties of hybrid carbonfiber-phenolic matrix composites containing graphene nano-platelets and graphite powder [J]. Plastics, Rubber and Composites, 2017, 46: 431-441.

[13] American Society for Testing and Materials. ASTM D790 standard test methods for flexural properties of unreinforced and reinforced plastics and electrical Insulating materials [S]. Meeting of Committee D30, 2006, 3.

[14] American Society for Testing and Materials. ASTM-D7905 standard test method for mixed mode I-mode I interlaminar fracture toughness of unidirectional fiber reinforced polymer matrix composites [S]. Florida: MACM Conference Melbourne, 2006, 3.

[15] American Society for Testing and Materials. ASTM-D7905 standard test method for mixed mode I-mode II interlaminar fracture toughness of unidirectional fiber reinforced polymer matrix composites [S]. Florida: MACM Conference Melbourne, 2006, 3.

[16] American Society for Testing and Materials. ASTM-D2863 standard test method for measuring the minimum oxygen concentration to support candle-like combustion of plastics [S]. Florida: MACM Conference Melbourne, 2006, 3.

Evaluation Surface Characteristics of Needle-Punched Nonwoven Polypropylene Sorbents

Abeer Alassod[1,2], **Guangbiao Xu**[1]*

[1] Key Laboratory of Textile Science and Technology, Ministry of Education, Shanghai 201620, China

[2] Department of Textile Engineering, Mechanical and Electrical Engineering University, Damascus, Syria

*Corresponding author's email: guangbiao_xu@ dhu. edu. cn

Abstract: The performance of needle-punched nonwoven polypropylene oil sorbents depend on surface properties like contact angle, surface free energy, wicking, and oil sorption capacity were investagted. The surface characteristics of the polypropylene nonwoven were determined by using the sessile drop and captive bubble methods, while the surface free energy was assessed using the basis of Owens-Wendt-Rabel and Kaelble (OWRK) method. Hence, the analysis revealed that highest water contact angle value (θ = 161. 1 °), lowest surface free energy (26. 9 mN/m) were recorded by sample F compared with other samples. The investigation manifested a significant influence of oil properties in oil sorption performance. The experimental results showed that the highest oil sorption rates of sorbents to Gasoline oil and soybean oil belong to sample B was 7. 6g/g and 7. 2g/g, respectively.

Keywords: Surface energy; Wicking; Polypropylene; Oil sorption; Contact angle

1 Introduction

Recently, researchers highlighted the high risk of oil spillage in the world. Oil spillage occurs during oil transport activities, storage, production or human-made errors. The danger of oil spills not only represents a loss of oil as a vital source of energy in the modern industrial world, but also often have harmful and long-term effects on the ecosystem, marine life, and human health[1-2]. When oil comes in contact with water it forms the oil in water emulsions or floating films, therefore, it is necessary to remove immediately. Various techniques have been adopted to clean the oil up and extract it from water bodies, for example, skimming, controlled burning, bioremediation, and uses of sorbents and dispersants[3]. Sorbents consider one of the most promising and feasible techniques. The typical sorbents are characterized by high hydrophobicity and oleophilicity, high oil sorption capacity, low water take up and inexpensive. Natural sorbents have been used for oil spill clean up, but this kind of sorbents pickup water capacity when used in polluted water bodies. Polypropylene (PP) fits this description as sorbents[4-6].

Nonwoven, on the other hand, provides high oil sorption capacity comparing with others conventional textile fabrics. Their construct depend on webs of individual fibers, which include small voids that offer facilitate way to transport liquids after sorption. Therefore, nonwovens polypropylene sorbents would appear to be ideal materials for the oil spill in the marine environment[7-8].

In this paper, the authors investigated the surface characteristics of different needle-punched polypropylene nonwoven sorbents from oil sorption capacity, wicking rate, contact angle and surface energy.

2 Experiments

2.1 Materials

In this paper, six needle-punched nonwoven polypropylene fabrics were used, A to F(Tab. 1). The parameters of these samples including, thickness (ASTM D 5729-

97), and mean pore diameter were recorded from Capillary flow porometry. The porosity of nonwoven fabric is given by

$$\varepsilon = \left(1 - \frac{n^\rho}{f^\rho}\right) \times 100\% \tag{1}$$

Where ε is the porosity of nonwoven fabric, n^ρ and f^ρ are the densities of nonwoven fabric and fiber (kg/m^3), respectively.

Tab. 1 Sorbent properties

	Thickness (mm)	Calculated porosity (%)	Mean porediameter (μm)
A	3	99.74	24.6
B	3.5	99.81	32.78
C	3.3	99.78	22.69
D	3.4	99.83	27.83
E	3.7	99.84	31
F	2.2	99.77	21.02

2.2 Preparation of test oils

Two types ofoils, namely gasoline oil and soybean oil were used in the contamination process of artificial seawater (3.5% salt). The densities and surface tensions of oils were examined using Dynamic contact angle tester (DCAT 1). A SNB2 Digital Rotary Viscometer tested the viscosities. The properties of the tested oil are listed in the Tab. 2.

Tab. 2 Properties of studied oils at room temperature (20℃)

Oil	Soybean	Gasoline
Viscosity(MPa/s)	64.8	32.2
Density(g/cm^3)	0.92	0.86
Surface tension(mN/m)	30.1	28.5

2.3 Contact angle and wettability measurement

Contact angle values have a considered effect on the wetting properties of the surface and defines the capability of a surface to face against the movement of a droplet liquid.

It has been stated that highest wetting (spreading), the contact angle is ($\theta = 0°$). Between $\theta = 0°$ and $\theta =$ 90°, the solid material is wettable and above 90° suggested to poor wetting.

Three different value of contact angle for water and oil were taken by measuring at places in the same sample to calculate the average. By using most popular goniometry methods the sessile drop (SD) and the captive bubble (CB) static contact angle was performed on optical contact angle meter (OCA15EC, Data Physics, Germany). The nonwoven fabric was firstly horizontally suspended by fixing two ends of the fabric with double-sided tape on to a special sample frame. Various oils and water were examined to the nonwoven fabric by a syringe needle (Hamilton, 1750, TLL) and their data capture was registered using CCD camera and software OCA20.

2.4 Surface free energy calculation

Surface energies of different samples for nonwoven polypropylene sorbents were determined based on the Owens – Wendt – Rabel – Kaelble method (OWRK)[9], which gives the following relationship between the surface energy of liquid

$$\sigma_1(1 + \cos\theta) = 2\sqrt{\sigma_1^d \sigma_s^d + \sigma_1^p \sigma_s^p} \tag{2}$$

Where superscript p and d represent polar and dispersion component, respectively. The contact angle of the liquid on solid. By further transforming Eq. (2) into the following form:

$$y = \sqrt{\sigma_s^p \cdot x} + \sqrt{\sigma_s^d}$$

$$y = \frac{(1 + \cos\theta)}{2} \cdot \frac{\sigma_1}{\sqrt{\sigma_1^d}}$$

$$x = \sqrt{\frac{\sigma_1^p}{\sigma_1^d}}$$

Surface free energies and their components of different samples of nonwoven polypropylene sorbents were realized by using three liquids: water, Ethylene Glycol, and Ethanol[10]. The surface tensions of liquids are shown in Tab. 3. Their contact angles on fabric were recognized by an optical contact angle meter OCA15EC.

Tab. 3 Properties of liquids for surface energy measurement of nonwoven polypropylene sorbents

Liquid type	Surface tension (mN/m)	Polar component (mN/m)	Dispersion component (mN/m)
Water	72.10	52.20	19.90

Liquid type	Surface tension (mN/m)	Polar component (mN/m)	Dispersion component (mN/m)
Ethylene glycol	48.00	29.00	19.00
Ethanol	22.10	4.60	17.50

Continued

2.5 Measurement of vertical wicking

Wicking is considered the essential parameters for absorption and transportation of liquid in fabric[11]. in nonwoven fabric wicking of liquid takes place through a capillary system. Generally, wicking affected by a series of factors such as properties of the liquid, absorption capacities and surface characteristics (hydrophilicity or hydrophobicity).

Vertical wicking (rising height) of fabric was used according to DIN 53924.

Five nonwoven strips size of (200mm × 25mm) of fabric was clamped, and 30mm of the sample length was kept in the immersed condition in the 250mL oil in glass beaker, and at the same time stopwatch was activated. After 10 seconds, the increased in length was recorded at different intervals of time, and the average value of all measurements was calculated.

2.6 Oil sorption experiments

The sorption capacity of needle-punched polypropylene nonwoven sorbents was evaluated using two kinds of oil. Samples were conditioned at (21 ± 2)℃ and (70 ± 10)% RH. The size of tested sorbents specimen was (10cm × 10cm).

For the sorption of the oil spill, known weight of sorbent material was put into the test cell containing 600mL of artificial seawater (3.5% NaCl) with 60 grams of oil for duration 5min. The specimens were neither pressed (by hand or external weights) nor immersed in water. After 5min, specimens were removed from the oil and water mixture surface and kept for 1min. To drain the weight of wetted sorbent was determined and recorded. The oil-loaded sorbents were dried at 100℃ for 40min and reweighed. The oil sorption capacity was calculated as follows:

$$\text{Oil sorption capacity } (g/g) = \frac{(s_f - s_0)}{s_0} \quad (3)$$

Where s_0 the weight of dry sorbent (g) is, s_f is the weight of sorbent with oil (g).

3 Results and Discussion

3.1 Contact angle and wettability

In order to know the behavior of water and oil on the surface of sorbents, a study of the surface properties of was carried out by using tow kind of method sessile drop and Captive Bubble as clarified in Fig. 1. Initially, the effect of water drops onto the sorbents surfaces was evaluated, as shown in Fig. 1 (a). A water droplet about 5μL allowed to contact the surface of sample F, the value of water contact angle (WCA) was θ = 161.1° without changing in the drop shape. In contrary, a when 5μL droplet of Soybean oil was dropped on its surface; oil droplet immediately spread on the fabric with oil contact angle (OCA, Soybean oil) of θ = 0° which refer that the sample F is superoleophilic. as shown in Fig. 1(b).

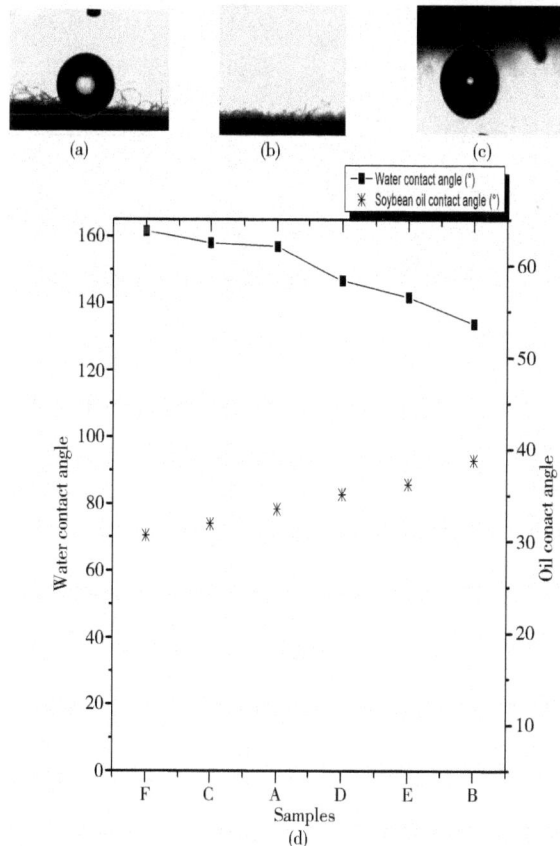

Fig. 1 Wettability of samples (a) Water droplet on sample F; (b) Oil droplet (soybean oil) on the sample F; (c) Droplet oil droplet (soybean oil) on sample F using captive bubble; (d) Hydrophobic and oleophilic properties of samples according to contact angle

The shape of drop soybean oil using Captive Bubble Method was recognized in Fig. 1 (c) , and registered oil contact angle value was $\theta = 30.5°$.

Two pure less polar liquids compared to water were evaluated to give more support for this hypothesis. These liquids were ethylene glycol and ethanol, respectively. Constant values of the liquids used during the test are given above in Tab. 3. The obtained results of contact angle values are summarized in Tab. 4

Tab. 4 Contact angle values of water ethylene glycol and ethanol

	Contact angle(°)		
Sample	Water	Ethylene glycol	Ethanol
A	148.2	117.35	36.1
B	138.56	105.7	30.1
C	144.1	119.8.2	39.6
D	142.9	114.4	34.3
E	140.6	105.9	31.2
F	151.1	123.1.8	46.3

3.2 Surface energies

As observed from result in the Tab. 4 and Tab. 5 the sorbent F show high water contact angle and very low surface energy compared with other 26.96mN/m this is in range the surface energy of oils 20–30mN/m and far below of water 72mN/m with contact angle $\theta = 161.1°$ as shown in Fig. 1 (a). The surface energies of other samples followed by sample C, sample A, sample D, sample E, sample B, respectively.

Tab. 5 Surface energy of polypropylene nonwoven fabric

	Surface Energy(mN/m)		
Sample	Total	Dispersion components	Polar components
A	29.85	22.39	6.74
B	48.9	26.02	2.91
C	28.93	26.02	2.91
D	32.34	26.18	6.16
E	47.8	39.42	8.38
F	26.9	21.93	5.04

3.3 Vertical wicking rate

The wicking behavior is investigated by contact angle and pore diameter of samples. A low contact angle causes higher wicking rates. Oil flow would be faster in the pores with a larger diameter than that in a small one. Also the smaller diameter pores can transport oil to a greater height as clarified in Fig. 2 and Fig. 3.

If we analyzed the results, sample F in both two types of oil showed higher performance with height value (54.1mm) using Gasoline, Oil and (77mm) using Soybean Oil followed by samples C, A, D, E, B, respectively. Due to low contact angle for both kinds of oil and small pore diameter as evident in the Tab. 1. Also, it was noticed that Soybean oil recorded highest wicking height than Gasoline oil.

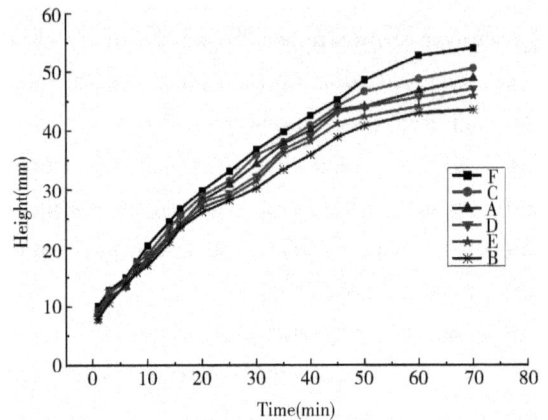

Fig. 2　Gasoline oil wicking rate

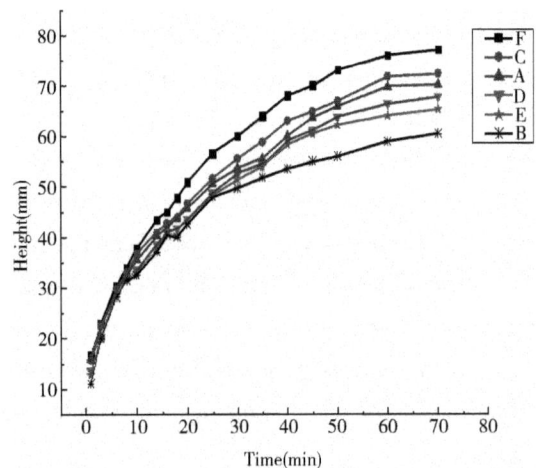

Fig. 3　Soybean oil wicking rate

3. 4 Sorption of needle-punched polypropylene nonwoven to different oils

The results of sorption of the samples are demonstrated in Fig. 4. Both kinds of oil followed the same arrange: B > E > D > A > C > F.

Oil sorption capacity of sample F by using gasoline and soybean oil were (7.6g/g, 7.2g/g) respectively.

In case of samples C, A, D, E and B, the oil sorption capacity were about (6.8g/g, 6.5g/g), (5.9g/g, 5.7g/g), (5.5g/g, 5.3g/g), (5.3g/g, 5.3g/g), (5g/g, 4.8g/g) for casoline oil and soybea oil, respectively.

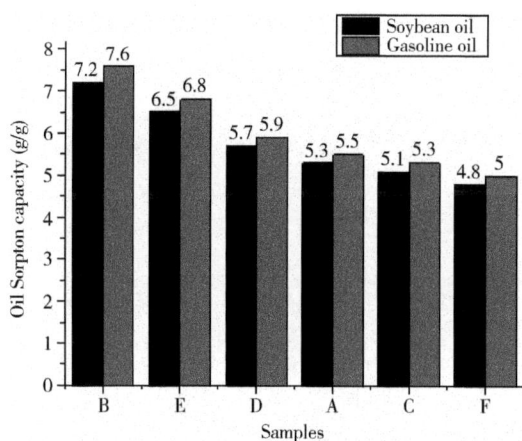

Fig. 4 Oil sorption capacities of different samples of polypropylene nonwoven

Oil with high viscosity attended to have higher initial sorption capacity. However, from the results concluded from the Fig. 4, oil with high viscosity has the opposite impact on the capillary penetration of oil into small pores of nonwoven sorbents[12].

Darcy's lawiproofs when the oil is more viscous; pores may become obstructed and therefore, sorption capacity decreases, this is what expected to have happened during the experiment. The oil sorption capacity decreased with soybean oil, and the same effect goes on gasoline oil. In addition, the samples with a small pore diameter led to less oil penetration compared with larger pore diameter.

Also, from the Fig. 4 as shown, oil sorption capacity for Gasoline oil for the same sample is slightly higher than soybean oil, the difference between these set of values according to different oil viscosity.

4 Conclusions

Characteristics of surface needle-punched nonwoven polypropylene sorbents were investigated in this study. Some conclusion can be made based on the results. Measured values of contact angles and surface free give better descriptions of Surface characteristics of sobents. Also, oil properties have essential effect in oil sorption capacity of sorbents based on pore diameter.

The highest sorption capacity of both kinds of oil was registered by sample F, and decreased with decrease pore diameter and high oil viscosity of the oil. In contrary, the highest wicking rate, water contact angle and low surface energy were recorded by sample B for oil with high oil viscosity and small pore diameter.

References

[1] Abdelwahab O. Assessment of raw luffa as a natural hollow oleophilic fibrous sorbent for oil spill cleanup [J]. Alexandria Engineering Journal, 2014, 53(1): 213-218.

[2] Nwadiogbu J V. Ajiwe, P Okoye. Removal of crude oil from aqueous medium by sorption on hydrophobic corncobs: Equilibrium and kinetic studies [J]. Journal of Taibah University for Science, 2016, 10(1): 56-63.

[3] Karan C P, Rengasamy R S, Das D. Oil spill cleanup by structured fibre assembly [J]. Indian Journal of Fibre & Textile Research, 2011, 36(2):190-200.

[4] Ceylan D, Dogu S, Karacik B, et al. Evaluation of butyl rubber as sorbent material for the removal of oil and polycyclic aromatic hydrocarbons from seawater [J]. Environmental Science & Technology, 2009, 43(10):3846-3852.

[5] Lim, T T, X Huang. Evaluation of kapok (Ceiba pentandra (L.) Gaertn.) as a natural hollow hydrophobic-oleophilic fibrous sorbent for oil spill cleanup [J]. Chemosphere, 2007, 66(5): 955-963.

[6] Guo M, et al. Study on melt-blown processing, web structure of polypropylene nonwovens and its BTX adsorption [J]. Fibers and Polymers, 2016, 17(2): 257.

[7] Choi H M, Needle punched cotton nonwovens and other natural fibers as oil cleanup sorbents [J]. Journal of Environmental Science & Health Part A, 1996, 31(6): 1441-1457.

[8] Choi H M, Kwon H J, Moreau J P. Cotton nonwovens as oil spill cleanup sorbents [J]. Textile Research Journal, 1993,

63(4): 211-218.

[9] Owens D K, Wendt R. Estimation of the surface free energy of polymers [J]. Journal of Applied Polymer Science, 1969, 13(8): 1741-1747.

[10] Roy M D, Sinha S K. Performance of wicking through yarn and fabric made from polyester fibres of different cross-sections [J]. International Journal of Textile Science, 2014, 3 (3): 44-50.

[11] Simile C B. Critical evaluation of wicking in performance fabrics [J]. Georgia Institute of Technology, 2004.

[12] Husseien M, et al. Availability of barley straw application on oil spill clean up [J]. International Journal of Environmental Science & Technology, 2009, 6(1): 123-130.

Extraction and Characterization of Cellulose Nanocrystals from Ethiopian Corn Silk

Mengistu Tessema[1,2], **Xue Yang**[1,2], **Hassan Mussana**[1,2],
Shuai Jiang[1,2], **Jianyong Yu**[1,2], **Lifang Liu**[1,2]*

[1] *College of Textiles, Donghua University, Shanghai 201620, China.*
[2] *The Key Lab of Textile Science & Technology, Ministry of Education, Shanghai 201620, China.*

* *Corresponding author's email*: lifangliu@ dhu. edu. cn

Abstract: This study aimed to characterize cellulose nanocrystals extracted from corn silk, which was abundant and had not been investigated as a raw-material option to produce cellulose nanocrystals. Cellulose microfibril (CMF) was obtained after ethanol, alkali (NaOH) and bleaching treatments of corn silk (CS). Cellulose nanocrystal (CNC) was extracted from CMF using sulphuric acid (H_2SO_4) hydrolysis treatment. The characterization was performed by using scanning electron microscopy (SEM), Fourier transform infrared (FT-IR) spectroscopy, X-ray diffraction (XRD), thermogravimetric analysis (TGA) and transmission electron microscopy (TEM). After chemical pretreatments, the lignin, hemicelluloses and other non-structural components were removed. The degree of crystallinity and thermal stability of CMF and CNC were increased compare to raw CS. The crystallinity indexes of CS, CMF and CNC were 34.65%, 64.78%, and 74.52%, respectively. The CNC was exhibited flat and roads like shape with diameter and aspect ratio range of 24.47–43.33nm and 31.57–16.03, respectively. The nanocrystals had an alternative potential to be used as reinforcing filler for bionanocomposites preparation.

Keywords: Agricultural waste; Cornsilk; Cellulose microfibril; Cellulose nanocrystal; New cellulose source

1 Introduction

In recent decades, Lignocellulose byproducts have taken the attention of researchers due to abundant in agricultural residuals and industrial wastes, low in cost, renewable, biodegradable and valuable source for cellulose microfibril (CMF) and cellulose nanocrystal (CNC) extraction[1-3]. From the literature reviews, CNC have been extracted from corn husk[4], rice husk[5], garlic skin[6], discarded cotton fibers[7], etc. The CNC is applied in a wide range of different fields, such as engineered nanocomposites, construction materials, porous materials, intelligent or active packages, electronics, membranes, supercapacitors, functional surfaces, biomedical, pharmaceuticals, bioimaging, cosmetics, and others. This is due to the special features of CNC, such as high surface area to volume ratio, biodegradable, excellent mechanical properties, low co-efficient of thermal expansion, non-toxicity, chemically functional and easy modified[2-3, 8-10].

From lignocelluloses studies, there has been extensive CNC extraction from non-conventional cellulosic sources of agriculture residuals[11]. However, there are still various unexplored and underutilized valuable cellulose sources have not consider as raw material for CNC isolation to fill market and application demand of nanocelluloses. Among those, corn silk (CS) is one of the promising materials. In Ethiopia, corn is the second most cereal product in the country[12-13]. Even if the corn is the second largest production in the country, the byproduct of corn mainly CS is usually discarded as wastes. In many parts of the world such as China, Turkey, United States and France use bioactive CS extractives as one of the herbs of pharmaceutical and traditional medicine for a therapeutic remedy of various illnesses such as kidney stones, diuretic, prostate disorder, urinary infections etc. CS is a thread like strands from the female flower of corn and it is consists of crude fiber, extractives (such as flavonoids, steroids, alkaloids and terpenoid), protein, wax and ashes[14-17]. However, in Ethiopia and in other countries still, yet no one consideres CS uses as new sources of cellulose materials for isolation of nanocrystals to fill nanocellulose market demand and their applications. The aim of this study is extraction and characterization of CMF and CNC from CS to test their potential as a new source of cellulose for CNC isolation.

2 Experiments

2.1 Materials

The dried CS was obtained from Wonberma Woreda, Amhara region, Ethiopia. Ethanol, Sodium hydroxide (NaOH), hydrogen peroxide (H_2O_2) and Sulphuric acid (H_2SO_4) chemicals were purchased from Sinopharm Chemical Reagent Co., Ltd., Shanghai, China.

2.2 Isolation of CMF and CNC

The CS was cleaned with tap water and then dried in an air oven at 60℃. To isolate CMF and CNC, CS was treated with 60% of ethanol for 1h at 70℃ to remove extractives[18]. After drying, it was milled with amilling machine and sieved with 80 mesh sieve. Hemicelluloses, lignin, and remaining non-cellulosic components were removed by alkali and bleaching treatments[5]. Alkali treatment was performed with 4% of NaOH for 1h at 80℃ and then washed with distilled water. After filtering alkali treated CS, bleaching was achieved by 4% of NaOH and 4% of H_2O_2 for 20min at 70℃. The bleached CS was washed with distilled water till the pH reached to 7 and filtered to get CMF for further hydrolysis. The acid hydrolysis treatment was performed with sulphuric acid (45% solution of H_2SO_4 with CS to liquor ratio of 1:20) for 2h at 60℃ under continuous stirring to get CNC. After 2h, hydrolysis was quenched by adding an excess of distilled water to the reaction mixture and the resulting mixture was cooled to room temperature. Then, the suspension was centrifuged using H1650 supercentrifuge (Hunan Xiangyi Laboratory Instrument Development Co., Ltd., Changsha, China) at 5000rpm for 15min and the supernatant was discarded

until it became turbid. The colloidal suspension was then homogenized for 5min using an IKA (T25 Digital Ultra Turrax, Laboratory technology Co., Ltd., Staufen, Germany). This centrifugation step was repeated several times before the suspension was dialyzed against distilled water for several times until pH reached neutral.

2.3 Characterization

The morphology of CS and freeze-dried CMF were characterized by scanning electron microscopy (JSM–5600LV, JEOL Ltd., Tokyo, Japan). Apparent shape and size of CNC were determined by transmission electron microscopy (JEM–2100, JEOL Ltd., Tokyo, Japan). FT-IR spectra of the samples were obtained by Fourier transform infrared (FTIR) spectrometer (Nicolet 8700, Thermo Fisher Scientific Co., Ltd., Waltham, MA, USA) in the range of 4000-500cm^{-1}. The X-R diffraction of the samples were examined by X-ray diffraction (XRD) diffractometer (D/MAX 2550 PC, Rigaku, Tokyo, Japan) at room temperature with a monochromatic CuKα radiation source ($\lambda = 1.54056$Å) in the step-scan mode with a 2θ angle ranging from 5° to 90° with a step of 0.02 and scanning time of 5.0min. The crystallinity index (CrI) was calculated using the following equation[19].

$$CrI(\%) = [(I_{002} - I_{am})/I_{002} \times 100 \qquad (1)$$

where I_{002} is the maximum intensity of lattice diffraction peak (at $2\theta = 22°$) and I_{am} is the intensity scattered by the amorphous part of the sample at $2\theta = 18°$. The thermal stability of the samples was tested with thermogravimetric analyzer (TG209F1, NETZSCH Instrument trading Ltd., Selb, Germany). About 5mg of each sample was heated from 30℃ temperature to 600℃ at a heating rate of 10℃/min under a nitrogen flow rate of 19.8cm^3/min.

3 Results and Discussion

3.1 The apparent shape and morphology

The apparent shape and morphology of the CS, CMF, and CNC were shown in Fig. 1. Originally the CS was a brownish color, but both of the CMF and CNC are white. Morphologically, the CS was thick, opaque and bundles of the fibrils bundled with lignin. However,

CMF was thin and a sheet of fibrils seem like alight transparent mainly due to the removal of lignin, hemicelluloses and wax bound firmly to the α-celluloses[14]. The CNC exhibited flat and road like shape with diameter and aspect ratio (L/d) as, shown in Fig. 1.

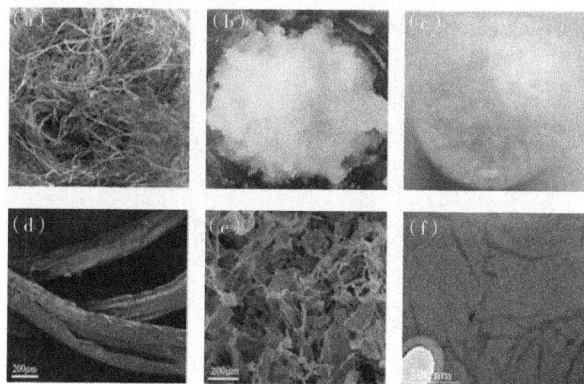

Fig. 1 (a) Raw CS; (b) CMF; (c) freeze dried CNC; (d) SEM image of CS; (e) freeze dried CMF; (f) TEM image of CNC

3.2 FT-IR analysis

The FT-IR spectra of CS, ethanol-treated CS, CMF and CNC were shown in Fig. 2. The intensity peaks at 3650–3200cm^{-1} (O—H stretch), 2850cm^{-1} (sp^{3}C—H stretch), 1770–1728cm^{-1} (C＝O stretch), 1640–1530cm^{-1} (C＝C aromatic stretch), 1460–1316cm^{-1} (sp^2 and sp^3 H—C bend), 1245–1238cm^{-1} (C—O phenol stretch) presented on CS spectrum but not on ethanol treated CS spectrum, which were indicated that extractives removed (such as flavonoids, alkaloids, etc.) after ethanol treatment of CS[20]. The intensity peaks at 3500–3300cm^{-1} (C—N stretch), 1301–1229cm^{-1} (C-N bend), 1770–1728cm^{-1} (C＝O stretch), 1640–1530cm^{-1} (C＝C aromatic stretch), 1245–1238cm^{-1} (C—O acetyl stretch) existed on ethanol treated CS spectrum but not appeared on CMF spectrum, which were range of 24.47–43.33nm and 31.57–16.03, respectively.

Protein, hemicelluloses and lignin were completely removed after bleaching of CS[21-22]. The peaks 1700–1630cm^{-1} (O—H bend and absorption of water), 1150–1100cm^{-1} (C—C ring linkage stretch), 1060–1019cm^{-1} (C—O glycosidic bond stretch) and 905–

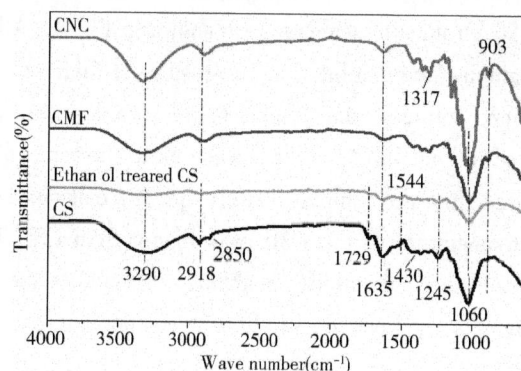

Fig. 2 FT–IR spectra of CS, ethanol–treated CS, CMF and CNC

890cm^{-1} (C—H rocking vibration) were maintained in all spectra[5,11]. The CMF and CNC had similar spectra patterns but CNC intensity peaks were higher than CMF. This was due to the degree of crystallinity of the CNC was higher than the CMF evidenced by XRD results (Section 3.3).

3.3 XRD analysis

The XRD diffraction of CS, CMF and CNC were shown in Fig. 3. The diffraction intensity peaks of CMF and CNC at around $2\theta = 16°$, 18° and 22° were distinctively changed. Especially at 22°, the peak of CNC was shapely hydronium ions to break amorphous regions of CMF and finally released the individual crystallites[23]. Thus, the crystallinity index values of raw CS, CMF, and CNC calculated using the Eq. (1) are 34.65%, 64.78%, and 74.52%, respectively increased. The changes were due to the removal of non-cellulosic components from CS and acid hydrolysis.

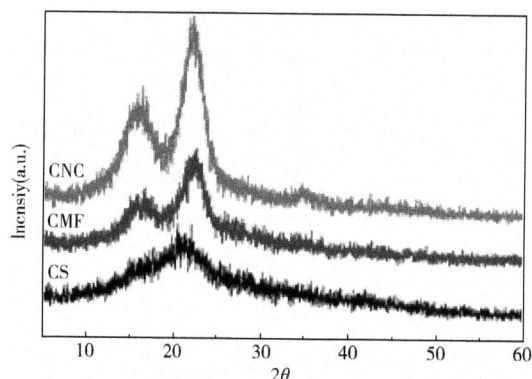

Fig. 3 XRD patterns of CS, CMF and CNC of CS

3.4 Thermogravimetric analysis

The TGA values of samples were shown in Fig. 4. All of the samples had exhibited multiple steps of thermal degradation. Initially, the weights of the samples were decreased around 100℃, which was due to the removal of moisture from the samples. The major thermal degradation temperature of the CMF was higher than CS. The increased thermal stability might be attributed to the removal of amorphous non-cellulosic components as evidenced by FT-IR and XRD results. From Section 3.3, it showed that the crystallinity of CNC was higher than CMF. However, the thermal stability of CNC was nearly similar to CMF. This was probably due to the introduction of sulfate groups into cellulose crystals during sulfuric acid hydrolysis. The sulfate groups introduced to the surface of cellulose crystals caused dehydration and reduced the CNC thermal stability[24].

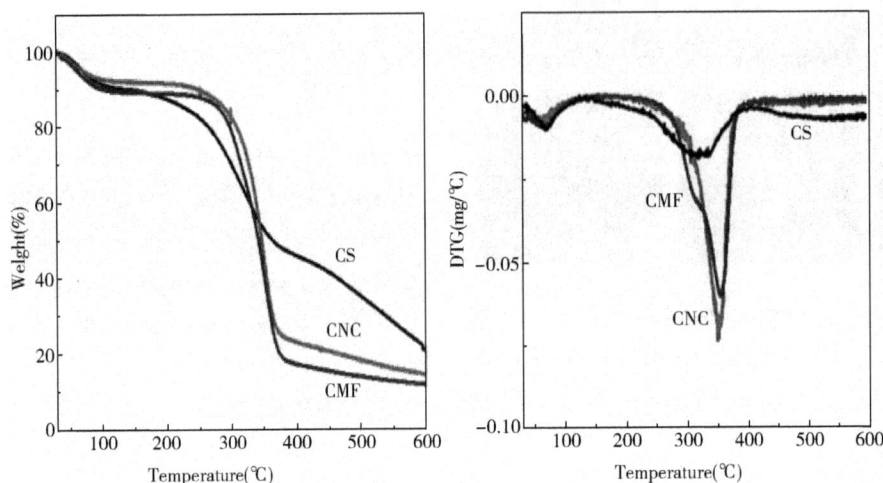

Fig. 4 TGA and DTG curves of CS, CMF and CNC of CS

4 Conclusions

The CMF and CNC were extracted from Ethiopian CS by alkali and acid hydrolysis. Morphologically, the CMF was flat and, the CNC was flat and road like shape with diameter and aspect ratio range of 24.47–43.33nm and 31.57–16.03, respectively. The degree of crystallinity and thermal stability of the CMF and CNC were increased. Conclusively, Ethiopian CS can consider as a new source of cellulose and is expected to have a high potential for the value-added utilization in the form of CMF and CNC as eco-friendly cellulosic nanofillers for diverse areas such as ascaffold, drug delivery, biomedical food packaging and other applications.

References

[1] Chirayil C J, Mathew L, Thomas S. Review of recent research in nano cellulose preparation from different lignocellulosic fibers [J]. Reviews on Advanced Materials Science, 2014, 37:20-28.

[2] Brinchi L, Cotana F, Fortunati E, et al. Production of nanocrystalline cellulose from lignocellulosic biomass: Technology and applications [J]. Carbohydrate Polymers, 2013, 94: 154-169.

[3] Eichhorn S. Cellulose nanowhiskers: Promising materials for advanced applications [J]. Soft Matter, 2011, 7: 303-315.

[4] Mendes C A C, Ferreira N M S, Furtado C R G, et al. Isolation and characterization of nanocrystalline cellulose from corn husk [J]. Materials Letters, 2015, 148: 26-29.

[5] Johar N, Ahmad I, Dufresne A. Extraction, preparation and characterization of cellulose fibres and nanocrystals from rice husk [J]. Industrial Crops and Products, 2012, 37: 93-99.

[6] Reddy J P, Rhim J W. Isolation and characterization of cellulose nanocrystals from garlic skin [J]. Materials Letters, 2014, 129: 20-23.

[7] Nascimento JHOd, Luz R F, Galvão FMF, et al. Extraction andcharacterization of cellulosic nanowhisker obtained from discarded cotton fibers [J]. Materials Today: Proceedings, 2015, 2: 1-7.

[8] Chirayil C J, Mathew L, Thomas S. Review of recent re-

search in nano cellulose preparation from different lignocellulosic fibers [J]. Reviews on Advanced Materials Science, 2014, 37: 20-28.

[9] Lin N, Dufresne A. Nanocellulose in biomedicine: Current status and future prospect [J]. European Polymer Journal, 2014, 59: 302-325.

[10] Ioelovich M. Cellulose as a nanostructured polymer: A Short review [J]. BioResources, 2008, 3:1403-1418.

[11] Reddy JP, Rhim JW. Isolation and characterization of cellulose nanocrystals from garlic skin [J]. Materials Letters, 2014, 129: 20-23.

[12] Alemayehu S, Taffesse P, Dorosh S, et al. Crop production in ethiopia: Regional patterns and trends[J]. Essp Working Papers, 2011.

[13] Abu Tefera Q G. Ethiopiagrain and feed annual report. USDA staff and not necessarily statements of official U. S. Government POLICY. 2013.

[14] Gwendlin V, Induja T, Manoj J, et al. Recent trends in effective utilization of by-product of corn [J]. Indian Journal of Science, 2015, 22: 18-26.

[15] Hasanudin K, Hashim P, Mustafa S. Corn silk (stigma maydis) in healthcare: A phytochemical and pharmacological review [J]. Molecules, 2012, 17: 9697-9715.

[16] Hu Q L, Zhang L J, Li Y N, et al. Purification and antifatigue activity of flavonoids from corn silk [J]. International Journal of Physical Sciences, 2010, 5: 321-326.

[17] Ebrahimzadeh M A, Pourmorad F, Hafezi S. Antioxidant activities of Iranian corn silk [J]. Turkish Journal of Biology, 2008, 32: 43-49.

[18] Yang G, Jaakkola P. Wood chemistry and isolation of extractives from wood [J]. Literature Study for BIOTULI Project-Saimaa University of Applied Sciences, 2011:10-22.

[19] Park S, Baker J O, Himmel M E, et al. Cellulose crystallinity index: Measurement techniques and their impact on interpreting cellulase performance [J]. Biotechnology for Biofuels, 2010, 3: 10.

[20] Oliveira R N, Mancini M C, Oliveira F C S, et al. FTIR analysis and quantification of phenols and flavonoids of five commercially available plants extracts used in wound healing [J]. Matéria (Rio de Janeiro), 2016, 21: 767-779.

[21] Kong J, Yu S. Fourier transform infrared spectroscopic analysis of protein secondary structures [J]. Acta Biochim Biophys Sin (Shanghai), 2007, 39: 549-559.

[22] Soni B, Hassan E B, Mahmoud B. Chemical isolation and characterization of different cellulose nanofibers from cotton stalks [J]. Carbohydr Polymers, 2015, 134: 581-589.

[23] Lee H V, Hamid S B, Zain S K. Conversion of lignocellulosic biomass to nanocellulose: structure and chemical process [J]. Scientific World Journal, 2014, 2014: 20.

[24] Roman M, Winter W T. Effect of sulfate groups from sulfuric acid hydrolysis on the thermal degradation behavior of bacterial cellulose [J]. Biomacromolecules, 2004, 5: 1671.

Fabric Classification Using Three Dimensional Drape Model

Azmat Hussain[1, 3], **Tayyab Naveed**[1], **Amjad Farooq**[1],
Shahid Siddique[4], **Zhicai Yu**[1], **Ge Wu**[1], **Yueqi Zhong**[1,2 *]

[1] *College of Textiles, Donghua University, Shanghai 201620, China*

[2] *Key Lab of Textile Science and Technology, Ministry of Education, Shanghai 201620, China*

[3] *Bahauddine Zakariya University College of Textile Engineering, Multan 54000, Pakistan*

[4] *Masood Textile Mills, Faisalabad*

* *Corresponding author's email:* zhyq@ dhu. edu. cn

Abstract: The paper presents a method of fabric hand classification through the exploration of three dimensional (3D) drape models objectively. Fabric drape models were developed using windows kinect scanners and point cloud data were processed with code developed in Matlab software to extract drape indicators. Thirty-seven woved fabrics were divided into different classes based on their tactile feel of fabrics softness and stiffness hand as a ground truth. Objectively processed fabric drape models were hierarchicaly clustered to match the subjective clusters of fabric hand. Results revealed that fabric drape indicators were able to classify (objectively) the unknown woven fabric samples in the same manner as did the subjectively judged hand attributes with 81% matching accuracy when processed on same fabric samples. These results will be a better reference in fabric hand evaluation from its drape vision for application such as online shopping and computer simulations.

Keywords: Fabric classification; Fabric 3D; Drape model; Principal component analysis

1　Introduction

Convenience and economy of fabric e-shopping booming business in generally is an acceptable fashion; however, the intangibility of virtual environment contrary to offline makes business to be restricted due to unavailability of fabric hand sensation. Non availability of the objective method to select fashion garments from the vision that customer can use to match its subjective preferences is the hindrance to the expansion of textile e-business.

Drape is an important characterstic of fabric appearance. The area under the draped fabric (Two dimensional outline considered in computing DC), node number and their shapes were considered the most important features[1]. Efforts have been made by scientists to classify fabrics using drape parameters such as researchers[2] used 2D fabric drape information obtained by Cusick drape tester to discriminate fabric samples. Despite 36 drape indicators have been discussed in litraure from 1950 to 2013, the drape coefficient (DC) continues to

be the most widely used. However, it has proved inadequate to explain drape shape and does not correlate completely fabric classification based on fabric hand[3]. Although, fabric drape is realised long before a complex 3D phenomenon, now a days, emerging technologies have been used by some researchers to determine the 3D drape of fabric as scientists used 3D scanned image for the prediction of fabric drape parameters[4]. A new 3D drape measuring concept in which force of gravity acts perpendicular to fabric plane contradicting with the traditional drape measuring method along with new parameters was presented by scientists[5], claimed to be more conforming with actual aesthetics of fabric drape. However, there is a need to delve deeper into 3D characteristics of fabric drape.

Since 80% of our daily perception is based on eye, we study the fabric hand from the angle of visual (3D fabric drape) perception.

We propose a new method for the measurement of fabric

hand from 3D drape image captured by Kinect scanner, point cloud data processed in Geomagic software to attain the triangular mesh and analyzed in Matlab software to extract drape indicators. The acquired data was classified using Hierarchical clustering technique and validated with the subjective evaluation of fabric hand.

2　Experiments

Thirty-seven different commercial fabric samples (woven) were collected from the different markets of Shanghai. The 3D fabric-drape data realized by Windows Kinect scanner were evaluated to classify fabrics. The main steps of the current study were shown in Fig. 1. The fabric samples of 240mm diameter were hanged freely in umbrella shape under gravitational force by the support of disk diameter i. e. 12cm. Fabric drape 3D images were processed in Geomagic software to get the refined polygonal mesh. Four drape variables i. e., drape coefficient, minimum drape, average trough and hand radius were assessed through clustering technique (Hierarchical).

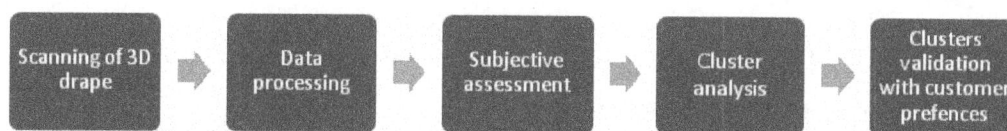

Fig. 1　Main stages of the study

2.1　Scanning of 3D drape

Fabric-drape 3D point cloud data were captured with cheaper Windows Kinect sensor. The sensor used infrared rays to capture the depth image and was controlled by the computer. Kinect sensor required to scan image at different locations. Therefore, we arranged the equipment to get the depth image at various locations with four cameras.

2.2　Data processing

Three dimensional point cloud data were processed by different software packages. First, the data were imported into the Geomagic software for noise removal and polygonal mesh refinement as shown in the Fig. 2. The code was generated in the Matlab software for further processing of the 3D drape images for extraction of the indicators.

2.3　Dimensionality reduction

Number of drape indicators to predict the shape of each fabric type would create difficulty to understand the position of each sample in the multidimensional space. Dimensionality reduction (principle component analysis) increased the perception between samples and multi-dimensional drape space without the loss of much information[6-7].

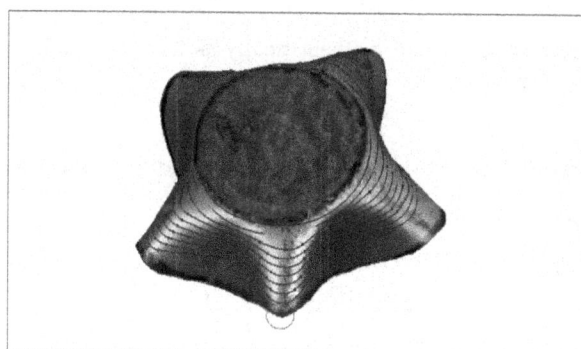

Fig. 2　Three dimensional drape model

2.4　Subjective assessment

For the assessment of fabric subjective hand of softness and stiffness sample size of 300mm × 300mm was taken[8]. Each customer was guided to washing hands with soap and drying them with paper towel before going to the evaluation table placed in the laboratory. A training session was organized to help the jury familiar with the descriptors, as well as the methods of handling the samples for the required properties[9-11].

2.5　Cluster analysis

To deal with the multi-dimensionality of 3D drape model data a clustering technique, i. e. Polythetic Agglomerative Hierarchical Clustering (PAHC) was chosen to classify the data. The algorithm started from singleton clusters and merges those clusters with minimal distances (linkage) until all objects were included in one cluster. The average linkage (L), defined below mathematically in Eq. (1);

$$L = \frac{1}{|A||B|} \sum_{a \in A} \sum_{b \in B} d(a,b) \qquad (1)$$

Where d is a metric selected as Euclidian Distance.

The clustering procedure was completed in the n-dimensional space (n is the number of variables), which meant during clustering the difference of every parameter between samples was considered so the results were much more realistic and definite, when this unique advantage of clustering compared to other statistical approaches[12].

For the validation of classified results, we adopted an external criterion which measures the performance of the hierarchical clustering algorithm in terms of matching accuracy. Let a_i denote the number of objects correctly matched to the ith cluster C_i then d "matching accuracy" could be described mathematically as follows:

$$d = \frac{1}{n} \sum_{i=1}^{k} a_i \qquad (2)$$

Where k is the number of clusters and n is the total number of samples assessed.

3 Results and Discussion

Four drape indicators were evaluated with principle component analysis (PCA) to reduce the dimensionality to be classified according to the customer subjective preferences of fabric hand in terms of softness and stiffness. Two principle components explained 94.78% data variability were selected. Fig. 3 depicted the Eigen

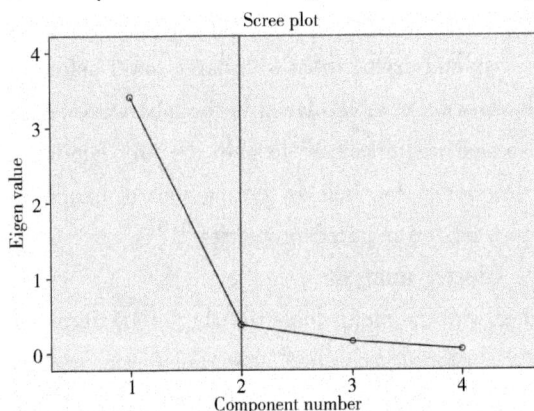

Fig. 3　Scree plot of principle component analysis

values of each component.

Requirement of data sphericity was also checked with Bartlett's test, the results proved the significant (Sig. = 0. 00) sphericity of the data as shown in Tab. 2. Kaiser-Mayer-Olkin sampling adequacy was also measured (0.79) which is more than 0.5, as shown in the Tab. 1. Hence, the number of the sample selected for the study were statistically large enough for further processing of data.

Tab. 1　KMO and Bartlett's test for sampling adequacy and data sphericity

KMO and Bartlett's test	
Kaiser-Meyer-Olkin　Sampling adequacy	0.79
Bartlett's test of sphericity	Sig. 0.00

3.1　Matching accuracy of classification

Matching accuracy of the objective (PCA components of drape indicators) classification with subjective hand evaluations of fabric softness and stiffness combined was examined $d = 81\%$ (i. e. 30 out of 37 samples matched correctly with 2nd clustering in respective clusters) using equation Eq. (2). The entire sample was divided into three hierarchical clusters objectively as shown in the Fig. 4 and Tab. 2. Cluster 1 represented the soft, cluster 2 represented the stiff and cluster 3 represented the moderately stiff fabrics. Overall, seven out of thirty seven specimens were miss classified in different clusters as shown in Fig. 4 and Tab. 2. It meant fabric hand from fabric 3D drape was classified successfully based on the customer subjective preference.

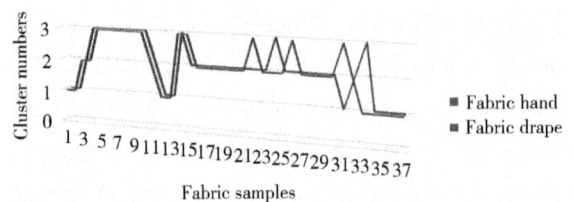

Fig. 4　Pair wise matching accuracy of clustered values based on subjective assessment and 3D drape indicators

Tab. 2 Cluster validation of 3D drape with fabric hand

Sample No.	Cluster numbers	
	Fabric hand	Fabric drape
1	1	1
2	1	1
3	2	2
4	2	3
5	3	3
6	3	3
7	3	3
8	3	3
9	3	3
10	3	3
11	2	2
12	1	1
13	1	1
14	3	3
15	3	2
16	2	2
17	2	2
18	2	2
19	2	2
20	2	2
21	2	2
22	3	2
23	2	2
24	2	3
25	2	2
26	3	2
27	2	2
28	2	2
29	2	2
30	2	2
31	3	1
32	2	2
33	1	3
34	1	1
35	1	1
36	1	1
37	1	1
Matching accuracy	30/37 =81%	

4 Conclusion

This paper presents efficaciously an objective method for the classification of fabric-hand from three dimensional (3D) drape models. Fabric 3D drape models were scanned using a method developed in our earlier research with the cheaper device (Kinect scanner). Classification based on 3D drape was significantly matched with fabric subjective hand assessment. In future, more 3D drape indicators are needed to explore to enhance the matching accuracy of the drape with fabric hand.

Acknowledgements

This work is supported by National Natural Science Foundation of China (Grant No. 61572124).

References

[1] Cusick G. The dependence of fabric drape on bending and shear stiffness [J]. J Text Ins, 1965. 56(11): 596-606.

[2] Lai S S. Using drape form to establish discriminant models of fabric characteristics [J]. Indian Journal of Fibre & Textile Research, 2004, 29(2): 143-148.

[3] Carrera-GallissÄ E, Capdevila X, Valldeperas J. Evaluating drape shape in woven fabrics [J]. Journal of the Textile Institute Proceedings & Abstracts, 2017, 108(3): 325-336.

[4] Glombikova V, Kus Z. Drape evaluation by the 3D drape scanner [J]. Tekstil Ve Konfeksiyon, 2014, 24(3): 272-278.

[5] Mei Z, Shen W, Wang Y, et al. Unidirectional fabric drape testing method [J]. Plos One, 2015, 10(11): e0143648.

[6] Morrison, D. F. Multivariate statistical methods [B]. 3. New York, NY. Mc, 1990.

[7] Kanai H, Morishima M, Nasu K, et al. Identification of principal factors of fabric aesthetics by the evaluation from experts on textiles and from untrained consumers [J]. Textile Research Journal, 2011, 81(12): 1216-1225.

[8] Zhang P, Liu X, Wang L, et al. An experimental study on fabric softness evaluation [J]. International Journal of Clothing Science & Technology, 2005, 18(2): 83-95.

[9] Ryu H S, Roh E K. Preference and subjective evaluation of washed fabric hand using conjoint analysis [J]. Textile Research Journal, 2010, 80(20): 2167-2175.

[10] Bertaux E, Derler S, Rossi R M, et al. Textile, physiological, and sensorial parameters in sock comfort [J]. Textile Research Journal, 2010, 80(8): 1803-1810.

[11]Grineviciūtè D, Gutauskas M. The comparison of methods for the evaluation of woven fabric hand [J]. Materials Science (Medžiagotyra), 2004. 10(1).

[12]Pan N, Yen K C, Zhao S J, et al. A new approach to the objective evaluation of fabric handle from mechanical properties Part I: Objective measure for total handle [J]. Textile Research Journal, 1988, 58(8): 438-444.

Fabrication of Fiber-Based Woven Triboelectric Nanogenerators and Study on Influential Factors for Output Performance

Ying Chen[1], Zhi Zhang[1], Chaoqun Zhong[1], Jingyi Li[1], Jiansheng Guo[1]*

[1] *College of Textiles, Donghua University, Shanghai 201620, China*

* *Corresponding author's email*: jsguo@ dhu. edu. cn

Abstract: Fiber-based triboelectric nanogenerators have attracted increasing attention by virtue of its small size, high flexibility, sensitivity and promising applications. It can be woven or knitted into wearable, comfortable and breathable fabrics to harvest human body energy. However, there are few researches on the parameters of energy-harvesting woven fabrics made from fiber-based triboelectric nanogenerators. Here in this paper, the properties of PU and PTFE threads and their corresponding fabrics are presented, and the impact of spatial density of warp and weft and different woven structures on electrical outputs are also investigated. The results show that the open-circuit voltage (V_{OC}) increases with the increase of warp and weft density. Better performance is obtained from woven TENG with Plain and twill structures compared with stain structure. However, no obvious change has been found between woven TENGs of warp-faced and filling-faced twill or stain.

Keywords: Woven fabric; Fiber-based; Triboelectric nanogenerators; Structural parameters

1 Introduction

Nowadays, traditional batteries are widely used for supporting wearable devices, but they are too bulky and rigid to be integrated into smart textiles for further usage. Meanwhile it is really inconvenient for people to constantly replace or recharge the used batteries. Moreover, the possible leakage of wasted batteries may cause serious environmental pollution as well[1]. For these reasons, traditional batteries can not meet the needs of flexible and wearable electronic devices sustainably, which highlights the superiority and significance of triboelectric nanogenerators(TENGs).

TENGs can convert the tiny mechanical energy around us into electrical energy based on the dual effects of triboelectrification and electrostatic induction[2]. A new epoch of research on TENGs has been opened since the invention of TENGs by professor Wang's team in 2012[3]. TENGs have been praised as one of the top ten innovative technologies in twenty-first Century by virtue of its small size, high efficiency and sensitivity[4]. More importantly, TENGs can collect energy from human body adequately and power the wearable electronics more conveniently and constantly instead of conventional batteries[5]. Given the above, TENGs have gradually become a novel sustainable green energy.

Recently, fiber-based TENGs are drawing more and more attention both in academy and industry because of the wide application possibilities, such as medical monitoring, sensors, portable military equipment intelligent electronicsand smart textiles[6-9]. Furthermore, textile-based TENGs are proved to be miniature, light and flexible[10]. In particular, energy-harvesting woven fabrics made from fiber-based TENGs combine the merits of textiles which are lightweight, breathable as well as comfortable and TENGs which are structure-simple, real-time and cost effective together[11].

However, there are a few researches on structural parameters of woven fabrics which can also impact electrical outputs[12-13]. Therefore, the effects of various parameters for woven energy-harvesting fabrics based on fiber-structured TENGs have been systematically studied in this paper. Specifically, Polyurethane (PU) threads and PTFE threads were prepared at first and then woven into PU and PTFE fabrics with different structures and parameters, separately. Then the combined woven TENGs in the contact-separation mode were fabricated and measured.

2 Experiments

2.1 Materials

Cotton threads (JC21S/2) were provided by Fukun Textile Co., Ltd. (Hangzhou, China). Silver paste was obtained from Lide electronic slurry Co., Ltd. (Hunan, China). Water borne polyurethane (PU) was supplied by Huakai Resin Co., Ltd. (Jining, China). And polytetrafluoroethylene (PTFE) as liquid was purchased from Qiming Engineering plastics Co., Ltd. (Dongguan, China).

2.2 Preparation of PU and PTFE threads

At first, cotton threads were coated with Ag using the silver paste with a homemade machine, of which the working principle was just like sizing method, given in Fig. 1. There was a self-driving roller at a constant speed of 0.1m/s. Besides, there was no need to place the Ag-coated cotton threads into an oven to dry for the machine had a dry unit of an air heating, and the temperature for coating Ag was set at 80℃. After that, the silver paste was replaced by PU solution and then PU threads were obtained after the coating process at 60℃. Likewise, PTFE was coated onto the surface of PU threads at 80℃, acquiring PTFE threads. The preparation illustration was shown in Fig. 2 (a).

The reason for using PU to separate PTFE and Ag was that the solvent of PTFE solution was able to dissolve the cured Ag. In this case, the surface of the coated thread might be conductive as well, which was not what we want. What's more, PTFE threads were easily to be broken without the existence of PU coating. Based on the mechanism of TENGs[14], even if PU coating separated PTFE coating and conductive Ag coating, there would still be equivalent but opposite charges inducted when the surface of insulating PTFE was polarized during the continuous contact-separation process.

2.3 Preparation of energy-harvesting fabrics

The PU threads were woven into PU fabrics with a cus-

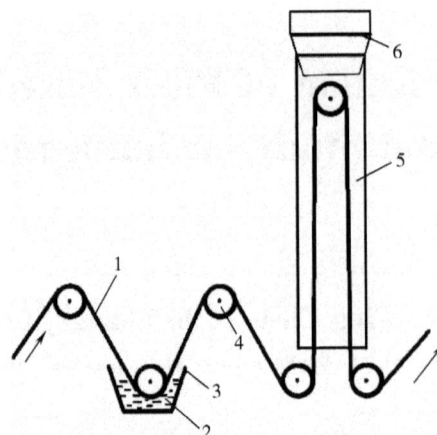

Fig. 1　Homemade machine
(1) Threads to be coated; (2) Coating material; (3) Container;
(4) Rollers; (5) Heating pipeline; (6) Air heater

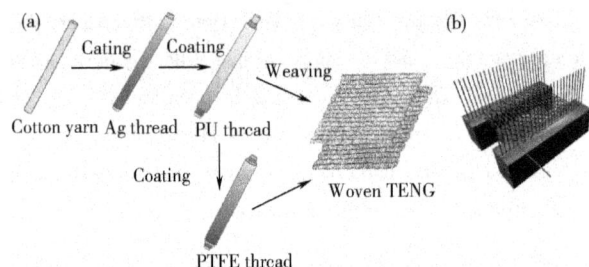

Fig. 2　(a) Schematic illustration of the preparation of fiber-based woven TENG; (b) Customized device for weaving fabrics

tomized device, as shown in Fig. 2 (b). In order to study the impact of density of warp and weft as well as structures, various PU woven fabrics were adopted as presented in Tab. 1. All the samples were with the same size (5cm × 5cm). For all tests, PTFE fabric was controlled of 5cm × 5cm, 56 ends per 10cm and 30 picks per 10cm.

Tab. 1　Various PU woven samples

No.	Warp count (ends/10cm)	Weft count (picks/10cm)	Structure
PU1	20	30	plain
PU2	40	30	plain
PU3	56	20	plain
PU4	56	30	plain
PU5	56	40	plain
PU6	56	60	plain

No.	Warp count (ends/10cm)	Weft count (picks/10cm)	Structure
PU7	56	40	twill
PU8	56	40	stain

2.4 Characterization and measurements

A field emission scanning electron microscope was used to observe the morphology of PU and PTFE threads (Hitachi S-4800, Japan). The resistance of threads was characterized by a digital multimeter (Agilent 34401A, America). And the electrical signals were obtained from a digital oscilloscope (ZDS2022 Plus, China) assisted by a high resistance box (ZX1G, China). A digital fabric thickness gauge with a load of 200N was used to measure the thickness (YG141N, China). Mechanical property of the corresponding thread samples were measured through Yarn strength tester (XL-1A, China) following ISO 2062: 2009. The clamp distance was 500mm. Since the elongation range was 3%–8%, the sliding rate of the lower clamp was set to 250mm/min. All samples were conditioned at 20℃ and 65% relatively humidity for 24h before testing.

3 Results and Discussion

3.1 Morphology and mechanical property

The fabrication process of energy-harvesting woven TENGs are illustrated in Fig.2. Ag thread is used as an electrode material because that Ag coating renders better fastness and a much lower resistance of $1\Omega/cm$ after coating 3 times.

From Fig.3 (a) we can see that the surface of Ag thread is rough before coated by PU and becomes smoother after coating. Fig.3 (b) shows scanning electron microscopy (SEM) images of the cross section of PU thread which comprises multiple cotton fibers inside, Ag coating in the middle and PU coating outside. The SEM images Fig.3 (c) illustrates the cylindrical shape of as-prepared PTFE thread with a radius of about 770μm. Cotton fibers, Ag, PU and PTFE distribute from inside to outside of the threads respectively. As displayed in Fig.3 (d), PU and PTFE threads exhibit

excellent flexibility under various external forces, including folding, knotting, and bending. Fig.3 (e) demonstrates two of the fabric samples, indicating thickness uniformity, great flexibility and comfort.

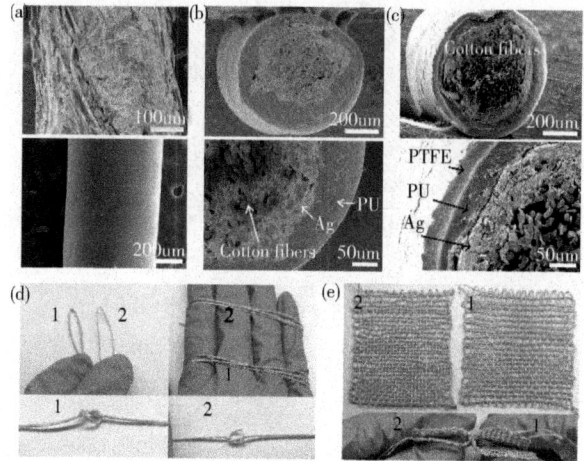

Fig.3 (a) Top-view SEM images of Ag thread (upper) and PU thread (lower); (b) Cross-section view SEM images of PU thread; (c) Cross-section view SEM images of PTFE thread; (d) Images of as-fabricated PU and PTFE threads under variousadditional forces including folding, knotting, and bending; (e) Images of PTFE fabric which is marked as 1 and PU fabric marked as 2

The thickness of woven PU and PTFE fabrics are depicted in Fig.4, where few regulations have been found with the increasing filling or warp count. However, by comparing sample PU5, PU7 and PU8, we can see the thickness of PU fabric increases when the structure starts from plain, and then twill to stain, correspondingly. Moreover, there is flexibility of movement for threads when it comes to stain structure. That is to say, the threads in stain are able to move more freely and randomly than those in plain or twill, as long as there is an external force applied on them. Therefore, threads might overlap and the stain fabric may get thicker than other structures.

As depicted in Fig.5, the tensile strength of cotton yarn, PU thread and PTFE thread are 667.2cN, 1391.6cN and 1718.2cN, respectively. Correspondingly, their elongations at break are 4.5%, 5.1% and 7.2%. It is worth mentioning that the core thread, cotton yarn, takes the advantage of the property of polymer and both of the as-fabricated PU and PTFE thread exhibit superior mechanical properties.

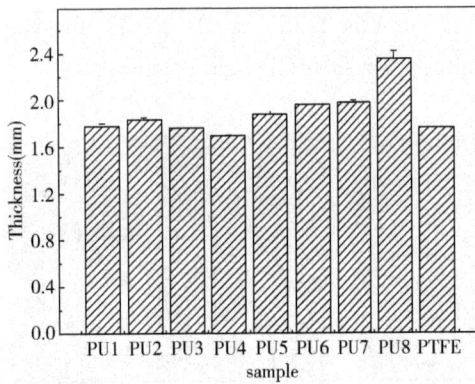

Fig. 4　Thickness of woven PU and PTFE fabrics

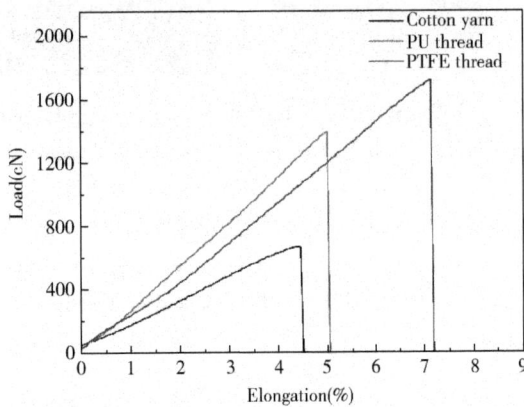

Fig. 5　Strength property of cotton yarn, PU thread and PTFE thread

3.2　Warp-count effect on output performance

The open-current voltage (V_{OC}) of all the TENG samples was tested on an external load resistance of 100MΩ under the tapping frequency of 3Hz or so. The warp count dependence of woven TENGs was explored and the results are shown in Fig. 6. It shows that with higher density of warp, the woven TENGs are able to generate higher voltage. As the warp count increases, the contact are as between PU threads and PTFE threads increases, resulting in more transferred charges between PU and PTFE. Accordingly, the increased open-current voltage can be observed.

3.3　Weft-count effect on output performance

Fig. 7 shows the open-current voltage of woven TENGs with the weft count of 20, 30, 40, and 60 picks per 10cm. It is the same phenomenon just like the impact

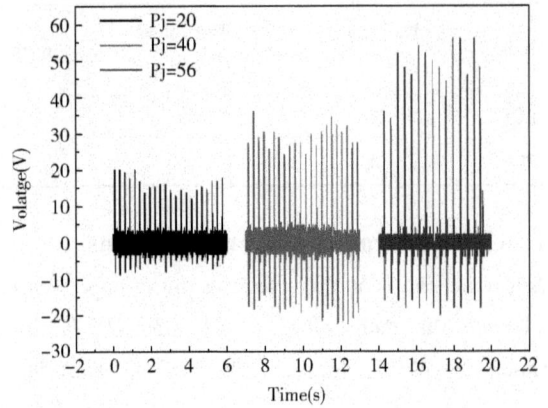

Fig. 6　Output performance of woven PU fabrics with different density of warp

of warp density. To put it to say, the more filling PU threads there are, the better V_{OC} it can obtain. Clearly, the effective contact areas between friction materials are on the increase, leading to a larger amount of transferred charges.

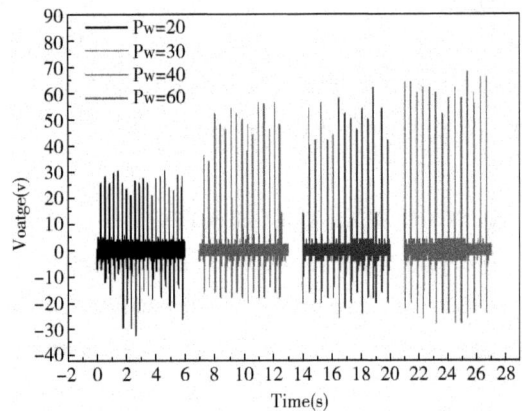

Fig. 7　Output performance of woven PU fabrics with different density of weft

It is noteworthy that the electrical signals of woven TENGs are lower and less stable compared with film TENGs[15]. Obviously, the open-current voltage of woven TENGs is based on the contact area between warp and filling yarns. Therefore, the area is limited and much less than that of film TENGs. As mentioned above, the flexibility and promising space possibility of PU and PTFE threads contribute to the improvement of output performance, which accounts for the changeable behavior each time. However, the greatest strength of woven TENGs is that the TENGs with woven structure ensure good flexibity, great comfort and superior permeability.

3.4 Structural effect on output performance

As we all know, basic woven structures are plain, twill and stain, and twill and stain are both wrap-faced and filling-faced. To further explore the influence of the structures on output performance, the V_{OC} with different structures were measured subsequently.

The relationship between the structure and electrical signal of woven TENGs is revealed in Fig.8. With the same density of warp and weft, woven TENGs of plain and twill structures bring about higher output voltages than stain structure, significantly. It demonstrates warp-faced and filling-faced twill or stain has no notable influence on the final electrical outputs. That's ascribed to the contacting chances for opposite threads of the two faces are almost the same.

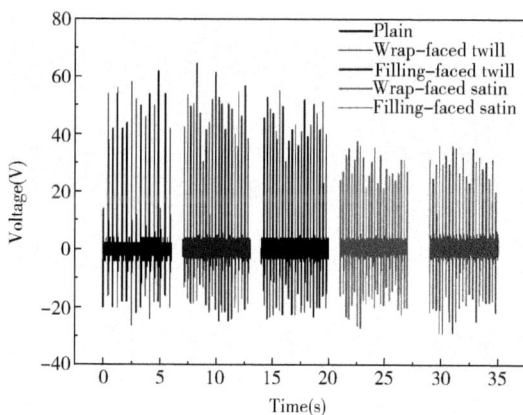

Fig.8 Output performance of woven PU fabrics with different structures

4 Conclusions

This study has focused on the effect of structural parameters on electrical output performance. First, the energy-harvesting threads present great flexibility and bring about excellent comfort and breathability for woven TENGs afterwards. Second, the PU and PTFE coatings strengthen the mechanical property of the whole thread, resulting in a higher tensile strength and a longer elongation at break. Third, higher warp and weft count can enhance electrical signals. Fourth, stain

structure for woven TENGs shows no superiority in thickness and generates less voltage than plain or twill. Thus, woven TENGs with relatively higher warp and weft density and a plain or twill structure could obtain better electrical output performance and ensure superior flexibility, comfort and permeability for further usage in wearable electronics and smart clothing.

References

[1]Xi F, Pang Y, Li W, et al. Universal power management strategy for triboelectric nanogenerator [J]. Nano Energy, 2017, 37: 168-176.

[2]Wang S, Lin L, Wang Z L. Triboelectric nanogenerators as self-powered active sensors [J]. Nano Energy, 2015, 11: 436-462.

[3] Fan F R, Tian Z Q, Wang Z L. Flexible triboelectric generator [J]. Nano Energy, 2012, 1(2): 328-334.

[4] Yoo D, Choi D, Dong S K, et al. Comb-shaped electrode-based triboelectric nanogenerators for bi-directional mechanical energy harvesting [J]. Microelectron Eng, 2017, 174: 46-51.

[5] Li Z, Shen J, Abdalla I, et al. Nanofibrous membrane constructed wearable triboelectric nanogenerator for high performance biomechanical energy harvesting [J]. Nano Energy, 2017, 36: 341-348.

[6] Zhong J, Zhang Y, Zhong Q, et al. Fiber-based generator for wearable electronics and mobile medication [J]. ACS Nano, 2014, 8(6): 6273-6280.

[7]Pu X, Li L, Liu M, et al. Wearable self-charging power textile based on flexible yarn supercapacitors and fabric nanogenerators [J]. Adv Mater, 2016, 28(1): 98-105.

[8]Wang J, Li X, Zi Y, et al. A flexible fiber-based supercapacitor-triboelectric-nanogenerator power system for wearable electronics [J]. Adv Mater, 2015, 27(33): 4830-4836.

[9]Lai Y, Deng J, Zhang S L, et al. Single-thread-based wearable and highly stretchable triboelectric nanogenerators and their applications in cloth-based self-powered human-interactive and biomedical sensing [J]. Adv Funct Mater, 2016, 27(1):1604462.

[10]Yue K, Bo W, Dai S, et al. Folded elastic strip-based triboelectric nanogenerator for harvesting human motion energy for multiple applications [J]. ACS Appl Mater Inter, 2015, 7(36): 20469-20476.

[11] Mallineni S S K, Behlow H, Dong Y, et al. Facile and robust triboelectric nanogenerators assembled using off-the-shelf materials [J]. Nano Energy, 2017, 35: 263-270.

[12] Dong K, Deng J, Zi Y, et al. 3D Orthogonal woven triboelectric nanogenerator for effective biomechanical energy harvesting and as self-powered active motion sensors [J]. Adv Mater, 2017, 29(38): 1702648.

[13] Kwak S S, Han K, Seung W, et al. Fully stretchable textile triboelectric nanogenerator with knitted fabric structures [J]. ACS Nano, 2017, 11(11): 10733-10741.

[14] Wang Z L. Triboelectric nanogenerators as new energy technology for self-powered systems and as active mechanical and chemical sensors [J]. ACS Nano, 2013, 7(11): 9533-9557.

[15] Zhang Z, Chen Y, Debeli D K, et al. A facile method and novel dielectric material using nanoparticles doped thermoplastic elastomer composite fabric for TENG applications [J]. ACS Appl Mater Inter, 2018, 10: 13082-13091.

Fabrication and Properties of Apocynum Venetum Bast Fibers Reinforced Polylactic Acid Composites

Ahsan Ali[1,2] , **Lantao Wu**[1,2] , **Lan Yao**[1,2] , **Yiping Qiu**[1,2]* , **Fuhu Zhang**[1,2]

[1] *Key Laboratory of Textile Science & Technology, Ministry of Education, Shanghai 201620, China*

[2] *Department of Technical Textiles, College of Textiles, Donghua University, Shanghai 201620, China*

* *Corresponding author's email*: ypqiu@ dhu. edu. cn

Abstract: This research was based on the fabrication and assessment of biodegradable Natural Fiber Composites (NFC) which possesses good mechanical properties potentially applicable to the bio-medical textiles, automobiles, civil engineering and cosmetics. This research was carried out by using extracted bast fibers from Apocynum Venetum (AV) plant as a reinforcement material for composites, the polymer matrix selection for composites was Poly Lactic Acid (PLA). There were two groups of composites including untreated and treated AV bast fibers reinforced PLA composites. The tensile strength both groups was analyzed following ASTM D3039 standard, in which the untreated AV bast fibers reinforced composite showed 80. 25MPa while 2% alkali treated fibers reinforced composite showed 103. 67MPa tensile strength. The bending test has been done by following ASTM D790 standard for both groups of samples, which showed 86. 38MPa and 195. 02MPa bending strengths respectively. The morphological analysis of composites for fiber-matrix adhesion characteristics has been obtained by using Scanning Electron Microscope (SEM).

Keywords: Apocynum venetum; Bast fibers; Polylactic acid; Green composites

1 Introduction

These days, Natural Fiber Composites (NFC) is one of the very hot topics in research studies, there are many research papers publish every year for the innovation and development of NFC's. As they possess potential applications and a wide number of great advantages[1] those are highly needed in this era like environment-friendly, low cost, low density, variable properties, biodegradability, good mechanical properties and less damage to equipment in processing than in case of synthetics fibers in composites.

There are several factors that affect the properties of natural bast fibers going to be used for a composite material. Pickering et al. figured out the tensile strength of hemp was changed during the flowering stage of plant[2]. However, alkali treatment showed the decreased lignin content with easiness in separation of bast fiber and uniform strength. Study shows that the tensile strength of composite materials can be improved due to reinforcement of natural fibers with polymers, and it was improved more after the surface treatment with alkali[3]. Sullins et al. investigated the effect of different concentrations of an alkali for the treatment on hemp fibers to make a composite with polypropylene as a matrix and found that the mechanical properties were improving with the concentration of NaOH[4]. It has been studied that the surface properties of kenaf was improved after the treatment with alkali[5]. The removal of hemi-cellulose content, lignin content and other impurities from the surface of fiber by an alkali treatment resulted in increased amount of cellulose[6], but the action of removal of impurities highly depends on the parameters of process and the concentration of alkali[7].

For this research work Apocynum Venetum (AV) plant was used, which is a small wild shrub obtained from the Xinjiang province of China, it has been used widely in past for the production AV fibers after degumming of its peeled off bast from plant and the fibers were found to be directly usable for the textile products. Besides the fiber produced by bast of AV plant, the peeled off bast from AV plant can also being considered itself directly for the application in textile composites area, while considering its good mechanical properties and antibacterial function. Study has been done for the production of fibers from AV bast and the traces of the anti-bacterial component found in the bast of AV[8]. Chemical and bacterial degumming have also been done for the comparative study of the functionality of AV fibers after degumming[9]. Although those are very few studies found on the bast of AV for the production of fibers, it is very difficult to find the work done on AV plant for the use of its bast as a reinforcement material for composite.

This research work has been carried out to use PLA as matrix and the bast of AV plant directly as a reinforcement material for natural fiber composites, in the light of previous studies and knowledge, the treatment of AV bast fibers has been carried out with alkali and the effect of treatments on tensile and bending properties of composites with their morphology characterization through SEM has been investigated.

2 Experiments

2.1 Materials

AV plant: AV plant has been sourced from Xinjiang. The cut stems and branches were mostly dried and contained leaves.

Polymermatrix: PLA (Nature Works © 4032D) was provided as pellets by Zhonghua Suhua Co., Ltd. (Guangdong). Its melting temperature was 166℃.

Alkali: Analytical grade, was supplied by Pinghu Chemical Reagent Factory (Zhejiang).

2.2 AV bast fiber preparation

AV bast fibers were firstly extracted from AV stems and branches by peeling off them manually, then converted into fiber bundles and then into bundle boards made of polypropylene, onto which the bundles were arranged linearly, the boards were immersed in alkali (NaOH) aqueous solution (2%) for 1h, then neutralized with acetic acid (1%) for 20min, and finally rinsed with distilled water to pH = 7, all the treatments were done at room temperature.

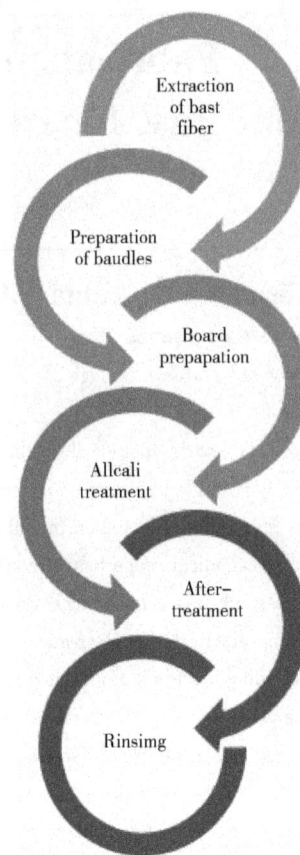

Fig. 1　Process flow for the preparation of AV bast fibers

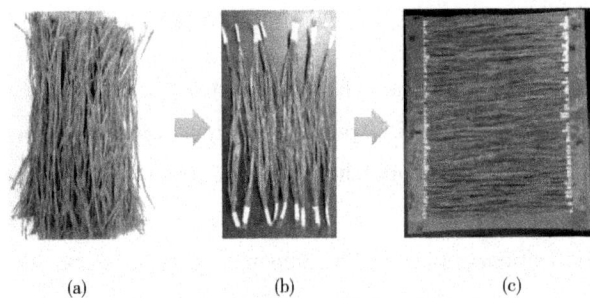

(a)　　　　　　(b)　　　　　　(c)

Fig. 2　(a) AV bast fibers; (b)Fiber bundles; (c) Bundle board

2.3 Preparation of reinforcement material

The reinforcement material was unidirectional AV bast fiber mat, which was prepared by using hand loom. The fiber bundles had been used as a weft and polyester yarns were used as warp during weaving process, the weft insertion into the weaving shed was done by hand and the selection of weaving pattern was plain weave. As the bast fiber bundles were thick enough, it was made sure that the beat-up motion by loom reed had been properly done to get the desired compactness.

2.4　Preparation of PLA laminations

For the preparation of PLA laminations hot press compression molding machine was used, PLA pallets were heated to make the flat and thin laminations under the maintained pressure and temperature of 3MPa and 180℃ for 3min, respectively. The weight age of PLA sheets in composites was set according to the percentage of matrix in composites during fabrication.

2.5　Composite fabrication

The PLA laminations were cut and set into a 5mm thick square steel mold layer-by-layer with AV bast fibers, which were in the form of unidirectional AV bast fiber mats. The stacking sequence of materials for composites fabrication was set like PLA – AV – PLA – AV – PLA, shown in Fig. 3. In such a way the two AV bast fiber mats were sandwiched between several PLA lamination layers to cover the fibers from the top, middle and the bottom adequately.

Fig. 3　Stacking sequence of AV/PLA composites

The whole system was put into the hot press compression molding machine to fabricate the composites at the pressure and temperature of 3MPa and 180℃ for 3min, respectively. The process was done twice at the same time. The composites were designed to cover the most area of fibers to be interacted with matrix so that the maximum force of adhesion and penetration during hot pressing can be occurred. And the weight distribution of composite panels was set accordingly, shown in Fig. 4.

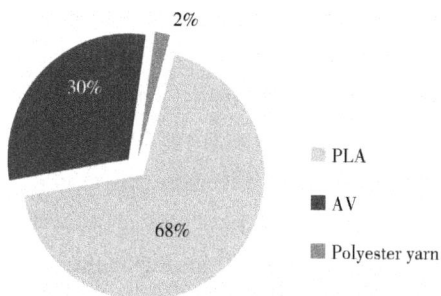

Fig. 4　Weight distributions of composite panels

3　Testing and Analysis

3.1　The tensile strength test

The samples were cut in the length of 100mm and having 10mm width and conditioned under lab standard environment for 24h, then set to the standard parameters according to the ASTM 3039 method[10], the composite samples were prepared by adhering an 25mm aluminum tabs at the end of top and bottom each side to avoid the gripping damage. The samples of each group were tested on INSTRON 4302 machine. The sample was clamped in the jaws of machine and allowed to stretch at a constant speed of 2mm/min, while the gauge length was set to 50mm.

Fig. 5　Samples for tensile and bending test

3.2　The bending strength test

The bending test was done using ASTM D790 standard[11] on the same INSTRON 4302 machine for the bending test the sample was prepared like in tensile test, the equipment was changed to hold the samples along horizontal so that the force can be applied over sample in the middle.

3.3　SEM analysis

The SEM analysis was done using "HITACHI TM3000" table microscope to analyze the fiber matrix interface of the AV/PLA composites, the micrographs of composites were taken after break. The samples of both groups including untreated and treated bast fiber reinforced PLA composites were cut accordingly and fixed with the equipment followed by gold spray over the samples. The magnification used for micrographs was X50.

4　Results and Discussion

4.1　The tensile strength of AV/PLA composites

The graph obtained from different groups tested for the

tensile strength showed in Fig. 6, reflected that the untreated fibers used in composites for reinforcement had tensile strength of 80.25MPa. However, the treated fibers reinforced composites have shown 103.67MPa strength. The improvement intensile strength of composites was because of improved strength of bast fibers after alkaline treatment and their unidirectional arrangement in composites.

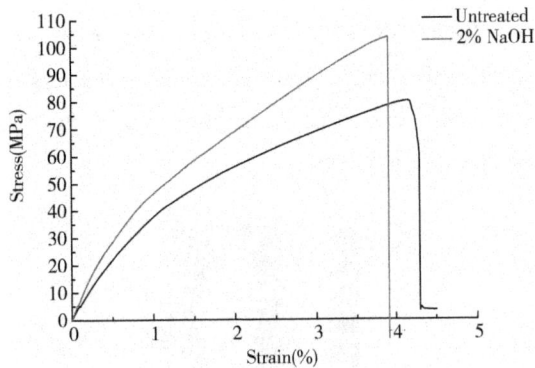

Fig. 6　Typical graphs for the tensile strength of untreated and treated AV fibers reinforced PLA composites

4.2　The bending strength of AV/PLA composites

The untreated one had shown the strength of 86.38MPa while treated one had shown 195.02MPa bending strength. The point of failure of composites reinforced with treated fiber was higher than the untreated reinforced one, shown in Fig. 7. The improvement in bending strength of composites after reinforcing treated AV bast fibers ensured good fiber - matrix adhesion.

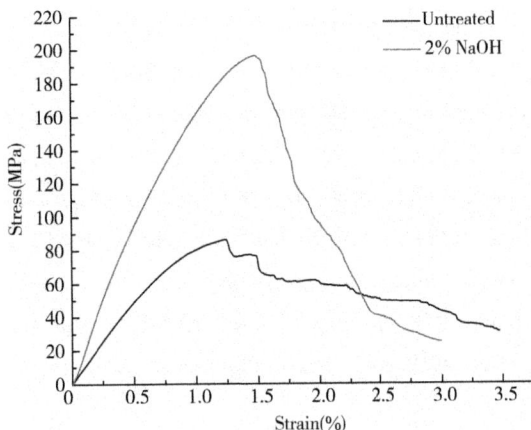

Fig. 7　Typical graphs for the bending strength of untreated and treated AV fibers reinforced PLA composites

4.3　Characterization of AV/PLA composites

Fig. 8 showed that the PLA matrix had been interacted with the AV bast fibers during melting at a constant higher temperature in molding machine and had flowed into the cavities of bast fibers through the openings in bast fiber mats under the applied pressure with respect to time.

Fig. 8　SEM micrographs of (a) untreated AV bast fibers reinforced PLA composite; (b) treated AV bast fibers reinforced PLA composite

5　Conclusions

This study has been done using the AV plant, by which the bast fiber was peeled off from the stems and branches of plant after boiling, and then treated with alkali to prepare the reinforcement material for the PLA composites, the two groups including untreated and treated bast fibers were used to prepare the unidirectional AV bast fiber mat by using hand loom and fabricated with PLA laminations in such sequence so that the bast fibers can be embedded properly with PLA matrix. Fabrication was done in a hot press compression molding machine under optimized pressure, temperature and time in a steel mold to get the composite panels. The samples were prepared for tensile, bending and SEM analysis, in which the alkali treated ones have showed the significant improvement in their mechanical properties (tensile and bending). The improved results reflect the increased use of natural resources for the development of natural fiber reinforced biodegradable composites. However, further research is also required.

References

[1] Pickering K L, Efendy M G A, et al. A review of recent developments in natural fibre composites and their mechanical performance [J]. Composites Part A: Applied Science and Manufacturing, 2016. 83: 98-112.

[2] Pickering K L, Beckermann G W, et al. Optimising industrial hemp fibre for composites [J]. Composites Part A: Applied Science and Manufacturing, 2007. 38(2): 461-468.

[3] Preet Singh JI, Dhawan V, et al. Study of effect of surface treatment on mechanical properties of natural fiber reinforced composites [J]. Materials Today: Proceedings, 2017. 4(2, Part A): 2793-2799.

[4] Sullins T, Pillay S, et al. Hemp fiber reinforced polypropylene composites: The effects of material treatments [J]. Composites Part B: Engineering, 2017. 114: 15-22.

[5] Edeerozey A M M, Akil H M, et al. Chemical modification of kenaf fibers [J]. Material Letters, 2007, 61: 2023-2025.

[6] Kabir M M, Wang H, et al. Tensile properties of chemically treated hemp fibres as reinforcement for composites [J]. Composites Part B: Engineering, 2013. 53: 362-368.

[7] Hossain M K, Dewan M W, et al. Mechanical performances of surface modified jute fiber reinforced biopol nanophased green composites [J]. Composites Part B: Engineering, 2011. 42(6): 1701-1707.

[8] Han G, Wang L, et al. Component analysis and microfiber arrangement of apocynum venetum fibers: The MS and AFM study [J]. Carbohydrate Polymers, 2008. 72(4): 652-656.

[9] Wang L, Han G, et al. Comparative study of composition, structure and properties of apocynum venetum fibers under different pretreatments [J]. Carbohydrate Polymers, 2007. 69(2): 391-397.

[10] ASTM, D 3039/D 3039M - 00, Standard test method for tensile properties of polymer matrix composite materials [S]. 2002.

[11] ASTM, D 790 - 03, Standard test methods for flexural properties of unreinforced and reinforced plastics and electrical insulating materials [S]. 2002.

Intelligent Plantar Pressure Monitoring Insole Based on 3D Printing and Flexi Force Sensor Technology

Min Gao[1,2], Yifan Zhang[1,2,3]*, Chengyu Hong[4], Xiuli Gao[5]

[1] *College of Textiles, Donghua University, Shanghai 201620, China*

[2] *Engineering Research Center of Technical Textiles, Ministry of Education, Shanghai 201620, China*

[3] *School of Textiles, Zhongyuan University of Technology, Zhengzhou 450007, China*

[4] *Department of Civil Engineering, Shanghai University, Shanghai 200444, China*

[5] *School of Textiles , Henan University of Engineering, Zhengzhou 450007, China*

* *Corresponding author's email*: zhangyifan@ dhu. edu. cn

Abstract: Using 3D printing and Flexi force sensor technology to measure the foot pressure of the body under different movement conditions, the plantar pressure distribution was mainly measured at the thumb, the first metatarsal, the fifth metatarsal and the heel. The results showed that the plantar pressure under different exercise conditions will change significantly. Thumb was first contact ground during running, followed by the forefoot and the heel, and the heel pressure is always the largest. During the upstairs and downstairs, the plantar pressure distribution will change with the movement of the gravity. When the person goes upstairs, the center of gravity moves forward. The pressure on the plantar forefoot is a bit more pressure than going downstairs, but the heel pressure increases dramatically when he goes downstairs, which explained people center of gravity is moving backwards during the downstairs.

Keywords: 3D printing; Flexi force sensor; First metatarsal; Fifth metatarsal

1 Introduction

Flexi force sensors have been widely used as an effective method for health monitoring. Flexi force offers a number of advantages such as super thin, highly Flexible, and almost able to measure the pressure between all plane contact surfaces comparing traditional sensors[1]. Flexi force sensors has been applied in telemedical and a large number of monitoring system. Timely and accurate data from these Flexi force sensors provide reasonable performance assessment, so that medical staff can adopt immediate and effective measures to deal with potential safety issues.

3D printing technique is becoming more and more popular among engineering communities particularly for the design and fabrication of novel structural components in recent years[2-3]. 3D printing is mostly realized by fused deposition modeling (FDM) method. Main advantages such as mass customization, rapid manufacturing, low production cost, great precision and rapid prototyping enable 3D printing technique wide scientific and industrial applications[4-5]. Insole pressure measurement systems have been have widely used in clinical and research environments, and many studies based assessment system. An insole focused on plantar pressure measurements in healthy and hemiparetic adults or in healthy children[6-8]. The F-Scan mobile system (Tekscan, Inc, Boston, USA) is one of the most commonly used in-sole pressure measurement system for gait analysis. Several studies have evaluated the accuracy and reliability of force and pressure measurements using the F-Scan© system and reached different conclusions. Pedar mobile system is a relatively new product among the insole pressure measuring devices. Although these devices have contributed to the basic analysis of human gait, some limitations have been noted from a therapeutic viewpiont. In particular, they are not designed for daily, real-time, and feedback use in therapy-directed research[8-9].

The sensors used for plantar pressure measurement mainly include polyvinylidene fluoride (PVDF) piezoelectric film type plantar pressure sensors. Due to the presence of electrical resistance, they are very susceptible to temperature and humidity. After many times of pressing, there will be a response delay, and the linearity will be degraded, which will result in a large test error. This paper selects 3D printing and Flexi force pressure sensors to improve the sensitivity, accuracy and hysteresis of the sensor. By collecting and analyzing the plantar pressure of the testers, the foot pressure distribution concentration and the plantar pressure distribution characteristics under the exercise state are fully reflected.

2 Sensors for Monitoring Plantar Pressure

2.1 Sensing principle of Flexi force sensors

Different types of pressure sensors; such as strain gage, piezoelectric force sensor, optical force sensors and FSR are available. Strain gage are used in robotic applications. Piezoelectric sensors are used in dynamic forces[10]. Optical sensors are used to measure intensity of light. The Flexi force sensors are used in this scheme for measurement of the foot pressure. It made up of two layers of substrate (polyester/polyimide) film. On each layer, a conductive material (silver) is applied, followed by a layer of pressure-sensitive link[11].

Flexi force sensor act as force sensing resister in an electrical circuit. Sensor in the circuit diagram is shown in Fig. 1. When the force sensor is unloaded, its resistance is very high (around 5 mega ohm) and when a force is applied to the sensor, its resistance decreases with respect to applied force. This sensor can be used to measure force above 100 lbs by applying driving voltage and reducing feedback resistance. Sensitivity of sensor can be changed according to requirement of the system[12].

When the sensing area is under pressure, the lines that

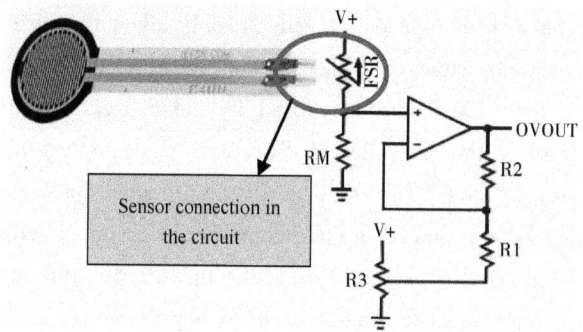

Fig. 1　Sensors and circuit diagrams

are disconnected from each other at the bottom layer will conduct through the top layer's pressure sensitive layer, and the resistance output of the port will change with pressure.

$$R = \rho \frac{L}{S} \tag{1}$$

ρ——resistivity, $(\Omega \cdot mm^2)/m$;

L——the length of the wire, m;

S——cross-sectional area of the wire, mm^2.

Because the resistivity and the length of the wire do not change under normal circumstances, the resistance of the sensor and the weight being tested are in the form of a power function and the reciprocal of the resistance of the sensor is proportional to the weight being tested. Therefore, we can use the weight of the pre-known weight loaded on the sensor and measure the resistance of the sensor to obtain a constant for calibration.

2.2 Fabrication of Flexi force sensors using 3D

A polylactic acid (PLA) flexible printing material is selected. Compared to other materials, polylactic acid is soft and bendable. It is placed in the insole without affecting the normal distribution of the plantar pressure, and the shape and size can be adjusted at any time. The 3D printer adopts a FDM (Fused Deposition Modeling) molding technology with a printing accuracy of 100 μm and a print volume of 410 cubic inches. Under the control of the computer, the printer outlines the model based on the 3D modeling software. The print head of the printer selectively applies the material to the work table and waits for rapid cooling to form a layer of cross section until the print job is completed.

Due to the use of a flexible 3D printing material, since

the flexible material can generate a synchronous deformation with the sensor, it will not only affect the detection performance of the sensor, but also protect the sensor from the distortion caused by the distortion. This improves the accuracy of the sensor and protects the sensor. The CATIA software is used to model the sensor model. A 1 mm or so cofferdam is built up on the edge of the sensor, on the basis of the measured round sensor, and a slot for entering and exiting the sensor is reserved at the bottom of the sensor to facilitate a more stable coupling with the sensor, and we call this piece the bottom of the sensor. Fig. 2 shows 3D printing and sensors design.

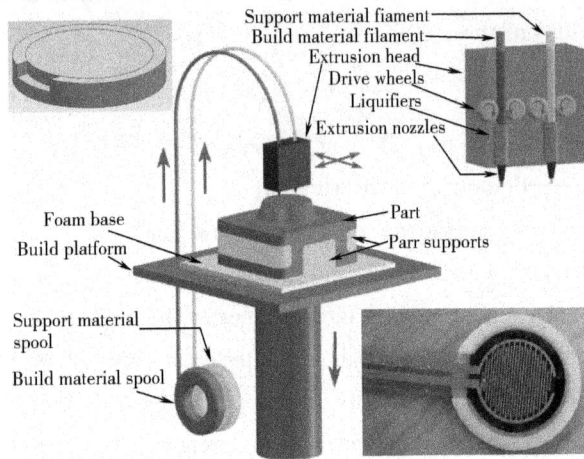

Fig. 2　3D printing and sensors design

2.3　Calibration test

Calibration test was carried out in an isolated laboratory at room temperature to validate the performance of a single Flexi force sensors based pressure sensor for pressure measurement. A calibration device electronic strength tester (No: HD026G with a measurement accuracy of 1 N) was used for the application of vertical load. In calibration test, the Flexi force sensors based pressure sensor was placed between two loading plates for pressure measurement.

By changing the loading force, the sensor is calibrated, adding 1kg at a time, using Origin to fit the data, first select the formula to be fitted, because we know in advance that the two are inversely proportional, so choose $y = a \times x^{\wedge} b$. The form of x performs a least-squares curve fit on the data. The least squares method can conveniently calculate the unknown fitting parameters and make the fitted data and the actual data produce the sum of the squares of the minimum errors. The Fig. 3 shows the images displayed after fitting.

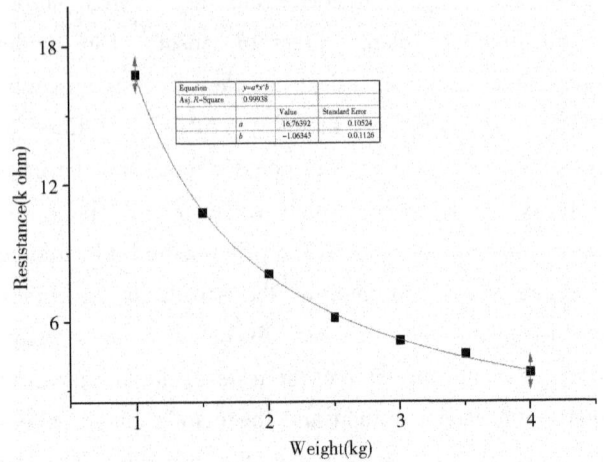

Fig. 3　Sensor fitting curve

From this figure it can be concluded that the fitting function between resistance and weight is $y = 16.76\ x^{\wedge}(-1.06)$, R-Square $= 0.99938$. Among them, R-Square, also called COD determination coefficient, the closer the coefficient is to 1, the better the correlation of the curve. The following formula is known.

$$TSS = \sum_{i=1}^{n} (y_i - \bar{y})^2 \tag{2}$$

$$SSreg = \sum_{i=1}^{n} (\hat{y}_i - \bar{y})^2 \tag{3}$$

$$RSS = \sum_{i=1}^{n} (y_i - \hat{y}_i)^2 \tag{4}$$

$$R^2 = \frac{SSreg}{TSS} = 1 - \frac{RSS}{TSS} \tag{5}$$

Where: R^2——The coefficient of determination;
　　　SSreg——Sum of squares for regression;
　　　RSS——Sum of squares for error;
　　　TSS——Total sum of squares.

The coefficient of determination here is 0.99938, which shows that the curve fits well. Then in later experiments it was decided to use this parameter to invert the pressure value.

3　Plantar Pressure Measurement

3.1　Smart insole design

In the process of the human body, the heel and forefoot

are the main body full weight. Therefore, the thumb, the first metatarsal, the fifth metatarsal and the heel are selected as measurement points in this test. The physical map of the insole is shown in Fig. 4 (a). The position of the sensor can be adjusted according to the size of the foot code to ensure the accuracy of the measurement. During the measurement process, the sensor and the collection box are connected. Fig. 4 (b) shows the smart insole in shoes. The data collected by the collection box is displayed on the computer interface through Microsoft C# programming. Fig. 4 (c) shows the display of the computer interface.

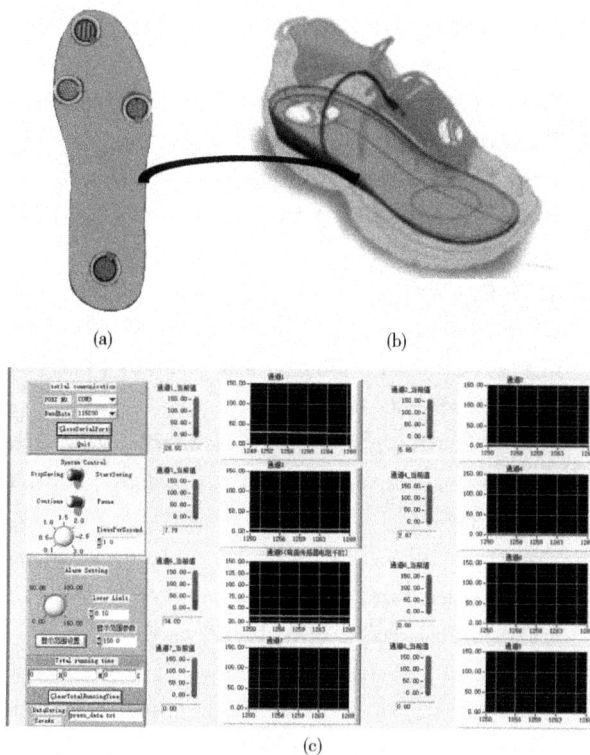

(a)   (b)

(c)

Fig. 4 Smart shoe and acquisition interface

3.2 Experimental procedures

In order to measure the measurement effect of the pressure insole, ten volunteers with a foot size of 37 yards (235 mm) were subjected to foot pressure measurement in 10 patients with no foot disease and hallux valgus. The measurement was at the thumb, the first metatarsal, the fifth metatarsal and heel. Ten volunteers have BMI values ranging from 18 to 25.

The subjects put on the shoes with pressure insole and kept the movement state. At the same time, the data

acquisition button of the computer interface was turned on to obtain the pressure data measured by the sensors of the soles. The height, weight and exercise habits of each person were different, and the measured data existed significant differences. The plantar pressure distribution at the measuring point during running is shown in Fig. 5.

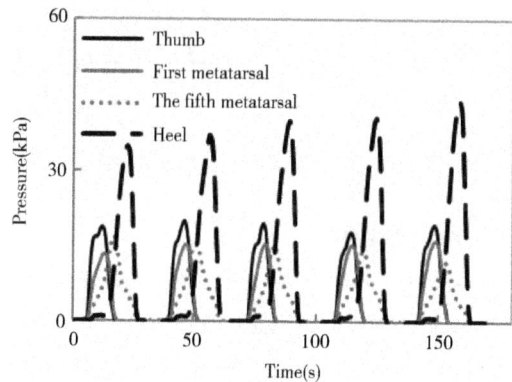

Fig. 5 Plantar pressure distribution

3.3 Data analysis and discussions

From Fig. 5, the fifth metatarsal can reach the pressure peak first, which indicate the toe first touches the ground, and the heel finally touches the ground during the walking process. The entire pressure data shows that the pressure at the heel remains the maximum data, but with the running the plantar pressure at the measurement point has an upward trend. At the same time, as the speed increases, there is no significant change in the time the front foot touches the ground, but the back heel is the latest contact with the ground, and the pressure value is still. The largest of all measuring points shows that the contact between the human body and the ground will produce an impact momentarily, resulting in an increase in the pressure value.

It can be seen from Fig. 6 that the contact time between the foot and the ground is different in the state of movement. When going upstairs and going downstairs, the thumb firstly comes into contact with the ground, then the front foot sole, finally the heel. Compared with the time when going downstairs, due to the forward shift of the center of gravity, the plantar pressure of the forefoot is relatively large, but the pressure at the heel increase sharply. This indicates that there is a tendency of backward movement of the body's center of gravity during the   downstairs.

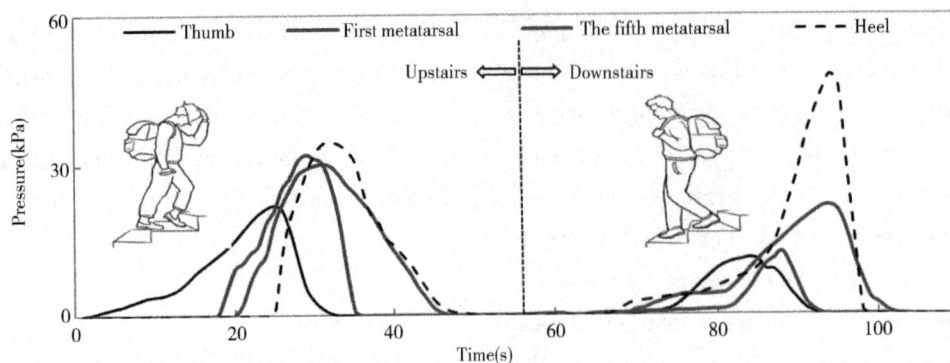

Fig. 6　Plantar pressure distribution upstairs and downstairs

4　Conclusions

This paper describes the use of 3D printing and Flexi force sensors for the human body in the running state and simulation of plantar pressure distribution in the upstairs, the main conclusions are: walking state, upstairs and downstairs, the contact is not synchronized. The thumb is first contact with the ground, and the heel follows.

In the process of going upstairs, the person of gravity moves forward, and the pressure in the forefoot is relatively large, almost equal to the pressure in the heel; the weight of the person in the process of going downstairs concentrates on the heel, so the heel pressure increases significantly. During the entire test, the heel pressure has been the largest, indicating that the heel is the main load-bearing part of the body during movement.

References

[1] Fang L, Chen T, Li R, et al. Application of embedded fiber bragg grating (FBG) sensors in monitoring health to 3D printing structures [J]. IEEE Sensors Journal, 2016, 16 (17): 6604-6610.

[2] Grimmel Sann N, Meissner H, Ehrmann A. 3D printed auxetic forms on knitted fabrics for adjustable permeability and mechanical properties [J]. IOP Science, 2016, 137 (1): 012011.

[3] Zhang Y F, Hong C Y, Rafique A, et al. A fiber Bragg grating based sensing platform fabricated by fused deposition modeling process for plantar pressure measurement [J]. Measurement, 2017, 112.

[4] Llacouras P C, Grant G T, Choudhry K, et al. Fiber bragg gratings embedded in 3D-printed scaffolds [J]. Ncsli Measure, 2015, 10(2): 50-52.

[5] Hong C Y, Zhang Y F, Zhang M X, et al. Application of FBG sensors for geotechnical health monitoring, a review of sensor design, implementation methods and packaging techniques [J]. Sensors and Actuators A: Physical, 2016, 244: 184-197.

[6] Naemi R, Chevalier T L, Healy A, et al. The effect of the use of a walkway and the choice of the foot on plantar pressure assessment when using pressure platforms [J]. Foot, 2012, 22(2): 100-104.

[7] Pa D, T L, B V, et al. Plantar pressure relief using a forefoot offloading shoe [J]. Foot and Ankle Surgery, 2010, 16 (4): 178-182.

[8] Zhao J, Guo Y, Wang L. An insole plantar pressure measurement system based on 3D forces piezoelectric sensor [J]. Sensors & Transducers, 2013, 160(12): 49-54.

[9] Hurkmans H L, Bussmann J B, Benda E, et al. Accuracy and repeatability of the Pedar Mobile system in long-term vertical force measurements [J]. Gait & Posture, 2006, 23 (1): 118-125.

[10] Chang C C, Lee M Y, Wang S H. Customized foot pressure redistribution insole design using image-based rapid pressure measuring system[C]. Proceedings of the IEEE International Conference on Systems, Man and Cybernetics, F, 2008.

[11] Zhu H, Maalei N, Webster J G, et al. An umbilical data-acquisition system for measuring pressures between the foot and shoe [J]. Biomedical Engineering IEEE Transactions on, 1990, 37(9): 908-911.

[12] Yurish S Y. Development of planter foot pressure distribution system using flexi force sensors [J]. Sensors & Transducers Journal.

Man's Web-Tailor-Making Shirt Demand Appeal to Integrated Technology and Business Solution

Xu Ming[1]*, **Syed Ahtsham Ali**[1], **Muhammad Ali**[1], **Hafiz M. Ilyas**[1], **Li Xiaolin**[1], **Yingfeng Zhou**[1]

[1]*Glorious Sun Institute of Management, Donghua University, Shanghai 200051, China*

* *Corresponding author's email*: xuming@ dhu. edu. cn

Abstract: Based on the analyses of increasing trend of web-tailor-making-shirt inglobal markets, this article has analyzed one of the key technologies in the modern apparel industry that is "man's body measurement technologies" although existing in firms but need to be re-innovated through integration. First, this article has offered results of marketing survey of web-tailor-making-shirt price range and delivery time and measurement technology used, which covers 11 web tailor making firms in China and 15 international suppliers. Second, body measurement technology patents suitable for web tailor making shirts have been dig in China Patent Bank, and a technique and operation transition analysis for a traditional apparel manufacturing (V 1.0) to web tailor making (V 2.0) has been offered. Third, based on web tailor supply price difference and China's capabilities of apparel manufacturing and logistics operation and some African Nation's linguistic convenience to the European market, a joint venture solution, with the sense of V 3.0 targeted with overseas market, for China and Africa firms to develop web-tailor-making-shirt business has been suggested out.

Keywords: Man's web-tailor-making-shirt; Body measurement technology; AI; Apparel firm transition; China-Africa cooperation

1 Introduction

From the last couple of decades, the living standard in a community has been increased and consumers have increasing interests to have some of their apparel be tailor making for more fitting. There are several reasons for this including the fact that tailor-made dress shirts really allow them to express their true identity and wear something that fits their body perfectly. According to recent reports, some experts estimate that tailor making apparel requirements in China is approximately RMB 5.3 billion (2015) while in 2018 the international market is about USD 10 billion[1]. Man's shirt sector is one of tailor making apparel industries, which is relatively easier for normal traditional manufacturing firms to transit in. As those firm usually faced great pressure in inventory and e-commerce shock[2].

2 Man's Web Shirt Market in China

The Man's shirts tailor making is anewly emerged segment in the apparel industry, which has developed with suit tailor-made and greatly become as an independent sector, because of shirts' styles are relatively easy to be standardization. In China, Shanghai and other main city people are still having the memory of PPG's efforts inshirts web retailing, which had some venture capital support and once was regarded as number one largest shirts supplier in 2006[3]. After PPG's story, there have been booming in web retailing for apparel, main web platforms to sell shirts are as shown in above Tab. 1. All these e-commerce sites sell shirts, but shirts tailoring suppliers are mostly concentrated on Tmall. com (Chinese largest web retailing platform), and the main suppliers and their characteristics of customized shirts have been collected for the year of 2014 survey, shown in below Tab. 2. Four points can be analyzed from Tab. 2.

(1) Price analysis: The price of Jieshimai is the lowest 99 – 149 RMB (\$16 – 24) per piece. This company targets the low-end market segment, focuses on the group of a college student and provides customized shirts for their job interviews. Whereas, Longqingxiang charged the highest price, as high as 6688 RMB (\$1096) per piece. And the other two suppliers, Ushan Bespoke and Saint Angelo, also offer the price over 2,000 RMB (\$328) per piece. More specifically, Ushan Bespoke has a larger price range, while Saint Angelo only focuses on the high-end market of the price above 1500RMB (\$246) per piece.

(2) Delivery time analysis: We can see from Tab. 2 that the shortest time is 7 days, and the longest is 15 days. There are 7 suppliers whose delivery time is over 10 days. The logistic time in China is usually about 2 or 3 days, so we know that the time spent on the production process is 7 or 8 days. And the suppliers targeting the high-end market may need 2 weeks for their delivery time.

Tab. 1　The main web platform to sell shirts in China

Taobao	Tmall	Jingdong	Weipinhui	Yihaodian	Maikaolin	Vancl
taobao. com	tmall. com	jd. com	vip. com	yhd. com	m18. com	vancl. com

Tab. 2　The main suppliers and their characteristics of customized shirts in tmall. com

Sr. #	Supplier	Price (¥/\$)	Delivery time (day)	Ordering process			Detailed body measurement guide
				Self-service	Online real-time service	One-on-one	
1	IWODE	198–998/32–163	14	—	√	—	√
2	I. D. S	158–398/26–65	7–10	—	√	—	√
3	Mono Formal	219–299/36–49	7	√	—	—	√
4	LONQN	298–788/48–128	15	—	√	—	√
5	Baaler	295–336/48–55	7–10	—	√	—	√
6	Ushan Bespoke	598–2698/97–440	10–14	—	√	—	√
7	Jieshimai	99–149/16–24	7	—	√	—	—
8	Longqing xiang	588–6688/96–1091	—	—	√	—	—
9	Yuanxiang	200–278/32–45	14	—	—	√	√
10	Saint Angelo	1580–2280/258–372	14	—	—	√	—
11	Collectrouge	349/57	7	—	—	√	—

(3) Analysis of customization process service: There is only one supplier, MONO FORMAL, of all the 11 shirts customization suppliers, that can totally let customers complete the ordering process by web computer system with no need of supplier's web real-time customer service, a kind of AI tech. And seven suppliers of them guide customers to measure and order online, which obviously needs to input more human resource, but it helps to place orders and improves the quality of ordering and customer satisfaction. And the remaining three suppliers offered the higher form of service, that is, sending staff to customers' place or invite them to the local store to measure the size, which costs more and requests more in hardware (e. g. store arrangement).

(4) Analysis of online measurement guidance service: Among all the 11 shirts web tailoring suppliers, six suppliers provide online measuring software with the form of

pictures and videos. Especially, what MONO FORMAL offers is the most user-friendly of all the suppliers. What's more, it can reduce human resource input, and it may indicate the direction of development in the future and play an important role especially in cross-region (country) business.

3 Lack of Professional Suppliers with Suitable Tech in this Field

In order to get the knowledge of this relatively new apparel industry's development situation, we have made an investigation in the web-tailor-making-shirt field in recent May 2018 and get some understandings in following.

Tab. 3 Supplier Information with a price range and delivery time (2018)

Supplier	Price range ($)	Average price ($)	Delivery time (days)
Italo Ferretti	1495–1195	1345	14
Indochino	$ 129– $ 79	104	21
Black Lapel	$ 179– $ 99	139	21
Modern Tailor	$ 79– $ 59	69	28
Dolce & Gabbana	$ 503. 99– $ 99. 99	301. 99	10
j. ver	$ 8– $ 20	14	7
Ralph Lauren	$ 799– $ 24	411. 5	not given
Thomas Pink	$ 250– $ 130	190	10
T. M. Lewin	$ 175– $ 34	104. 5	14
Charles Tyrwhitt	$ 129– $ 29	79	7
j. Crew	$ 189– $ 99	144	14
Ledbury	$ 165– $ 59	112	7
Mizzen + Main	$ 145– $ 69	107	7
Club Monaco	$ 130– $ 80	105	7
Brooks Brothers	$ 348– $ 69. 5	208. 75	10

There are about 10 network platforms for web-tailor-making-shirt suppliers in China, among which Tmall. com is the main representative. But when you really want to find some suitable network to make an order, you may get confused to choose a proper supplier, plenty of ready making products are full of screens.

There is still lack of suitable body measurement tools in web situation to guide customer easily to get precise data to put into supplier's customer system. We have found that a newly developed web-tailor-making-shirt supplier, MatchU, web name as iammatchu. com, is a good solution in this field. It has got two runs of venture investments, which is developed by a group of Shanghai Jiao Tong University Alumni. The price scope is from RMB 200–700. This is a kind of semi web body measurement way, which could be improved further. This

company announced that during their first-year operation, there are about 13000 customer's body size data, and they also claim that they have the access to the big body database of 40 million, with this support they have not made any unfitted products to their customers.

4 Technology Needs and Requirements

In tailor making apparel field, human body measurement technology is really important for the supplier who wants to offer individualized service, so a lot of experts have been involved to develop suitable technologies. We had searched Chinese Patent Web Site for body measurement technology in 2014 and founded that there were about 31 technique patents appeared in China Patent Administration Bureau Web Site, among them there were four patents from Donghua University. Unfortunately, when we visited some tailor making apparel firms, such as Red Collar, which is the most powerful suit tailor making firm in China, got the information that those firms are still faced achallenge to develop suitable tech to serve for their customized tailor making needs. Most of the technique patents are just keeping silent on the patent web site.

Concerning the manufacturing operation in apparel firms, we have made an analysis, and develop a comparison requirement table for traditional apparel manufacturing (V 1. 0) to the tailor making apparel firms (V 2. 0) which are mainly for the domestic market in Tab. 4 above.

Tab. 4 Comparison of two models with the new requirements of flexible production line of new model (web tailoring supply)

Features	Traditional model	New model	New requirements
Fabric purchasing	Large quantity	Small quantity	Need to set up a quick response system with suppliers to offer asmall quantity of fabrics
Warehouse management	Large quantity stacking	Small piece put on shelves	Need more capable precisely computer management software
Production line material supply	Large bulk arriving	Small piece	Need special turnover plate or cart, need more workers for material supply to individual working positions
Design	Designing first	Getting customer needs first, then making design	Need to have acomputer-based designing bank, which can support fast design process and provide technical instructions quickly
Cutting	Large quantity, use paper pattern	Automatic tailor cutting machine	Need to equip such newfacility and training operators
Sewing	Flow line production	Circle line production	—
Buttoning	Same in large quantity	Small quantity in deferent items	Precise supply to special worker position just in time
Finishing and packaging	Line packaging, few categories, and standard pieces for apackage	Single or small quantity may need to put accessories	Special printing or embroidery machines and materials needed for the individualized offering.
Quality management	Sampling inspection	Self-inspection	Need to indicate the specifications on working position, RFID attached chips
Transportation	Package boxes with few destinations	Single piece or small quantity	—
Worker training	Single working position	Multiple working positions	—
Production line management	Focused on shift and quantity	Focused on production team and quality	More attention to conformance to requirements

5 Transition from Version 2. 0 to Version 3. 0

We have gone through the survey conducted in the year 2014 and make a comparison with the year 2018. Zang for contrast, from Tab. 3, we know that international suppliers' average price is about $115, in which extremely high and low price are also removed. Obviously, Chinese price is about half of international ones, so even with added each shirt with $ 20 logistic cost and more delivery time 3–4 days, we still could develop following thinking in a viable way.

From our survey, we know that there are some existing web tailor making suppliers in China as V 1.0, which is mainly for domestic markets, as there are price margins, explore oversea high-end markets could be an opportunity.

As there are existing many good suppliers for domestic markets as mentioned above as V 2.0, we have a good chance to transit from V 2.0 to V 3.0, which means mainly for international markets, say in Europa and North America.

Real solution could be like following:

There is need powerful entrepreneur innovative efforts to develop a systematic integrated solution which composed of a semi web-tailor-making-shirt body measurement easy use tooling (similar to MatchU, not waiting for getting advanced technology, first need to have a market supply solution), an AI-customer database treatment system, which needs to be developed further, some well-talented shirt manufacturing firms, which could be found in China's east coast area, and a dedicated innovative team, which is the key.

For such circumstance, Donghua University has some advantage to promote this solution specifically under the background of two first classes construction initiative from China central educational administration.

As the geographic and linguistic advantages in Africa (some nation has official language same as European nation), we may think about to build a supply chain targeted in European markets, first produce web-tailor-making-shirt in China, marketing and customer service jointly offered in China and Africa, fully to make use of linguistic and logistic advantages in Ethiopia and Kenia. Next step we need to looking forward to transferring more functions in the supply chain to Africa.

References

[1] Zhiyan Consulting Group. Prediction to tailor making apparel market from 2016–2022, 2016.

[2] Zhao Y. (2017). Model innovation of cotte: Data driven clothing mass customization, 285(1): 26–30.

[3] Zhang X, Zhang S, Liu C. Red collar group: Leading in internet + apparel tailor making. Economic Daily. 2015.

Overview About the Co-Branding Development of Fashion Brands

Ziwei Ye[1]*

[1]*Donghua University, Shanghai 20051, China*

* *Corresponding author's email*: yeziweiziv@ foxmail. com

Abstract: Under the influence of the trend of world economic integration, the world economy, trade and commercialization are developing rapidly. Brand management is becoming more and more popular and valued in the era of enterprise brand. And brand includes all, in the whole process of sales and service, tangible or intangible benefits are part of the brand influence. The brand image of an enterprise represents the industry advantage of clothing brand in the minds of consumers, and it is an important strategic resource for enterprises to stand in the industry. Now the business gradually began to join the new ways of cooperation in brand building, new operating mode, based on the importance of the brand and universality of the two important under the present conditions. Many clothing brands also have similar intention that is to establish a joint venture or cooperation partners to form the brand, for the two sides to achieve win-win future. Brand alliance has become the focus of competition among enterprises, and it has strategic significance for business owners. The paper sums up the business cases of existing brand alliances and makes hypothesis tests to find the logical essence behind the business and provides some guidance for the joint branding of garment enterprises.

Keywords: Brand combination; Consumer demand; Clothing brand; Enterprise interests

1 Introduction

1.1 Research background

With the development of economic integration, world trade economy is developing rapidly. Brand management is becoming more and more popular and valuable in the enterprise brand. And brand includes all. In the process of selling goods and servicing customers, producing tangible or intangible benefits are part of the brand influence. The business brand image represents the industry advantage of fashion brand in the mind of consumers, which is an important strategic resource for enterprises to keep a foothold in the industry.

Now, enterprise operation has gradually begun to add new ways of cooperation and operation in brand construction[1]. Under the two important conditions of brand significance and universality, many garment enterprises form cooperative or joint venture brands with similar intention partners, which provides the possibility for a win-win result. Co-branding is a universal expression of fashion industry companies. The brand has become the key point of competition between enterprises, which is provided with strategic significance for business owners, therefore it more be viewed as a dominant commercial property.

Co-branding has been applied early to commercial combat. In the 1961, the U. S. General Mills and Sunkist companies relied on co-branding causing a new trend in the industry. However, Mc Kinsey consulting company has done a study which found with the development of the world trade economy, the brand's way of operation had become increasingly diverse, and brand alliance was one of them[2].

Many famous international brands such as Nutra Sweet, Microsoft and Intel have achieved some commendable achievements in the industry by co-branding. In recent years, the apparel industry has a large number of joint brands. For example, H&M would be combined with different fashion brands on each season. LOUIS VUITTON launched different series with Kusama Yayoi and Da Vinci, and even was united with the high fashion street brand Supreme to launch a new style. And ADI-DAS created the co-branding Y-3 with Yohji Yamamoto, which still operated with Kanye West for "YEEZY" collections. But there are also some practical experiences in Chinese, such as HLA cooperated with young designer Xander Zhou to producing the new style. On the whole, it still has great development space that for garment enterprises.

1.2　Research purpose and significance

With the development of new media, building brand actively or passively both faced big challenges and opportunities, the old branding development mode has come across the bottleneck. At the same time, with more and more brands grow, how to integrate brand marketing resources, rich and meet consumer needs at different levels has become an important step of brand building. However, co-branding meets the businesses or spiritual needs of businesses and consumers in this direction, starting making great efforts on business[3].

Appropriate and win-win brand alliance can come into each other's market gradually, expanding their market influence.

Each brand has its own loyal consumer groups. When consumers see their cognition within the scope of the brand and other brands to cooperate with each other, the subconscious of another brand acceptance will also increase[4]. Thus, it is easier to graft consumer consciousness onto the new joint brand and build a new consumption bridge with each other through the positive grafting of both sides. At the same time, all the brands have their own good or is said to have unique resource. This personalized and unique resources will become the foundation of enterprise core competitive advantage.

And in the development of marketing, co-branding can be very useful and effective to reduce all brands share economic costs. Costs and risks to share with each other for both economies are greatly benefited.

1.3　Research methods

Using literature research and case analysis, we will analyze and interpret the joint brand.

2　Paper Review and Theoretical Basis

2.1　Concept of co-branding

Co-branding refers to short-term or long-term cooperation between brands of different business companies. On brand characteristics, joint between brands mainly in the product or service business in simple while the use of multiple or common brands, such as Adidas and Yohji Yamamoto combined with commercial brand "Y-3" as a common commercial brand. On brand resources, brand alliance through the use of resources integration, between different brand resources to change the original image or brand cooperation to strengthen the brand, deepens the impression in the minds of consumers.

The concept of co-brand in business is very early. In recent years, with the joint brand has appeared more and more, in order to meet the different needs of consumers, brand alliance cooperation is becoming more and more diversified, such as American singer Rihanna and the famous sports brand PUMA. Rihanna as the designer launched a number of series that let PUMA sales growth for several consecutive quarters. The cooperation between the stars or some fashion influence people and business brand, not only meets the information age characteristics of consumers who want to follow the trend, but also is good to strengthen the brand image features, made success in commercial practice frequently.

2.2　Analysis on the consumer attitudes

Consumer purchasing behavior can be effectively summed up and perceived. In the same way, brand alliances can also predict the consumer behavior effectively by studying consumer attitudes.

Attitude is mainly the expression of human emotions, but consumer attitudes mainly reflect consumer's emotional expression of the market. The emotional response to an objective object or thing is based on the subjective perception of the object.

Consumer attitudes are seen as the first factor affecting consumer buying behavior, and are more pronounced in the three aspects of their purchasing process:

The first process is the consumer's initial brand judgment and evaluation of the goods after contact. In the process, "compliance" is a common attitude of consumers, and social media, public opinion these media tend to play an active guiding role.

The second process is attitude, which influences learning interest and cognitive effects. At this stage, the "identity" is the commercial value of the pursuit of consumer psychology. In the attitude of not stable, consumers are willing to put into their own brand value or effect of learning and cognitive structure.

The third process is the consumer attitude to decide the purchase intention, thus promoting the choice of purchasing behavior. This process is the most critical stage of "assimilation", which affects the consumer contact in the active or passive media, the concept of the brand or product attitude into a part of their own personal value system, the formation of emotion and behavior tendency of commodity market stability.

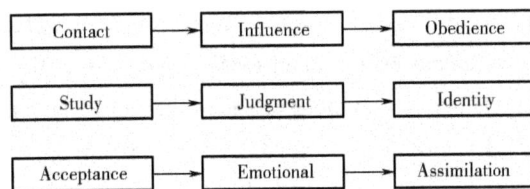

The "shaping" process of consumer attiudes toward behavior

With the value of the brand, the brand is the use of the customer's attitude and behavior preference to bring commercial profit. On the one hand, has the brand preferences have an influence on consumer attitudes. On the other hand, the consumer attitude still represent brand conversely.

3 Case Analysis of Co-Branding

3.1 The state of co-branding

The example of co-branding has appeared in the commercial field long ago. The first appeared in the automobile industry in the United States. Since 1980's, the number of joint brands has gradually increased. Facing the phenomenon of co-branding emerge in an endless stream, the opportunities and challenges are coexisting for brands.

Now, through the observation of existing co-branding business cases at home and abroad, brand alliance still belongs to the developing stage.

In the early stage, it has good market prospects. High social concern and cooperation have not reached the saturation of the market, a certain extent for satisfying consumer more and more critical taste, taking advantage of this complex and multi-tier consumer choice, which's reaction more strongly in the form of commercial performance in each enterprise. The response was very effective.

In the middle stage, co-branding has the strong momentum of development. All enterprises feel satisfied with the economic benefits and have started to try to use a joint approach to brand promotion of new brand. It not only has a breakthrough in the form of cooperation, but also has repeatedly breakthrough in terms of cooperation. However, this process will inevitably lead to the phenomenon of uneven in quality.

In the later stage, the trend in development of co-branding is the way to integrate resource, which will not meet consumer demand as a part of the brand out. Co-branding is the essence of the rational use of resources integration and sharing of internal balance between two brands to seek higher interest, so the co-branding will solve the problem how to keep the uniqueness of face and balance the internal system.

What kind of co-branding is in accord with the development of modern economic society? What kind of impact has a positive co-branding with what kind of impact, and what's the affection between each other? Those are worthy of our serious consideration. The rapid change and growth of brand association in business practice make it very necessary for enterprises to realize the necessary for researching and investigating this problem.

3.2 Classification of co-branding

With the development of business, in order to meet the needs of different consumers, the form and types of brand alliances are changing. This chapter classifies and summarizes the specific types of alliances.

3.2.1 A combination of clothing brands

The clothing brand internal combination makes cooperation between brands with similar characteristics to a certain extent, that's why co-branding known as the good match between the partners, from that partners can maximize the transmission of information and consumers can more easily accept the new co-branding.

The cooperative partner selected by H&M fit in easily with own brand positioning. H&M is located in the civilian consumption level and aimed at those hearts for fashion and luxury demand, but these people often do not have the ability to consume real luxury goods. H&M amplifies consumers' inner desire for obtain luxury, through a variety of cooperation with luxuries to have a robust business. The opportunities of the win-win cooperation can bring fresh consumer groups for both parties, and improve the value of the product itself, attracting more attention and hot spots.

3.2.2 A combination of clothing brands and celebrity individuals

It is often seen that brand invite for celebrity to represent, for celebrity's influence is obvious to everyone. From the Super Star shell head shoe, the Adidas Stan Smith shoes, NMD shoes and Kanye West "Yeezy" series, Adidas constantly created social public opinion which in the commercial market momentum cannot be underestimated.

Different from the traditional way, Kanye West made new way of cooperation with Adidas by being a hiphop's fashion icon. In accordance with the same method of marketing, Rihanna and Puma cooperation is also the new wave of fashion sports style.

Fig. 1 The co-branding by Yayoi Kusama and LV

The artists and the brands are also having a lot of collision sparks, such as LV and have Kusama Yayoi, Mu-

rakami Takashi, COMME des GARCONS and other industries artists had launched many times. The most famous co-branding is Murakami Takashi's "Murakami Multicolore" series, that took LV from the traditional old flower series into the colorful world and created the unbelievable profit in business.

3.2.4 Acombination between rows

We call the garment industry and other industry cooperation as "cross-border cooperation". To become a commercial value of the cross-border cooperation, which requires not only the product of highly involved matching, is in each other between the brand business model or brand market value more or less complementary to each other together[5], the role of growth. For example, the famous Korean cosmetic brand "Innisfree" into the coffee shop in the flagship store, and Starbucks and UNIQLO's cooperation, the domestic well-known brand exception to joint side of the bookstore, the clothing to introduce the concept of culture. Through the development of cross industry, clothing brands penetrate into other industries, extend the brand concept and influence, and stimulate the growth of economic demand.

3.3 Concrete case analysis of co-branding

The concept of co-branding is more and more widely cited in various fields. Brands need to consider not only the commercial value but more the future direction and connotation of the brand. Rihanna and Puma's cooperation is just fit the contemporary young consumer psychology. It may be said as win-win situation.

Net profit growth of 68% and the fixed exchange rate of Puma's business performance on the fourth quarter of steady growth was recorded 10.1% meter growth that changed the fate of being sold off form "kering" to being the brand of leading sport fashion trend in young generation.

Puma has now from "helpless" to "fast", at any time to guide the discussion and trend in a large number of major social media. No matter the financial statements or fashion industry, the role of Rihanna in this changecannot be ignored.

In the incentive of the sports apparel market, Puma is congenitally deficient, the conditions are not good, but in the information age just seize the love of fashion cir-

Fig. 2 PUMA's creeper became "shoes of the year" in the selection of "Footwear News"

cles, selection and Rihanna cooperation, will be on the streets wind movement. Gorgeous and rebellious girl Palace are integrated into their design philosophy, which has become one of the leading brand of fashion brand. The way of cooperation with celebrities, on the one hand will be part of a star's influence absorption into the brands, on the other hand selected representative is the connotation of the brand needs, more in consolidating the brand image and characteristics in the minds of consumers.

The co-branding in garment industry also emerges in an endless stream of clothing brand cross-border cooperation. When we talk about the co-branding, we have to mention the love of high street fashion and big tied fast fashion brand H&M, had a trickle and Versace, Karl Lagerfeld, Lavin Maison, Martin Margiela, Stella Mc Cartney, Alxander Wang, Kenzo launched a number of joint series, which let consumers with a relatively cheap price to enjoy similar luxury series. H&M uses strongly customer psychology of the strength of the general consumer but also for fashion and luxury goods, that known as cross-border cooperation in the industry classic.

While UNIQLO is the cross-border cooperation extended to all walks of life, from Starbucks to app LINE application of new media communication, from the Disney cartoon image to Kusama Yayoi, from luxury brand "LEMAIRE" to street artist Kaws. UNIQLO is able to find the public opinion climax point of cooperation in

every brand and arouse common interest and topic of the millennial generation to cause the hot tide. And recently, Louis Vuitton and Supreme cooperation series released. This is almost regarded as the 2017 most successful cross-border series.

Fig. 3 LV and Supreme combined series

4 Research Conclusions and Outlook

4.1 Conclusions

Whether brand alliances can eventually be accepted by consumers and accepted as a change in confidence depends on consumer attitudes. The brand alliance also plays a role in changing consumers' symbiotic brand of joint brand, and studies the law of brand association from three variables[6].

4.1.1 Co-branding assets

According to the research and study of brand equity brand induction cooperation between reputation, visibility and quality influence on joint cooperation, the concept of these factors are attributed to the partnership owned brand assets.

Before the joint brand, the attitude of consumers to the previous brand often influences the direction of brand alliance. Through the reasonable cable simply pursuit, we can find that from the perspective of consumer attitudes, so as to extract consumer memory and the brand impression. According to this, we can say that the more positive brand cooperation in combination, consumer evaluation on CO branding is more popular.

When goods quality is not easily observed, the brand will be used as an important criterion for judging quality problems. So the brand value is seen as an important part of quality inspection. From this point we can guide consumer attitudes, obtain the trust of consumers. According to this, we can think that cooperation brand reputation is higher and the degree of trust by consumers will be higher.

According to the analysis, we divided brand equity into two parts can be predicted. Thus put forward the different angle assumption from two aspects. Finally summarize the front of the two premise, and we can sum up that the combination of brand cooperation before the brand equity is more strong, the more positive attitude will be.

4.1.2 Matching between brands

Brand matching degree is the degree of matching between cooperative brands, which is divided into two attitudes complementary or similar in consumer perception. More precisely, the two cooperation brands have common similarities or different areas. Each has its own advantages. Use of these similar or complementary, choose together or complement each other, resulting new attractive to consumers. Therefore, the joint brand is only based on good matching and the cooperative brand will be able to give full play to "1 + 1 > 2" subjective initiative[7].

4.1.3 Coverage of collaboration products

The selection and evaluation of visual branding by consumers for brand effect is related to the degree of information processing and modification of absorption. When demand is simple, easy to satisfy, consumers of information processing and easyself-reaction in this process do not need to pay too much understanding of the structure. According to the situation, choosing the strength of the high visibility of the brand which even is lack of branding matching can still get the success. However, when consumers purchase consciousness very tortuous, consumers need to pay a certain degree of analysis in the purchase process. In the process of cognition in selecting ideology which is very complex, uncertain, and modification of the information, the brand provides not only needs to be read by more consumers accept, but also should have a certain uniqueness and certainty to lead consumers to make stable choice. So just choosing a high profile brand won't give you a convincing answer

at all times. Under these circumstances, the matching degree is very necessary.

4.2 Co-branding trend and suggestion

4.2.1 Choose the right brand to work with

Choosing the right brand partners is an important guarantee for the success of brand alliances. Consumers have the same attitude to brand combination fore-and-aft. So the higher the evaluation before the joint, the more the consumers are welcome after the joint. At the same time, only a high degree of matching between brand alliances, will be able to maximize the cooperation of brand information and ideas to consumers to deepen consumer awareness from acceptance to emotional identification process.

4.2.2 Choose the positive way

Consumer's evaluation and acceptance of brand alliances are also related to the way of brand alliances. Vertical cooperation category is more easily accepted by consumers and will bring obvious profit in business. Horizontal cooperation expanding the cooperation form and scope, need to have strong complementarity, professionalism and word of mouth for each other. Only in that way can we push the co-branding to positive way.

4.2.3 Establish good brand awareness

Considering by consumer, the co-branding awareness largely depends on prior brand recognition. So in order to cultivate the consumer trust, the most important mean is to establish self brand awareness, strengthen the brand's cognitive framework in the minds of consumers and form a unique mind mapping. Cultivating customers' consumption loyalty and building good brand cognition are two inseparable relations.

4.2.4 Choose a unique marketing tool

According to the relevant content of the study, consumer groups have a higher degree of dependence on the apparel industry, and the desire to consume groups is becoming more and more difficult to consider. In order to meet consumer demands for fresh and desire, we can use the characteristics of the new media to create public opinion and topic, stir up public interest and desire for co-branding, so as to focus on social concerns, expand brand influence and stimulate commercial consumption.

References

[1] Dan Yuanyong, Liu Ruiming, Jin Yufang, et al. Brand alliance research progress [J]. Journal of Management, 2007 (2).

[2] Guangxi University. Brand Wenbin joint decision model and empirical study based on brand alliance success rate perspective.

[3] Zhou Chunyuan. Based on consumer decision-making information of different industries brand joint difference study [J]. Management Journal, 2009(3).

[4] Lu Juan. Lu Juan's summary and conception of brand joint research [J]. Business Economics and Management, 2009 (3).

[5] Feng Hao. Explores the construction of the theoretical model of component brand combination [J]. Modern Business Industry, 2013(2).

[6] Flowers. Feifei factors influencing brand joint and Countermeasures Research[J]. Business Herald, 2015(23).

[7] Wu Fang. 1 + 1 = ? A joint exploratory research.

Preparation and Properties of ZnO–Ag–CeO$_2$/PI Composite Films

Jiaojiao Sui[1], Huaping Yin[1], Qing Li[1]*

[1]*China Academy of Dress Science and Technology, Beijing Institute of Fashion Technology, Beijing 100000, China*

* *Corresponding author's email*: LiQing409@ souhu. com; 18801006317@ 163. com

Abstract: In this paper, ZnO–Ag–CeO$_2$/PI composite films were prepared by doping ion-exchange method with Zn, Ag, and Ce ions onto the polyimide surface. The structural and topographic of the synthesized composite were characterized by X-ray diffraction (XRD), scanning electron microscopy (SEM) and energy dispersive X-ray spectroscopy (EDS). The photocatalytic capacity of ZnO–Ag–CeO$_2$/PI was further evaluated by methylene blue (MB) degradation experiments and the results indicated that ZnO–Ag–CeO$_2$/PI composite films exhibited higher photocatalytic activity than ZnO/PI and ZnO–Ag/PI. When the ion exchange time was 1.5h, the ratio of three ions was 7:10:3, the total ion concentration was 0.3mol/L, and the calcining temperature was 390℃ for 3h, the degradation rate reached 96.6% after 2.5h. The composite film still had high photocatalytic activity after 5 cycles of degradation, and also had photocatalytic activity for different organic pollutants.

Keywords: Polyimide; Pon-exchange; Semiconductor composite; Precious metal deposition; Photocatalysis; Methylene blue

1 Introduction

ZnO has a wide band gap and cannot effectively use sunlight. At the same time, photoelectron-hole pairs are easy to recombine, which affects the photocatalytic activity of ZnO. The precious metal Ag has a plasma resonance effect. When Ag and ZnO are combined, the electrons on the ZnO conduction band can be promoted to migrate into the Ag medium, and the holes remain on the ZnO valence band, thereby inhibiting the recombination of the photoelectron-hole pairs. CeO$_2$ is a rare earth metal oxide. Due to its unique pore structure, surface cavities show good oxygen storage capacity[1] and are often used as co-catalyst. Polyimide (PI) is used as a photocatalyst carrier, and the catalyst of light is easier to recycle and reuse. At the same time, there is a mechanical interlocking effect between silver and the PI matrix, which strengthens the adhesion between the catalyst of light and the carrier, making the catalyst difficult Shedding from the carrier improves the recyclability of the composite film.

In this study, ZnO–Ag–CeO$_2$/PI composite films were prepared by loading zinc, silver and gallium on the surface of PI films by ion exchange method. In order to obtain composite films with higher photocatalytic activity, Ag and CeO$_2$ were added.

2 Experiments

2.1 Materials and apparatus

Commercial polyimide film (50μm, Jiangsu Liyang Huajing Electronic Materials Co., Ltd.); Zinc nitrate (AP, Aladdin Industrial Company); Silver nitrate (AP, Guangdong Guanghua Technology Co., Ltd.); Barium acetate (AP, Aladdin Industrial Company); Methylene Blue (AP, Beijing Chemical Plant).

UV–7504C UV–Vis Spectrophotometer (Shanghai Xinmao Instrument Co., Ltd.); KQ5200DE Digital Control Ultrasonic Cleaner (Kunshan Ultrasonic Instrument Co., Ltd.); SX2 – 4 – 10 Box Resistance Furnace (Tianjin Zhonghuan Electric Furnace Co., Ltd. X-ray diffractometer (XRD, Bruker D8 Advance type); Scanning electron microscope (SEM, JSM–7500Ftype, Japan Co., Ltd.); Energy dispersive X-ray spectrometer (EDS, Hitachi Model S–4007).

2.2 Preparation of ZnO–Ag–CeO₂/PI composite film

The PI film was placed in a Petri dish containing anhydrous ethanol, placed in a 4mol/L potassium hydroxide solution after ultrasonic cleaning, and reacted for 0.5h. After washing with distilled water, it was used for ion exchange in a mixed solution of 0.3mol/L silver nitrate, zinc nitrate, and cesium acetate in different proportions. Silver nitrate, zinc nitrate and lanthanum acetate mixed solution for ion exchange; Finally, it was placed in a muffle furnace and calcined. The temperature was raised from room temperature to 140℃ for 1h and the temperature was maintained for 1h, and then within 1h from 140℃ to a certain temperature Insulation was performed to obtain a ZnO–Ag–CeO₂/PI composite film.

2.3 Characterization of composite films

X-ray diffraction (XRD) was used to determine the crystal structure of the sample. The Cu target was used as the radiation source. The scanning range was 5° to 90°, the tube pressure was 40.0kV, and the tube current was 40mA. Scanning electron microscopy (SEM) was used to observe the surface morphology of the sample. The filament voltage was 5.0kV and the current was 10μA. The energy dispersive X-ray spectrometer (EDS) was used to analyze the surface elements of the samples.

2.4 Photocatalytic performance test

To 10mg/L methyleneblue solution of simulates the dye wastewater as a degradation target. A certain size of the composite film was placed in a methylene blue solution, and air was allowed to pass through for 30 minutes in the dark, and the lamp was irradiated under a UV lamp of 365nm and 500W. Samples were taken at regular intervals to measure the absorbance of the degradation solution. The degradation rate was used to evaluate the photocatalytic activity of the composite film under different reaction conditions.

3 Results and Discussion

3.1 Structural analysis of composite films

Fig. 1 shows the XRD patterns of ZnO/PI, ZnO–Ag/PI, and ZnO–Ag–CeO₂/PI films. As can be seen from Fig. 1, there is no characteristic diffraction peak of ZnO in the line a, which may be due to the low content of zinc on the surface of the PI, which is beyond the detection limit of the instrument and can not be detected, or ZnO is on the surface of the PI film. Amorphous or highly dispersed state exists. Lines b and c show characteristic diffraction peaks at 2θ of 38.1°, 44.3°, 64.4°, 77.4° and 81.6°. Compared with the standard card (JCPDS 89–3722), they correspond to the face-centered cubic structure Ag (111), (200), (220), (311), (222) crystal faces. The characteristic diffraction peak of CeO₂ is detected on line c. There is a weak diffraction peak at 23.4 for 33.4°, corresponding to the CeO₂ (220) crystal plane of the cubic fluorite structure[2]. Comparing the intensity of the peaks of Ag in the spectral lines b and c, the diffraction peak of Ag in the ZnO–Ag–CeO₂/PI composite film is more acute, which indicates that the addition of CeO₂ increases the particle size of Ag.

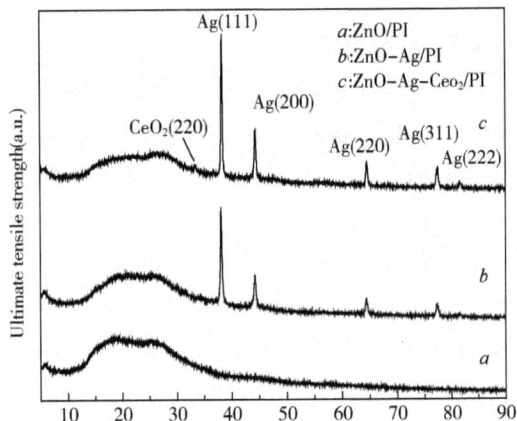

Fig. 1 XRD patterns of different composite films

3.2 Morphology and composition analysis of composite films

Fig. 2 shows the EDS spectra of ZnO/PI, ZnO–Ag/PI and ZnO–Ag–CeO₂/PI films. It can be seen from Fig. 2(c) that the ZnO–Ag–CeO₂/PI film is composed of C, N, O, Zn and Ag, Ce, etc. 6 elements. When the ZnO–Ag–CeO₂/PI composite film was prepared, the molar ratio of zinc nitrate, silver nitrate and antimony acetate is 10:7:3, which is obtained from the proportion of the atomic elements in Fig. 2(c), and is attached to PI. The atomic ratio of Zn, Ag, and Ce on the surface is approximately 3 : 14 : 2. The number of Ag atoms is approximately 5 times that of Zn and 7 times that of Ce. The reason for the analysis should be that Ag with a lower valence state is more likely to exchange K^+ with the surface of PI.

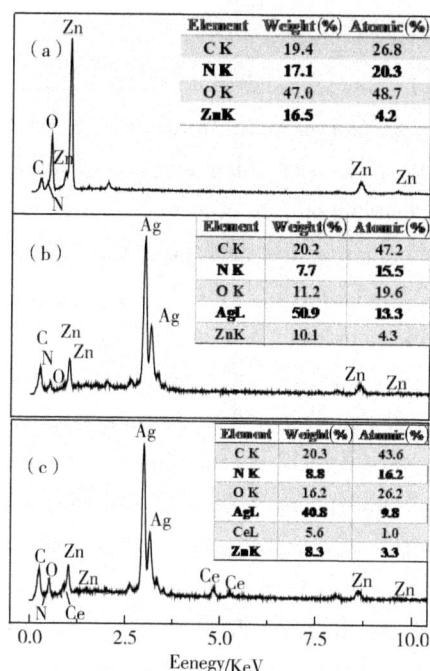

Element	Weight(%)	Atomic(%)
C K	19.4	26.8
N K	17.1	20.3
O K	47.0	48.7
ZnK	16.5	4.2

Element	Weight(%)	Atomic(%)
C K	20.2	47.2
N K	7.7	15.5
O K	11.2	19.6
AgL	50.9	13.3
ZnK	10.1	4.3

Element	Weight(%)	Atomic(%)
C K	20.3	43.6
N K	8.8	16.2
O K	16.2	26.2
AgL	40.8	9.8
CeL	5.6	1.0
ZnK	8.3	3.3

Fig. 2 EDS spectra of composite films (a) ZnO/PI; (b) ZnO-Ag/PI; (c) ZnO-Ag-CeO$_2$/PI

Fig. 3 (a), (b), and (c) are SEM images of ZnO/PI, ZnO–Ag/PI, and ZnO–Ag–CeO$_2$/PI composite films under the same preparation conditions. As can be seen from Fig. 3(a), particles are generated on the surface of the PI, and the particles do not completely grow out of the PI matrix and exist on the surface of the PI in a semi-coated form. The particle size of the particles is about 30nm and the dispersion is high. From Fig. 3 (b), it can be seen that the precious metal Ag has good compatibility with the PI matrix. The analysis may be due to the fact that the Ag^+ in the lower valence state is easily exchanged with the K^+ on the PI surface

Fig. 3 SEM image of composite film (a) ZnO/PI; (b) ZnO-Ag/PI; (c) ZnO-Ag-CeO$_2$/PI

(results obtained from the EDS spectrum), resulting in a uniform silver layer. The silver layer has a mechanical interlocking effect with the PI matrix so that the silver layer is firmly attached to the PI surface. Nanoparticles are loaded on the surface of Ag and PI, but there is a certain degree of agglomeration. In Fig. 3 (c), the particle size of the spherical particles is increased as compared with that of Fig. 3(a) and Fig. 3 (b), and the particles are uniformly dispersed without obvious agglomeration.

3.3 Photocatalytic activity of different composite films

Fig. 4 shows the degradation curves of ZnO/PI, ZnO–Ag/PI, and ZnO – Ag – CeO$_2$/PI to methyleneblue. Comparing the three degradation rate curves, we can conclude that the order of photocatalytic activity of the three samplesis: ZnO/PI < ZnO – Ag/PI < ZnO – Ag – CeO$_2$/PI, in which ZnO–Ag–CeO$_2$/PI composite films exhibited higher photocatalytic activity. After photocatalytic degradation for 2.5h, the degradation rate of methyleneblue reached about 96.6%. From the order of the photocatalytic activity of the sample, it can be seen that the addition of Ag and CeO$_2$ improves the photocatalytic activity of the ZnO/PI composite film. The photocatalytic activity of ZnO–Ag/PI is higher than that of ZnO/PI. This is because when ZnO is in contact with Ag, electrons will migrate from ZnO with high Fermi level to noble metal Ag until the Fermi level reaches equilibrium to form Schottky. Potential barrier, when ZnO is irradiated with ultraviolet light, electrons are captured by the Schottky electrode, and then transferred to Ag, which separates photoelectrons and holes on ZnO, inhibits their recombination, and improves the photocatalytic activity of the composite film. The photocatalytic activity of ZnO – Ag – CeO$_2$/PI is higher than that of ZnO–Ag/PI, probably because the band gap of CeO$_2$ is narrower than that of ZnO, and it is easier to generate electrons under the excitation of ultraviolet rays. Thas, more photoelectrons participate in the reaction. The photoelectrons are captured by the metal Ag, further improving the photocatalytic activity of the catalyst[3-6].

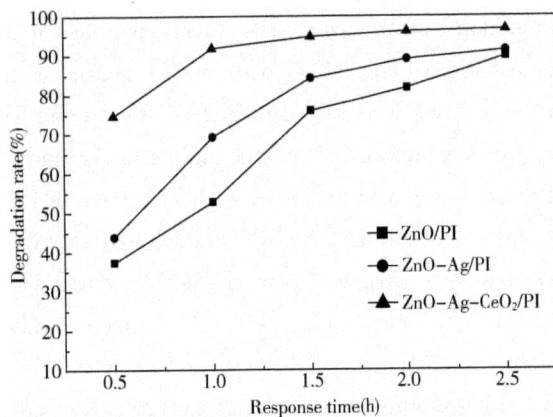

Fig. 4 Comparison of photocatalytic activity of different samples

3.4 Effect of preparation conditions on photocatalytic performance of composite thin films

3.4.1 Ion exchange time

A series of composite membranes with different ion exchange times were prepared under the condition that the molar ratio of zinc nitrate, silver nitrate and antimony acetate was 2 : 1 : 1, the total ion concentration was 0.3mol/L, the calcining temperature was 350℃, and the temperature was kept for 3 hours. The degradation rate of methylene blue is shown in Tab. 1. From the data in Tab. 1, it can be seen that as the ion exchange time increases, and the degradation rate of methylene blue increases first and then decreases. When the ion exchange time is 1.5 hours, the degradation rate reaches a maximum of 96.2%. The surface of the carrier PI film is etched by a certain concentration of KOH to form a polyamic acid salt, and the exchangeable K^+ content is constant. When the ion exchange is completed, the amount of metal ions exchanged to the PI surface no longer increases, and the reaction tends to be complete. The photocatalytic activity of the composite film is no longer improved.

Tab. 1 Effect of ion exchange time on photocatalytic performance of ZnO-Ag-CeO$_2$/PI composite films

Ion exchange time(h)	Degradation rate(%)				
	0.5h	1h	1.5h	2h	2.5h
1	39.3	69.1	84.5	91.4	95
1.5	54.8	84.1	91.9	94.4	96.2

Continued

Ion exchange time(h)	Degradation rate(%)				
	0.5h	1h	1.5h	2h	2.5h
2	44.8	74.2	87.3	92.6	94.7
2.5	38.5	68.9	80.3	86.8	90.7

3.4.2 Matching ratio

A composite film with different ratios was prepared at an ion exchange time of 1.5h, a total ion concentration of 0.3mol/L, and a calcining temperature of 350℃ for 3h. The degradation rate of methylene blue is shown in Tab. 2. Comparing the data, when the molar ratio of Ag^+, Zn^{2+} and Ce^{3+} is 7 : 10 : 3, the photocatalytic activity of the composite film is the highest. When light was irradiated for 2.5h, the degradation rate of methylene blue reached 97%. When Ag content further increases, excessive Ag will become the recombination center of photoelectrons and holes, at the same time, the amount of Ce will decrease and the effect of CeO$_2$ will weaken, resulting in a decrease in the photocatalytic activity of the composite film.

Tab. 2 The effect of the ratio of three components on the photocatalytic performance of ZnO-Ag-CeO$_2$/PI composite films

The molar ratio of (Ag^+:Zn^{2+}:Ce^{3+})	Degradation rate(%)				
	0.5h	1h	1.5h	2h	2.5h
1:10:9	53.3	81.9	92	95.1	96.3
3:10:7	45.1	79.1	91.2	95	96.6
1:2:1	44.8	74.2	87.3	92.6	94.7
7:10:3	56.4	85.1	94.1	95.9	97
9:10:1	39.8	61.6	76.9	84.8	88.9

3.4.3 Calcining temperature

Fig. 5 is a graph showing the degradation rate of methylene blue with UV irradiation time for ZnO-Ag-CeO$_2$/PI composite films prepared at calcining temperatures of 350℃, 390℃ and 430℃. The preparation conditions of the composite film were ion exchange 1.5h, three ion ratios 7 : 10 : 3, total ion concentration 0.3mol/L, calcining temperature 350℃, 390℃, 430℃, and holding time 3h. It can be seen from Fig. 5 that the photocatalytic activity of the composite film is higher at the calcining temperature of 390℃. The proper temperature can get the complete crystalline metal oxides and Ag particles. With the further increase of the temperature, the PI film may undergo some degradation under the action of the metal oxides, reducing the photocatalytic activity of the composite film.

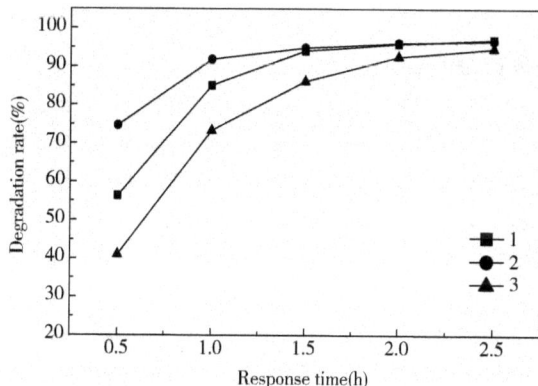

Fig. 5　Effect of calcining temperature on photocatalytic performance of ZnO – Ag – CeO₂/PI composite film (1) – 350℃ (2) –390℃ (3) –450℃

3.4.4　Holding time

Preparation of ZnO–Ag–CeO₂/PI Composite Films with Holding Time of 1h, 2h, 3h, 4h and 5h, under the conditions of ion exchange time of 1.5h, three ion ratios of 7 : 10 : 3, total ion concentration of 0.3mol/L and calcining temperature of 390℃. It can be analyzed from the curve in Fig. 6, before the holding time of 3h, the metal oxide ZnO and CeO₂ continue to shape, Ag ions are continuously reduced to elemental Ag, and the composite film continuously improve the photocatalytic properties. As the holding time continues to increase, the ZnO, CeO₂, and Ag elements will agglomerate and the photocatalytic activity of the composite film will decrease. When the holding time was 3h, the photocatalytic activity of the composite film was the highest, and the degradation rate of methyleneblue was 96.6%.

3.4.5　Recycling

Fig. 7 shows the effect of ZnO–Ag–CeO₂/PI film on the degradation of methylene blue. After 5 cycles of composite film, the degradation rate of methyleneblue can still reach 96%, indicating that ZnO–Ag–CeO₂/PI film

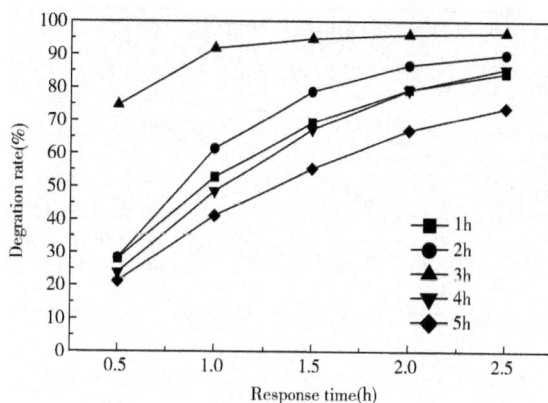

Fig. 6　Effect of holding time on photocatalytic performance of ZnO–Ag–CeO₂/PI composite film

has good photocatalytic stability and can be recycled and reused.

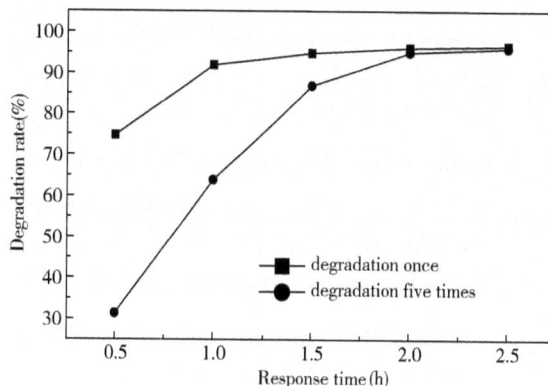

Fig. 7　ZnO–Ag–CeO₂/PI Composite film recycling efficiency

3.4.6　Photocatalytic degradation effect of different dyes

In order to investigate the photocatalytic degradation rate of ZnO–Ag–CeO₂/PI films for different dyes, two other dyes were selected for the degradation experiments. The results are shown in Fig. 8. As can be seen from Fig. 8, the degradation rate of methylene blue by the film is high, and the degradation rate reaches 97% after 2.5 hours of degradation. The azo dyes methyl orange and Congo red also have certain degradation effects, but they are lower than methylene blue.

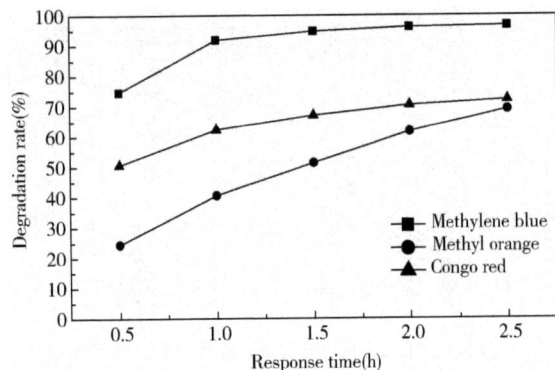

Fig. 8　Photocatalytic performance of ZnO-Ag-CeO₂/PI com-posite films on different dyes

4　Conclusions

ZnO/PI, ZnO-Ag/PI and ZnO-Ag-CeO₂/PI composite films were prepared by ion exchange method. Three-component modified ZnO-Ag-CeO₂/PI composite films were obtained by photocatalytic activity test. The photocatalytic efficiency of methylene blue is the highest.

Using XRD, SEM, EDS and other characterization means, Ce modification increased the particle size of Ag. ZnO-Ag-CeO₂/PI composite film contained six elements such as C, N, O, Zn, Ag, and Ce. Ag was more easily attached to the PI surface. Ag$^+$ was reduced to a face-centered cubic structure of Ag by ion exchange and high-temperature calcination, and Ce^{3+} formed a cubic fluorite structure of CeO₂.

Through the study of the preparation conditions, the best preparation conditions were ion exchange 1.5h, three ion ratios 7 : 10 : 3, total ion concentration 0.3mol/L, and calcining temperature 390℃ for 3h. The degradation rate of methylene blue by the composite film reached 96.6% after 2.5 hours. The composite film has good photocatalytic stability, can be recycled, and has a certain photocatalytic degradation effect on different dyes.

References

[1]Li Y, Luo L T, Li C Q. Effect of ZnO on the partial oxidation of methanol to partial oxidation of Au-Pd/CeO2 catalysts [J]. Molecular Catalysis, 2009, 23(5): 448-453.

[2] Cao G L, Pan G F, He P, et al. Preparation of CeO₂ doped ZnO thick film and its gas sensitivity [J]. Functional Materials, 2013, 44(5): 682-684+688.

[3] Zhang Z F, Liu H R, Zhang H, et al. Synthesis and photocatalytic performance of ZnO/Ag microspheres [J]. Chemical Journal of Chinese Universities, 2013(12): 2827-2833.

[4] Liang J, Zhang C X, Dong H L, et al. Synthesis and visible light photocatalytic activity of Ag/ZnO/ZnSe ternary heterojunctions [J]. Journal of Inorganic Chemistry, 2015, 31(2): 260-266.

[5] Li C Q, Luo L T, Xiong G W. Preparation and photocatalytic properties of CeO₂/ZnO composite nanotubes [J]. Chinese Journal of Chemical Chemistry, 2010, 68(10): 1028-1031.

[6] Wang X W, Fan Y, Chen Y, et al. Dielectric and thermal properties of nano Mg(OH)₂-ZnO/polyimide composite films [J]. Acta Materiae Compositae Sinica, 2018, 35(01): 30-34.

Ramie Fabrics Fixed with TiO_2 NPs for Formaldehyde Elimination

Innocent Toendepi[1,3], Fangfang Weng[1,3], Yani Feng[2], Quan Zhu[5],
Wanshuang Liu[4], Yiping Qiu[1,3,4], Qiuran Jiang[1,3]*

[1] Key Laboratory of Textile Science & Technology, Ministry of Education, Shanghai 201620, China

[2] Guangzhou Fiber Product Testing and Research Institute, Guangzhou, GuangDong 511447, China

[3] Department of Technical Textiles, College of Textiles, Donghua University, Shanghai 201620, China

[4] Donghua University Center for Civil Aviation Composites, Donghua University, Shanghai 201620, China

[5] Department of Applied Chemistry, College of Chemistry, Chemical Engineering and Biotechnology, Donghua University, Shanghai 201620, China

* Corresponding author's email: jj@ dhu. edu. cn

Abstract: Formaldehyde is a prevalent compound in indoors air pollution. Photocatalysis has proven to be amongst the most effective approach to eliminate formaldehyde. In this research, a low temperature treatment was developed to fix titanium dioxide nanoparticles (TiO2 NPs) on ramie fabrics to produce fabrics with formaldehyde elimination function. The treatment made the ramie fabric stiffer. The treated fabric was able to remove 77% of formaldehyde after 120min when the initial formaldehyde concentration was 4.4mg/m^3. The maximum removal efficiency was achieved in the environment with a relative humidity of 50%. A higher relative humidity elicited reduction in the formaldehyde removal efficiency. These results indicate that the developed low temperature treatment can be used to produce textile products with efficient formaldehyde elimination function.

Keywords: Formaldehyde removal; Photocatalysis; TiO2 nanoparticles; Low temperature fixation

1 Introduction

Formaldehyde is one of the major indoors air pollutants, which can cause nausea, skin rashes and chest tightness at a relatively low concentration or with a short exposure time[1]. With a high concentration or a long exposure time, formaldehyde can elicit cancer, and is classified as a carcinogen[2]. Therefore, to effectively control and eliminate the indoor formaldehyde is of great importance to secure public health.

Efforts have been made to develop the indoor formaldehyde removal approaches. Ventilation is an efficient method, but only suit for unsealed space with relatively low formaldehyde concentration. Physical adsorption is currently widely used and effective, but this method lacks gas molecule selection and sensitive to environment parameters. The effect of this approach is restricted by its adsorption upper limit. More importantly, the adsorbed molecules have the possibility to be released

from adsorbents and cause the secondary pollution[3]. Other radiative methods including plasma or anion treatment technologies can eliminate formaldehyde by oxidation, but might create other toxic gases[4]. Photocatalysis is a method to oxidize toxic gases into harmless small molecules, such as CO_2 and H_2O[1,4-6]. However, the fixation of TiO2 NPs on substrates is a concern. The common approaches include padding[7], coating with toxic binders[4], sol-gel fixation[6]. However, these methods suffer problems, including the agglomeration of nanoparticles, the weak fixation which cannot withstand abrasion and washing processes, or the toxicity caused by the binders.

Professor Lina Zhang's group developed a cellulose dissolution method using alkaline and urea at a low temperature below −5℃[8]. However, this method can only dissolve cellulose smaller than 11.4×10^4[9]. The selective dissolution properties of this method inspired us to develop a low temperature fixation method.

In this research, ramie fabrics with porous structure were selected as the substrates. By the low temperature fixation method, the components with small molecular weights could be dissolved from ramie fibers and serve as the binder between TiO_2 NPs and fibers. The formaldehyde elimination function, the changes in the morphology and mechanical properties were evaluated before and after the treatments.

2　Experiments

2.1　Materials

The plain-woven ramie fabrics were provided by Hunan Dongting Ramie Textile printing and dyeing factory. Titanium dioxide nanoparticles (TiO_2 NPs, Degussa, P25) and formaldehyde were purchased from Beijing Entrepreneur Science & Trading Co., Ltd. Polyethylene glycol (PEG) 1000 dispersant was bought from Shanghai Sinopharm Chemical Reagent Co., Ltd. The rest of the chemical reagents were purchased from Shanghai Lingfeng Chemical Reagent Co., Ltd.

2.2　Fixation of TiO_2 nanoparticles

The one-pot suspension of TiO_2 NPs was prepared by mixing 7% NaOH chips, 12% urea granules, 3% TiO_2 NPs and 0.75% PEG in distilled water, then stirring at 600r/min for 30mins and sonicating in anultrasonic cleaner bath (SK7200B Instrument) at 350W for 30mins. The suspension was pre-cooled to -10 ℃. Ramie fabrics (30cm × 40cm) were immersed into the TiO_2 NPs suspension at a liquor ratio of 50 : 1 for 10mins at -10 ℃. Excess suspension was squeezed out by a mini-mangle (LP, Nantong Sansi Electromechanical Science & Technology Co., Ltd.) under a pressure of 400N/cm. The fabrics were dried at 100 ℃ for 2mins, post-cured at 170 ℃ for 1min and washed for three times in distilled water to remove soluble agents and unfixed particles. Fabrics immobilized with TiO_2 NPs were dried at 60 ℃ for 24h.

2.3　Morphological observation

The surface morphological differences of the ramie fabrics before and after treatments were observed under a scanning electron microscopy (SEM, JSM-5600LV). The samples were sputtered coated with gold at a cur-

rent of 8mA for 10s and observed under the SEM with an acceleration voltage of 15kV. The magnifications were set at 7000 × and 4000 ×.

2.4　Evaluation of the formaldehyde removal performance

A self-designed system was used to test the formaldehyde removal performance of ramie fabrics. This system constitutes a 64L glass chamber, inside the chamber contains a mounted fabric holder, a UV light source, formaldehyde injection system, an air agitation device, heating unit, hygro thermometer and formaldehyde detector. The environment inside the chamber was preset at room temperature and relative humidity was varied from 30% –70%. The initial concentration in the chamber was kept at around 4.4mg/m^3. During the formaldehyde elimination tests, the fabric samples were mounted on the frame vertically. The concentration of formaldehyde in the chamber was measured every 30mins by a formaldehyde tester (LB-HD, Lanbao Eletrotech Ltc.). The UV-light at 15 watts was mounted 23cm away from samples and pre-set at awavelength of 253.7nm.

2.5　Evaluation of mechanical properties

Tensile test was performed to investigate the influence of the treatment on the mechanical properties of ramie fabrics. The tensile strength and the elongation of the fabrics (5cm × 25cm) were measured according to the standard of GB/T 3923.1—2013 on the tensile tester (YG026MB) with a gauge length of 20cm and a crosshead speed of 100mm/min.

3　Results and Discussion

3.1　Surface morphology of untreated and treated ramie fabrics

Fig.1 showed the SEM images of the untreated and the TiO_2 NPs fixed ramie fabrics. The fibers in the raw ramie yarns were clearly separated with smooth surface (Fig.1(a)), while the treated yarns were covered with a coating layer, which was composed with TiO_2 NPs and the dissolved or partially dissolved components from fibers (Fig.1(b)). The dissolved substances might be lignin, pectin, hemicellulose, wax and cellulose with small molecular weights. Since these components were dissolved from the ramie fibers, they have inherent high affinity to the yarn body, which may form strong fixation between TiO₂ NPs and the fibers. Besides, though the yarns in the treated fabric were coated, the pores in the fabric were maintained indicating the permeability could be kept.

Fig. 1   Surface morphologies of ramie fabrics. The SEM images of (a) untreated fabric and (b) TiO₂ fixed ramie fabric

3.2   Formaldehyde removal performance

Fig. 2 revealed the formaldehyde removal performance of the TiO₂ NPs fixed ramie fabric.

It was shown that the formaldehyde concentration could be efficiently reduced by the TiO₂ NPs fixed ramie fabric. In the first 30min, the treatment rate was around $0.107mg/m^3/min$. From 30min to 120min, the treatment rate slightly reduced to $0.024mg/m^3/min$, but kept a linear trend. After 120min, the formaldehyde concentration was $1.025mg/m^3$, close to the indoor critical formaldehyde concentration ($1.07mg/m^3$).

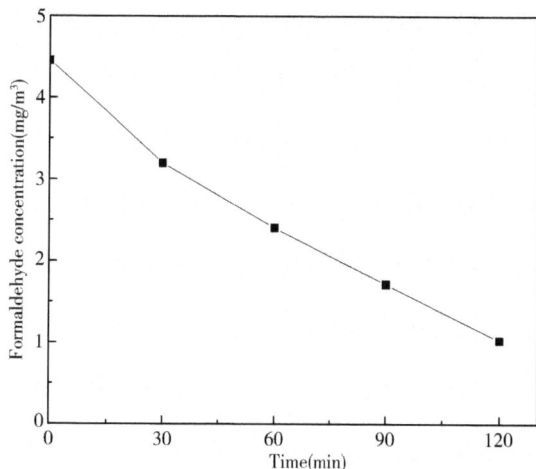

Fig. 2   Formaldehyde removal performance of the treated fabric during 120min

3.3   Effect of the relative humidity on formaldehyde removal

Fig. 3 showed the formaldehyde removal efficiency of the treated fabric in the environment with different relative humidifies. When the relative humidity increased from 30% to 50%, the formaldehyde removal efficiency was slightly raised from 82% to 87%, but the change was not significant. However, the formaldehyde removal efficiency reduced linearly as the relative humidity was elevated from 50% to 70%. Water molecules with a small amount provided hydroxyl radicals, which improved the activity of the photocatalyst[5]. However, excessive water suppressed the photocatalysis reaction and even covered the surface of TiO₂ NPs to block and quench the hydroxyl radicals[2].

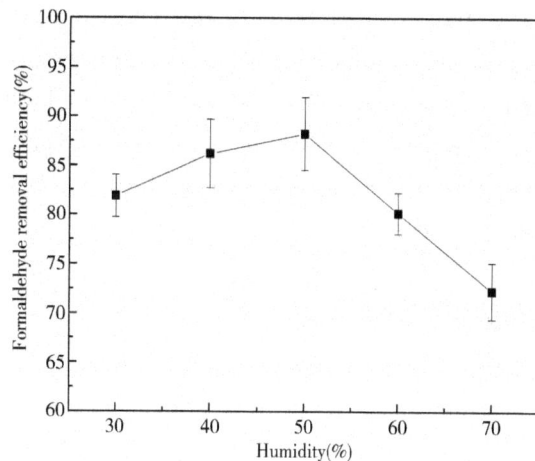

Fig. 3   Effect of the relative humidity on formaldehyde removal performance

3.4   Mechanical properties

To maintain the mechanical properties of the treated fabrics is important for practical applications. The tensile strength of the original fabric was 651.43N. After the treatment, the strength of the fabric was enhanced 4% to around 676.86N. The elongation was reduced from 7.93% to 7.50%, about 5.4%. The results indicated that the low temperature treatment could make the fabric stiffer. As seen from Fig. 1(b), the connections were built among fibers in the treated fabrics by the coatings. By this way, the fabrics were strengthened, and the movement of fibers was restricted.

Tab. 1 Mechanical properties of the
original and the treated ramie fabric

Sample	Stress (N)	Elongation (%)
Original	651.42 ± 23.70	7.93 ± 0.19
Treated	676.86 ± 13.86	7.50 ± 1.97
P-Value	0.184	0.729

4 Conclusions

In this research, a low temperature treatment was developed to fix TiO_2 NPs on ramie fabrics for indoor formaldehyde removal. The treated fabrics became slightly stronger and stiffer. The formaldehyde concentration could be efficiently reduced from $4.4 mg/m^3$ to $1.025 mg/m^3$ in 120min. The relative humidity above 50% reduced the efficiency of the treated fabrics, but an efficiency around 80% could still be achieved at RH 70%. Therefore, the low temperature treatment for ramie fabrics can be used to develop formaldehyde removal products.

Acknowledgements

This research was supported by the research project of the Guangzhou Fiber Product Testing and Research Institute (2016PZ04) and the NSFC Project (51503031), and the Fundamental Research Funds for the Central Universities (2232017A-09).

References

[1] Ao C H, Lee S C, Yu J Z, et al. Photodegradation of formaldehyde by photocatalyst TiO_2: Effects on the presences of NO, SO_2 and VOCs [J]. Applied Catalysis B: Environmental, 2004, 54(1): 41-50.

[2] Gary A, Krzyzanowsk M, Naohide S, et al. WHO Guidelines for indoors air quality [M]. 2010.

[3] Bellat J P, Bezverkhyy I, Weber G, et al. Capture of formaldehyde by adsorption on nanoporous materials [J]. Journal of Hazardous Materials, 2015, 300: 711-717.

[4] Liang W, Li J, Jin Y. Photo-catalytic degradation of gaseous formaldehyde by TiO_2/UV, Ag/TiO_2/UV and Ce/TiO_2/UV [J]. Building and Environment, 2012, 51: 345-350.

[5] Abdullah H, Khan M M R, Ong H R, et al. Modified TiO_2 photocatalyst for CO_2 photocatalytic reduction: An overview [J]. Journal of CO_2 Utilization, 2017, 22: 15-32.

[6] Hathway T, Rockafellow E M, Oh Y C, et al. Photocatalytic degradation using tungsten-modified TiO_2 and visible light: Kinetic and mechanistic effects using multiple catalyst doping strategies [J]. Journal of Photochemistry and Photobiology A: Chemistry, 2009, 207(2): 197-203.

[7] Kundu S, Kafizas A, Hyett G, et al. An investigation into the effect of thickness of titanium dioxide and gold-silver nanoparticle titanium dioxide composite thin-films on photocatalytic activity and photo-induced oxygen production in a sacrificial system [J]. Journal of Materials Chemistry, The Royal Society of Chemistry, 2011, 21(19): 6854-6863.

[8] Qi H, Chang C, Zhang L. Effects of temperature and molecular weight on dissolution of cellulose in NaOH/urea aqueous solution [J]. Cellulose, 2008, 15(6): 779-787.

[9] Cai J, Zhang L. Rapid Dissolution of Cellulose in LiOH/Urea and NaOH/Urea Aqueous Solutions [J]. Macromolecular Bioscience, Wiley-Blackwell, 2005, 5(6): 539-548.

Research on Surface Properties of Cotton Fabrics Coated with Nano-TiO₂ Particles

Na Zhang[1,2]* , **Yanping Yu**[1,3], **Rong Huang**[1,2], **Tianyu Xia**[1,2]

[1]*Key Laboratory of Textile Science & Technology, Ministry of Education, Shanghai 201620, China*

[2]*Department of Textile Engineering, College of Textiles, Donghua University, Shanghai 201620, China*

[3]*Department of Textile Materials, College of Textiles, Donghua University, Shanghai 201620, China*

* *Corresponding author's email*: 2420331251@ qq. com

Abstract: Nano-TiO₂ particles are loaded onto cotton fabric by the cavitation effect of ultrasonic wave, which is a combination of nano-technology and ultrasonic technology. The concentration of nano-TiO₂ solution (1%, 2%, 3%, 4%, 5%) was determined for the three variables of the experiment and their respective experimental levels. The time of ultrasonic action is (10min, 20min and 30min) and the power of ultrasonic wave is (30%, 50%, 70%, 100%). The results show that the water repellency and water resistance of cotton fabric treated by nano-TiO₂ are improved remarkably, and the pilling phenomenon on the surface is improved obviously, but the antistatic property of cotton fabric is decreased.

Keywords: Cotton fabrics; Ultrasonic finishing; Nano-TiO₂; Surface properties

1 Introduction

The E502 nanometer TiO₂ finishing agent is an anatase nitrogen-doped quantum dot. TiO₂ nano-composite solution is produced by a nanometer self-assembled liquid phase synthesis technology. Its composition is mainly 6–8 nanoparticles and some quantum dot-grade TiO₂ nanoparticles. All crystal structures are anatase, doped with nitrogen, and the solution and its drying powder are yellowish. The TiO₂ solution is designed by electric double-layer self-stabilizing design; without dispersant, steric hindrance agent and other additives. All colloidal particles are dispersed by the surface charge layer at the time of synthesis, and the dispersion is almost single. Even if the centrifugal force is over 1000g, no delamination and precipitation will occur. Nano-particles attached to the fiber can form a porous structure with porosity up to 50% –90%, further improving the surface area and working efficiency.

The traditional nanoparticle finishing processes are complicated, also the conventional finishing agents cause environmental pollution, and the binding forces between the nanoparticles and the fabric are relatively weak, resulting in poor wash-fastness[1]. The ultrasonic effect can effectively transport the nanoparticles into the inside of the fibers. Inside the fibers, the nanoparticle has strong binding forces with the fibers' structure. Thus, the functional effect of fabric (i. e. washing fastness) can withstand multiple washings.

In this study, we used the E502 nano-TiO₂ finishing agent and the "cavitation effect"[2] by means of ultrasonic treatment. The nano-TiO₂ particles were loaded on the surface of the cotton fabric and even penetrated into the interior structure of fiber. Then, the samples were tested for surface properties such as water repellency, pilling and antistatic properties. Finally, the effects of different factors on the surface properties of the fabrics were investigated.

2 Experiments

2.1 Materials

White cotton fabrics were provided by Guangdong Forward Cowboy Co., Ltd. (Guangdong). Nano-TiO₂

Finishing Agent (Model E502) was provided by Huzheng Nano Technology Co. , Ltd. (Shanghai).

2.2 Ultrasonic treatment

TiO_2-1 solution was prepared using 5g of TiO_2 Taknano-particles dissolved in deionized water, dubbed 1% TiO_2 solution, and stirred by ultrasonic weare 10min. TiO_2-2 solution, TiO_2-3 solution, TiO_2-4 solution and TiO_2-5 solution were obtained in the same way. Then cotton fabrics with a size of 100mm × 100mm were immersed into a nano-TiO_2 solution (at a liquor ratio of 100 : 1) for 10 minutes, 20 minutes and 30 minutes at 35℃, separately. Next, the ultrasonically finished cotton fabrics were taken out of the system and placed in an oven for drying at (150℃) for 30 minutes. The pristine cotton fabric was as a comparison.

2.3 Test methods

2.3.1 SEM test

Scanning electron microscopy (SEM) was used to observe the surface of ultrasonically treated cotton fabrics to examine the distribution of nano-TiO_2 particles in cotton fabrics.

2.3.2 Contact angle test of cotton fabrics coated with-nano-TiO_2 particles

The water repellency performance of cotton fabrics coated with nano-TiO_2 particles was evaluated measuring the water contact angle using OCA15EC contact angle measuring instrument at room temperature. Tests were performed using international standard ISO 27448 : 2009[3].

2.3.3 Spray rating test of cotton fabric of cotton fabrics coated with nano-TiO_2 particles

The water resistance performance of cotton fabrics coated with nano-TiO_2 particles was evaluated measuring the spray rating using Y813 fabric water degree tester at room temperature using ISO 4920 : 2012 test method[4] where 1 grade indicated completely wetted, 3 grade indicated rarely wetted and 4 grade indicated no wettability but little drops of water on the surface.

2.3.4 Anti-pilling test of cotton fabrics coated with nano-TiO_2 particle

This study covers the GB/T 4802.2—2008 methods for testing textile anti-pilling using YG401E type fabric flat grinding instrument (Martindale Pilling Tester).

2.3.5 Antistatic test of cotton fabrics coated with nano-TiO_2 particle

The Antistatic properties of cotton fabrics coated with nano-TiO_2 particles were determined according to testing standard FZ/T 01042—1996 using a Model 6105 fabric static instrument.

3 Results and Discussion

3.1 Analysis of SEM

Fig. 1 shows the SEM analysis of the pristine cotton fabric and the coated fabrics with nano-TiO_2 particles. As shown in Fig. 1 (a), the surface of pristine cotton fabric is smooth, and there are few impurities on the surface of the fiber and in between the fibers. However, it is thoroughly possible to recognize the titanium dioxide nanoparticles on the surface of all samples by comparing Fig. 1 (b) – Fig. 1 (f) and Fig. 1 (a). With the increase in the concentration of nano-solutions, the number of nano-particles between the fibers is increased and some fiber surfaces also appear cracked, as shown in Fig. 1 (f). When the material is subjected to ultrasonic waves, part of the energy in the ultrasonic process is transmitted to the fiber, which accelerates the crack propagation on the surface of the fiber and causes the fiber surface to be eroded. The specific surface area of the fiber that adsorbs the nano-dispersion is greatly increased, which leads to the penetration of fine particles into the gaps of the fibers. It also facilitates the finishing process and processing of textiles after dyeing and functional treatments[5].

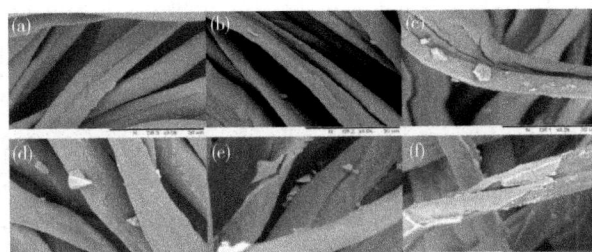

Fig. 1 SEM micrographs of (a) untreated; (b) 20% TiO_2 treated; (c) 40% TiO_2 treated; (d) 60% TiO_2 treated; (e) 80% TiO_2 treated; (f) 100% TiO_2 treated

3.2 Contact angle analysis of cotton fabrics coated with nano-TiO₂ particles

When ultrasonic power is 100% and ultrasonic time is 30min, comparison of water-repellent contact angles of cotton fabrics coated with nano-TiO₂ particles are shown in Fig. 2. It can be seen that the contact angle of untreated cotton fabric is less than 90°. However, the surface contact angle of nano-finished cotton fabric is more than 90°. Due to the roughness, if the surface of the solid is hydrophilic, the surface will be more hydrophilic; if the surface of the solid is hydrophobic, the surface will be more hydrophobic[6]. For hydrophobic fabrics, the contact angle is higher, the water repellency isbetter. Research shows that untreated cotton fabric is hydrophilic. However, ultrasonically treated specimens have increased contact areas between water and the material due to the rough surface, and due to the surface tension of water, its surface area is reduced.

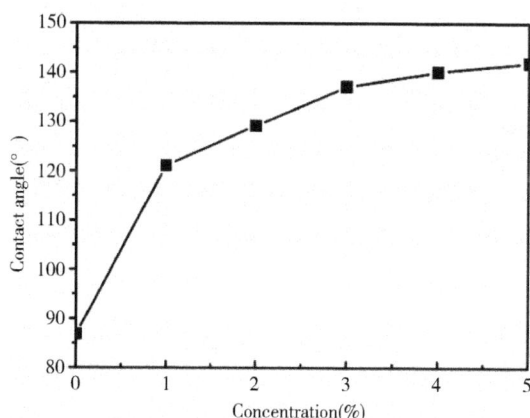

Fig. 2　Comparison of water-repellent contact angles of different fabric samples with different concentrations of titanium dioxide nanoparticles when ultrasonic power is 100% and ultrasonic time is 30min

Water droplets will reduce their surface area by increasing the contact angle[7]. As a result, a hydrophobic surface is formed, which has a water and oil repellency function. When the concentration of nano-TiO₂ is 3%, the contact angle has reached to 137.1°. The contact angle changes slowly when the nano-TiO₂ continue to increase, indicating that the nano-TiO₂ has reached saturation at this time.

3.3 Spray rating analysis of cotton fabrics coated with nano-TiO₂ particles

When ultrasonic power is 100% and ultrasonic time is 30min, spray rate of cotton fabrics coated with nano-TiO₂ particles are shown in Tab. 1. Cotton fabricsunt reated with nano-TiO₂ are completely wetted. In contrast, with the untreated fabric, the cotton fabrics coated with nano-TiO₂ particles have good water repellency with around 3 – 4 grade, because nano-TiO₂ solution leads to rough surface. Besides, with the increasing concentration of nano-TiO₂ solution, the water repellency of nano-cotton fabric strengthens to a certain extent, which can block some liquid contaminants and achieve a self-cleaning effect.

Tab. 1　Spray rating of different fabrics treated with different concentrations of titanium dioxide nanoparticles

Nano-TiO₂ concentration (%)	Ultrasonic power (%)	Ultrasonic time (min)	Spray rating
0	100	30	1
1	100	30	3
2	100	30	3
3	100	30	3
4	100	30	4
5	100	30	4

3.4 Anti-pilling analysis of cotton fabrics coated by nano-TiO₂ particle

According to Tab. 2, when rubbed 10 to 60 times, all samples show only slight fluffing, but the pristine hairiness is significantly more and denser. The effect after rubbing 350 times is shown in Fig. 3, It can be clearly seen that the pilling phenomenon is not serious on the surface of the nano-treated fabric, and the sample with nano-concentrations of 4% and 5% have almost no pilling phenomenon and only slightly fluffing (Fig. 3). This is because cotton fabrics coated with nano-TiO₂ particle have nano-adhesion on its surface, which is equivalent to a layer of nano-films, enveloping hairiness and improving the abrasion resistance of the fabric.

Tab. 2　Fabric pilling rating

Number of friction	Pilling rating*					
	Pristine	1%	2%	3%	4%	5%
10	4	4	4	4	4	4
30	4	4	4	4	4	4
60	4	4	4	4	4	4
100	3	4	4	4	4	4
150	2	3	3	4	4	4
200	1	2	2	3	4	4
300	1	2	2	3	4	4
350	1	2	2	3	4	4

* Ultrasonic power is 100%, ultrasonic time is 30min.

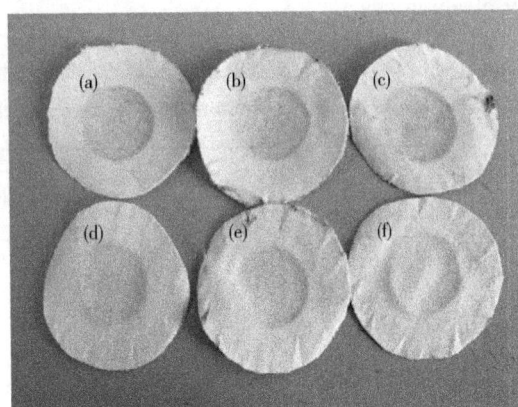

Fig. 3　Friction and pilling effect after rubbing 350 different samples of (a) untreated, (b) 1% TiO_2 treated, (c) 2% TiO_2 treated, (d) 3% TiO_2 treated, (e) 4% TiO_2 treated, (f) 5% TiO_2 treated

3.5　Antistatic analysis of cotton fabrics coated with nano-TiO₂ particle

Fig. 4 shows the antistatic performance test results of cotton fabrics coated with nano-TiO_2 particle prepared under different process conditions. It can be seen that the nano-cotton fabrics finished with nano-TiO_2 have longer decay time and worse antistatic performance than the pristine. This is because the cotton fabric itself has a good anti-static effect, the charge stays on the surface of the fabric, the static voltage decay time is fast, and its original half-life has reached the level of anti-static A (less than 5s). After nano-finishing the samples, the half-life time increases with the increase in concentration. This is due to the fact that nano-TiO_2 is a semi-

conductor. After finishing, the specific resistance of the fabric is larger and the charge stays slightly more[8]. The attenuation time of the nano-TiO_2 cotton fabric without ultrasonic treatment is almost unchanged. The longer the ultrasonic time, the smaller will be the electrostatic decay time with the concentration change trend. This is because when the ultrasonic treatment time is relatively short, the instability caused by the high-voltage discharge of the measuring instrument is caused.

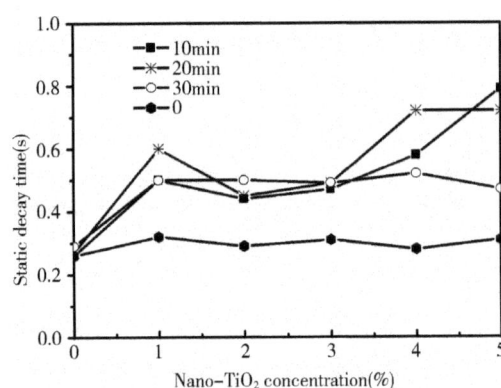

Fig. 4　Comparison of electrostatic decay time of different fabric samples with different concentrations of titanium dioxide nanoparticles and different ultrasonic time when ultrasonic power is 100%

4　Conclusions

Cotton fabrics coated with nano-TiO_2 particle were prepared by combining nano-technology and ultrasonic technology. Using the scanning electron microscope, it was observed that the nano-particles were entered into the fabric. With the increase of concentration of nano-solution and ultrasonic time, the adhesion of nano-particles to the yarn and even between the fibers was increased. Research showed that nano-TiO_2 treated cotton fabric formed a hydrophobic surface, and both the water repellency and the water-stain resistance were improved significantly. The highest contact angle was 143. 6°, which is very good for the fabric to block some liquid pollutants. In addition, the fabric showed a layer of nano-film covering the hairiness. The higher the concentration of nano-solution, the lower would be the pilling effect. Because nano-TiO_2 was semiconductor, the antistatic property of cotton fabric after nano-TiO_2 finishing was reduced.

References

[1] Macwan D P, Dave P N, Chaturvedi S. A review on nano-TiO_2 sol - gel type syntheses and its applications [J]. Journal of Materials Science, 2011, 46(11): 3669–3686.

[2] Guo C, Zhu X J. Effect of ultrasound on dynamics characteristic of the cavitation bubble in grinding fluids during honing process [J]. Ultrasonics, 2018, 84.

[3] ISO 27448–2009 Fine ceramics (advanced ceramics, advanced technical ceramics)—Test method for self-cleaning performance of photocatalytic materials—Part 1: Measurement of water contact angle [S].

[4] ISO 4920 ISOS. Textile fabrics - Determination of resistance to surface wetting (spray test) [J]. 2012.

[5] Gong Z L, Luo C M, Wu S Z, et al. Effects of ultrasound-combined microbubbles on hippocampal AchE fibers in rats [J]. Asian Pacific Journal of Tropical Medicine, 2014, 7 (5).

[6] Wenzel R N. Resistance of solid surfaces to wetting by water [J]. Industrial & Engineering Chemistry, 1936, 28(8): 988–994.

[7] Ni B, Zhang P. Experimental study on fabric surface wettability based on contact angle and surface energy [J]. 2017 (apetc).

[8] Asagoe K, Ngamsinlapasathian S, Suzuki Y, et al. Addition of TiO nanowires in different polymorphs for dye-sensitized solar cells [J]. Central European Journal of Chemistry, 2007, 5(2): 605–619.

Research on Moisture Absorption and Transmitting Perspiration Performance of Cotton Fabrics

Xinying Ji[1]*

[1]*Department of Textile Engineering, College of Textiles, Donghua University, Shanghai 201620, China*

* *Corresponding author's email*: jixinyingdhu@ 163. com

Abstract: Cotton fabrics are popular with consumers because of their excellent wearability, but its defects in thermal-wet comfort affect the wearer's comfortable experience. Through proper finishing technology, it can greatly improve the thermal-wet comfort of cotton fabric. The purpose of this text is to use finishing agent with Environment-friendly and washable to finishing cotton fabrics. The study verified the optimal finishing conditions: Concentration of finishing agent is 1g/L; pH = 5; The dipping time is 10min, Dipping or one dipping and one rolling. Under the condition that cotton fabric had little influence on moisture absorption and wicking properties, the performance of moisture permeability and quick-drying improved significantly.

Keywords: Cotton fabric; Thermal-wet comfort; Silicon finishing agent; Finishing

1 Introduction

"Health dress" has already become an important consumption concept of fashion apparel in the new period. Returning to the "pure cotton era" is inevitably becoming the most intense desire in people's hearts[1]. Pure cotton clothing is widely welcomed by consumers because of its good moisture absorption, soft, natural, ecological, healthy, nonirritating to skin and excellent air permeability. However, with the in-depth study of clothing comfort theory and the improvement of apparel performance requirements, it is found that the cotton fabric is not satisfactory in terms of thermal-wet comfort[2]. When the body surface is sweating, the pure cotton fabric is slow to guide and release moisture, and the fiber expands after the moisture absorption, blocking the blowhole, obstruct the heat and moisture exchange between the microclimate zone formed between skin and clothing and the external environment. When the sweat is scattered, the moisture will squeeze out the interior air of the fabric[3-4], reduce the heat preservation and produce a negative coldness, which seriously affects the comfort performance of the cotton fabric[3]. Therefore, achieving dry fit of cotton fabrics is the key to solve the

thermal-wet comfort. The purpose of this study is to use finishing agent with Environment-friendly and washable to finishing cotton fabrics, giving cotton fabric good effect of moisture absorption and transmitting perspiration.

2 Experiments

2.1 Materials

The Materials include cotton fabric (32[S], were obtained from market), hydrophobic finishing agent of silicon, Glacial aceticacid (shanghai Ling Feng chemical agent Co., Ltd.), sodium carbonate (shanghai Ling Feng chemical agent Co., Ltd.), potassium dichromate (National drug group chemical reagents Co., Ltd.).

2.2 Preprocessing of fabric

In order to remove the residual oil, wax and other auxiliaries on the surface of cotton fabric, the fabric should be cleaned with detergent first and the cleaning condition is 50℃, 30min. Then, rinse with clean water and dry at room temperature. Finally, iron will be used to iron the washed cotton fabric.

2.3 Specimen preparation with different finishing agent concentration

The concentration gradients of silicon finishing agent

were 0, 0.5g/L, 1g/L, 2g/L, 5g/L and 10g/L. 36 pieces samples of 10cm × 10cm, 12 pieces of 25cm × 3cm samples including warp and weft were cut off on the pretreated pure cotton fabric. After cutting, the samples were divided into six groups according to the concentration gradient. The different concentration finishing liquid was prepared, the cut fabric was impregnated with 20min and suspended vertically until no more dripping water. Then put them into the 105℃ constant temperature oven and drying 30min and the sample preparation was completed.

2.4 Specimen preparation with different finishing liquid pH

The gradients of pH were set to 3, 5, 7, 9 and 11. 20 pieces samples of 10cm × 10cm, 10 pieces of 25cm × 3cm samples including warp and weft were cut off on the pretreated pure cotton fabric. After cutting, the samples were divided into five groups according to the pH gradient. The finishing liquid with a concentration of 1g/L was prepared, two groups were treated with glacial acetic acid to adjust pH to 3 and 5, the other two groups adjusted pH with sodium carbonate to 9 and 11. The cut fabric was impregnated with 20min and suspended vertically until no more dripping water, then put them into the 105℃ constant temperature oven and drying 30min. The sample preparation was completed.

2.5 Specimen preparation with different dipping and rolling process

This experiment intended to explore the effects of three processes (impregnation, one dip and one rolling, two dip and two rolling) on moisture absorption and transmitting perspiration of cotton fabric. 12 pieces samples of 10cm × 10cm, 12 pieces of 25cm × 3cm samples including warp and weft were cut off on the pretreated pure cotton fabric. After cutting, the samples were divided into three groups according to the different processes. The finishing liquid with a concentration of 1g/L was prepared, dealing with different processes, then put them into the 105℃ constant temperature oven and drying 30min. The sample preparation was completed.

2.6 Specimen preparation with different dipping time

The gradients is of dipping time were 1min, 3min,

5min, 10min and 30min. 10 pieces of 25cm × 3cm samples including warp and weft were cut off on the pretreated pure cotton fabric. After cutting, the samples were divided into five groups according to the dipping time gradient. The finishing liquid with a concentration of 1g/L was prepared, dealing with different dipping time, then put them into the 105℃ constant temperature oven and drying 30min. The sample preparation was completed.

2.7 Water absorption testing on fabrics

The sample was cut into the size of 10cm × 10cm, making sure that the surface of the sample is smooth. The sample were placed in the standard condition environment to adjust humidity. Then weigh the original weight A and the unit was g, and 3 decimal digits were reserved. After that, the samples were completely immersed in beaker containing distilled water. After 5min, clamp the natural suspension with tweezers and let the water drip continuously until more than 30s. Than weigh B.

$$\text{Water absorption }(\%) = \frac{B(\text{g}) - A(\text{g})}{A(\text{g})} \times 100\%$$

2.8 Wicking effect testing on fabrics

The sample was cut into a strip of 25cm × 3cm, along the longitude and latitude. One end was fixed on the device, suspended vertically, and the other end was fixed with the tension clip of around 3g and submerged in the water. Adjust the level of liquid level so that the top end of the tension clip was about 1cm from the water surface. The capillary height of 30min fabric was recorded. The potassium dichromate solution of 5g/L was used as capillary height developer in this experiment.

2.9 Evaporation rate of water testing on fabrics

The sample was cut into the size of 10cm × 10cm, making sure that the surface of the sample was smooth. The sample were placed in the standard condition environment to adjust humidity. Then weigh the original weight a. After that, the samples were completely immersed in beaker containing distilled water. After 5min, use pneumatic small rolling mill rolling out excess water and weigh the weight b. The sample were placed in the standard condition environment to release moisture, A quality c was called once every 10min, until the adjacent two times weighing change did not exceed 1%. Relative moisture content at a certain time = (c−a) / (b−a).

2.1 Moisture permeability testing on fabrics

The sample was cut into the size of 10cm × 10cm, making sure that the surface of the sample was smooth. The sample were placed in the standard condition environment to adjust humidity, Silica gel desiccant, 35g, which had been dried to absolute drying, was added to the beaker of the same specification. After the weighing scales were used, the samples with moisture balance were covered with a leather band.

After beaker was placed in the 95% constant humidity box, and then weighed after 1h. After reprocessing 24h, after weighing and measure the water absorbed by 1h and 24h silica gel desiccant, we can calculate the amount of water vapor passing through the sample per unit time.

3 Results and Discussion

3.1 Concentration of finishing agent effect on fabric moisture absorption and transmitting perspiration performance

3.1.1 Water absorption and capillary effect

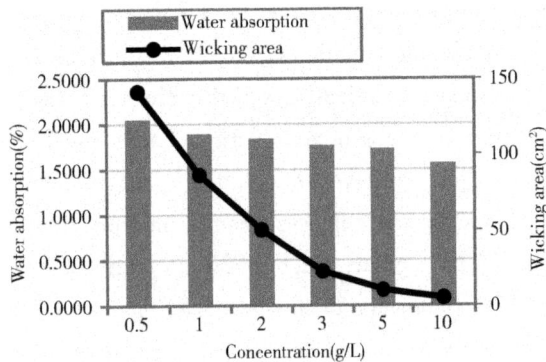

3.1.2 Evaporation rate of water

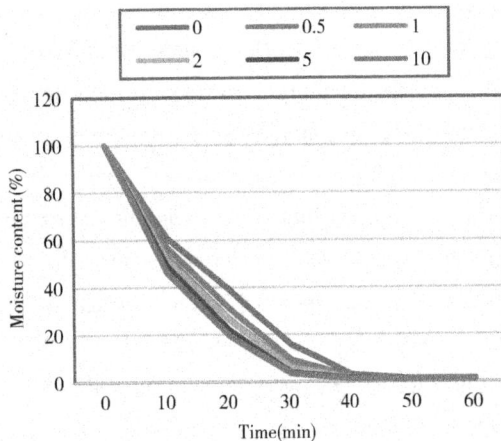

3.1.3 Moisture permeability

The results show that the water absorption and wicking area of cotton fabrics decrease with the increase of the concentration of the finishing solution. The influence of the core suction area is slightly larger. The moisture content of the fabric decreases with the increase of concentration. It is beneficial to the quick drying of the fabric. The moisture absorption and quick drying of the fabric is taken into consideration. When the finishing agent concentration is 1g/L, the moisture permeability and quick drying property can be enhanced, and the moisture absorption and the wicking effect can hardly be affected. Therefore, the optimum concentration of the finishing agent is 1g/L.

3.2 Finishing liquid pH effect on fabric moisture absorption and transmitting perspiration performance

3.2.1 Water absorption and capillary effect

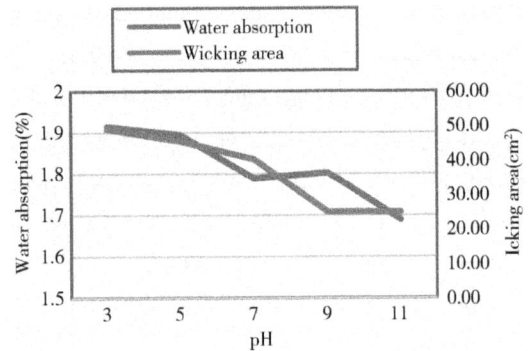

3.2.2 Evaporation rate of water

Group	1h moisture permeability(g)	24h moisture permeation(g)	Unit moisture permeation(%)
0	0.0764	0.6799	1.94
0.5g/L	0.0821	0.6926	1.97
1g/L	0.0768	0.7199	2.05
2g/L	0.0732	0.7045	2.02
5g/L	0.0736	0.7219	2.06
10g/L	0.0703	0.6904	1.98

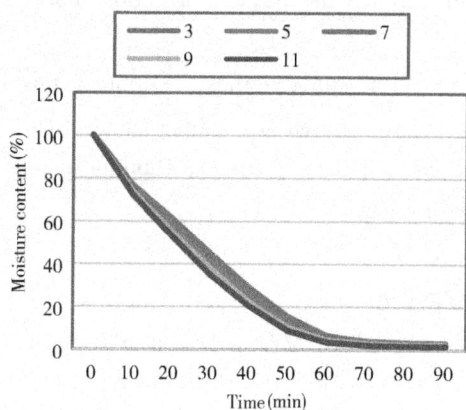

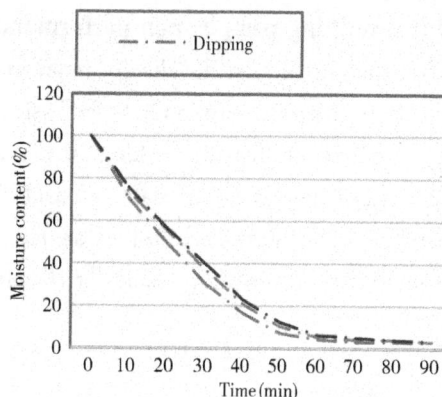

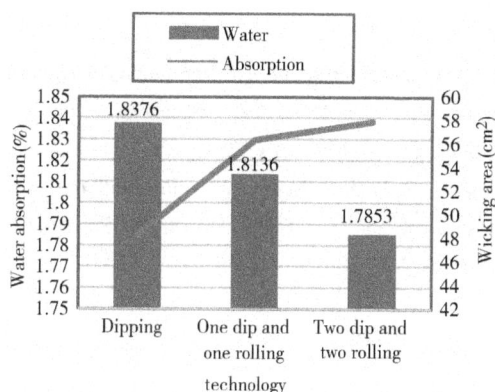

3.3.3 Moisture permeability

Group(pH)	22h moisture permeability(g)	Unit moisture permeation(%)
3	0.6025	1.71
5	0.5991	1.70
7	0.6186	1.77
9	0.6337	1.81
11	0.6219	1.78

Group	26h moisture permeability(g)	Unit moisture permeation(%)
Dipping	0.8235	0.0235
One dip rolling	0.8143	0.0233
Two dip rolling	0.7936	0.0227
Non fabric control	0.8328	0.0238

3.2.3 Moisture permeability

The results show that the water absorption and wicking area of cotton fabrics are better than those of alkaline conditions under acidic and neutral conditions. The pH has little effect on the moisture content. The drying performance is the worst in neutral condition, and the alkaline condition is slightly better than the acidic condition. Considering the moisture absorption and quick drying properties of cotton fabrics, cotton fabric has the ideal moisture absorption and quick drying energy when pH is 5.

3.3 Dip rolling process effect on fabric moisture absorption and transmitting perspiration performance

3.3.1 Water absorption and capillary effect

3.3.2 Evaporation rate of water

The analysis shows that the impregnation effect of the soaking process can make the core sucking effect slightly enhanced. However, the times of soaking and rolling are not good for the moisture permeable and fast drying performance, and the time and cost are wasted in the production process. Therefore, two dipping and two rolling are not considered. Impregnation is beneficial to the moisture permeable drying of the fabric. One dipping and one rolling can enhance the wicking effect and subsequent washability of fabrics. In production, dipping or one dipping and one rolling can be selected according to actual demand.

3.4 Dipping time effect on fabric moisture absorption and transmitting perspiration performance

The analysis shows that after the time of impregnation is 10 minutes, the water absorption rate is basically not changing, which shows that the soaking 10 minute fabric almost reaches the saturation state. Considering the requirement of saving time and cost in actual production, the impregnation time is selected for 10 minutes.

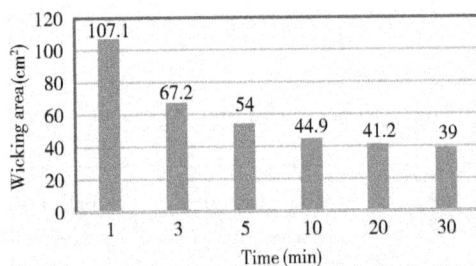

4 Conclusions

According to the results of the test, it can be seen that after proper moisture absorption and perspiration finishing, the moisture permeability and drying performance of thin cotton fabric are obviously improved. It is beneficial to improve the comfort of cotton fabric everyday wear.

To sum up, the study verifies the optimal finishing conditions: Concentration of finishing agent is 1g/L; pH = 5; The dipping time is 10min; Dipping or one dipping and one rolling.

References

[1] Li C G, Li Y H. Moisture absorption and transmitting perspiration performance of cotton fabrics [J]. Textile Dyeing and Finishing Journal, 2015, 37(10): 20–22.

[2] Mohsin M, Farooq A, Abbas N, et al. Environment friendly finishing for the development of oil and water repellent cotton fabric [J]. Journal of Natural Fibers, 2016, 13(3): 261–267.

[3] Li T. Moisture absorption and transmitting perspiration performance of cotton fabrics [J]. Shandong Textile Science & Technology, 2011, 52(1): 25–27.

[4] Wang Y, Fang F. Discussion on three different wet drying finishing agents [J]. Textile Dyeing and Finishing Journal, 2007, 29(7): 35–39.

Study on Stress Relaxation of High Stitch Density Biaxial Warp Knitted Polyester Fabric Reinforced PVC

Jiajia Hou[1,2], Nanliang Chen[1,2], Jinghua Jiang[1,2]*, Enquan Hao[3], Renbiao Zhang[3]

[1] *Engineering Research Center of Technical Textiles, Ministry of Education, Donghua University, Shanghai 201620, China*

[2] *College of Textiles, Donghua University, Shanghai 201620, China*

[3] *Zhejiang MSD New Material Co. ,Ltd. ,China*

* *Corresponding author's email*: jiangjinhua@ dhu. edu. cn

Abstract: The relaxation modulus of PVC membrane again time was obtained by the uni-axial stress relaxation tests. The generalized linear viscoelastic model, fractional model and fractional exponential model were adopted to simulate the teat curves and comparisons. The analysis results showed that both models could predict the stress relaxation modulus. Generalized Maxwell model has a high accuracy while Fractional model can hardly simulate the short-term relaxation modulus well.

Keywords: Reinforced PVC membrane; Stress relaxation; Viscoelastic model; Fitting

1   Introduction

In actual membrane structure, creep and stress relaxation reduce the initial tension on the surface of membrane with time, which causes surface relaxation and reduction on structural stiffness of the membrane[1]. Therefore, the viscoelastic properties of the membrane materials have a great influence on the long-term use performance of the membrane structure.

The study of viscoelastic properties of membrane generally utilizes viscoelastic models. Maxwell and Kelvin models are classic viscoelastic model. Extending the classical viscoelastic model infinitely, we can get generalized Maxwell and Kelvin Models[2]. However, with the increasing of basic components, the number of unknown parameters consequently increasing causes inconvenient application. To solve this problem, Schiessel[3] replaced springs and dashpot in classic models with viscoelastic fractional elements. The above models are based on the Boltzmann superposition principle to describe the linear viscoelastic behavior of materials. For non-linear viscoelastic behaviors, the constitutive equations can be expressed as multi-integral, single-integral, differential types based on theoretical, empirical, or semi-empirical correction theory. Weiming Zhang[4] proposed a practical expression of relaxation modulus and creep modulus and named it Sub-index model. But so far, there has not much use of mathematical models to study the viscoelastic properties of membranes. The applicability of various models and the simulation accuracy still lack the verification of tests and numerical calculations[5-8].

Biaxial warp knitted fabric reinforced PVC coating composites were used to do uniaxial stress relaxation tests in this paper and the classical Generalized viscoelastic model and the Fractional model were utilized to perform numerical fitting. Then, comparison of these two models were obtained. At last, this paper obtained a better equation to simulate the stress relaxation modulus.

2   Experiments

2.1   Materials

The experiment was done at room temperature of 24℃ ±1℃. The specimen were from biaxial warp knitted fabric reinforced PVC laminated composites and the specification was shown in Tab. 1.

The ground cloth was produced by Zhejiang MSD New

Material Co. ,Ltd. Warp and weft linear density: 1111 picks/inch.
dtex; Warp density: 36 picks/inch; Weft density: 21

Tab. 1   Sample specifications

| Sample No. | Areal density (g/m²) | Thickness (mm) | Breaking strength(MPa) | | Elongation(%) | |
			Warp	Weft	Warp	Weft
1	1557.20	1.68	203.47	139.189	11.43	13.18

2.2 Relaxation testing

In the test, two strips of specimen were cut along the warp and weft of the material. The distance between gauges was 200mm × 50mm. Experiments were done on Instron 5967 with a speed of 100mm/min to stretch to 10mm. Then the strain (ε) at this time was recorded. The displacement was fixed and the changes in stress (σ) over time (t) were recorded. The whole test lasted 6 hours. The result of warp and weft was consistent, so this paper took the warp sample for example.

3 Results and Discussion

3.1 Result of stress relaxation testing

The results of stress relaxation testing and relaxation modulus are shown in Fig. 1 and Fig. 2 by calculating. It can be seen that stress of reinforced PVC membrane is nonlinear with time. The stress relaxation rate become slower in long term.

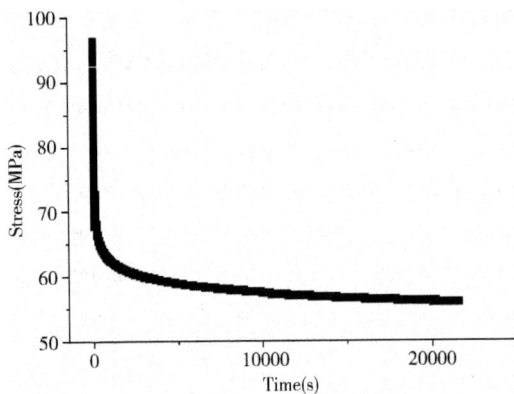

Fig. 2   Typical curve of relaxation modulus

3.2 Generalized viscoelastic model

Generalized Maxwell model is a combination of some Maxwell units connected in parallel. Studies have found that the model can describe stress relaxation behavior well. In this model, the relaxation modulus can be described as:

$$Y(t) = E_e + \sum_{i=1}^{n} E_i e^{-t/\tau_i} \qquad (1)$$

$Y(t)$ —Relaxation modulus;

$\tau_i = \eta_i/E_i$ —Relaxation time;

E_i —The elastic modulus of the spring;

η_i —Sticky coefficient of dashpot;

E_e —Balanced modulus.

Generalized Maxwell model is a combination of 3 Maxwell units in this paper. The fitting results of model parameters were shown in Tab. 2 and Fig. 3.

It can be seen that the relaxation modulus calculated by Generalized Maxwell model is closer to the modulus curve measured by experiment and also has a high accuracy.

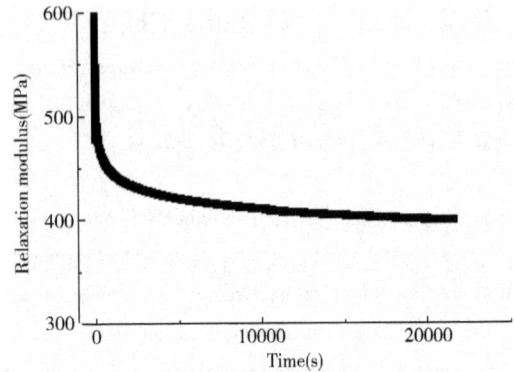

Fig. 1   Typical curve of stress relaxation

Tab. 2   Fitting results of model parameters

E_e	E_1	E_2	E_3	τ_1	τ_2	τ_3
394.67	54.80	32.80	42.64	127.75	1050.37	9851.66

3.3 Fractional model

The constitutive equation described by fractional elements is:

$$\sigma(t) = E\tau\alpha\frac{d^\alpha\varepsilon(t)}{d^\alpha t} \tag{2}$$

The relaxation modulus expression of the Fractional model can be obtained through the Fourier transform and the Mellin inverse transform:

When $0 \leqslant \beta < \alpha < 1$

$$Y(t) \cong \frac{E}{\Gamma(1-\beta)}\left(\frac{t}{\tau}\right)-\beta \ (t \ll \tau) \tag{3}$$

$$Y(t) \cong \frac{E}{\Gamma(1-\alpha)}\left(\frac{t}{\tau}\right)-\alpha \ (t \gg \tau) \tag{4}$$

$$\text{Let } k_1 = \frac{E\tau\beta}{\Gamma(1-\beta)},$$

Then (3-2) can be transformed to

$$Y(t) = k_1 t - \beta \tag{5}$$

The fitting results of model parameters: $k_1 = 570.03$, $\beta = 0.036$. The fitting curve is shown in Fig. 4. It can be seen that there is a big difference from the experimental value with a short time. However, it can simulate relaxation modulus well in long term.

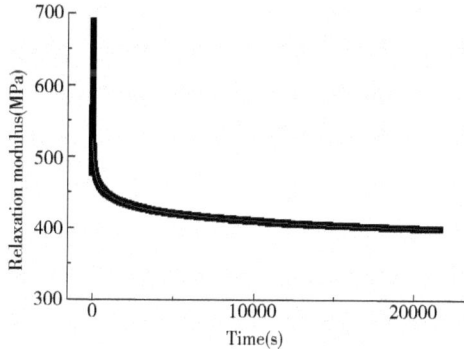

Fig. 3 Fitting curve of Generalized Maxwell model

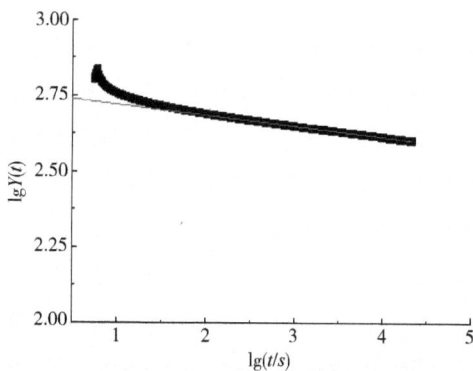

Fig. 4 Fitting curve of Fractional model

3.4 Comparison

Two equations are obtained by fitting process above:

$$Y(t) = 394.67 + 54.80 e - t/127.75 + 32.80e -$$
$$t/1050.37 + 42.64 e - t/9851.66 \tag{6}$$

$$Y(t) = 570.03 t - 0.036 \tag{7}$$

Generalized Maxwell model gives the steady-state modulus of relaxation modulus, which can reflect the memory characteristics of materials, so it has a better fitting effect. For Fractional model, it has a good fitting result in long term. But it can hardly simulate the short-term relaxation modulus well due to its form of the linear function. So, the equation (5) can be used to simulate the relaxation modulus trend of high density biaxial warp knitted polyester fabric reinforced PVC. Generalized Maxwell model has a better fitting effect.

4 Conclusions

The relaxation curve above indicates that stress of reinforced PVC membrane is nonlinear with time. The stress relaxation rate becomes slower in long term. Both models can predict relaxation. For Fractional model, it has a good fitting result in long term. But it can hardly simulate the short-term relaxation modulus well due to its form of the linear function. The equation $Y(t) = 394.67 + 54.80 e-t/127.75 + 32.80 e-t/1050.37 + 42.64 e-t/9851.66$ is selected to predict stress relaxation modulus.

Acknowledgements

This work was financially supported by National Key R&D Program of China (2016YFB0303300), and National Natural Science Foundation of China (NSFC 11472077), the Fundamental Research Funds for the Central Universities (2232018G-06).

References

[1] Lei M, Wu M. Stress relaxation and creep properties of PTFE membrane for building [J]. Journal of Architectural Materials, 2012, 15(02): 206-210.

[2] Nielson L E. Mechanical properties of polymers and composites [M]. Translated by DING Jia-ding. Beijing: Light Industry Press, 1981: 50-68.

[3] Schiesseil H, Metzler R, Blumen A, et al. Generalized visco-

elastic models: Their fractional equations with solutions [J]. J Phys(A):Math Gen,1995, 28(23): 6567-6584.

[4] Zhang W M. Practical expressions of relaxation modulusand creep compliance[J]. Natural Science Journal of Xiangtan University, 1999, 20(3):26-28.

[5] Shuai C J. A generalized Maxwell model for viscoelastic materials [J]. Journal of Mechanics, 2006,38(4): 565-569.

[6] Zhou G Q,Liu X M. Viscoelastic theory [M]. Hefei: University of Science and Technology of China Press, 1996: 36-44.

[7] Li Z, Xu B Y. Finite element method for the viscoelastic fractional derivative model [J]. Engineering Mechanics, 2001, 18(3):40-44.

[8] Zhang C Y, Zhang W M. Elastic recovery correspondence principle for solving a class of nonlinear viscoelastic problems [J]. Engineering Mmechanics, 2002, 19 (1): 139-146.

Study on Properties of Bamboo Yarn Knitting Products

Min Gao[1]* , Yifan Zhang[1] , Xiaoyan Ren[2] , Xiuli Gao[3]

[1] *College of Textiles, Donghua University, Shanghai 201620, China*

[2] *Hangzhou Second Middle School in Baima Lake, Hangzhou 310053, China*

[3] *School of Textiles, Henan University of Engineering, Zhengzhou 450007, China*

* *Corresponding author's email*: gmalice@ 126. com

Abstract: Through the mechanical properties of bamboo fibers, the thermal and wet comfort of bamboo fabrics was tested and discussed, and the bamboo fibers were subjected to electron microscopy and infrared spectroscopy. A bamboo knitting products was designed on a seamless underwear machine. Studies have shown that the surface morphology of bamboo fibers is mainly vertical and cross-sectional. The infrared spectrum of bamboo fibers shows that there are more hydrophilic groups of bamboo fibers, which is the main reason why bamboo fibers are better in hygroscopicity. Using fuzzy comprehensive evaluation, it is concluded that the bamboo-drier knitted fabrics have good heat and wet comfort, especially taking well, and are widely used in underwear and sportswear.

Keywords: Bamboo fiber; Scanning electron microscope; Infrared spectrum; Fuzzy comprehensive evaluation

1 Introduction

In China, Bamboo has been used in agriculture, handicraft, paper-making, furniture and architecture for thousands of years[1]; however, it is only recently that attempts have been made to produce textile fiber from bamboo[2]. At present, there are two ways to utilize bamboo in the textile in dustry in China. One is to produce natural fiber from bamboo by chemical and physical treatment (this material is called bamboo fiber)[3]. Bamboo fiber is developed by China's Tangshan Sanyou Group Xingda Chemical Fiber, and independently developed and developed a new environmental protection green textile with higher wet modulus. Bamboo fiber is a biodegradable regenerated cellulose fiber made from natural bamboo using modal processing technology[4]. It retains the advantages of bamboo fiber in terms of strength, dry and wet modulus, and inherits the important characteristics of modal fibers. This makes the bamboo fiber with good natural antibacterial, anti-mite, deodorant, pest control function. These properties make Bamboo Fiber widely used in underwear and sportswear[5].

The performance analysis of bamboo knitted fabrics made from bamboo fabrics and cotton yarns, polyester yarns, silk yarns, and viscose yarns was evaluated using a fuzzy comprehensive evaluation[6-7]. The results showed that: Knitted products have better moisture perspiration and soft skin-friendly properties. This provides a theoretical basis for the development of Bamboo knitwear products.

2 Experiments

2.1 Bamboo fiber properties

Bamboo fiber belongs to regenerated cellulose fiber, its chemical composition is cellulose, so the structure of cellulose is the structure of bamboo fiber. Bamboo fiber has the same molecular structure as natural cellulose fiber, which determines its good moisture absorption and moisture permeability.

2.2 Cross section analysis of bamboo fiber

The analysis of the morphological characteristics of the bamboo dale was performed using the Quanta 250 scanning electron microscope of the FEI company in the Czech Republic and recorded its longitudinal and transverse morphological structure with a magnification of 10000. The equipment sample preparation, the magnification can be continuously adjustable within a certain range, but also has a high resolution. The electronic scanning of the cross-sections of the bamboo fibers was mainly performed, and the vertical and horizontal surface morphologies at a magnification of 10000 were shown in Fig. 1.

(a) Longitudinal morphology

(b) Cross-sectional shape

Fig. 1　Bamboo 10000 times vertical and horizontal surface morphology

Bamboo fiber surface morphology is an important part of the fiber structure analysis. It can be seen from Fig. 1 that the fiber surface of the bamboo fiber is smooth and its cross section is non-circular. The cross-sectional shape of the fiber changes the gap between the fiber and the fiber. In the new product development shows a unique advantage. In terms of taking, unconventional cross-sectional shape fibers can give the fabric a special appearance and excellent moisture absorption performance. It increases the comfort properties of the knitted fabric, anti-pilling and good tactile sensation, comfort and high moisture, fast drying, breathable.

2.3　The infrared spectrum analysis of bamboo fiber

The infrared absorption spectrum was measured on a Nicolet 6700 Fourier Transform Infrared Spectrometer (Thermo Fisher Co., USA). A particular chemical bond or functional group in different molecules will always absorb infrared light in a certain frequency range. By observing the spectrum, it can be seen which groups are present, and the content of these groups can be roughly analyzed[8]. The amount of sample required for the experiment is small, the analysis speed is fast, and the destruction performance of the sample is minimized. Therefore, infrared spectrum is widely used to analyze and study the composition and structure of the molecules inside the fiber. Fig. 2 shows the infrared spectrum of bamboo fibers.

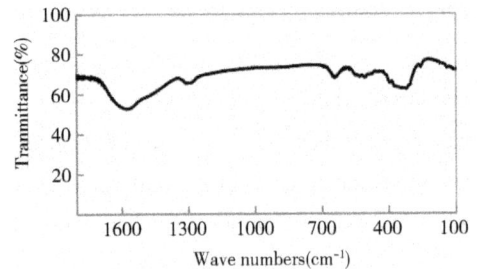

Fig. 2　The infrared spectra of the bamboo fiber

2.4　The physical properties of bamboo fibers

Data studies have shown that bamboo fibers have some advantages over cotton fibers and other regenerated cellulose fibers. Tab. 1 compares the physical and mechanical properties of bamboo fibers and other fibers. The moisture absorption rate of bamboo fiber is higher than that of cotton fiber, which indicates that the bamboo hair products have good hot and humid comfort in taking the product, and the products with high moisture regain rate will not have static electricity effect, so the bamboo hair product's taking performance is relatively high.

Tab. 1 Comparison of physical and mechanical properties of bamboo fibers and other fibers

Property	Bamboo fibers	Bamboo modal fibers	Modal fiber	Viscose fiber	Cotton fiber
density(g/m^3)	1.46–1.52	1.33	1.52	1.52	1.58
Water swelling rate(%)	70	80	70	90	45
Moisture absorption rate(%)	10–12	12	12	11–13	7–7.5
Length(mm)	38 ± 3	38 ± 3	25~35	38 ± 3	25–35
Fineness(dtex)	1.33	—	1.4–2.16	1.33–2.22	1.56–2.12
Dry strong(cn/dtex)	3.5	2.20–2.5	3.4–3.6	2.1–2.5	1.8–3.1
Dry stretch rate(%)	14–16	—	—	20–24	8–15
Wet strength(cN/dtex)	2.0	1.3–1.7	2–2.2	1.2–1.6	2.2–4.0
Wet modulus(cN/dtex)	0.6	—	0.65–0.70	0.2–0.3	0.3–0.65

3 Results and Discussion

The mechanical properties and thermal and humid comfort of the fabric are important factors in the intake. The bursting strongly affects the durability of the fabric, and the breathability and moisture permeability affect the comfort properties of the fabric. The results of the four knitted fabricsare shown in Tab. 2.

Tab. 2 Measured results of mechanical and thermal comfort properties of four knitted fabrics

Fabric	Bamboo knitting fabric	Modal knit fabric	Viscose knitted fabric	Cotton knitted fabric
Breaking strength (N)	403.82	459.00	295.54	436.98
Picking and pilling (level)	2.5	3.5	3.5	3
Breathability (mm/s)	1168	741.2	768.3	804.4
Moisture permeability [$g/(m^2 \cdot h)$]	98.53	101.35	99.79	99.37
Moisture conductivity (cm)	12.5	10.5	11.5	10.7

Analyze the test results of the comfort properties of the four types of fabrics. The bamboo wick fabric has good wicking properties. The modal fabric has good moisture permeability. The bamboo fabric has the best breathability among the four fibers. Pilling is better for Modal knit fabrics and ordinary viscose knit fabrics, and Modal fabrics have higher burst strength. Thermal insulation test results of four types of knitted fabrics, as shown in Tab. 3.

Tab. 3 Thermal insulation test results of four kinds of knitted fabrics

Fabric sample	Thermal resistance [$(m^2 \cdot K)/W$]	Heat transfer coefficient U [$W \cdot (m^2 \cdot \text{℃})$]	CLO	Insulation rate Q (%)
Bamboodale knitting fabric	0.0373	26.76	0.241	43.41
Modal knit fabric	0.0383	25.97	0.248	44.15
Viscose knitted fabric	0.032	30.41	0.212	40.30
Cotton knitted fabric	0.0344	29.08	0.221	41.38

3.1 Desizing effect on composite tensile properties

Determine the evaluation object of each evaluation index factor, $U = \{U_1, U_2, \cdots, U_m\}$ and then determine the evaluation level of the domain $V = \{V_1, V_2, \cdots, V_m\}$. It first determines the evaluation domain of the evaluation object m evaluation index, $U = \{u_1, u_2, \cdots, u_m\}$ and then determines the comment level domain $V = \{v_1, v_2, \cdots, v_m\}$. The fuzzy subsets correspond to it, and the single factor fuzzy evaluation of the j factors is the fuzzy subset R on $V = \{ri_1, ri_2, \cdots, ri_m\}$, and the direction of the evaluation factors is determined. Determine the e-valuation factor weight vector $B = (b_1, b_2, \cdots, b_m)$, the elements of the weight vector are essentially the factors that correspond to the degree of membership of the fuzzy subset {for the evaluation of important things} and finally establish the fuzzy relation matrix E, for the evaluation object comprehensive review. The result of the judgement is a fuzzy set $E = A \cdot R$, where the single factor judgment matrix

$$R \begin{cases} r_{11} & r_{12} \cdots\cdots r_{1j} \\ r_{21} & r_{22} \cdots\cdots r_{1j} \\ \cdots & \cdots\cdots \\ r_{m1} & r_{m2} \cdots\cdots r_{mj} \end{cases}$$

This is the comprehensive evaluation of the acceptability of four knitted fabrics. The comprehensive evaluation field of the fabric's performance is $U =$ (top break strength, pilling performance, thermal conductivity, warmth retention, breathability, moisture permeability, etc.) reflecting the above performance indicators, among which 3, 4 (take two Mean). These indicators are slightly better, using formulas.

$$r_{ij} = \frac{X_{imax} - X_{ij}}{X_{imax} - X_{imin}} \tag{1}$$

The bigger the four indicators 1, 2, 5 and 6, the better, using the formula

$$r_{ij} = \frac{X_{ij} - X_{imin}}{X_{imax} - X_{imin}} \tag{2}$$

Among them, X_{ij} is the actual value of each element. X_{imin} is the minimum value. X_{imax} is the maximum value.

The test values of the performance indicators in the table into equations (1) and (2), the fuzzy relationship between the evaluation effect of fuzzy performance and the index is calculated.

$$R_1 \begin{cases} 403.83 & 436.98 & 295.54 & 459.0 \\ 0.0373 & 0.0383 & 0.032 & 0.0344 \\ 43.41 & 41.38 & 40.30 & 44.15 \\ 2.5 & 3.5 & 3 & 5 \\ 1168 & 741.2 & 768.3 & 804.4 \\ 98.53 & 101.35 & 99.79 & 99.37 \end{cases} \Rightarrow$$

$$R \begin{cases} 0.66 & 0.86 & 0 & 1 \\ 0.16 & 0 & 1 & 0.62 \\ 0.19 & 0.71 & 1 & 0 \\ 0 & 1 & 0.4 & 0.4 \\ 1 & 0.14 & 0.06 & 0 \\ 0 & 0.30 & 0.44 & 1 \end{cases}$$

Then examine the set of weight coefficients for each performance. Among them, b_1, b_2, b_3, b_4, b_5, and b_6 indicate the weight of the top breaking strength, the weight of the pilling level, the weight of the breathability, the weight of the moisture permeability, the weight of the thermal coefficient, and the weight of the warming rate. When using two indicators for comparison, if the index j is more important than the index k, then the index is 1 and the equal importance is 0.5, otherwise it is 0, the score is λ_{jk}, and the weight of the index j is denoted as b_j.

$$b_j = \frac{\sum_{k=1}^{m} \lambda_{jk}}{m(m-1)/2 + 0.5m} \tag{3}$$

$j = 1,2,3,\ldots,m$; $k = 1,2,3,\ldots,m$.

On the basis of consulting relevant data, according to the requirements of good permeability and moisture permeability of underwear, substituting the formula (3) to calculate the index weights of the four fabrics are shown in Tab. 4

Tab. 4 Weight coefficient results for each indicator

Index(k)	Index(j)						Proportion
	Breaking strength	Thermal resistance	Warmth rate	Picking and pilling	Air permeability	Moisture permeability	
Breaking strength	0.5	0	0	0	0	0	0.03
Thermal resistance	1	0.5	0	0	0	0	0.09
Warmth rate	1	1	0.5	1	0	0	0.19
Picking and pilling	1	1	0	0.5	0	0	0.14

Index(k)	Index(j)						Proportion
	Breaking strength	Thermal resistance	Warmth rate	Picking and pilling	Air permeability	Moisture permeability	
Air permeability	1	1	1	1	0.5	0	0.25
Moisture permeability	1	1	1	1	1	0.5	0.30

The weight of the top breaking strength is 0.03, the weight of the thermal resistance is 0.09, the weight of the warming rate is 0.19, the weight of pilling and pilling is 0.14, the weight of the ventilation is 0.25, and the weight of the moisture permeability is 0.30. Dampness is the most important part of this experiment so it has the highest weight. It was found that the acceptability of the four fabrics was bamboo > cotton > modal > viscose.

4   Conclusions

The appearance and morphology of bamboo fibers and the comparison of the wet and dry strengths of bamboo fibers and other regenerated cellulose fibers show that bamboo fibers have a relatively smooth morphology as the new fibers, but their friction coefficient is large. Spinning performance has been greatly improved, which makes the design of knitted products have better performance, and because bamboo itself contains bamboo shoots this antibacterial material, which also gives bamboo fiber good antibacterial and antibacterial function, while seamless underwear. With full molding and no side seams, Bamboo Knitting is widely used in underwear.

References

[1] Wang Y, Ge W, Tian G, et al. Structures of bamboo fiber for textiles [J]. Textile Research Journal, 2010, 80(4): 334-343.

[2] Zhang W, Yao W, Li W. Research and development of technology for processing bamboo fiber [J]. Transactions of the Chinese Society of Agricultural Engineering, 2008, 24 (10): 308-312.

[3] Chen F, Wang G, Cheng H, et al. Development of advanced bamboo fiber based composites material [J]. Journal of Northeast Forestry University, 2016.

[4] Zakikhani P, Zahari R, Sultan M TH, et al. Extraction and preparation of bamboo fibre-reinforced composites [J]. Materials & Design, 2014, 63(2): 820-828.

[5] Erdumlu N, Ozipek B. Investigation of regenerated bamboo fibre and yarn characteristics [J]. Fibres & Textiles in Eastern Europe, 2008, 16(4): 43-47.

[6] Jin J L, Wei Y M, Jing D. Fuzzy comprehensive evaluation model based on improved analytic hierarchy process [J]. Journal of Hydraulic Engineering, 2004(2): 144-147.

[7] Cai W, Dou L, Si G, et al. A principal component analysis/fuzzy comprehensive evaluation model for coal burst liability assessment [J]. International Journal of Rock Mechanics & Mining Sciences, 2016, 81(June): 62-69.

[8] Khan Z, Yousif B F, Islam M. Fracture behaviour of bamboo fiber reinforced epoxy composites [J]. Composites Part B Engineering, 2017, 116:186-199.

Study on the Integration of Sizing and Dyeing of Medium and Coarse Yarn

Yue Zhang[1], Lamei Guo[1]*, Bijun Li[1], Yanzhen An[1]

[1]*Department of Technical Textiles, College of Textiles, Donghua University, Shanghai 201620, China*

* *Corresponding author's email*: lmguo@dhu.edu.cn

Abstract: This paper presents a new method for the integration of sizing and dyeing and weaving without desizing of medium and coarse yarn. The polyacrylate adhesive was synthesized by emulsion polymerization and mixed with nano-scale paint and cross-linking agents, etc. and then the multifunctional color size was made to size and dye the cotton yarn at the same time. The effect of polyacrylate adhesive with a different mass fraction on the sizing and dyeing properties of yarns was discussed. The results showed that when the mass fraction of polyacrylate adhesive was 6%, the weaving requirements, sizing performance and dyeing effect of yarn can be guaranteed.

Keywords: The integration of sizing and dyeing; Polyacrylate adhesive; Non-desizing; Sizing properties; Dyeing properties

1 Introduction

In the era of rapid development of modern textile technology, thedyeing, desizing, scouring and bleaching process of yarns in traditional textile industry consume much water and time, low production efficiency. And this do not conform to the environmental protection concept of modern cleaner production. Therefore, it is the only way to carry out clean production, save water, promote the sustainable development of textile dyeing. It is the trend of modern industry and the only way to achieve sustainable development[1].

Sizing process is one of the important processes for preparation before weaving, especially for natural cellulose-based yarns such as cotton and hemp. This process is mainly to enhance the warp yarn weavability by enhancing the strength, abrasion resistance, and wearing hairiness of the yarn[2]. However, currently used textile sizing mainly includes starches, polyvinyl alcohol (PVA) and acrylic sizing materials, which all have their own problems. Therefore, in addition to the need to meet the warp yarn weaving performance requirements, the development of new sizing techniques needs to be less polluted, low energy consumption, easy bio-degradation, and the harmful substances that remain on textiles meet the specified requirements[2-3], and the price is low.

In the yarn-dyed process, after the yarn is pre-treated, it needs to be dyed withthe traditional dyestuff, then the warp sizing and desizing process is carried out. The traditional yarn-dyed technology has the disadvantages of a complicated process and high energy consumption. But the pigment dyeing has the advantages of simple process, cost saving, and short process flow, etc. Therefore, the application of a new type of pigment dyeing method combined with the sizing process is developed. A process which can eliminate intermediate multi-step processes, reduce wastewater discharge and resources[4].

2 Experiments

2.1 Materials

Yarn 16^s Cotton Yarn, 16^s Cotton Bleached Yarn Drugs n-butyl acrylate, acrylic acid, methyl methacrylate, styrene (all chemically pure), sodium dodecylbenzene sulfonate, ammonium persulfate, anhydrous sodium carbonate, ammonia (all are analytical grade), nano-scale paint, cross-linking (Shanghai Xirun Chemical Technology Co., Ltd.), penetrant JFC (Shanghai Rufa Chemical Technology Co., Ltd.)

2.2 Synthesis of polyacrylate adhesive

After mixing sodiumdodecylbenzenesulfonate and anhydrous sodium carbonate, dissolve it in a flat-bottomed flask with deionized water, and measure acrylic acid, n-butyl acrylate, methyl methacrylate, and styrene mixed monomers. Added half of the mixed monomer to a flat-bottomed flask with stirring at 60℃ in a water bath. The temperature was raised to 70℃, and ammonium persulfate was diluted with deionized water. And diluted ammonium persulfate was slowly poured into the flask. After 30 minutes of reaction, the temperature was raised to 80℃. The remaining mixed monomer was slowly dropped into the flask. After reaction for 1 hour, the temperature was raised to 90℃ and the remaining persulfuric acid was injected. Ammonium solution, reaction 30min. Then it was cooled to 45℃, and the pH was adjusted to 6-7 with ammonia water. The material was filtered to obtain a polyacrylate adhesive.

2.3 Modulation of color size

Prepare 5 parts of 500mL color size solution with 2%, 4%, 6%, 8%, 10% mass fraction of the obtained polyacrylate adhesive, and add 0.5% of a cross-linking agent under high-speed stirring at 50℃. And 0.3% of the penetrant, and then adjust the pH to 7-8 with ammonia, then add 3% of the nano-scale paint, stirring 30min after the filter material, to obtain a different mass fraction of polyacrylate adhesive size.

2.4 The integration of sizing and dyeing

The prepared color size with different mass fractions was injected into the slurry tank of the GA392-2 single-spindle sizing machine which pre-heated for 20 minutes, and the sizing and dyeing were performed in one step. Sizing machine speed 70m/min, moderate pressure, drying room temperature 70℃. After the yarn is dried by a sizing machine, it is taken out into a 140℃ oven and baked at a high temperature for 3 minutes to be fixed.

2.5 Performance testing

2.5.1 Performance test of color size

(1) Viscosity

The emulsion viscosity was measured by NDJ-79 rotary viscometer.

(2) Storage stability

The viscosity of the emulsion was measured at room temperature for one months and the caking or delamination was observed. If there is no obvious change, the storage stability is good.

2.5.2 Sizing properties of yarn testing

(1) Sizing rate

In this test, the sizing rate of the yarn was estimated using a weighing method. Measure 100m long original yarn, calculate the corresponding sizing length according to sizing elongation and measure the corresponding length of sizing. Through the quality test before and after the slashing of the original yarn, the sizing rate was calculated.

(2) Enhancement rate and elongation reduction rate

The XL-1C sizing elasticity tester was used to measure the sizing reinforcement ratio and elongation reduction rate.

(3) Wear resistance

The abrasion resistance was measured by Y731 fiber cohesion forcetester.

(4) Hairiness reduction rate

The hairiness index was measured by YG173 hairiness tester and the hairiness reduction rate was calculated.

2.5.3 Dyeing properties of yarn testing

(1) Color fastness of yarn to soap washing

The soap color fastness tester was used according to the GB/T 3921—2008 "Textiles color fastness test soaping fastness" standard.

(2) Color fastness of yarn to rubbing

The rubbing color fastness tester was used according to the GB/T 3920—2008 "Textiles color fastness test rubbing fastness" standard.

(3) Apparent color and vividness of yarn

Datacolor colorimeter was used to test the yarn's apparent color depth K/S value (coloring amount), using a D65 light source, 10° viewing angle.

3　Results and Discussion

3.1　Viscosity and stability of color size

The polyacrylate emulsion synthesized by emulsion polymerization has a glass transition temperature of 20 degrees, a solid content of 30%, and a viscosity of 7. In the past, the new type of polyacrylic acid slurry was used for the purpose of replacing the traditional starch or PVA slurry. It is still based on the consideration of its easy desizing property. It often introduces too many hydrophilic groups to increase its water solubility, resulting in its low adhesion properties; or in order to improve its adhesion characteristics, the polyacrylic acid slurry designed with the very low glass transition temperature, prone to hygroscopicity and re-adhesion phenomenon[5]. Therefore, the new sizing-dyeing integrated non-desizing process is adopted.

From Tab. 1, it can be seen that with the increase of the mass fraction of the polyacrylate adhesive in the color size, the viscosity of the color size is also increasing and the stability of the color pulp is better. When the mass fraction of the polyacrylate adhesive is over 8%, delamination occurs after a long period of time. This is due to the fact that the binder concentration in the size is too high, and the cross-linking and nano-scale paint aggregates are attracted together by electrostatic attraction, resulting in the formation of large particles that aggregate and precipitate delamination.

Tab. 1 Effect of mass fraction of polyacrylate adhesive on color size performance

	2%	4%	6%	8%	10%
Viscosity(MPa · s)	1.5	3	4	4.5	5
Stability	Stabilization	Stabilization	Stabilization	Delamination	Delamination

3.2 Yarn sizing performance

(1)The effect of a mass fraction of polyacrylate adhesive on yarn sizing rate

The warp dyeing is mainly based on the coating color of the warp yarn by the slurry. Therefore, the sizing rate of the warp yarn is one of the key factors that determine thedyeing quality, the weaving efficiency, and the wearing comfort[6].

From Fig. 1, it can be seen that the sizing rate of the yarn increases as the mass fraction of the polyacrylate adhesive increases. The conventional desizing process starch slurry is controlled at 8%-12% in order to ensure the weaving performance of warp yarns. Therefore, it is necessary to control the low sizing rate as much as possible to achieve the weaving requirements. As can be seen from Fig. 1, when the mass fraction of the polyacrylate adhesive is 6%, the sizing rate of the yarn is controlled at about 5%, which is a relatively suitable sizing rate for the new-type sizing and dyeing integration process.

(2)The effect of the mass fraction of polyacrylate adhesive on the yarn reinforcement rate and elongation reduction rate

From Fig. 2, it can be seen that the yarn reinforcement rate increases with the mass fraction of the polyacrylate adhesive, and the reinforcing rate of the 16^s cotton yarn is much greater than that of the 16^s bleached yarn. This is because the surface of the cotton yarn contains some impurities such as cottonseed, which prevents the polyacrylate adhesive from entering the inside of the yarn and forms a relatively complete film on the surface of the yarn, thereby increasing the breaking strength of the original cotton yarn.

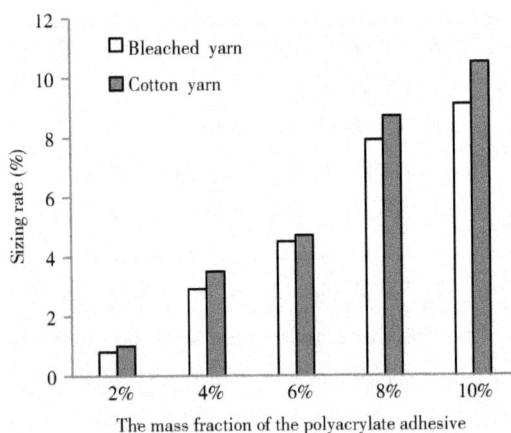

Fig. 1 Effect of mass fraction of polyacrylate adhesive on yarn sizing rate

From Fig. 3, it can be seen that the mass fraction of polyacrylate adhesive has little effect on the yarn elongation reduction rate, but the reduction rate of 16^s

bleached yarn is much larger than that of 16ˢ cotton yarn. This is due to the fact that the polyacrylic adhesive has entered more of the interior of the bleached yarn and has a greater permeability to the yarn. The adhesive does not have too many original cotton yarns. It only covers the surface of the yarn, and there is no fiber slipping inside the bound yarn. Therefore, the original cotton yarn has good elongation retention performance.

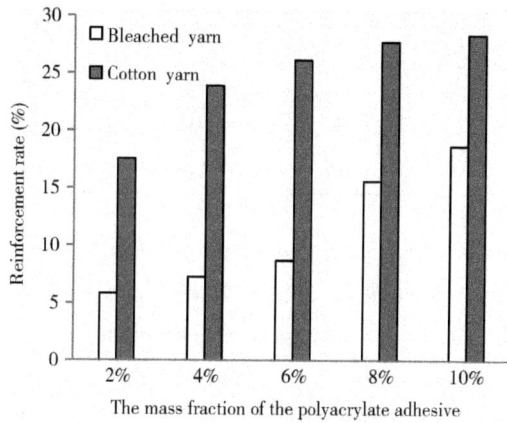

Fig. 2　Effect of mass fraction of polyacrylate adhesive on yarn strength

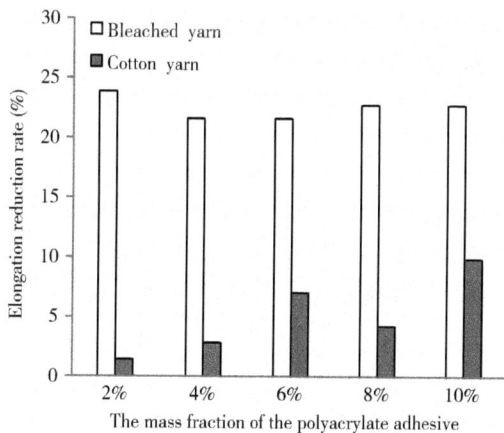

Fig. 3　Effect of mass fraction of polyacrylate adhesive on yarn elongation reduction rate

(3) The effect of the mass fraction of polyacrylate adhesive on the abrasion resistance of the yarn

From Fig. 4, it can be seen that the abrasion resistance of the yarn increases with the mass fraction of the polyacrylate adhesive, and the wear resistance of the 16ˢ cotton yarn is better than that of the 16ˢ bleached yarn. The low wear resistance of the cotton yarn itself is due

to the fact that the surface of the yarn has a lot of hairiness, which deteriorates the abrasion resistance of the yarn. The higher abrasion resistance of the bleached yarn itself is due to the fact that the surface of the yarn becomes smooth and tough after the pretreatment.

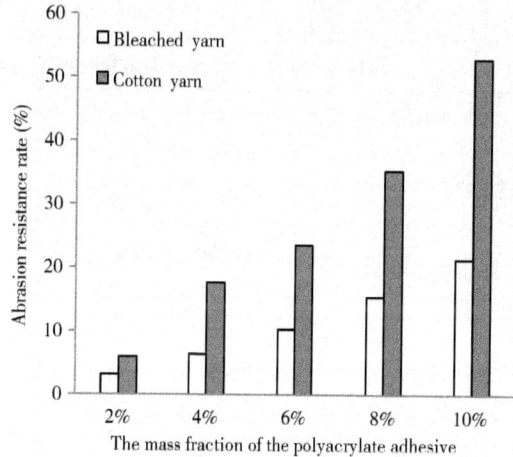

Fig. 4　Effect of mass fraction of polyacrylate adhesive on yarn abrasion resistance rate

(4) The effect of a mass fraction of polyacrylate adhesive on yarn hairiness

From Fig. 5, it can be seen that the reduction rate of the yarn hairiness increases with the increase of the mass fraction of the polyacrylate adhesive, and the degree of coverage of the hairiness of the two yarns by the polyacrylate adhesive is better. This is because the higher the binder concentration, the more pigment is absorbed by the yarn, and the thicker the film is formed on the surface of the yarn, which effectively covers the hairiness of the yarn surface.

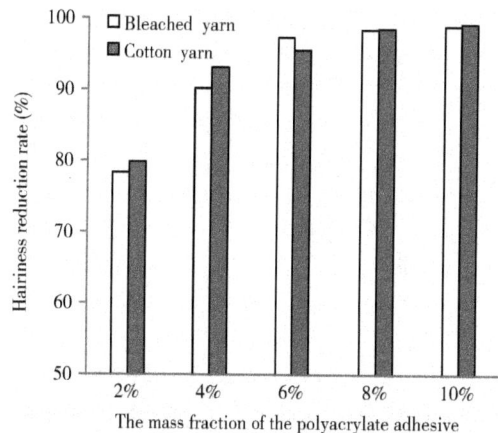

Fig. 5　Effect of mass fraction of polyacrylate adhesive on yarn hairiness reduction rate

3.3 Yarn dyeing performance

(1) The effect of a mass fraction of polyacrylate adhesive on the fastness to rubbing of yarns

From Tab. 2, it can be seen that the color fastness to rubbing of the yarn becomes better as the mass fraction of the polyacrylate adhesive increases. The color fastness to dry rubbing is better than that of the wet rubbing, and the 16ˢ bleached yarn's color fastness to rubbing is better than that of 16ˢ cotton yarn. This is due to as the increase in the amount of polyacrylate adhesive, the better the adhesion and coating of the yarn to the nano-pigment so that the color fastness is good.

Tab. 2 Effect of mass fraction of polyacrylate adhesive on the fastness to rubbing of yarns

The mass fraction of the polyacrylate adhesive		2%	4%	6%	8%	10%
Dry rubbing / series	16ˢ bleached yarn	3	3	3	3-4	3-4
	16ˢ cotton yarn	3	3	3	3-4	3-4
Wet rubbing / series	16ˢ bleached yarn	2	2-3	3	3	3
	16ˢ cotton yarn	2	2	2-3	2-3	2-3

(2) The effect of the mass fraction of polyacrylate adhesive on thecolor fastness to soaping of yarns

From Tab. 3, it can be seen that the mass fraction of the polyacrylate adhesive has little effect on the staining, and the soaping performance of the two yarns does not differ much. Among them, the color fastness of cotton stained is better than that of wool. This is due to the fact that the temperature and pH are relatively high during the soap color fastness test. The pigments detached from the yarns have poor adsorption capacity to cotton and good adsorption capacity to wool. Therefore, the color fastness to cotton is better.

Tab. 3 Effect of the mass fraction of polyacrylate adhesive on the color fastness to soaping

The mass fraction of the polyacrylate adhesive		2%	4%	6%	8%	10%
Cotton staining/ series	16ˢ bleached yarn	4	4	4	4-5	4-5
	16ˢ cotton yarn	4	4	4-5	4-5	4-5
Wool staining/ series	16ˢ bleached yarn	3-4	3-4	4	4	4
	16ˢ cotton yarn	3-4	3-4	3-4	4	4

(3) The effect of a mass fraction of polyacrylate adhesive on apparent color and vividness of yarn from Fig. 6, it can be seen that the apparent color of the yarn dyeing gradually deepens as the mass fraction of the polyacrylate adhesive increases. Among them, when the binder concentration reached 10%, the K/S value of the 16ˢ cotton yarn decreased on the contrary. This was due to the increase in the amount of binder, the thick polymer film formed by the binder.

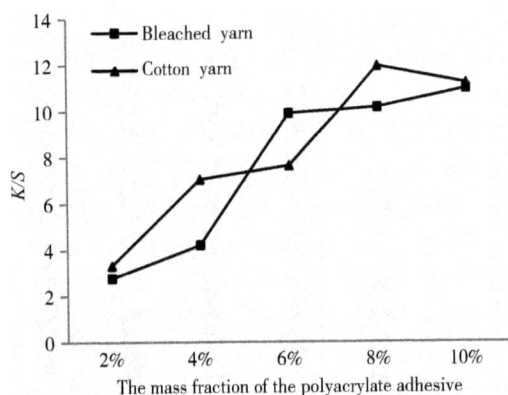

Fig. 6 Effect of mass fraction of polyacrylate adhesive on apparent color of yarn

4 Conclusions

(1) When the 16ˢ cotton yarn is processed by the integrated of sizing anddyeing, the mass fraction of self-synthesized polyacrylate adhesive is controlled at 6%, and the yarn sizing rate is controlled at about 5%, which can meet the requirements for weaving. The sizing performance and dyeing performance of the yarn are all well.

(2) After 16ˢ raw cotton yarn was treated with the inte-

grated of sizing and dyeing process, the sizing performance was generally better than 16^s bleached yarn, but for the dyeing performance, the 16^s bleached yarn was better. It can be selected based on follow-up needs and actual use.

(3) The sizing and dyeing integration process is short, the energy consumption is less, and the environment is clean. For the subsequent use of the actual weaving process can be further explored.

References

[1] Wu Q Y, Wu X Y, Yang Y X. A new dyeing process for energy saving, precipitation, sewage, and emission reduction in coating yarn [R]. 2007.

[2] Chen S, Qiu Y P, Shi W, Jiang Q. Non-slurry sizing technology for natural cellulose fiber yarns [J]. Journal of Textiles, 2016, 02: 85-91.

[3] Cai J, Liu Y T, Zhang L. Dilute solution properties of cellulose in Li OH/Urea aqueous system [J]. Wiley Inter Science, 2006, 10: 3093-3101.

[4] Wu Q Y, Sun Z Z, Wu X Y, et al. Dyeing process of yarn coating [J]. Dyeing and Printing, 2008(10): 29-32.

[5] Zhang Z J. Study on sizing process of denim specialty pulp [C]. 2012: 346-348.

[6] Cheng J, Zhang Z J, Chang P, et al. Synthesis of special pulp for denim blended warp yarn and its one-step pulping process [J]. Dyeing and Finishing Technology, 2015(10): 26-29.

Surface Modification Analysis of Flaxseed Fiber Bundles

Sayed Waqar Azhar[1,2] , Fujun Xu[1,2] , Yiping Qiu[1,2] *

[1] *Key Laboratory of Textile Science & Technology*, *Ministry of Education*, *Shanghai 201620*, *China*

[2] *College of Textiles*, *Donghua University*, *Shanghai 201620*, *China*

* *Corresponding author's email*: ypqiu@ dhu. edu. cn

Abstract: Exceptional properties exhibited by natural fibers and strict legislations have been the key points to keep the recent research trends focused on their use in non-conventional textiles, such as biodegradable composite materials. However, residual biomass of agriculture crops has been continuously wasted despite possessing higher lignocellulose fiber content. Particularly, flaxseed crop, one of the most widely grown crop worldwide for seed and its oil derivative products, annually producing massive quantities of wasted straws, if utilized, can become an abundant and economical source of lignocellulose fibers. This study investigates the effects of surface modification of flaxseed fiber bundles by Sodium Hydroxide (NaOH) and Acetic acid (CH$_3$COOH) treatments. The Fourier Transform Infra-Red Spectroscopy (FTIR) characterization results revealed significant decrease in surface impurities and changes in structural composition after alkali treatments. Scanning Electron Microscopy (SEM) analysis revealed cleaner and improved surface roughness of the fiber bundles after treatments. This study provided preliminary insight regarding the fundamental data about the potential of flaxseed fiber bundles as reinforcement in green composite materials with acceptable mechanical and interfacial properties.

Keywords: Flaxseed fiber; NaOH treatment; Acetic acid; Green composites

1 Introduction

Flax are of two varieties, most common is fiber flax variety grown for the fine yarns and linen, whereas, flaxseed plants are the agricultural crop variety exclusively grown globally for seed and its oil derivative products. Fiber flax have also continuously been focused by numerous researches[1-3]. However, despite huge consumption of flaxseed products for human and animals as well as in industrial applications such as paints, varnishes, printing inks etc[4]. millions of metric tons of by-product flaxseed straws are still wasted annually due to lack of alternative uses. Globally, posing challenge to handle this waste management. The top two producers in world are Canada and China (FAOSTAT 1994—2016)[5]. In Canada, millions of tons of unused wheat straw[6] and flaxseed straw residues had stirred severe environmental concerns[7]. Longer degradation period required it to be only burnt[8], which in fact is an overall global pollution hazard reaching beyond the territorial boundaries of respective country.

Lignocellulosic fibers (LCFs) are microfibrils of cellulose implanted in an amorphous matrix of hemicellulose and lignin[9], derived from various sources such as bast etc. had been used as fillers in biopolymer composites in numerous applications[10]. LCFs are generally cultivated in developing regions. Therefore, the utilization of LCFs could be a significant source of income for local economically disadvantaged farmers[11]. These are renewable, degradable, recyclable and promote inalleviating pollution[12]. Hence, possess the environmental, economic and social advantages.

Therefore, reusing this valuable natural resource of shorter flaxseed fibers, which are abundant, reliable and economic lignocellulose fibers, could prove to be potential reinforcements in green composite material applications on commercial scale. For instance, in automotive industry, as natural fiber reinforced composite parts, which could replace glass fiber composite materials[13-15]. Improved adhesion in the flax fiber/PLA composites by the surface modification was observed[16], and improved interfacial adhesion was achieved by mercerization, benzoylation, acetylation and peroxide treatmentsin flax fiber reinforced composites[17]. Environmental protection lawsand legislative policieshas pushed the industry towards natural fiber biodegradable composite materials fabrication[18-19] and also promoting biodegradable polymer matrices with exceptional mechanical and processing attributes[1,19,20].

An extensive attempt to individualize fibers resulted in very short, non-spinnable, damaged flaxseed fibers and environmental pollution[21], revealing significant fiber damage and excess weight loss by higher alkali concentration treatment, whereas, lower concentrations showed negligible effect on fiber surface. NaOH + Acetic acid treatment showed improved surface roughness, higher mechanical properties and thermal degradation temperature, better delignification, adhesion and less hydrophilicity[22].

Therefore, this study aims at using fiber bundles instead of individualized fibers. The Evaluation and comparison of characterization of surface morphology and modification of untreated and treated flaxseed fiber bundles was carried out. Eventually, its potentialin valuable green composite products is investigated and ultimately utilizing a valuable but wasted resource.

2　Experiments

2.1　Materials

Flaxseed fiber bundles from plants obtained from Agriculture research academy, Inner Mongolia.

2.2　Procedure

2.2.1　Flaxseed fiber bundles

Untreated fiber bundles refer to manually peeled-off bast from retted flaxseed stems by water logging for 24 hours.

2.2.2　Alkali treatment

10g/L NaOH treatment of samples was carried out at boiling temperature for 1.5 hours, followed by rinsing thoroughly with distilled water and let dry for 24 hours. Second treatment was carried out in two steps; Firstly, sample was treated with 10g/L NaOH at boiling temper-

ature for 1.5hour, thoroughly rinsed with distilled water and the resultant sample was further treated with a solution of 2% Acetic acid for 1hour at room temperature, rinsed thoroughly with water and let dry for 24 hours.

2.3　Characterization

2.3.1　Fourier transform infra-red spectroscopy

FTIR spectroscopy was performed to observe chemical compositional change after chemical treatment. 5% fiber was mixed with 95% kBr and passed through a disk of FTIR spectrometer (Nicolet 6700). Each spectrum was recorded at $4cm^{-1}$ resolution within the range of $4000-400cm^{-1}$.

2.3.2　Scanning electron microscopy

Samples were gold coated by sputter coating with evaporated gold. Subsequently their morphology was examined by using HITACHI TM3000 Scanning Electron Microscopy (SEM) systemat an acceleration voltage of 13kV.

3　Results and Discussion

3.1　Fourier transform infra-red spectroscopy

FTIR was conducted to analyse structural composition and corresponding changes before and after the treatment. Fig.1 illustrates FTIR spectra of treated and untreated fibers. The peak of $3200-3600cm^{-1}$ indicates axial deformation of the —OH group. The peak found at $3411cm^{-1}$ denotes hydrogen bonded —OH stretching. The C—H stretching was observed at $2918cm^{-1}$ and $2850cm^{-1}$ for both cellulose and hemicellulose, as C—H is a common element for both materials. Hence, after chemical treatment, the C—H absorbance peak decreased. The peak at $1633cm^{-1}$ is for C ═O band with carboxyl and ester group in hemicellulose and the absorbance peak is observed to decrease in treated fibers. The absorbance peak at $1427cm^{-1}$, $1375cm^{-1}$ and $1065cm^{-1}$ are for —CH₃ asymmetric, —CH symmetric stretching and —CH aromatic stretching in lignin, respectively. These peak values also get reduced with alkali treatment. The absorbance peak at $1249cm^{-1}$ is for —CH and C—O stretching in acetyl group in hemicellulose. The absorbance peak of $898cm^{-1}$ was for glucosidic linkage. These results indicate that a significant amount of hemicellulose and lignin has indeed been removed through our chemical treatment process. The acetic acid helped to remove the residual-Na from fiber bundles and enhanced delignification better surface morphology.

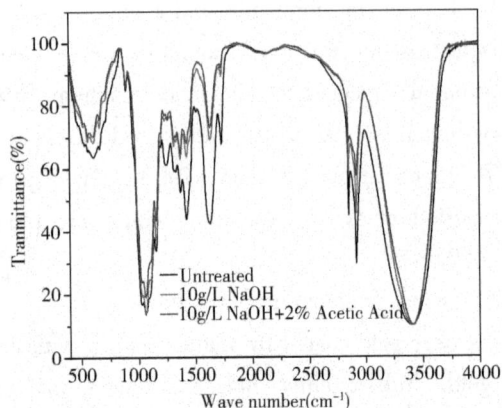

Fig. 1   FTIR spectra of (a) Untreated; (b) 10g/L NaOH treated and; (c) 10g/L NaOH + Acetic Acid treated flaxseed fiber bundles

3.2   Scanning electron microscopy

The surfaces morphology of the untreated and treated samples was investigated.

The SEM Micrographs showed that the untreated fiber bundles were completely embedded ingummy materials and impurities (Fig. 2). 10g/L NaOH treatment superficially removed the surface gum but the inter-fiber impurities were not removed (Fig. 3), however, comparatively rougher surface was observed but the fibers were still intact in bundles. Surface of the 10g/L NaOH and acetic acid treated fibers was significantly cleaner and rougher after removal of the superficial cementing materials and the fibers were distributed in much smaller bundles (Fig. 4). The acetic acid helped to remove the residual-Na from fiber bundles and enhanced delignification and surface morphology. It was assumed that 10g/L NaOH and acetic acid treatment resulted in significant surface modification due to improved surface morphology, roughness and more fiber surface contact area available, which is key for superior interfacial properties and fiber-matrix interlocking.

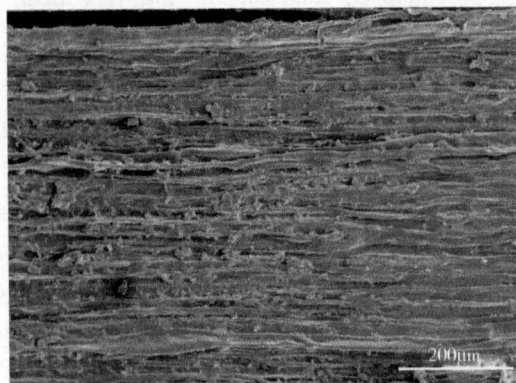

Fig. 2   SEM micrograph of untreated flaxseed fiber bundles

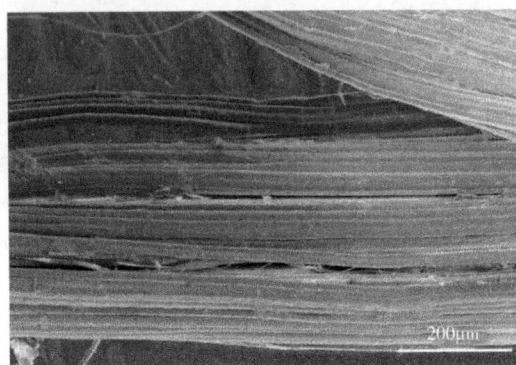

Fig. 3   SEM micrograph of 10g/L NaOH treated flaxseed fiber bundles

Fig. 4   SEM micrograph of 10g/L NaOH + Acetic acid treated flaxseed fiber bundles

4   Conclusions

It's been observed that the untreated fiber surface morphology was not very clean and found to be covered with gummy materials. However, the 10g/L NaOH treated fiber bundles showed improved fiber surface morphology and roughness. The 10g/L NaOH + Acetic acid treated samples showed much smaller fiber bundles with significant removal of surface impurities and residual-Na, improved surface morphology and availability of more reactive sites for fiber wetting and matrix interaction. Hence, better interfacial properties are expected inresultant composite materials. It is concluded that the fundamental data obtained in this study is very significant, highlighting the potential of flaxseed fiber bundles as prospective reinforcement in green composite materials.

Future Work

Carry out further characterizations, evaluation of mechanical properties and fabrication of composites.

References

[1] Oksman K, Skrifvars M, Selin J F. Natural fibres as reinforcement in polyacetic (PLA) composites [J]. Compos Sci Technol, 2003, 63: 1317-1324.

[2] Goutianos S, Peijs T, Nystrom B, et al. Development offlax fibre based textile reinforcements for composite applications [J]. Applied Composite Materials, 2006, 13(4): 199-215.

[3] Kulma A, Skórkowska-Telichowska K, Kostyn K, et al. New flax producing bioplastic fibers for medical purposes [J]. Industrial Crops & Products, 2015, 68: 80-89.

[4] Singh K K, Mridula D, Rehal J, et al. Critical reviews in food science and nutrition flaxseed: A potential source of food, feed and fiber[J]. Critical Reviews in Food Science & Nutrition, 2011, 51(3).

[5] FAOSTAT, 2018. FAOSTAT forworld linseed production 1994—2016. Food and Agriculture Organization of the United Nations.

[6] Sain M, Panthapulakkal S. Bioprocess preparation of wheat straw fibers and their characterization [J]. Industrial Crops & Products, 2006, 23(1):1-8.

[7] Ulrich, A and Marleau, R. Using agronomic practices to increase the per hectare yield of flax[C]. 91st PAPTAC Annual Meeting, 2005.

[8] Anthony W S. Separation of fiber from seed flax straw [J]. Applied Engineering in Agriculture, 2002, 18(2): 227-233.

[9] Martínez A T, Ruiz-Dueñas F J, Martínez M J, et al. Enzymatic delignification of plant cell wall: From nature to mill [J]. Current Opinion in Biotechnology, 2009, 20(3): 348-357.

[10] Dweib M A, Hu B, O'Donnell A, et al. All natural composite sandwich beams for structural applications [J]. Composite Structures, 2004, 63(2): 147-157.

[11] Satyanarayana K G, Guimarães J L, Wypych F. Studies on lignocellulosic fibers of Brazil. Part I: Source, production, morphology, properties and applications [J]. Composites Part A, 2007, 38(7): 1694-1709.

[12] Monteiro S N, Lopes F P D, Ferreira A S, et al. Natural-fiber polymer-matrix composites: Cheaper, tougher, and environmentally friendly [J]. JOM, 2009, 61(1): 17-22.

[13] Zafeiropoulos N E, Williams D R, Baillie C A, et al. Engineering and characterization of the interface in flax fibre/polypropylene composite materials. Part I. Development and investigation of surface treatments [J]. Composites Part A Applied Science & Manufacturing, 2002, 33(8): 1083-1093.

[14] Gassan J. A study of fibre and interface parameters affecting the fatigue behaviour of natural fibre composites [J]. Composites Part A, 2002, 33(3): 369-374.

[15] Joshi S V, Drzal L T, Mohanty A K, et al. Are natural fiber composites environmentally superior to glass fiber reinforced composites? [J]. Composites Part A, 2004, 35(3): 371-376.

[16] Shanks R A, Hodzic A, Ridderhof D. Composites of poly (lactic acid) with flax fibers modified by interstitial polymerization [J]. Journal of Applied Polymer Science, 2010, 99(5): 2305-2313.

[17] Wang B, Tabil L, Panigrahi S. Effects of chemical treatments on mechanical and physical properties of flax fiber-reinforced composites [J]. Science & Engineering of Composite Materials, 2008, 15(1): 43-58.

[18] Netravali A N, Chabba S. Composites get greener, Materials Today, 2003, 6(4): 22-29.

[19] Mohanty A K, Misra M, Hinrichsen G. Biofibres, Biodegradable polymers and composites: an overview [J]. Macromol Mater Eng, 2000, 276/277: 1-24.

[20] Liu L, Yu J, Cheng L, et al, Biodegradability of poly (butylene succinate) (PBS) composite reinforced with jute fibre [J]. Polymer Degradation and Stability, 2009 (94): 90-94.

[21] Peter, R L, Ron J D. Flaxcottonised fibre from linseed stalks [M]. Australian Government Rural Industries Research and Development Corporation. RIRDC, 2004.

[22] Hossain M K, Karim M R, Chowdhury M R, et al. Comparative mechanical and thermal study of chemically treated and untreated single sugarcane fiber bundle [J]. Industrial Crops and Products, 2014, 58: 78-90.

Temperature-Sensitive Garment for Real-Time Monitoring of Human Skin Temperature

Hui Chen[1,2], Ruifang Xiang[1,2], Qiao Li[1,2]*, Xin Ding[1,2]

[1] Key Laboratory of Textile Science & Technology, Ministry of Education, Shanghai 201620, China

[2] College of Textiles, Donghua University, Shanghai 201620, China

* Corresponding author's email: qiaoli@dhu.edu.cn

Abstract: Chronic diseases have become a huge challenge in public healthcare, many of which can make regulation mechanism obstacles and cause changes in human skin temperature. This paper presents a temperature-sensitive garments comprised of fabric temperature sensors to monitor human skin temperature in a comfortable way. The fabric temperature sensor was made by integrating a continuous metal fiber into woven structure. It has good softness, breathability and good Resistance-Temperature relation. What's more, woven sensitive-networks which are integrated 7 temperature sensors at different locations has excellent elasticity, then integrating sensitive-networks into a garment. The design of next-to-skin of garment will make people comfort. To demonstrate its applicability, a smart garment integrated the assembly has been used for in-situ detection of skin temperature while normal respiration and deep breath.

Keywords: Chronic disease; Skin temperature; Temperature sensors; Sensor network; Real-time monitoring

1 Introduction

In the latest decades, chronic diseases have become a huge challenge in public healthcare in many countries. Many chronic diseases can make human regulation mechanism obstacles and cause changes in human skin temperature. As a basic physiological parameter, skin temperature can reflect human health status[1-3]. Thus, it is necessary to design and create new medical system which can real-time monitor the temperature of patients and normal people in daily life. At present, several technologies have been developed, for example, smart wearable devices, electronic textiles and textile sensors[4]. In clinic or hospital, doctors will track someone's health then make diagnosis and feedback. However, so far, a number of technologies are confined to the room for complex body networking structure and complicated operations. It is difficult, hence, to carry the whole system. What's more, the existing temperature sensors such as conductive composite coating, stitching and weaving have some problems: low accuracy, high price, easy to be influenced by external environments and making human prickle sensation. Recently, several scholars have created wovenor knitted[5] fabric sensors, and the former have more advantages, such as tight structure, good air permeability and lower cost. Thus, the development of a woven temperature sensor would be a valuable innovation. In terms of current problems, it is necessary to combine textile sensors with body area networks to construct a wearable-temperature-sensitive. It contains flexible textile sensors around a person, which has good all-fabric materials won't make people uncomfortable.

The project aims to do research on temperature-sensitive garment for real-time monitoring. To achieve these aims, several comprehensive studies need to be conducted. Weaving the full-fabric temperature sensors and packaging them for later experiment. Integrating sensors into woven fabric-sensitive-network at different locations. Integrating networks into garment and making realtime monitoring.

2 Textile Sensors

In the current study, we developed a textile sensor with soft structure, small scale, and high sensitivity. The cotton yarns (280D, from Hangzhou Zhangfu Textile Co., Ltd.) are chosen for warp and weft to weave through a conventional weaving technology by using a semi-automatic weaving machine (Model: SGA598, Jiangyin Tongyuan Textile Machinery Co., Ltd.). In addition, every other piece of cotton yarn is woven with a continuous metal fiber—(Platinum, Pt)—(from Shanghai Shenjie Instrument Co., Ltd.) as a weft to weave a 10mm × 10mm sensor unit and weaving more than 5mm of Pt fiber in the diagonal position of the sensing unit (Fig. 1). The average total length of the metal fiber is about 150mm; the spacing between each line is 800 μm.

The sensor will be packaged for later environments: binding a certain length of silver yarns to Pt fiber which is on back side of sensor and drop the conductive silver paste, as shown in Fig. 2(a), putting the sensor into an oven at 60 ℃ for 30 minutes then let it cool naturally to room temperature. After that, a 5mm diameter thermoplastic polyurethanes film (TPU, d = 0.08mm, from Shanghai ShiYe Adhesuve Products Co., Ltd.) will be placed on the area of the conductive silver paste, then covering a 5mm diameter synthetic fabric (d = 0.08mm) on it and ironing (Model: RH183, from Shanghai Hongxin Appliance Co., Ltd.) it to paste firmly, as shown in Fig. 2(b). The same method is used at the other Pt fiber, as shown in Fig. 2(c). Fig. 3 shows the packaged sensor.

Selected thermal resistance fiber-Pt fiber possesses linear relationship between resistance and temperature. Thus, to get accurate data, calibration of "Resistance-Temperature, $R-T$" relationship is especially important. We place the sensor on a digital hot plate with temperature ranging from 30 ℃ to 50 ℃ to calibrate the $R-T$ relationship. Fix the sensor on insulating paper and keep the sensor close to the insulating paper. Connect the two silver wires to the probe of the resistance tester and acquired continuously by Agilent 34970A. Exact conditions of the test must be specified together with the time constant when apply a temperature sensor

to an application[6]. Fig. 4 shows the result: R = 0.207T + 66.676, R − Square = 0.9999, which R is the resistance of the fabric sensor; T is the temperature. It proves that the packaged sensor is equipped with good $R-T$ linear relationship.

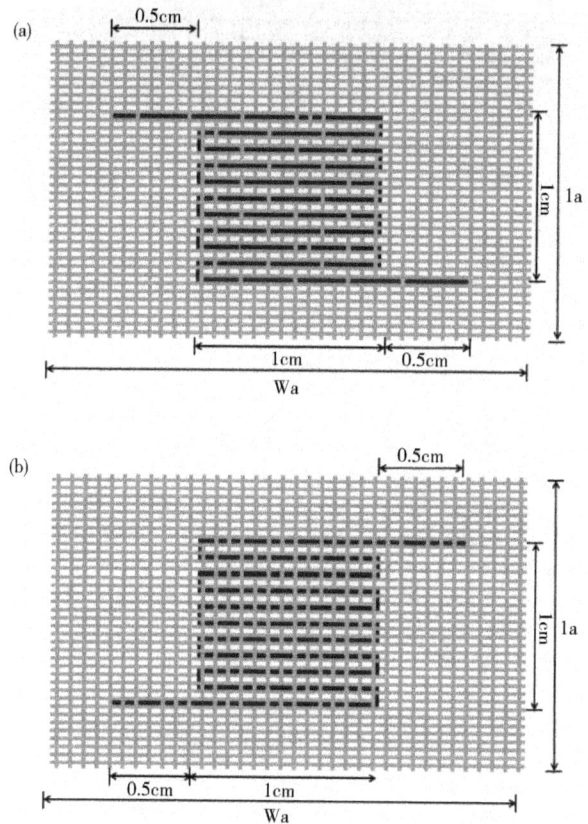

Fig. 1 Structure of the sensor (a) Front side; (b) Back side

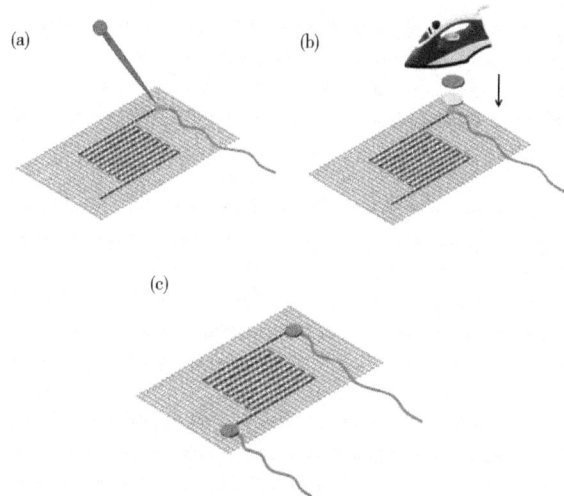

Fig. 2 Packaging process (a) Dropping the conductive silver paste; (b) Ironing; (c) The finished product

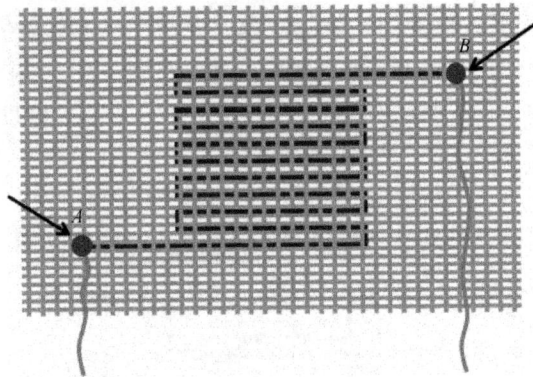

Fig. 3　Packaged sensor

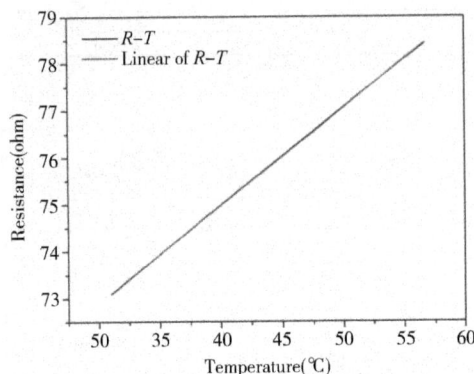

Fig. 4　*R-T* linear fitting

3　Temperature-Sensitive Garment

3.1　Selection of location

As a basic physiological parameter of the human body, body temperature can reflect human health. Many diseases will make the temperature regulation mechanism obstacles and change the body temperature[7-8]. Thus, we need to choose the suitable location to monitor.

Generally speaking, more test points will be good to monitor. The current study selects test points according to ISO 9886: 2004 (ergonomics-evaluation of thermal strain by physiological measurement), we adopted the 14 measuring points: there are differences in the skin temperature in different parts of the human body, but the difference between the left and right sides of the same part is not obvious. Meanwhile, considering the experiments requirements, we decided to choose 7 points (Fig. 5): scapula, armpit, upper chest, upper

arm, paravertebral, lower arm and abdomen.

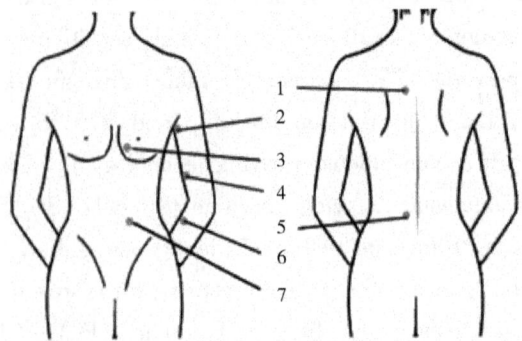

Fig. 5　Location of measuring sites
1—Scapula; 2—Armpit; 3—Upper chest; 4—Upper arm;
5—Paravertebral; 6—Lower arm; 7—Abdomen

3.2　Design and fabrication

In order to reduce the constraints of complex wires on human activities and ensure simultaneous monitoring of multiple points, we respectively integrated 7 sensors into two fabricated flexible and stretchable platform as a wearable assembly to be used for in-situ detection of human skin temperature[9-11]. Fig. 6 (d) presents the distribution of the fabric sensing network on garment.

Fabric circuit based on woven fabric which used elastic yarn as warp and weft, and use incorporating silver nano-particles coated polyurethane yarns (Young's modulus: 0.531GPa, tensile stress: 159.2MPa with 30% strain) as the conductive tracks. To ensure the quality of the connection between the fabric circuit and sensor, each circuit is separated by 10mm, as shown in Fig. 6 (a).

3.3　Connection of sensors

We implement the sensors on the corresponding locations of the undistorted woven fabric circuit board (FCB) so that the temperature sensors form checkerboard patterns in a precision method. Firstly, knotting the silver wire on the sensor with the silver wire on the network and dripping the conductive silver paste on it, and put it into the oven until dried. The next procedure is to place TPU between sensor and network, and press firmly. The exterior of network with sensors is showed in Fig. 6(b). Then, the silver wires of the respective circuits are connected to the aluminum conductor and tied firmly. At last, using a piece of synthetic fabric to cover the TPU which is put on knotting area and ironing to paste firmly to protect the knot points, as shown in Fig. 6(c).

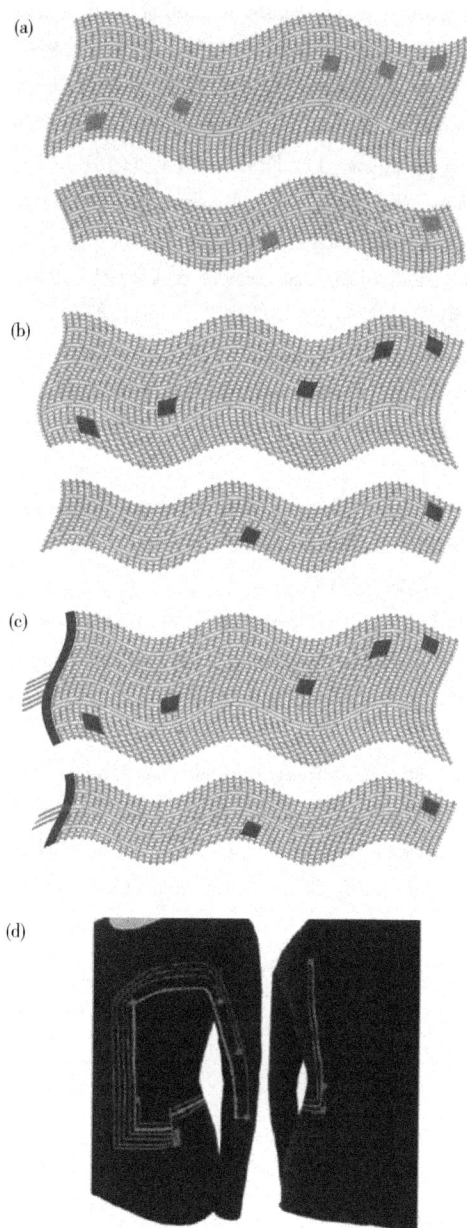

Fig. 6 The sensor networks (a) Fabric circuit distribution; (b) Networks with sensors; (c) Packaged networks; (d) Temperature-sensitive garment

4 Measurement of Skin Temperature

To investigate the applicability of the network with sensors, the packaged assembly is integrated into a garment for monitoring the skin temperature in different lo-

cations of a young and healthy female subject, as shown in Fig. 6(d). The front side of the sensor directly contacts non-flat human skins to detect the physiological temperature changes in the selected regions, which won't cause physical damage to the skin. Before measurement, sensors were calibrated by using a non-contact infrared digital thermometer (Berrcom JXB-182, China). All temperature sensors on the networks are functional and the packaged network worked well without any mechanical and electrical failure. Fig. 7 exhibits the temperature sensed by the fabric sensor array with respect to eupnea and deep breathing, respectively. The skin temperature differs on separate places of the human body, armpit has higher temperature and upper arm has lower temperature.

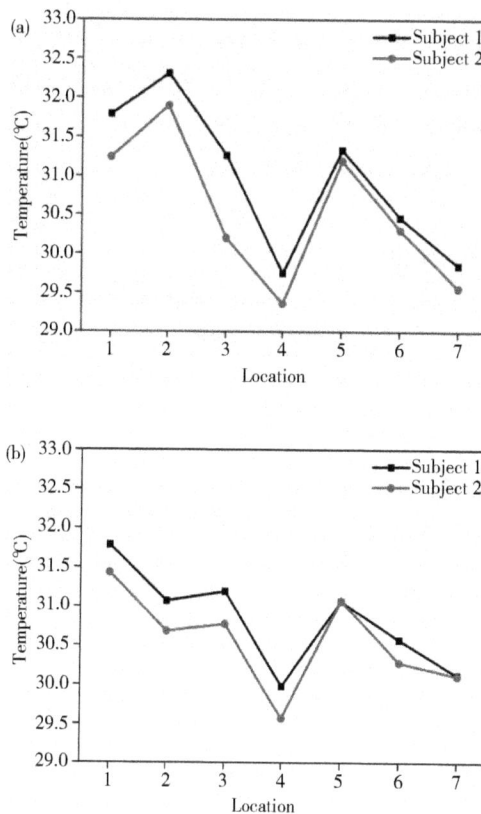

Fig. 7 Temperature distribution in different locations at normal respiration (a) and deep breath (b)

5 Conclusions

In this paper, the temperature-sensitive garment provides the best performance for wearable electronic applications when compared with previously thin films. The temperature sensor has good softness, breathability, and good $R - T$ relation. The network with excellent flexibility and superior breath ability could be attached conformably on a curved surface without any physical damage. This precise temperature sensing capability of the fabric sensor array demonstrates its potential to be applied in prosthetics and wearable skin electronics for monitoring of skin temperature variation during daily activities.

Acknowledgements

The authors acknowledge funding support fromthe National Science Foundation of China (Grant No. 51603039), the Fundamental Research Funds for the Central Universities, the Key Laboratory of Textile Science and Technology (Donghua University), Ministry of Education (Grant No. KLTST201623), and the Initial Research Funds for Young Teachers of Donghua University for this research.

References

[1] Trung T Q, Lee N E. Flexible and stretchable physical sensor integrated platforms for wearable human-activity monitoringand personal healthcare [J]. Advanced Materials, 2016, 28(22): 4338-4372.

[2] Law M K, Lu S, Wu T, et al. A 1.1 mu W CMOS smart temperature sensor with an inaccuracy of +/-0.2 degrees C (3 sigma) for clinical temperature monitoring [J]. IEEE Sensors Journal, 2016, 16(8): 2272-2281.

[3] Lee F F, Chen F, Liu J. Infrared thermal imaging system on a mobile phone [J]. Sensors, 2015, 15(5): 10166.

[4] Meyer J, Arnrich B, Schumm J, et al. Design and modeling of a textile pressure sensor for sitting posture classification [J]. IEEE Sensors Journal, 2010, 10(8): 1391-1398.

[5] Hhsain M D, Kennon R. Preliminary investigations into the development of textile based temperature sensor for healthcare applications [J]. Fibers, 2013, 1(1): 2-10.

[6] Chohan R K, Kerlin T W. Experimentation for the dynamic response of industrial temperature sensors [J]. Transactions of the Institute of Measurement & Control, 1986, 8(2): 58-60.

[7] Sadasivunik KK, Kafy A, Kim H C, et al. Reduced graphene oxide filled cellulose films for flexible temperature sensor application [J]. Synthetic Metals, 2015, 206: 154-161.

[8] Yang J, Wei D, Tang L, et al. Wearable temperature sensor based on graphene nanowalls [J]. Rsc Advances, 2015, 5 (32): 25609-25615.

[9] Kimd I, Trung T Q, Hwang B U, et al. A sensor array using multi-functional field-effect transistors with ultrahigh sensitivity and precision for bio-monitoring [J]. Sci Rep, 2015, 5: 12705.

[10] Wang Q, Yu Y, Yang J, et al. Fast fabrication of flexible functional circuits based on liquid metal dual-trans printing [J]. Advanced Materials, 2016, 27(44): 7109-7116.

[11] Wang X, Liu J. Recent advancements in liquid metal flexible printed electronics: Properties, technologies, and applications [J]. Micromachines, 2016, 7(12): 206.

Tensile and Flexural Properties of Sisal Reinforced Unsaturated Polyester Composite: For Furniture Manufacture

Anbesaw Muket[1], Adino Getie[1], Ashenafi Gashaw[1], Rotich k. Gideon[2] *

[1] *Textile Engineering, Ethiopian Institute of Textile and Fashion Technology, Bahir Dar University, Ethiopia*

[2] *Textile Chemistry, Ethiopian Institute of Textile and Fashion Technology, Bahir Dar University, Ethiopia*

* *Corresponding author's email: rotichgideon@ yahoo. com*

Abstract: Recently, natural fibers are increasingly replacing synthetic fibers as polymer composite reinforcement due to their benefits of low density, environmental friendly, low cost and high specific mechanical performance. This study aims at manufacturing and characterizing sisal reinforced unsaturated polyester composite. Sisal fibers were sun-dried after extraction and characterized on their strength, elongation and fineness. The composites were manufactured by combination of hand lay-up technique and compression molding by stacking woven sisal fabrics at different stacking sequence (0°, 90°, 90°/0°, +45°/ −45°) but equal number of layers. The tensile and bending strength of the manufactured composite was tested. The results showed that stacking sequence greatly influences the strength properties of the composite. Tensile and bending strength results of 0° stacked composite were 67MPa and 64MPa, respectively. The produced composite was used in the manufacture of tabletop proving that it can replace conventional timber in furniture manufacture.

Keywords: Sisal fiber; Unsaturated polyester resin; Composite; Furniture; Tensile and bending strength

1 Introduction

Development of natural fiber reinforced composite materials or eco-friendly composites have been gathering momentum recently due to the increasing environmental awareness. Natural fibers can replace synthetic fibers in composite reinforcement due to their low cost, easy availability, low density, satisfactory specific properties, enhanced energy recovery, carbon dioxide neutrality, biodegradability and being recyclable in nature[1-7]. Natural fiber reinforced polymer composites are finding application in furniture manufacture and automotive industries.

Among the several natural fibers, sisal is of utmost interest. The processing ways for extracting sisal include retting followed by scraping and mechanical means using decorticators. It is shown that the mechanical way gives about 2% ±4% fibers with excellent quality having a lustrous color while the retting process yields a large quantity of poor quality fibers. After extraction,

the fibers are washed thoroughly in plenty of clean water to remove the surplus wastes such as chlorophyll, leaf juices and adhesive solids[8]. Sisal composites boast of high impact strength in addition to having moderate tensile and flexural properties as compared to other ligno-cellulosic fibers[9-10]. There is an immense awareness in the use of sisal fiber as an alternative to glass fibers, driven by its light weight, lower price, and environmental advantage of being renewable and eco-friendly[11]. The hybrid composites of sisal/glass fiber and jute/glass fiber has been studied and found that although their strengths are slightly low, they offer the advantages of lower costs and environmentally friendly composites[2]. Sisal fiber constitutes cellulose (65%), hemicelluloses (12%) and lignin (10%) plus other water-soluble compounds. The proportion of these three constituents affects the mechanical and physical characteristics of the fibers.

The key setback with the use of natural fibers as reinforcements for thermoplastics matrix composite material has been identified as their poor wettability and weak interfacial bonding with polymer[12]. This is because of the intrinsically low compatibility as well as spread-ability of the hydrophilic cellulose fibers in the hydrophobic thermoplastics resin[9]. In addition, as a result of a higher processing viscosity of thermoplastic polymers, suitable wetting of fibers is not easy and the high temperatures can also cause unnecessary modification of the fiber surface or yet weaken the fibers[13]. Chemical surface treatment improves fiber-matrix interface. The chemical used for surface treatment of natural fiber include alkali, anhydride, resorcinol, amine, silanes or acrylates[6, 12]. For this reason, this work uses thermoset unsaturated polyester resin.

This research aims at manufacturing and characterization of sisal fiber reinforced thermoset composites which are made using untreated natural sisal fibers by a combination of normal hand lay-up procedure and compression molding process. The mechanical behavior of the manufactured composite was evaluated by testing their tensile and flexural strength. The damage morphology was also studied to understand how the forces are propagated during use.

2 Experiments

2.1 Materials

Both sisal fibers and cotton warp yarns were sourced locally in Bahir Dar market. Sisal fibers were dried to ensure that the moisture was removed. Tab. 1 shows the mechanical and physical properties of sisal fiber and Fig. 1 shows dried sisal fibers. Unsaturated polyester resin and its hardener was source from glass fiber tank manufacturers.

Fig. 1   Sisal fibers

Thermoset unsaturated polyester resin is one of the cost-effective resins when compared to other resins because of its less water absorbing capacity and outstanding bonding affinity plus good mechanical properties. The characteristic properties of the unsaturated polyester resin are shown in Tab. 1.

Tab. 1   Mechanical, physical and chemical properties of sisal fiber and unsaturated polyester

Properties sisal fiber[14]		Properties of the unsaturated polyester resin[15]	
Diameter (μm)	100–300	Specific gravity	−1.1–1.46
Density (g/cm^3)	1.45	Density	1125kg/m^3
Cellulose (%)	65–78	Tensile strength	18MPa
Hemicellulose (%)	10–14	Tensile modulus	0.8 – 1.1GPa
Pectin (%)	10	Compressive strength	90–250MPa
Lignin (%)	9.9	Flexural strength	30 MPa
Wax (%)	2	Flexural modulus	1.2–1.5GPa
Elongation at break (%)	4–9	Shrinkage	0.004%–0.008%
Tensile strength (MPa)	511–635		
Young's modulus (GPa)	9.4–22		

2.2   Experiment prosedures

2.2.1   Sisal woven fabric

Cotton yarns were used as warp yarns at a density of 2 yarns/inch. Sisal fibers were used as weft yarns and they were woven together in plain structure by using

handloom as shown in Fig. 2 (a). The handloom was used because the sisal weft yarn used was coarse and could be handled well in this way.

2.2.2   Composite manufacture

The composite samples were manufactured following the

Fig. 2 (a) Woven fabric preparation; (b) Manufacture composite; (c) MDF board; (d) Plastic table top

steps shown in Fig. 3. Four samples were manufactured with different stacking sequence as shown in the Tab. 2. The sisal fiber to resin ratio used was 1 : 3 while the resin to hardener ratio used was 10 : 1 and curing was done at room temperature. Stainless steel plates having dimensions of 50cm × 50cm was used and a releasing agent was applied to facilitate easy removal of composite from the plates after curing. Spacers of 2cm were used to set the thickness of the samples and each composite was cured under a load of 50kg for 24 hours before removing from the plates. Specimens of suitable dimensions were cut using diamond cutter for flexural and tensile test from the manufactured sample as shown in Fig. 2 (b).

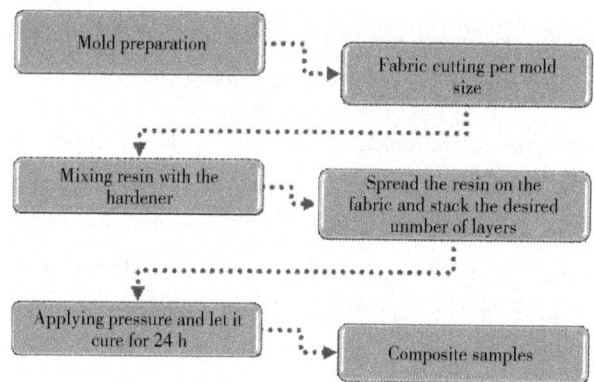

Fig. 3 Steps of composite manufacture

Tab. 2 Composite manufacture stacking sequence

Sample no.	Stacking sequence (°)	Sample no.	Stacking sequence (°)
Sample 1	90	Sample 2	0
	90		0
	90		0
	90		0
Sample 3	0	Sample 4	−45
	90		+45
	0		−45
	90		+45

2.3 Testing

2.3.1 Characterization of sisal fiber and cotton warp yarn

The tensile strength and elongation of the single sisal fiber and the cotton warp yarn was tested. A single column tensile strength testing machine with a load cell of 5 kN was used as shown in Fig. 4. The rate of testing was 5 mm/min and the samples were conditioned before testing in a standard testing condition.

2.3.2 Tensile strength testing of composite samples

The composite tensile strength test was done on a universal testing machine as shown in Fig. 4 (b). The specimen was gripped pneumatically and the test performed until fracture. The composite specimen size was 200mm × 10mm and gauge length was 85 mm. The specimen with desired dimension was fixed in the grips of the WAW − 1000 B microcomputer controlled UTM machine with 70 mm gauge length. The corresponding

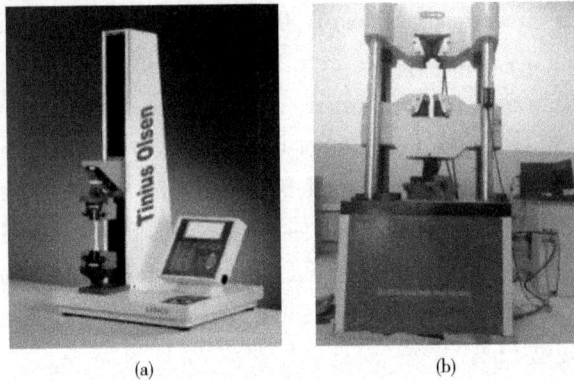

Fig. 4 (a) Tensile strength testing machine; (b) WAW-1000B Microcomputer controlled Universal testing machine

load and strain obtained was recorded and reported. Five separate specimens were tested for each test and the average value is reported. The composite tensile strength was also compared with commercially available medium-density fiberboard (MDF) and polypropylene plastic table top as shown in Fig. 2 (c) and Fig. 2 (d).

2.3.3 Bending test of composite samples

The composite bending test was done on a universal testing machine as shown in Fig. 4 (b) as per the ASTM: D790 standards. This test determines the behavior of a specimen when it is subjected to simple flexural loading. The dimensions of the rectangular shaped bending specimens was 150mm × 10mm with a span length of 48 mm. Five separate specimens were tested for each test and the average value is reported.

Calculation of flexural strengthand flexural modulus were performed by using equation (i) and (ii) respectively.

$$\text{Flexural strength} = \frac{3FL}{2b\,d^2} \qquad (\text{i})$$

$$\text{Flexural modulus} = \frac{m\,L^3}{4b\,d^3} \qquad (\text{ii})$$

Where: F is the ultimate failure load (N), L is span between center of supports (mm), b and d are width and thickness respectively, m is the slope of tangent to the initial straight-line portion of the load-deflection curve.

3 Results and Discussion

3.1 Tensile strength and elongation of sisal fiber and cotton yarn

Commonly, the strength and stiffness of plant fibers are affected by the cellulose content and the spiral angle which the bands of microfibers in the inner secondary cell wall make with the fiber axis. That is, the structure and properties of natural fibers depend on their source, age and which part of plant it's from. The tensile properties of sisal fiber are not uniform along its length. The lower part has low tensile strength and modulus but high fracture strain. It becomes stronger and stiffer at midspan and the tip has moderate properties as shown in Fig. 5.

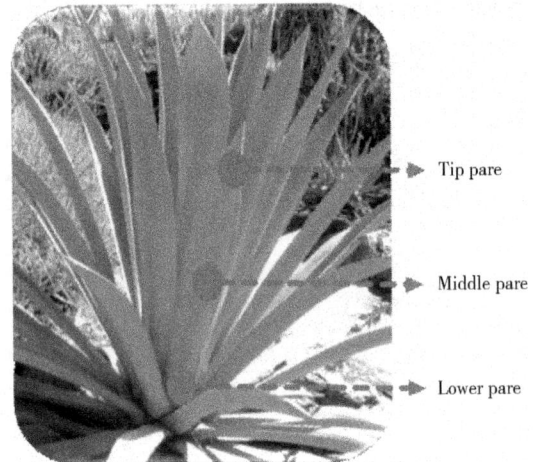

Fig. 5 Sisal plant

Tab. 3 shows the tensile strength and elongation of the sisal fibers that were used. As seen, it is slightly lower than the sisal strength and elongation reported in the literature as seen in Tab. 1.

Tab. 3 Tensile test result of sisal fiber

	Mean	Median	Std. Dev
Max stress (MPa)	410	416	169
Force at break (N)	102	75	320
Elongation at break (%)	2.541	2.510	0.794

Tab.4 shows the tensile strength and elongation of the cotton yarn used as warp yarn. The yarn was a plied yarn, therefore had high strength and high elongation.

Tab. 4　Tensile test result of cotton warp yarn

	Mean	Median	Std. Dev
Max stress (MPa)	6896	6800	2035
Force at break (N)	6750	6600	1995
Elongation at break (%)	13.559	12.730	2.060

3.2　Composite tensile strength

The tensile strengths of sisal reinforced composite within different stacking sequence are shown in Fig. 6. As seen sample 2 with stacking sequence of (0°/0°/0°/0°) had the highest tensile strength as expected because the sisal fibers was aligned to the direction of the force. The lowest was sample 1 with stacking sequence of (90°/90°/90°/90°) which only represented the strength of the unsaturated polyester resin because the fibers did not bear any force. The combination of different orientation improves the tensile strength of sample 1 (90°/90°/90°/90°). When the manufactured sample was compared with commercially available plastic chair top and Medium-density Fiberboard (MDF), the composite was three times strong than both as shown in Fig. 6.

It is evidenced from Fig. 6 that the stacking sequence greatly affects the tensile properties and the performance of sisal fiber reinforced unsaturated polyester composites.

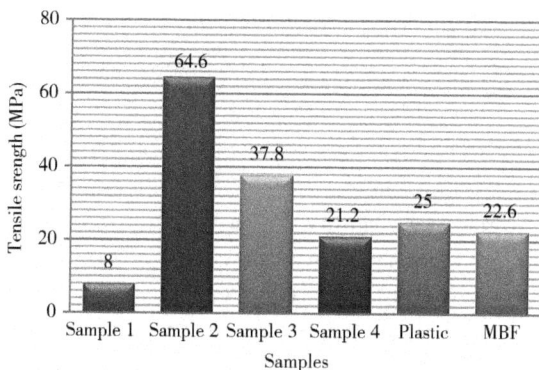

Fig. 6　Tensile strength of sisal reinforced composite, plastic table top and MDF

3.3　Composite bending strength

Fig. 7 shows the bending strength of the manufactured composite with different stacking sequence.

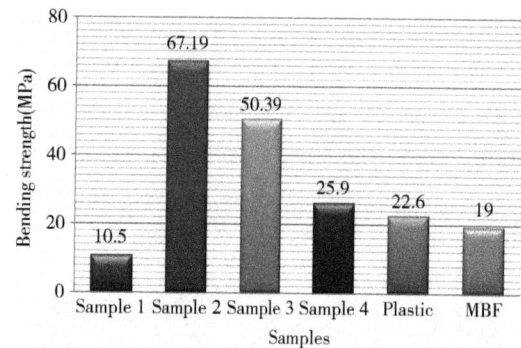

Fig. 7　Bending strength for sisal reinforced composite, plastic table top and MDF

As observed, sample 2 with fiber orientation of 0° had the highest bending strength followed by 0°/90° stacking sequence. This could be explained by the fact that the fibers oriented at 0° provide the resistance to the flexural loading. When compared with plastictable top and MDF, the manufactured composite had almost three times the bending strength especially 0° stacked.

3.4　Damage morphology

The damage morphology revealed by the manufactured composite after fracture is shown in Fig. 8.

As seen from Fig. 8, the damage morphology include matrix cracking along the fiber direction, fiber breakage and fiber pull out. This damage was pronounced by the fact that the samples were manufactured by hand layup method which exacerbates the existence of voids and poor interface between the fiber and the resin.

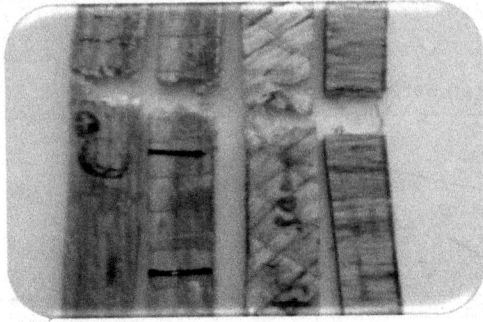

Fig. 8 Damage morphology of the specimen

3.5 Application area

A new potential application of sisal reinforced composite is the manufacturing of furniture top that are strong, cheap with good water resistance and replacing the use of timber. An example of manufactured table top is shown in Fig. 9. The other possible applications include fencing, roofing, pavement tiles, outdoor furniture and partition boards.

Fig. 9 Table top manufactured with sisal reinforced unsaturated polyester composite

3 Conclusions

This research successfully manufactured and characterized sisal reinforced unsaturated polyester composite. It has been shown that the stacking sequence affects both the strength and the damage morphology of the manufactured composite. The composite has the potential of be-

ing used in the manufacture of furniture replacing the dwindling timber. It can be conclude that sisal fiber can productively be exploited to manufacture composite by properly bonding with resin for the development of value-added products.

References

[1] Mohini Saxena A P, Anusha Sharma, Ruhi Haque, et al. composite materials from natural resources [J]. Recent Trends and Future Potentials, Int J, 2011, 43.

[2] Ramesh M P K, Reddy K, Hemachandra. Comparative evaluation on properties of hybrid glass fiber-sisal/jute reinforced epoxy composites [J]. Procedia Engineering, 2013, 5: 1745-1750.

[3] Alves F M E P, Thatiana V C G, Otávio d F M, et al. The effect of fiber morphology on the tensile strength of natural fibers [J]. J of Materials Research and Technology, 2013, 2 (2): 149-157.

[4] Verma D G P C, Shandilya A, Gupta A, et al. Coir fibre reinforcement and application in polymer composites: A review [J]. J. Mater. Environ. Sci. , 2013, 4(2): 263-276.

[5] Sandhyarani M V B. Physical and mechanical properties of bi-directional jute fiber epoxy composites [J]. Procedia Engineering, 2013, 51: 561-566.

[6] D. Nabi Saheb J P J. Natural fiber polymer composites: A review [J]. Advin Polymer Tech, 1999, 18(4): 351-363.

[7] Fatinah T, Majid M A, Ridzuan M, et al. Tensile properties of compressed moulded napier/glass fibre reinforced epoxy composites [J]. Journal of Physics: Conference Series: IOP Publishing; 2017: 012-013.

[8] Li Y, Mai Y W, Ye L. Sisal fibre and its composites: A review of recent developments [J]. Composites Science and Technology, 2000, 60(11): 2037-2055.

[9] Kuruvilla J, Beena J, Sabu T, et al. A review on sisal fiber reinforced polymer composites, R. Bras. Eng [J]. Agríc. Ambiental, Campina Grande, 1999, 3(3): 367-379.

[10] Partha H, Nipu M, Sutradhar G. Comparative evaluation of mechanical properties of sisal-epoxy composites with and without addition of aluminium powder [J]. Materials Today: Proceedings, 2017, 4: 3397-3406.

[11] Milanese Andressa Cecília CMOH, Voorwald, Herman Jacobus Cornelis. Mechanical behavior of natural fiber composites [J]. Procedia Engineering, 2011, 10: 2022-2027.

[12] Kanny TPMK. Chemical treatment of sisal fiber using alkali and clay method [J]. Composites: Part A, 2012, 43: 1989-1998.

[13] Mitra B C. Environment friendly composite materials: bio-composites and green composites [J]. Defence Science J, 2014, 64(3): 244-261.

[14] Srivastava M K, Ga R K. Tensile and flexural properties of sisal fiber reinforced epoxy composite: A comparison between unidirectional and mat form of fibers [J]. Procedia Mat Sci, 2014, 5: 2434-2439.

[15] Sathishkumar T, Navaneethakrishnan P, Shankar S. Tensile and flexural properties of snake grass natural fiber reinforced isophthallic polyester composites [J]. Comp Sci and Tech, 2012, 72(10): 1183-1190.

The Effect of Different Female Body Shape Patterns on Marker Efficiencies at Dissimilar Fabric Width in the Garment Production

Tayyab Naveed[1, 2], Azmat Hussain[1], Yu Zhicai[1], Wu Ge[1],
Xi Zhang[1], Kai Lu[1], Xin Wang[1], Haoyang Xie[1], Yueqi Zhong[1, 3]*

[1] College of Textile Engineering, Donghua University, Shanghai 201620, China

[2] School of Fine Arts, Design & Architecture, GIFT University, Gujranwala, Pakistan

[3] Key Lab of Textile Science and Technology, Ministry of Education, China

*Corresponding author's email: hyq@ dhu. edu. cn

Abstract: :The purpose of this study is to investigate the effect of body shape patterns and marker efficiency on fabric utilization at different fabric width. Patterns and markers of the fitted shirt are generated conventionally for four women body shapes i. e. triangle, square, oval and circle. The results reveal that there is a linear relationship between pattern marker efficiency and fabric width (sig. < 0.05). The regression analysis (*p*-value) is also statistically significant. All body shapes have more marker efficiency results at larger fabric width however amongst all; Square shape female body is the most efficient and cost-effective in fabric utilization for a fitted dress shirt.

Keywords: Female body shapes; Fabric width; Marker efficiency; Garment production

1　Introduction

Patterns are drawn by a patternmaker according to the specifications of the designer for a specific style[1]. When the patterns are arranged altogether precisely as a single diagram, it is called a marker[2]. How well all the pieces of patterns are arranged on the fabric to achieve the most efficient layout is called marker efficiency[3]. Thus the marker efficiency is determined from the fabric utilization. In other words, it is the percentage of the total fabric actually consumed in garment component parts in a maker[4]. The pattern making and maker efficiency are the major activities that contribute mainly to the fabric consumption and wastage in the cutting-room of apparel firm. Thus saving an inch of a fabric through the efficient placement of pattern pieces in a maker has a pronounced effect on company profits[1]. Therefore in the growing environment of competition, garment industries are always looking forward to solutions in optimizing the fabric utilization, operations and manufacturing processes to overcome the challenges.

Optimization of fabric utilization has long been an important topic of discussion in the cutting-room of the apparel industry. In the literature review, many studies have focused on cutting software, instruments and systematic procedures for fabric savings[5-7]. However very limited study with the combined effect of body shapes and fabric width on fabric utilization. The aim of this research is to determine the effects of different body shapes at different fabric width (127 – 216cm) on the marker efficiency. For this purpose, fitted dress shirt was studied. 144 markers were prepared (each body shape has 36 markers) on the Gerber Technology (GGT; V10.351) software system and the marker plan efficiencies were compared.

2　Experiments

2.1　Materials and equipment

100% cotton woven fabric with a plain weave of warp-66, weft-36, and fabric density (10 ×10) is selected. The fabric has 2% shrinkage in both warp and weft yarns. Four different female body types (as shown in Fig. 1) are selected for producing close fitted shirts. The features of the fitted shirt are displayed in Fig. 2. The tools and equipment used for making the patterns are pattern making toolkit and GGT software for pattern grading and construction of marker plans.

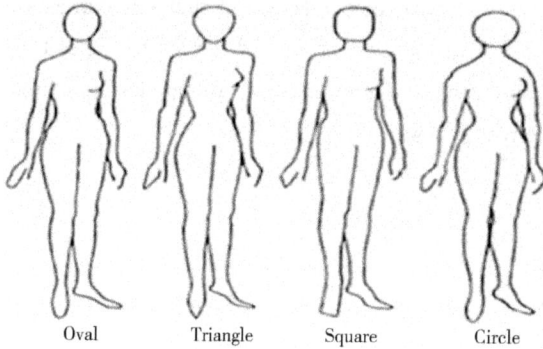

Fig. 1　Four different female body types[8]

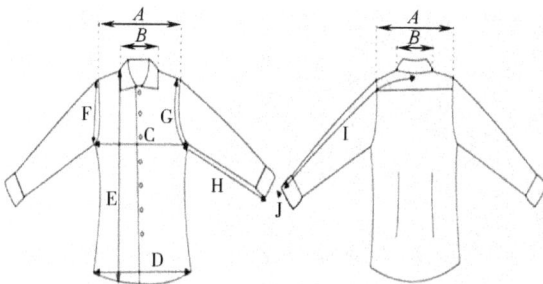

Fig. 2　Technical drawing of women fitted shirt

2.2　Experimental work

The patterns of garment style (shown in Fig. 2) are drawn comparatively to each selected female body type on thirty-six different fabric widths i. e. 127 – 216cm (50 – 85 inches) for the assessment of the fabric consumption.

Triangle shape body is considered well proportional body amongst all body types. The reason is equal in bust and hip size with the narrowest waist. The proportional grading skills among the sizes (extra-small, small, medium, large, extra-large) are applied according to the rule of ASTM D5585 – 95 standard. With the help of GGT software, 20 patterns (each shape five sizes of shirt) are constructed. The size ratios (XS : S : M : L : XL; 1 : 1 : 1 : 1 : 1) of all body shapes are kept constant. This is done in order to explore precise utilization of the fabric with equal quantity and sizes of garments in all body types. Fig. 3 has shown the pattern marker of the shirt of four female body shapes as for an example. These are auto pattern markers drawn with the help of GGT software. The detailed marker efficiency values of all body types in different fabric widths are enlisted in Tab. 2 (in the appendix).

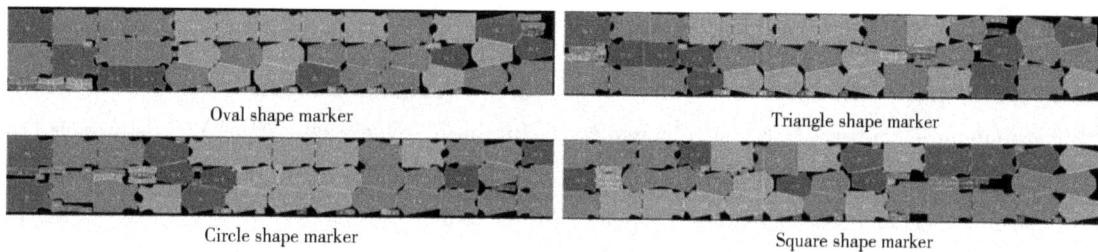

Fig. 3　Patter markers of the fitted shirt of four body types

3　Results and Discussion

From the investigation displayed in Tab. 1 (in the appendix), it is determined that the marker efficiencies varied with body types and fabric width. It has been observed that there are an increase and decrease in values of fabric consumption efficiencies. Fabric construction, fabric width (127 – 216cm), four different body shapes, fabric shrinkage, the total number of pattern pieces of each shape, the total number of patterns in each marker and number of fabric plies are the factors

which are kept constant. The data is analyzed to determine the significance level of difference and the relationship between the variables.

3.1　Marker efficiency

Fig. 4 has shown the fitted shirt marker efficiencies (ME) of four body types. The variations in the bar graph of the Fig. 4 illustrate that the general trend (black dotted line) in the marker efficiency increases with the increase of fabric width in all body shapes.

The Fig. 4 illustrates that the triangle shape body has the most marker efficiency (90.33%) at 205.7cm (81 inches) fabric width, the circle shape body has the most marker efficiency (90.03%) at 200.7cm (79 inches) fabric width, the oval shape body has the most marker efficiency (90.7%) at 203cm (80 inches) fabric width and square shape body has the most efficiency (89.34%) at 190.5cm (75 inches) fabric width. Thus in women fitted shirt, the fabric width ranges from 200.7cm to 205.7cm (79 inches to 81 inches) has

provided the best and maximum marker efficiency results in most of the body shapes. However in manufacturing the women fitted shirt, square shape body is the best type as it has good results with minimum fabric width utilization. Thus square shape body is the most efficient and cost-effective than the other body types. The results have also discovered that companies which are set of using fabrics with 147cm (58 inches) width are operating at lesser marker efficiencies and thus ineffective in cost.

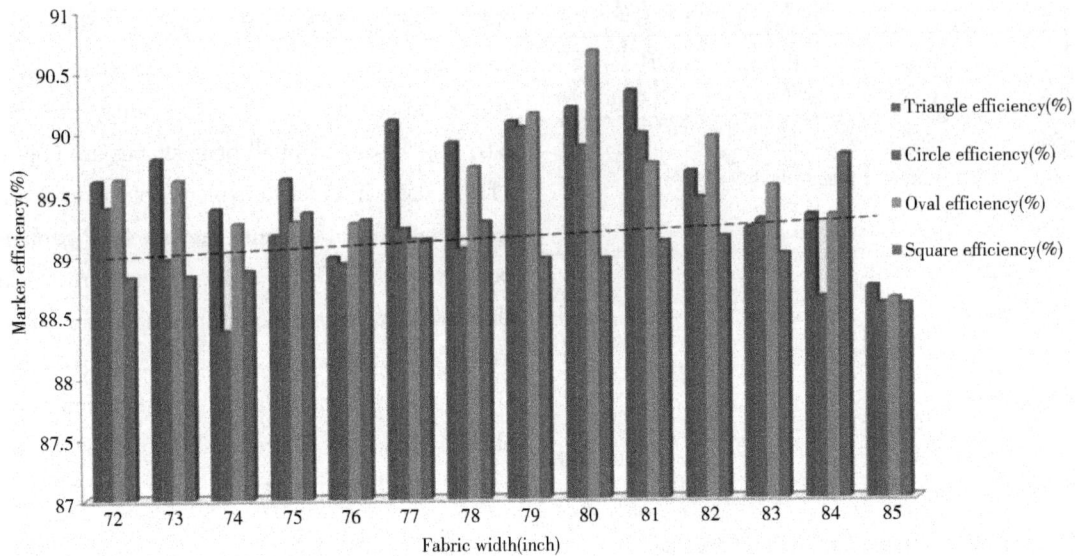

Fig. 4　Marker efficiencies of the fitted shirt at different fabric width

3.2　Fabric consumption efficiency

The fabric consumption efficiency(FCE) also increases with the increase in fabric width. The triangle shape body has the most fabric consumption efficiency (87.6%) at 205.7cm (81 inches) fabric width, the circle shape body has most fabric efficiency (87.25%) at 200.7cm (79 inches) fabric width, the oval shape body has the most fabric efficiency (87.9%) at 203cm (80 inches) fabric width and square shape body has the most fabric efficiency (86.6%) at 190.5cm (75 inches) fabric width. Thus the fabric width ranges from 203–205.7cm (79–81 inches) has provided the best and maximum fabric consumption efficiency results for most of the body types. However, from the investigations, the square shape body is the most cost-effective in fabric consumption efficiencies.

3.3　Variance analysis

In Tab. 2 (One-way ANOVA), it is observed that there is a statistically significant effect on the marker efficiency, fabric consumption efficiency and fabric width, given the significant value (below 0.05) in the ANOVA Table. The regression analysis (p-value) between dependent variables and predictor variables is also statistically significant.

3.4　Correlation analysis

Tab. 3 confirm a linear relationship between marker efficiency and fabric width (sig. < 0.05). Pearson correlation coefficient is 0.858. The results are also similar in fabric consumption efficiency. Thus both have a strong and positive relationship with marker efficiency and fabric consumption efficiency and are affected by the variations in fabric width.

Tab. 2　One-way ANOVA analysis

One-way ANOVA analysis		Df	Sum of squares	Mean square	F	Significance(p)
Women fitted shirt	ME	3	3.317	1.1057	3.15	0.027
	FCE	3	3.654	1.2181	3.47	0.018
Fabric width	ME	15	21.42	1.4278	5.32	0.00
	FCE	15	21.42	1.4278	5.32	0.00

ME: Marker efficiency; FCE: Fabric consumption efficiency.

Tab. 3　Correlation analysis

Correlation analysis		Fabric width	Women fitted shirt
Marker efficiency (%)	P value	0.00	0.00
	Correlation coefficient	0.858	0.762
Fabric consumption efficiency (%)	P value	0.00	0.00
	Correlation coefficient	0.858	0.762
	Correlation	Strong	Not quite strong
	Linear relationship	Positive	Medium

4　Conclusions

In this study, fabric consumption was investigated with the variations in fabric width (127–216cm). For this purpose, fitted dress shirt patterns were cut and marker plans were completed for four different female body types i. e. triangle, circle, oval and square. The research reveals that the pattern markers are more productive and cost-effective with larger fabric width. There is a linear relationship between marker efficiency and fabric width (sig. < 0.05). The regression analysis (p-value) between dependent and independent variables is also statistically significant. Furthermore, the square shape female body is the efficient and cost-effective in fabric utilization for fitted dress shirt manufacturing amongst all body types.

Acknowledgements

The research is supported by National Natural Science Foundation of China (61572124).

References

[1] Kayar M, Ozel Y. Using neural network method to solve marker making "calculation of fabric lays quantities" efficiency for optimum result in the apparel industry [C]// Conference on Simulation, Modelling and Optimization. World Scientific and Engineering Academy and Society (WSEAS), 2008: 219–223.

[2] Bilgic H, Baykal P D. The effects of width of the fabric, fabric and model type on the efficiency of marker plan in terms of apparel [J]. Tekstil Ve Konfeksiyon, 2016, 26 (3): 314–320.

[3] Amaral C, Bernardo J, Jorge J. Marker-making using automatic placement of irregular shapes for the garment industry [J]. Computers & Graphics, 1990, 14(1): 41–46.

[4] Bennell J A, Oliveira J F. The geometry of nesting problems: A tutorial [J]. European Journal of Operational Research, 2008. 184(2): 397–415.

[5] Czarnecki C. Integrating the cutting and sewing room of garment manufacture using mechatronic techniques [J]. Mechatronics, 1995. 5(2): 295–308.

[6] Wong W K. A selection of a fabric-cutting system configuration in different shapes of apparel manufacturing environments [J]. The International Journal of Advanced Manufacturing Technology, 2003, 22(9–10): 641–648.

[7] Naveed T, Hussain A, Zhong Y. Reducing fabric wastage through image projected virtual marker (IPVM) [J]. Textile Research Journal, 2017, 0040517517703605.

[8] Irenee Riter. The science of personal dress complete study: Body shapes. Amazaon. com. 2015.

Appendix

Tab. 1 A comparison study of shirt marker efficiencies at 36 different fabric widths

		Women's fitted Shirt			
Sr. no.	Fabric width (inches)	Triangle efficiency (%)	Circle efficiency (%)	Oval efficiency (%)	Square efficiency (%)
1	50	87.591	87.431	88.136	88.216
2	51	87.537	88.428	88.026	88.21
3	52	87.842	88.797	88.759	88.113
4	53	88.525	88.192	88.921	88.361
5	54	88.057	88.111	89.238	88.364
6	55	88.794	88.581	89.015	88.314
7	56	88.705	88.392	88.077	88.805
8	57	88.506	88.335	88.64	88.55
9	58	90.041	89.417	89.647	88.943
10	59	89.247	89.373	89.461	89.006
11	60	88.974	88.431	88.861	88.773
12	61	88.169	88.199	89.113	88.716
13	62	88.249	87.801	88.82	88.749
14	63	88.246	87.827	88.389	88.976
15	64	89.417	89.073	89.617	88.705
16	65	88.744	89.123	88.954	88.989
17	66	88.763	88.595	89.107	89.113
18	67	89.243	88.253	88.59	89.223
19	68	88.855	88.679	88.205	88.738
20	69	89.057	88.155	88.974	88.782
21	70	89.134	88.598	89.628	88.952
22	71	89.512	88.487	89.424	88.964
23	72	89.602	89.385	89.613	88.812
24	73	89.784	88.962	89.606	88.825
25	74	89.373	88.375	89.249	88.862
26	75	89.156	89.616	89.265	89.341
27	76	88.978	88.923	89.253	89.283
28	77	90.089	89.207	89.119	89.119
29	78	89.907	89.041	89.707	89.264
30	79	90.078	90.029	90.142	88.959
31	80	90.194	89.874	90.652	88.957
32	81	90.329	89.975	89.731	89.098
33	82	89.669	89.453	89.95	89.137
34	83	89.208	89.275	89.548	88.991
35	84	89.313	88.638	89.308	89.802
36	85	88.724	88.585	88.626	88.577

The Preparation and Hydrophobic Test
of PTFE/PAM Electrospinning Membrane

Xiangfei Xu[2], Jinhua Jiang[1,2]*, Nanliang Chen[1,2]

[1] *Engineering Research Center of Technical Textiles, Ministry of Education, Donghua University, Shanghai 201620, China*

[2] *College of Textiles, Donghua University, Shanghai 201620, China*

* Corresponding author's email: jiangjinhua@ dhu. edu. cn

Abstract: Electrospinning technology could be used to form membranes applied to the hernia mesh, which would achieve an effect of anti-adhesion. Polytetrafluoroethylene (PTFE) as a material with good adhesive and nontoxicity, but it's difficult to reach the electrospinning. Polyacrylamide (PAM) is not expensive and not harmful, which was selected to as the assistant to achieve the spinning. When the injector speed was 0. 8mL/h, the spinning voltage was adjusted to 18kV, the distance between the fiber collector and the needle of spinneret was 10cm, the concentration was 17.5%, the solute mass ratio of PTFE : PAM was 84 : 16, the forming electrostatic spinning membrane was achieved with a fine construction and its hydrophobic property presents good. Through further study, this membrane would be used to hernia mesh for anti-adhesion.

Keywords: PTFE; PAM; Electrospinning; Membrane; Hydrophobicity

1 Introduction

Electrospinning is a spinning technology, using the polymer solution or melt to form fibers and membranes in a strong electric field. In that electric field, the drops at the needle will change from sphere to cone, and as a result from the conical cusp to form the nanoscale fiber. In these years, electrospinning technology has an increasing development, which has been applied to many fields, including biomedical materials, energy sources, filtration, food engineering and so on. Especially, the most of applications are in the biomedical field[1], because of its simplicity and cost-effective. Also the electrostatic fibers and membranes have many excellent properties of high surface-to-volume ratio andhigh porosity, which are benefit from the mutual effect of cell-cell and cell-matrix[2]. So it is effective and important to develop this technology.

Hernia is a severe illness and is bad for human body, which has not the self-healing capability. Hernia mesh is a production for repairing this illness, but the common mesh that is made of polypropylene fiber has many problems, such as adhesion to tissue. Nowadays, some people use the electrospinning to make an anti-adhesion membrane applied to the hernia mesh, and have reached some good goals. But this technology is not ripe that also need to be improved constantly. Xu[3] used the electrospinning to get polycaprolactone (PCL) membrane attached to the PP warp knitting fabric, thus forming the anti-adhesive composite hernia mesh.

Polytetrafluoroethylene (PTFE) commonly referred to as "non-stick coating" or "clean material", which is non-toxic and tasteless. This material has high temperature resistance and low friction coefficient, even it is not change at low temperature[4]. At the same time, it is resistant to acids and bases, and almost insoluble in all solvents, so it's difficult to form PTFE fiber with solution spinning. As for the molten PTFE, which will be break rather than forming fiber when it's prolonged[5]. It's impossible to form pure PTFE fiber in electrospinning technology[6]. Adding some easy-spinning material to the PTFE spinning solution could make it possible to product the PTFE fibers and membranes with electrospinning. Sun[7] utilized the polyvinyl alcohol (PVA) as carrier to product PTFE electrostatic spinning membrane. Feng[8] used polyethylene oxide (PEO) to mix with PTFE to accomplish the electrostatic spinning, and the dosage of PEO is very low.

In this study, a new spinning solution was invented to get the membranes with PTFE. Polyacrylamide (PAM), which as an easy-electrospinning material and could to be the assistant to mix with PTFE to form the membrane. Because of the special performance of the PTFE, the membrane of PTFE/PAM has some excellent properties. And by means of the contact angle test to judge membrane's hydrophobic, consequently to reflect its anti-adhesive, the good hydrophobicity isn't conducive to cell adhesion. What's more, the electrospinning conditions were changed to get the PTFE/PAM membranes with the best hydrophobic.

2 Experiments

2.1 Materials

PTFE water miscible liquid (60% solid-containing content) was bought on the internet. PAM particles (nonionic, the molecular weight is 5 million) were bought on the internet. The deionized water was provided by the Donghua University.

2.2 Preliminary experiment

Changing the conditions of electrospinning, including the concentration and solute mass ratio of spinning solution, as well asspinning parameters, used the electrostatic spinning machine model QZNT-E01 (Qingzi Precision Test Technology Co., Ltd., Foshan, China) to spinning.

When the temperature was 25-35℃, the humidity was 30%-35%, the injector speed was 0.7-0.9mL/h, the voltage was 15-20kV, the distance of needle to receiver plate was 5-15cm, the concentration of spinning solution was 15%-20% and the solute mass ratio of PTFE:PAM was 80:20 to 90:10, it could form fibers membrane with the good appearance.

2.3 Methods

2.3.1 Different concentration

Keeping others' conditions, the same except the concentration of spinning solution, this part of the experi-

ment chose three different concentrations: 15.5%, 17.5%,19.5%. The solute mass ratio of PTFE:PAM was 84:16. The injector speed was controlled in 0.8mL/h. The spinning voltage was adjusted to 18kV. The distance between the fiber collector and the needle of spinneret was 10cm.

First of all, having a calculation about the formulation of spinning solution, the total mass of the solution was 10g. And on the basis of the concentration and the solute mass ratio to know the weight of PTFE, PAM and water that needed. The calculation results are listed in Tab.1.

Tab. 1　Ingredients of spinning solution

Concentration	PTFE (60%)	PAM	Water
15.5%	2.17g	0.248g	7.582g
17.5%	2.45g	0.28g	7.27g
19.5%	2.73g	0.312g	6.958g

Then, the PAM what needed was added to the water in a glass bottle with stirring at 300r/min for 12h on the magnetic stirrer model 524G (Shanghai, China), until this solution was mixed uniformly. Similarly, the PTFE water miscible liquid was added to bottle at 300r/min for 6h, let the whole solution be homogeneous.

Next, the 5mL injectors with size 20 syringe needles, which were used to absorb spinning solution. With aluminum foil as plate to receive the electrostatic spinning membranes, by means of some tests and to know which concentration was the best.

2.3.2 Different solute mass ratio

On the basis of previous experiment, this part of the experiment chose three different solute mass ratios: 82:18, 84:16, 86:14 (PTFE:PAM), while with other conditions same. The same experimental steps were done.

2.4 Test on membranes

The electrostatic spinning membranes needed to have the treatment in the vacuum drying chamber model DZF-6030B (Yiheng Technology Co., Ltd., Shanghai, China) with 70℃ for 5h. In order to eliminate the remainder water that existed in membranes, and let them convenient to test.

2.4.1 SEM analysis

Scanning electron microscope was used to observe the morphological features of forming fibers. Each sample of membrane was dealt with the metal spraying.

2.4.2 Contact angle test

Contact angle tester model OCA15EC (Instruments GMBH, Germany) was used to measure the contact angle of membrane with the sessile drop method, and got the result of hydrophobic.

3 Results and Discussion

3.1 Micromorphology of spinning membrane

From Fig. 1, it could be seen that the membranes between different conditions of solution concentration have some different constructions. With the concentration increases, the construction of membrane becomes dense. Fig. 1 (a) shows the forming fibers are not regular and gap between fibers is so large, also the connection of fibers is not tightness and leads to the instability of membrane. But Fig. 1 (b) and Fig. 1 (c) show that these forming fibers are more tightness and gap between fibers is so inerratic, and the fibers of 19.9% are thinner than 17.5%. So relatively speaking, when the concentration of spinning solution is around 17.5%, the forming fibers and membranes are finer and solid.

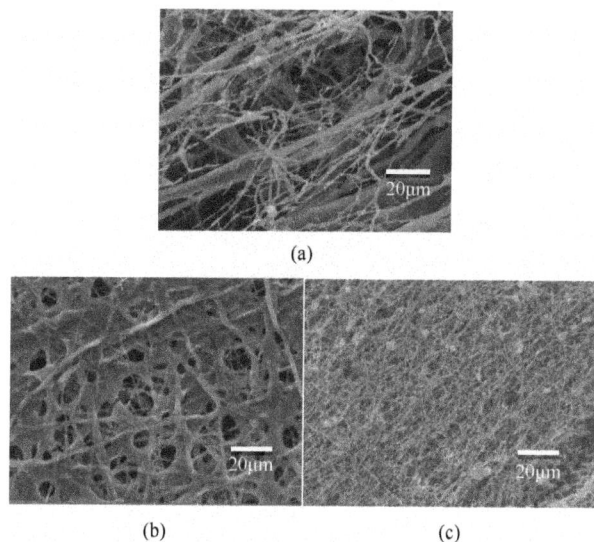

(a)

(b)   (c)

Fig. 1 Morphological comparison between three different concentrations (a) The membrane made from solution with 15.5%; (b) 17.5%; (c) 19.5%

Fig. 2 displays the morphological changes of membranes with different solute mass ratios and same concentration of 17.5%. Fig. 2 (a) and Fig. 2 (b) show that there are strings of beads in the membranes, so the forming fibers are not smooth. Compared with Fig. 1 (b), their constructions aren't dense and tightness.

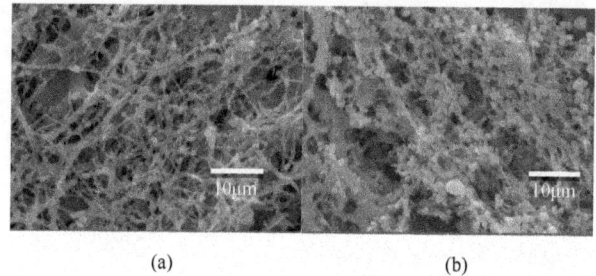

(a)   (b)

Fig. 2 Morphological comparison between different solute mass ratio of PTFE : PAM (a) The membrane made from solution with 82 : 18; (b) 86 : 14

3.2 Hydrophobic of spinning membrane

Three times test to every membrane, and choose three different positions on the membranes. As shown in Fig. 3, Fig. 4, Fig. 5, Fig. 6, Fig. 7, because of the different spinning conditions and different constructions between membranes, they have diversity hydrophobicity.

Fig. 3 The contact angle test of membranes that were made from solution with 15.5% and 84 : 16

Averaging to three test values, the results are presented in Fig. 8. As shown in Fig. 8 (a), when keeping the PTFE : PAM is 84 : 16, with the increase of concentration, the contact angle value of membrane is firstly

Fig. 4　The contact angle test of membranes that were made from solution with 17.5% and 84:16

Fig. 5　The contact angle test of membranes that were made from solution with 19.5% and 84:16

Fig. 6　The contact angle test of membranes that were made from solution with 17.5% and 82:18

increase and then decrease. And the contact angle is maximum when concentration is 17.5%, which also

Fig. 7　The contact angle test of membranes that were made from solution with 17.5% and 86:14

presents this membrane has fine hydrophobic property. Fig. 8 (b) shows that when the concentration is 17.5%, with the change of PTFE:PAM, there is an alteration of the contact angle value. And while the solute mass ratio of PTFE:PAM is 84:16, the membrane has the fine hydrophobicity.

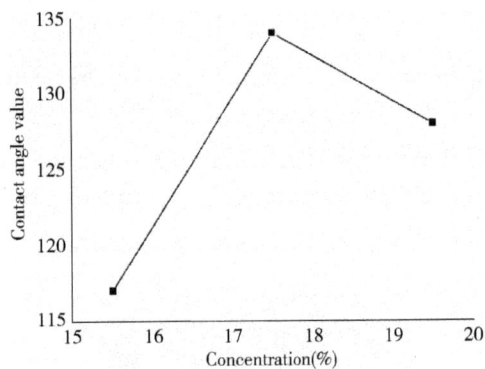

(a)

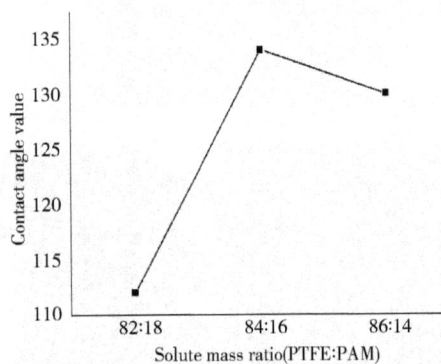

(b)

Fig. 8　Contact angle values between different concentrations and solute mass radios

4　Conclusions

This study selected the PTFE and PAM to prepare of electrostatic spinning solution. In which, the PAM is to the benefit of the forming fibers and membranes. As a result, this solution could spin successfully, and the membrane had fine construction, also with excellent hydrophobicity. What's more, when the injector speed was controlled in 0. 8mL/h, the spinning voltage was adjusted to 18kV, the distance between the fiber collector and the needle of spinneret was 10cm, the concentration was 17. 5%, the solute mass ratio of PTF : PAM was 84 : 16, the hydrophobic property of electrostatic membrane presented best. This experiment proved of through the electrospinning that it can form PTFE/PAM membranes with good properties. Through further study, this membrane would be used to hernia mesh with anti-adhesion.

Acknowledgements

This work was financially supported by National Key R&D Program of China (2016YFB0303300), and National Natural Science Foundation of China (NSFC 11472077), the Fundamental Research Funds for the Central Universities (2232018G-06).

References

[1] Bhardwaj N, Kundu S C. Electrospinning: a fascinating fiber fabrication technique [J]. Biotechnology Advances, 2010, 28(3): 325-347.

[2] Villarreal-Gómez L J, Cornejo-Bravo J M, Vera-Graziano R, Grande D. Electrospinning as a powerful technique for biomedical applications: A critically selected survey [J]. Journal of Biomaterials Science Polymer Edition, 2016, 27 (2): 157-176.

[3] Xu R. Preparation and performance evaluation of PP/PCL anti-adhesive composite hernia mesh [D]. Donghua University, 2017.

[4] Goessi M, Tervoort T, Smith P. Melt-spun poly(tetrafluoroethylene)fibers [J]. Journal of Materials Science, 2007, 42 (19): 7983-7990.

[5] Borkar S, Gu B, Dirmyer M, et al. Polytetrafluoroethylene nano/microfibers by jet blowing [J]. Polymer, 2006, 47 (25): 8337-8343.

[6] Zhou B B, Xu W Z, Feng Q, et al. Preparation and performance evaluation of PTFE/PVP electrospinning composite fiber [J]. Journal of Anhui Polytechnic University, 2016, 31(5): 6-9.

[7] Sun C Q, Liu C K, Hong Y M. Electrospinning of PTFE/PVA blend Fiber membrane[J]. Shanxi Textile, 2009(1): 8-10.

[8] Feng Yan. Preparation and modification of PTFE fiber membrane[D]. Jiangxi Normal University, 2016.

The Study on the Variance of Fabric Drape Based on the Three-Dimensional Mesh Model

Zhicai Yu[1]* , Rong Gong[3] , Haoyang Xie[1] , Azmat Hussain[1] , Yueqi Zhong[1,2]

[1] *College of Textiles, Donghua University, Shanghai 201620, China*

[2] *Key Lab of Textile Science and Technology, Ministry of Education, China*

[3] *The School of Material, University of Manchester, Manchester, UK*

* *Corresponding author's. email*: zhyq@ dhu. edu. cn

Abstract: The 3D point cloud of draped fabric was obtained with the self-developed 3D scanning instrument. A new method based on the Embedding Algorithm was proposed to analyze the variance of fabric drape. Thirty-four indicators characterizing the drape performance were extracted from the 3D model. The variance of thirty-four indicators was analyzed. The result shows that: Area/Perimeter ratio, Peak Drape Angle, Circularity, Fitness Factor, Percent Radial Distance ratio, Drape Coefficient, Equivalent Circle Radius, Fold Height, Average Radius and Mean Valley Length were comparatively small in coefficient of variance. A final feature vector was composed with the indicators with a small coefficient of variance. A supporting vector machine model was constructed to establish the relationship between the selected feature vector and total hand value of draped fabric. The result shows that the accuracy of the classification of fabric hand with the SVM model could reach 75%.

Keyword: Fabric drape; Variance of fabric drape; Drape coefficient; 3D triangle mesh

1 Introduction

Fabric hand is a comprehensive physical, psychological and social response to touching a fabric[1]. It is concerned with the subjective judgment of roughness, smoothness, harshness, pliability, and thickness[2]. In the item of objective measurement of fabric hand, Peirce[3] first proposed bending length to evaluate the fabric hand. The shortness of this method is that he treated fabric drape as a cantilever beam. In factor, fabric hand is a kind of comprehensive properties of the fabric. In evaluating fabric drape performance in a general and objective way, the Kawabata Evaluation System for Fabrics (KES-FB) was invented to test 16 mechanical and surface parameters of fabric. The 16 parameters could be used to compute primary hand value and total hand value. Following the KES-FB, a system termed Fabric Assurance by Simple Testing (FAST) was developed by CSIRO. With the FAST system, fabric tailoring performance and the appearance of garments in wear can

be predicted[4]. Alternative simple approaches have been investigated by many researchers to predict fabric hand from the properties of fabric extraction through a ring or orifice. The Phabr Ometer™ Fabric Evaluation System was developed by Nu Cybertek Inc, based on the research by Pan and his co-workers[5]. This instrument could obtain a complicated curve. By analyzing the curve, the fabric hand could be predicted. To simply the evaluation method of fabric hand further, researchers attempt to predict fabric hand with some simple parameters. For example, Xue[6] proposed a novel algorithm based on rough set theory and fuzzy set theory to measure relations between fabric hand and the visual perception of flared skirt fabric. The base of this kind of researches lies that woven fabric is a kind of complex assembly of fiber, and it has complex hierarchy construction. Friction between fibers makes the fiber assembly stay balance under external load. When the load was applied to the woven fabric, the fiber and yarn would slip and bend to resist the external forces. The fiber assembly would update again and again, which makes woven fabric different from regular rigid, fluence and elastic solid. Fabric hand is the display of comprehensive properties of fabric in tactile. Fabric drape is the display of comprehensive properties of fabric in vision. Therefore, there is a specific relationship between fabric drape and fabric hand. At present, studies about fabric drape most lie how to optimize the mechanical properties and constructor parameters as well as maintaining fabric drape performance. However, the study about fabric drape and fabric hand is quite rare. Drape performance was visible, and the hand of fabric was invisible. If a system on which designers can select the desired fabric accurately and quickly were developed, it would be a significant breakthrough. Therefore, Capdevila[7] proposed a linearity model based on seven variables to discriminate the fabric Drapery or Lining. Kuijpers[8] recruited a panel to predict the rigid of woven fabric by viewing the fabric drape. Despite this, another problem important was the variance of fabric drape. Niwa[9] tested 145 fabrics for female dress and 138 fabrics for the male shirt. The result revealed that the same fabric could possess different drape coefficient under the same experimental condition. For the variance of fabric drape, Kenkare[10] pointed that fabric drape is dependent on fabric properties, the shape of the object over which it is draped, and the environmental conditions. Each of these is in turn dependent on more variables, which exhibit chaotic behavior. Therefore, fabrics do not fall in the same configuration each time they are draped. The variance of fabric drape generates some obstacle for the connection between fabric hand and fabric drape. Therefore, it is difficult to find stable parameters of fabric drape.

Therefore, in this study, 35 indicators summarized by Carrera-GalissÃ[11], as well as the radius of the minimum bounding sphere of 3D fabric (R_{sph}) proposed ourselves be extracted and analyzed. We aim to select some indicators which were small in coefficient of variance for the same fabric and great in variance for different fabrics.

2 Experiments

2.1 The obtain of the 3D point cloud of fabric drape

Fifty-three commercial fabrics with a wide range of fabric hand were purchased from the market. Five fabrics, whose construction parameters were shown in Tab. 1, were selected from the fifty-three fabrics for the further use. All fabrics were ironed to remove wrinkles before conditioned under constant temperature and constant humidity (Temperature: 23℃ ±2℃, Humidity: 65% ± 2%) for 48 hours. A panel of 6 postgraduate students with textile background 49 was recruited to classify the fabric into six classifications by total fabric hand value. Each fabric was cut into a circular specimen with a radius of 120 mm. The fabrics were put on a supporting disk with a radius of 60 mm. The center of the specimen was aligned with the center of the supporting disk as shown in Fig. 1.

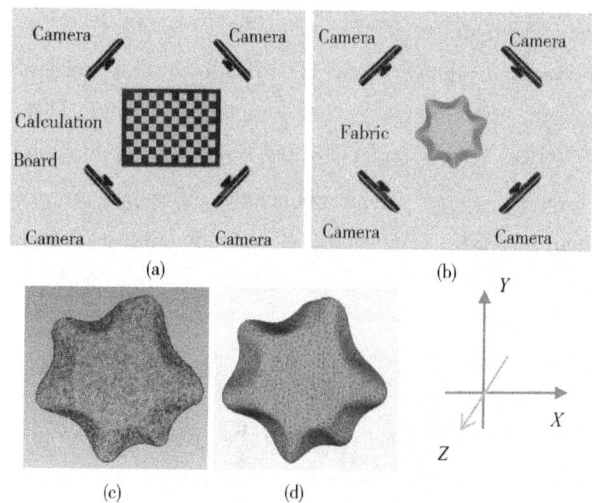

Fig. 1 The workflow of scanning fabric drape

Four depth cameras were positioned around the fabric specimen (Fig. 1). Each camera captures a 3D point patch of fabric from a given direction. As shown in Fig. 1, the angle between neighbor cameras was 90°. Before scanning fabric, four cameras should be calculated. In this study, Zhang's[12] calculation method and a checkboard, as shown in Fig. 1 (a) were used to register four cameras. After scanning, Iterative Closest Point method was used to register these points patches to generate a completed point cloud, as shown in Fig. 1 (c).

The corresponding 3D point cloud was wrapped into triangle mesh by surface reconstruction, as shown in Fig. 1 (d). For the selected five fabrics, each fabric was draped nine times under the same condition. The rest of fabrics were draped two times under the same circumstance.

Tab. 1   The parameters of five selected fabrics

	1	2	3	4	5
Component	Cotton	Polyester	Silk	Linen	Cotton
Mass(g/m^2)	97.91	101.54	72.24	257.15	380.21
Thickness (mm)	0.191	0.228	0.176	0.532	0.731

2.2   The further analysis of variance of fabric drape with a new method

The woven fabric is a kind of complex assembly of fibers. The friction between fibers makes the fiber assembly stay balance state. When the load was applied to the woven fabric, the fiber and yarn would slip and bend to resist the external forces. Therefore, the structure of fabric would change after draping. Sometimes, the change was slim and invisible. As shown in Fig. 2, fabric with drape coefficient of 39.71%–40.03% was draped four times. Four 3D triangle meshes were obtained. The differences between their DC (39.71%–40.03%) were slim. Their drape nodes were the same. However, there was a noticeable difference between them in shape. Therefore, it is challenging to descript the variance of fabric drape with DC or drape nodes.

variance of fabric drape. The method contains three steps.

(1) Compute the 2D embedding of a 3D triangle mesh. As shown in Fig. 3, (a) is the 3D triangle mesh of fabric drape. The embedding algorithm[13] was used to compute the 2D embedding of (a), as shown in Fig. 2(b).

(2) Generating concentric circles. Five concentric circles, which have the radiuses of R, $0.9 \times R$, $0.8 \times R$, $0.7 \times R$, $0.6 \times R$, were drawn, as shown in Fig. 3 (b), where, R is the radius of Mesh 1.

(3) Computing the intersection between concentric circles and Mesh 1. The intersection between the concentric circles and Mesh 1 were recorded, as well as the geometry information of edges in Mesh 1. Because Mesh 1 has the same topology with Mesh, the intersection points in Mesh could be computed reverse according to the geometry information of edges in Mesh 1.

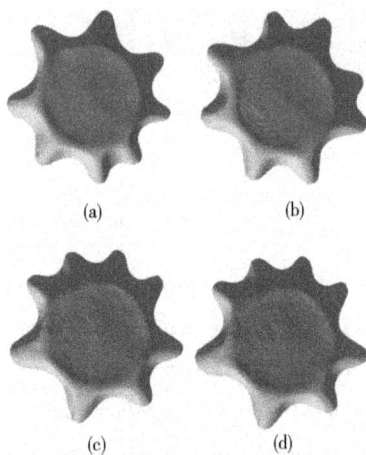

Fig. 2   The different top view image of the same fabric in different draping tests

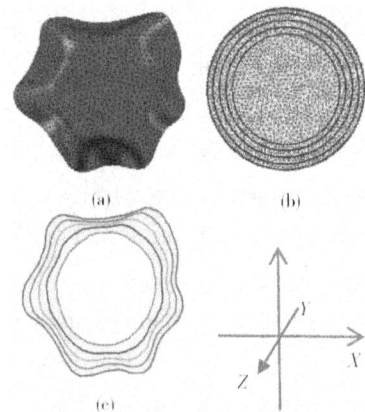

Fig. 3   The schematic diagram of computing of isopleths on 3D triangle mesh (a) The 3D triangle mesh; (b) The 2D embedding of a; (c) The top view of isopleths

In this study, a new method based on "Embedded Algorithm" and "Isopleth" was proposed to analyze the

As shown in Fig. 3 (b), there were five closed curves.

After draping, the geodesic distance between original point and points on the same closed curve were constant[14]. We call it isopleths. However, the straight distance between original point and points on the same closed curve would change. The harder the fabric drape, the smaller the straight distances were. Therefore, the distances between the original point and the points on isopleth could be used to evaluate the drape performance. Because the fabric specimen was smooth and continuous, the whole draped fabric could be represented by several isopleths, as shown in Fig. 3 (c). Therefore, the distances between original point and points on isopleths could be used to compare the similarity between different specimens.

2.3 The computation of coefficient of variance of drape indicators

Based on the 3D triangle mesh, thirty-five indicators, R factor, Fold Number (FN), Shape Factor (SF), Drape Coefficient (DC), Mean Length between neighboring Peaks (FAPR), Mean Valley Length (VAFR), Peak Drape Angle (α^{FPR}), Valley Drape Angle (α^{VFR}), Fold Peak Variance (FP_{var}), Average Radius (R_{avg}), Percent Radial Distance ratio (DDR), Fold Depth Index (FDIDe), Radius Variance (VR_i), Circularity (CIRC), Mean Node Severity (MNS), Variability of Node Severity (VS), Mean Fold Width (FW), Mean Fold Height (FH), Fold Distribution (G_p), Mean Fold Depth (ECR), Maximum Drape (F_{max}), Minimum Drape (F_{min}), Fitness Factor (D/O), Equivalent Circle Radius (ECR), Mean Radius Amplitude (A/R), Angle between consecutive Folds (α), Percent Fold Depth (FDIDE), Radius Half-amplitude (ARR), Drape Unevenness (DU), Fold Height (H), Amplitude (WAM), Height-to-Angle ratio (RH/α), Area/Perimeter ratio (A/P), Fold Profile (F_{sp}) [12] were extracted. Besides, a new 3D indicator based on 3D triangle mesh proposed in this study was the Minimum Radius of Bounding Sphere of draped fabric (R_{sph}).

3 Results and Discussion

As shown in Fig. 4 (a1) and (a2) are two triangle meshes of fabric a in different drape test times. The Fig. 4

(b1) and (b2) are two triangle meshes of fabric b in different drape test times. It is evident that Fig. 4 (a1) and Fig. 4 (b2) have the same drape nodes. As shown in Tab. 2, with the method proposed in this study, the similarity between Fig. 4 (a1) and Fig. 4 (b2) reaches 0.853. It is higher than the similarity between Fig. 4 (a1) and Fig. 4 (a2). The similarity between Fig. 4 (a2) and Fig. 4 (b1) reaches 0.860. It is higher than the similarity between Fig. 4 (b1) and Fig. 4 (b2). The result identifies the fact that Fig. 4 (a1) and Fig. 4 (b2) are more similar than Fig. 4 (a1) and Fig. 4 (a2).

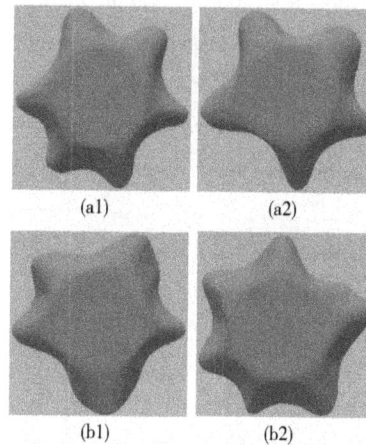

Fig. 4 The top view images of two fabrics in different draping tests

Tab. 2 The similarity between fabric a and fabric b

	a-1	a-2	b-1	b-2
a-1	1	0.598	0.625	0.853
a-2	0.598	1	0.860	0.829
b-1	0.625	0.860	1	0.758
b-2	0.853	0.829	0.758	1

As shown in Fig. 5, fabric 1 was comparatively large in coefficient of variance of α, A/P, ARR, α^{VFR}, ECR, FDIDE, FH, F_{min}, G_p, VR_i, VS, WAM; Fabric 2 was comparatively large in coefficient of variance of α^{VFR}, FH, FP_{var}, F_{sp}, G_p, VS; Fabric 3 was comparatively large in coefficient of variance of α^{VFR}, DU, FP_{var}, F_{sp}, VS. Fabric 4 was comparatively large in coefficient of variance of A/R, ECR, FDIDE, FH, F_{min}, FP_{var}, G_p, VS, WAM; Fabric 5 was comparatively large incoefficient of variance of α, A/R, ARR, ecr, FDIDE,

FH, F_{min}, FP_{var}, F_{sp}, G_p, R factor, VS, WAM;

As shown in Fig. 5 and Fig. 6, the A/P, α^{FPR}, CIRC, D/O, DDR, DC, ECR, H, R_{avg}, VaFR of same fabric was comparatively small incoefficient of variance. The, A/P, α^{FPR}, CIRC, D/O, DDR, DC, ECR, H, R_{avg}, VaFR of different fabrics were comparatively large incoefficient of variance.

For the rest fabric specimens (48 fabrics, drape twice), the A/P, α^{FPR}, CIRC, D/O, DDR, DC, ECR, H, R_{avg}, VaFR were extracted and composed a feature vector. The vector of the 72 out of 96 specimens was used to train a supporting vector machine model as the input. The result of classification of fabric was output. The vector of the 24 out of 96 specimens was used as test specimens. The overall accuracy of clustering for the testing specimens could reach 75% ;

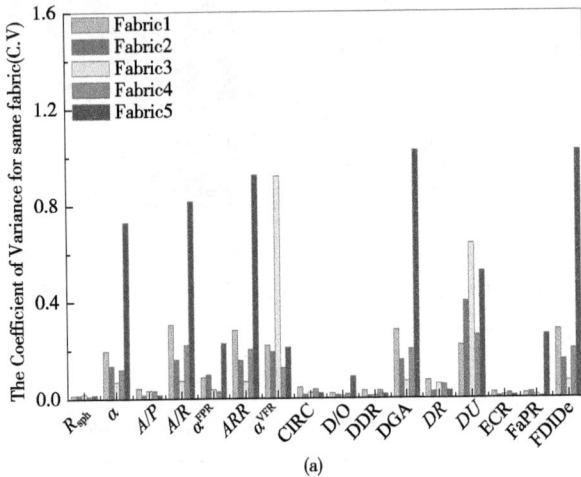

(a)

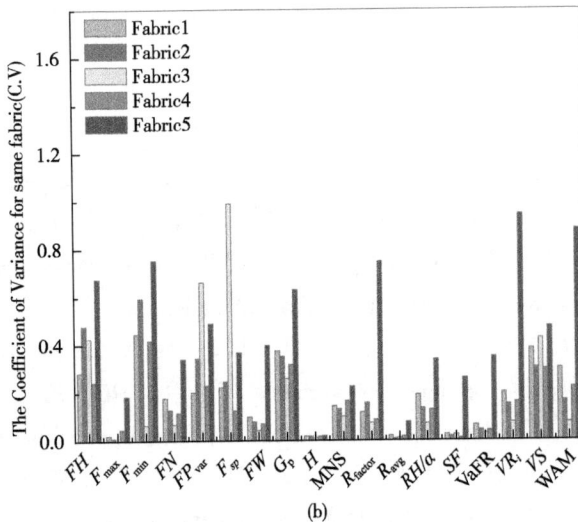

(b)

Fig. 5   The coefficient of variation of indicators of the same fabric

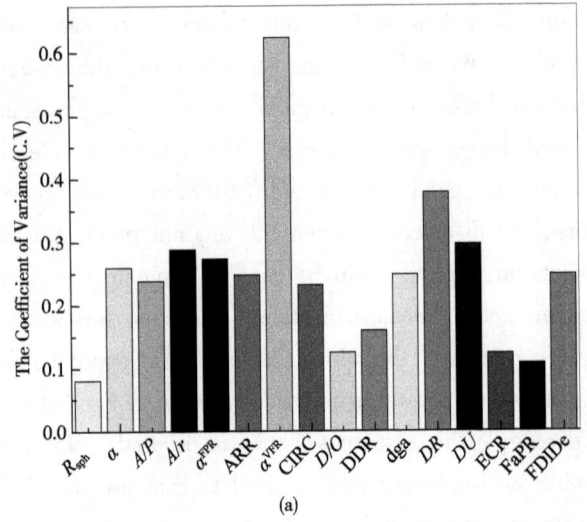

(a)

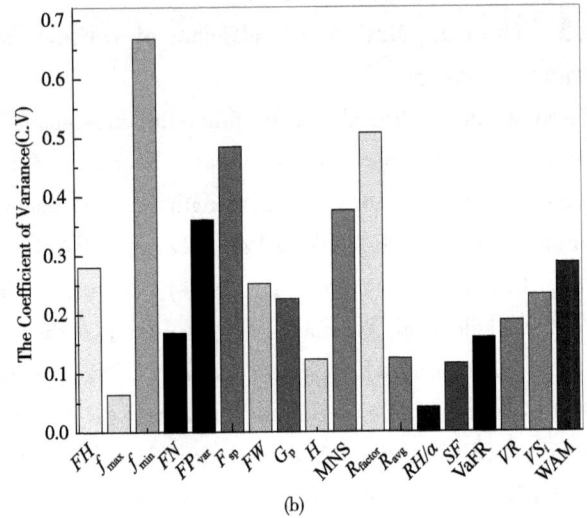

(b)

Fig. 6   The coefficient of variation of indicators of different fabrics

4   Conclusions

The variance of five kinds of fabrics was studied in this research. Thirty-four indicators characterizing fabric performance were extracted. The result of coefficient of variance shows that the variance of fabric shape lies in Mean radius amplitude (A/R), Valley drape angle (α^{VFR}), Mean fold depth (DGA), Fold depth index (FDIDE), Mean fold height (FH), Minimum drape (F_{min}), Fold peak variance (FP_{var}), Fold profile (F_{sp}), Fold distribution (G_p), Variability of node severity (VS), Amplitude (WAM). The A/P, α^{FPR}, CIRC, D/O, DDR, DC, ECR, H, R_{avg}, VaFR were small in coefficient of variance between the same fabric and were significant in coefficient of variance between different kind fabrics. The A/P, α^{FPR}, CIRC, D/O, DDR, DC, ECR, H, R_{avg}, VaFR of draped fabric were assembled to a feature vector, and it was used to classify fabric by hand. The accuracy of 24 specimens was 75%.

Acknowledgements

This work is supported by National Natural Science Foundation of China (Grant No. 61572124).

References

[1] Mahar T J, Wang H. A review of fabric tactile properties and their subjective assessment for next-to-skin knitted fabrics [J]. Journal of the Textile Institute Proceedings & Abstracts, 2013, 104: 572-89.

[2] Withers J C. Textile terms and definitions, Aslib proceedings [J]. 2013, 4: 95-100.

[3] Adams D P, Schwarz E R. The Relationship between the structural geometry of a textile fabric and its physical Properties [J]. Textile Research Journal, 1956, 26 (9): 653-665

[4] Minazio P G. FAST -fabric assurance by simple testing [J]. International Journal of Clothing Science & Technology, 1995, 7: 43-48

[5] Pan N, Yen K C. A new approach to the objective evaluation of fabric handle from mechanical properties Part I: Objective measure for total handle [J]. Textile Research Journal, 1988, 58: 438-444.

[6] Xue Z, Zeng X. Extracting fabric hand information from visual representations of flared skirts [J]. Textile Research Journal, 2014, 84: 246-266.

[7] Capdevila X, Carrera-Gallissà E. Application of discriminant analysis to parameters describing the drape for two types of woven fabrics [J]. Journal of the Textile Institute Proceedings & Abstracts, 2016, 107: 784-790.

[8] Kuijpers A. Evaluation of physical and virtual fabric draped from objective fabric properties [D]. UK, Manchester, the University of Manchester, 2017: 18-25.

[9] Niwa M, Seto F. Relationship between drapability and mechanical properties of fabrics [J]. Sen I Kikai Gakkaishi, 1986, 39(11): 43-50.

[10] Narahari K. Enhancing accuracy of drape simulation. Part I: Investigation of drape variability via 3D scanning [J]. Journal of the Textile Institute Proceedings & Abstracts, 2008, 99: 211-218.

[11] Carrera-Gallissà E, Capdevila X, Valldeperas J. Evaluating drape shape in woven fabrics [J]. Journal of the Textile Institute Proceedings & Abstracts, 2017, 108: 325-336.

[12] Zhang Z. A flexible new technique for camera calibration [J]. IEEE Computer Society, 2000, 22 (11): 1330-1334.

[13] Sam T. Roweis, Lawrence K. Saul. Nonlinear dimensionality reduction by locally linear embedding [J]. Science, 2000(290): 2323-2326.

[14] Sze K Y, Liu X H. A co-rotationalgrid-based model for fabric drapes [J]. International Journal for Numerical Methods in Engineering, 2003, 57: 1503-1521.

Using Different Mordanting Methods for Tencel Fabric Dyeing with Pomegranate Peel Extracted Dye

Faisal Rehman[1], Tayyab Naveed[2], Noor Sanbhal[2], Zamir Ahmed Abro[3], Wei Wang[1, 4]*

[1] *College of Chemistry, Chemical Engineering and Biotechnology, Donghua University, Shanghai 201620, China*

[2] *College of Textile Science and Engineering, Donghua University, Shanghai 201620, China*

[3] *Departments of Textile Engineering, BUITEMS, Quetta, Pakistan*

[4] *Saintyear Holding Group Co. , Ltd. , China*

* *Corresponding author's email*: wangv@ dhu. edu. cn

Abstract: Natural dyeing is a technique to dye the textile fabrics from the natural sources like plants. In this study dyeing of tencel fabric with punica granatum peel extracted dye has been examined with the effect of different mordanting methods and different chemicals. The mordanting methods are pre-mordanting, simultaneous mordanting and post-mordanting. Dyed tencel fabric analyze color efficiency, color coordinates on CIELab and color fastness to washing, light, rubbing and perspiration. Solvent extraction method is utilized for the extraction of natural dye. Copper sulfate and stannous chloride are consumed as a mordanting agent. The results reveled that dyeing tencel without mordants has good color fastness properties i. e. washing (4), light (4), dry and wet rubbing (4) and perspiration (4), but exhibit poor color efficiency (1. 6). Moreover, the mordants have improved the color efficiency with stannous chloride (from 1. 6 to 6) and copper sulfate (4). They also enhanced the color fastness properties on pre-mordanting method. Thus pre-mordanting method has good results in all mordanting methods with all chemicals.

Keywords: Punica granatum; Tencel fabric; Solvent extraction; Color efficiency

1 Introduction

The non-biodegradable waste released from leather and textile industries has key role in the water pollution of the world. The aquatic ecosystems are seriously disturbed by the water pollution due to hindrance in photosynthesis and carcinogenicity. This has become problematic for the environment and aquatic system. Therefore has attracted the attention of researchers to adopt a friendly product for the color pigment in different textile industries during the dyeing process.

Dyeing is an old skill which is studied since Bronze Age[1]. The dyes are used for different color shade of textiles materials. Natural dyes are eco-friendly, while synthetic dyes are not[2]. Synthetic dyes are broadly and commercially used to give solid color to textile fibers and fabrics. However, they are very toxic and causes inhibition of benthic photosynthesis and carcinogenici-

ty[3]. Many countries have banned the various particular azo-dyes ($-N=N-$) for their applications and manufacturing[4]. Therefore the trend towards natural dyes (obtained from plants) have been increased in all over the world because of their low toxicity, green approach, biocompatibility and eco-friendly nature[5].

Natural dyes contain colorants that are attained from vegetable and animal matter without applying any chemicals. In plants, coloring agents are obtained from roots, leaves, flowers, barks and fruits e. g. pomegranate, eucalyptus, kamala, madder, henna, turmeric etc. As compared to the synthetic dye, the pure dye content and color yield in dye plant is typically very low[3-6]. Nature has gifted us about 500 types of plants to produce different colors[7].

A number of researchers have made significant efforts on the influence of dyeing properties and natural dyes at different conditions. In the last one decade and more, research has been carried out in plants for natural dyes in comparative to synthetic dyes as they do not require any strong acids and alkalis in their applications and productions[1]. Natural dyes provide attractive shades with acceptable levels of color fastness. They are also renewable[8-10]. Natural dyes have limitations in color yield, reproducibility results, difficulties of dying procedure, mixing problems and poor fastness properties[11-12]. The chemicals which are used to solve these issues are called mordants. Natural dyes when used without mordants have very low fastness properties because it has very low affinity towards fibers and fabrics[8].

Mordants are metal salts which increase dye uptake properties between the dye and fabric[13-14]. Moreover they give different shades to the fabric with different concentrations. The better color strength depends upon the concentration of metal salts used[15]. Metal ion of mordants form co-ordinate bond with dye molecule and not soluble in water[16]. These metallic salts combine with the dyestuff to produce dye aggregates, which are not removed easily from the cloth. The mostly used mordantsare alum, ferrous sulfate, copper sulfate, chrome and stannous chloride etc[12,14,17].

The botanical name of Pomegranate is " Punica granatum "[18]. Granatonine is the main coloring component which is present in the form of N-methyl granatonine[1-19,20]. This compound provides color to the dye and the study of this enable to know the structural chemistry of the coloring compound[2]. In the current research work, three different mordanting methods are used with three different mordants for mordanting and dyeing tencel fabric to evaluate shade depth, color range values and color fastness properties with extracted dye from punica granatum.

2 Experiments

2.1 Materials

Punica granatum (Pomegranate Peel) has shown in the Fig. 1, were collected from local market in, Shanghai. 100% Tencel fabric of weight 160g/m² and fabric den-

sity 128 × 82 was used for dyeing, which is obtained from Hangzhou Xinsheng Printing and Dyeing Co., Ltd., (Hangzhou). Laboratory grade metallic salts such as coppers (II) sulfate and stannous chloride manufactured by (Sinopharm Chemical Reagent, Co., Ltd.) were used as a chemical mordants and ethanol as a solvent.

Fig. 1   Pomegranate peel

2.2 Methods

2.2.1   Powder preparations

The peels were separated from punica granatum and then washed with water to remove the dust particles and other impurities. They are kept for drying in direct sunlight or at room temperature for 24-48 hours. After drying, the samples were grind into powder form with the help of grinder. The grinded powder was further used for dye extraction process.

2.2.2   Extractions

Solvent extraction method was used to extract dye from punica granatum peel and Soxhlet apparatus was used for extraction. 10g powder of punica granatum peel was placed in round bottom flask and 200mL solvent (120mL ethanol and 80mL distilled water) was added into flask with material to liquor ratio 1 : 20. The flask was heated in water bath for 100 minutes at temperature 95℃. After extraction, the solution was filtered through what man filter paper and rotary evaporator was used to evaporate the remaining solvents to make it pure dye.

2.2.3   Mordanting

Mordanting is a process which increases a chemical reaction between fibers and dye. Pre-mordanting, simultaneous and post-mordanting methods were used. In pre-mordanting method, fabric treated with different chemicals and then dyed. In simultaneous mordanting, the fabric treated with different chemicals and dyed in one dyeing bath at the same time. In post-mordanting method, fabric dyed with extracted dyed and then treated with different chemicals. After mordanting process, the samples were taken out, squeezed, dried at room temperature and the sample further used for dyeing process. Tab. 1 shows the recipe of mordanting process.

2.2.5 Dyeing

Dyeing is a process used to add color to the fabric and this process is carried out after mordanting process. Punica granatum peel dye was used for tencel fabric dyeing. The water shaker machine was utilized for this process. After dyeing process, the dyed fabric was washed with cold water and soaping agents, and then dry in oven or at room temperature. Tab. 1 shows the recipe of dyeing process.

Tab. 1 Recipe of extraction, mordanting and dyeing process

Methods	Temperature (℃)	Time(mms)	$L:R$ (Liquor Ratio)
Extraction	95	100	1:20
Mordanting	90	60	1:30
Dyeing	90	60	1:30

2.2.4 Shade depth and color measurements

Dyed samples were prepared for shade depth (K/S) and color range values (L^*, a^*, b^*, C^* and h), were carried out by standard procedure. Color shade and color range values were evaluated by Data Color SF600 spectrophotometer.

2.2.6 Color fastness

The dyed sample was tested for different color fastness according to ISO standards like color fastness to light (ISO 105-B02), washing (ISO 105-C10), rubbing (dry and wet) (ISO 105-X12) and perspiration (ISO 105-E04).

3 Results and Discussion

In this study, three different mordanting methods with punica granatum peel extracted dye are used for tencel fabric dyeing. Samples are dyed without mordants and with mordants to evaluate different color shade and color fastness properties.

3.1 Color shade and color measurements

The dyed tencel fabric was assessed for their color shade and color coordinates as reported in Tab 2. Data Color, SF-600 spectrophotometer is used to calculate the dye absorption on the tencel fabric surface by using K/S values, and also measure the color range values on tencel fabric by using L^*, a^*, b^*, C^*, h^*. Tab. 2 indicates the CIE LAB values and L^*, a^*, b^* are the three axis of CIE LAB system. It explains that higher value of L^* shows lighter shade and lower value of L^* shows darker shade. Values of a^* shows color from red to green and b^* value indicates color from yellow to blue.

Tab. 2 shows that dyed sample with no mordant has (1.6) K/S. In pre-mordanting method the K/S values recorded were (6), (4) for stannous chloride and copper sulphate respectively. In simultaneous mordanting, K/S values were (4), (2.8) for stannous chloride and copper sulphate respectively and for post-mordanting the K/S values were (5), (3.2) for stannous chloride and copper sulphate respectively. The overall result of Tab. 2 indicates that pre-mordanting method with both mordants showed good color shade values.

Tab. 2 K/S and L^*, a^*, b^*, C^* and h values of dyed tencel

Mordants	Methods	K/S	L^*	a^*	b^*	C^*	h
No mordant		1.6	85.02	1.73	12.31	12.44	81.98

Mordants	Methods	*K/S*	*L**	*a**	*b**	*C**	*h*
SnCl₂	Pre-mordanting	6	73.75	2.87	34.44	34.56	85.24
	Simultaneous	4	80.59	3.63	30.60	34.71	84.00
	Post-mordanting	5.5	75.10	2.42	32.88	32.97	85.79
CuSO₄	Pre-mordanting	4	73.07	2.95	25.74	25.91	83.47
	Simultaneous	2.8	76.07	1.38	21.45	23.47	87.63
	Post-mordanting	3.2	74.10	2.86	24.53	24.69	83.36

3.2 Color fastness properties of dyed tencel

3.2.1 Washing fastness

Fig. 2 shows the results of washing fastness of tencel fabric without mordant and with three mordanting methods. It shows that sample with no mordant possess good washing fastness properties (4). But when the fabric was treated with mordants stannous chloride and copper sulphate in all mordanting methods, the washing fastness was improved from good to excellent (4–5). It is concluded that tencel fabric has excellent washing fastness in all mordanting methods with extracted dye from pomegranate peel.

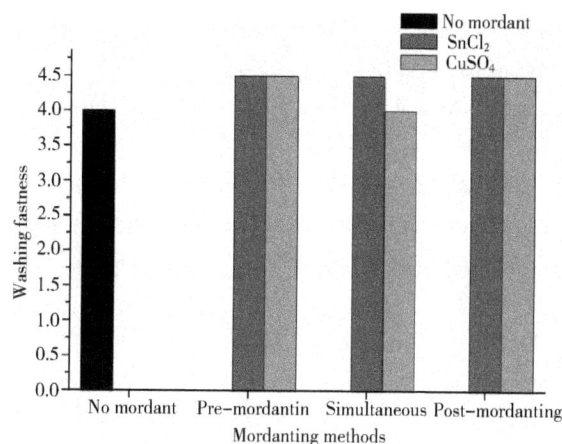

Fig. 2   Washing fastness of dyed sample

3.2.2 Light fastness

Fig. 3 indicates the light fastness results of dyed tencel with punica granatum peel extracted dye. Sample without mordant show moderate light fastness but improved with chemical treatment. The figure shows that light fastness of tencel fabric with mordant stannous chloride in pre-mordanting method is highest i. e. [6] and light fastness in post-mordanting method is good i. e. [5].

Mordant copper sulphate also possess moderate to good light fastness in all mordanting methods. The overall result shows that light fastness of tencel fabric improved from moderate to better with different mordant treatments and methods.

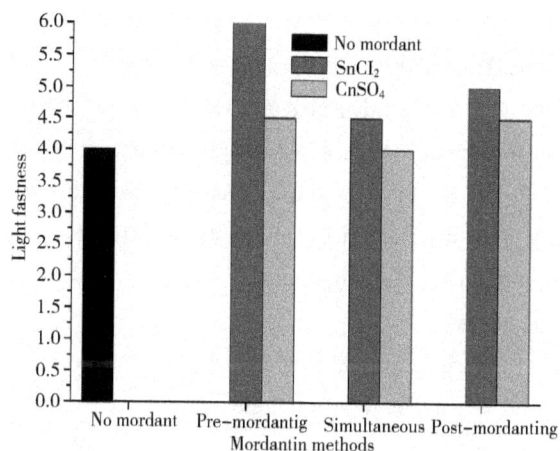

Fig. 3   Light fastness of dyed sample

3.2.3 Rubbing fastness (dry & wet)

Tab. 3 indicates the dry and wet rubbing fastness results of tencel fabric with extracted dye. It shows that wet rubbing results are same (very good) in all mordanting methods, with both chemicals and without mordants. Mordant stannous chloride and coppers sulfate exhibit very good to excellent[4-5] dry rubbing in pre-mordanting and post-mordanting methods. The overall results of rubbing fastness shows that pre-mordanting and post-mordanting with both mordants has improved the dry rubbing fastness.

3.2.4 Perspiration fastness

Tab. 3 presented the results of perspiration fastness (acidic and alkali) with punica granatum peel extracted dye. Tencel fabric dyed without mordants have good perspiration fastness however the fastness improved from good to excellent in all mordanting methods with both chemicals. The results in the tab. concluded that tencel fabric dyed with punica granatum peel extracted dye exhibited good to excellent perspiration fastness[4-5] in all mordanting methods.

Tab. 3　Rubbing and perspiration fastness of dyed sample

Mordant	Methods	Rubbing fastness		Perspiration fastness	
		Dry	Wet	Acidic	Alkali
No mordant		4	4	4	4
SnCl₂	Pre-mordanting	4-5	4	4-5	4-5
	Simultaneous	4	4	4-5	4-5
	Post-mordanting	4-5	4	4-5	4-5
CuSO₄	Pre-mordanting	4-5	4	4-5	4-5
	Simultaneous	4	4	4-5	4-5
	Post-mordanting	4-5	4	4-5	4-5

4　Conclusions

In the current study, solvent extraction method was used to extract dye from punica granatum peel for dyeing the tencel fabric. Fabric was dyed with two mordants (stannous chloride and copper sulfate) and without mordants. The important results of the paper are abridged as:

(1) Experimental outcome show that pre-mordanting method is good choice for better results in comparison with simultaneous and post-mordanting methods.

(2) Both mordants stannous chloride and copper sulfate show good color shade and color fastness properties. However, stannous chloride gives better results than copper sulfate.

(3) Washing and light fastness results of stannous chloride in all methods are better. However the rubbing and perspiration fastness results of both mordants are same in all methods.

(4) Sample dyed without mordants shows good color fastness properties but exhibit poor color shade.

Tencel fabric dyeing through punica granatum peel extracted dye is biodegradable, helpful to environmental safety and protection purposes for the surrounding community.

References

[1] Kulkarni S S, Gokhale A V, Bodake U M, et al. Cotton dyeing with natural dye extracted from pomegranate (punica granatum) peel [J]. Universal Journal of Environmental Research & Technology, 2011.

[2] Goodarzian H, Ekrami E. Wool dyeing with extracted dye from pomegranate (Punica granatum L.) peel [J]. World Applied Sciences Journal, 2010, 8(11): 1387-1389.

[3] Adeel S, Ali S, Bhatti I A, Zsila F. Dyeing of cotton fabric using pomegranate (Punica granatum) aqueous extract [J]. Asian Journal of Chemistry, 2009, 21(5): 3493.

[4] Patel N. Natural dye based sindoor [J]. Life Sciences Leaflets, 2011, 11: 355-361.

[5] Shahid M, Mohammad F. Perspectives for natural product based agents derived from industrial plants in textile applications – a review [J]. Journal of Cleaner Production, 2013, 57: 2-18.

[6] Kechi A, Chavan R B, Moeckel R. Dye yield, Color strength and dyeing properties of natural dyes extracted from ethiopian dye plants [J]. Textiles & Light Industrial Science & Technology, 2013, 2(3): 137-145.

[7] Mahanta D, Tiwari S. Natural dye-yielding plants and indigenous knowledge on dye preparation in Arunachal Pradesh, northeast India [J]. Current Science, 2005, 88(9): 1474-1480.

[8] Farooq A, Ali S, Abbas N, et al. Optimization of extraction and dyeing parameters for natural dyeing of cotton fabric using Marigold (Tagetes erecta) [J]. Asian Journal of Chemistry, 2013, 25(11): 5955.

[9] Pruthi N, Chawla G D, Yadav S. Dyeing of silk with barberry bark dye using mordant combination [J]. Indian Journal of Natural Products & Resources, 2008, 7(1): 40-44.

[10]Win Z M, Swe M M. Purification of the natural dyestuff extracted from Mango bark for the application on protein fibers [J]. World Acad Sci Eng Technol, 2008, 22: 536-540.

[11]Sachan K, Kapoor V P. Optimization of extraction and dyeing conditions for traditional turmeric dye [J]. Indian Journal of Traditional Knowledge, 2007, 6(2): 270-278.

[12]Siva R. Status of natural dyes and dye-yielding plants in India [J]. Current Science Bangalore, 2007, 92(7): 916.

[13]Vankar P S, Shanker R, Wijayapala S. Dyeing cotton, silk and wool yarn with extract of garcinia mangostana pericarp [J]. Journal of Textile & Apparel Technology & Management, 2009(1).

[14]Samanta A K, Agarwal P. Application of natural dyes on textiles [J]. Indian Journal of Fibre & Textile Research, 2009, 34(4): 384-399.

[15]Kamel M, Helmy H, El Hawary N. Some studies on dyeing properties of cotton fabrics with crocus sativus (Saffron flowers) using an ultrasonic method [J]. Journal of Natural Fibers. 2009, 6(2):151-170.

[16]Mongkholrattanasit R, Kryštufek J, Wiener J, et al. Dyeing, fastness, and UV protection properties of silk and wool fabrics dyed with eucalyptus leaf extract by the exhaustion process [J]. Fibres Text East Eur, 2011, 19(3): 94-99.

[17]Mahangade R R, Varadarajan P V, Verma J K, et al. New dyeing technique for enhancing colour strength and fastness properties of cotton fabric dyed with natural dyes [J]. Indian Journal of Fibre & Textile Research, 2009, 34 (3): 279-282.

[18]Sheets M, Du Bois M, Williamson J. The pomegranate: University of florida cooperative extension service [J]. Institute of Food and Agriculture Sciences, EDIS, 1994.

[19]Mishra P K. Evaluation of various techniques for extraction of natural colorants from pomegranate rind-ultrasound and enzyme assisted extraction [J]. Indian Journal of Fibre & Textile Research, 2010, 35(3): 272.

[20]Rehman F, Naveed T, Ullah W, et al. Extraction and dyeing behavior of pomegranate dye on tencel fabric [J]. Universal Journal of Environmental Research & Technology. 2016, 6(4).

An Investigation on Crashworthiness of Carbon-Glass Hybrid Composites

Khalil Ahmed[1], Jing Xu[1], Yan Ma[2], Hiroyuki Hamada[3], Yuqiu Yang[1]*

[1] *College of Textiles, Donghua University, Shanghai 201620, China*

[2] *Maruhachi Corporation, Fukui 910-0276, Japan*

[3] *Advanced Fibro-Science, Kyoto Institute of Technology, Kyoto 606-8585, Japan*

* *Corresponding author's email*: amy_yuqiu_yang@ dhu. edu. cn

Abstract: Composite materials have attracted much attention because of their light weight and excellent energy absorption properties. Carbon fiber is most widely used in the composite where the above mentioned properties are required however, due to high price of carbon fiber, hybrid method should be taken into consideration. Therefore, in the present study, Carbon/glass hybrid composite tubes were designed and fabricated by using prepreg method. These tubes were divided into two groups (heated and non-heated) and finally experimented by quasi static compression test to find out their energy absorption capabilities. Results revealed that under heated and non-heated conditions, G4−C3−G4 and CFRP absorbed the highest amount of energy among others with a stable failure mechanism.

Keywords: Crashworthiness; Hybrid composites; High-temperature properties; *Es*

1 Introduction

Composite materials possess light weight, high strength, high modulus and good impact resistance characteristics as compared with the metals and plastics[1-2]. Fiber reinforced plastics (FRPs) can be utilized in automotive cover parts, structural components and functional parts and studies have shown that FRPs can be used as energy-absorbing components as well[3-4]. For this purpose various composite structures with different fiber orientations[5-7], lay-up[8] resin types[9] etc. had been tested. Thornton and Edwards[10-11], Mamalis[11-12], and Kindervater[12-13] found energy absorption properties of composite tube with circular cross section to be higher than the square-section composite tubes. Single/multi axial fiber reinforced composite tube in axial direction has excellent compression performance, but prone to de-lamination in the thickness direction[13]. Therefore, textile fabric introduced as reinforcement composite products can improve performance of composite material in non-axial direction[14-15].

It is well-known that carbon fiber tube with the same design has stronger energy absorption ability than its counterpart glass fiber. However, carbon fiber can be expensive and less worldwide than glass fiber. As a result, hybrids are good way to achieve both low price and good energy absorption capability[16]. In this study, carbon and glass fiber were chosen as reinforcement and epoxy was used as resin to manufacture circular tubes by using prepreg warping method and their energy absorption performance was calculated through quasi-static compression test.

2 Experiments

2.1 Material and design

In the present study, three different types of tubes were prepared with different fiber composition as shown in Tab. 1.

Each specimen was composed of 11 prepreg layers with an average tube wall thickness of (1.8 ± 2) mm. For CFRP and GFRP tubes 11 layers of carbon, glass fiber prepreg were stacked and wrapped above each other at 0° stacking angle, respectively. For hybrid tubes one kind of laminate layers were sandwiched in between equal layers of the other fiber laminates. For example, C4–G3–C4 is a hybrid tube with 4 internal carbon layers, 3 sandwiched glass layers and 4 external carbon layers as shown in Fig. 1.

Tab. 1 Specimen details

Type	Reinforcement	Reinforcement form (Prepreg)
CFRP tubes	Carbon fibers	Unidirectional
GFRP tubes	Glass fibers	Woven (1/1 plain)
G–C–G group G4–C3–G4/G3–C5–G5	Carbon/glass fibers	Woven glass/ unidirectional carbon
C–G–C group C4–G3–C4/C3–G5–C3	Carbon/class fibers	Unidirectional carbon/ woven glass

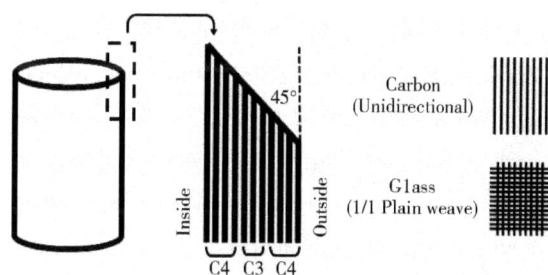

Fig. 1 Schematic diagram of a hybrid tube (C4–G3–C4)

2.2 Manufacturing and temperature treatment

Specimens were manufactured by prepreg lamination molding process. All the specimens were tapered from one end at around 45° angle to generate progressive crushing by collapse trigger mechanism rather than catastrophic failure which is undesirable. Then half of the specimens were treated under 100℃ for 200 hours (about 8.33 days) to investigate the effect of temperature treatment on the crashworthiness. Specimens after heat treatment didn't show any remarkable difference in the appearance. In the present study, non-heat treated specimens are referred as "NHT" while heat-treated as "HT".

2.3 Quasi-static compression test

All composites tubes were axially compressed using a WDW-100KN universal testing machine. Tubes were compressed up to 30 mm at a constant cross-head speed of 5 mm/min. Energy absorbed by specific length of the tube was calculated by using this formula.

Specific Energy Absorption (kJ/kg) :

$$Es = \frac{\text{Total Energy(kJ)}}{\text{Crushed Mass(kg)}}$$

3 Results and Discussion

Representative crushing behavior of different FRP tubes before and after heat treatment is shown in Fig. 2, Fig. 3 respectively. Almost all the tubes exhibited splaying mode by forming internal and external fronds along with central crack generated below the debris wedge in longitudinal direction. Representative load-displacement curves of the specimens before and after heat treatment are shown in Fig. 4 and it can be clearly seen that all the specimens showed increment in Es value except that of GFRP.

3.1 Effect of structure

Representative crush zones of tubes and their schematic diagrams are shown in the Fig. 2. Among all the types, CFRP showed highest amount of energy absorption and among both hybrid groups (C–G–C and G–C–G), the later one showed better energy absorption, in both heated and non–heated state. G4–C3–G4 showed highest SEA value among hybrid groups afterheat treatment as shown in Tab. 2. The overall energy absorbed by any tube was the sum of energies absorbed by different type of fractures occurred inside the tube wall like central crack, inter-laminar crack, intera-laminar crack, transversal crack etc. From the microscopic examination of the specimens, it was found that all the specimens showed progressive crushing by splitting into internal and external fronds. CFRP and G-C-G group tubes showed debris wedge below which a longitudinal central crack was formed as shown in Fig. 2 (a), Fig. 2 (b). There was not such an obvious difference found in the crushing behavior of the tubes belonging to the same group.

Tab. 2 SEA values before and heat treatment

| No. | Specimen | SEA(kJ/kg) | | SEA difference(%) |
		NHT	HT	Before and after heat treatment
1	C4-G3-C4	95.42	109.97	13.3
2	C3-G5-C3	97.26	102.11	4.7
3	G4-C3-G4	102.60	124.20	17.4
4	G3-C5-G3	107.84	116.43	7.7
5	CFRP	100.48	136.01	26.1
6	GFRP	80.69	74.19	-8.8

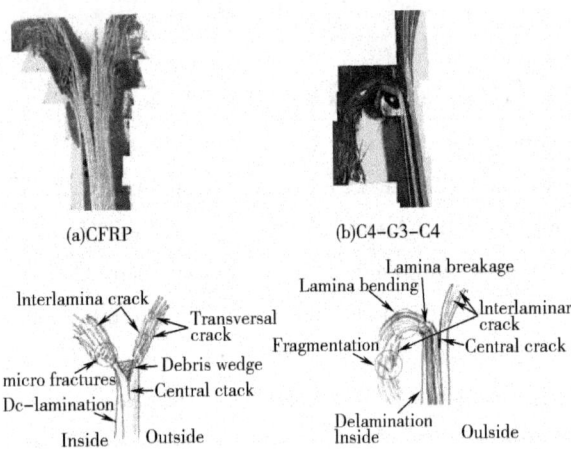

Fig. 2 Cross sectional view of crushed NHT tubes and their schematic diagrams

The reasons for lower SEA value of C-G-C group are predicted to be the lower strength of carbon fiber in transversal direction. It is supposed when the tube started splaying, it formed internal and external fronds, because glass fiber is highly brittle so as the load was applied it must have broken earlier, and the whole load would have been carried by only carbon fibers as shown in Fig. 2 (b). As carbon fiber laminate were at the outer most sides of the tube so they bent with a larger radius thus being compressed in almost non-axial direction by the compression head. Carbon fiber has low strength in transverse direction thus ultimately leading the whole tube to less energy absorption. Moreover, some shearing cracks were also found indicating the presence of shear stresses inside the structure. For G-C-G group, higher hoop to axial fiber ratio and small bending curvature of internal and external fronds is considered to be the main reason for high energy absorption. However, further investigation still needs to be done to fully understand the detailed mechanism.

GFRP tube showed buckling behavior and possessed lowest energy absorption in both heated and non-heated states because of glass fiber's low strength and brittle nature.

3.2 Effect of temperature

It's very obvious from the Tab. 2 that all the specimens showed increment in the energy absorption after heat treatment except GFRP which showed decrement by 8.8%. Among all the tubes, CFRP showed the highest energy difference after heat treatment which was 26.1%. However, among hybrid tubes G4-C3-G4 showed the highest Es difference which was 17.4% while C3-G5-C3 and G3-C5-G3 didn't show any remarkable difference. From the microscopic observation of CFRP tube, it is considered that fracture toughness of CFRP tube might have increased after heat treatment as it showed comparatively smaller central and transversal cracks along with micro fragmentation in the inner fronds as shown in Fig. 3 (a). There were few transversal cracks found in the HT G3 – C5 – G3 tube and the outermost glass laminae showed buckling behavior after heat treatment. Crushing behavior of HT C4 – G3 – C4 tube was different than in non‑heated state as after heat treatment lamina splitting, many micro fragments and transversal cracks were found in the crush zone which is considered to be one of the reasons for higher E_s value of C4–G3–C4. Overall, the reason for higher E_s value of most of the composite tubes after heat treatment might be attributed to the brittle nature of the resin at elevated temperature. Meanwhile, fracture toughness of the composites also makes positive contribution to control the propagation of longitudinal crack which is responsible for the higher or lower energy absorption[16].

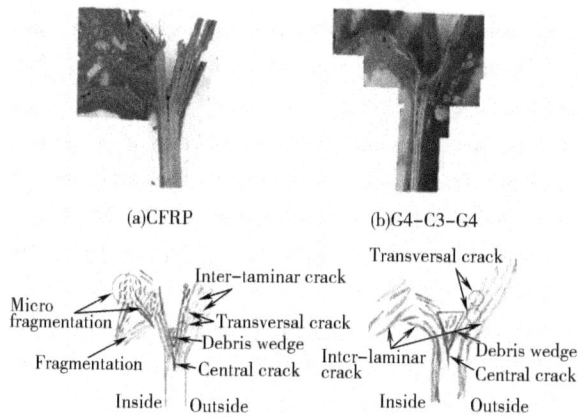

(a)CFRP (b)G4–C3–G4

Fig. 3 Crush behavior of various HT tubes and their schematic diagrams

However, for GFRP, after heat treatment intra-laminar type of fractures were observed in both inner and outer fronds, and lamina de-bonding dominated throughout the tube wall along with a comparatively long central crack than non-heat treated state, which ultimately led to an overall lower energy absorption. Further investigation is being done to fully understand the effect of heat on the crushing behavior of these tubes. Load-displacement graphs obtained from the compression data are shown in Fig. 4. All the tubes showed progressive crushing in which load firstly rose to a peak value and then dropped off and remained almost constant. It can be seen that load fluctuated in a quasi-random fashion with serrations of very small amplitude.

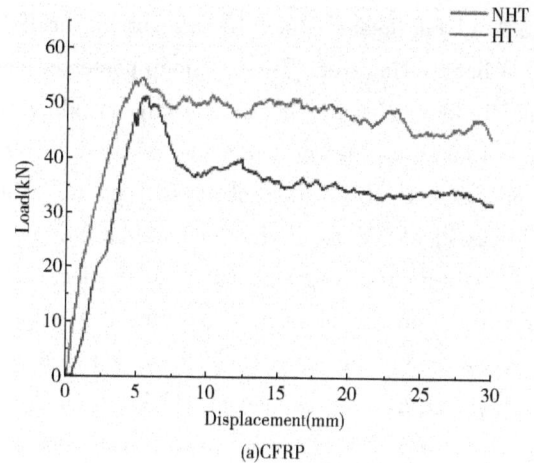

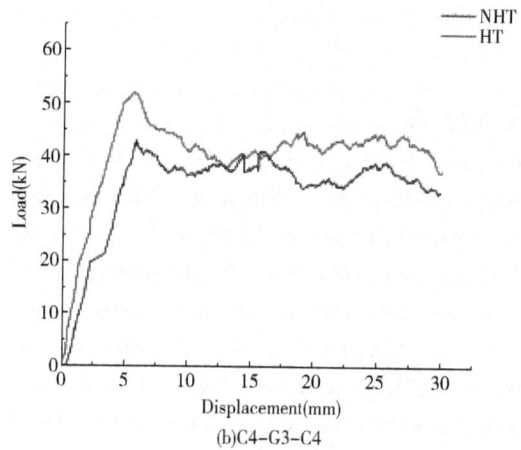

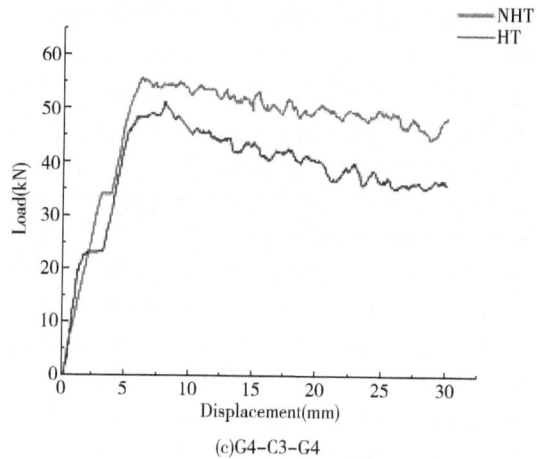

(a)CFRP

(b)C4–C3–C4

(c)G4–C3–G4

Fig. 4 Typical load-displacement curves of different FRPs

4 Conclusions

From the carried-out research it was found that all composite tubes showed better energy absorption properties after heat treatment except GFRP. Among hybrid groups, G – C – G group exhibited higher E_s value in heated and non-heated states because of higher H : A ratio of fibers. However, C–G–C group possessed comparatively lower E_s value because of large bending curvature of outermost carbon laminates. Meanwhile, from the microscopic observation of cross section, failure mode was identified for each kind of tube and it was found that structural geometry has a great effect on the energy absorption capabilities of the tubes. As this experimental study was aimed to achieve a hybrid tube with the same E_s value as that of CFRP but with lower cost, so G4–C3–G4 was found to be having nearly the same E_s value and might be considered as a replacement of CFRP.

References

[1] Brooks R, Shanmuga Ramanan S M, Arun S. Composites in automotive applications: Design, reference module in materials science and materials engineering[J]. Elsevier, 2017.

[2] Liu Z, Lu J H, Zhu P. Lightweight design of automotive composite bumper system using modified particle swarm optimizer[J]. Composite Structures, 2016, 140: 630–643.

[3] Alkbir M F M, Sapuan S M, Nuraini A A, et, al. Fibre properties and crashworthiness parameters of natural fibre-reinforced composite structure: A literature review [J]. Composite Structures, 2016, 148: 59–73.

[4] Yang Y Q, Wu X F, Hamada H. Application of fibre-reinforced composites beam as energy absorption member in vehicle[J]. Int J Crashworthines, 2013, 18(2): 103–109.

[5] Mahdi E, Hamouda A M S, Sebaey T A, The effect of fiber orientation on the energy absorption capability of axially crushed composite tubes [J]. Mater Design, 2014, 56: 923–928.

[6] Okano M S K, Saito H, et al. Effect of the braiding angle on the energy absorption properties of a hybrid braided FRP tube [J]. Journal of Materials Design and Applications, 2005, 219(1): 59–66.

[7] Okano M N A, Hamada H, Axial crushing performance of braided composite tubes[J]. Int J Crashworthines, 2005, 10(3): 287–294.

[8] Mirzaei M, Shakeri M, Sadighi M, et al., Experimental and analytical assessment of axial crushing of circular hybrid tubes under quasi-static load [J]. Composite Structures, 2012, 94(6): 1959–1966.

[9] Hamada H, Coppola J C, Hull D, et, al. Comparison of energy-absorption of carbon epoxy and carbon peek composite tubes[J]. Composites, 1992, 23(4): 245–252.

[10] Edwards P H T J. Energy absorption in composite tubes [J]. 1982, 16(6): 521–545.

[11] Mamalis A G Y Y B, Viegelahn G L. Collapse of thin-wall composite sections subjected to high speed axial loading [J]. International Journal of Vehicle Design, 1992, 13(5–6): 564–579.

[12] K C M. Energy absorption of composites as an aspect of aircraft structural crash-resistance[J]. 1990: 643–651.

[13] Sridharan S L Y. FRP de-lamination under lateral impact and In plane compression [J]. St. Louis, MO, 2006: 1663–1670.

[14] Kobayashi H N N, Maekawa Z, et al. Fabrication and mechanical properties of braided composite truss joint [J]. Anaheim, California 1: 1089–1103.

[15] R. E. W. Krebs N E, Aerospace application of braided structures[J]. Journal of the American Helicopter Society, 1989, 34(3): 69–74.

[16] Xu J, Ma Y, Zhang Q J, et, al. Crashworthiness of carbon fiber hybrid composite tubes molded by filament winding [J]. Composite Structures, 2016, 139: 130–140.

Automatic Classification of Fabric Flatness Templates Based on Deep Learning

Wenjun Zhang[1], Zhu Zhan[2], Jun Wang[1,2]*

[1] *College of Textiles, Donghua University, Shanghai 201620, China*

[2] *Key Lab of Textile Science and Technology, Ministry of Education, Shanghai 201620, China*

* Corresponding author's email: junwang@ dhu. edu. cn

Abstract: The automatic classification of fabric flatness levels has a great influence on the garment industry. The extraction of features based on artificial or neural networks has problems such as time-consuming and low accuracy. For this reason, deep convolutional neural network models are used to deeply learn the data of fabric templates. In this paper, the gray value and height of the fabric template are selected as the input of the model, and a convolutional neural network model is constructed to train the data. The experimental results show that the height value is easier to extract features, the classification accuracy can reach 98% , and it has good robustness and generalization.

Keywords: Flatness rating; Deep learning; Convolutional neural network; Template height

1　Introduction

The surface properties of fabrics can be evaluated with a number of indicators. The fabric flatness grade after repeated washing is one of the indicators. The flatness grade of the fabric directly affects the clothing effect after the garment is processed and formed. Textiles and clothing are affected by many factors in the daily home care and industrial washing process. Changes in the appearance will affect the appearance of the clothes and their performance. At present, the testing organizations mostly use the artificial vision evaluation method to give the grade value of the flatness of the fabric appearance[1] , that is to visually compare the sample and the flatness stereoscopic model under the specified lighting conditions. However, this assessment method will be affected by the inevitable factors in the visual inspection of psychological factors, environmental factors, ambiguity and fault tolerance of the human eye, and the results of subjectively assessed textile fold levels are often uncertain and not uniqueness.

With the development of computer vision technology and neural networks, some new theories have begun to be applied to the flatness rating of fabrics. Chang K P et al. used neural networks combined with fuzzy theory to evaluate fabric flatness[2] ; Tsunhciro et al. applied wavelet theory to the evaluation of the flatness of fabrics and Daubehcies wavelet to extract the flatness eigenvalues[3] ; Shiloh invented a wrinkle tester to evaluate fabric wrinkling. He used geometric parameters such as height, slope, and density to define wrinkling[4] ; Xu B used a scanner to collect wrinkled samples to obtain a uniform background. The Grayscale image proposes a method for grading wrinkles using creased grayscale surface areas and shaded areas[5] ; Stylios G and his team first used CCD (Charge Coupled Device) photography to obtain garment surface seams[6]. All of the above methods are based on the extraction characteristics of the fabric surface. Due to the complexity of the fabric appearance, the feature extraction process has brought great difficulties, and it also directly affects the evaluation accuracy.

In view of the above problems, this paper adopts a deep learning model to automatically extract features of the AATCC fabric stereo standard model to avoid the complexity and limitations of themanual extraction features, and to establish an electronic template for assessing the fabric flatness rating to achieve automatic classification of the tested fabrics. The deep learning data includes the height and gray value of the template, and further improves the recognition rate of the rating by adjusting the parameters of the model.

2 Experiments

Deep learning includes multi-layered artificial neural networks[7]. By constructing a neural network model with multiple hidden layers, the low-level features are transformed through layer-by-layer non-linear feature combinations to form more abstract high-level feature expressions to discover data[8]. In this paper, we obtain the surface data of the fabric flatness template, including the gray value of the template and the height of the surface of the template, and do deep study on the data to obtain a model with a higher correct rate for the classification of the fabric to be tested.

2.1 Convolutional neural network

As one of the most commonly used deep learning models, convolutional neural networks can avoid the complex feature extraction process in traditional machine learning algorithms. Compared with fully connected neural network models, convolutional neural networks have local connections, weight sharing, and multi-convolution kernels. The down sampling feature reduces the number of network parameters and further reduces the computational complexity. The convolutional neural network directly takes the form of images or data as the input of the network. It extracts features and classifies them through the functions of the input layer, convolution layer, pooling layer and fully connected layer.

2.2 Network architecture

Input layer: Responsible for loading images or data, to get the output vector as input to the convolution layer. The data loaded by this model includes gray values and height values, which are converted into matrices and then cut into small blocks of different sizes as input.

Convolutional layer: Learn about the characteristics of data. There are different sizes of convolution kernels on the convolution layer, and one convolution kernel is shared by the same feature. The convolution kernel is actually a set of weights, which is mainly used as a filter. When training a picture, these weights will constantly change. A learnable convolution kernel is convolved with a number of features obtained in the previous layer, and the corresponding elements are accumulated and then biased, which means that feature extraction can be achieved.

The activation function is added in the convolution layer, the features are retained and mapped by the function. The purpose is to increase the nonlinearity of the model and remove the redundancy in the data. The commonly used activation function in convolutional neural networks is the ReLU function, which is defined as $f(x) = \max(0, x)$. The ReLU function as an activation function has the following advantages: (1) The use of ReLU converges faster than other functions, and the gradient does not saturate; (2) ReLU only needs a threshold to get the activation value, speeding up the calculation of forward propagation; (3) ReLU will make a part of the neuron output is 0, which causes the network's sparsity, and reduce the interdependence of parameters, ease the occurrence of over fitting problems. The ReLU function image is shown in Fig. 1.

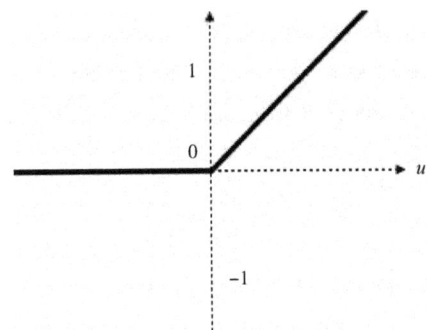

Fig. 1 ReLU function image

Pooling layer: Responsible for the aggregate statistics of the characteristics of adjacent areas. The pooling layer is similar to the convolutional layer and is also moved with a convolution kernel on the map. The feature of the convolutional layer is down-sampled by taking the region's maximum value or average value to reduce the input size of the next layer, thereby reducing the number of parameters and the amount of calculation of the network. The maximum pooled max-pooling is used in this model. The largest number in the picture window covered by the current kernel is selected, the pooled receptive field is set to 2 × 2, and the moving step length is 2.

Fully connected layer: Connects all the input features and sends the output values to the soft max classifier for classification. Each layer in the fully connected layer is a tiled structure made up of many neurons and is responsible for fully connecting the pooled features. The entire convolutional neural network model structure is shown in Fig. 2.

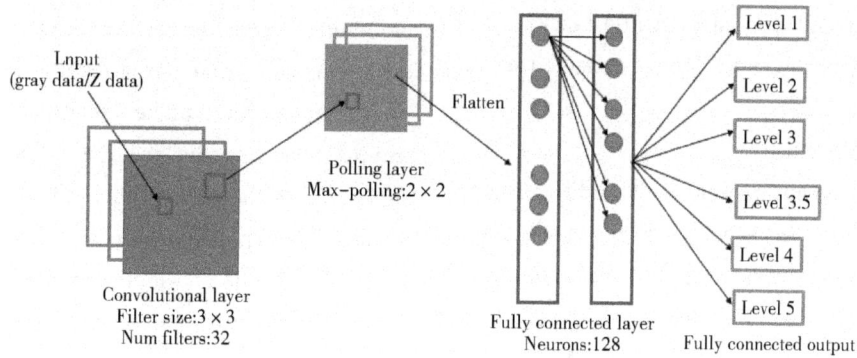

Fig. 2　Convolutional neural network framework

2.3　Data collection

The data of the fabric fold sample template is used as the input value of the convolutional neural network. There are six AATCC samples corresponding to different levels of flatness. In order to achieve good classification purposes, the data between different blocks should be ensured as much as possible. In this paper, the model's gray value and surface height are used as input data.

For grayscale values, the template can be photographed with a Canon 80D camera under natural light conditions. Fig. 3 shows the grayscale of the template one. The undulation of the template surface can be clearly seen in the figure, the fluctuation of the image brightness occurs locally in the wrinkle change. The wrinkles on the same template are relatively uniform, so the gray value can be selected as the feature for deep learning.

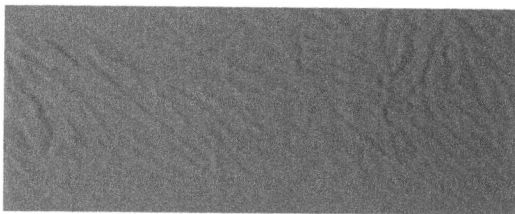

Fig. 3　Flatness level 1 template grayscale

For the height value, a binocular camera is used to shoot the template, an obj format file containing the three-dimensional coordinate values of the template surface is obtained, and the Z value of each point is extracted. The Z value can reflect the fluctuation of the point. Binocular camera equipment is shown in Fig. 4.

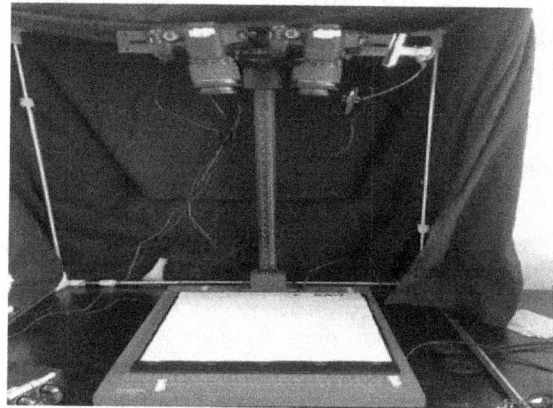

Fig. 4　Binocular camera equipment

3　Results and Discussion

3.1　Data processing

The grayscale image of the template shot by the digital camera can be converted into a matrix of gray values. The gray value range is relatively small. In order to make the difference in gray values of different templates more obvious, the gray value is normalized. The formula is: $X_i = (X_i - X_{min}) / (X_{max} - X_{min})$, multiplied by 255. The grayscale range is extended to $0-255$, then the matrix is cut into pieces, the maximum value of each block is calculated and the first 20% value is extracted. The corresponding small block serves as input for deep learning. For the height value, it is also converted into a matrix and then divided into blocks, and the maximum value of the first 20% is extracted as an input.

3.2 Model adjustment

In the convolutional neural network model, different parameters directly affect the accuracy of the model, including the size of the matrix cut, the offset, the data set split ratio, the number of iterations. After repeated parameters adjustment, compare the accuracy of each model, and get the optimal parameter configuration as follows: small block size is 100×100, offset is 10, number of iterations is 3000, training strategy is 60% of training set, validation set 20% and test set 20%, in which the training set is used for model training and parameter learning; the validation set is used to optimize the model, the model is tested during the training process, and the parameters are automatically fine tuned according to the test results; test set used to test model identification and generalization capabilities. In order to ensure the model's ability to generalize unknown data, data sets do not cross each other.

3.3 Comparative results

Using the above model, the grey value and height value are continuously trained to select the optimal result. The optimal classification accuracy of gray value is 78%, and the optimal classification accuracy of height value is 98%. For the gray value, since the shooting of the template image is greatly affected by the natural light, and the difference in the gray value between the templates is not obvious, the accuracy rate is not high. For the height value, there is a clear step-like distribution between the templates, with easier differentiating the characteristics, the recognition rate is higher, and it has better robustness and generalization.

4　Conclusions

In this paper, the deep learning method is used to achieve the automatic classification of the fabric flatness template, and the grey value and height of the template are selected as the input. Compared with traditional machine learning algorithms, the deep convolutional neural network model has a deeper and more complex structure, which avoids the complexity and limitations of the manual extraction of features, and the fewer model parameters and higher accuracy. The experimental results show that the accuracy of the model can reach 98% due to the more obvious differences in the height values between templates, and it has good robustness and generalization, which satisfies the requirements of automatic identification of templates to some extent.

References

[1] Ajayi J O. Fabric smoothness, friction, and handle [J]. Textile Research Journal, 1992, 62(1): 52-59.

[2] Chang K P, Kang T J. Objective evaluation of seam pucker using artificial intelligence part I: Geometric modeling of seam pucker [J]. Textile Research Journal, 1999, 69 (10): 735-742.

[3] Aibara A T, Mabuchi T, Ohue K. Automatic evaluation of the appearance of seam puckers on suits [J]. Proceedings of SPIE-The International Society for Optical Engineering, 2000, 83(7): 1346-1352.

[4] Shiloh M. The evaluation of seam-puckering [J]. Journal of the Textile Institute, 1971, 62(3): 176-180.

[5] Xu B. An overview of applications of image analysis to objectively evaluate fabric appearance [J]. Textile Chemist and Colorist, 1995, 28(5): 18-23.

[6] Sotomi J O. Investigation of seam pucker in lightweight synthetic fabrics as an aesthetic property part II: Model implementation using computer vision [J]. Journal of the Textile Institute, 1993, 84(4): 593-600.

[7] Shen D, Wu G, Suk H I. Deep learning in medical image analysis [J]. Annual Review of Biomedical Engineering, 2017, 19(1): 221-248.

[8] Bengio Y, Delalleau O. On the expressive power of deep architectures [C]. International Conference on Algorithmic Learning Theory. 2011: 18-36.

Classification of Scarf Printing Pattern Based on Perceptual Cognition

Yue Han[1,3] , Xiongying Wu[2] * , Xuemei Ding[3,4]

[1] Textile Institute, Donghua University, Shanghai 201600, China

[2] Shanghai Entry-Exit Inspection and Quarantine Bureau, Shanghai 200135, China

[3] Fashion & Art Design Institute, Donghua University, Shanghai 200051, China

[4] Key Laboratory of Clothing Design & Technology, Shanghai 200051, China

* Corresponding author's email: wuxy@ shciq. gov. cn

Abstract: Printed scarves are the important accessory for women, and the highlight of the scarf design is the pattern design. The diversity and prevalence of print patterns make it difficult to clearly classify them, but for consumers who want to purchase silk scarves online, and those designers who search the design material on the website, a clear classification of Scarf Printing Pattern can make the search process more efficient. The article analyzes 2210 sample pictures, firstly taking "modeling" as the main consideration, combining color, composition, and performance techniques to classify sample pictures. Then, the focus group discussion of 10 experts make the secondary classification, which is based on the tester's perceptual cognition of the whole perception of pictures, recording each participant's perceptual description of adjectives. Finally, summarize the perceptual characteristics of each secondary classification.

Keywords: Printed scarves; Pattern classification; Perceptual cognition

1 Introduction

Scarves are the best accessory for fashion lady to show their aesthetic taste. They often play the role of finishing touch in the whole looking. Because of the changeable pattern styles, Printed scarves become the main products of contemporary scarf market. The pattern design process of printed silk scarves not only follows the design principles of general textiles, but also has unique design features. Color, modeling and composition of the pattern are the key points of the design, and the performance techniques, edges and subjects will also be related to make effect to the overall perception of the print pattern.

The diversity and prevalence of the print patterns make it difficult to be clearly classified, usually based on the factory's printing process system. However, many scholars have tried to discuss the classification of print patterns from the design theory. Domestic scholars, suchas Tian, trying to divide the women scarves into four categories: figurative pattern, abstract pattern, traditional pattern and popular pattern. Xu divides textile patterns into 8 categories: flower patterns, monochrome patterns, ethnic patterns, patch patterns, paisley patterns, geometric patterns, folk patterns, and new movement art patterns[1-2]. Foreign scholars, such as Alex Russell, divided textile printing patterns into six categories: floral patterns, geometric patterns, graphic designs, motif elements, historical style patterns, regional style patterns[3]. Current printing pattern classification methods are obviously miscellaneous, or contain printing patterns that do not apply to scarves, and there are also phenomena that the classification is too fine. These problems may not disturb the producers, but for consumers, especially when purchasing silk scarves online, or designers searching design materials on related websites, will not do favor to help them find what they want quickly and easily.

2 Experiments

2.1 Image data analysis

2500 pictures of silk scarves are collected by searching

domestic and foreign scarf brands, official websites, shopping sites and material gallery websites. Then get rid of those pictures do not clearly enough. At last, 2210 images were left as experimental samples. The experimental sample pictures contain as many different combinations of various design elements as possible.

In the experimental samples, a number of pictures are from the brand's official websites, and most of the foreign brands have main type scarves pattern. such as floral pattern is widely used in brands Salvatore Farragamo, MARJA KURKI, Liberty London. Burberry, Alexander McQueen mainly use geometric figures, ethnic pattern is the main style of Echo, while Versace is mainly decorated with decorative patterns. The most famous silk scarf brand, Hermes, is involved in all topics.

2.2 Expert focus group discussion

The actual research methods use expert focus group discussions, which consisted of 10 members, all from the textile and clothing field. In the focus group discussion, the team members first browse the sample pictures that have been initially classified according to the styling elements, discuss the samples that have objections, and obtain a first-level classification of the sample pictures. After the agreement is reached, secondary classifications are based on participants' perceptual perceptions of the pictures, and the adjectives of each expert are recorded. Themoderator guides the focus discussion, and finally summarizes the secondary classification and perceptual semantics describes of each secondary classifications.

2.3 Pattern design elements

Print design elements include color, modeling, composition, performance techniques, edge relationships, and printing processes. In the pattern design of scarves, the first three elements are the key points.

Color consists of four elements: hue, lightness, purity, and warmth. There are six kinds of basic hue, and a rich color system is obtained by increasing the intermediate colors. Brightness is divided into a bright hue, a middle hue, and a dark hue. Purityis divided into brilliant colors, gray tones, and pure gray tones. The color warm and cold refers to the emotional expression caused by the attributes of color materials, which are divided into cool colors, neutral colors, and warm colors. There

are four kinds of color matching designs for scarlet printing patterns, the same color matching, similar color matching, contrast color matching and complementary color matching[4].

According to the correlation between the expression and the natural objects, the modeling is divided into figurative imagery and abstract. The concrete shape in the design scope refers to the form that can be identified; the abstract shape refers to the geometric shape that pleases people in a pure form; imagery is a special form of figuration, usually using creative means such as exaggeration, deformation, and addition to conceptualize the realistic style, so that the pattern has a plausible visual effect[5-6].

Composition is the form of a pattern, which means that the elements are combined within a certain range of specifications according to certain form. According to the laws of symmetry and equilibrium, the common compositional forms are classified into four categories: equal-to-edge equilibrium, quadrangular equilibrium, specific composition, and comprehensive composition. Each major category can be further subdivided[7].

2.4 Perceptual cognition of design elements

When people browse silk scarf pictures, they will inevitably pay attention to the pattern of scarves. The color, modeling, and composition of the patterns will bring about different levels of visual stimuli, and this stimulation will take place in the psychological level with the inherent experience of the past. The connection leads to a series of association and emotional experiences, and the experience is similar in a certain group of people. The emotional resonance brought by association is the perceptual perception of design elements.

For most people, color is the first design element to enter the visual channel. Bright, high-purity warm colors can form a bright, lively color tone, making people feel relaxed and happy. Brightness, higher purity cold colors often form a glamorous, deep color tone, giving people a quiet, elegant feel. Colorlessness often gives people a low-key, neutral, simple, classic impression. Composition and modeling complement each other in visual effects. Usually the figurative shape has more delicate and abundant feelings due to more details. The abstract shape makes people to feel simple, elegant and structured perceptual cognition. Different composition forms can bring different feelings, such as scattered and radial usually make people feel concise, loose, independent style has a sense of freedom, sense of change, four-corner balanced composition has obvious Balance, gives people a stable feeling.

3 Results and Discussion

3.1 First-class classification and design features of pattern

According to the design elements, and taking modeling as the primary consideration, the experimental sample-images are classified into five categories: flower & plant, abstraction & texture, realistic & theme, ethnic & traditional, decorative style.

The floral & plants pattern is mainly composed of realistic flowers and freehand flowers. The single leaves and individual plants usually appear in the form of a combination of flowers. The color is bright and vivid, also the extremely cool and warm colors are rare. Similar color match is used mostly as overall color match, while the contrast color, complementary color with only embellishment. "Flower field", single pattern, scattered pattern, corner pattern, and combination pattern in a balanced are common patterns.

Abstract & textured patterns' modeling include plaids, line patterns, letter patterns, geometric shapes, color blocks, abstracted concrete figures, and visual graphics in popular designs, animal fur and natural texture patterns. There are two kinds of performance techniques. One is include linear arrangement of regular/irregular points, simple sketching of lines, or painting of color blocks. The other is the special use of tools, materials and means, including natural texture. The overall color matching is mainly composed of contrast color and similar color, and the color is used with a certain gray scale. The use of no color system is more than other pattern types.

In the realistic & thematic patterns, the realistic styling is refers to the figurative forms other than plants and flowers. Animal shapes are used widely, especially the image of the beast. Other modeling, such as architectural and landscape, fashion accessories, figures, fruits and vegetables are also used. It is usually represented by a realistic depiction or cartoon image with detailed features. There are also many watercolor paintings. Due to the wide range of subject matter of such patterns, almost all kinds of colors are present, and extreme cold and warm colors are also used.

In the national & traditional patterns, common patterns include cashew-shaped paisley patterns, life-tree patterns, and Chinese traditional auspicious patterns. Also include African tribal totems, Japanese Bushido, and new Art movement pattern. The national pattern often uses contrasting color matching and high-brightness color tones, with a cumbersome pattern and a strong visual impact. Decorative style patterns mainly focus on the modeling and composition. There are few types of styling, such as carriages, metal ornaments, and ribbons. At the same time, it should satisfy the balanced equation on the composition.

3.2 Secondary classification based on perceptual cognition

Secondary classification is based on perceptual cognition. Firstly, classify the collected sensible vocabulary according to the design elements. Then experts selected those adjective according to the perceptual cognition. Analyze the vocabularies with more ticks and sum up the perceptual features, as summarized in Tab. 2 below.

Tab. 1 Example of primary classification

Flower & plant	Abstraction & texture	Realistic & theme

Ethnic & traditional	Decorative style

Tab. 2　Example of secondary classification

	(a) Gorgeous	(b) Elegant	(c) Simple
Flower & plant			
Modeling:	Complicated	Gentle	Simple, conservative
Color:	Bright	Elegant, plain	Pure
Composition:	Compact	Changed, flat	Succinct, loose
	Exaggerated	Modern	Conservative
Abstraction & texture			
Modeling:	Wild, illusory	Gentle, calm	Sluggish, still
Color:	Bright, hit color	Pure, elegant	Dim, conservative
Composition:	Free, rhythmic	Harmonious	Tethered, monotonous
	Wild	Romantic	Childish
Realistic & theme			
Modeling:	Nature, fine	Elegant, exquisite	Cartoon
Color:	Conflicting, full	Dreamlike	Lively, pure
Composition:	Free	Harmonious	Messy

	Traditional	Contemporary
Ethnic & traditional		
Modeling:	Classical, complicated	Modern, light
Color:	Bright, intense	Elegant, intellectual
Composition:	Compact	Free
	Gorgeous	Elegant
Decorative style		
Modeling:	Complicated	Exquisite
Color:	Luxurious, mysterious	Soft, gentle
Composition:	Balanced, suitable	

4 Conclusions

This paper summarizes and analyzes a large number of pictures of printed silk fabrics. Based on the design elements, the pictures are classified into five categories. Then we can base on perceptual cognition to make secondary classification. From the perspective of the "people-oriented" design philosophy, the use of a perceptual and rational thinking approach to explore the classification of silk scarf prints can improve the search efficiency of scarves, and make the search process more responsive to the perceptual needs of people, which have bright prospect in marketing application.

References

[1] Tian X. Design and research of women's scarf pattern [D]. Shanghai: Donghua University, 2013.

[2] Xu B J. Textile pattern design [M]. Beijing: China Textile & Appard Press, 2009.

[3] Alex R. Textile print design [M]. Beijing: China Textile & Appard Press, 2015.

[4] Dai A. Hermes silk pattern design and art research [D]. Wuhan: Hubei University of Technology, 2016.

[5] Zhu G X. Pattern design principles [M]. Suzhou: Jiangsu Fine Arts Publishing House, 1991.

[6] Liu X B, Dai A. Hermes's wisdom and art － Scarf ornament pattern study [J]. Yi Hai, 2015(11):76-78.

[7] Sun J G. Appreciation of textile pattern design [M]. Beijing: Chemical Industry Press, 2013.

Design and Experimental Data Analysis of Four-Wing Split-Type Multifunctional Pillow Based on Ergonomics

Xueqin Wang[1,2]* , Lei Zhang[2]

[1] Silk and Fashion Culture Research Center of Zhejiang Province, Hangzhou 310018, China

[2] College of Materials and Textiles, Silk Institute, Hangzhou 310018, China

* Corresponding author's email: 917589373@qq.com

Abstract: People's sleeping time occupies about one third of their life time. Well-designed sleeping pillow is a guarantee of good sleep. However, the function of most pillows is relatively simple at present, and there is a lack of study on the compression of the pillow on the side of the face and cheek when sleeping on the side. Therefore, it is necessary to study an innovative multifunctional pillow with anti-wrinkle on face and neck, health care and sleep aids. In order to solve the above problems, this paper designed a four-wing split-type multifunctional sleeping pillow for adult women based on ergonomics principle, and used tactilus pressure mapping system for body pressure distribution test. The innovative design of four-wing split-type structure meets people's various needs of sleeping on the back, lying on the side, and reclining, and can prevent the formation of facial furrows when lying on the side, and can avoid the formation of the cervical stripe when reclining. The results of body pressure distribution test showed that compared with the common and well-designed S-shaped latex pillow on the market, the four-wing split-type pillow was more effective when sleeping on the side.

Keywords: Ergonomics; Multifunctional pillow; Anti-wrinkle; Body pressure distribution test

1 Introduction

Sleeping takes about one-third of one's life. People need good sleep after a busy day in this fast-paced urban life. However, according to the investigation of the author of this paper, there are the following deficiencies in sleeping pillows on the market: Firstly, the squeezing of sleeping pillows on the user's side face and cheeks when sleeping on the side was not considered, which had the potential to cause wrinkles; Secondly, the function is relatively simple, and cannot fully meet consumers' high demand for sleeping. Therefore, it is of great significance to design a multifunctional pillow that is ergonomic, with anti-wrinkle on face and neck, health care and sleep aids.

The design of a highly comfortable pillow should be considered from three aspects: structure design, parameter settings and material selection. This paper mainly studies the structure design and parameter settings.

Structure design mainly refers to the shape design of the pillow. Hou Jianjun[1], a domestic scholar, classified the pillow type into five types: flat, cubic, S-shaped, concave, and convex. Combined with a series of related experimental analysis, He found that when using S-shaped pillow or convex pillow, spinal deformation is relatively small, and subjective comfort is higher. He Yanmei[2] conducted a series of related tests for the flat, S-shaped and cubic, and found that S-shaped pillows had the best effect. Parameter settings mainly refer to the setting of height, length and width of pillow. Foreign scholars Erfanian[3] and Bernateck[4] and others studied the height separately. They pointed out that the pillow's height is closely related to the shoulder width. If the pillow is too high, it will change the normal physiological curve of the cervical vertebra. If the pillow is too low, it will make the head engorged, leading to snoring. According to the investigation, measurement and analysis of the zygomatic distance and shoulder width of

68 adults, Xu Linhai[5] concluded that the appropriate height of pillow was 0.167 times of shoulder width plus 4.633cm. Professor Su Youxin[6] concluded that the suitable height of supine pillow was (6.54 ± 0.63)cm, the suitable height of the supine position pillow was (11.23 ± 1.08)cm, and the suitable height of the lateral position pillow was (15.10 ± 1.67)cm, according to bio-mechanical analysis and measurement of the head and neck features of human body. Su Cuijuan[7] proposed that the pillow height should be 6cm to 12cm when lying supine and 7cm to 15cm should be appropriate when lying on the side. The study on the length of the pillow and the width of the pillow is relatively lacking. Generally, the length of the adult's pillow is 15cm over its shoulder width, and the length is between 50cm and 70cm. The width of the pillow should be more than 25cm[8].

2　Design

2.1　Structure design

Based on the above problems and current researches, this article takes ergonomics as the basic concept and innovatively designs a four-wing split-type multifunctional pillow, as shown in Fig.1. As you can see in Fig.1: 1 is pillow body; 2 is a flexible deformed wire embedded in the interior of the pillow; 3 is the depressed head area in the upper center of the pillow; 4 is the cervical support area; 5 is the curved support on both sides of the pillow; 6 is the connecting and fixing part on the two arc-shaped supports.

This design can change the shape of four-wing of the pillow by bending the wire and the four-wing structure to adapt to different sleeping habits and needs. The shape of the upper and lower part of the pillow can be changed by the flexible deformation of metal wire in the body of the pillow, to adapt to different sleeping habits. When sleeping on your back, your back brain is slightly lower, which increases blood flow to your brain and prevents snoring. The depressed head area also can fix the head and prevent it from leaving the pillow. When the wings on both sides of the pillow become curved arcs, the support body can be connected through Velcro, invisible fastenings and son on, and can be sup-

ported under the neck chin to support the neck, and can also be used for fixing the pillow and preventing stiff neck, when lying flat. In addition, it is more suitable for those who like to lean on the bed to read a book and play with a mobile phone. When the pillow is placed obliquely, the pillow wings, insert the neck, under the chin, can avoid the formation of cervical stripe and reduce the neck bending angle and fatigue. When lying on the side, the supporting body on both sides of the pillow can support the head, so that most of the side of face can be suspended, avoiding the squeeze of cheek on the corner of the eye and the lower eyelid, which slows the generation of furrows, and appropriate for all kinds of people with poor sleep quality and suffered from cervical pain, as well as to people have high demand for sleep and want to be pretty.

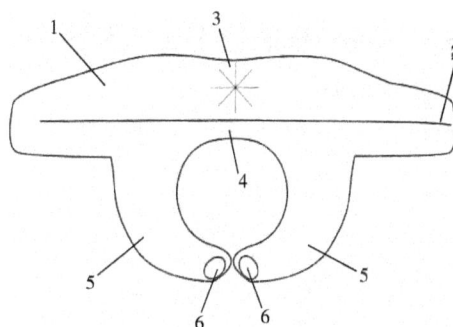

Fig.1　Structure of pillow body

2.2　Parameter settings

After the structure of the pillow is determined, parameters are set in this paper based on the above research, as shown in Fig.2. The study found that the shoulder width of Chinese adult females is approximately (34.35 ± 2.13) cm[9]. In this study, the shoulder width is 35cm. According to the above description: "Appropriate pillow height is approximately 0.167 times the shoulder width plus 4.633cm", this paper calculates a suitable height is 10.478cm, so the highest pillow height in this study is 10cm. Since the back-sleeping height is generally 3cm to 6cm[10] lower than the side sleep height, so the lowest height of the sleeping pillow is 7cm. In consideration of the actual use experience, the width of the cervical spine support area is 18cm, the length of the two-support body is 22cm, and the width is 8cm. The upper width of the pillow body is set to a minimum width of 25cm. Considering the overall shape of the sleeping pillow, the length of the sleeping pillow is set to 68cm.

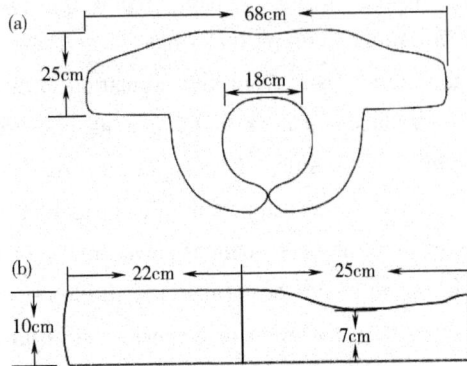

Fig. 2　(a) Size of the front of the pillow; (b) Size of the profile of the pillow

3　Experiments and Data Analysis

3.1　Experiments

According to the above design, a multifunctional pillow which is simply "sample" for short was preliminarily produced with cotton grey cloth as fabric and imported 3A pearl cotton as the filler. The pressure on the back of the head and neck of the user was measured in this sample while sleeping on the back and side (as shown in Fig. 3). The comparison of this experiment is a comfortable S-shaped latex pillow, abbreviated as "contrast". Considering that individuals with different body weights and heights have different sleeping pillow parameters, there are three subjects in this experiment. Subject A has a body weight of about 80kg, a height of about 155cm, and a very thin body type; the weight of the subject B is about 55kg, and the height is about 170cm, body size is thin; subject C has a weight of about 50kg, and a height of 160cm, and her body size is moderate. A has a large body type difference with B and C, while B have a small body type difference with C. The instrument used in this experiment is the Tactilus Pressure Mapping System. It is mainly composed of software and rectangular sensor pads. There are a total of 50×50 sensor elements on the sensor pad. At the end of each experiment, an excel file can be exported from the software to record the pressure of each induction element, as well as the maximum, minimum and average values of the experiment. A total of three groups of experiments were conducted. Each subject was a group. Each subject was tested 4 times in total, using the "sample" and "contrast", respectively, in a lying and side state. At the end of the experiment, a total of 12 Excel experimental data files were obtained.

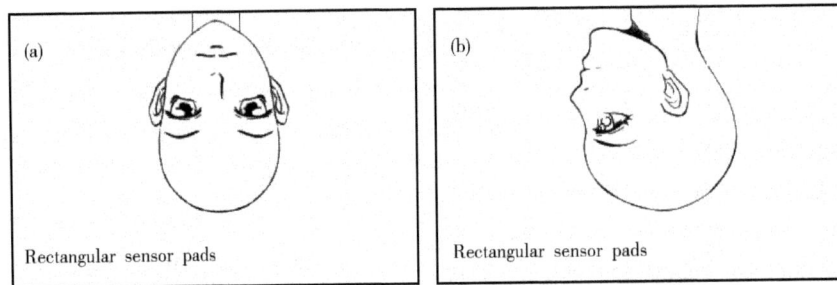

Fig. 3　(a) Sleeping on one's back; (b) Lie on the side

3.2　Data analysis

Limited by the experimental equipment, the original experimental data presented are not intuitive. Therefore, the experimental data are processed and made into "excel thermodynamic chart", and then compared and analyzed. In excel thermodynamic chart, color can reflect the degree of pressure, with red as the highest value, yellow as the middle value, and blue as the lowest value. After processing, there are 12 Excel thermodynamic charts in this paper, as shown in Fig. 5 and Fig. 6, and the maximum value of single experimental data is made into Tab. 1.

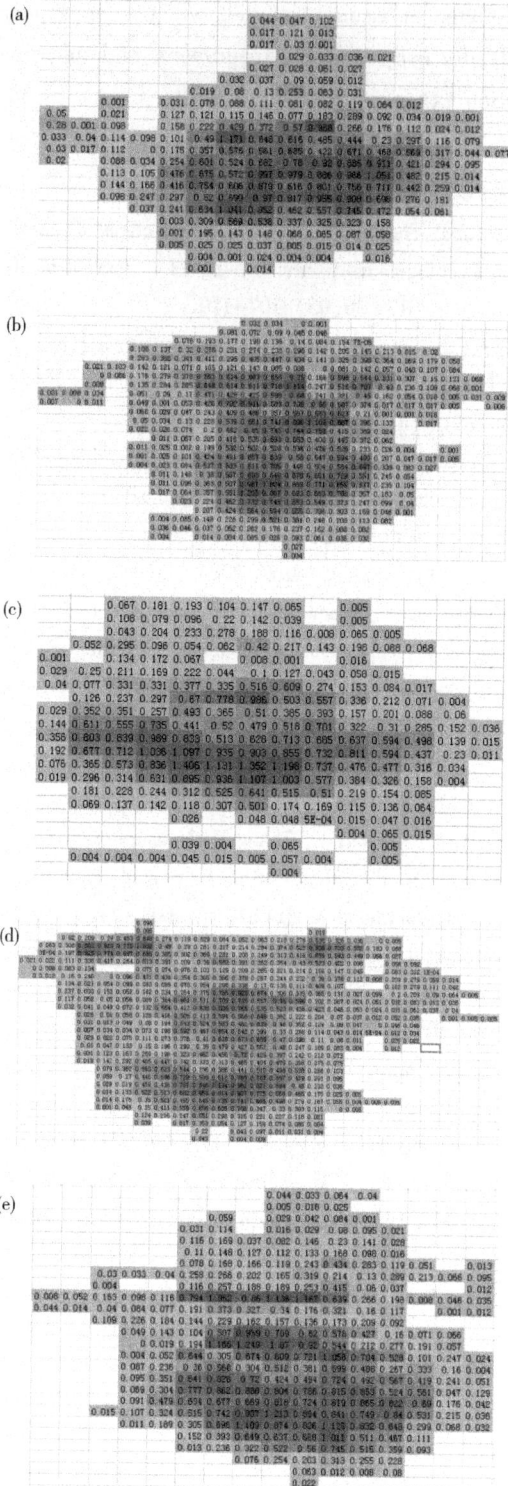

Fig. 4 (a) Subject A's Thermodynamic Diagram of the use of "sample" in a flat state; (b) Subject A's Thermodynamic Diagram of the use of "contrast" in a flat state; (c) Subject B's Thermodynamic Diagram of the use of "sample" in a flat state; (d) Subject B's Thermodynamic Diagram of the use of "contrast" in a flat state; (e) Subject C's Thermodynamic Diagram of the use of "sample" in a flat state; (f) Subject C's Thermodynamic Diagram of the use of "contrast" in a flat state

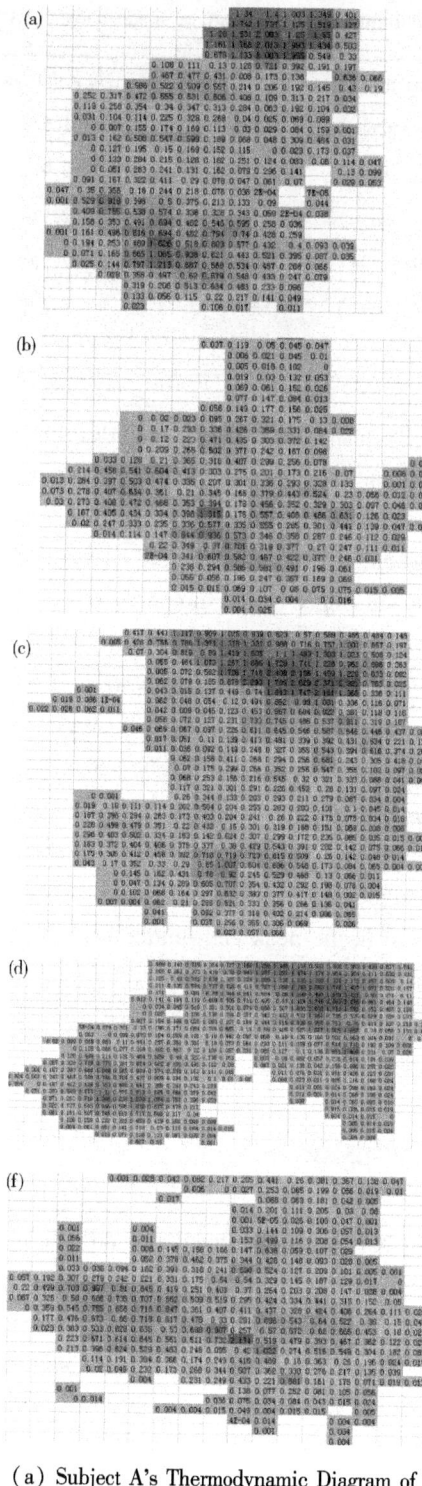

Fig. 5 (a) Subject A's Thermodynamic Diagram of the use of "sample" in a side sleep state; (b) Subject A's Thermodynamic Diagram of the use of "contrast" in a side sleep state; (c) Subject B's Thermodynamic Diagram of the use of "sample" in a side sleep state; (d) Subject B's Thermodynamic Diagram of the use of "contrast" in a side sleep state; (e) Subject C's Thermodynamic Diagram of the use of "sample" in a side sleep state; (f) Subject C's Thermodynamic Diagram of the use of "contrast" in a side sleep state

Tab. 1 Maximum pressure value of single body pressure test

Maximum	In a flat state	In a side state
Subject A (contrast)	1.203	1.626
Subject A (sample)	1.171	2.013
Subject B (contrast)	1.134	2.176
Subject B (sample)	1.406	2.408
Subject C (contrast)	1.143	2.171
Subject C (sample)	1.213	2.501

From the thermodynamic chart analysis, the following conclusions can be drawn: (1) From the pressure area analysis, compared with the "contrast", the area under pressure when using the "sample" is relatively small; (2) In the side sleep state, in combination with the actual situation, when subjects used the "contrast", the pillow caused a large area of squeezing on the side of the face, and when subjects used "sample", the side face was largely suspended, which effectively prevent the pillow from squeezing the side of the cheek; (3) From the pressure position analysis, whether it is the use of "sample" or "contrast", most of the pressure is concentrated in the neck and hindbrain; (4) From the maximum pressure value in Tab. 1, the pressure of the "contrast" is smaller than the "sample", which does not exclude the factor of the latex material.

4 Conclusions

The four-wing split-type multifunctional pillow studied in this paper has various functions and can be adapted to different sleeping needs, such as sleeping on the back, lying on the side, and reclining. It has been proved by experiments that the four-wing split-type multifunctional pillow can effectively avoid the formation of facial wrinkles when lying on the side, and compared with the S-shaped pillow, it has a smaller area under pressure. However, this multifunctional pillow is also inadequate. Subsequent studies will use more accurate samples for body pressure experiments and subjective evaluation experiments.

References

[1] Hou J J, Shen L M. Research on the effect of pillow shape on sleeping comfort on side lying [J]. Journal of Machine Design, 2013, 30(03):107–110.

[2] He Y M. The influences of pillow type on sleeping comfort [J]. Journal of Beijing Institute of Clothing, 2005(12): 40–47.

[3] Erfanian P, Tenzif S, Guerriero R C. Assessing effects of a semi-customized experimental cervical pillow on symptomatic adults with chronic neck pain with and without headache [J]. J Can Chiropr Assoc, 2004, 48(48): 20–28.

[4] Bernateck M, Karst M, Merkesdal S, et al. Sustained effects of comprehensive inpatient rehabilitative treatment and sleeping neck support in patients with chronic cervicobrachialgia: a prospective and randomized clinical trial [J]. International Journal Rehabilitation Research, 2008, 31 (4): 342–346.

[5] Xu L H, Chen H L, Zhang F. Measurement of 68 adults' shoulder width and proper pillow-related parameters [J]. Chinese Journal of Rehabilitation, 2009, 24(5): 310–311.

[6] Su Y X, Lin S L, Liu X X. Discussion on pillow and sleeping causing spinal disease [J]. Chinese Medicine, 1998, 10 (3): 9–10.

[7] Su C J, Sun G W. Suggestions on the Scientific application of pillow to prevent cervical spondylosis[J]. Chinese Journal of Orthopaedic Surgery, 2002, 10(11): 1143–1144.

[8] Wang M, Li J. The application of ergonomics in the design of pillows [J]. China Personal Protective Equipment, 2008 (05): 19–21.

[9] Mu R R. Analysis on the change of the morphology character of 20–25 years old urban adults in China [D]. Shanghai: Shanghai University of Sport, 2017.

[10] Sleep needs to use "core" [J]. Textile Decoration and Technology, 2013(04): 26–28.

Effects of Graft Modification on Water-Solubility and Adhesion Property of Chitosan for Warp Sizing

Shiyao Chen[1], Enqi Jin[1]*, Bojun Xi[1], Manli Li[1], JianguoLu[2], Juan Wang[2]

[1] *College of Textiles and Garments, Shaoxing University, Shaoxing 312000, China*

[2] *Zhende Medical Co. , Ltd. , Shaoxing, Zhejiang 312035, China*

* *Corresponding author's email*: jdkxxh_2001@163. com

Abstract: Unmodified chitosans exhibit poor water-solubility, are unable to meet the water-based sizing requirement satisfactorily, and have limited industrial application as warp sizes. In order to impart good water-solubility to chitosans and extend their practical utilization in textile field, various amounts of hydrophilic vinyl monomers-acrylamides (AM) were grafted onto the molecular chain of chitosan. A series of chitosan–g–PAM with different grafting percentages were prepared and the composition of the graft copolymer was characterized by FTIR. Then effects of the graft modification on main sizing properties of chitosan were surveyed in terms of water-solubility and adhesion to fibers. It was found that, by grafting appropriate amounts of AM onto the molecular chain of chitosan, the water-solubility and adhesion to fibers were improved markedly. In view of overall performance of the grafted chitosan sizes, the optimum value should be 11.90% when the grafting percentage was in range of 0–26.89%.

Keywords: Chitosan; Graft polymerization; Acrylamide; Water-solubility; Adhesion property

1 Introduction

Chitosan is a kind of high molecular weight polysaccharide composed mainly of β–(1,4)–linked 2–deoxy–2–amino–D–gl–ucopyranose units and partially of β–(1,4)–linked 2–deoxy–2–acetamido–D–glucopyranose ones. Chitosan prepared from chitin through deacetylation using hot alkali solution is a more versatile form, which is an abundant natural polymer and ranks only second to cellulose on the earth[1]. In recent years, chitosans have been employed as new warp sizes and exhibited many good characteristics, such as high film-forming property, abrasion resistance, antibacterial property, and biodegradability. Modern sizing operation is based on an aqueous paste and this requires sizing agents to possess water-solubility or at least water-dispersibility. However, the poor water-solubility, which results from high regularity and rigidity of the molecular chains and strong intramolecular and intermolecular hydrogen-bond interactions, is becoming a fundamental constraint on the utilization of chitosan as a sizing agent with high performance in textile field[2].

In the present study, different amounts of acrylamide (AM) monomers were grafted onto chitosan through $K_2S_2O_8/NaHSO_3$ redox system to develop sizing agents since previous investigations proved that polyacrylamide (PAM) showed good water-solubility and might be able to make the substrate more water-soluble as grafted branch[3-4]. A series of chitosan–g–PAM with various grafting percentages were prepared and their water-solubility was evaluated compared with unmodified chitosan.

In terms of the apparent viscosity, mechanical properties and water dissolution rate of the chitosan film, and adhesion-to-fibers, effects of the graft modification on the properties of the chitosan for warp sizing were evaluated systematically. Finally, appropriate grafting percentage was recommended for the preparation of chitosan–g–PAM for enhancing its serviceability as a bio-based sizing agent.

2 Experiments

2.1 Materials

Chitosan was prepared from chitin through deacetylation using hot alkali solution and degree of deacetylation of the chitosan was 60%. The deacetylated chitoson was dried completely, pulverized and stored in desiccator. AM, potassium persulfate, sodium bisulfite and paradioxybenzene, which were provided by Sinopharm Chemical Reagent Co., Ltd. (Shanghai), were used as monomer, oxidant, reductant and terminator in the graft polymerization, respectively. All the reagents used were chemically pure. Pure cotton rovings (479tex) were obtained from Qingfeng Textile Co., Ltd. (Jiangsu). The parameters of cotton fibers in the rovings were 27mm × 1.91dtex.

2.2 Graft polymerization

Before grafting, 5g of native chitins were dispersed with distilled water. Then, the dispersion was transferred into a 500mL four-neck flask. Acetic acid was added to adjust the dispersion to a desired pH (4.5 – 6.5). The flask was maintained at a specific temperature (30 – 70℃) in a water bath. The mixture was deoxygenated by passing N_2 for at least 30min. The initiators including the oxidant ($K_2S_2O_8$) and the reductant ($NaHSO_3$) with varying concentrations were dissolved in distilled water, respectively. The initiator solutions and various amounts of MMA monomers in range of 20%–60% (MMA/chitin) were added into the flask through three funnels simultaneously. The addition was completed in 10–20min and final weight ratio of the chitin to water was 1:7. The graft polymerization was carried out in the flask under vigorous stirring using a mechanical stirrer at 1000r/min under nitrogen atmosphere for a predetermined time (0.5 – 4h). Finally, 2% of paradioxybenzene solution was added to terminate the polymerization. The product was neutralized to about pH 7.0, filtered, washed thoroughly with distilled water and the filtrate was saved to determine the amount of residual monomer. At last, the product was dried at 105℃ in an oven. Each graft polymerization was repeated 3 times.

2.3 Determination of water-solubility

The chitosan sample was suspended into acetic acid solution to form 6% dispersion. Then the dispersion was heated to 95℃ and maintained at the temperature under stirring to make the sample dissolved completely. After that, the solution was cooled to room temperature without stirring and kept under the condition for 3 days for the observation of the solubility stability. During the days, the appearance time and the amount of the precipitation in the solution were recorded.

2.4 Measurement of adhesion property

The chitosan was suspended into acetic acid solution to form 1% dispersion. The dispersion was heated to 95℃ and maintained at the temperature under mechanical stirring for 1hour. Then the chitosan solution obtained was decanted into a stainless steel box placed in water bath at 95℃. The roving carefully wound onto a special frame was impregnated with the chitosan solution for 5min. The frame was hung and dried in air. Finally, the rovings were kept at 65% RH. and 20℃ for 24 hours before tested. Tensile strength and elongation of the roving samples were measured on a BZ2.5/TNIS Zwick Material Tester with 100mm in initial chuck-distance and 50mm/min in drawing speed[5].

3 Results and Discussion

3.1 Effects of grafting percentage on water-solubility

Tab.1 shows the water-solubility of the non-grafted and grafted chitosans. Grafting appropriate amounts of AM had a great contribution to the improvement on the water-solubility of chitosan. With the increase in the grafting percentage, water-solubility and solubility stability of the modified chitosan initially increased, reached the maximum when grafting percentage was 11.90%, and then decreased.

Tab.1 Water-solubility and apparent viscosity of chitosan sizes

Grafting percentage	Water solubility	Solubility stability
0	+	+
2.06%	+	+ +
4.37%	+ +	+ +
11.90%	+ + +	+ + +
26.89%	+	+

3.2 Adhesion to fibers

Effects of the graft modification on the adhesion properties of chitosan sizes to cotton fibers are presented in Fig. 1. Compared to the non-grafted samples, the graft modification could improve the adhesion of the chitosan due to the increased tensile strength and elongation of the sized roving. With the increase in the grafting percentage, the tensile strength of sized cotton rovings gradually increased. As for the tensile elongation, it initially increased, leveled off when grafting percentage ranged from 4.37% to 11.90%, and then decreased substantially.

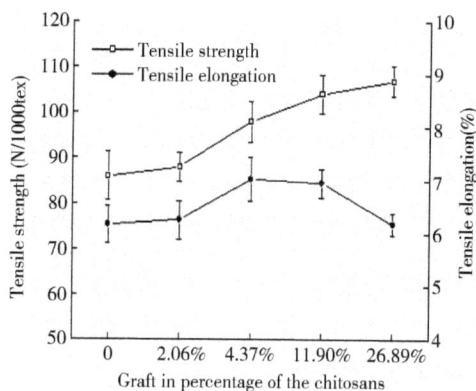

Fig. 1　Adhesion of the chitosan sizes to cotton fibers

4　Conclusions

The serviceability of chitosan used as sizing agents was remarkably improved through grafting appropriate amounts of AM onto the molecular chains of chitosan. Water-solubility, apparent viscosity, mechanical properties of sizing film, and the adhesion to fibers depended directly on the grafting percentage of chitosan-*g*-PAM. The grafted chitosan showed better water-solubility and sizing properties when grafting percentage was 11.90%. If the percentage exceeded this value, the water-solubility would decrease and the decrease led to the deterioration of sizing properties, such as mechanical properties of the sizing film and tensile elongation of the sized roving. This denoted the grafted chitosan possessed better adhesion to cellulose fibers. The graft modification endows the grafted chitosan with good water-solubility under weak acid condition and contributes to a wider use of chitosan as an inexpensive bio-based sizing agent in textile industry.

Acknowledgements

The work was supported financially by Technological Research Project for Public Welfare of Shaoxing (No. 2017B70047) and Science and Technology Planning Project (collaboration between institutions) of Shaoxing (No. 2017710). Financial sponsors do not endorse the views expressed in this publication.

References

[1] Don T M, King C F, Chiu W Y. Synthesis and properties of chitosan-modified poly(vinyl acetate) [J]. J. Appl. Polym. Sci, 2002, 86(12): 3057-3063.

[2] Shen F. Study on improving water-solubility of chitin size by enzyme [D]. Shanghai: Donghua University, 2010:6.

[3] Francolini I, Taresco V, Crisante F, et al. Water soluble usnic acid-polyacrylamide complexes with enhanced antimicrobial activity against staphylococcus epidermidis [J]. Int. J. Mol. Sci, 2013, 14(4): 7356-7369.

[4] Harutyunyan R S. Molecular interactions in a surfactant-water-polyacrylamide system, according to densimetry, viscometry, conductometry, and spectroscopy data [J]. Russ. J. Phys. Chem. A, 2013, 87(8): 1319-1328.

[5] Jin E Q, Zhu Z F, Yang Y Q. Structural effects of glycol and benzenedicarboxylate units on the adhesion of water-soluble polyester sizes to polyester fibers [J]. J. Text. I, 2010, 101(12): 1112-1120.

Fabrication of Electrospun PA6 Nanofibrous Porous Membrane

Wenwen Li [1,2,3], **Jiaona Wang**[1,2,3]*, **Jiamin Zhang**[1,2,3], **Xiuyan Li**[1,2,3]

[1] *College of Material Science and Engineering, Beijing 100029, China*

[2] *Beijing Key Laboratory of Clothing Materials R&D and Assessment, Beijing 100029, China*

[3] *Beijing Institute of Fashion Technology, Beijing 100029, China*

* *Corresponding author's email*: jnwangjn@ sina. com

Abstract: Polyamide 6/polyvinylpyrrolidone (PA6 / PVP) composite nanofibrous membrane was prepared by using PA6 as raw material and PVP as a pore forming agent. Porous PA6 nanofibrous have been prepared via electrospinning after washing PVP off in this study. The structure and morphology were characterized by scanning electron microscopy (SEM). The effects of different average molecular weights of PVP, different soaking times, and different mass ratios of PA6/PVP on the morphology of nanofiber membranes were explored. The results showed that the surface features of the nanofibrous became evident when average molecular weights of PVP is 24000, the surface roughness was large and the pore number were increased with soaking time going, the pore number were increased with the increase of the content of PVP, and the PVP could be washed off for preparing PA6 porous nanofibrous membrane. The porous membrane has a great application prospect in adsorption, filtration, smart garment and other fields.

Keywords: Polyamide 6; Polyvinylpyrrolidone; Electrospinning; Porous nanofibrous membrane

1 Introduction

Nanofibrous porous materials, as the forefront of the fundamental materials nowadays, provide one of the greatest potential in a number of industrial sectors, which are gradually accessing into our daily life. In comparison with other methods of fiber fabrication such as template synthesis, drawing, and phase-separation, electrospinning techniques[1] have emerged as straight forward approaches to the fabrication of nanofibers with high specific surface areas, high porosities, and controllable compositions for a wide range of applications[2-3]. A variety of advanced techniques have already been developed to fabricate nanostructures with porous[4], ribbon-like[5], necklace-like[6-7]. Due to its high specific surface area, nanofibrous materials have a certain application prospect in filtration[8], smart garment[9] and other fields.

Electrospinning methods for producing porous nanofibers include direct and post-treatment methods. Post-treatment refers to the treatment of fibers after electrospin-

ning to obtain porous structures[10-11]. In this paper, two kinds of PA6 and PVP polymer solutions were prepared and mixed into a uniform solution without precipitation. After electrospinning, acetic acid solvent was used to selectively dissolve and remove PVP. The effects of the average molecular weight of PVP, the solvent soaking time and the ratio of spinning solution on the porous structure of the fiber were studied.

2 Experiments

2.1 Materials

PA6 pellets (number-average molecular weight = 20000g/mol) were purchased from Yueyang BaLing ShiHua Chemical & Synthetic Fiber Co. , Ltd. Polyvinylpyrrolidone (PVP), average molecular weight = 24000g/mol, was purchased Shanghai Macklin Biochemical Technology Co. , Ltd. Polyvinylpyrrolidone (average molecular weight = 130000g/mol) was purchased Shanghai Macklin Biochemical Technology Co. , Ltd. Formic acid was purchased from Beijing Tongguang

Fine Chemicals Co., Ltd. Acetic acid was purchased from Beijing Tong Guang Fine Chemicals Co., Ltd. All chemicals were of analytical grade and were used without further purification.

2.2 Preparation of the PA6/PVP membranes

Polymer solution was preparation by the dissolution of PA6 in formic acid. The solution was prepared by magnetic stirring at room temperature. The concentration of PA6 was 28%. The PVP was dissolved in an acetic acid solvent and magnetically stirred at room temperature to prepare 30% PVP spinning solution. The two spinning solutions were mixed at different mass ratios and the mass ratio of PA6 to PVP were 9:1, 7:3, 5:5 and 3:7 respectively. The mixed spinning solutions were loaded into syringes and injected through metal needles with a controllable feed rate of 1mL/h. The collector drum, which rotated at a speed of 60r/min and was coated with nonwovens were made of polyethylene terephthalate (PET). During electrospinning, the applied voltage was held constant at 20kV, and the receiving distance between the polymer solution and the polyethylene foil collection screen was kept at 15cm. The relevant temperature was 45℃. The prepared nanofibrous membranes were separately soaked in acetic acid solution and then given an airing at room temperature.

2.3 Characterization

The surface morphology of nanofibrous membranes was studied by using scanning electron microscopy (JSM-7500F, JEOL, Japan). All samples were sputtered with gold under vacuum before the SEM measurements.

3 Results and Discussion

3.1 Morphology of nanofibrous membranes with different average molecular weight of PVP

Fig. 1 is SEM images of nanofibrous membranes with different average molecular weight PVP, the mass ratio of PA6 to PVP was 9:1. Fig. 1 (a#) – (d#) on the right were the enlarged view of Fig. 1 (a) – (d) on the left. Fig. 1 (a) and Fig. 1 (b) showed the morphology of PA6 / PVP nanofibrous membranes, in which the average molecular weight of PVP was 24000. Fig. 1 (c) and Fig. 1 (d) showed the morphology of PA6 / PVP nanofibrous membranes, in which the average molecular

weight of PVP was 1300000. Fig. 1 (b) and Fig. 1 (d) were acetate-soaked PA6 / PVP nanofibrous membranes for 24h. It can be seen from the Fig. 1 that the PVP component in nanofibrous membranes after acetic acid soaking treatment was dissolved and the average molecular weight of PVP had a great influence on the morphology. The PA6 / PVP nanofirous membranes with PVP average molecular weight of 1300000 had certain level aggregate phenomenon after immersing in acetic acid and had significantly less porous structure. The PVP component in the membrane is not easily dissolved, because the average molecular weight of PVP is too large. The morphology of PA6 / PVP nanofibrous membranes with the PVP average molecular weight of 24000 after immersing in acetic acid was superior to that with the PVP average molecular weight of 1300000.

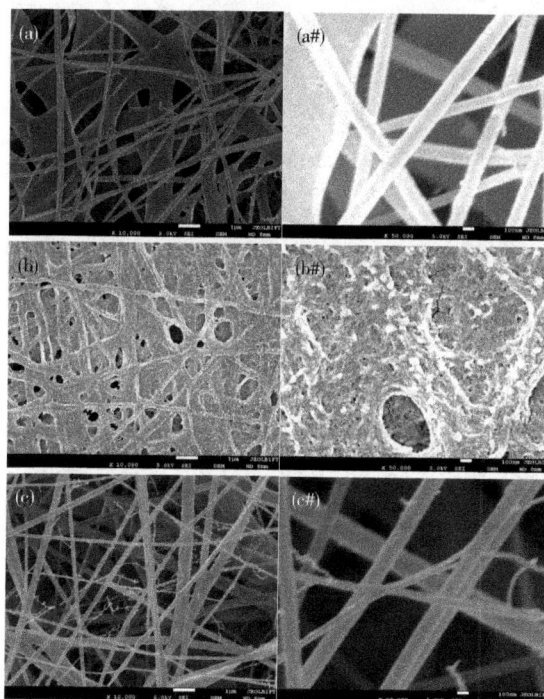

Fig. 1 SEM images of the PA6 / PVP nanofibrous membranes with different average molecular weight PVP. PA6 : PVP (*Mn* = 24000) = 9 : 1 (a) PA6/PVP nanofibrous membranes; (b) Acetate-soaked PA6 / PVP nanofibrous membranes for 24h; PA6 : PVP (*Mn* = 1300000) = 9 : 1; (c) PA6 / PVP nanofibrous membranes; (d) Acetate-soaked PA6 / PVP nanofibrous membranes for 24h; (a#) – (d#) on the right were the enlarged view of (a) – (d) on the left

3.2 Morphology of nanofiber membranes with different soaking time

The prepared PA6 / PVP nanofibrous membranes were separately soaked in acetic acid solution. Fig. 2 showed SEM images of nanofibrous membranes with different soaking time (3h, 6h, 9h, 12h, 36h and 48h respectively), in which the average molecular weight of PVP was 24000. The mass ratio of PA6 to PVP was 9 : 1. Fig. 2 (a#) – (f#) on the right were the enlarged view of Fig. 2 (a) – (f) on the left. As shown in Fig. 1 and Fig. 2, with the soaking time going, the porous structure of the nanofibrous membranes was significantly increased, which indicated that the PVP component in the nanofibrous membranes was more completely dissolved with longer soaking time. However, when the soaking time was 48h, the porous structure of the nanofibrous membrane was reduced and the membrane aggregation was severe. Therefore, the PVP in the nanofibrous membrane was fully dissolved when the soaking time was 36h.

3.3 Morphology of PA6/PVP nanofibrous membranes with different mass ratios

Fig. 3 showed SEM images of nanofibrous membranes with different mass ratios of PA6 / PVP (7 : 3, 5 : 5

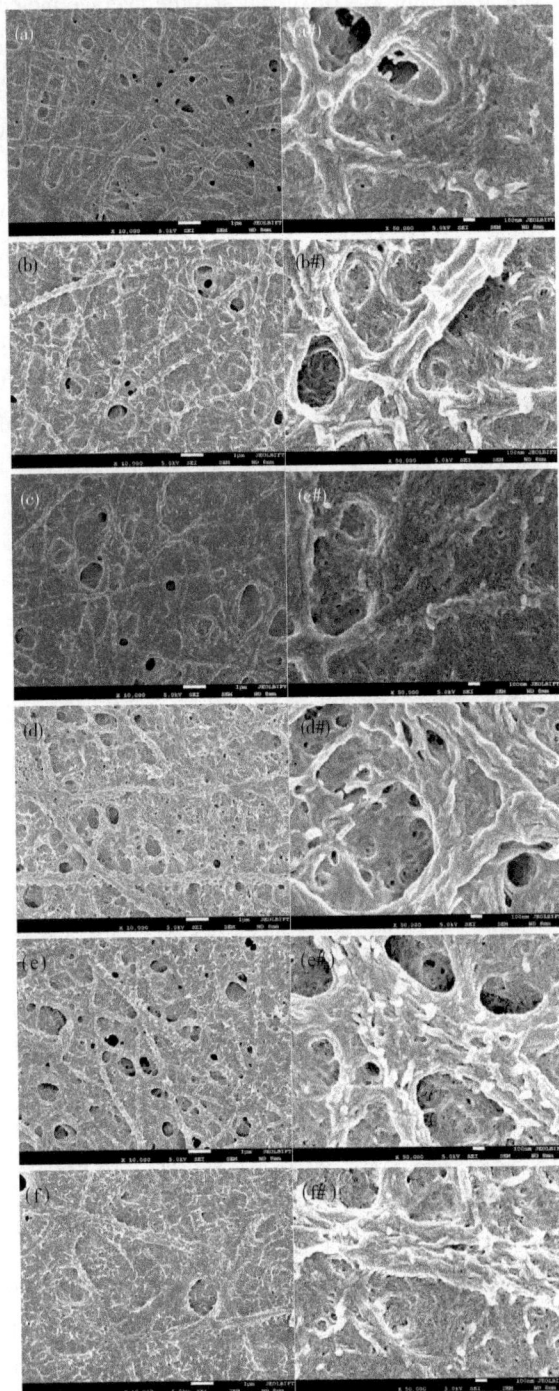

Fig. 2 SEM images of the PA6 / PVP nanofibrous membranes with different soaking time (a) 3h; (b) 6h; (c) 9h; (d) 12h; (e)36h; (f) 48h; (a#) – (f#) on the right were the enlarged view of (a) – (f) on the left

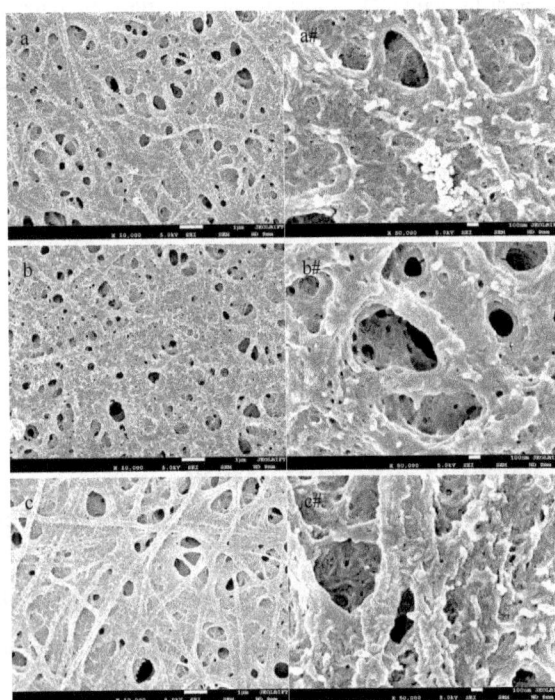

Fig. 3 SEM images of the PA6/PVP nanofibrous membranes with different mass ratios (a) The mass ratio of PA6 / PVP = 7 : 3; (b)The mass ratio of PA6 / PVP = 5 : 5; (c) The mass ratio of PA6 / PVP = 3 : 7; (a#) – (c#) on the right were the enlarged view of (a) – (c) on the left

and $3:7$ respectively), in which the average molecular weight of PVP was 24000. The soaking time of nanofirous membranes in acetic acid was 36h. The mass ratio of PA6 to PVP was $9:1$. Fig. 3 (a#) – (c#) on the right is an enlarged view of Fig. 3 (a) – (c) on the left. From Fig. 3, Fig. 2 (e) and Fig. 2 (e#), we can explore the effect of different mass ratios of PA6 / PVP on morphology. By comparison, it can be seen that the porous structure of the nanofiber membrane gradually increased with the mass ratio of PA6 / PVP decreasing. At the same soaking time, with the increase of PVP content, it can be seen from the surface morphology that the surface roughness of the membrane becomes significantly larger. When the mass ratio of PA6 to PVP is $3:7$, the fiber surface roughness changes most significantly.

4 Conclusions

The PA6 / PVP composite nanofibrous membranes with different mass ratios were spun by electrospinning. After immersing in acetic acid, the PVP components were dissolved and PA6 nanofibrous porous membranes were successfully prepared. Compared with the average molecular weight of 1300000, the surface morphology of PA6 porous membranes after acetic acid soaking is better when the average molecular weight of PVP is 24000. After PA6 / PVP composite nanofiber membranes were immersed in acetic acid for 36h, the PVP components were removed more completely and finally the nanofibrous porous membranes were obtained. When the mass ratio of PA6 to PVP was $3:7$, the membrane surface roughness changed most significantly, and the fiber surface presented a porous structure.

Acknowledgements

This study was partly supported by Nature Science Foundation of China (Grant No. 51503005), Beijing Nature Science foundation (2182014), General Program of the Science and Technology Development Project of the Beijing Municipal Education Commission of China (SQKM201710012004), High levels Teacher's Team Construction Special Funds of Beijing Institute of Fashion Technology (BIFTQG201801), Beijing Municipal Association for Science and Technology " golden bridge engineering seed money" (H2017-42), Beijing Science and Technology Leading Talent Project (grant no. Z161100004916168), Beijing Outstanding Talents Cultivation (contract grant numbers 2017000020124G089).

References

[1] Jiang L, Zhao Y, Zhai J. A lotus-leaf-like superhydrophobic surface: a porous microsphere/nanofiber composite film prepared by electrohydrodynamics [J]. Angew Chem Int Ed, 2004, 43(33): 4338-4341.

[2] Ding B, Wang M, Yu J, et al. Gas sensors based on electrospun nanofibers [J]. Sensors, 2009, 9(3): 1609-1624.

[3] Wang X, Ding B, Yu J, et al. Engineering biomimetic superhydrophobic surfaces of electrospun nanomaterials [J]. Nano Today, 2011, 6(5): 510-530.

[4] Lin J, Ding B, Yu J. Direct fabrication of highly nanoporous polystyrene fibers via electrospinning [J]. Acs Applied Materials & Interfaces, 2010, 2(2): 521.

[5] Koombhongse S, Liu W, Reneker D H. Flat polymer ribbons and other shapes by electrospinning [J]. Journal of Polymer Science B Polymer Physics, 2001, 39(21): 2598-2606.

[6] Jia C, Yang P, Huang B. Uniform Ag/AgCl necklace-like nano-heterostructures: Fabrication and highly efficient plasmonic photocatalysis [J]. Chemcatchem, 2014, 6 (2): 611-617.

[7] Jin Y, Yang D, Kang D, et al. Fabrication of necklace-like structures via electrospinning [J]. Langmuir the Acs Journal of Surfaces & Colloids, 2010, 26(2):1186-90.

[8] Kaur S, Sundarrajan S, Rana D, et al. Review: The characterization of electrospun nanofibrous liquid filtration membranes [J]. Journal of Materials Science, 2014, 49(18): 6143-6159.

[9] Fang D, Shen L, Zhe HU, et al. Review of smart garment materials and wearability thereof [J]. Journal of Textile Research, 2015.

[10] You Y, Ji H Y, Lee S W, et al. Preparation of porous ultrafine PGA fibers via selective dissolution of electrospun PGA / PLA blend fibers [J]. Materials Letters, 2006, 60 (6): 757-760.

[11] Li X S, Nie G Y. Nano-porous ultra-high specific surface ultrafine fibers [J]. Chinese Science Bulletin, 2004, 49 (22): 2368-2371.

Incorporation of Metal Ions into Hydrogen-Bonded Polymer Complex Film

Rehan Kiran[1,2]*, **Ali Altam**[1,2], **Chao Su**[1,2], **Hajo Yagoub**[1,2], **Shuguang Yang**[1,2]

[1] *State Key Laboratory for Modification of Chemical Fibers and Polymer Materials & College of Material Science and Engineering, Donghua University, Shanghai 201620*

[2] *Center for Advanced Low-dimension Materials, Donghua University, Shanghai 201620*

* *Corresponding author's email*: kiransaif11@ gmail. com

Abstract: Incorporation of metal ions in polymers might give rise to some functionality which onld be explored in some useful applications. Keeping this in view, we were able to incorporate lanthanide ions into poly (vinyl-pyrrolidone)/ poly (acrylic acid) (PVPON/PAA) films. The films were LBL (layer by layer) assembled and lanthanide ions were introduced into the films at different pH. The concentration of Ln ions was increased gradually. Effect of incorporation of lanthanides was investigated at different molar solutions. Finally the metal-polymer films were characterized by UV-Visible and FT-IR. The emission and excitation spectra were also recorded.

Keywords: PVPON/PAA; LBL (layer by layer); Luminescence

1　Introduction

PVPON is a neutral and chemically stable polymer and its chain conformation can be considered to not change[1]. In contrast to PVPON, Poly (acrylic acid) (PAA) is a water soluble polymer and is the simplest synthetic poly (carboxylic acid). PAA and its derivatives are widely used for thickening, dispersing, suspending and emulsifying agents in pharmaceuticals, cosmetics and paints[2]. One PAA chain can provide many carboxylate groups which are among the most suitable ligands for lanthanide ions. Studies on PAA help more specifically in the interpretation of the behavior of polymers containing carboxylic acid group, such as acidic poly-saccharides, humic substance and proteins[3].

PAA is a weak polyelectrolyte and its ionization degree depends on pH[4]. The ionization degree strongly affects the chain mobility of PAA in aqueous solution[5-6]. As the pH elevated, the ionization of PAA will increase and there will be more COO^- groups present. COO^- shows stronger interaction with lanthanide ions than COOH does. At the same time hydrolysis of lanthanide will strength as pH increases, i. e. lanthanide ions would form $Ln(OH)_3$ to precipitate out from the solution. So if the pH in the solution is too high, COO^- and OH^- will have competition to interact with lanthanide ions.

In this paper, we investigate the incorporation of lanthanide ions into hydrogen-bonded PVPON/PAA film and investigated the effect of pH and molar concentration of lanthanide solution. Lanthanides show characteristic properties on optics, electrics, and magnetics[7-8]. Hence, the film is endowed with properties of the lanthanides, which enable potential applications, such as in luminescence or catalysis.

2　Experiments

2.1　Materials

Poly(vinyl-pyrrolidone) (PVPON, M_w 360000), Poly (acrylic acid) (PAA, M_w 450000) were purchased from Sigma-Aldrich. Cerium chloride heptahydrate (CeCl$_3$ · 7H$_2$O), Europium chloride hexahydrate

($CeCl_3 \cdot 6H_2O$), Terbium chloride hexahydrate ($CeCl_3 \cdot 6H_2O$), were bought from Aladin, Alfa Aesar and J&K chemicals respectively.

2.2 Preparation of hydrogen-bonded thin film

The films were deposited on quartz substrates (1mm thick, 12mm wide and 45mm long) which were rigorously cleaned before use. The substrates were immersed in a boiling H_2SO_4/H_2O_2 mixture (7/3, v/v) for 30min, followed by thorough rinsing with deionized water and dried in a stream of pure N_2. The substrates were alternately immersed into PVPON and PAA solutions, with three rinses in the interval. The assembling and rinsing time were set to 4min and 1min, respectively. Assembling solutions (PVPON and PAA) were prepared at a concentration of 10mg/mL.

2.3 pH dependence

Lanthanide solutions at different pH (pH 2.5, 3.0, 3.5 and 4.0) were prepared to study the effect of pH on incorporation of lanthanides into hydrogen-bonded PVPON/PAA films. As PVPON/PAA film was prepared at pH 2.0.

2.4 Molar ratio

At different pH (pH 2.5, 3.0, 3.5 and 4.0) the concentration of Ln ions were increased gradually. Effect of incorporation of lanthanides was investigated at different molar solutions (0.001M, 0.01M and 0.1M).

2.5 Characterization

The thin films deposited on a quartz substrate were analyzed with an UV-visible spectrometer (Shimadzu UV-2550). The films deposited on silicon wafer were characterized with a Nicolet 87 FT-IR spectrometer (a clean silicon wafer was used as blank). The emission and excitation spectra were recorded at room temperature with Shimadzu 5301-RF machine.

3 Results and Discussion

The PVPON/PAA LbL films were previously studied by several groups[9]. It could be well said that incorporation of lanthanide ions into hydrogen-bonded thin film was strongly dependent on pH of lanthanide solution. As (PVPON/PAA)$_{20}$ films were fabricated at pH = 2, where ionization of PAA was prohibited. When pH of lanthanide solution was increase, then interaction be-

tween carbonyl group of PAA and metal atom would take place. The metal ions in aqueous solution had trend to hydrolyze. When pH of the solution increases, lanthanide ions would form Ln(OH)$_3$ and the solution would become cloudy and finally there would be precipitation. When pH was higher than 7.5, the LnCl$_3$ solutions became cloudy and absorbance signal in UV-Visible region suddenly increased, indicating Ln(OH)$_3$ formed. In the pH region, it showed that the interaction of metal ions within hydrogen-bonded PVPON/PAA film would not facilitate the Ln(OH)$_3$ formation.

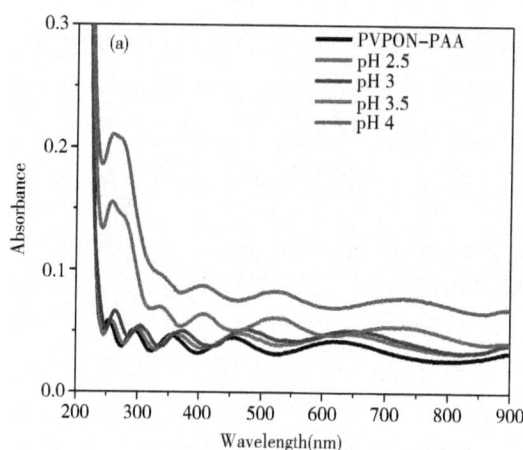

Fig. 1 UV-Visible spectra of PVPON/PAA film at different pH of Ce ion solution

As shown in Fig. 1, at pH 2.5 and 3.0 of lanthanide solution had no effect on the film and film remained the same as in this pH region. Ionization of PAA was very less, so metal ion could not make interaction in the film. Rubner, et al. confirmed that ionization degree of PAA increased with the increase in pH[10]. With the increase in pH hydrogen bonding, interaction decreased gradually and coordination interaction increased. The Ce content in the film increased with the increase in the pH of Ce-ion solution which was due to the increase in the ionization of PAA. As the ionization of PAA increased, the ratio of COO$^-$ also increased. COO$^-$ had stronger interaction with lanthanides than that of COOH. Ce ion content increased with the increase in pH.

FT-IR spectroscopy was further utilized to characterize the PVPON/PAA films after basic vapor incubation.

The IR absorbance peaks of free PAA and PVPON were located at 1706cm^{-1} and 1680cm^{-1}, respectively. However, in PAA there were several hydrogen bonding modes among COOH groups, which resulted in a C=O stretching vibration located at 1709cm^{-1}. In LBL assembled PVPON/PAA film, PAA's peak shifted to higher frequencies (1721cm^{-1}), while PVPON's peak shifted to lower frequencies (1640cm^{-1}) due to hydrogen bonding between PVPON and PAA.

FT-IR spectra of PVPON/PAA film after incorporation of lanthanide ions showed that at pH 2.5, C=O group stretching vibration of PAA and C=O group stretching vibration of PVPON did not show any significant displacement as shown in Fig. 2. As the pH increased to 3.5, due to ionization of PAA, intensity of the peak at 1722cm decreased and new peak appeared at 1545cm. With the further increase in pH 4.0, the intensity of peak at 1545cm increased gradually, which indicated the interaction of lanthanide ions with COO$^-$ groups of PAA.

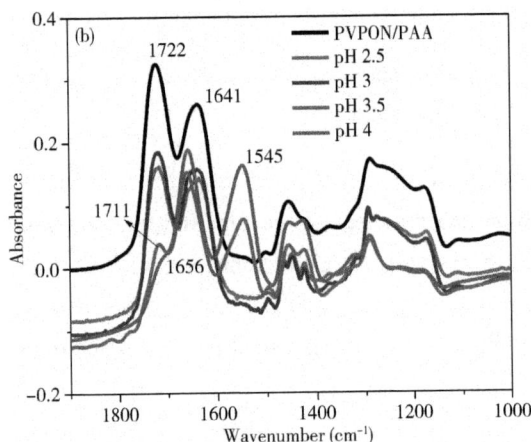

Fig. 2   FT-IR spectra of Lanthanide ion Ce ion after incorporation into hydrogen-bonded PVPON/PAA film at different pH

The degree of ionization could be calculated by eq. (1) with the help of the absorbance strength of COOH and COO$^-$ on IR spectrum.

$$\alpha = \frac{v_{COO^-}}{v_{COOH} + v_{COO^-}} \tag{1}$$

Where α was ionization degree, v_{COO^-} was absorbance peak strength of COO$^-$, and v_{COOH} was absorbance peak strength of COOH. PAA was a kind of weak polyelectrolyte and only partially ionizes. When pH of lanthanide solution rised up, ionization degree of PAA would increase. The fluorescence property of [PVPON/PAA]$_{20}$-Ce film was also investigated. Under UV light (254 nm) irradiation, the film showed a tint of blue color (Fig. 3).

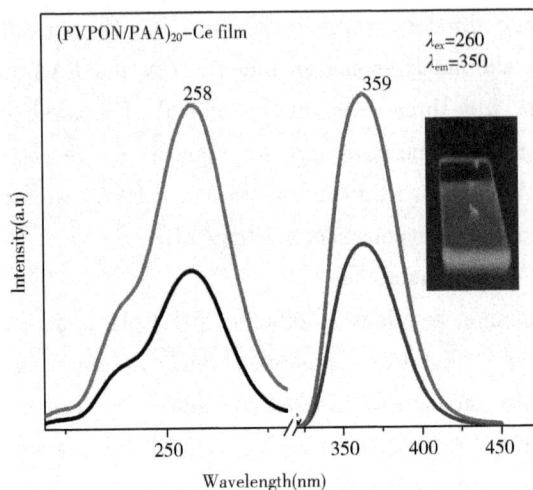

Fig. 3   Fluorescent excitation spectra of lanthanide ion Ce ion

The [PVPON/PAA]$_{20}$-Ce film showed a fluorescent excitation peak at 260nm, which was ascribed to the 4f-5d transition of Ce^{3+} ions. Under excitation at 260nm, the fluorescent emission peak was located at 357nm. Compared with Ce^{3+} ions in the solution, the excitation and the emission peaks showed several nanometers red shift, which was due to the coordination with PAA. Other lanthanide ions, Eu^{3+} and Tb^{3+}, were also incorporated into hydrogen bonded PVPON/PAA films.

4   Conclusions

This study had focus on the co-ordination of Ln ions with hydrogen bonded PVPON/PAA films. When pH of lanthanide solution was increased, then interaction between carbonyl group of PAA and metal atom took place. This interaction was confirmed by UV-Visibe and FT-IR spectrum. At a higher pH region, we explored that the interaction of metal ions within hydrogen-bonded PVPON/PAA film would not facilitate the Ln(OH)$_3$ formation. The fluorescence property of [PVPON/

PAA $]_{20}$-Ce film was also investigated. The results had shown that, fabricated metal-polymer films had very attractive luminescence properties.

References

[1] Yang S, Zhang Y, Zhang X, et al. The influence of pH on a hydrogen-bonded assembly film [J]. Soft Matter, 2007, 3 (4): 463-469.

[2] Bromberg L. Properties of aqueous solutions and gels of poly (ethylene oxide)-b-poly (propylene oxide)-b-poly (ethylene oxide)-g-poly(acrylic acid) [J]. Journal of Physical Chemistry B, 1998, 102(52): 1956-1963.

[3] Petrov A I, Antipov A A, Sukhorukov G B. Base-acid equilibria in polyelectrolyte systems: From weak polyelectrolytes to interpolyelectrolyte complexes and multilayered polyelectrolyte shells [J]. Macromolecules, 2003, 36 (26): 10079-10086.

[4] Philippova O E, Hourdet D, Audebert R, et al. pH-Responsive gels of hydrophobically modified poly (acrylic acid) [J]. Macromolecules, 1997, 30(26): 8278-8285.

[5] Sulatha M S, Natarajan U. Origin of the difference in structural behavior of poly (acrylic acid) and poly (methacrylic acid) in aqueous solution discerned by explicit-solvent explicit-ion MD simulations [J]. Industrial & Engineering Chemistry Research, 2011, 50(21): 11785-11796.

[6] Garcés J L, Koper G J, Borkovec M. Ionization equilibria and conformational transitions in polyprotic molecules and polyelectrolytes [J]. Journal of Physical Chemistry B, 2006, 110(22): 10937-10950.

[7] Binnemans K. Lanthanide-based luminescent hybrid materials[J]. Chemical Reviews, 2009, 109(9):4283-4374.

[8] Lin W, Guan Y, Zhang Y, et al. Salt-induced erosion of hydrogen-bonded layer-by-layer assembled films [J]. Soft Matter, 2009, 5(4): 860-867.

[9] Yang S, Tan S, Zhang Y, et al. Fabry-Pérot fringes of hydrogen-bonded assembly films [J]. Thin Solid Films, 2008, 516(12): 4018-4024.

[10] Choi J, Rubner MF. Influence of the degree of ionization on weak polyelectrolyte multilayer assembly [J]. Macromolecules, 2005, 38(1):116-124.

Influence of Polymerization Conditions on Grafting of Methyl Methacrylate onto Native Chitin for Melting Spinning

Bojun Xi[1], Shiyao Chen[1], Enqi Jin[1]*, Manli Li[1], Jianguo Lu[2], Juan Wang[2]

[1] *College of Textiles and Garments, Shaoxing University, Shaoxing 312000, China*

[2] *Zhende Medical Co., Ltd., Shaoxing, Zhejiang 312035, China*

* *Corresponding author's email:* jdkxxh_2001@163.com

Abstract: Since native chitins exhibit poor thermoplasticity, they cannot meet the requirement of melt spinning and have limited industrial application as thermoplastic fibers. In order to endow the chitins with good thermoplasticity, various amounts of vinyl monomers-methyl methacrylate (MMA) were grafted onto molecular chains of the chitins. In this research, effects of polymerization conditions, such as concentration and molar ratio of initiators, pH, temperature and time on grafting parameters, i. e., conversion of monomer to polymer, grafting percentage and grafting efficiency, were studied. MMA was proved to be successfully grafted onto the molecular chains of the chitin and appropriate graft polymerization conditions were obtained. It was found that the grafted chitins developed exhibited favorable thermoplasticity and were expected to be suitable for melt spinning.

Keywords: Chitin; Melt spinning; Thermoplastic fiber; Graft polymerization; Methyl methacrylate

1   Introduction

Nowadays, most of thermoplastic fibers in textile field are petroleum-based synthetic polymers, such as PET, PE, and PP. They exhibit good mechanical and thermal properties and thus are widely used as chemical fibers for decades. However, their poor biodegradability caused by high molecular weight, low specific surface area, high chemical stability and resistance to microorganism erosion leads to growing concern to the environment. In recent years, increasing interests have been aroused on the investigations on bio-based thermoplastic fibers able to take place of the synthetic ones completely or partly at least[1-3]. Chitin is a kind of linear polysaccharide composed of $\beta-(1,4)$-linked 2-deoxy-2-amino-D-glucopyranose and $\beta-(1,4)$-linked 2-deoxy-2-acetamido-D-glucopyranose repeating units and is an abundant natural polymer ranking only second to cellulose on the earth. It is estimated that 38 thousand tons of chitin-contained fishery byproducts (e. g. shrimp and crab shells) are generated annually only in Hainan, an island of China[4]. For a long time, the fishery byprod-

ucts are usually disposed in landfills or dumped into the sea as wastes. However, more than one fifth of the byproducts are chitin. So traditional disposal methods result in the tremendous waste of chitin resources.

In order to combine the advantages of both natural and synthetic polymers, graft polymerization is often chosen from various chemical modifications due to its high efficiency and easy operation. Redox, oxidation, and radiation are three main ways, in which vinyl monomers can be initiated to graft onto molecular chains of natural polymer and form branches with different chain lengths. Due to the generation of numerous free radicals under mild conditions, redox system is utilized the most widely for the initiation of graft polymerization of chitin with vinyl monomers.

A $K_2S_2O_8$/NaHSO$_3$ redox system was used to initiate the graft polymerization of native chitin with methyl methacrylate (MMA) as reference vinyl monomer in the study. Although PMMA is a synthetic non-biodegradable thermoplastic polymer, starch-*g*-polyacrylate is still easy to be attacked by microorganisms in the nature and retains good biodegradability in the case of low grafting percentage (% Grafting) according to Chen's investigation[5]. In our research, graft polymerization conditions such as molar ratio of $K_2S_2O_8$ to $NaHSO_3$, initiator concentration, pH, polymerization temperature and time were varied to obtain high conversion of monomer to polymer (% monomer conversion), % Grafting, and % Grafting Efficiency. The preparation of modified chitin with high grafting yield will not only reduce the cost of disposing fishery wastes but also help to retain the unique structure of chitin for melt spinning.

2 Experiments

2.1 Materials

Native chitin from crab shells was provided by Yuhuan Sea Biochemical Co., Ltd. (Zhejiang). MMA, potassium persulfate, sodium bisulfite and paradioxybenzene purchased from Sinopharm Chemical Reagent Co., Ltd. (Shanghai) were used as monomer, oxidant, reductant and terminator in the graft polymerization, respectively. All the reagents used were chemically pure.

2.2 Graft polymerization

The graft polymerization of chitosan with AM was carried out in accordance with previous study[5]. Before grafting, 10g of chitosan prepared were dispersed in 1% of acetic acid solution (1/99, V_{HAc}/V_{water}). The concentration of all the acetic acid solutions except the solution used in the measurement of the water dissolution time of chitosan film in this study was 1%. Then the dispersion was transferred into a 250mL four-neck flask. The flask was maintained at 60℃ in a water bath and the dispersion was deoxygenated by passing N_2 for at least 30min. The initiators including the oxidant ($K_2S_2O_8$) and the reductant ($NaHSO_3$) were dissolved in the acetic acid solution, respectively. The oxidant solution, reductant solution, and various amounts of AM monomers in range of 5%–40% (AM/chitosan) were added into the flask simultaneously. The addition was completed in 10–20 min and final bath ratio of chitosan to acetic acid solution was 1 : 10. The concentration of $K_2S_2O_8$ was 0.0370mol/L and the molar ratio of $K_2S_2O_8$: $NaHSO_3$ was 1 : 1.5. The graft polymerization was carried out under vigorous stirring using a mechanical stirrer at 1000r/min under nitrogen atmosphere for 2h. Finally, 2% of paradioxybenzene solution was added to terminate the polymerization. The product was filtered and washed thoroughly with distilled water. The filtrate was saved to determine the amount of residual monomer. At last, the product was dried completely and stored in desiccator.

2.3 Measurement of water-solubility

The chitosan sample was suspended into acetic acid solution to form 6% dispersion. Then the dispersion was heated to 95℃ and maintained at the temperature under stirring to make the sample dissolved completely. After that, the solution was cooled to room temperature without stirring and kept under the condition for 3 days for the observation of the solubility stability. During the days, the appearance time and the amount of the precipitation in the solution were recorded.

3 Results and Discussion

3.1 Effects of initiator concentration on grafting parameters

Effects of initiator concentration on the grafting parameters were shown in Fig. 1. With the increase in the concentration of $K_2S_2O_8$, % monomer conversion increased continuously when the concentration was in range of

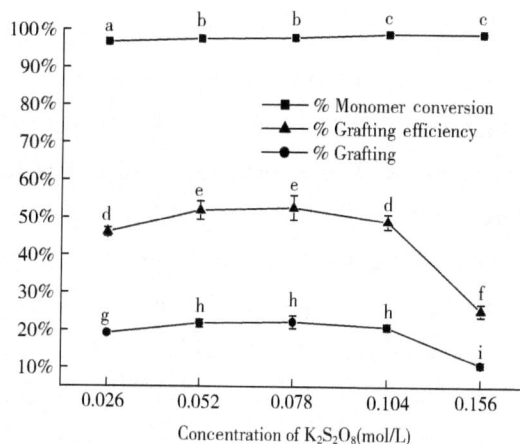

Fig. 1 Effect of initiator concentration on grafting parameters (The grafting was carried out at 60℃ and pH 5.5 for 4h; The molar ratio of $K_2S_2O_8$/$NaHSO_3$ was 1 : 1 and the monomer concentration was 40% to chitin)

0.026–0.104mol/L and then leveled off. In addition, % Grafting initially increased and then decreased after an optimum range of 0.052–0.078mol/L. As to % Grafting Efficiency, it initially increased slightly, then leveled off when the concentration ranged from 0.052mol/L to 0.104mol/L, and then decreased substantially when the concentration reached 0.156mol/L.

3.2 DSC analysis

DSC thermograms of native chitin and chitin–g–PMMA were shown in Fig. 2. No endothermic peaks appeared in the curve of native chitin due to its poor thermoplasticity. The curve of chitin–g–PMMA exhibited a broad endothermic peak around 110℃ attributed to the melting of the grafted chitin. The presence of the melting peak showed that the thermoplasticity of the chitin was improved markedly due to the grafting of MMA.

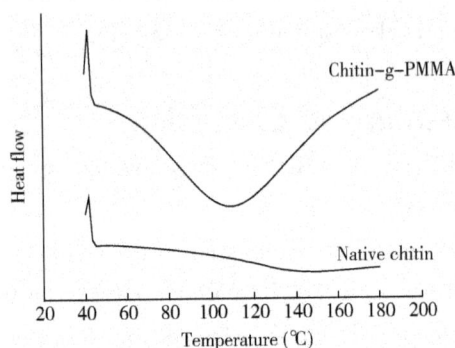

Fig. 2　DSC spectra of native chitin and chitin–g–PMMA (% Grafting of the chitin–g–PMMA was 26.8%)

4　Conclusions

Native chitin could be modified to be thermoplastic by grafting MMA using $K_2S_2O_8$/NaHSO$_3$ redox system. Polymerization variables, such as initiator concentration, molar ratio of oxidant to reductant, pH, temperature and time, had remarkable influence on grafting parameters. High % Monomer Conversion, % Grafting and % Grafting Efficiency were obtained when the grafting was performed in aqueous dispersion under the protection of nitrogen gas at 40℃ in pH range of 5.0–5.5

for 2h by using $K_2S_2O_8$/NaHSO$_3$ redox system. Preferred concentration of $K_2S_2O_8$ was 0.052mol/L and molar ratio of $K_2S_2O_8$: NaHSO$_3$ was 1 : 1. The modified chitin was endowed with favorable thermoplasticity and had a broad melting peak around 110℃. The films developed from the chitin–g–PMMA after heat molding had good tensile properties and water-resistance. Therefore, the chitin–g–PMMA had great potential as an environment-friendly and inexpensive thermoplastic polymer to replace common petroleum-based ones for commercial applications.

Acknowledgements

The work was supported financially by Technological Research Project for Public Welfare of Shaoxing (No. 2017B70047) and Science and Technology Planning Project (collaboration between institutions) of Shaoxing (No. 2017710). Financial sponsors did not endorse the views expressed in this publication.

References

[1] Hu C Y, Reddy N, Yan K L, et al. Acetylation of chicken feathers for thermoplastic applications [J]. J. Agr. Food Chem, 2011, 59(19): 10517–10523.

[2] Reddy N, Jin E Q, Chen L H, et al. Extraction, characterization of components, and potential thermoplastic applications of camelina meal grafted with vinyl monomers [J]. J. Agr. Food Che, 2012, 60(19): 4872–4879.

[3] Jin E Q, Li M L, Zhang L Y. Effect of polymerization conditions on grafting of methyl methacrylate onto feather keratin for thermoplastic applications [J]. J. Polym. Mater, 2014, 31(2): 169–183.

[4] Shi J. Studies on shrimp and crab shell waste of the resource utilization [D]. Master's thesis, Hainan University: Haikou, China, 2011, 1.

[5] Don T M, Chen Y R, Chiu W Y. The synthesis of chitin-g-poly(vinyl acetate) copolymers with a redox initiator [J]. J. Polym, Res. 2002, 9(4): 257–263.

Pilling Image Grade Evaluation of Round Fabric Area with Deep Convolutional Neural Networks

Zhu Zhan[1], Kaixin Lu[1], Jun Wang[1,2] *

[1] *College of Textiles, Donghua University, Shanghai 201620, China*

[2] *Key Laboratory of Textile Science & Technology, Ministry of Education, Shanghai 201620, China*

* Corresponding author's email: junwang@ dhu. edu. cn

Abstract: The pilling of fabrics can seriously affect the performance and value of fabrics, so the evaluation of the grade of pilling has become increasingly important. This study proposed an automatic method for evaluating the pilling image grades based on the deep convolutional neural networks. Firstly, determine the center and radius of the pilling area, remove the fabric texture in this pilling area, and divide the round pilling area into sub-windows to obtain the training sets and the test sets. Secondly, create a convolutional neural network consisting of five convolutional layers and three fully connected layers for pilling grade evaluating. Finally, the subsample size is optimized by predicting the accuracy index. The experimental results show that the accuracy of the evaluation of fabric pilling grade using the deep convolutional neural network can reach 98.5%. This method is feasible and effective.

Keywords: Pilling fabric; Image processing; Deep convolutional neural networks

1　Introduction

Under excessively frequent frictional forces, the fibers begin to slide to escape the control of the yarn or the fiber bundle to be exposed on the surface of fabric and form fluff. If the fluff is not removed in time in the subsequent friction process, the fluff will be intertwined and interlocked with each other. These fluffs on the surface of the fabric form pilling balls, not only destroying the appearance, but also reducing the contact comfort of the fabric, and ultimately leading to a decrease in the value of the fabric. When the factory begins to select apparel fabrics, its production department will strictly control the quality of the products. The anti-pilling performance of fabrics has become one of the necessary assessment indicators for measuring fabric quality. However, the anti-pilling performance of fabrics is mainly reflected by evaluating the pilling grade of the fabrics after pilling test. Therefore, the accuracy of the evaluation results is more and more important. It affects the grade and use of the fabrics.

The art pilling grade evaluation methods are mostly image processing methods based on artificial feature extraction. These methods can be roughly divided into two categories. One uses the differences in hairballs and fabric grayscale information in the spatial domain for rating[1-3], and the other uses frequency information to remove the fabric background in the frequency domain and then rank them[4-6]. Deep learning methods based on self-extracting high-level abstract features are rarely studied. Deep convolutional neural networks are rarely studied. Convolutional neural networks are a special type of feed forward networks which perform very well on visual recognition tasks[7].

This study establishes a method for objectively assessing fabric pilling images using deep learning techniques, including image acquisition, extraction of round pilling area, textures removing, and construction of deep neural networks. The evaluation of pilling grade for different types of fabrics is realized.

2 Experiments

2.1 Materials and hardware

Wool pilling standard template was 11.3 cm × 11.3 cm and 5 total levels. The scanner model used to scan the standard template is MICROTEK. The workstation for deep learning is equipped with an Intel i7-6850k six-core CPU, 64G Hynix DDR4 2400Hz memory, 512G Intel SSDPEKKW51 solid state drive, 2T Seagate hard drive, and four NVIDIA GeForce GTX1080Ti 12G GPUs. The software operating system is Ubuntu 18.04, and the deep neural network is based on Caffe.

2.2 Image acquisition

Since the standard template is saved in the form of a paper picture, digital images can be obtained by a scanner with parallel light sources to reduce the influence of other factors. The selected resolution is 600dpi (600 pixels per inch). The size of the scanned image is 11.5 cm × 11.5 cm with the corresponding pixels 2717 × 2717 as shown in Fig.1.

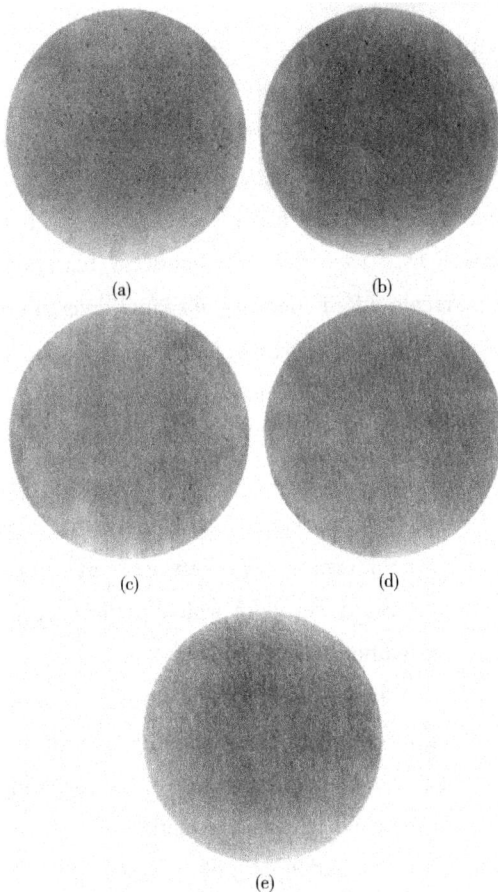

Fig. 1 Standard template acquisition image (a) Grade 1; (b) Grade 2; (c) Grade 3; (d) Grade 4; (e) Grade 5

2.3 Extraction of round pilling area

In the current fabric pilling image processing, there has been no study on the round pilling area of the fabric, but either intercepting part of it or intercepting its largest inscribed square as shown in Fig.2. Such an operation is obviously unreasonable, even if the largest inscribed square will also lose some pilling information, causing errors in the evaluation stage.

As the difference between fabric area and background area is significant, the fabric area can be extracted by image binarization operation. And then a Matlab function (Region props) can be used to find the center of the round pilling area as shown in Fig.3.

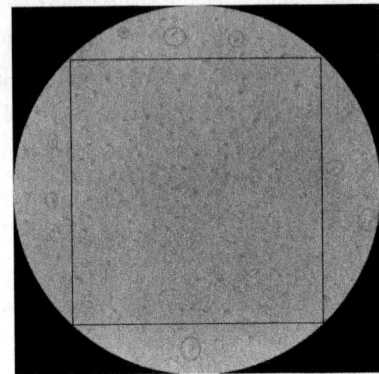

Fig. 2 The largest inscribed square lose pilling information

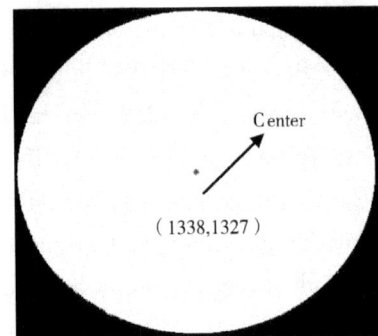

Fig. 3 Mark out the canter of the round pilling area

2.4 Textures removing

The evaluation of the pilling grade mainly based on the presence of hairballs will destroy the uniform grayscale distribution of the image, and the fabric texture will interfere with the later-stage deep learning algorithm, so fabric texture removal is required.

The main process is as follows: A fast fourier transform

is performed on the standard template image to obtain a spectrum map, zeroing the brightness of points greater than 8, and the middle bright point is retained, and then the texture-removed image is obtained through inverse Fourier transform. The processed spectrum diagram is shown in Fig. 4.

2.5 Construction of deep neural network

Five levels of pilling template images are divided into sub-windows of different sizes by overlapping, and training sets and test sets are obtained according to a ratio of 5:1. Fig. 5 shows a schematic diagram of dividing sub-windows. The principle of dividing requires that each sub-window contains a full pilling area without background pixels.

The constructed deep convolutional neural network framework is based on AlexNet[8] which contains five convolution layers and three full connected layers as shown in Fig. 6. The algorithm has two phases: In training phase, classification model is trained using a date set comprised of the images and their corresponding labels. In prediction phase, the trained model is used to predict labels of unseen images.

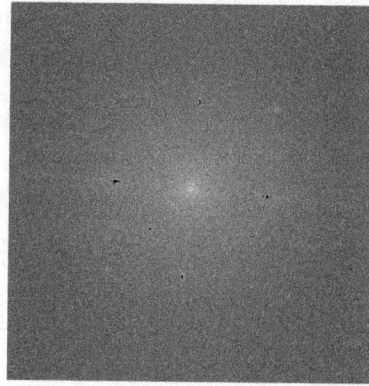

Fig. 4   The processed spectrum diagram

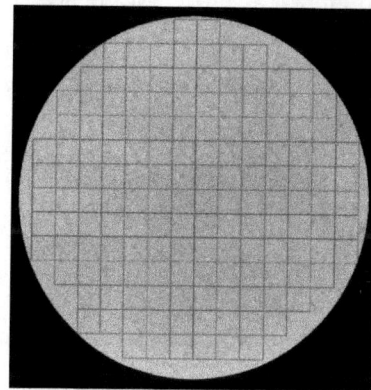

Fig. 5   A schematic diagram of dividing sub-windows

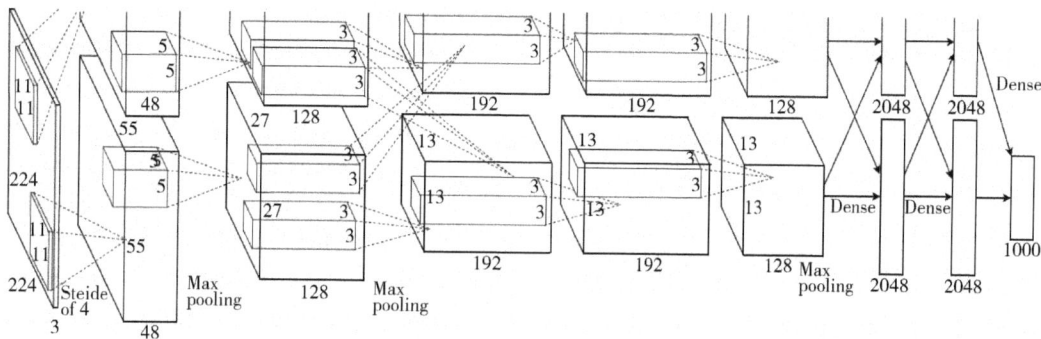

Fig. 6   AlexNet structural model

3   Results and Discussion

3.1   Center coordinates of round pilling area

Tab. 1 shows the center coordinates of round pilling area (grade 1 to grade 5). The image resolution is 600dpi, 2.54cm corresponds to 600 pixels. While the real pilling area radius is 4.5cm, the radius of the pilling area in the image can be calculated to correspond to 1063 pixels.

3.2   Sub-window size optimization

Four different sub-window sizes were set up according to section 2.5 to build the train sets andtest sets. Tab. 2 shows the number of samples for the train sets and test sets. The influence of the sub-window size on pilling grade evaluation accuracy shows in Fig. 7. It can be seen that the sample set with the size of 600 × 600 pixel has the highest accuracy. This is because too large a sample will result in the data set being too small for neural network training. If the sample is too small, over fitting will occur. Fig. 8 shows the training curve with the size of 600×600 pixels' samples.

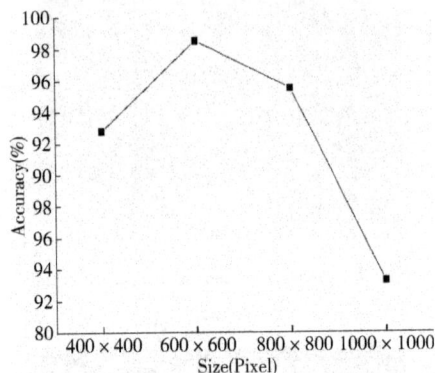

Fig. 7 The influence of the sub-window size on pilling grade evaluation accuracy

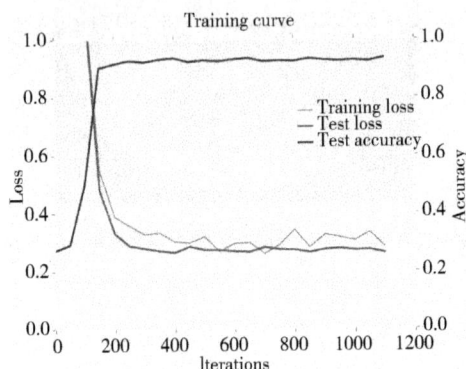

Fig. 8 The training curve with the size of 600×600 pixels samples

Tab. 1 Center coordinates of round pilling area

Coordinates Grade	X(pixel)	Y(pixel)
1	1327	1338
2	1356	1338
3	1315	1343
4	1333	1344
5	1338	1345

Tab. 2 The number of samples for the train sets and test sets

Sub-window size (pixels)	Train sets	Test sets
400×400	23804	3967
600×600	10020	1670

		Continued
Sub-window size (pixels)	Train sets	Test sets
800×800	3982	664
1000×1000	2431	406

4 Conclusions

This study has focused on the deep convolutional neural networks applied to fabric pilling image. A method for determining the center and radius of the pilling area is proposed. The texture of the fabric is effectively removed, and the sub-sample size is optimized. The experimental results show that this method can effectively evaluate the pilling grade, but its generalization performance needs further study.

References

[1] Mendes A D O, Fiadeiro P T, Rui A L M. Virtual subjective pilling evaluation: An alternative [J]. Textile Research Journal, 2011, 81(9): 892-901.

[2] Xu Z B, Yang H S. Fabric pilling object detection based on scale-space extremum [C]. International Conference on Information Science and Control Engineering, IEEE, 2015: 229-233.

[3] Technikova L, Tunak M, Janaek J. New objective system of pilling evaluation for various types of fabrics [J]. Journal of the Textile Institute, 2016, 108(1): 123-131.

[4] Kim S C, Kang T J. Fabric surface roughness evaluation using wavelet-fractal method-Part II: Fabric pilling evaluation [J]. Textile Research Journal, 2005, 75(11): 761-770.

[5] Jing J, Zhang Z, Kang X, et al. Objective evaluation of fabric pilling based on wavelet transform and the localbinarypattern [J]. Textile Research Journal, 2012, 82(18): 1880-1887.

[6] Guan S, Shi H, Qi Y. Objective evaluation of fabric pilling based on bottom-up visual attention model [J]. Journal of the Textile Institute, 2016, 108(4): 597-604.

[7] Lecun Y, Boser B, Denker J S, et al. Back propagation applied to handwritten zip code recognition [J]. Neural Computation, 1989, 1(4): 541-551.

[8] Krizhevsky A, Sutskever I, Hinton G E. Imagenet classification with deep convolutional neural networks [C]. Advances in Neural Information Processing Systems, 2012: 1097-1105.

Preparation of Anti-Bacterial Cotton/willow Non-Woven Composites via Needle Punching Process

Xiaojie Guo[1], Kunlei Luo[2], Juan Wang[3], Bojun Xi[2]*

[1] *College of Materials and Environment Engineering, Hangzhou DianziUniveristy, Hangzhou 310018, China*

[2] *College of Textiles and Garments, Shaoxing University, Shaoxing 312000, China*

[3] *Zhende Medical Co., Ltd., Shaoxing, Zhejiang 312035, China*

* *Corresponding author's email:* xiaojie. guo@ hdu. edu. cn

Abstract: In this research, cotton/willow non-woven composites were successfully prepared using cotton and willow fiber through needle punching process. The effects of cotton/willow fiber ratio and post-treatment using chitosan on the surface density and mechanical properties of cotton/willow non-woven fabrics were thoroughly studied. The results showed that surface density, tensile strength and bursting strength were slightly decreased with willow fiber loading, while the pharmacological value was introduced by the addition of willow fiber. After post-treatment using chitosan, the mechanical properties of modified cotton/willow non-woven composites were obviously improved. Furthermore, the cotton/willow non-woven composites exhibited prominent antibacterial activity against E. coli (Escherichia coli) and S. aureus (Staphylococcus aureus). The novel cotton/willow non-woven composites could be utilized as potential medical dressings materials.

Keywords: Willow fiber; Non-woven composites; Mechanical properties; Chitosan; Anti-bacterial

1　Introduction

Non-renewable petroleum resources have brought many environmental issues such as global warming and resource depletion, which lead to the shift of replacing the petroleum-based synthetic materials with renewable bio-based materials. Ligno cellulose is the most abundant biomass on earth. Recently, there is an increasing interest of using ligno cellulosic materials in textile composites to substitute synthetic fiber. This is mainly ascribed to the inherent properties of low-cost, biodegradability and biorenewability of ligno cellulosic materials[1]. Unlike viscose and cotton which are widely utilized in our daily life, willow fiber has not been used in fabrics due to its short/thin fiber and relatively low tensile strength[2]. However, according to the ancient medical literatures, willow fiber contains the hemostatic properties[3]. Hence, willow fiber is a new type fiber with medical value and is of great potential to be used in medical dressing composites.

Chitosan is a high molecular weight polysaccharide composed mainly of $\beta-(1, 4)$-linked $2-deoxy-2-amino-D-glucopyranose$ units and partially of $\beta-(1,4)$-linked $2-deoxy-2-acetamido-D-glucopyranose$. Chitosan is prepared from chitin, an abundant natural polymer and inferior only to cellulose on the earth[4]. Due to the antibacterial property and biodegradability, chitosan has been widely used in textiles and medical supplies[5].

In the research, anti-bacterial cotton/willow non-woven composites were fabricated through needle punching process. Chitosan was used as a biodegradable anti-bacterial additive during post-treatment. The effects of cotton/willow fiber ratio and post-treatment on the surface density, mechanical properties and anti-bacterial activity of the cotton/willow non-woven fabrics were thoroughly investigated, and the results indicated that the novel cotton-willow non-woven fabrics could be used as promising medical dressing materials.

2 Experiments

2.1 Materials

Willow fiber was collected from willow tree. Willow fiber was washed with water three times to remove dust and impurities, and was dried at 55℃ in a vacuum oven. Cotton fiber was provided by Fulida Textile Co., Ltd. (Zhejiang). The parameters of cotton fiber were 25mm × 1.7dtex. Chitosan (the degree of deacetylation was 95%) was purchased from Shenjiade Biotechnology Co., Ltd. (Shandong). Acetic acid was purchased from Huadong Medicine Co., Ltd. (Zhejiang). All the reagents were utilized without further purification.

2.2 Preparation of cotton/willow non-woven composites

In order to meet the requirement of medical dressings (thickness, weight and mechanical properties), the punching processing parameters were explored prior to the preparation. The determined processing parameters during needle punching were: feed/output speed, 20 m/min; punching frequency, 33 times/min, and number of acupuncture, 2 times. Willow was mixed with cotton with the cotton/willow ratios of 100/0, 95/5, 90/10, 85/15, 80/20 and 75/25 by weight. The punching processes of cotton/willow non-woven fabrics were as follows: opening and mixing process (WL-GK-1 and WL-GK-2), carding process (WL-GS-A), cross lapping process (WL-GP-C) and needle-punching process (WL-ZGS-Z-Y, WL-ZGS-Z-D and WL-ZGS-Z-Z).

2.3 Post-treatment of non-woven composites using chitosan

1.67g chitosan was added into 1% acetic acid solution, the dispersion was heated up to 65℃ and stayed for 1.5h under stirring to make the chitosan dissolved completely. Then, the mixture solution was diluted into 0.167% chitosan solution using 1% acetic acid solution. After that, 30g non-woven fabrics were immersed in 0.167% chitosan solution. The mixture was heated up to 60℃ and maintained for 30min to make the chitosan covered evenly on the fabrics. After first compression, the fabrics were immersed in 60℃ water bath for 30min. after second compression, the fabrics were dried in an oven at 80℃ for 5min and 105℃ for 3min.

2.4 Characterization

2.4.1 Surface density

10cm^2 samples of cotton/willow non-woven fabrics were sampled using Z(B)01B disk sampler and measured according to FZ/T 60003—1991 standard.

2.4.2 Tensile strength

According to FZ/T 60005—1991 standard, fabric strength tester (YG026H-250) was used to measure the tensile strength of cotton/willow non-woven fabrics. The sample dimension was 200mm × 50mm.

2.4.3 Bursting strength

According to GB/T 19976 standard, bursting strength of cotton/willow non-woven fabrics was measured using fabric strength tester (YG026H-250) through steel ball method. Sample was placed in the circular base, the steel ball drop vertically at the speed of 30mm/min to make the sample rupture.

2.4.4 Anti-bacterial activity

Staphylococcus aureus and Escherichia coli were selected as gram positive and negative bacterial, respectively. According to GB/T 20944.3—2008 standard, agar was prepared in petri dish to activate the bacterial in 37℃. A colony taken from activated bacterial was inoculated in nutrient broth at 37℃. The colony was incubated in a gas bath thermostat oscillator (130r/min) for 24h to obtain bacterial suspension. The cotton/willow non-woven fabrics before and after post-treatment were placed in the bacterial suspension to observe.

3 Results and Discussion

3.1 Effects of fiber ratios and post-treatment on mechanical properties of cotton/willow non-woven composites

The effects of cotton/willow fiber ratio and post-treatment on the surface density and mechanical properties were illustrated in Fig. 1. As shown in Fig. 1(a), the surface density decreased monotonously with willow fiber content regardless of the post-treatment. This phenomenon was mainly ascribed to the light-weight and hollow structure of willow fiber. Since the willow fiber was easily broken during carding process and formed into scattered fibers, which led to the decline in the total amount

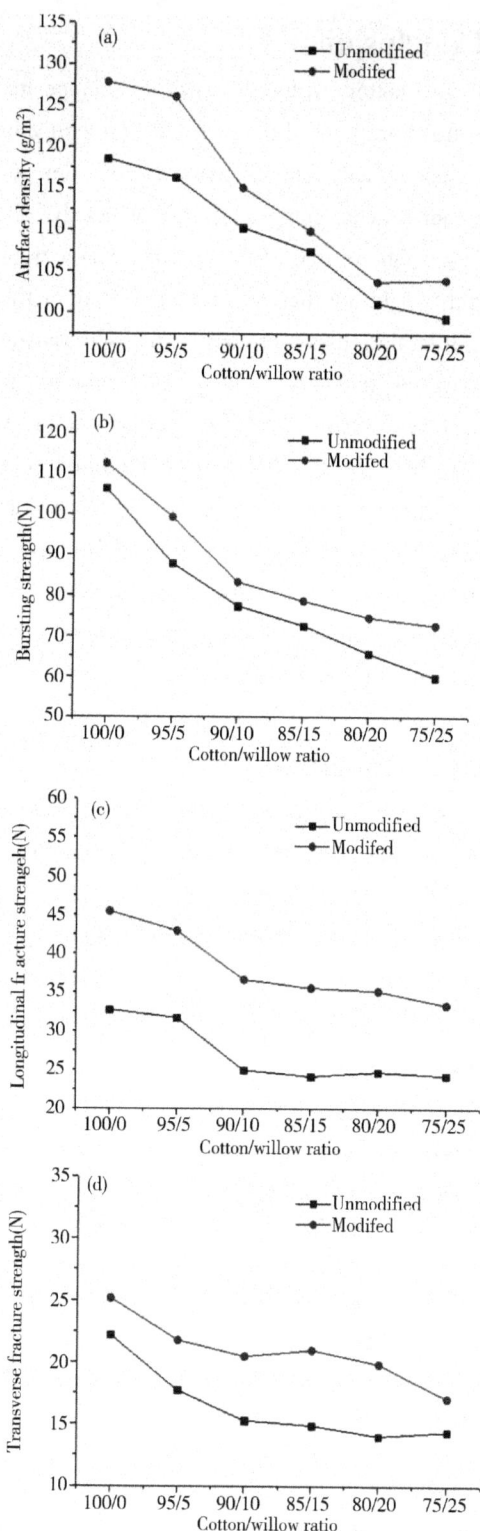

Fig. 1 Curves of (a) surface density, (b) bursting strength, (c) longitudinal fracture strength and (d) transverse fracture strength of cotton/willow non-woven fabrics before and after modification using chitosan versus cotton/willow ratio

of fiber during lapping process and lower surface density. In addition, the surface density of cotton/willow non-woven composites was improved after modification using chitosan, which was attributed to the coated chitosan on the composites. As the willow content increased from 20% to 25%, the surface density of modified composites leveled off. Fig. 1 (b), (c) and (d) indicated that the mechanical properties of cotton/willow non-woven composites gradually decreased with willow fiber content due to the low tensile strength and of willow fiber and poor cohesive force between cotton and willow. Therefore, the mechanical properties decreased with the surface density decreasing. Furthermore, the mechanical properties of cotton/willow non-woven composites were significantly improved after modification using chitosan, which resulted from the compression processes during post-treatment.

3.2 Anti-bacterial activity of cotton/willow non-woven composites

Inhibition zone test was utilized to evaluate the anti-bacterial activity of the cotton/willow non-woven fabrics before and after modification with chitosan. As shown in Fig. 2 and Fig. 3, the unmodified cotton/willow non-woven fabrics showed no boundary around the fabric sample, while the chitosan-modified cotton/willow non-woven fabrics showed the inhibition zone round the fabric sample. This phenomenon exhibited that the chitosan-modified cotton/willow non-woven fabrics composites showed prominent anti-bacterial activity against E. coli and S. aureus. It was probably due to the released cation groups from chitosan. These released cation groups could interact with ions in the cellwall and led to the apoptosis of bacterials. In addition, the coated chitosan prevented the growth and immigration of bacterials via wrapping the whole bacterial cell to isolate the nutrients and water. Hence, the chitosan-modified cotton/willow non-woven composites with satisfactory anti-bacterial activity had great potential to be utilized as medical dressing materials.

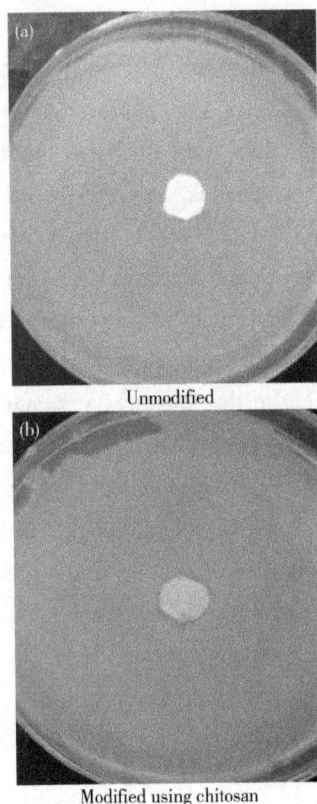

Fig. 2 Inhibition zone against E coli of cotton/willow non-woven composites before and after post-treatment

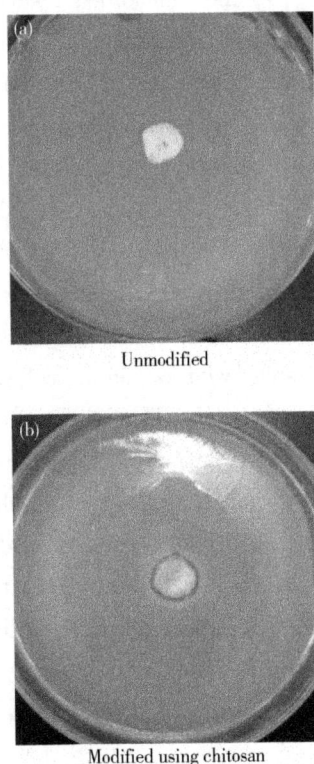

Fig. 3 Inhibition zone against S aureus of cotton/willow non-woven composites before and after post-treatment

4 Conclusions

The novel cotton/willow non-woven composites were successfully prepared through needle-punching process. The surface density and mechanical properties of cotton/willow non-woven composites monotonously decreased with increasing willow fiber content, which was due to the light-weight and hollow structure of willow fiber. After modification using chitosan, the chitosan-modified cotton/willow non-woven composites showed improved the surface density, tensile strength and bursting strength. In addition, the chitosan-modified cotton/willow non-woven composites exhibited significant anti-bacterial activity. With the prominent anti-bacterial properties and pharmaceutical value of willow fiber, the novel cotton/willow non-woven composites could be utilized as medical dressing materials.

Acknowledgements

The work was supported financially by Science and Technology Planning Project (collaboration with Zhende Medical Co., Ltd.) of Shaoxing (No. 2017710). Financial sponsors do not endorse the views expressed in this publication.

References

[1] Don T M, King C F, Chiu W Y. Synthesis and properties of chitosan-modified poly (vinyl acetate) [J]. J. Appl. Polym. Sci, 2002, 86(12): 3057-3063.

[2] Zafar M T, Zarrinbakhsh N, Mohanty A K. Biocomposites based on poly (lactic acid)/willow-fiber and their injection moulded microcellular foams [J]. Express Polymer Letters, 2016, 10(2): 176-186.

[3] 邬浩杰. 止血中药作用机理研究概况[J]. 新中医, 2009, 41(4): 116-117.

[4] Fernandes M M, Francesko A, Torrent-Burgués J. Effect of thiol-functionalisation on chitosan antibacterial activity: Interaction with a bacterial membrane model [J]. Reactive & Functional Polymer, 2013, 73(10): 1384-1390.

[5] Rabea E I, Badawy E T, Stevens C V. Chitosan as antimicrobial agent: Applications and mode of action [J]. Biomacromolecules. 2003, 4(6): 1457.

The Present Situation of Cashmere Market and Consumer Behavior in Shanghai

Xinyi Chen[1a,1b], Min Li[1c,2] *

[1a] *College of Fashion and Design, Donghua University, Shanghai 20051, China*

[1b] *Key Laboratory of Clothing Design and Technology, Ministry of Education, Shanghai 200051, China*

[1c] *Shanghai Style Fashion Design & Value Creation Collaborative Innovation Center, Donghua University, Shanghai 200051, China*

[2] *Tongji University Shanghai Institute of Design and Innovation, Shanghai 200092, China*

* *Corresponding author's email*: fidlimin@ dhu. edu. cn

Abstract: As one of the high-grade products in knit wears, cashmere sweaters are very popular. China, as a big cashmere production, processing and trading powers, has the absolute advantage geographically. Although there are numerous local brands, the number of those truly competitive is very less. Thus, if the brand wants to own a place in the changing market, one must have an insight into the change of consumer demand and refresh the information of consumer behavior. The paper is based on this purpose, hoping to provide the reference basis for brand's marketing and product development. Though literature consulting, consumer behavior theory and the achievements of related cashmere consumption literature research from home and abroad are set as the theoretical basis. Then by means of marketing research and in-depth interviews, the consumer questionnaire is designed and statistically analyzed to release the cashmere consumption situation and product preference in Shanghai, combining the population statistics to find the key factors that influences consumer behavior.

Keyword: Shanghai market; Cashmere; Consumer behavior; Present situation of market; Product preference

1 Introduction

China, as a big cashmere production, processing and trading powers, has about 70% of the world's production and 90% of raw materials, and also most of the cashmere products in the international market come from China. The globalization and innovation of science and technology have already changed the demand of market and people's consumption preference[1].

For consumers, this study can provide a more comprehensive and systematic analysis of the brand cashmere-sweaters in Shanghai's top business circles, meeting their shopping needs. For enterprises, this paper studies the determinants of buying behavior and summarizes the consumer's opinions on the existing cashmere sweater and different demands of different consumers, putting forward the improvement measures and the possible future development trend.

2 Literature Review

The history of cashmere industry development, the change of trade pattern, consumption preference and characteristics are studied though second-hand materials. In order to overcome the homogeneity of products, the cashmere industry has changed its pattern from the simple quantitative growth in 2003 to both inheriting and innovating[2]. The business model has changed from the disorder rules into careful management, and even begin to expand scales into shopping malls, outlets and online services. The global value chain is also gradually improving[3].

Consumers of cashmere products appears younger[4]. Changes in consumption characteristics are concentrated in vague seasonality[5], and the product definition has gone through a period of high price of rarity, low price epidemic, and high quality rarity[6]. Overall innovation can attract more consumers than a simple price tug.

3 Research on the Market Status of Brand Cashmere Sweaters

3.1 The design of research tables

Based on the 4Ps basic marketing strategy, considering the product, price, distribution, promotion four points of view, the research includes the basic situation of the shop, assistants, customer, overall product, shop promotion, the condition of fitting room, and the details of both classic and specially styles.

3.2 Research object and research scope

The research object refers to those that specialized in products and sales of cashmere sweater brand, such as Deer King, Pipidog and so on. Considering the particularity of its category as well as the investigation time, research chose 7 big business Circles, including North Sichuan Road, East Nanjing Road, West Nanjing Road, Middle Huaihai Road, Wujiao Square, Lu Jia Zui and Zhongshan Park, according to Shanghai Commercial Network Planning (2013—2020).

3.3 Analysis on brand cashmere sweaters

By means of field visits, on-site interviews and second-hand data collection, the research collected the information of 45 cashmere sweater brands and 113 stores in 28 shopping malls.

The physical stores are mainly concentrated in the location that has more people and more department stores. Most decoration styles are simple, which may bring visual fatigue to consumers. Different shops differ from display and area, but the same brand has the same decoration style, paying more attention to their brand establishment. Consumers' characteristics concentrate in the middle-aged, friends, couples and family form.

Brand cashmere shops always like to display more styles and colors in limited area by hanging, only the hot-selling products and new arrivals can be showed on plastic models in special area. Cashmere sweater shops in Mid-range shopping center always choose to display more goods, but in fact it's not conducive for consumers to choose and purchase.

Same brands may have different categories of products and discount methods in different locations to attract different consumers, such as new product discounts, the overall price discount or participating in the shopping malls' seasonal activities. Middle-grade stores always have serious product homogeneity, so the focus of shop promotion is still on brands and prices.

3.4 New trend of cashmere market

Some clothing brands which are not exclusive cashmere agencies such as Uniqloexp and their basic consumer groups by releasing more styled and cheaper cashmere sweaters. Individualized clothing shops either have brands or personally offers more personalized choices, and they're welcomed by local residents nearby. The increase of personalized customization is market-oriented, meeting the needs of a multi-level of crowds[7]. Online sales increased, but regardless of the amount of consumption, quantity or consumer preferences, the consumption status of cashmere products in China is in a disadvantageous position compared with other competing products, such as cotton[8].

4 Model Construction and Questionnaire

4.1 Model construction

Combined the Howard-Sheth model with the 5W1H analysis method for consumer purchase behavior, the research confirmed the part of the consumer behavior analysis model of cashmere sweater buyers in Shanghai, which consists of five parts, such as basic situation, stimulating factor, external factor, internal factor and reflection factor. Tab. 1 shows the detailed indicators.

Tab. 1 Detailed index for model

First class index	Second class index	Third class index
Basic situation	Population statistics(who)	Age, gender, marriage, culture, career, average monthly disposable income and outcome, expense condition

First class index	Second class index	Third class index
Stimulating factor	Physical stimuli(what)	Brand, quality, materials, color, style, decoration, price, comfort level, after – treatment technology shopping guide, reputation promotion, advertisement
Exetmal factor	Time(when) , place(where)	Shopping environment
Intemal factor	Mind of consumpition need(why)	Buying motive, consuming preference, shopping psychology
Reflection factor	Use of experience	Shopping experience, after – sales service, satisfaction degree

4. 2　Questionnaire

The respondents were divided into two categories, which were and were not purchased or wore cashmere-sweaters, and the former was divided into three parts: respondents' basic information, purchase behavior of those who had bought or worn cashmere sweaters, preference and influence factors of all. The formal research time was set between March 20th, 2017 to March 26th, 2017. The questionnaires were distributed on line, and paper forms were provided for consumers over 50 years old for convenient. In the end, 327 effective questionnaires were collected. Excel and SPSS 22. 0 were used to describe statistical analysis of the collected data.

At the beginning of the questionnaire, loyal consumers of cashmere sweaters and the professors in the product industries were interviewed in depth, hoping to set the basic form of the questionnaire. The preliminary ones were distributed to different age groups for tests and supplement. The formal-designed questionnaires found that the most profound experience of the consumers to cashmere sweater was its warm and soft dressing experience, and the summer cashmere market had a great development space.

The Cronbaca of questionnaire was 0. 975, showing the good reliability, and the KMO was 0. 969, the Bartlett was 0. 000, which indicated the structure validity. Using exploratory factor analysis to further verify the validity, the model was proved to be reasonable.

5　Analysis on the Data of Cashmere Sweater Consumption Behavior

5. 1　Sample analysis

Most of the respondents prefer to buy 3 – 6 cashmere sweaters with a frequency of 1−3 purchases a year. For products with high prices, most consumers prefer to buy in physical stores or online official stores, and do not believe in unofficial channels or products below average prices. Most consumers are sure that cashmere sweaters are warm, comfortable, and always experience, but they are not very satisfied with their styles and after-sales service.

Active purposes of purchasing are the majority of all the consuming behaviors, and those who purchased passively such as attracted by the display or activities of shopping malls count for a small proportion. Those who purchase through media or recommendation are less.

The most popular brands are those that have already been famous such as ERDOS and Heng Yuan Xiang and then followed by the fast-growing brands such as Spring Bamboo and Deer King. Consumers have the preference for a clean and color such as black and gray, instead of pink or purple. Most of them like simple and generous styles, and some of them prefer noble, elegant and personalized styles. The decoration methods for cashmere sweaters are numerous. Younger consumers prefer embroidery and color bar, and the older ones have more acceptable choices.

5. 2　Group classification and marketing suggestion

According to the result of factor analysis Tab. 2, the important factors of cashmere sweater are divided into two categories.

Tab. 2　Rotation factor analysis

Influencing factor	Factor one	Factor two
Brand	0. 360	0. 318
Quality	0. 911	0. 200
Material	0. 900	0. 203
Style	0. 521	0. 600

According to the results of investigation and analysis, the consumers are classified into three types (Tab. 3): "Functional Type" "Appearance Type" and "Middle Type".

Tab. 3 Consumer classification

Types	Features	Population characteristics
Functional Type	①Pay attention to brand, quality, material, comfort ②Emphasis on wearing experience ③Have no particular requirements to low price and styles ④Prefer reputable brand with good reputation	①More average expenditure monthly(clothing category) ②White - collar workers, married women, retired consumers
Appearance Type	①Pay attention to styles, color, decoration, price, cleaning and nursing ②Have no particular requirements to brand ③Prefer to dress and buy clothes by trends	Females
Middle Type	①Stay between the "Functional" and "Appearance" types ②Prefer the classic style ③Concemed more about the durability and the ease of nursing	Males

The room for development for cashmere sweater market is large, and some marketing suggestions are given bellow. For example, for brand development, attention must paid both on high-end and low-end prices. On the one hand, for "Middle Type" consumers, the brand should provide for a more cost efficient solution, increasing the popularity of cashmere sweater. On the other hand, for "Functional Type" consumers, imitating foreign luxury brands, to develop the brand to high-quality casual luxury and establish its own status and aesthetic symbol.

6 Conclusions

The main conclusion of marketing research: With the convergence of product quality, the emphases of advertisements still come to brand and price. Physical stores sometimes choose to display more goods, and it turns to be inconvenient for consumers to choose and purchase. The decoration style is simple and similar, easily causing visual fatigue, but the service attitude and the promotion method act as stimulus to consumers which will buy the products in the physical stores.

The main conclusion of the sample analysis:

(1) Consumers have a positive attitude towards the shopping experience of cashmere sweater.

(2) Consumers' demands and purposes are simple, and active purposes of purchasing are the majority of all the consuming behaviors.

(3) Consumption preferences count less than the previous research. The factors affecting the consumers' purchasing behavior are gender, occupation, education, marriage, monthly disposable income, monthly average expenditure (clothing category).

According to the research results, the group is classified into three categories: "Appearance Type" "Function Type" and "Middle Type".

References

[1] Ou Y. Study on international management of cashmere enterprises in Mongolia [D]. Capital University of Economic and trade, 2014.

[2] Chu X, Zhang L P, Ye D M, et al. Study on sustainable development of cashmere industry in China [J]. Journal of Gansu Agricultural University, 2003, 01: 62-67.

[3] Shen L, Li J. Comparative study on design characteristics of Chinese and Western cashmere sweate r[J]. Journal of Textile Industry, 2010, 09: 100-103 + 108.

[4] Zhang Z X, Mao L L, Liu J. Investigation and analysis on consumption behavior of women's sweater in Xi'an city [J]. Journal of Textile Industry, 2008, 02: 29-33.

[5] Xu H Q, Yang L H. Study on the innovation of Enterprise's marketing strategy basing on the changes of the consumption characteristics of cashmere products [J]. Economic Forum, 2008, 20: 94-95.

[6] Xi N. Let cashmere follow the pace of fashion [J]. Textile Research, 2015, 12: 80-81.

[7] Fang W. Shanghai cashmere sweater set to do business fire [N]. Journal of Textile Industry, 2002-12-13.

[8] Chen T, Xiao H F. Analysis on the consumption competition of Chinese cashmere products and other textile raw materials [J]. Agriculture Outlook, 2014, 08: 69-75.

Structure and Mechanical Properties
of Polyamide 56 (PA56) Fibers

Yassir A. Eltahir[1,2]*, **Haroon A. M. Saeed**[1,2], **Yumin Xia**[2], **Yong He**[2], **Yimin Wang**[2]

[1] *Faculty of Industries Engineering and Technology, University of Gezira, Wad-Medani, P. O. Box 20, Sudan*

[2] *State Key Laboratory for Modification of Chemical Fibers and Polymer Materials, College of Materials Science and Engineering, Donghua University, Shanghai 201620, China*

* *Corresponding author's email*: yassir_eltahir@ yahoo. com

Abstract: Polyamide 56 (PA56) and polyamide 6 (PA6) fibers were prepared by melt spinning process and drawn by a thermal drawing at different draw ratios (DRs). PA56 and PA6 fibers were characterized by means of differential scanning calorimeter (DSC), wide-angle X-ray diffraction (WAXD), sonic velocity, and tensile testing measurements. DSC results revealed that the melting temperature had no considerable variation, while the heat of fusion increased with increments in the draw ratio. This could be due to the existence of crystals with lower perfection and sizes. The equatorial WAXD revealed that PA56 as-spun fibers exhibit α-like crystal structure, while PA6 as-spun fibers observed γ-form structure. The WAXD results showed that the crystallinity and crystal size of PA56 and PA6 fibers were directly proportional to the draw ratio. This could be attributed to the molecular chain and adjacent crystals and small crystallite in the amorphous region transforming from a random state and becoming densely packed. The orientation factor was increased as expected upon drawing. However, the tenacity and Young's modulus were found to be significantly increased, while the elongation at break decreased as the draw ratio increased. The improved mechanical properties were attributed to the improvement of molecular orientation along the fiber axis, the development of more ordered crystalline structure, and the crystallinity. Compared with PA6, PA56 fibers showed a little lower mechanical property at different draw ratios. Polyamide 56 spun fibers presumably a competitive fiber and the above results could help to optimize their manufacturing. Further research was under way to compare different chemical and physical properties of polyamide 56 with other polyamide fibers.

Keywords: Polyamide 56; Melt spinning; Fibers; Tenacity; Modulus

1 Introduction

Polyamides (PAs), commonly referred as nylons, are semi-crystalline polymers that can be used as fibers and engineering plastics because of their outstanding strength and toughness along with excellent resistance to abrasion[1]. Since the invention of nylon 66 by Carothers in 1934[2], many kinds of nylons have been developed, and most of them have been commercialized in the past 80 years. Polyamide fibers are generally produced by melt spinning, which is the most common process for producing synthetic fibers. The effect of melt spinning and drawing variables on the crystalline orientation and mechanical properties of synthetic fibers were devised by Carothers and Coworkers in 1932[3]. Since this work, many studies were carried out to investigate the effect of drawing of polyamide fibers on the structure and mechanical properties. The aim of this work is to prepare PA56 fibers and study on the structure and properties of novel PA56 fibers.

2 Experiments

2.1 Materials

Polyamide 56 (PA56) pellets with an intrinsic viscosity 0. 68dL/g were kindly supplied from Guangdong Xinhui Media Nylon Co. , Ltd. , China. Polyamide 6 (PA6) pellets were kindly supplied from Guangdong Xinhui

Media Nylon Co. , Ltd. , China. Model: Bright R. V. 2.4-2.8.

2.2 Apparatus and procedures

Melt spinning was carried out in a lab melt-spinning machine (Polymer ABE Engineering MATE-V, Co. , Tokyo, Japan) at a spinning temperature of 285℃ and a take-up speed of 1000m/min for PA56 and PA6.

The melting point temperatures and heat of fusion of all the fibers were determined by Perkin-Elmer DSC-Q20 (TA Instruments, USA) differential scanning calorimeter.

X-ray diffraction (WAXD) measurements were performed in a Bruker AXC (D2 Phaser, Lynx EyeTM, Germany). Samples were scanned using an incident X-ray with a Ni-filtered CuKα radiation with a wavelength of (0.1542nm) in 2θ ranges from 10° to 60° at a step interval of 0.02°.

The orientation factors (f_0) of the fibers were measured using a model SCY-III sonic velocity apparatus, manufactured by Donghua Kaili Chemicals and Fiber Technology Corporation, Shanghai, China.

Mechanical properties were measured at 25℃ and 65% RH using ASTM D 3822 with a XL-2 Yarn Elongation Tester, from Shanghai New Fine Instrument Co. , Ltd. with a crosshead speed of 400mm/min and a gauge length of 250mm. The results were reported as the average of 20 measurements.

3 Results and Discussion

DSC thermograms of PA56 and PA6 fibers displayed a single endothermic melting peak as shown in Fig.1 and Fig.2, respectively. The melting temperature showed no considerable variation for both PA56 and PA6 fibers with increasing draw ratio. However, the heat of fusion increased with increments with the draw ratio. These results suggest that the crystallinity increased with the increase in draw ratio, without any improvement in crystal size and crystal perfection.

Fig. 3 and Fig. 4 show the wide-angle equatorial (WAXD) scanning patterns for PA56 and PA6 fibers drawn at different draw ratios at same drawing temperature, respectively. It can be seen that all the patterns of PA56 fibers show the same diffraction peaks which

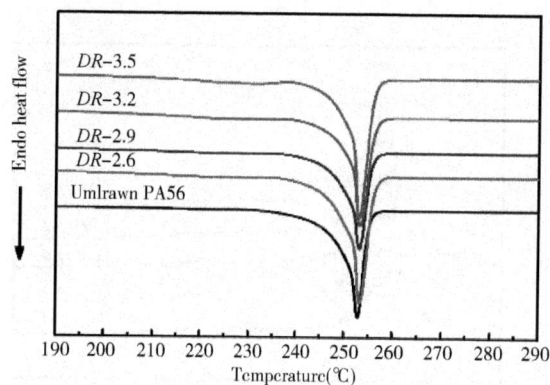

Fig. 1　Thermograms of polyamide 56 fibers at different draw ratios

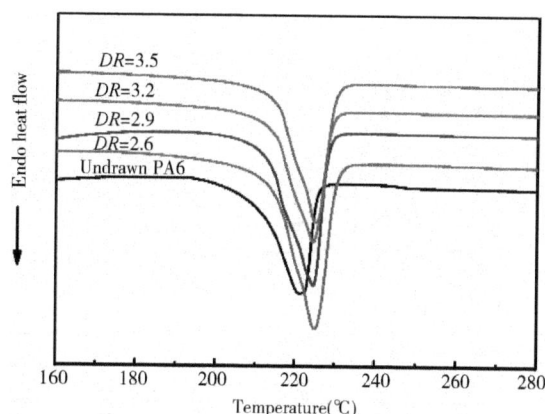

Fig. 2　Thermograms of polyamide 6 fibers at different draw ratios

meant that they have the same crystal structure in spite of the drawing conditions. The main characteristic diffraction peaks located approximately at $2\theta = 20.6°$ and 22.7° were assigned to the 020 and 110 planes, respectively[4]. On the other hand, the PA6 fibers after drawn show two strong peaks approximately at 20.3° and 22.8° characteristic of the thermodynamically favorable α-form with crystalline peaks of 200 and mixed 002/202 planes, respectively. It was found that the relative crystallinity of drawn PA56 and PA6 fibers were increased continuously with the draw ratio. These results suggest that the high ratio drawing increased the degree of fiber orientation and led to a more orderly arrangement of macromolecular chains. Moreover, the molecular chain transforms from a random state to extended form and densely packed, which results in an increase in crystallinity.

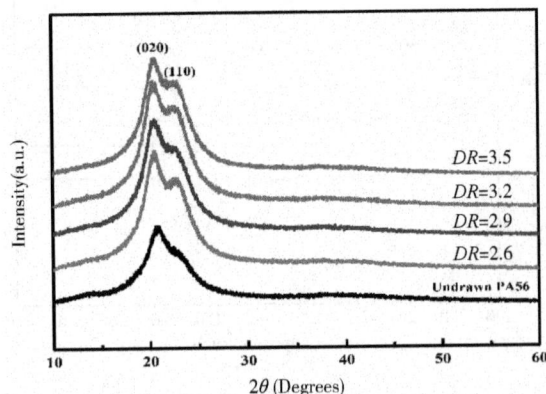

Fig. 3   WAXD patterns for PA56 fibers drawn at different draw ratios

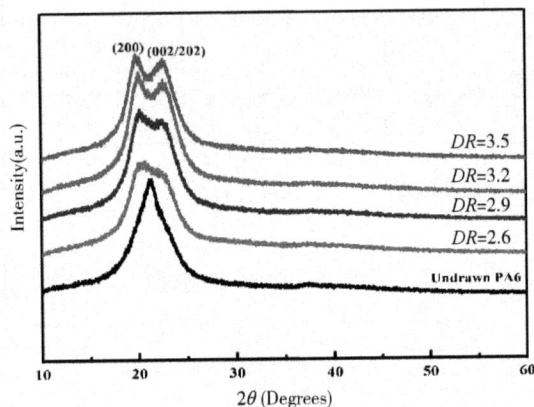

Fig. 4   WAXD patterns for PA6 fibers drawn at different draw ratios

The orientation factor (f_0) values of PA56 and PA6 fibers at different draw ratio measured by sound velocity apparatus are summarized in Tab. 1. The results show that the orientation factor (f_0) of PA56 and PA6 fibers increase continuously with the draw ratio. This is because the drawing process will align the molecular chain along the drawing direction.

Tab. 1   Sound orientation factor (f_0) of PA56 and PA6 fibers at various draw ratios

Draw ratio (DR)	Orientation factor (f_0)	
	PA56	PA6
2.6	0.75	0.68
2.9	0.77	0.70
3.2	0.80	0.72

Continued

Draw ratio (DR)	Orientation factor (f_0)	
	PA56	PA6
3.5	0.83	0.75

Tab. 2 shows the mechanical properties of PA56 and PA6 fibers obtained at a different draw ratio. As shown in Tab. 2, the tenacity and tensile modulus of the PA56 and PA6 drawn fibers increased continuously with the drawing process, while the elongation at break decrease at the same drawing temperature. The improvement of molecular orientation along the drawing direction, the development of more ordered crystalline structure and the increase in crystallinity, have a good influence on the mechanical properties of PA56 fibers when subjected to the drawing process. It is worthy of noting that the PA6 fibers show high tenacity and tensile modulus than PA56 fibers at different draw ratios. This can be attributed to the regularity of molecules conformation and crystallinity of PA6.

4   Conclusions

Polyamide 56 (PA56) and polyamide 6 (PA6) have been successfully spun as fibers through the melt-spinning process. DSC results reveal that the melting temperature has no considerable variation, while the heat of fusion increase with increments in the draw ratio. The equatorial WAXD reveal that PA56 as-spun fibers exhibit α-like crystal structure, while PA6 as-spun fibers observe γ-form structure. The WAXD results show that the crystallinity of PA56 and PA6 fibers are directly proportional to the draw ratio. The orientation factor is increased as expected upon drawing. However, the tenacity and Young's modulus are found to be significantly increased, while the elongation at break decrease as the draw ratio increased. Compared with PA6, PA56 fibers show a little lower mechanical properties at different draw ratios. Polyamide 56 spun fibers presumably a competitive fiber and the above results can help to optimize their manufacturing.

Tab. 2　The effect of draw ratio on the mechanical properties of PA56 and PA6 fibers

Draw ratio	Tenacity (cN/dtex)		Elongation at break (%)		Modulus (cN/dtex)	
	PA56	PA6	PA56	PA6	PA56	PA6
2.6	2.09 (0.14)	2.54 (0.20)	44.24 (3.2)	25.90 (3.7)	13.8 (0.7)	18.9 (0.9)
2.9	2.16 (0.11)	3.10 (0.17)	28.00 (3.5)	21.31 (2.4)	19.6 (1.1)	24.9 (0.7)
3.2	2.42 (0.12)	3.66 (0.15)	14.60 (2.6)	14.0 (2.4)	22.5 (0.9)	33.3 (1.0)
3.5	2.72 (0.14)	4.26 (0.20)	12.21 (1.6)	8.85 (1.1)	28.4 (1.5)	48.6 (1.3)

Note: The numbers in parentheses are standard deviation.

References

[1] Kohan M I. Nylon plastics handbook [M]. Hanser Publishers, Hanser/Gardner Publications, 1995.

[2] Carothers W H. U. S. Patent (1938); 2,130,948.

[3] Carothers W, Hill J W. Studies of polymerization and ring formation. XV. Artificial fibers from synthetic linear condensation superpolymers [J]. J. Am. Chem. Soc. , 1932, 54: 1579-1587.

[4] Puiggalí, J, Franco L, Alemán C, et al. Crystal structures of nylon 5, 6. a model with two hydrogen bond directions for nylons derivedfrom odd diamines [J]. Macromolecules, 1998, 31: 8540-8548.

Study on Properties of Nano-TiO$_2$ Glass Fiber Cloth

Guoqing Zhang[1] , Yanping Yu[1] , Xiatian Yu[1] ,Rong Huang[1] *

[1] *Department of Textile Materials , School of Textiles , Donghua University , Shanghai 201620 , China*

* *Corresponding author's email*: 1115479494@ qq. com

Abstract: In this project, the method of ultrasonic treatment was adopted. Glass fiber cloth was selected as the substrate, and nano-TiO$_2$ particles were loaded on the surface of the glass fiber cloth to form a layer of Nano coating. Through the research on the concentration of nano-TiO$_2$ solution, ultrasonic treatment time, ultrasonic power, drying temperature and other technological conditions, the influence of various technological conditions on the performance of glass fiber cloth was discussed. In view of the unfavorable factors that may be encountered during the actual use of glass fiber filter cloth, this subject tests the water repellent performance of glass fiber cloth loaded with nano-TiO$_2$ particles. The experimental results show that the air permeability of glass fabrics prepared by different process conditions does not change significantly, but the water repellent properties have been improved to some extent.

Keyword: Glass fiber cloth; Nano-TiO$_2$; Ultrasonic finishing

1 Introduction

The filter cloth is the key part of the bag filter, which has great influence on the dust removal effect of the high temperature smoke. However, due to the continuous impact of the high temperature dust gas during the use of the filter cloth, as well as the changeable external environment, it needs to have excellent properties such as water and oil repellent, antis, high temperature resistance, corrosion resistance and high strength. The ordinary glass fiber cloth has good corrosion resistance, heat resistance, dimensional stability, and high strength, especially its low cost, and the addition of glass fiber cloth on the basis of the filter cloth is anexcellent choice[1-2]. In addition, due to the high-temperature dust-laden flue gas, impurities may adhere to or even penetrate the interior of the filter cloth when passing through the filter cloth, resulting in the filter cloth losing its original performance. Frequent cleaning or replacement of the filter cloth not only consumes labor costs but also affects the normal operation of the factory. Therefore, it is of great significance to impart water repellent properties to textile filter cloths.

In view of the unfavorable factors that may be encountered during the actual use of glass fiber filter cloth, these subject tests the water repellent performance of glass fiber cloth loaded with nano-TiO$_2$ particles[3-5]. The experimental results show that the air permeability of glass fabrics prepared by different process conditions does not change significantly, but the water repellent properties have been improved to some extent[6-7].

2 Experiments

2.1 Materials

Glass fiber cloth provided by Shanghai Xiangli Filter Material Co. , Ltd. and its thickness was 0. 18mm. It could be used for low temperature (-180℃), high temperature (550℃), and the color was white. Nanometer TiO$_2$ solution was supplied by Shanghai Huzheng Nanotechnology Co. , Ltd. According to the information provided by the company, the model of nano-TiO$_2$ solution used was G380.

2.2 Fabric treatment

At room temperature, 1000mL of pre-configured different concentrations of G380 nano-TiO$_2$ solutions were added to the ultrasonic instrument. Then, a pre-cut glass fiber cloth with a size of 10cm × 10cm was soaked in the nano-TiO$_2$ solution, and ultrasonic treatment was performed using an ultrasonic instrument. After the preset ultrasonic time, the glass fiber cloth was taken out of the ultrasonic apparatus and placed thereon. Drying in oven, drying time set to 15min.

In the preparation process, different samples to be tested were prepared by controlling variables such as the concentration of nano-TiO$_2$ solution, the size of ultrasonic power, the time of ultrasonic treatment, and the drying temperature, to examine the effect of each variable on the function of the sample.

The process conditions were as follows:

Nano-TiO$_2$ solution concentration: 60%, 80% 100%; Ultrasonic treatment time: 10min, 20min, 30min, 60min; Ultrasonic power: 60%, 80%, 100%; Drying temperature: 100℃, 150℃, 200℃. When one of the process conditions was studied, the other three process conditions were set to the maximum value. For example, when exploring the influence of nano-TiO$_2$ solution concentration, the time, power, and drying temperature were respectively set to: 60min, 100%, 200℃.

2.3 Surface water repellent measurement

According to ISO 4920: 2012(E) *Textile Fabrics-Determination of resistance to surface wetting (spray test)* skills requirement, the ultrasonically treated glass fiber cloths were cut to a size of 18cm × 18cm under different process conditions, and then the samples to be tested were placed in a constant temperature and humidity chamber for 24h pre-conditioning. The Y813 fabric water repellent tester was used as a test instrument. The sample was subjected to a water-spray test and compared with a standard picture by naked eyes to determine the water repellent rating of the sample. According to the water repellent of the sample surface, the water repellent rating of the sample could be divided into six levels of 0, 1, 2, 3, 4, and 5. Level 5 was the highest level, indicating that the surface of the sample was completely free of water. According to the actual situation, you could use the middle level, with 0.5 as the difference.

3 Results and Discussion

3.1 Effect of Nano-TiO$_2$ solution concentration on water repellent properties of glass fiber cloth

Test results are shown in Tab. 1.

Tab. 1 Concentration dosage and water repellent rating test results

No.	Nano-TiO$_2$ solution concentration (%)	Water repellent rating
Original sample	No	0
1	60	1-2
2	80	1-2
3	100	2

It can be seen that as the nano-TiO$_2$ solution concentration increases, the water repellent rating of the sample gradually increases.

3.2 Effect of ultrasonic treatment time on water repellent of glass fiber cloth

Test results are shown in the Tab. 2.

Tab. 2 Duration and water repellent test results

No.	Ultrasonic processing time (min)	Water repellent rating
Original sample	No	0
1	10	1-2
2	20	2
3	30	2
4	60	2

It can be seen that the sample water repellent level remains unchanged after the ultrasonic treatment time reaches 20min.

3.3 Effect of ultrasonic power on water repellent of glass fiber cloth

Test results are shown in Tab. 3.

Tab. 3   Power size and water repellent rating test results

No.	Ultrasonic power (%)	Water repellent rating
Original sample	No	0
1	60	1-2
2	80	2
3	100	2

It can be seen that after the ultrasonic power reaches 80% , the water repellent level of the sample remains unchanged.

3.4   Effect of drying temperature on water repellent of glass fiber cloth

Test results as shown in Tab. 4.

Tab. 4   Drying temperature and water repellent rating test results

No.	Drying temperature (℃)	Water repellent rating
Original sample	No	0
1	100	2
2	150	2
3	200	2

It can be seen that the sample water repellent level remains unchanged at 3 drying temperatures.

According to the results of the water repellent test of glass fiber cloth prepared under the above different process conditions, we can see out. No matter what conditions are changed, compared to the phenomenon of being completely wet, the ultrasonically treated glass fiber cloth has a certain level of water repellent to varying degrees. The drying temperature has almost no effect on the water repellent level of glass fiber cloth, The level of water repellent of glass fiber cloths increa-

ses to some extent with the increase of nano-TiO$_2$ solution concentration, ultrasonic processing time, and ultrasonic power.

4   Conclusions

In this topic, the glass fiber cloth is subjected to ultrasonic treatment and its "cavitation effect" is used to obtain a glass fiber cloth loaded with nano-TiO$_2$ particles, so that it has a water repellent function. Under different process conditions, its water repellent has improved to varying degrees. In the course of the experiment, it is also found that the nano-TiO$_2$ also improve the washing performance of the glass fiber cloth to varying degrees.

References

[1] Lin M Q, Wu H B, Zhang X D, et al. High temperature hot pressure coating process of PTFE film filter [J]. Journal of Donghua University (Natural Science Edition), 2017, 43 (05): 645-650 + 688.

[2] Zhang X L, Zhen P, Peng L, et al. PPS-based Mn-based catalytic denitration-dust removal integrated filter preparation and its low temperature SCR denitrification [J]. Functional Materials, 2015, 46(S2): 160-164.

[3] Wenzel R N. Resistance of solid surfaces to wetting by water [J]. Ind. Eng. Chem, 1936, 28(8): 988-994.

[4] Cassie A B D. Wettability of porous surfaces [J]. Trans Faraday Soc, 1944, 40(1): 546-551.

[5] Chong M N, Jin B, Chow C W, et al. Recent developments in photocatalytic water treatment technology: A review [J]. Water Research, 2010, 44(10): 2997-3027.

[6] Macak J M, Tsuchiya H, Ghicov A, et al. TiO$_2$, nanotubes: Self-organized electrochemical formation, properties and applications [J]. Current Opinion in Solid State & Materials Science, 2007, 11(1): 3-18.

[7] Mor G K, Varghese O K, Paulose M, et al. A review on highly ordered, vertically oriented TiO$_2$ nanotube arrays: Fabrication, material properties, and solar energy applications [J]. Solar Energy Materials & Solar Cells, 2006, 90 (14): 2011-2075.

The Ingenious Design in the Decoration of Ethnic Minority Costume in Southwest China

Xin Li[1] *

[1] *Beijing Institute of Fashion Technology (BIFT), Beijing 100029, China*

* *Corresponding author's email:* 75487609@ qq. com

Abstract: Combining primary sources obtained from physical measurements and field-study, this article interprets the design ingenuity in decoration of ethnic minority costume in southwest China, while combing the wisdom of ancestors and the concept of traditional creation, it also hopes to be able to inspire the modern fashion design.

Keywords: Minority; Dress; Cloth; Design

1　Introduction

Southwest of China is a minority region. Here, there are more than 50 different ethnic groups living together, presenting diverse costume cultures. Among the costumes of the southwest minority, the abundant decorations are the most outstanding feature; with different styles of embroidery, brocade, and batik jointly decorate a colorful "decoration" world. Under the gorgeous appearance, there are some little-known cultural connotations in the ornament[1].

2　Case Analysis of the Decorative Design of Ethnic Minority Clothing in Southwest China

2.1　"Hold-back" and "semi-finished" philosophy

Among the many Miao costumes, I discovere a special but common phenomenon: the decorative patterns on the costumes are often incomplete[2-4]. Take the cross stitch cloth from Guizhou Huaxi Miao in Fig. 1 as an example, in the top of the embroidered cloth, there is an obvious black background without any pattern; then if you carefully observe the octagonal pattern on it, many of the red and green lines for the outline drawing, which seems not have been sewn completely (Fig. 2 & Fig. 3). It may be because most of these costumes have

several decades of history. Therefore, they are partially off-line. But how can we explain why the batik patterns are not drawn completely? That may be because when the producers just do half of works, lines or wax was not enough, which caused regrets. And what do they think about the incomplete decoration?

Finally, I got the answer in the process of going to the Miao area for field-study. Miao's women like to "hold back" on the decoration of their costumes. They said, "My mom said, 'I'm going to be blind after finishing all sewing.' "If I've done it all my life, I would forget how to do it in my next life and become stupid." On the one hand, they believe that younger generations can learn how to make this pattern according to their own blanks and stitches left on the cloth. It is the heritance of wisdom which is full of mercy and love from the ancestors to their younger generations. On the other hand, these seemingly superstitious explanations have coincided with the traditional Chinese philosophy of "full is loss" and "making room for everything". So, these blanks are not caused by objective reasons "not done", but their subjective idea "do not fill up". In addition, from an aesthetic point of view, in a rich picture, proper windowing and blank space break the completely repetitive arrangement and density relationship, making the entire picture more lively and full of detail, but it eliminates the "airtight" atmosphere sense of tension and depression.

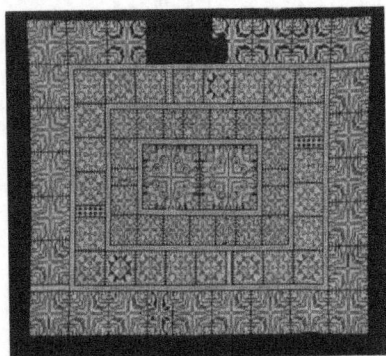

Fig. 1　The collection Huaxi Miao cross stitch cloth from ethnic costume museum of BIFT

Fig. 2　(Top) The details of Huaxi Miao cross stitch cloth

Fig. 3 (Bottom) The details of Huaxi Miao cross stitch cloth

2.2　The correct "wrong word"

Brocade is also one of the commonly used clothing decoration methods for minorities in China. The Tujia people mainly live in the Wuling mountainous areas in the border areas of Hunan, Hubei, Chongqing and Guizhou in China. Its brocade "Silankapu (Tujia Transliteration)" is dominated by geometric patterns with vivid and lively colors. It is typical of Chinese minorities brocades.

Due to the close relationship with the Han people, the Tujia Brocade also shows the imprint of the integration of many ethnic cultures. This is a piece of "Tujia Fu Lu Shou Xi pattern" (Fig. 4 and Fig. 5). At first glance, this is a brocade full of Chinese characters, but a close look reveals a lot of "wrong words" arranged above: "Fu" "Lu" and "Shou" were reversed, and the word "Guo" was missing one stroke. In fact, this is due to the unique phenomenon that the producer sees the words as a picture. It is not because the Tujia people do not have their own characters, or they are illiteracy for making the confusing jokes. Instead, the producers treat the words as patterns; they emphasize the expression of the auspicious connotations rather than the glyph. Therefore, the unconscious insist the inversion of the words. In their views, "Fu" "Lu" "Shou", "Xi" and the bats that refer to the good connotations

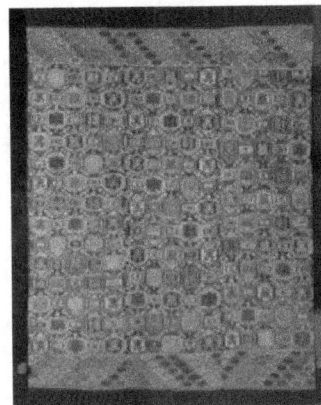

Fig. 4　The collection of Tujia Fu Lu Shou Xi pattern from ethnic costume museum of BIFT

Fig. 5　The Fu Lu ShouXi pattern of the partial

(according to homonyms, take the meaning of "Fu"), the deer (according to homophony, take the meaning of "Lu", the red-crowned cranes (symbols of longevity), the butterflies (metaphor for love, meaning the same as "Xi"), and the flowers (representing the beautiful) (Tab. 1). Therefore, the Chinese characters appearing in this brocade are actually equivalent to graphics. They are treated as graphic texts so they do not need to deliberately pursue positive and negative inversions, nor do they have such strict differences between right and wrong. It is neither affects people's reading nor changes the good wishes conveyed by the pattern. Since the pattern that symbolizes auspiciousness can be "positive means auspicious and so it reverses", then auspicious words do the same.

Tab. 1 Comparison of brocade pattern and chinese characters writing

The pattern on the brocade	The correct chinese character writing
福	福
禄	禄
壽	壽
国	国

2.3 The "good and fast" method

Every minority woman married must undertake the task of making the whole family's costumes while doing farm work and housework. Only by doing it fast can they ensure that all the old and young have clothes to wear; only if it be well done, the wearer will appear "honored" in social activities (this is the criterion for judging the minority society), and the women will also gain recognition from family and society. And the elaborate decoration often takes a lot of time and energy, so they can always come up with some clever labor-saving methods to deal with heavy manual labor.

There are many colorful triangular patchwork decorations on this Yi's blouse (Fig. 6). Take the patchwork area of the "Big white triangle" in Fig. 7 as an example, on the face of it, the "white triangle" is composed of 15 "red triangles" and 16 "white triangles", which is complex to operate, but the producer uses a clever method-first sewed a "red medium triangle" in the middle of the "white triangle", divided the frame into four medium triangles. Then sewed three "green small triangles" on the middle "red medium triangle" and finally sew three "red small triangles" on the three "white triangles" around (Fig. 8). The addition of a "red medium triangle" greatly reduces the frequency of stitching together one by one. This time-saving and labor-saving method does not affect the visual beauty, but is more durable than directly using the rags, which fully reflects the wisdom of the creator.

Fig. 6 (Top) The collection of patchwork blouse of Yi from ethnic costume museum of BIFT

Fig. 7 (Bottom) The detail of patchwork

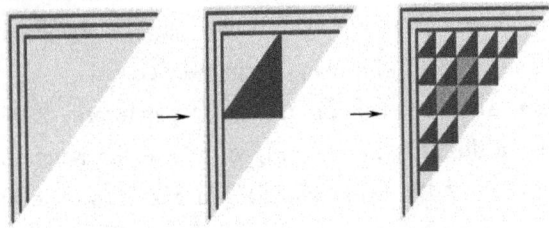

Fig. 8 Patching method analysis diagram

This "good and fast" skill was also used in the costume decoration of the Wudang Miao in Guiyang, Guizhou (Fig. 9 and Fig. 10). The square decoration color block at the back of the clothes is clear. It seems simple but contains the balance between the visual beauty,

Fig. 9 The collection of Guiyang Wudang Miao festival costume from ethnic costume museum of BIFT: front view (top) and rear view (bottom)

Fig. 10 The patch decoration of the dress-tails

craftsmanship and practically. At first sight, this set of patchwork decorations is made up of several triangles, but actually the visual effect is created by the superposition, decomposition, and reorganization of squares. Prefabricate each part, and then assemble according to a certain methods. When a part is damaged, it can be removed and replaced at any time without discard and waste. This is a modern modular method, which is hidden in the decoration of traditional minority costume. It makes a reasonable division of complex tasks and creates an efficient and effective working method that everyone can master.

The following is the graphic combination principle of the patch decoration that I restore according to the physical details.

(1) Decompose first

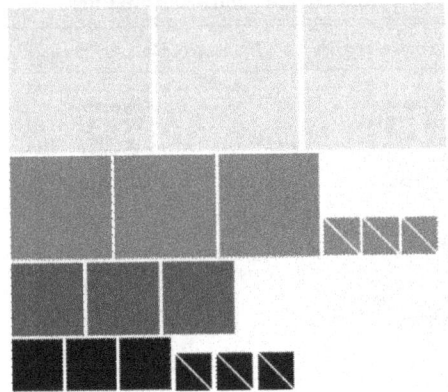

(2) Overlay combination

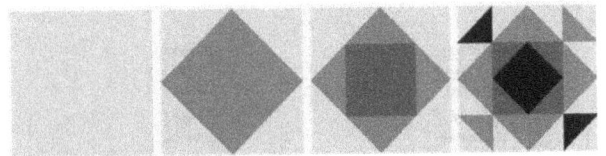

3 Conclusions

Because of the producers are not full-time embroiders and weavers, but who are mostly ordinary women with uneven levels of talent-in addition to the farm work in the fields and the housework in the house, these ordinary women had to take the task of making clothing for all family members are also required. This is the reason why it is difficult to find the perfect production of the minority costumes in the southwest. However, the energy and emotions devoted to the daily supplies from folks often allow us to feel more unique, love, warmth and humanities. From the above example analysis, we can find that the decoration of the minority costumes in southwest China not only includes the philosophy of life, but also reflects the integration of cultures, and it also shows the ingenious wisdom in the methods of decoration. The traditional folk costumes are not just " old antiques", but also a summary of the practical experience of labouring people for thousands of years. Nowadays, modern people are always racking their brains to innovate, but rarely looking back at the wisdom and aesthetics of our ancestors. The creativity and inspiration are never whimsical things, but the study of design ingenuity in traditional costumes may be a good source of innovation.

References

[1] Ledderose L. Ten thousand things——modularization and large-scale production in Chinese art [M]. Beijing: SDX Joint Publishing Company, 2012.

[2] Zeng X Y. Guizhou's hidden civilization [M]. Beijing: People's Fine Arts Publishing House, 1999.

[3] Zeng X Y. Miao zhuang [M]. Beijing: People's Fine Arts Publishing House, 1992.

[4] Deng Q Y. Yunnan minority art of dresses and decorative design [M]. Taipei: People Publishing House & Yongquan Publishing Business Co. , Ltd. , 1992.

Raw Material Analysis and Structure Properties Research on Hotan Traditional Etles Silk

Gulisitan Yigemu[1,2], Qiu Yiping[1]*

[1] *Donghua University, Textile college, Shanghai 201620, China*

[2] *Xinjiang University, Textile and Fashion college, Urumchi, Xinjiang 830046, China*

Corresponding author's email: ypqiu@dhu.edu.cn

Abstract: With reference of national, industrial standards and trade standards for Etles silk-Hotan cocoon, there were all kinds of indicators of testing, such as: moisture content, the cocoon rate, the cocoon layer thickness, oil content and glue rate of cocoon and compared with natural silk. This process involved a lot of exploratory and verification experiment. Raw silk and morphological structure, molecular structure, crystal structure performance of silk using traditional and modern method had been studied by electronic scanning microscope, infrared spectrometer, X-ray diffraction etc. On the premise of protecting and inheriting the exquisite technique and rich resources of Uyghur nationality's traditional silk crafts, it can provide the evidence for Etles silk production process specialization and standardization and also had significant meaning to optimize the original process and study the production of high quality.

Keyword: Traditional Etles silk; Hotan cocoon; Natural silk; Structure

1 Introduction

The main raw material for the Etles silk is natural silk from Hotan Xinjiang. The silk is endowed with special propertiesand characteristics by special geographical location, environment, and weather conditions in Hotan. By modern technology of exploratory testing and test methods, raw materials of traditional Etles silk, silkworm cocoons and silk structural properties were studied systematically in this article.

2 Experiments

2.1 Experiment material

Cocoon, silk (provided by Hotan Jiya beauty Eltes silk Ltd., made in Hotan)

2.2 Experiment reagent

Anhydrous sodium carbonate Na_2CO_3 (Shanghai Reagent Factory), picric acid (Guangzhou Chemical Reagent Factory), carmine (Sinopharm Chemical Reagent Co., Ltd.), trisodium phosphate, sodium bicarbonate $NaHCO_3$, industrial soap, three water (distilled water), petroleum ether.

2.3 Experiment equipment

2.3.1 Equipment device for raw materials analysis

Water bath of constant temperature, beakers, glass, thermometer, electronic balance, timer, fat extractor, 250mL balloons, plastic head dropper, filter paper, weighing paper, gas lights, analytical balance (maximum range 100g, minimum scale value 0.0001g), Y801A constant temperature oven, weighing bottles, dried containers

2.3.2 Equipment for fiber structure observation

Scanning electron microscopy-energy dispersive spectrometer (SEM-EDS)

Instrument Model: SEM: JSM-5600LV; Manufacturer: SEM: Japan JEOL;

FTIR-Raman spectroscopy (FTIR-Raman)

Instrument Model: NEXUS-670; Manufacturer: Nicolet

X-Ray diffraction (XRD)

Instrument Model: D / Max-2550 PC; Manufacturer: Japan RIGAKU

2.4 Method

2.4.1 Cocoon ratetest

GB/T 19113—2003[1]

Amount of dry shuck: 50g fresh cocoon, the weight measured in an hydrous state.

According to test result of amount of the dry shuck, fresh cocoon levels can be confirmed; the basic level conditions are shown in Tab. 1.

Tab. 1 Basic level classifications of cocoon

Level cocoon class	Amount of the dry shuck	Level of cocoon class	Amount of the dry shuck
Special 3	> 11.6	10	> 9.2
Special 2	> 11.4	11	> 9.0
Special 1	> 11.2	12	> 8.8
1	> 11.0	13	> 8.6
2	> 10.8	14	> 8.4
3	> 10.6	15	> 8.2
4	> 10.4	16	> 8.0
5	> 10.2	17	> 7.8
6	> 10.0	18	> 7.6
7	> 9.8	19	> 7.4
8	> 9.6	20	> 7.2
9	> 9.4		

Note: Classification of dry shuck amount listed in this chart is lower limit value, under level 20 is out of class.

Among tested fresh cocoons, by a multi-point random test method the cocoons were extracted out and tested and the number of samples was not less than 1kg. Mix test sample cocoons and extract 250g cocoon randomly, count the number (a double cocoon as two cocoons). These counted cocoons were used for testing. Measure its cocoon rate.

Cocoon rate formula:

Cocoon rate = (cocoon weight before peeling pupa-cocoon weight after peeling pupa)/ cocoon weight before peeling pupa

2.4.2 Moisture content test

GB/T 9995—1997

Under specified conditions moisture content in cocoon/ silk was measured.

Moisture content = (weight before drying-weight after drying)/ weight before drying[2]

2.4.3 Oil content test

Experiment condition: Water bath: 80℃

Reflux times: About 12 times

Reflux time: 2hour

Petroleum ether (boiling range: 60-90℃)

Experimental procedure: Get about 5g of the sample wrapped with filter paper bag, place it in fat extraction vessel, add 150mL petroleum ether, reflux along with balloons in water bath. After reflux, the sample was removed and placed in an oven to 105-110℃ to bake for 2 hours, weighed out with a bottle and placed in a dryer to cool to room temperature, and then weighed. The weight minus weight of weighing bottle was degreasing dry weight[3].

Oil content formula:

Oil content formula (%) = (dry weight before degreasing-dry weight after degreasing) / dry weight before degreasing × 100%

Notes:

(1) The sample cannot be placed immediately in the oven, because it contained organic solvents and it should be placed inside the fume hood to let the organic solvent evaporate and then placed in the oven.

(2) Normally Petroleum ether was not pure. There was water in balloon after recycling. Therefore it should be put into the oven after water evaporated in water bath.

2.4.4 Glue content test

2.4.4.1 Glue content of silkworm cocoon test

Scouring conditions:

First time: Industrial soap: 5g/L

Second time: Sodium carbonate: 1g/L

Sodium carbonate: 0.5g/L

Sodium carbonate: 1 : 100

Bathratio: 1 : 100

time: 20min

Time: 30min

Test procedure: Put the silkworm cocoons after degreasing into oven at the temperature of 105－110℃ for 2 hours; Put the cocoons into weighed bottle and then put it into dryer to cool down to room temperature; Weigh the weight that minus weighed bottle is the dry weight of cocoon. Scour cocoon under the scouring conditions and make it dehydration after scouring; Put it into oven for 2 hours; Weigh the mass that minus weighed bottle is the dry weight of cocoon after scouring.

Glue content formula:

Glue content formula = (dry weight before scouring-dry weight after scouring)/ dry weight before scouring × 100%

Notes:

(1) Weighing bottle should be dried and weight each time.

(2) During scouring process, pay attention to the evaporation of solvents and replenish the loss water.

2.4.4.2 Glue content of raw silk test

FZ/T 40004—2009

Test condition:

Na_2CO_3: 0.5g/L

Water: Three level water

Bath ratio: 1 : 100

Temperature: Boiling point

Time: 30min

Mark two samples and weigh the weight respectively; dry to constant weight according to the GB/T 9995 standard and weigh the dry weight before degumming. Degum two marked samples under test conditions in Na_2CO_3 solution; During degumming, stir with glass rod constantly to make the degumming even and wash the unscoured samples with three-level water. Repeat above procedures 3 times and wash samples with three-level water of 50–60℃; dry them to constant weight according to GB/T 9995 and weigh the weight after degumming[4].

Glue content formula = (dry weight before degumming-dry weight after degumming)/ dry weight before degumming × 100%

2.4.4.3 Preparation of picric acid carmine solution

Dissolve 1g picric acid into 100mL hot distilled water and cool it down; dissolve 1g carmine solution into 100mL distilled water and boil 5min, and put it into picric acid after cooling. After degumming, picric acid carmine solution can be used to test if silk was completely unglued after degumming. If the sample color was yellow it proved silk was degummed entirely and if color was red it indicated silk was degummed partially[4].

2.4.5 Observation method

2.4.5.1 Observe the silk surface and cross section

Observe surface morphology of silk sample with scanning electron microscope-energy disperse spectroscopy (SEM-EDS) and take photos with magnification times of 1000, 2000, 3000, 4000 etc.

Test conditions:

Temperature: 20℃

Relative humidity: 65%

2.4.5.2 Absorption spectrometry test

Make silk powder into samples with KBr tabletting and test on FTIR-Raman spectroscopy (FTIR-Raman), and the scanning range is between 4000 to $200cm^{-1}$.

Test method: Mixed abrasive particles screened by 80 mesh sieves with KBr, and then press them into a thin disk, and directly place them in the optical to be tested.

Test conditions: Temperature 20℃, relative humidity 70%.

2.4.5.3　X-ray diffraction analysis

The silk samples were prepared into powders and measured in the X-ray diffract meter. Tube voltage 4.0 kV, tube current 35 mA, scanning speed 2°/min, Ni filter, CuK radiation of the target, the scanning angle 5°–50°.

Test conditions: Temperature 20℃, relative humidity 65%.

3　Analysis of Etles raw materials

According to national standard, industrial standard, each indicator of cocoon that is also called Etles in Hotan area such as moisture content, cocoon rate, oil content, and glue content were tested and measured, which was also compared with cocoon and raw silk of southern area[5].

Based on test result, moisture content, oil content, glue content and cocoon rate were tested and results were shown in following Tab. 2.

Tab. 2　Comparisons of performance index of cocoon and raw silk in Hotan Xinjiang and southern area

Type Test index	Natural silk in Hotan Xinjiang		Natural silk in southern area	
	Cocoon	Raw silk	Cocoon	Raw silk
Moisture content (%)	9.29	9.52	11.15	
Oil content (%)	14.85	0.60	15.55	0.75
Glue content (%)	29.36	22.30	26.53 (yellow silk) 24.64 (white silk)	

As it shown in Tab. 2, moisture content of natural silk and cocoon in Hotan was lower than white cocoon in southern areas obviously, and oil content was less. The glue content of Hotan cocoon was about 30% which was higher than yellow and white silk in southern areas[6].

3.1　Morphological structure of Etles raw materials

3.1.1　Surface morphology of cocoon and silk before and after degumming

Sample preparation: To observe the surface morphology before and after degumming, seven kinds of samples were prepared. By cooking the cocoon, the silk was pulled out and some of silk were separated to make sample 1 that was called unscoured silk; part of extracted cocoon silk was degummed by degumming method was sample 2 which was called degummed silk. Single silk drawn out from raw silk of spring cocoon was made of sample 3, which was called unscoured raw silk (spring cocoon). By fat extraction process sample 4 was made, which was called degreasing and unscoured silk (spring cocoon). Some raw silk was made into sample 5 by degumming that was called degreasing and degummed silk. Single silk was extracted from summer cocoon to make sample 6 that was unscoured raw silk (summer cocoon). Scoured silk that was degummed and bleached provided by manufacture was sample 7.

As it can be seen in Fig. 1–Fig. 7, silk surface before degumming had a thick gum and was very rough with very obvious tearing cracks. Longitudinal surface of degummed silk was very smooth, clean and can be clearly seen that the lines and void was parallel to the axis. Unscoured silk of spring cocoon's surface was coated with gum whose appearance was rough, cracked with some granular substance. It had significant changes in raw silk surface after degreasing treatment with granular substance decreasing. After degumming, silk surface became smooth and clean. Monofilament can be more clearly observed. The longitudinal surface of unscoured summer silk cocoons was attached with a number of particlesand particles of the outer layer overlapped densely. Compared with spring silk, the surface gum and particulate impurities had a significantly difference. There were little particles along longitudinal surface of degummed and bleached silk provided by the manufacturer.

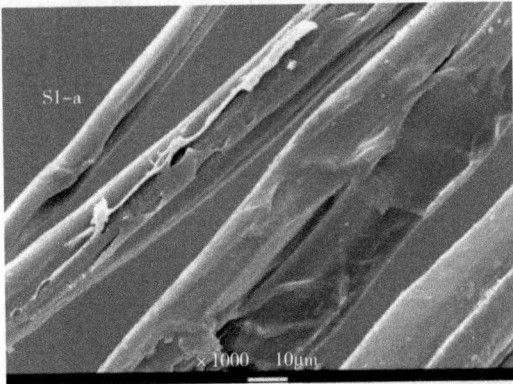

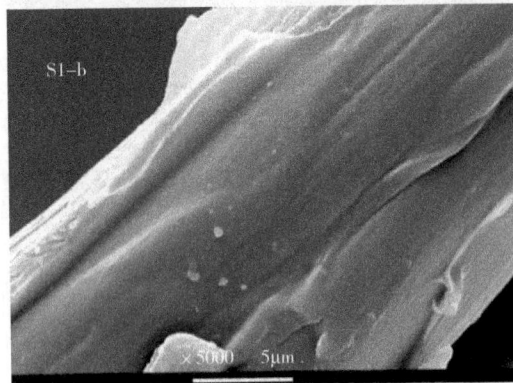

Fig. 1   Sample 1-unscoured silk

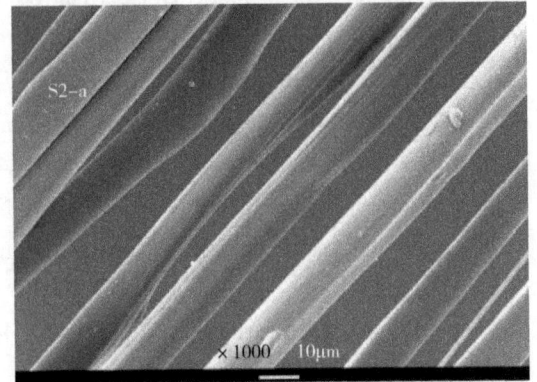

Fig. 2   Sample 2-degummed silk

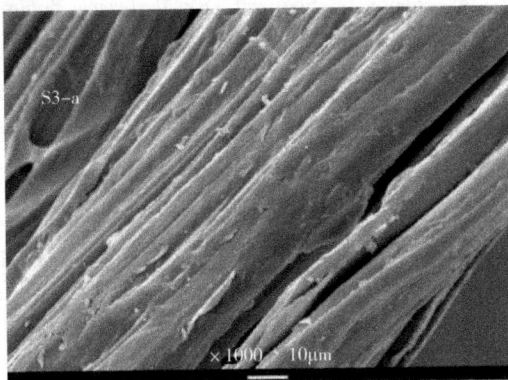

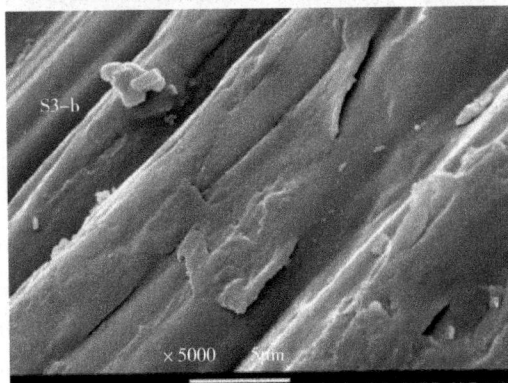

Fig. 3   Sample 3-unscoured raw silk (spring cocoon)

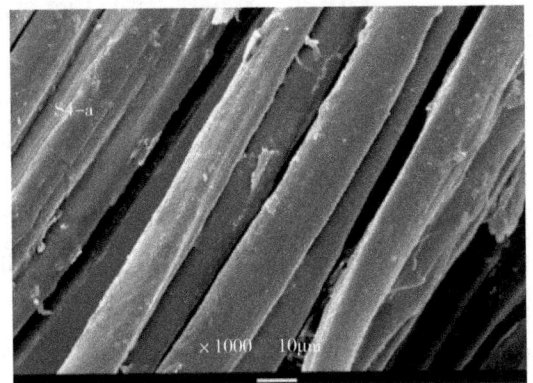

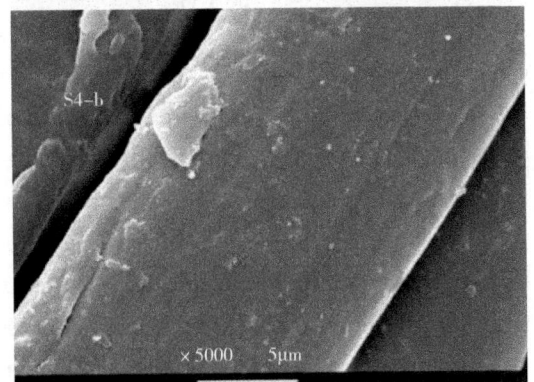

Fig. 4   Sample 4 - degreasing and unscoured raw silk (spring cocoon)

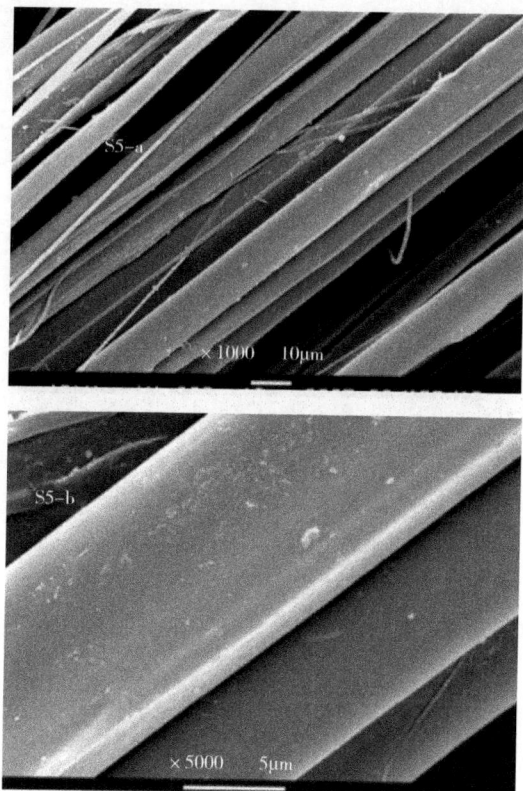

Fig. 5   Sample 5-degummed silk (spring cocoon)

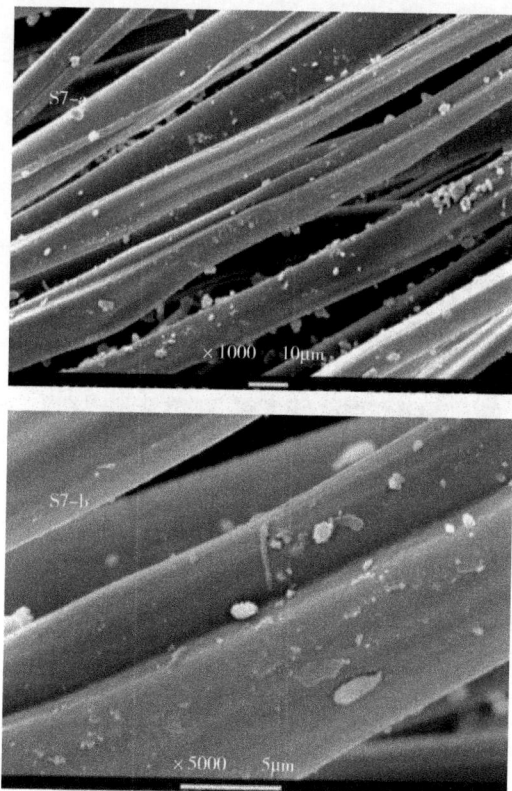

Fig. 7   Sample 7-degummed and bleached scoured silk

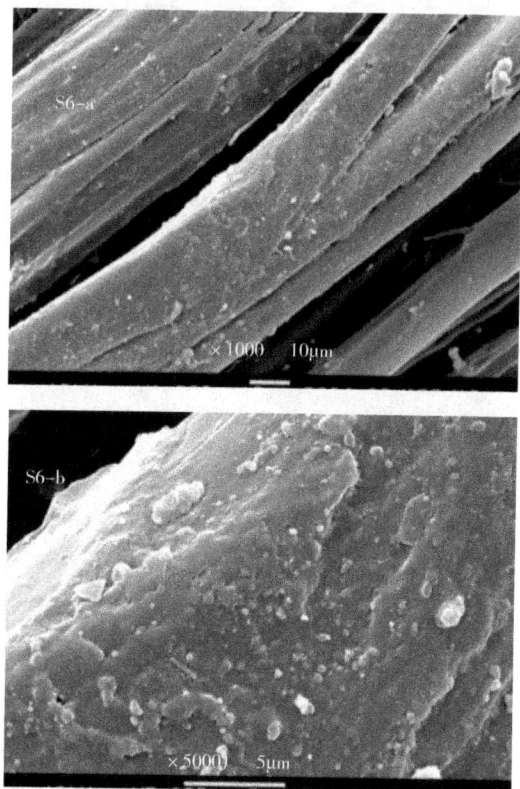

Fig. 6   Sample 6-unscoured raw silk (summer cocoon)

3.1.2   Cross section morphology of cocoon silk and silk before and after degumming

Sample preparation: To observe the cross-sectional shape before and after degumming seven kinds of samples were prepared. In order to observe surface morphology samples were prepared by Hardy's slicer and fixed with collodion, and transverse cross-section was cut as sample slice.

As it can be seen in Fig. 8 – Fig. 14 that the cross-sectional shapes of Hotan natural silk fibers were mainly irregular triangular whose edges were smooth and plump, similar to section morphology of southern white silkworm silk. There was a big difference of silk cross-section before and after degumming. Because the surface of unscoured silk was coated with sericin, although there was void between the fibers, they were not regular. After degumming the edge became smooth, clean, and there were more obvious gaps between the fibers. Compared with cross-sectional shape of no degreasing silk it can be found out that degreasing process can make debris and grease excluded. Due to different cross-sectional form

Fig. 8　Sample 1−unscoured silk

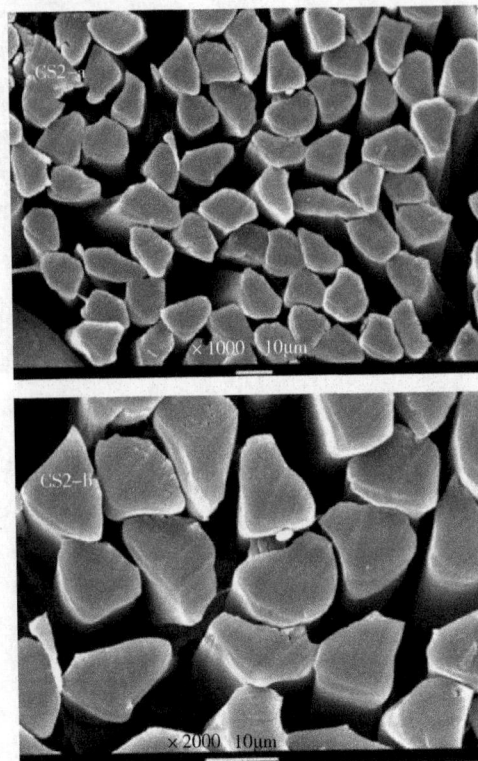

Fig. 9　Sample 2−degummed silk

Fig. 10　Sample 3−unscoured raw silk（spring cocoon）

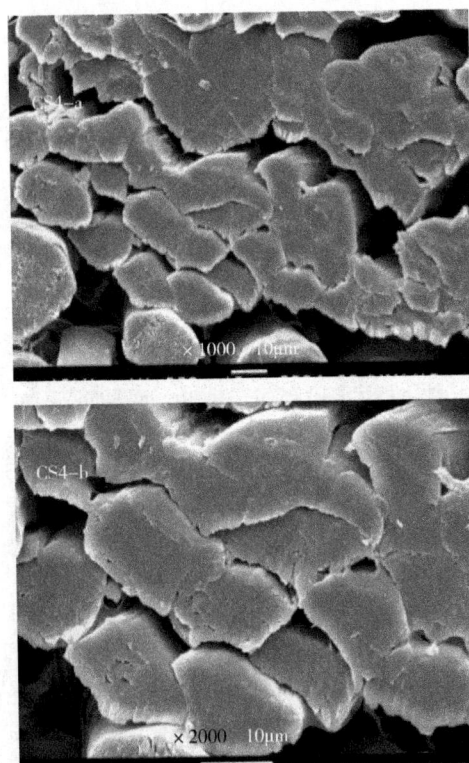

Fig. 11　Sample 4−degreasing and unscoured raw silk（spring cocoon）

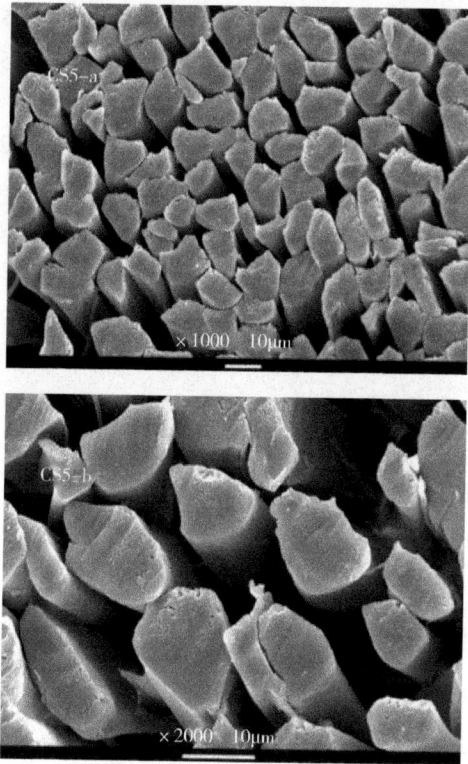

Fig. 12　Sample 5−degummed silk（spring cocoon）

Fig. 13　Sample 6−unscoured raw silk（summer cocoon）

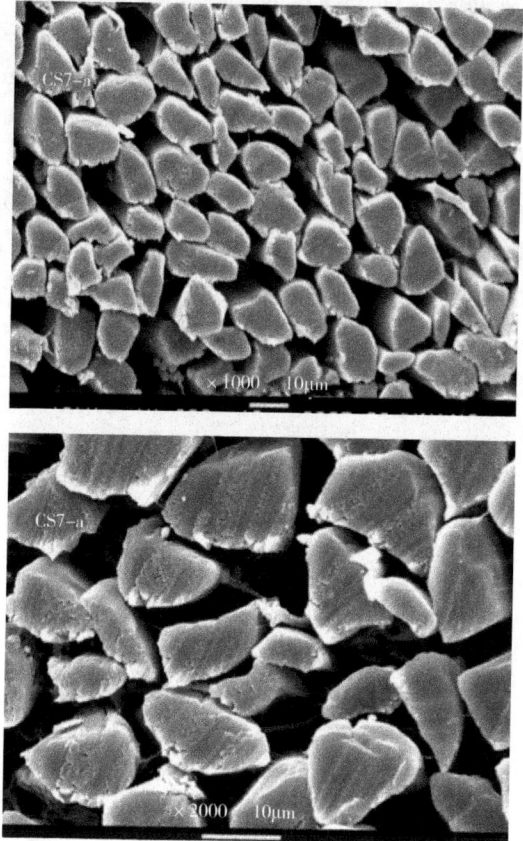

Fig. 14　Sample 7−degummed and bleached scoured silk

of spring cocoon silk and summer cocoon silk there were significant differences in adhesion degree under the interaction of sericin. Cross-sectional shape of degummed and bleached silk provided by the manufacturer was nearly triangle with some deformation. Single fibers were loose and among them there were some particles. And the edges were smooth.

3.2　Molecular structure analysis of Etles raw materials

To analyze the molecular structure of different silk before and after degumming, silk powder were prepared with KBr pellet and made of samples which were measured under Fourier transform infrared-Raman spectroscopy（FTIR-Raman）. The samples were sample 1−unscoured spring cocoon silk, sample 2 − degumming spring cocoon silk, sample 3 − unscoured summer cocoon silk, sample 4−degumming summer cocoon silk, sample 5−degummed and bleached silk. The samples were analyzed by infrared absorption spectrometry.

As it can be seen in Fig. 15 that according to the affiliation of protein characteristic absorption peaks, the infrared absorption spectrum absorption peaks appeared at (unscoured spring cocoon silk) 1655cm^{-1}, (degumming spring cocoon silk) 1647cm^{-1}, (unscoured summer cocoon silk) 1648cm^{-1}, (degumming summer cocoon silk) 1648cm^{-1}, (degummed and bleached silk) 1640cm^{-1} was amide I C ═O stretching vibration that was phthalimide I α-helical structure. Peaks appeared at 1535cm^{-1}, 1517cm^{-1}, 1515cm^{-1}, 1518cm^{-1}, 1517cm^{-1} were amide bond II C—N stretching and N—H bending

vibration that was phthalimide II α-helical structure. Peaks at 1235cm^{-1}, 1232cm^{-1}, 1231cm^{-1}, 1235cm^{-1}, 1232cm^{-1} were amide III. Peaks at 1165cm^{-1}, 1164cm^{-1}, 1163cm^{-1}, 1165cm^{-1}, 1167cm^{-1} were amide IV that was β-sheet structure. Peaks at 632cm^{-1}, 630cm^{-1}, 634cm^{-1}, 634cm^{-1}, 636cm^{-1} were amide V that was α-helical structure. Peak at 1070cm^{-1} was the characteristic peak of sample 1 and sample 2. Peak at 634cm^{-1} was the characteristic peak of sample 3 and sample 4[7].

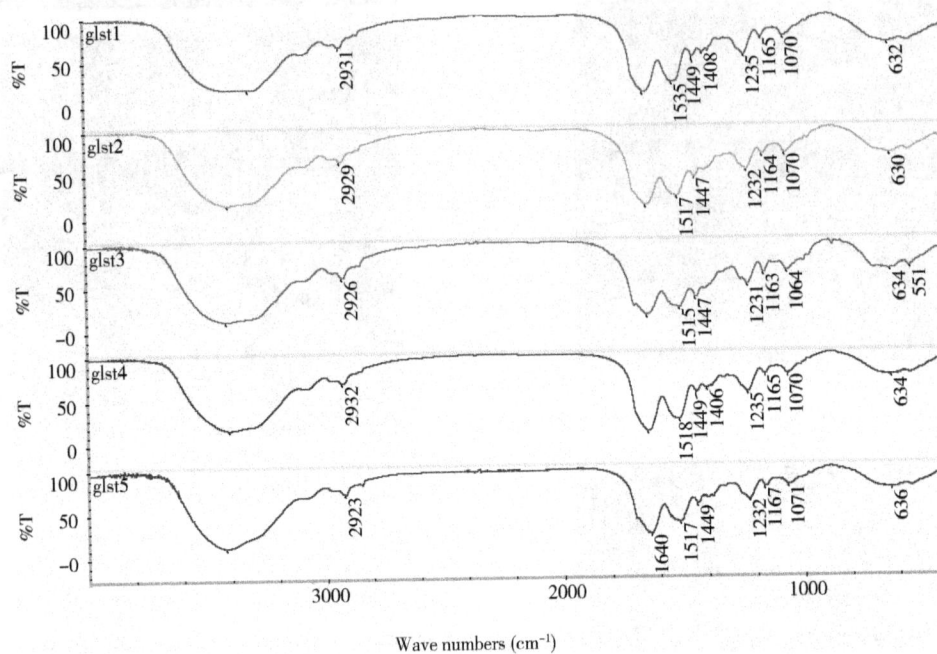

Fig. 15 Infrared absorption spectrum sample 1—unscoured spring cocoon silk, sample 2—degumming spring cocoon silk, sample 3—unscoured summer cocoon silk, sample 4—degumming summer cocoon silk, sample 5—degummed and bleached silk

Comparing IR spectra of spring cocoon silk and summer cocoon silk before and after degumming it can also be seen in the degumming process, the amino stretching vibration had displacement from 3311cm^{-1}, 3416cm^{-1} to higher wave number 3404cm^{-1}, 3407cm^{-1}, which indicated that silk sericin in silk were connected by hydrogen bonds and fibroin, and during degumming process hydrogen bonds had been destroyed[8].

3.3 Crystal structure of Etles raw materials

In Fig. 16 it was found out that diffraction curves of five kinds of silk were similar and each curve was overlapped by 3 diffraction peaks and 3 β-overlap peaks

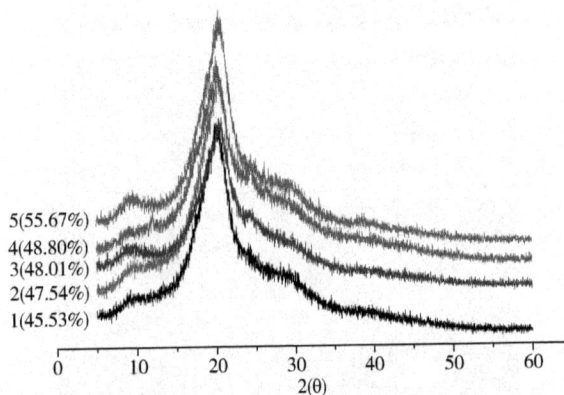

Fig. 16 X-ray diffraction spectrum sample 1—unscoured spring cocoon silk, sample 2—degumming spring cocoon silk, sample 3—unscoured summer cocoon silk, sample 4—degumming summer cocoon silk, sample 5—degummed and bleached silk

whose corresponding angles 2θ were 10°, 20° and 30°. It indicated that these five kinds of silk had the same crystal system. Two of these silk presented X-ray diffraction peaks at 20° which were characteristic peaks of higher-oriented fibroin structure.

The crystallinity of silk samples 1, 2, 3, 4, 5 was tested as 45.53%, 47.54%, 48.01%, 48.80%, 55.67% and crystallinity of normal silk was 48.53% ± 1.46% [9-10].

4 Conclusions

(1) Moisture contentof natural cocoon silk and raw silk in Hotan was significantly lower than natural white silkworm cocoons in the southern region and oil content was little less than the southern region. Glue content of Hotan cocoon was 30%, higher than yellow and white silk of the southern region.

(2) Surface of unscoured silk was rough, cracked wrapped with granular particles. Longitudinal surface of degummed silk was smooth and it can be clearly seen that lines and gaps were parallel to the fiber axis. Silk fiber surface morphology was mainly irregular triangles whose edges were smooth, plump and similar to southern white silkworm silk. There was a big difference of silk cross-section before and after degumming. Although the surface of unscoured silk was wrapped with sericin and space between fibers were not regular, after degumming the edge became smooth, clean, and space between the fibers were more obvious.

(3) Silk structure mainly contained amide I, amide II, amide III, amide IV, amide V and other amide group whose conformation was α-helical structure and β-sheet structure. During degumming process the molecular structure of α-helical structure silk before and after degumming transformed from α-helix to β fold.

(4) Hotan natural silk and normal silk had the same crystal construction and crystallinity differed before and after degumming, in different seasons. The crystallinity of the sample1, 2, 3, 4, and 5 were respectively 45.53%, 47.54%, 48.01%, 48.80%, 55.67%.

References

[1] GB/ T 19113—2003, Silkworm cocoon grading (shell dry Method) [S].

[2] GB / T 9995—1997, Textile material moisture content and moisture regain measurement (oven drying method) [S]

[3] Wang J. Scouring process of raw silk research [D]. Shanghai: Donghua University, 2008.

[4] FZ / T 40004—2009 13-14, Silk gum content experimental methods [S].

[5] Jiang X J, Hu Z Y, Ning W, et al. Research of scouring effect on the performance of Guangxi natural yellow cocoon [J]. Silk, 2010, (6): 4-8.

[6] Wang J N, Xu S Q, Yi H G. Study on quality properties of natural yellow silk cocoons [J]. Silk, 2004, (1): 27-29.

[7] Dong F C, Pan Z J, Gua Y T, et al. Structure and properties of wild silk [J]. Silk, 2006, (3): 18-20.

[8] Zhou X C, Chen G Q. Heptyl methyl acrylic twelve fluorine and cool grafted silk fiber textile structure[J]. Silk, 2008, 29 (3): 56-58, 62

[9] Gao X F, Zuo B Q. The effects of different degumming methods on silk mechanical properties [J]. Silk, 2008, (12): 30-33.

[10] Chen Y M, Cai Z S, Ding Z Y. Structure and properties of male cocoon silk [J]. Silk, 2010 (1): 23-26.